RHETORIC
and human consciousness

A HISTORY • 4th EDITION

CRAIG R. SMITH
California State University, Long Beach

WAVELAND

PRESS, INC.

Long Grove, Illinois

Consulting Editor: Robert E. Denton, Jr.

For information about this book, contact:
Waveland Press, Inc.
4180 IL Route 83, Suite 101
Long Grove, IL 60047-9580
(847) 634-0081
info@waveland.com
www.waveland.com

Photo credits
Cover, 101, 119 Craig R. Smith; **38** adapted from BryanEnders; **44** Culver Pictures; **73** Paos Karap-anagiotis; **85** TakB; **91** Library of Congress LC-DIG-pga-02972; **106** alessandro0770; **143** Steven Kordic; **157** Philippe de Champaigne, *Saint Augustine*, circa 1645-1650, il on canvas, 31 1/8 x 24 5/8 in. (78.7 x 62.2 cm), Los Angeles County Museum of Art, Gift of The Ahmanson Foundation (M.88.177); **179** Perig; **197** Tupungato; **207, 211, 219, 231, 235, 240, 247, 250** Georgios Kollidas; **223** Luis Garcia; **276** AP/WideWorld; **281** Rue des Archives / The Granger Collection, NYC—All rights reserved.; **283** © Bettmann / CORBIS; **292** © Scherl/SV-Bilderdienst / The Image Works; **304** Wolfram Huke; **341** Glynnis Jones / Shutterstock.com; **351** Library of Congress LC-DIG-ppmsca-09398; **352** © Sijmen Hendriks; **359** Woodfin Camp & Associates, Inc.; **369** David Shankbone; **377** Bracha L. Ettinger; **384** © Hulton-Deutsch Collection / CORBIS; **393** K. Kendall

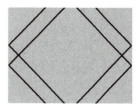

Contents

PART I
Rhetoric in the Ancient World   15

PART III
Rhetoric in the Age of Reason 231

PART IV
Rhetoric in the Contemporary World   341

Preface

As early as 2100 BC, wise men were advising select groups of aristocratic and noble pupils about the proper ways to live. The Egyptian vizier Ptahhotep wrote his advice into a book of maxims that includes advice about "fine speech," the role of silence, critical listening, and manners. Specifically, Ptahhotep advises his charges to avoid being arrogant about what they know; someone always knows more that you do. If you face a superior in argument, you should bow to him to gain his allegiance. If you face an equal, allow your silence to reveal your virtue: "Great respect is given to the quiet man." If you face one who is humble, instruct him. This rather passive philosophy recommends that speakers never revert to appeals to fear. Gossip and slander are condemned. Ptahhotep, however, did not provide detailed advice. Because he existed in an authoritarian regime, his theory was not broadened to include appeals to the population as a whole, nor was that population given access to his theory.

The same can be said of the rhetorical theory of the Chinese philosopher Confucius (Kung fu-tsu, 551–479 BC). He, too, was the captive of an autocratic leader and a society that sought to adapt to the environment rather than adapt the environment to it. However, a close reading of Confucius' *Analects* reveals that they were built on ancient sayings and meant to prepare the reader for "the way." At its base, the philosophy of Confucius resembles the advice of Plato, whom we will examine in this book. One should only speak to enlighten and only speak when enlightened. Very much like the Roman Quintilian (see chapter 5), Confucius attempts to construct a "great man" who speaks well. However, Confucius is not above audience adaptation. He recommends paying homage to the dead of the audience, taking their interests to heart, and speaking circumspectly about what is controversial. The uses of deception, role playing, and an appeal to manners are acceptable to create and maintain harmony. Confucius also tells his charges that word choice is important: "If the designators are not accurate, language will not be clear. . . . Great man is never careless in any respect" (XIII-3). While Confucius is making something of a comeback in contemporary China, the rulers in his time did not allow his teaching to reach the rest of the population. By 200 BC, the Chinese had developed categories for discourse that included oral persuasion *(shui)*, argumentation *(bian)*, and explanation *(ming)*. However, public speaking was not respected in this culture; in fact, no text on the subject would be developed in China until AD 1170.

In that year, Chen Kui's *Rules of Writing* went beyond mere spelling and grammar. The book's ten chapters included advice on the use of tropes, figures of speech, and form. However, the book was focused on the writing of literature as opposed to rhetoric. Catholic priests were the first to bring sophisticated theories of rhetoric from the West. Public speaking was not considered a survival skill until much later in China's history. In the twentieth century such persuasive speakers as Sun Yat-Sen and Mao Zedung would dramatically change the history of China.

Unlike the East, in the West most early philosophers recognized that persuasive skills are critical to survival in the world. Early references to speech can be found in the mythos of the West. For example, in the Old Testament in chapter 27 of Sirach, one reads at lines 4–7:

> When a sieve is shaken, the husks appear;
> So do a man's faults when he speaks.
> As the test of what the potter molds is in the furnace,
> So in his conversation is the test of man.
> The fruit of the tree shows the care it has had;
> So too does a man's speech disclose the bent of his mind.
> Praise no man before he speaks,
> For it is there that men are tested.

In fact, Deuteronomy, the fifth book of the Old Testament, is derived from the word for speeches and is said to be composed of the last five speeches of Moses. Many of the prophet Isaiah's speeches are policy statements, what Aristotle would call deliberative public address (see chapter 4).

This book describes and analyzes the evolution of rhetorical theory in Western civilization. In the process, the text illustrates the evolving definitions of rhetoric from myth and display to persuasion and symbolic inducement. The book closely examines the dialectic between rhetoric and other disciplines, notably philosophy and psychology. Some of these disciplines believe that rhetoric should be a servant that makes their findings understandable to an uninformed public. While this making-known function of rhetoric is important, I will argue that rhetoric is an art form with its own set of generative principles and its own pathways to the truth. I hope to demonstrate that rhetoric can be epistemic: it can find truths that elude other disciplines, particularly at times when science and reason fail to solve the most important crises facing humanity. Or rhetoric can inspire us to a transcendent spirit.

Sophisticated rhetorical theory is grounded in Greco-Roman principles; as it advances through history in fits and starts, it becomes deeper and more complex. This expansion was the case in the twentieth century, and we see more of its untapped dimensions emerge on the theoretical landscape of the twenty-first century. Thus, this book is mainly historical, though conceptual frameworks arise on each historical horizon. Essentially, this text uses history as a context for major figures who advanced rhetoric, and it analyzes developments in rhetorical theory that resulted from its interaction with other disciplines and the cultures that surrounded it. The illustrative examples in this book demonstrate the usefulness of rhetorical theory, especially its ability to inform and guide. By providing probes for rhetorical criticism, the book also demonstrates that rhetorical criticism illustrates, verifies, and refines rhetorical theory. Thus, the synergistic relationship between theory and criticism in rhetoric is no different than in other arts. *Theory informs practice; analysis of successful practice refines theory.*

The book begins with chapter 1, which lays the groundwork for the study by defining rhetoric as pragmatic and situational, and by illustrating how it works with a contemporary example of mediated and fragmented public discourse. After this introduction, the chapters are contained within four parts: Part I examines rhetoric in the ancient world; Part II looks at medieval and renaissance rhetorical theory; Part III focuses on rhetoric in the age of reason; and Part IV studies rhetoric in the contemporary world.

Chapter 2 begins Part I by exploring the mythic roots of rhetoric and its narrative qualities. These qualities are illustrated with one of the most enduring narratives in history, the Gospel of Matthew.

Chapter 3 traces the reaction to mythology in the thinking of pre-Socratics such as the naturalists, who are led by Thales, and the mystics, who are led by Parmenides. It examines the important contribution of the Sophists and the ethical debate they set off with Plato. For the first time, we see clearly how values and the methods of finding the truth affect the rhetorical theory espoused by its various creators. Rhetoric emerges as a techné—a discipline of its own.

Chapter 4 is a commentary on Aristotle's significant advancement of this discipline in his book on *Rhetoric*, the field-setting work that synthesizes so much of what was written and said before it. The chapter reveals that while Aristotle did not always provide the right answers in defining the art of rhetoric, he certainly asked the most important questions. The result is a set of generative and relevant principles that guide us in the craft of speech making, whether we are lawyers, politicians, preachers, salespersons, teachers, or suitors.

Chapter 5 reviews the contributions of Roman rhetorical theorists with an emphasis on the *Rhetorica ad Herennium*, Cicero, and Quintilian. Aside from codifying Greek theory into five canons, the Romans provided new inventive tools such as the *stasis* system for generating legal speeches. They also provided a sophisticated system of developing style in speech, using their concepts of *decorum* and *ornatus*. The importance of providing a proper education to future speakers is stressed along with rhetoric's relationship to civic virtue. Most important, careful consideration is given to the Roman contribution to the notion of style in language and its effect on speaker credibility and the emotional state of the audience.

Initiating the second part of the book, chapter 6 examines the impact of the Christianization of the Roman Empire on rhetorical theory. The chapter, which emphasizes Augustine's retrieval and reformulation of the classical system, makes the case that the Christian church advanced rhetoric for its own purposes while subjugating it to other forms of discourse, as dogma overcame tolerance in the medieval period. The chapter reveals that the humanists revived rhetoric near the end of the medieval period in spite of opposition by scholastics who usually sublimated rhetoric to other forms of discourse.

Chapter 7 discusses the rebirth of rhetorical theory in the Renaissance and its role in nation building and in the religious disputes among the factions jockeying for dominance. Most of the major figures of the Renaissance, from Machiavelli to Luther, had important advice to give on the role of persuasion in our lives.

At the beginning of Part III, chapter 8 looks at yet another turn in scholarship. Advances in science accelerated the examination of mental processes; a reformulation of rhetorical theory reflected these changes during the modern era. The emergence of faculty psychology on the one hand, and taste, eloquence, and delivery on the other demonstrates that rhetorical theory was rewritten to reflect the scientific and psychological breakthroughs of the seventeenth, eighteenth, and nineteenth centuries.

Chapter 9 defines "modern philosophy" to provide a backdrop for the existentialist revolt against it. The contributions of major existentialist thinkers such as Søren Kierkegaard, Jean-Paul Sartre, Martin Heidegger, Karl Jaspers, and Martin Buber are reviewed to deduce an existentialist theory of rhetoric. The chapter explores an ethical basis for determining what constitutes "authentic rhetoric." It also looks at rhetoric as an art form, arguing that rhetoric is capable of reflecting spirit and providing pathways to it.

Chapter 10 explores theorists who provide theories of their own while also laying the foundation for Kenneth Burke's work. Sigmund Freud and Karl Marx, one a psychological innovator and the other a political critic, had a major influence on Burke, and they provide major insights into various theories discussed in the remainder of the text. Burke drew from other theorists, as well, including Carl Jung, Jacques Lacan, and Jürgen Habermas, and their influential ideas are also discussed in this chapter. In chapter 11 we see how Burke absorbed the work of these great thinkers and applied their insights to his own innovative analysis of the communicative act.

The last part of the book, which focuses on the contemporary world, begins with chapter 12. It focuses on two new turns in the evolution of rhetoric. The first is Marshall McLuhan's examination of the impact of media on rhetoric. The second is I. A. Richards' semantic theory based on the electronic broadcasting model. The chapter then examines the more traditional advances of Chaim Perelman, Lucie Olbrechts-Tyteca, and Stephen Toulmin.

Chapter 13 examines the postmodern theories of such innovative thinkers as Michel Foucault and Jean-François Lyotard. It also deduces a feminist rhetorical theory from very diverse feminist critiques of society.

Chapter 14 highlights some the basic principles discussed previously and demonstrates their relationship to human consciousness and their usefulness for human interaction.

Because charting the evolution of rhetoric's many phases and stages can be daunting, I have included an appendix containing a timeline of events that influenced the relationships among rhetoric, events, and knowledge, which I hope provides a useful overview.

Some of my examples will have a political cast due to my experience as a researcher, writer, and analyst for CBS News for convention, election night, and inaugural coverage starting in 1968, and my role as a full-time presidential speechwriter and consultant to numerous political candidates. Moreover, political examples are easy to access should instructors desire to have their students use them in class papers and exercises. Many of our political leaders were well trained in rhetorical theory and have become its best exemplars. Presidents John Adams and his son John Quincy read the classics, particularly Cicero, as did James Madison, Thomas Jefferson, Daniel Webster, Woodrow Wilson, and Franklin Roosevelt. John Quincy Adams was a professor of rhetoric, and Woodrow Wilson taught courses in it. Students of political science will appreciate the contributions of persuasion theory to political science, which are examined in this text.

I am pleased to provide this fourth edition because it gives me the opportunity to correct minor errors, deepen areas of research, and include new items and characters in the story. In this edition, you will find new material on such theorists as Isocrates, Cicero, Machiavelli, Kenneth Burke, and Michel Foucault. I have also added material on the rhetoric of civil religion, ideological criticism, constitutive discourse and feminist rhetorical theory. There are many new examples to illustrate the material covered in this comprehensive study. Where appropriate, I have expanded the historical context for the creation of rhetorical theory and its use in public address.

The exploration undertaken in this text will challenge its readers, but rising to the challenge will prove rewarding. We encounter some of the most important minds in the history of the world and move through its most important epochs while exploring the relationship between rhetorical theory and the evolution of human consciousness. This book chronicles big ideas from ancient Greece and Rome through the rise of Islam and the Renaissance to Western civilization. I have tried to note connections that exist between great thinkers over huge periods of time. For example, Plato's ancient three parts of the soul—the charioteer (will), the white horse (conscience), and the dark horse (desire)—are reflected in Sigmund Freud's twentieth-century construction of the ego, the superego, and the id. Aristotle's system of commonplaces shows up in Michel Foucault's exploration of values. The virtues of interrelational existentialists reappear in feminist rhetorical theory.

I hope what is provided here lays a basis for an understanding of the history of rhetorical theory that is fair, comprehensive, and relevant. I hope to sustain the argument that rhetoric is a legitimate and evolving art form crucial to decision making—and hence an integral part of our lives from everyday discourse to the most important public address, whether that be the call of conscience on a lonely beach or a call for war before Congress.

Craig Smith
Long Beach, California

Acknowledgments

I want to thank Carol and Neil Rowe for raising important editorial questions and for bringing this edition to publication in a timely manner. No experience with a publisher has been better than this one. I also want to thank Jeni Ogilvie for her marvelous copyediting of this and previous editions.

ABOUT THE AUTHOR

Dr. Craig Smith, professor of Communication Studies, won the Douglas Ehninger Award from the National Communication Association for his lifetime achievement in research on rhetorical theory. Dr. Smith is the author of 15 books and over 60 scholarly articles. He also serves as the director of the Center for First Amendment Studies at California State University, Long Beach, and was a member of the Board of Trustees of the California State University system for four years. He has testified before Congress, the Federal Communications Commission, and state and local governments. He regularly writes editorials in such diverse publications as *TV Guide*, the Copley News Service, the Associated Press, the *Miami Herald*, the *Los Angeles Times*, and *Reason Magazine*. He has served as a consultant to CBS News for convention, election night, and inaugural coverage. He served as a full-time speechwriter for President Gerald Ford and Chrysler CEO Lee Iacocca, and as a consulting writer for George H. W. Bush. He has won many awards from his university including the Scholarly and Creative Activities Achievement Award, the Distinguished Faculty Teaching Award, the Outstanding Professor Award, and the Hardeman Award for Academic Leadership. The National Speakers' Association named him Outstanding Professor of the Year in 2006. Before coming to California State University at Long Beach, Dr. Smith taught at San Diego State University, the University of Virginia, and the University of Alabama at Birmingham.

An Introduction to
Rhetorical Theory

The Greek philosopher Aristotle defined humans as speaking animals and then concluded that rhetoric is instrumental in our most important decisions. He knew that rhetoric is pervasive. Whether it is in the form of a presidential speech, an advertisement for a car, an argument with a roommate, or the act of talking to ourselves, rhetoric operates to influence behavior, change attitudes, and articulate opinions. It has changed the world and our perception of it. Would the United States have been as willing to engage in a cold war with the Soviet Union had not Winston Churchill warned that an "Iron Curtain" had descended from the Baltic to the Adriatic Sea? Would John Kennedy have won his remarkably close election to the presidency had he not envisioned a "New Frontier" for America? If Martin Luther King Jr. did not "have a dream," would the civil rights movement have succeeded in getting legislation passed? If Barack Obama had not defended freedom of speech and religion in a speech in Cairo, Egypt, would there have been an Arab Spring filled with revolutions across North Africa? Had Mitt Romney not improved his debating skills in the spring of 2012, would he have become the Republican nominee?

Clearly, the strategies of persuasive communication are at work all the time; they are so close to us that we often take them for granted. In doing so we ignore how they shape our lives, and that is a mistake if we want to control our own destinies.

So let us begin with an important question: What makes rhetoric different from other forms of communication? One of the themes of this book is that rhetoric is a definable art form, and rhetorical studies therefore constitute a legitimate academic discipline. An art form, or what the Greeks called a *techné*, is a body of principles that can generate an artifact, a work of creation. *Technés* are teachable disciplines that enhance natural talent. Rhetoric is one of the oldest members of any curriculum since it was taught by the ancient Greeks, many of whom wrote books on the subject.

Since rhetoric is a kind of communication, it makes sense to determine what characteristics make it different from other forms of communication. In general, communication is the attempt to elicit and/or transfer meaning and can be broken into three major types: informative communication adds to our knowledge; entertaining communication holds our attention and fascinates our minds; rhetorical communication goes beyond both by attempting to persuade ourselves and others to change actions, beliefs, attitudes, and/or opinions. These divisions of communication are better seen as dimensions of discourse. That is, a lecture by an official of the National Aeronautics and Space Administration is mainly informational, but it can also contain a rhetorical dimension if the lecture *persuades* us to support a larger budget for NASA. Films such as *Saving Private Ryan* or *The Help* are mainly entertaining, but they also reinforce patriotism or raise questions about racial tolerance and thus have a rhetorical dimension. Jon Stewart of *The Daily Show* is amusing, but his purpose is to reveal the hypocrisy and errors of politicians and, hence, is mainly rhetorical. This book focuses on the rhetorical dimension of communication.

DEFINING RHETORIC

We need not venture beyond our own consciousness to find rhetoric functioning; rhetoric is rooted deep in our psyche and operates at very fundamental levels of our being. First, it helps us understand what we experience because we must convince ourselves that our experiences are true (this form of rhetoric is intrapersonal). When you see a rose, the process is simple. You align the vision before you with retrieved past knowledge of roses, make the comparison, and *persuade* yourself that you have indeed seen a rose. After a while, the process becomes intuitive, an automatic recognition takes place of which you are sure. In other cases, the persuasive process may take longer, as when we think we see friends at a distance but must catch up to them to confirm our conclusions.

When you smell an object, you decide if it has a pleasant fragrance based on an interpretation of sensed data. To accomplish this interpretation, you must compare the smell to the memory of smells stored in your brain. (In his famous book *Remembrance of Things Past*, Marcel Proust is reminded of his childhood when he smells the fragrance of a Madeleine cookie.) Based on that comparison, you assess the smell—that is, you *name* it to be pleasant if you persuade yourself that it qualifies for that label. The smell can also help you retrieve memories of times before when you have enjoyed or been annoyed by the smell. In short, you make a choice based on the probabilities available to you and then assign a word or phrase to that choice to make sense out of it.

As Aristotle noted, intrapersonal rhetoric is often converted to interpersonal persuasion: *the way we persuade ourselves is the way we persuade others*. If you decide to see a film because you believe it is well acted and entertaining, you may try to convince others to see the film for the same reasons. Listen to arguments over whether films are good or bad, and you will hear people talking about what convinced them of their opinion: "I couldn't follow the plot in *Harry Potter* so I wouldn't see it again if they paid me, and neither should you." "The graphics in *Avatar* were so awesome I could see it ten times. Do you want to come with me?" In most cases, the reason you like the movie is the reason you give to urge others to go see it.

Rhetoric is also *epistemic*, a way to come to know things that cannot be known through other types of discourse whether they be informative or entertaining. Rhetoric has a "making-known" function. It explains what we and others discover. This making-known function has very important everyday consequences as any doctor can tell you. For example, scientists developed a drug called risperidone to treat paranoia; in some cases it not only halts a person's delusions but reverses their dementia. The problem for doctors who prescribe the drug is how to convince a paranoid person to take a pill. One method many doctors use to convince a paranoid person to take risperidone is to compare the drug's effect on brain chemicals to the way insulin works on sugar levels in diabetics. The analogy is not exact, but it is persuasive. Many patients have been cured of their paranoia because doctors found a way to make known to them how risperidone works.

Rhetoric is also epistemic because it overcomes the limitations of other forms of discourse. For example, logical discourse is limited to proven and true premises, valid forms of reasoning, or accepted definitions and symbolic notations. However, when accurate and complete data are unavailable to us, rhetoric is essential to making sense out of a probabilistic and sometimes chaotic world. The world is not always a rational place, nor are individuals always open to reasonable appeals. Sometimes, as in the case of emergencies, we don't even have time to construct a logical appeal. Making a case out of syllogisms to convince people to clear an area containing an explosive device might not be efficient or safe. Instead, one assesses the emotional state of those in the room, edits the information to make a quick decision, and firmly and sincerely delivers it in an authoritative fashion. The delivery of that information, the tone of voice, the language selected, and the framing of the message are matters of life and death—they are rhetorical, not logical.

Rhetoric is essential to human existence because it can deal with the mental states that affect our perceptions. It is impossible not to be emotional in some way, whether that be a state of apathy or agitation. Our state of mind or mood affects how we hear and understand things. Thus, discourse that deals with human emotion is more effective than discourse that fails to take it into account. Since rhetoric does deal with psychological states, it is invaluable to survival and success in this world.

As an art form that facilitates persuasion of diverse populations, rhetoric recognizes that word choice and the building of images play an important role in gaining adherence to an idea, a policy, or a personal commitment. It recognizes also that the delivery of messages can influence how they are received. Because of its concern for style and oral delivery, rhetoric has sometimes been dismissed as a knack or mere sophistry, as we shall see when we examine Plato's theories. Because it can be used to advance an evil cause as well as a just one, it has been condemned as amoral. This text takes issue with both of these hypotheses by arguing that style and delivery are wedded to thought, particularly in the mind of the audience. If we fail to impart this art to those who seek to do good in the world, they might well fall victim to those who skillfully advance evil, particularly in societies that value freedom of expression. Even when rhetoric is used primarily for display or entertainment, artistic discourse can evoke emotions that lead to a deeper understanding of self, elicit a cathartic release, and/or inspire us to transcendent levels of spirituality.

Rhetoric is a keystone of education, a place of connection for many disciplines. That's why the study of it will introduce you to the major figures in Western civilization. Yet it is by no means an esoteric undertaking about an arcane art form. It is relevant to us every day of our lives. Recent surveys indicate that when hiring new employees, business leaders put communication skills above all others. The major cause of divorce is communication failure. Every time we vote for a political candidate, we do so in part because of our perception of that candidate. That perception is influenced by the candidate's rhetorical skills, from the mispronunciation of words to the ability to present accurate data effectively. Every time we make a presentation, whether it be at the dinner table, to a classroom full of students, or to the Joint Chiefs of Staff, we use our rhetorical talents.

This endorsement of the study of rhetoric is based on at least three very important phenomena. First, for the most part, the decisions that are made by societies and governments are based on probable, not certain, truths. Therefore, we need to be persuaded to accept them.

Second, what makes us human also makes us rhetorical. *We are decision-making creatures capable of overruling our own instincts.* Developing the habit of making good decisions is critical to human existence. We are constantly persuading ourselves, making and remaking decisions, debating and redebating actions. We are reflective; we can live in the past, present, and future. As a result, we are constantly thinking in ways that other creatures do not. Thus, humans need to become proficient in rhetoric if they are to be effective decision makers—that is, persons who lead authentic lives instead of being led by others.

Third, the need for rhetoric grows out of the fact that the human mind does not usually tolerate that which cannot be explained. For the most part, the human mind is offended by the irrational, the absurd, and the chaotic. Humans are unique because they wonder about things; they question; they are curious; and they need to make sense of what they perceive. Yet, the world is not always subject to a rational ordering. As symbol users, we have developed nonlogical discursive talents to cope with this condition.

The noted psychologist Bruno Bettelheim, in an interview before his death, weighed the alternatives he faced rhetorically as an aging person. In this interview the reasons to live are compared to the reasons to die.

> Things I enjoyed are no longer available to me. . . . I like to walk. I like to hike. Now when I read, I get tired. . . . Part of the problem is that our society doesn't know what to do with old people. We want to put them away. . . . It is very hard to go on living if you no longer feel useful or very important. . . . I've had some disappointments in my private life. There was the death of my wife, to whom I was deeply attached and whom I miss very much. . . . I envy those people who believe that in an afterlife you will be reunited with your loved ones. That's a very comfortable thought, but I can't believe it.[1]

Bettelheim survived the Nazi death camps at Buchenwald and Dachau but could not survive his own rhetoric. After this interview, Bettelheim talked himself into taking his own life. One wishes that Bettelheim would have understood the power of rhetoric to transcend logic and to "make sense" where other forms of communication fail. Many who have considered suicide have either talked themselves out of it or others have talked them out of it using rhetorical appeals. It is just that fundamental.

WHAT IS THEORY?

To this juncture, we have seen that rhetoric has many functions and touches on many different important philosophical questions. Bettelheim's case warns us that since rhetoric is involved in the most important decisions of our lives, it is *ontological;* that is, it concerns the "why" we exist and "how" we exist. Rhetoric's making-known function is epistemological because it helps us obtain knowledge. Thus, rhetoric touches on two of the most important branches of our lives: how we learn things and how we live. That is why we need to understand how it works.

Theories make sense of seemingly random phenomena and explain how things work. Geologists propose theories that make sense out of earthquakes. Physicists create theories that explain the smallest particles of the universe, even though they are not observable with the finest microscopes. Sociologists have theories about collective behavior that explain mob activity. A persuasive theory explains the relevant variables and overcomes contradictions. Theory explains gathered evidence in a compelling way. *Sound theories in some sense have been verified in reality and are very persuasive because they resonate with reality.*

This book presents theories about how rhetoric works and the relevance it has to our culture and ourselves. It examines the major theories about the rhetorical process. It explores the exciting relationship between rhetoric and philosophy. Philosophy is often critical of rhetoric because of rhetoric's bias for the pragmatic, the expedient, and the ongoing. Rhetoric is often so caught up with the everyday world that it does not have time for the reflection needed to pursue philosophical aims. Rhetoric is often critical of philosophy because it is too remote from the realities of existence. Philosophy's quest for the ideal limits its contribution to the real. As we shall see, David Hume's philosophical position (see chapter 8) that we cannot logically separate cause from coincidence is elegant but usually quite useless in everyday life, as Hume himself admitted. However, rhetoric and philosophy also have a synergy, with philosophy sometimes providing theory on which new rhetorics can be built. Rhetoric can hold philosophy's feet to the fire of the real world by showing how applicable or inapplicable philosophical positions can be.

For example, Albert Camus, the French existentialist of post–World War II France, asserted that humans are alone in an absurd universe and are forced to act without reasonable grounds for their most important decisions. For better or worse, rhetoric must be at the heart of the most important decisions we make because it is the only thing that can cope with the absurdity of the human condition. Hence, Camus' philosophical musings provide us with a new rhetorical theory that helps us cope with the absurdities of life.

This book is a history of rhetorical theory that illustrates how relevant it has been to important thinkers and their audiences. The more knowledgeable we become about the interaction between rhetoric and philosophy, the more we shall see the relevance of both to our lives. To punctuate this point, the book provides examples of the effective use of rhetorical principles to generate persuasive discourse. One theme will emerge early and remain with us throughout this study: in times when probability is emphasized, rhetoric flourishes; in times when the truth is "known," rhetoric is marginalized. Dogmatism is an enemy of the development of rhetorical theory. A supporting theme will also surface: where humans have more opportunity to speak freely, rhetorical theory flourishes; where humans are restricted in terms of freedom of expression, rhetorical theory tends to atrophy.

We begin our explorations at the macro level by establishing an all-encompassing view of rhetorical theory—in essence, it is a guidebook for the various theories and parts of theories we will encounter on the march from ancient Greece to contemporary society. This overview can best be accomplished by asking what makes something rhetorical. The answer is, when it is suasory; that is, when it tries to change an opinion, attitude, belief or behavior. Attempts to elicit change exist in time and space. Thus, we need to ask what makes a situation rhetorical.

Aristotle believed that rhetoric was situational and defined it as *"the art of finding in any given case the available means of persuasion."* Twenty-three centuries later, literary and rhetorical critic Kenneth Burke placed his dramatistic approach to rhetoric in the *scene,* which included not only the stage of action but the backdrop of values, attitudes, and opinions for the speech. Jean-François Lyotard, the postmodern critic, argued that universal contexts marginalized various groups and peoples; local and rhetorical contexts are required for the proper identification of all voices. These and other theorists understand that the situation limits the resources available to speakers and places prior constraints on them. But the situation also provides speakers with unique opportunities to engage in persuasion. The situation is the context, the setting, or the scene of the rhetorical event. Since rhetoric is pragmatic and about persuading someone, somewhere, with some message, it is always in some context.

A SITUATIONAL METATHEORY

The contemporary theorist Lloyd Bitzer helps us understand the art of rhetoric by synthesizing various theories that have preceded him into a metatheory of rhetoric, a kind of organizing platform that gives us an essential overview of the constituents of rhetoric.[2] Bitzer wrote that "a work of rhetoric . . . comes into existence for the sake of something beyond itself; it functions ultimately to produce action or change in the world; it performs some task."[3] He identified three features that encompass all of the relevant variables in a rhetorical situation: exigence, audience, and constraints. Creators of speeches, editorials, or any other rhetorical artifacts use these categories to construct their products. Because rhetoric is an art based on audience adaptation, the bulk of the theories we will examine concern the interaction of the situation, speaker, message, channel and audience.[4]

Is there a problem with the current situation that rhetoric could solve? The problem is an *exigence*—some sort of urgent deficiency, privation, or need. Bitzer called it an imperfection marked by urgency. Without an exigence, perceived or real, there is no need for rhetoric. The exigence can be as simple as a child begging for food. It can be as complicated as the desire to utter the proper eulogy for a slain leader.

If there is change to be made, there must be agents of change—the *rhetorical audience*, persons who can remedy the problem. The nearby parent can supply the child with food and becomes the audience when alerted by the cries or words of the child. The followers of the slain leader must be induced to mourn; they become the audience of the eulogizer's speech.

Audience is one of the most important elements of rhetorical studies because so many of the strategies used in persuasive situations are based on appeals to an audience. Furthermore, the audience can determine the context for the speech, or the audience can be a product of the context. If an audience has gathered to mourn someone who has died, the audience expects to hear a eulogy. If it has gathered to decide an issue, it expects rhetoric that addresses a policy decision. *Rhetoric works to constitute audiences;* that is, speakers often seek to bring kindred spirits together and to unify them into a public. Ralph Nader, for example, was more instrumental than any other speaker in creating a public out of consumers. The evangelist Billy Graham created a Christian public from the audiences for his "crusades." Finally, rhetorical theory often searches for ideal audiences that allow speakers to create ideal speeches. Some theorists such as Plato believe that the ideal audience consists of persons who are enlightened and well versed in logic and would decide every issue on reasonable grounds. For them, the ideal speech would appeal to reason only and present the most objective view possible. But for others, the ideal audience might be spiritual or emotionally sensitive, and an entirely different kind of speech would provide the ideal model. Thus, notions of audience are crucial to rhetorical studies.

If there is an exigence, and an audience that can act to solve the exigence, then there must be rhetorical strategies that will motivate the audience to action. These *constraints* arise out of the situation inclusive of the speaker and audience. Constraints are not only the limitations placed on speech by the situation, they are also the available means of shaping an appeal in a given situation. In this way, the situational model includes many of the elements of Aristotle's system of strategies (see chapter 4) under constraints; they are the shapers of the rhetorical appeal. For example, while the child begging for food has relatively few strategic options, the eulogizer probably has a great many, including recalling the life of the slain leader, playing on the emotions of the audience, delivering the speech in somber tones, or referring to the place of the eulogy and the events of the day. Speeches that remove the exigence, that is, that correct the imperfection, are fitting responses to the situation.

In general, then, the rhetorical situation consists of a problem, an audience, and constraints available to a speaker to help shape the message. However, there have been several correctives to Bitzer's model, one of the most important of which is to take into account audience and speaker perceptions.[5] Although Bitzer argued that exigences were real and could be determined objectively, some exigences perceived by an audience and/or created by a speaker may not be accurate or even real.[6] For example, in the 1960 presidential election, John Kennedy alleged that there was a "missile gap" between U.S. and Soviet forces. He created the perception of an exigence that required action, even though the exigence was exaggerated at best and contrived at worst. However, it was real enough to those who *perceived* the threat to our security to be real, and many of them voted for Kennedy because of it.

The introduction of perceptions creates the possibility for multiple exigences, multiple audiences, multiple constraints, and multiple responses that better reflect the dynamics of complex rhetorical situations likely to exist in the postmodern era. For example, the recommendation of postmodernist Michel Foucault (whose ideas we will examine in chapter 13) to analyze "power as diffused throughout multiple social sites"[7] would reduce the situational model to many smaller locations where speeches are performed to solve problems. Such a perspective would be useful in analyzing the ecological movement, since the fight is carried on at multiple sites—from nuclear dumps to beaches to courtrooms to international conferences. In this case, there are many audiences, and some of them are marginalized by the political process and might be ignored if we did not explore the multiplicity of the rhetorical situation.[8]

Rhetoric in the Contemporary World

As a preview to the many theories of rhetoric this book examines, we can analyze persuasion in the contemporary world and use the situational model to help catalogue the strategies employed. President George W. Bush declared a "war" on terrorism in several speeches delivered in September of 2001, the most important of which was given to a joint session of Congress on September 20, 2001. The first speech in this series was delivered on the night of September 11, 2001, following a horrific attack on the Twin Towers in New York City and on the Pentagon near the U.S. Capitol. This speech was delivered from the Oval Office after the president, who had been visiting Florida, was ferried in secure aircraft to several other locations. The first speech attempted to calm and assure the public while outlining an important problem that needed to be solved: the United States had been attacked with impunity on its own soil and nearly 3,000 people had been killed. Later, the president gave a eulogy at the National Cathedral and then the famous speech of September 20.

By the end of the speeches, the number of people who approved of President Bush's handling of the situation soared above 90 percent, the highest percentage enjoyed by any president in history. Congress promptly passed a number of measures that the president requested including strengthening homeland security, increasing spending on national defense, and stimulating the economy. By these measures, one would have to assume that Bush's speeches were very effective. However, the situation was much more complicated than that. Using the situational model, we can catalogue the complex dimensions of the president's rhetoric. He found an exigence (the terrorist attack) and explained it to the public and to Congress (how these audiences serve in a problem-solving capacity is discussed in the section on audiences). The speeches (using available constraints) seemed to be effective in terms of increasing awareness of the problem, achieving a national consensus, and convincing Congress to provide legislative aid. However, these standard means of assessing effectiveness fail to reveal the complexity of the situation. An analysis of its constituent parts demonstrates that the president's antiterrorist rhetoric was derived from the multiple exigences, audiences, and constraints involved in the rhetorical situation. An examination of each helps us to understand how rhetoric works in the real world.

Exigences

Given the gravity of the attack on the nation, the *controlling* exigence in this situation was readily apparent. Terrorism, which had mainly been experienced in other countries or in relatively few and isolated cases in the United States, such as Timothy McVeigh's attack in Oklahoma City, was now present in the United States on a larger scale than ever and was evidently the work of a long-term conspiracy directed by a fundamentalist fanatic operating from Afghanistan. In his September 20 speech, the president described the exigence in the following ways:

> Tonight, we are a country awakening to danger. . . . [E]nemies of freedom committed
> an act of war against our country. . . . There are thousands of these terrorists in more
> than 60 countries. . . . Our enemy is a radical network of terrorists and every govern-

ment that supports them. . . . These terrorists kill not merely to end lives but to disrupt and end a way of life.[9]

However, terrorism was only one of many exigences at the time of Bush's speeches. Given the United States' political system, Bush had to be concerned with his political popularity, a factor that constrained his purpose whether he wanted it to or not. To put it another way, *once we turn from a single exigence to consider multiple exigences, we open the door to the questions of intent and motive on the part of the speaker.* Of interest here is the fact that the same exigence that constrains Bush also constrains the audience. By the next election, those listening to Bush would assume the role of voters and would render a judgment about him. Their judgment about his ability to hold the office of president would be influenced by how he handled the terrorist crisis. It is easy to imagine that in a dictatorship, the orator (if constrained to speak at all) would merely lay out policy regardless of how the populace felt about it. However, given the institutional constraints from which Bush operated, his response to the crisis could place public opinion squarely behind his leadership and preempt Democratic efforts to use the issue to political advantage in the next congressional or presidential campaign. The fact is that Bush had barely won a questionable election that was not officially decided until December 13, 2000, by the Supreme Court. He was not known as an effective public speaker. According to press commentary and poll data, his speech from the Oval Office immediately after the attacks failed to unite or inspire the nation. Thus, a secondary exigence for the president, which greatly affected how well he would deal with the primary exigence, involved his ability to command respect and demonstrate leadership.

The rhetorical context frames the kind of speaking that will take place and carves out the audience that will receive it. In Athens, all the citizens of the city were allowed to come to the assembly to hear speeches and to vote on policy. In Imperial Rome, Caesars ruled by decree and speeches were mainly confined to the courts and forums of display. In a democracy, getting antiterrorist legislation through the congressional quagmire is a major undertaking. Perhaps this is why Bush engaged in a campaign of persuasion in several different venues.

President Bush may have realized that other exigences included terrorist-related crises in foreign nations, such as Turkey, Germany, and France, where government leaders had tried to stop terrorist attacks for years. To present a united front against terrorism, to use their bases for attacks, Bush had to appeal to their leaders or at least say nothing that might turn them against the United States. The terrorist leader claimed to have come from a Muslim sect; Bush faced the exigence of winning over Muslim states, particularly Pakistan, that would be essential to offensive operations against the Al-Qaeda network. The point is that the speaker's selection of an exigence or an aspect of a problem can make a great deal of difference in the message that is conveyed.

Audiences

The problem of multi-audiences in the contemporary world reinforces the fragmented nature of communication. For all the exigences that existed in this situation, there were several audiences that affected them and were affected by the exigences. For example, the American people were voters and taxpayers who helped shape public policy and kept the economy growing. Recognizing this fact, the president targeted an audience composed of those who could endorse his policies and influence their congressional representatives. On September 20, he appealed directly to them by organizing his speech around significant rhetorical questions, questions drawn from that public:

> Americans have many questions tonight. Americans are asking, "Who attacked our country?" . . . Americans are asking, "Why do you hate us?" . . . Americans are asking, "How will we fight and win this war?" . . . America is successful because of the hard work and creativity and enterprise of our people. These were the true strengths of our economy before September 11, and they are our strengths today.

Since these people could alter the crisis at a grassroots level and could pressure Congress to pass legislation, they formed a primary rhetorical audience. They were capable of modifying the situation in tangible ways, and they saw the problem as an immediate one.

The nation's lawmakers were also a rhetorical audience because of their ability to allocate funds and to strengthen laws that applied to terrorists. The president addressed them directly:

> I thank the Congress for its leadership at such an important time. All of America was touched on the evening of the tragedy to see Republicans and Democrats joined together on the steps of this Capitol singing "God Bless America." . . . We will come together to improve air safety, to dramatically expand the number of air marshals on domestic flights and take new measures to prevent hijacking. We will come together to give law enforcement the additional tools it needs to track down terror here at home.

The governments of foreign nations, especially Islamic countries (because of their direct contact with the Al-Qaeda syndicate and their knowledge of its leader, Osama bin Laden), were also rhetorical audiences. Bush addressed the United States' friends and allies by stating what he admired and wanted from these countries:

> We will not forget South Korean children gathering to pray outside our embassy in Seoul, or the prayers of sympathy offered at a mosque in Cairo. . . . Dozens of Pakistanis, more than 130 Israelis, more than 250 citizens of India, men and women from El Salvador, Iran, Mexico, and Japan, and hundreds of British citizens. . . . An attack on one is an attack on all. The civilized world is rallying to America's side. They understand that if this terror goes unpunished, their own citizens may be next.

The president also addressed the leadership in Afghanistan, the Taliban, who were protecting bin Laden. They certainly formed a rhetorical audience since they could surrender him and ease the terrorist situation.

> By aiding and abetting murder, the Taliban regime is committing murder. And tonight the United States of America makes the following demands on the Taliban. Deliver to United States' authority all of the leaders of Al-Qaeda who hide in your land. Release all foreign nationals, including American citizens you have unjustly imprisoned. Protect foreign journalists, diplomats and aid workers in your country. . . . Give the United States full access to terrorists' training camps. . . . These demands are not open to negotiation or discussion.

At the same time, the president separated the extremists from the rest of the Muslim world, and made a special appeal to another audience, Muslims.

> Al Qaeda is to terror what the Mafia is to crime. . . . The terrorists practice a fringe form of Islamic extremism that has been rejected by Muslim scholars and the vast majority of Muslim clerics. . . . The enemy of America is not our many Muslim friends. It is not our Arab friends. Our enemy is a radical network of terrorists and every government that supports them.

The speech of September 20, then, is much more comprehensive than earlier speeches given by the president on this crisis. Its effectiveness is in part due to its inclusive nature with regard to relevant audiences and its carving away of extremist groups.

Constraints

Rhetorical strategies should be based on situational factors that impinge on the message, the speaker, and/or the audiences. In the September 20 address, President Bush referred to many in the audience who were present to reinforce his message. He thanked the leadership of Congress; he acknowledged the presence of Prime Minister Blair from Great Britain; he asked the wife of one of those killed by terrorists to stand. He also referred to the occasion itself, acknowledging that normally when a president comes before a joint session of Congress, it is to present the State of the Union address: "We have seen the state of our union in the endurance of rescuers working past exhaustion." Aristotle called references to items external to the speech "inartistic proofs"; those who advance theories of courtroom speaking call them evidence; modern media theorists call them props. They are drawn from the context of the speech and provide one of the many bases of argument for persuasion.

Situational constraints were also used to strengthen the president's credibility in terms of his appearing to demonstrate expertise. This particular constraint served to overcome critics who charged that the president was not up to the job. For example, the president's description of the enemy and its host was highly detailed:

> This group and its leader . . . are linked to many other organizations in different countries, including the Egyptian Islamic Jihad, the Islamic Movement of Uzbekistan. . . . Women are not allowed to attend school. You can be jailed for owning a television. Religion can be practiced only as their leaders dictate. A man can be jailed in Afghanistan if his beard is not long enough.

This sense of expertise was enhanced by another constraint arising from the situation, the president's delivery. He overcame a reputation for being a self-conscious and mispronouncing speaker by delivering his speech in a periodic cadence with hardly a misstep. His delivery was no doubt aided by rehearsal, and the appearance of fluency was induced by the use of teleprompters.

Constraints are also used to carve out an audience and manipulate its opinions. Bush and his advisors knew that the office of the presidency and the unique nature of the crisis presented them with opportunities to shape public opinion. They used constraints that were based on audience perceptions of the problem. To the extent that Bush was able to draw a congruent picture of the problem using these constraints, he was successful in keeping his audience with him.

Bush's success may also be explained by a close reading of his word choice. It was well adjusted to the situation. For example, to conclude his description of the terrible events of September 11, he said: "Americans have known the casualties of war, but not at the center of a great city on a peaceful morning. Americans have known surprise attacks, but never before on thousands of civilians. All of this was brought upon us in a single day, and night fell on a different world." We have already examined his use of rhetorical questions to organize the speech for his audience. His use of parallel structure and repetition also gave the speech a unity and solemnity to meet the occasion. Most of all, the imagery in this speech brought many scenes alive for his audiences in ways that made the speech the most vivid of his career.

> Afghanistan's people have been brutalized, many are starving and many have fled. . . . By sacrificing human life to serve their radical visions, by abandoning every value except the will to power, they follow the path of fascism, Nazism, and totalitarianism. And they will follow that path all the way to where it ends: in history's unmarked grave of discarded lies.

These images helped to bring the emotions of the audience closer to the surface and helped identify with the president. They also presented a vivid picture of the enemy, one that alienated the audience from it.

This example reveals how complicated a rhetorical situation can be and how important it is to sort it out properly. While there may be a controlling exigence in any rhetorical situation, there are likely to be other exigences in play, some perceived by the speaker and some perceived by the audience. There are also likely to be multiple audiences in a world fragmented by media. That condition leads to many available modes of persuasion that can be drawn from any rhetorical situation. Thus, rhetoric is a complex art form that requires much study to master so that we can provide responses that are not only effective but fitting.

CONCLUSION

Problems searching for solutions are not always objective realities; they may be created by speakers and/or perceived by audiences. Just as a speaker may have more than one controlling motive, a situation may have more than one exigence. Thus, we ought to examine each exigence not only in terms of its objectivity arising out of the situation but also in terms of its subjectivity from the speaker's and the audiences' points of view. As poll data and other indices reveal, audience and speaker perceptions can alter reality in complex ways that must be dealt with by sophisticated speakers and critics. Constraints need to be particularized in terms of these multiple perspectives and should incorporate more than the strategic uses of language that we will examine in this text.

Beginning with the platform of the rhetorical situation, we can examine what parts of which rhetorical theories prove relevant to our lives. Some theorists will focus on the role of the speaker in the rhetorical situation; they are likely to emphasize how one builds a reputation or provides a model for persuading an audience. Other theorists will focus on the audience, arguing that what makes rhetoric a unique art form is how the strategic use of language arises from the audience. Other theorists will focus on constraints, studying style in language, delivery techniques, or organizational strategies. Still others will focus on the situation itself, turning it into a set of questions that can be asked to generate a speech or a scene from which the speaking occasion can be viewed as a drama or a story. What unifies these theories is their contribution to a unique art form that seeks to find the available means of persuasion in any given situation. From the analysis of such situations we can generate new theories and refine ancient ones.

Study Questions

1. Provide specific examples of intrapersonal, interpersonal, and mass media uses of persuasion.

2. Is Aristotle correct to assert that the way we persuade ourselves is the way we persuade other people? How would you modify his theory?

3. Demonstrate three ways in which rhetoric is more useful in the everyday world than logic.

4. What is the relationship between rhetoric and decision making?

5. Define the constituents of situational rhetoric using a contemporary problem that needs a solution.

Notes

[1] In Celeste Fremon, "Love and Death," *Los Angeles Times Magazine* (January 17, 1991): 20. The interview was published after his suicide.

[2] Immediately following its publication, Bitzer's "The Rhetorical Situation" was absorbed into the consciousness of rhetorical theorists and critics; it was used to determine whether speeches were "fitting responses" to certain events. Lloyd F. Bitzer, "The Rhetorical Situation," *Philosophy and Rhetoric,* 1 (1968): 1–14.

[3] Ibid., pp. 3–4.

[4] Ibid., p. 8.

[5] Richard E. Vatz, "The Myth of the Rhetorical Situation," *Philosophy and Rhetoric,* 6 (1973): 155; Craig R. Smith and Scott Lybarger, "Bitzer's Model Revised," *Communication Quarterly,* 44 (1996): 197–213.

[6] Scott Consigny, "Rhetoric and Its Situations," *Philosophy and Rhetoric,* 7 (1974): 176.

[7] S. Best and D. Kellner, *Postmodern Theory: Critical Interrogations* (New York: The Guilford Press, 1991), p. 39.

[8] In 1980, Bitzer published a revision of his original article "to remove ambiguities and difficulties identified by colleagues." L. F. Bitzer, "Functional Communication: A Situational Perspective," in *Rhetoric in Transition: Studies in the Nature and Uses of Rhetoric,* E. White, ed. (State College: Pennsylvania State U. Press, 1980), p. 21.

[9] President George W. Bush, "Address to Joint Session of Congress," (September 20, 2001), reprinted in the *Los Angeles Times* (September 21, 2001): A5. All the quotations that follow are from this transcript.

PART I

Rhetoric in the Ancient World

Plato and Aristotle walking through the stoa.

Rhetorical Dimensions of Myth and Narrative

The use of sounds as symbols for objects, feelings, perceptions, and so forth—that is, language—may have developed over 60,000 years ago. That led to the formation of communities and to the development of the first myths at a time when both storytelling and argument were considered forms of *logos*, words that made sense of the world. Unable to tolerate the random nature of the stars, our ancestors, whether European or Native American, African or Asian, imposed patterns on the heavens and attached meaning to them. The elements of nature were often given god-like standing. Ehécatl was the Aztec god of wind; Chaac was the Mayan god of rain; Illapa was the Incan god of thunder.

Myth is a meta-language that crosses cultures as it makes sense of the nonrational. For example, while evidence of reasoning exists in the earliest Greek texts, *mythos* rationalized a world where logic failed to provide rational order. While the term "rhetoric" did not appear until fourth century BC, rhetorical discourse had already rationalized the absurd and the unexplainable. In fact, the Greeks even had a goddess named Peitho who gave the gift of persuasion; appropriately, her daughter, Pheme, gave the gift of fame. As another example of myth, take the case of the array of stars known by the metaphorical phrase, the Milky Way; the stars are so thick they appear almost as if they were thin clouds. In studying the sky at night, the early Romans had trouble accounting for this Milky Way. So they built a myth that would make sense of this phenomenon. They claimed that Jupiter fathered Hercules by the mortal Alcmene, an act of adultery. To assure Hercules would be immortal, Jupiter took the babe to Jupiter's sleeping wife, Juno, and had the child suckle her breast. Since Juno had not had a baby, when she awoke she pulled the babe from her breast, spraying the heavens with her milk thereby creating the Milky Way.[1] And if you do not think that myth and metaphor ever rule our thinking, just listen to talk about the moon "rising" and the sun "setting."

17

In our time, myth imbues rules of society with moral force. It transforms the vague thought into the clear sentence, the unexplainable scientific theory into the understandable metaphor, and the unmotivated into the proactive. It connects us with the metaphysical and grounds us in the material. In the preliterate world, rhetoric served to rationalize the environment in mythic terms, and it converted naked desire into acceptable cultural values. Psychologists have demonstrated that fantasy chains can motivate group cohesion and action. Writing in 1972, Ernest Bormann converted this finding to a method for explaining rhetorical vision; rhetorical critics quickly began to examine "fantasy themes" in persuasive speeches. Akin to Kenneth Burke's dramatistic approach (see chapter 11), Bormann saw a rhetorical world of heroes and villains, sinners and saints created by a speaker seeking to convince an audience to accept his or her fantasy. America becomes the "promised land." The Soviet Union becomes an "evil empire." The race in space takes place on a "new frontier."[2]

Humans, unable to tolerate irrational and anarchic impulses, devised myths to teach lessons to communities badly in need of order. Myths that meet this exigence are more than good stories; they have a moral. Oedipus kills a man he later learns was his father; he marries a woman he later learns is his mother. The moral: he could not escape the fate that had been predicted at his birth. Human decision making can't overcome the will of the gods.

One of the earliest Judeo-Christian myths is about the development of diverse languages. Imagine that in your explorations from village to village you discovered that each used a different language, a language that was unintelligible to you. Baffled, you would seek an explanation. The explanation provided by the writers of the Old Testament was that humans in their arrogance attempted to build a tower to reach the place where God dwelled. To punish this insult, God caused them to speak in different tongues, reducing their communication to babble, thereby preventing completion of their tower. The story not only provides a rationale for the many languages one encounters in the world, it provides a moral: do not attempt to become an equal with God.

Whether we read the *Iliad* and the *Odyssey* of Homer or Aesop's fables, we find lessons that endorse particular values. In fact, the early Greek and Roman teachers of speech often required their students to build a story around a saying, making up their own fables. They understood that stories we spin into myths are not always national or cultural; they can be personal and serve as guides in our personal decision making. The great warrior Achilles was taught to speak by Phoenix, who also taught Achilles to be a doer of great deeds. Homer believed that speaking persuasively is almost as important as acting heroically; he combined the two in his ideal hero Odysseus. Homer popularized his own stories by reciting them from memory since he was blind. He became so popular that he was invited to Athens and Argos and to many other cities in the Greek world.

Perhaps the best-known speech written by Shakespeare is Hamlet's soliloquy on suicide. In his anguish after learning that his uncle killed his father, Hamlet vacillates between suicide and revenge, posing the major question "to be or not to be." Hamlet's intrapersonal debate contains several arguments, but none of his evidence is sufficient to justify either taking his life or killing his uncle. Under the circumstances, the rhetorical arguments and pictures Hamlet draws help him make up his mind. He opts for the "slings and arrows of outrageous fortune" in this world rather than "perchance to

Athena, protector of Athens, is honored in cities around the world.

dream" forever in some hellish unconscious state. Hamlet thereby demonstrates that rhetoric is crucial to decision making and inherent in the most important decisions of our lives.

Like Hamlet, we are often compelled to act even though we do not have sufficient evidence for our decisions. Dealing with probabilities is one of the most important—if not *the* most important—things we do. We want to make the sensible decision, but how is that to be determined in an irrational world where information is incomplete? The role of language in decision making is obvious: the symbolic use of language is intimately linked to making sense of the world. Our very survival depends on our ability to cope with an ever-changing, often irrational environment. It has been that way since the beginning of time, and that is why storytelling is the oldest form of rhetoric.

MYTH AND NARRATIVE AS RHETORIC

The purpose of this chapter is to explore the rhetorical dimensions of myth and narrative. How do myths function to make sense of the world? How does narrative make a collection of facts into a coherent and persuasive story? Myths are stories that have taken on historic and cultural dimensions; they are narratives that have become part of the fabric of our lives. They are often the docudramas of the actions that gods have taken on this earth. It is important to note that narratives are a way of remembering events. By telling the story, we recall what happened, for example, at the battle of

Gettysburg during the Civil War. But we also need to note that narrative functions to help us forget. By reshaping events into narratives, speakers often leave certain unpleasant or disagreeable facts out. Speakers can stress what they believe are good things, such as heroism in battle, and/or leave out bad things, such as cowardice or carnage that occurred on the battlefield.

Since prehistoric times myths and narratives have been used for entertainment, but they also built tribes, cultures, and nations. Myths were used to advance values and to order lives, villages, and the world. Schoolchildren in the United States were taught that General and then President George Washington had never told a lie, and, therefore, neither should they. He was called the "Father of our country" and exemplified the virtue of a national culture. Whether true or not, one of mythology's most important functions is to inspire great creativity. The mythology of the Germanic peoples inspired the operas of Richard Wagner; the mythology of the "Old West" inspired countless classic films in America. Imaginative myths inspire imaginative responses, which can be even more inspirational than the original story.

Even today, mythmaking serves many of the same purposes.[3] The Harry Potter children's stories, which have been converted into films, may be seen as modern myths because they endorse certain transcendent values that help children cope with the world. For example, in *Harry Potter and the Sorcerer's Stone*, the high-flying soccer-like game demonstrates the importance of teamwork, the rewards of competition, and the importance of natural talent. Later in the story as Harry and his two friends seek the stone, they cooperate but each one of them must use his or her unique knowledge and talent to get Harry to the stone. In this way, individualism, an important Western value, is balanced against teamwork, an important Eastern value. Throughout, courage emerges as a touchstone value; no great deed is accomplished without it.

Kenneth Burke (see chapter 11) wrote, "To derive a culture from a certain mythic ancestry, or ideal mythic type, is a way of stating that culture's essence in narrative terms."[4] He claimed that myths were usually based on nature and served to explain first happenings or "origins," for example, the first flood, the first marriage, the first birth.[5] Contemporary theorist Walter Fisher reinforced this point; narrative "constitutes stories we tell ourselves and each other to establish a meaningful life-world."[6] How did these talents evolve?

In most societies, the first sign of sophistication in symbol using begins with a mythology to explain the past, make sense of the present, and give mission to the future. Around 3000 BC, the Sumerians of Mesopotamia were the first to invent writing. In those fragments myths have argumentative force. However, the Mesopotamians downgraded public speaking. Greek society, which emerged later, was more oral. In fact, its most famous myths begin with a prayer asking the gods to speak to the writer. The gods also inculcated virtues: Ares inspires the war hero Achilles; Aphrodite inspires the lovesick Paris.[7] In Greek society, the myths were memorized and handed down orally by Hesiod in his *Theogony* and by Homer in the *Iliad* and the *Odyssey* before 700 BC—about the time when the Olympic Games were founded, Panhellenism was developing, the city-states were forming colonies, and a female oracle took a seat in Delphi.[8] In fact, in Homer's writings, the word for "words" is "mythos." However, Hesiod's work speaks to the eloquence of the prince and differentiates it from the poetry of the minstrel:

> Words from his mouth flow honeyed: the people all look toward him discerning
> precedents with straight justice, and with unfaltering address he quickly and skill-
> fully settles even a great dispute; thus there are sagacious princes, for when the
> people are misguided in assembly these end the wheeling recriminations easily,
> persuading with gentle words.[9]

While rhetoric would not become a discipline until Socrates' time, it is clearly part of Greek consciousness and mythology that would eventually become a counterpart to rational order or chaos.

The process of creating stories began in early Greece. By 700 BC the Greeks had adopted Phoenician spelling. Rhyme served to make memorization easier, much the way a song sticks in the mind today.[10] Homer's rival, Archelochos of Paros (714–676 BC), invented iambic meter and perhaps the elegy, a meditative poem of lament. He also dabbled in satire, which added a second rhetorical edge to his stories. Other societies have their myths; Virgil's *Aeneid* (see chapter 5) for the Romans, *Gilgamesh* for the Sumerians, and the *Bible* for the Judeo-Christian world serve a similar purpose. *Gilgamesh* was an oral epic eventually rewritten into Assyrian. It is the story of an arrogant king who seeks complete divinity, but his earthly desires for women and men keep him from his goal. All hope is not lost, however, because a more virtuous character, Utnapishtim, does achieve immortality. The myth also includes Shamash, the masculine sun god, and Enkidu, the feminine goddess of intuition. Notice that each of these characters represents an essential element of what it is to be human.

While myths may be based on fictional characters, they always contain a kernel of truth. They are the way by which a society inculcates values, the guides for decision making. *Mythos* (sometimes rendered *muthos*) functions rhetorically to achieve its ends because religion and rhetoric are inextricably bound together in the discourse of the nonrational. If you cannot live with the crushing absurdity of the fact that a storm rose out of the ocean and killed a hundred sailors, then the tale that Poseidon stirred up the sea in retribution for some act rationalizes what happened and provides some sense of order where none existed before. If you cannot live with the irrational fact that you are a captive in a strange land, it helps to believe that you are one of God's chosen people and your offspring will be redeemed.

Each work of mythology is inspired by forces greater than humans and beyond their control. However, humans can control the *interpretation* that is put on these events; that interpretive function is also rhetorical because it allows us to *take something as something else*. Interpretation allows comparison, which is sometimes figurative in order to make meaning clear. Thus, successful narratives, many of which become myths, have at least two rhetorical dimensions: they advance a moral and they are subject to interpretation by an audience. The story's credibility is enhanced and its interpretation is made easier if it meets certain requirements: it must not abide contradiction; it must be internally coherent and seamless; it must elicit meaning in its audience by relating to its culture; it must speak the audience's language; it must resolve a conflict; it must reinforce its values; it must have credibility; it must be better than competing illusions spun by others. Should a story fail these rhetorical tests, it is doomed. That is why such early writers as Thucydides and Herodotus were trained as rhetors before they became famous historians. History was their story of events, especially in the case of Thucydides who wrote about the downfall of Athens. In telling that story, the narrator can emphasize, shade, delete, and edit as he or she sees fit.

ARCHETYPAL METAPHORS

We have seen that myths are rhetorical fantasies that often have religious overtones.[11] They arrange the world into acceptable stories and often provide a society with compelling comparisons. Walter Fisher explains why myths were so powerful to the ancients:[12] they embodied "symbolic actions [that] have a sequence and meaning for those who live, create or interpret them."[13] To put it another way, stories are adapted to a people's values and then reconstitute that people into a public—a coherent audience with fairly consistent beliefs, a coherent audience that can deal with the absurdities of the world. Marxists (see chapter 10) sometimes object to these public myths because their "ideological" overtones may create false consciousness. However, Marxist critics can deny neither their existence nor their necessity. The public will always need some mythology to live by; the question is which mythology will prevail.

They are often marked by *archetypal metaphors*, wellsprings into which speakers can tap to make their appeals more accessible to an audience. For example, the myth of the Phoenix that arises anew out of its own ashes or the resurrection of Jesus told in the New Testament are two stories that lend support to the birth, death, and rebirth cycle, which is refashioned into many speeches and works of literature. You have to hit bottom before you can recover; all must be lost before you can be saved. The birth, death (or defeat), rebirth cycle is incorporated into such popular movies as *Gone with the Wind* (a new South emerges out of the ashes of the old one). It is also used by Alcoholics Anonymous to persuade alcoholics to embrace a new spirituality to save their troubled lives.

The myth about Prometheus bringing fire and artistic skill to humans and the writings of Enlightenment thinkers such as Francis Bacon or John Locke create the association between light and knowledge, another popular archetypal metaphor. The idea is understood; the light comes on; darkness is dispersed.

Every culture is filled with such archetypal metaphors that play across our consciousness and give connotations to what we hear. Connotation is an attached, implicit meaning—as opposed to denotation, which is the official or dictionary definition of a word. For example, the denotation of water is the combination of two hydrogen atoms with one oxygen atom usually found in liquid form. The *connotation* of water, however, is diverse; it can be connected to baptism and new beginnings, to consciousness, or to the unknown beneath the surface.[14] In its connotative sense, water represents many archetypal metaphors from the sea to purification. Context is often crucial for understanding connotative meaning. For example, if you go into a music store and ask for a "CD," the clerk will understand you to be looking for a compact disc; if you ask for a "CD" in a bank, the teller will understand you to be looking for a certificate of deposit—different contexts, different meanings. Just try figuring out what "bad" and "cool" mean without knowing the context in which those words were uttered. If such simple words require context to be understood, think how much more important context is to complicated discourse.

Archetypal metaphors ground myths and help them convey their morals. The psychologist Carl Jung believed these "archetypes" grew out of a "collective unconscious." They provided "pathways" toward ingrained expressions in the human psyche. Claude Lévi-Strauss, who studied the formation of language, examined myths for their "deep structure" to see how they controlled cultural activity.[15] Roland Barthes saw myths as a way by which "a natural and eternal justification" masks a hidden "historical intention."[16] He claimed that myths could be used as "perpetual alibis" in which "the reader lives the myth as a story at once true and unreal."[17] Joseph Campbell traced many of these pathways to spirituality across very diverse cultures.[18]

What makes metaphors archetypal?[19] First, they are popular; they show up frequently and are easily accessible to the mass of the public. Second, they last over time. They are passed along in the culture. What is "hot" and what is "cool" may change from generation to generation, but each generation still uses these two words to evaluate various fads, movies, lifestyles, and the like. Third, archetypal metaphors are grounded in major experiences, conditions, or objects. Death, for example, plays a large role in our lives. Thus, it is commonly used as a metaphor: for example, "sudden death overtime," "she's to die for," and "it was a killer exam." Fourth, archetypal metaphors carry messages about humanity. Mountains can be metaphors for obstacles or problems in our way through life. Thus, we are urged metaphorically to "climb every mountain." Darkness can serve as a metaphor for a mystery or a symbol of evil, such as "the dark side" in the case of the *Star Wars* films.

Like the ancient storytellers, speakers who fail to avail themselves of such metaphors likely will be less successful than those who do. Worse, if a speaker fails to learn about the audience's interpretation of such archetypal metaphors, he or she can make startling and embarrassing declarations. "Playing it by ear" does not mean putting your ear on the keys of the piano.

Rhetoric can remake reality and re-create a sense of publicness because it maintains the power of myths.[20] Presenting a narrative of events is important to the message one wishes to convey. One can easily discern this rhetorical use of mythos in the ongoing debate over how to deal with illegal immigrants. One side demonizes the immigrants as "aliens" who are taking jobs from legal workers and receiving undeserved medical and welfare benefits for themselves and their children. The use of the term "aliens" associates immigrants with predators in science fiction films. The other side praises illegal immigrants as hard-working individuals who take jobs no one else wants. They are part of the mythos that can be traced back to other immigrants such as Pilgrims, Italians, and Irish who came into the country, proved their worth, and created the "melting pot" of our culture.

While science, technology, and the rational mind may have distanced us from nature and its cruel condition, they have brought their own absurdities that require the very same strategies of mythos used by the Greeks, Hebrews, Hindus, and all preliterate publics. We still rely on heroic and demonic characters that are larger than life, born in times of mythic import, transcending time and place. The clashes between these characters help reinforce the values we embrace by representing them in their purest form. They are essential elements in nation building. The moralism of the Declaration of Independence is manifest in its advocacy of tolerance, happiness, freedom, compassion, and respect for the rights of others. When Lincoln reasserted it in the Emancipation Proclamation and the Gettysburg Address, he purified the dream of the founders and became a mythic hero himself.

In order to avoid mindless manipulation, we need to understand the dialectical nature of values and how they are served by the rhetorical dimensions of mythmaking.[21] Films and speeches reflect, reinforce, project, and alter our values by placing them in opposition to other values and then characterizing the conflict. The drama holds our attention, but it also can change our values or intensify our belief in them. While films may be fictional, and some political and eulogistic speeches "mere rhetoric," they also function to undermine or reinforce our values and our view of the world. Many people believe that filmic narratives are true simply because they are coherent. Movies and novels thus become what is taken for history by many of our citizens.

More than that, actors and speakers may serve as models. The better their personas are rhetorically constructed—that is, adjusted to an audience and crafted in language—the more likely we are to identify with them and to embrace their values. Luke Skywalker's high-minded yet naive individualism appeals to the hero in all of us and reinforces a sense of right and wrong, no matter the odds. Mother Teresa's compassion for the poor in India inspires countless acts of charity around the world. ACLU President Susan Herman's impassioned critique of the Patriot Act inspires citizens to think about the repercussions when constitutional rights are compromised by a government that has been charged with upholding them. Without these heroes, our sense of communal values would erode. These leaders would not have been recognized had they not been rhetorically attuned to their audiences. Myths create a sense of community; however, they must be rhetorical—audience oriented—to be effective. Thus, the first theory we need to embrace as we equip ourselves rhetorically is the theory of the storyteller, the mythmaker, the narrator.

There are at least three types of narrators: first person, second person, and third person. A first person narrator is a character in the story that tells about events from the personal level. The credibility of this narrator comes from his or her eye-witness account. In the film version of *Lord of the Rings*, the audience generally sees things from the point of view of Frodo, whom we come to trust as the film progresses because of the heroism he displays.

A second person narrator shares the story with another; the story is told from a "you" point of view. Witnesses in court cases, for example, share their impression of events with the court. In his address to the UN calling for armed intervention in Iraq, Secretary of State Colin Powell narrated a story about genocide, biological warfare, violations of UN resolutions, and weapons of mass destruction. In F. Scott Fitzgerald's *The Great Gatsby*, Gatsby's friend Nick tells the story, observing events in chronological order from his perspective.

Third person narrators can be divided into at least three types. The omniscient narrator is all-knowing and can tell us about everything that takes place. Ernest Hemmingway is often an all-knowing narrator in his great novels such as *The Sun Also Rises* wherein he can even relate to the reader the intimate feelings of the characters. The partially omniscient narrator knows everything about some people, events, and places. Director Robert Altman has made at least two successful films using this device: *Nashville* and *Gosford Park*. The camera moves from scene to scene in Nashville extending mini-biographies of the characters who come together in a surprise ending. In the mansion at Gosford Park, the audience is allowed to see the activities of the wealthy as contrasted with the servants while a murder mystery unravels. The observant narrator knows everything that can be seen from his or her perspective. Any of these narrators can be manipulated to bring them closer to or distance them from characters or readers. For example, Shakespeare has Richard III, from the play by that name, and Iago, from *Othello*, speak to the audience directly and reveal their evilness. In this way, we learn about their values. In the film *Sunset Boulevard*, the narrator is found dead in the pool in the opening scene; he then tells the story revealing his love affair with the leading lady, thus becoming closer to the characters as the story unfolds. Proxemics, distance from or nearness to characters in time and space, is another way to deepen the narrator's persona.

Of course narrators control the timing of the story in another way; they can take time to reveal many details, as does Charles Dickens, or they can hurry us along as Nick does in the short novel, *The Great Gatsby*. That is, narrators can synthesize events into a quick sentence or two, or they can describe things as they would appear in actual time (impressionistic), or they can use a great amount of detail to retard the development of the story while developing a scene or character.

While we have examined the general characteristics of solid storytelling and mythmaking, we have not looked at the specifics of story building. The example study that follows examines the nuts and bolts of narrative in a detailed way.

The Gospel Narrator

The narrators of the four gospels serve as persuasive purveyors of the life and preaching of Jesus. Mark is symbolized by the lion because his gospel opens in the desert. Luke is symbolized by the ox because of his construction of the manger scene. John's symbol is the eagle because of a transcendent (high-flying) theme on wisdom. And Matthew is symbolized by a man because he is known for his humanistic approach. If they were not effective storytellers, Jesus' lessons might have been lost for future generations since he wrote nothing down except for one note in the dust. If the storytellers contradicted one another, their credibility might have suffered. Walter Fisher has paid special attention to the question of narrative credibility; here, we examine some of the prevailing strategies for obtaining it. The measures of effective narrative that he establishes are particularly useful in assessing narrative skills.[22] This approach will help determine not only whether narrators are credible but what case they are trying to make.[23] As Fisher makes clear, "dramatic and literary works do, in fact, argue."[24] Matthew's gospel, for example, makes the case that Jesus is the son of God. Mark's "biography of Jesus adapted an existing narrative tradition to his rhetorical purposes, shaping each of the stories to his own persuasive ends."[25] The gospel writers were converting an oral tradition into the written word.[26]

Fisher examines three key terms for measuring the effectiveness of a narrative: *rationality, fidelity,* and *coherence.* The rationality of a narrative depends on its truthfulness, reliability, and probability in terms of its unique culture and history.[27] For example, the killings that take place in Shakespeare's *Henry IV* often appear irrational in today's world; however, in Shakespeare's time when audiences had faith in St. Augustine's belief that all activity was the work of God, the killings during the War of the Roses had a rationale. Characters believed they were being guided by a higher power. Thus, in the culture of its time, *Henry IV* was an effective narrative.

Fidelity concerns truth-value beyond form, function, and validity. Fidelity relates to how well audiences can resonate with the story based on their own values and experiences.

When examining the fidelity of the story, we try to determine how it weighs, implies, and argues values. It is the job of the critic to ferret out what is being argued and how the values make the narrative hang together.

Coherence is demonstrated structurally, materially, and characterologically. Structural coherence concerns internal consistency; it is in fact the launching pad for fidelity. Material coherence concerns how the narrative relates to other credible narratives in the world, or what we could call external credibility and congruence with an audience's worldview. Characterological coherence concerns the *ethos* of the author; that factor allows the narrative to support "moral inducements."[28]

The word "narrators" describes the writers of the four gospels because they have a voice and a persona. They are not mere chroniclers because they do not always present events in the same order they occur, nor do they present events without commenting on their persuasive appeal. More than biographers, they are advancing an ideology for their respective audiences.

To reinforce this point, I focus on the gospel according to Matthew. I chose it for a number of reasons, not the least of which is its credibility. Papias, the Bishop of Hierapolis in South Phrygia, refers to Matthew in the *Exposition of the Oracles of the Lord* in AD 140. He is also cited in the work of Irenaeus, the Bishop of Lyons, written before AD 200.[29] Studies of the Dead Sea Scrolls from the Qumran community of Essenes also lend credence to the authenticity of this gospel;[30] they indicate that Matthew caught the temper of the times and knew the lay of the land. To date, nothing in the scrolls contradicts his account.[31]

But who was this Matthew? Some scholars believe Matthew the writer is not Matthew the tax collector whom Jesus chose to be an apostle.[32] However, most early church scholars including Papias, Irenaeus, Origen, and Eusebius, a fourth-century historian, reach the opposite conclusion; they believe the obscure author was the apostle Matthew who labored among the Parthians, Persians, and Medes after the ascent of Jesus and is referred to in Mark 3:18.[33] Barnabas, Paul's companion, also referred to Matthew. Irenaeus claimed that Matthew first wrote his gospel in Hebrew while Peter and Paul were preaching in Rome.[34] Since they were martyred in AD 64, Matthew's gospel might have preceded Mark's, hence the established order Matthew, Mark, Luke, and John. Forty

St. Matthew and the Angel, Stefano Trapanese.

years after the reported ascension of Jesus, Ignatius quoted Matthew, as did the Shepherd of Hermas and Polycarp, a disciple of the apostle John.

The Qumran scroll fragments of Mark's Gospel were written before AD 68, and the Magdalen Papyrus of Matthew's Gospel was written around AD 66. The Jewish Temple was not destroyed until AD 70, and Jesus had predicted such an eventuality in these gospels. If they were written after the fall of the Temple, the writers could have put the prediction in Jesus' mouth to make him appear more divine. If they were written before the fall, then Jesus' prediction has much more credibility. This may explain why Matthew's Gospel was the most quoted by early church fathers.[35]

Putting this historic evidence aside, Matthew's credibility depends on his narrative skills, which I examine closely to discover what they can teach us about narrative technique. Translated into Hellenistic Greek, Matthew's gospel is a full account.[36] Many consider it to be the best written, the most comprehensive, and the one most concerned with ethical questions.[37] George Kennedy demonstrates that it "makes the widest use of all aspects of rhetoric," and reveals that Matthew borrowed devices from Greek religious rhetoric.[38] It clearly creates dialectical tensions between the rich and the poor and Jesus and the Pharisees as it tells its story in an effort to support Christian values.[39]

An important aspect of Matthew's success is his ability to focus on a specific audience. Matthew's gospel was directed at Jewish and Gentile audiences that were not part of the Jewish leadership.[40] Matthew narrowed his rhetorical audience by eliminating the Pharisees, Sadducees, Herodians, chief priests, scribes, and elders.[41] While Matthew does not cater to the Zealots and Essenes, some of them probably identified with his portrayal of a Messiah. In any case, Matthew's manner of telling his story induced large numbers of non-Jews to join the Christian movement.

Matthew's rhetorical problem was to persuade his audience, including the followers of John the Baptist, that Jesus was the promised Messiah. He attempted to do this by writing a story in which Jesus fulfills the Old Testament scriptural predictions and specifications, performs miracles, resists the temptation of Satan, exposes the corruption of the Jewish leadership,[42] dies to redeem sins, rises from the dead, and ascends into heaven. These events required a coherent narrative. Matthew provided one that is credible, reinforces identification with the intended audience, and creates sermons that are appealing and catch the spirit of a strong religious leader.

Matthew began his construction of the narrative using the *pericope*, which relates an incident or event.[43] Pericopes are like beads in varying sizes that must be strung together to complete the story. Other than transitions, each gospel is composed entirely of pericopes. Some contain sermons; some relate miracles; some re-create disputes; some are parables. The transformation of Jesus while he stands with Elijah and Moses is a pericope; the miracle of the fishes and loaves is a pericope.

Within pericopes are substructures. For example, one of the most common ways of delivering a message is to have Jesus speak an *apothegm*, a Greek term for an aphorism, an instructive pronouncement or lesson embedded in a rhetorical situation.[44] When Jesus says, "My kingdom is not of this world," he is making such a pronouncement. The Sermon on the Mount in Matthew's gospel begins with nine *apothegms*, which we commonly call the beatitudes.

Parables, another form of pericopes,[45] are stories within the narrative that also carry a lesson at the end, shorter than but very like the fables of Aesop. Parables are also used to link Jesus to the Old Testament. The symbology of parables can be deep and requires careful deconstruction. That is why parables need to be seen against the field from which they are drawn if we are to understand how they help create *narrative congruence*. Understanding the culture of Jesus' time helps readers interpret the parables in ways that give them immediacy and relevance. For example, the many references in Matthew's gospel to sheep and shepherds are due in part to the fact that the hills of Judea and the surrounding states were often dotted with sheep. They provided food and wool to the society and were thus integral to the lives of the Semites. Stories referencing sheep had a deep impact. The same can be said of wedding feasts, of harvesting wheat, and of fishing. Parables are also helpful in identifying the intended audience of the narrator. Matthew directed parables to the mass of Jews that he hoped to convert.

Other pericopes relate actions and create conflicts that are essential if any narrative is to hold attention and advance plot for an audience. These often have symbolic importance. For example, when Jesus uses a rope to clear the money changers from the Jewish Temple, the action is dramatic, emotional, and tense, but the cleansing of the Temple may also symbolize the purification of the body or the soul by expunging material influences.

Another example is the withering of the fig tree. Because the tree is barren, Jesus condemns it, and to the astonishment of the apostles, it withers when he strikes it (Matthew 21:19). Jesus then draws an *apothegm* from the event, claiming that those who have faith not only can wither trees, they can also move mountains. Since the fig tree was the traditional symbol of the nation of Israel, Jesus may have been symbolically predicting the demise of that nation if it did not revive its faith.

Once the pericopes have been organized, narrators should develop the credibility of characters. Matthew attempts in several ways to establish the claim that Jesus was the Messiah. First, his gospel began by tracing Jesus' lineage back to Abraham through King David.[46] In verse 22 of chapter 1, he wrote, "that it might be fulfilled which was spoken by the prophet," Joseph married Mary and named their child Jesus. This process introduced a second technique, the use of *intertextual material* from the Old Testament. Matthew's account is an echoing of the rhetoric of Chronicles I of the Old Testament. The attempt to establish congruence is not without its problems as several scholars have noted.[47] If Joseph descended from David, and Jesus is not Joseph's natural son, then how can Jesus claim direct lineage to David? Matthew overcame these difficulties by showing that the lineage is symbolic given that in every other way Jesus is Joseph's son.

To enhance congruence, Matthew mentioned the fulfillment of prophecy more often than the other three gospel writers. Matthew's Jesus was on a mission defined by Old Testament scriptures.[48] Jesus often referred to the prophets of old, and Matthew often claimed that certain events took place to fulfill certain prophecies, particularly those of Isaiah. For example, when Jesus resisted Satan's temptations, the three responses he used were drawn from Deuteronomy 8:3, 6:16, and 6:13. Jesus' name is the Greek form of the Hebrew Joshua (Y'shua), which relates Jesus to Joshua of the Old Testament, who brought the Hebrews back into the Promised Land. The name means "Yahweh is salvation."[49]

Reinforcing this strategy of fulfillment is the use of *paroemia*, proverbial expressions as intertextual support. More than in the other gospels, Matthew used sayings that were no doubt common in his day. The use of these expressions probably made Matthew's gospel more accessible to his audience while reinforcing a feeling of fidelity among all readers over time.[50]

Finally, the credibility of Jesus' character is increased by playing on Old Testament *mythos*, the stories the Jewish people knew well. When Jesus spends forty days and nights in the desert, the event recalls Moses and the Jews wandering for forty years in the Sinai. When Jesus delivers the beatitudes to the apostles and the gathered crowd in the Sermon on the Mount, it recalls Moses coming down the mountain and delivering the Ten Commandments. When Jesus feeds the five thousand with bread and fish, the event recalls Elijah being fed by ravens. Even Jesus' bodily ascension into heaven reminds the faithful of Elijah being carried to heaven in a chariot drawn by horses and a whirlwind.

Matthew's narrative is also strengthened by its stress on personality characteristics that induce identification with the Jewish audience. For example, in Matthew's account Jesus was well versed in the Old Testament and very familiar with Jewish law and tradition. He was often called Rabbi and preached in the synagogues. He outwitted the Pharisees, the Sadducees, the Herodians, the scribes, the chief priests, and the elders.

Another characteristic that enhances character identification is mysteriousness. This strategy helped the faithful overcome certain paradoxes. Readers were often left free to put their own interpretations on Jesus' remarks and life because there is much to fill in about his persona.[51] We learn only late in the gospel that Jesus may have had brothers and sisters. His stepfather is not mentioned after the early chapters. Matthew did not write about the period between the return from Egypt during Jesus' childhood and his sudden appearance at the river where John is baptizing.

Matthew relates other qualities that enhance this mysterious side of the persona: Jesus was of divine birth; angels attended him and brought messages to his parents; he worked miracles;[52] he spoke in parables;[53] he rose from the dead and claimed that he would return "in the clouds of heaven."

Another factor that contributes to Matthew's rhetorical effectiveness is that unlike the other gospel writers, he grouped Jesus' sayings into coherent speeches that revolve around a set theme: for example, authentic faith in the Sermon on the Mount,[54] evangelical duties in the advice to his disciples in chapter 10, and the apocalyptic future in chapters 24 and 25. Each of the five major sermons is immediately followed with the phrase, "And it happened when Jesus finished. . . ."[55] In this way, Matthew created a cyclical formula that delineates the five divisions of his story.[56] This formal progression further strengthens the coherence of the story and helps it argue that Jesus' life is a natural outgrowth of the Old Testament.

This analysis reveals that Matthew was a skilled narrator who created a sense of credibility for himself and for Jesus. His effective uses of intertextual and geographic references make his story congruent for his target audience. He created speeches with an authentic feel and a cyclical narrative that holds attention as it persuades.

ESSENTIAL ELEMENTS OF EFFECTIVE NARRATIVES

Storytelling helps to transform a set of facts, which might otherwise be unpersuasive, into a coherent narrative that advances a point of view. In this sense, history is rhetorical, for there are many interpretations that can be put on events; the most persuasive will be the most coherent, the one that hangs together the best for its audience, and is congruent with the audience's understanding of the world. To review the elements of strong narrative persuasion, let's demonstrate their contemporary relevance by looking at some important rhetorical moments.

First, the narrator needs to select an audience. To whom is this story being told? As we saw in chapter 1, President George W. Bush tried to unite the country behind his war on terrorism using a nationally televised speech delivered to a joint session of Congress. He recognized the immediate audience, a joint session of Congress with its visitors in the galleries, but also targeted the national audience watching the speech on

TV or listening to it on the radio, foreign allies, and enemies. Which audiences we select determines many of the rhetorical strategies we use to build our story, from word choice to intertextual allusions. So it was with Bush as he gave examples of how citizens had shown bravery during the attacks of September 11 and how foreign allies had rallied to our cause.

Second, any good storyteller needs to understand how to structure the pericopes of the narrative. What are the events that take place, how will they be sequenced, and how will they be represented? The first Harry Potter film proceeds from the oppressed life of a young boy living with unenlightened foster parents to his new home, a school for wizards, to his ultimate triumph in procuring the sorcerer's stone. The audience keeps track of the story because the film carefully assembled the pericopes in a compelling way. Using the same technique, modern advertisers set out the pericopes of a commercial on a storyboard. Each roughly drawn picture on the board represents a pericope. The plot advances, and a moral is asserted.

Third, intertextual allusions are important to narrators for several reasons. They provide a way by which speakers can tie their stories to outside materials with which the audience is familiar. For example, when President Reagan referred to America as "a shining city upon a hill," he was referring to a sermon by Puritan John Winthrop. Winthrop in turn was quoting scripture to give his audience a sense of mission. During his campaigns for the presidency in 2008, Barack Obama recalled the *words* of the Declaration of Independence and of Martin Luther King Jr. Intertextuality can increase credibility by demonstrating knowledge of other texts, but it can also function to make a thought more accessible to a given audience by using texts with which audience members are familiar. Daily we hear maxims, verities, proverbs, ideographs, and sayings: "The squeaky wheel gets the grease." "Money can't buy happiness." They work to include members of audiences into the public the speaker wishes to address. The use of intertextuality creates a subtext that provides both open and subliminal support for a speaker's claims. It also reveals to us the need to understand that no rhetorical text, whether a speech or a newspaper editorial, stands as an artifact in isolation. If effective, the text usually has intertextual allusions that need to be traced.

Fourth, character credibility enhances the likelihood that an audience will identify with a story. Conversely, the narrator may wish to destroy the credibility of characters to alienate the audience from those characters and thereby draw them to an alternate story. In no arena are these two strategies of story building more obvious and more important than in legal battles. Prosecutors emphasize the bad deeds and immoral characters of defendants. In turn, their lawyers emphasize the good deeds and virtues of their clients. President John Quincy Adams, who had been a teacher of rhetoric, once claimed that the lawyer who usually carries the day with the jury is the one who tells the best story.

Fifth, fulfillment of prophecy or foreshadowing is an effective narrative technique because it meets an expectation that is already in the mind of the audience. Speakers can also plant seeds in the minds of their listeners and then return to them to produce a feeling of expectations being met. In Shakespeare's famous play, the witches assure Macbeth that he will rule until the forest comes to Dunsinane. He feels safe. How could the forest move to a castle? But when the opposing army chops down the forest, uses it as cover, and moves toward the castle, the audience knows that Macbeth is doomed.

Finally, speakers and writers can advance themes in a cyclical progression by using narration; using this technique, they can be very effective at getting their argument across. Few speakers are more skilled in this than Jesse Jackson. Perhaps the most prominent use occurred at the 1988 Democratic Convention. Jackson's theme—that unless the Democrats unify, they would not defeat the Republicans—was advanced cyclically through different stories. First, he talked about how the Democrats won when they united behind John Kennedy in 1960. Then, he told them the story of how they lost when they were divided over the candidacy of Hubert Humphrey in 1968. At the climax of the speech, he told the story of how his grandmother made a quilt from small, insignificant pieces of cloth. He compared each of the constituencies in the Democratic Party to one of those patches. Alone no patch was "big enough" to do the job; but united they could make a quilt of many colors that would produce victory. This passage was the most memorable moment of the convention that year.

CONCLUSION

I began this chapter by analyzing how mythology functioned rhetorically to rationalize the inexplicable, to promote values, and to build a sense of tribe, culture, or nation. Speakers can use their knowledge of lore to impress and persuade an audience to become one with their stories. Myths are rhetorical fantasies that become legends and spin out archetypal metaphors that help bind a people together. Archetypal metaphors also imbue words and phrases with connotative meaning that, because of its illusive nature, requires rhetorical skill to tap and use.

One of the most common uses of storytelling to make an argument is the *personal narrative*. We often speak from our own experience to support a point we want to make or to refute someone else's point. Motivational speakers inspire us with their personal stories. Families argue around the dinner table, speaking from their own experiences. Students assess professors in terms of their history with them. In each case, a personal narrative is used to make a point, and its effectiveness depends on the principles examined in this chapter.

The narrative strategies that conclude the chapter review the elements of a coherent and congruent story. Historians or storytellers build sound narratives and make them persuasive with rhetorical tools. Speakers who ignore the venerable narrative fail to take advantage of a compelling persuasive technique.

Study Questions

1. What myths guide you in your everyday decision making? How do myths help you make sense out of the world? Give an example of a personal narrative that you have used to advance an argument.

2. Why should historians be skilled in rhetoric?

3. What are archetypal metaphors? How do they relate to myths?

4. Determine the difference between the denotative and connotative meanings of "family," "love," and "sport."

5. What measures of effectiveness does Fisher establish to explain the success of narratives?

6. In what ways does the phrase "family values" function as an "ideograph" in American society?

7. How does the editorial slant of the narrator affect the story?

8. What is a "pericope"?

9. What is an "apothegm"?

10. What is the rhetorical dimension of a "parable"?

11. What is the rhetorical dimension of "intertextuality"?

Notes

[1] The Romans borrowed these gods from the Greeks and renamed them, as we shall see.

[2] Ernest Bormann, "Fantasy and Rhetorical Vision: The Rhetorical Criticism of Social Reality," *Quarterly Journal of Speech*, 59 (1972): 396–407.

[3] See, for example, Michael McGuire, "Ideology and Myth as Structurally Different Bases for Political Argumentation," *Journal of the American Forensic Association*, 24 (1987): 16–26; Stephen O'Leary and Michael McFarland, "The Political Use of Mythic Discourse: Prophetic Interpretation in Pat Robertson's Presidential Campaign," *Quarterly Journal of Speech*, 75 (1989): 433–52.

[4] Kenneth Burke, "Ideology and Myth," *Accent*, 7 (1947): 200.

[5] Ibid.

[6] Walter Fisher, *Human Communication as Narrative* (Columbia: U. of South Carolina Press, 1989), p. 62. See also, Robert C. Rowland, "On Mythic Criticism," *Communication Studies*, 41 (1990): 101–16.

[7] These moods eventually become the pathé of Aristotle, the states of mind of the audience and the speaker.

[8] The priestesses were known as the Pythia and may have achieved mystical states because the stream running through Delphi emits the gas ethylene, which can induce euphoria or delirium. The rhetoric of the Pythia was vague, allowing for interpretation; however, some predictions were rather precise as they channeled for Apollo.

[9] As quoted in and translated by Jeffrey Walker, "Before the Beginnings of 'Poetry' and 'Rhetoric': Hesiod on Eloquence," *Rhetorica*, 14 (1996): 244.

[10] It is no accident that rhetoric, rhyme, and rhythm all begin with the same Greek letter.

[11] Rhetorical efforts can be made more effective when they play to fantasy themes. See Bormann.

[12] Fisher, p. 57.

[13] Ibid., p. 58.

[14] We will return to the concepts of connotation and denotation in the concluding chapter of this book.

[15] See Claude Lévi-Strauss, *Structural Anthropology*, C. Jacobsen and B. G. Schoeff, trans. (New York: Basic Books, 1963).

[16] Roland Barthes, "Myth Today," *A Barthes Reader* (New York: Hill and Wang, 1982), pp. 130–32.

[17] Ibid., p. 115.

[18] See Joseph Campbell, *The Inner Reaches of Outer Space: Metaphor as Myth and as Religion* (Novato, CA: New World Library, 2002).

[19] See Michael Osborn, "Archetypal Metaphor in Rhetoric: The Light-Dark Family," *Quarterly Journal of Speech*, 53 (1967): 115–26.

[20] See for example, Michael McGuire, "Mythic Rhetoric in *Mein Kampf*: A Structural Critique," *Quarterly Journal of Speech*, 68 (1977): 1–13.

[21] See, for example, Walter R. Fisher, "Rhetorical Fiction and the Presidency," *Quarterly Journal of Speech*, 66 (1980): 119–26.

[22] Fisher in *Human Communication* readily acknowledges that his "narrative paradigm" is based on the work of others. I have also examined those works to buttress what is done here. Of particular help were Stanley Hauerwas, *A Community of Character: Toward a Constructive Christian Ethic* (Notre Dame, IN: U. of Notre Dame Press, 1981); M. Goldberg, *Theology and Narrative* (Nashville: Parthenon Press, 1982); Frederick

Jameson, *The Political Unconscious: Narrative as a Socially Symbolic Act* (Ithaca: Cornell U. Press, 1981); and Robert Alter, *The Art of Biblical Narrative* (New York: Basic Books, 1981). Fisher rightly points out that none of these writers see the rhetorical import of narrative; see pp. 57–84. See also G. Genette, *Narrative Discourse* (Oxford: Oxford U. Press, 1980) and *Narrative Discourse Revisited* (Ithaca: Cornell U. Press, 1989); D. Carr, *Time, Narrative and History* (Bloomington: Indiana U. Press, 1986).

[23] Fisher, *Human Communication,* p. 57.

[24] Ibid.

[25] Robert S. Reid, "When Words Were a Power Loosed: Audience Expectation and *Finished* Narrative Technique in the *Gospel of Mark,*" *Quarterly Journal of Speech,* 80 (1994): 433.

[26] W. R. Farmer, *The Synoptic Problem* (Dillsboro: Western North Carolina Press, 1976), p. 31.

[27] Fisher, *Human Communication,* p. 47. See also his "Narrative Rationality and the Logic of Scientific Discourse," *Argumentation,* 8 (1994): 21–32.

[28] Fisher, *Human Communication,* p. 58.

[29] E. P. Sanders and Margaret Davies, *Studying the Synoptic Gospels* (London: Trinity Press International, 1991), p. 7. See Irenaeus, *Against Heresies.*

[30] James H. Charlesworth, *Jesus and the Dead Sea Scrolls* (New York: Doubleday, 1992), p. 9ff.

[31] Further weight has been given to the gospel based on a new carbon dating of the Magdalen Papyrus. German papyrologist Carsten Peter Thiede in *Eyewitness to Jesus* (Doubleday, 1996) argues that this fragment of Matthew's gospel is from AD 66, and thus Matthew must have been writing before the fall of the Jewish Temple in Jerusalem. That would also support the contention of others that Matthew is actually the apostle of Jesus recruited from amongst the tax collectors.

[32] Hendrickus Boers sums up the modern position this way: "Mark is the oldest Gospel and . . . Matthew and Luke, independent of each other, used Mark as one of their sources. In addition, Matthew and Luke used a second common source, generally referred to as Q, from the German *Quelle,* meaning simply source." In *Who Was Jesus* (New York: Harper and Row, 1989), p. xviii. See also E. F. Scott, *The Literature of the New Testament* (New York: Columbia U. Press, 1963), pp. 66–67. But Boers also recognizes the "possibility" that Matthew's gospel was written first and Mark abridged it; see page 27. And distinguished scholarship in Germany supports the view that the author of the gospel was the apostle; see T. Z. Zahn, *Das Evangelium des Matthäus* (Kommentar Zum Neuen Testament I; Leipzig: A. Duchert, 1910); A. Schlatter, *Der Evangelist Matthäus* (Stuttgart: Calwer, 1959). Farmer takes the strongest position claiming that Matthew was not only the apostle of Jesus but wrote the first gospel before AD 70 (see *The Synoptic Problem*).

[33] The case for the Apostle Matthew as author is persuasive for several reasons: A tax gatherer might be educated in Greek, Hebrew, and Aramaic, which this author was. He would also have a much more sophisticated knowledge of currency than the other gospel writers, and this author did. Unlike the other gospels, which refer to the Apostle as Levi, Matthew would refer to himself by the name Jesus gave him. See W. Graham Scroggie, in *A Guide to the Gospels* (London: Pickering & Inglis Ltd., 1948), pp. 246–47, 273; Scott, pp. 42–49; *Dartmouth Bible* (New York: Houghton Mifflin, 1950), p. 858; Robert Eisenman, *Maccabees, Zadokites, Christians and Qumran: A New Hypothesis of Qumran Origins* (Leiden: Brill, 1983), p. 30; Jack Dean Kingsbury, *Jesus Christ in Matthew, Mark, and Luke* (Philadelphia, PA: Fortress Press, 1981), pp. 67–69.

[34] Sanders and Davies, p. 7.

[35] See H. Swete, *The Gospel According to St. Mark* (London, 1905), pp. xxxii, xxxiv–xxxix.

[36] If Matthew was the tax collector named Levi that Jesus called, then he was an eyewitness to much of what was written. If he is another Matthew, then he is retelling the story. Scroggie writes, "We may assume that the chronological order of the Synoptic Gospels is Mark, Matthew, and Luke. Mark may well have been written as early as AD 50 . . . Matthew's Record was written probably about AD 58, shortly before Luke's," p. 249.

[37] The *Dartmouth Bible* reads, "[Matthew], more skilled in writing than Mark, presents the moral and religious teachings of Jesus so effectively that his Gospel is regarded to this day as the best compendium of Christian ethics" p. 860. Scott writes, "Matthew has been by far the most important" gospel; "it has been accepted in all times as the authoritative account of the life of Christ, the fundamental document of the Christian religion," p. 65.

[38] George Kennedy, *New Testament Interpretation Through Rhetorical Criticism* (Chapel Hill: U. of North Carolina Press, 1984), pp. 101–2. See also, Rollin Grams, "The Temple Conflict Scene: A Rhetorical Analysis

of Matthew 21–23," in *Persuasive Artistry: Studies in New Testament Rhetoric in Honor of George A. Kennedy, Journal for the Study of the New Testament,* Suppl. 50 (Sheffield, Eng.: Sheffield Academic Press, 1991), pp. 41–65.

[39] This form of discourse is called *epideictic*, as we shall learn when we focus on Aristotle. See Philip Shuler, *A Genre for the Gospels: The Bibliographical Character of Matthew* (Philadelphia, PA: Trinity Press International, 1982).

[40] The attacks on the Pharisees, Sadducees, chief priests, and elders would indicate that the gospel was written before the destruction of Jerusalem at the hands of Titus in AD 70 and aimed at the Essenes and John the Baptist's followers. Scroggie writes, "Irenaeus says: 'Matthew issued a written Gospel among the Hebrews,' and 'The Gospel of St. Matthew was written for the Jews.' Origen says: 'St. Matthew wrote for the Hebrews.' Eusebius says: 'Matthew . . . delivered his Gospel to his countrymen.' The complexion and content of the Gospel abundantly confirm this view," p. 248.

[41] The Pharisees, literally the "separate ones," were a conservative group who led the opposition to the even less flexible and aristocratic Sadducees. The Sadducees were closely allied with the followers of King Herod, known as Herodians. The Sadducees numbered only 5,000 but had gained power by supporting the Maccabean Kings and coming to terms with the Romans. The Sadducees accepted the written law of the Old Testament, believed in a Messiah, demons, and angels; they were annihilated in the holocaust of AD 70. See the *Dartmouth Bible,* pp. 850–51. In Acts 23:6, Paul says, "I am a Pharisee, the son of a Pharisee."

[42] The Maccabees and Josephus talk about the growing corruption of the Jewish priesthood. These crimes provide the backdrop for Jesus' attack on the Jewish clergy. See also Emil Schurer, *The History of the Jewish People in the Age of Jesus* (175 BC to AD 135), vols. I & II (Edinburgh: T. & T. Clark, 1979).

[43] The landmark work on pericopes has been done by Rudolf Bultmann and Karl Knudsin in *Form Criticism: Two Essays on New Testament Research* (New York: Harper & Row, 1962).

[44] This term is also known as *chreia*. See Klaus Berger, *Einfuhrung in die Formgeschichte* (Tubingen: U. of Tubingen Press, 1987), especially pp. 80–93; Farmer, *The Synoptic Problem,* pp. 266–67.

[45] See, for example, Joachim Jeremias, *The Parables of Jesus* (New York: Scribner, 1963); Adolf Julicher, *Die Gleichnisreden Jesu,* 2 vols. (Tubingen: U. of Tubingen Press, 1910); J. D. Kingsbury, *The Parables of Jesus in Matthew 13* (St. Louis: Clayton Publishing House, 1977).

[46] See First Chronicles 2:1–15 and 3:5–19; Ruth 4:12–22. The numerology here provides some of the magical identification. The count is 14 generations times three; hence, the three of the trinity and the magic of seven multiplied.

[47] See, for example, Stephen Mitchell, *The Gospel According to Jesus* (New York: Harper Perennial, 1993), pp. 22–28.

[48] See Scroggie, p. 270; Boers, p. 11. There are 129 references to the Old Testament that cover 25 books of the 39 that make up the canon.

[49] See the *Dartmouth Bible,* p. 963.

[50] See E. W. Bullinger, *Figures of Speech Used in the Bible Explained and Illustrated* (Grand Rapids: Baker Book House, 1968), pp. 760–64, and Matthew 3:10–11, 7:12, 12:25, 12:34, 13:57, 15:14, 21:21, 24:28. See also W. D. Davies and Dale Anderson, *The Gospel According to St. Matthew,* v. I. (Edinburgh: T. & T. Scott, 1988) for a close examination of literary style and structure.

[51] An enthymeme is a syllogism based on probability that usually has a premise suppressed so that the audience must fill it in. A full-blown enthymeme is an epichireme. The device was named by Aristotle, as we shall see later in this text. But for now, by enthymematic character, I mean one that requires the audience member to fill in something about him or her.

[52] See Morton Smith, *Jesus the Magician* (New York: Harper & Row, 1968), pp. 8ff.

[53] Speaking in parables fulfills a quotation from Psalms 78:2, "I will open my mouth in parables, I will utter what has been hidden since the foundation of the world."

[54] "The Sermon on the Mount . . . is so well constructed that it might easily pass for an organic whole," Scott, p. 69.

[55] 7:28, 11:1, 13:53, 19:1, and 26:1.

[56] Scott contends that Matthew meant to "parallel the five books of Moses," p. 70. Such a subliminal device might make the story more appealing to the Jewish audience. For a neo-Aristotelian analysis of the Sermon as a deliberative speech, see Kennedy, chapter 2.

The Development of Rhetorical Theory in Greece

As humans gained some control over their environment, mythologizing gave way to explaining the world in objective, scientific ways. Paradigm shifts are common in Western civilization; *for every school of thought, another school is established in reaction.* In this chapter, we will examine how the naturalists reacted to the mythologists to establish an empirical basis for knowledge. Then we will see how the mystics reacted to the naturalists by establishing an internal basis for the discovery of transcendent truth. That led to an offshoot of mystical philosophy known as Sophistry. Sophists synthesized the foregoing schools of thought into a skeptical yet tolerant approach to knowledge. The Sophists usually began their quest by doubting what was common wisdom; the result was a relativism, in which humans became the standard by which all things were measured, and truth was based on individual perception.

Plato reacted to this subjective approach by trying to establish an objective method of finding the truth in its perfected nature in a transcendent world, one that is outside and beyond the physical world, one that can only be reached through the soul. Thus, this chapter takes us on a unique journey through the development of Greek notions of consciousness. The journey begins where mythology is left behind to pursue scientific observation and then scientific observation is left behind for a metaphysical understanding of knowledge.

Each of these schools produced a different theory of rhetoric that exists in some form to this day. As we have seen, the mythologists established the importance of narrative in everyday affairs, trials, and even nation building. The *naturalists'* preference for an empirical method (a theory based on observation of what exists around us) can be seen in modern quantitative studies including the social sciences. The naturalists believed that if the world could be reduced to substance, then the need for mythology might be replaced with a new, more objective rhetoric. Instead of explaining the world by creating myths, rhetoric would be dedicated to explaining nature in terms of scientific evidence obtained from observation through seeing, smelling, hearing, touching, and tasting. Humans would be persuaded that certain scientific "facts" are true, and these facts would be woven into a believable, coherent theory that explains them. If there were any loose ends, the theory would unravel.

The Sophist position that the truth is relative (that is, based on individual perception) has been revived, as we shall see, throughout history most notably by David Hume, Freidrich Nietzsche, many existentialists, and some postmodern thinkers. In contrast was Plato's notion that truth is permanent, infinite, perfect (ideal), and recollectable by the soul. He believed that there are perfect ideas in a *noumenal* world that serve as models for this world of shadows and copies. Platonism served as a sounding board of normative standards for many new theories over the last two millennia, and continues to do so in the third. It is the rock upon which idealism is constructed.

The debates among these schools took place in part as a result of organizing various tribes into the city-states of ancient Greece. Tradition has it that King Theseus made Athens into a small kingdom in 700 BC. By 621 BC, this early Greek city-state was codifying its laws. Solon (c. 639–c. 559 BC) helped Athens recapture the Salamis Islands and was elected head of the city in 594 BC. However, he is remembered more for his refining the laws into a civil code in 593 BC that became a model for Western civilization. His new code created the venue for litigation, and hence persuasive speaking skills in the courts. Solon gave power to the lowest classes by allowing them to be placed in the *heliaea*, a pool of 6,000 jurors.[1] This reform meant that juries would be more diverse than ever before, making speaking before them even more of a challenge.

Solon clipped the powers of the Athenian senate *(Areopagus)*, which many believed had been created by the gods.[2] He then opened the assembly to all free men and created a Council of Four Hundred for the propertied classes; it was composed of 100 members from each of the four founding tribes. Solon ruled that in order to speak before the council, a citizen needed to be at least fifty years of age. The council's job was to create an agenda for the assembly, which was also given the authority to select magistrates *(archons)*, a task formerly performed by the Areopagus. His laws incorporated some long-standing practices, such as individual ownership of property, but he also created new laws, such as reporting wealth annually (which he borrowed from the Egyptians) and legalizing wills. The great historian Herodotus tells us that Solon left Athens for a decade after putting his laws into effect so that he would not violate them, so that Athens would prove its commitment to the laws, and so that Solon might absorb the knowledge of other countries. Soon after his return, Solon became known as the lawgiver.

When, in 572 BC, Solon retired to write poetry, declining offers to resume leadership in Athens, infighting among the three political groups broke out. The aristocrat Peisistratus rallied the commoners behind him and became dictator. At first he rejected Solon's reforms, but when this proved enormously unpopular, he consolidated them. Peisistratus soon died and was succeeded by his son Hippias, who ruled for thirteen years.

As the political system became more sophisticated so did rhetorical practices and philosophical debates. This chapter explores the new theories of rhetoric created by the post-mythological thinkers of ancient Greece. In some cases, these theories are stated outright; in other cases they are implied; and in some cases, they must be deduced. They are part of a debate between philosophy and rhetoric that rages to this day. Those who view the world as objectifiable often do not see the need for the development of rhetorical skills. They believe the facts speak for themselves. Those who see the world in subjective or relative terms argue that rhetoric is essential. And then there are those who believe that rhetoric is useful in explaining scientific and philosophical discoveries and theories to lay audiences.

We begin with the scientific thinkers such as Thales, move to mystics such as Parmenides, and then to the Sophists, the great teachers who dominated Athenian culture in its golden age. The chapter concludes by examining the backlash against the Sophists first by Isocrates and then by Plato, whose main character Socrates dominates the *Dialogues*, some of the most important philosophical works in the history of civilization. Because each of these schools defined the universe in a different way and saw the way humans determine the truth differently, they have very different theories about rhetoric and its uses.

THALES AND THE NATURALIST SCHOOL

What kind of rhetorical theory can be deduced from science? At first the two seem incompatible. Science attempts to reduce phenomena to their simplest explanations, while rhetoric often establishes elaborate rationalizations. Thales of Miletus (c. 636–546 BC), often called the father of philosophy,[3] was a brilliant advisor to political and military leaders. He predicted the eclipse of 585 BC and diverted a river when his leader's army could not find a way to cross it. Thales argued that "water is the origin of all elements; water is the principle of all things." Thales was thus the first known reductionist; Aristotle called him the first cosmologist. Thales was so taken with the heavens, that while looking up at them he fell over backward into a well and died. Despite his demise, many followed his lead. Anaximander of Miletus, a contemporary of Thales, wrote the first scientific study, *On the Nature of Things*. Perhaps it contains the first written sentences preserved in Western thought, one of which reads: "Out of those things from which beings are generated, into these again does their perishing take place according to what is needful and right; for they pay the penalty and make atonement for one another for their wrongdoing, according to the ordinance of time."[4] He claimed all things could be traced back to the infinite, the limitless, the eternal *(apeiron)*. But his physics is symmetrical and dialectical; elements divide out into hot and cold, dry and wet, high and low. He viewed the earth as a huge disk, and the sun and stars as wheels of fire.

Anaximenes (c. 546 BC), also of Miletus, was a devoted follower of Anaximander. Anaximenes believed all things could be reduced to air, which he said was infinite and supported the earth-disc. Democritus of Abdera 460–370 BC, like his teacher Leucippus, accepted Anaximenes' theories and expanded them by arguing that atoms were the essential smallest unit. Democritus admitted that the senses were easily fooled; thus it was important that scientists generate theories that are rational and consensual. Leucippus divided the universe into Being (matter) and Nonbeing (empty space, void). He, too, sought theories that would overcome the plurality of descriptions that could be generated by the senses.

These pre-Socratic thinkers shifted the concern of humans from mythology to questions of reality, particularly material reality, leaving much less wiggle room for rhetorical explanations. In short, they changed the focus of human attention from the

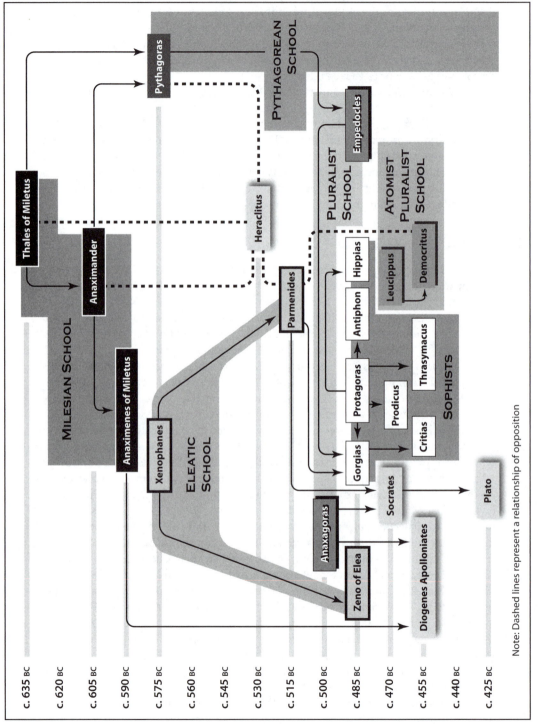

Relationship among pre-Socratic philosophical schools.

Note: Dashed lines represent a relationship of opposition

gods to matter—and hence to earthly externalities. In such a world, rhetoric served only secondary purposes. Rhetoric could help explain what science discovered. It could be used to convince opinion leaders that the material view made more sense than a mythological one.[5] However, rhetoric itself could not discover truth in the scientific world because Thales and his "naturalist school" rejected subjective and metaphysical explanations for phenomena.[6] Theirs was a world of observable truths.

The problem with such a worldview is that it assumes that discovered truth does not require persuasive skill. Even those scientists who see a need for the explanatory functions of rhetoric often deny its ability to provide hypotheses, to discover and invent. Scientists would discover the truth or demonstrate it; teachers would explain it to the rest of the world sometimes relying on rhetoric. The danger of this alternate view of rhetoric is that it inhibits the scientist from developing the rhetorical skills he or she needs to cope with contingent life-and-death situations. For example, when is an abortion a legitimate option? When is euthanasia justified? When is a space shuttle ready for launch?

ATHENIAN REFORM AND THE RISE OF RHETORIC

The increased importance of the contingent world as opposed to the scientific saved rhetoric in its first battle with objectivist philosophers. The mystics and the relativists were rescued in part because Athens underwent a dramatic change under the leadership of a popular aristocratic Archon named Kleisthenes (also Cleisthenes).[7] Between 510 and 502 BC and after the exile of Hippias (see above), he completed a series of governmental reforms that put limited democracy into force. A populist, Kleisthenes himself was then exiled when a coup led by his opponents succeeded; 700 Athenian families loyal to Kleisthenes also were sent into exile. The coup leaders quickly became unpopular when the citizens of the city realized that their rights were being eroded. The leaders of the coup sought refuge in the Acropolis. They surrendered after a siege and were bound hand and foot. Kleisthenes and the families loyal to him were recalled to power. The reforms of Kleisthenes were reestablished, and he expanded Athenian territory in the wake of a subsequent division amongst the allies of his enemies, namely Sparta.

Kleisthenes' reforms included abolishing the four-tribe system and replacing it with ten territorial divisions or *demes*, each of which would provide a general for the army and fifty members over the age of thirty for the new Council of Five Hundred *(boulé)*.[8] Those who spoke before the council had to demonstrate persuasive prowess, especially knowledge of subject matter, or they would be shouted down. Out of Athens' population of 250,000, only 35,000 or so were citizens. Six thousand were needed to constitute a quorum in the assembly, which was given new powers. Herodotus praises this new equality and free speech as the key to Athenian greatness.

Other reforms soon followed. In 462 BC, for example, Ephialtes changed the judicial system by creating courts for the lower levels of society and restricted the power of magistrates. The council further reduced the influence of the Areopagus, confining it to regulation of religious practice.

By the Sophists' time, a government of the citizens was in full operation; it was the freedom in Athens that attracted many of the Sophists to the city. In this "democracy," all male citizens over the age of eighteen could attend the assembly that regularly drew 6,000 to 9,000 persons depending on the importance of the issue being debated. The Council of Five Hundred determined what items were to be considered; a simple majority decided the policy to be followed. In both the council and the assembly, skill in public speaking was important not only because of the orality of Greek culture but because of the necessary give-and-take of political debate. Hence, speech was made part of the schooling of young men, along with athletics, reading, writing, mathematics, and music. Haggling over what should go into that curriculum was intense. Should rhetoric serve cultural mythology, create new art forms, explain scientific discoveries, or encourage mystical explorations?[9]

This free thinking was encouraged by Pericles, who ruled Athens during its golden age from 461 BC to 429 BC. He benefited from the success of the Delian League of Greek city-states that had won an important victory over the Persians and provided the Greeks with a modicum of security. New architecture dominated the Athenian skyline as Pericles ordered the re-creation of the Acropolis; more realistic statues reflecting the beauty of the body dotted the temples. Phidias, who was chosen to sculpt the goddess Athena for the Parthenon, created many of these statues. In this golden age, there was also a flowering of rhetorical theory, which Pericles clearly understood. One of the most important ceremonial speeches ever given was his funeral oration during Athens' tragic war with Sparta. Its theme—never fight for material gain, only for noble goals in the name of those who have given their lives in battle—has carried on through history, surfacing in Abraham Lincoln's Gettysburg Address and Ronald Reagan's salute to the astronauts who died in the *Challenger* explosion.

The Mystics

In this period, Parmenides emerged as the most radical mystic. In his most spiritual work, *On Nature*, he argued that the only thing worth doing was attending on Being: "All things that mortals have established, believing in their truth, are just a name."[10] Yet in fragment 6 he implied that words have the power to discover existence by bringing its reality and permanence to light. He defined his reality when he wrote that "Being has no coming-into-being and no destruction, for it is whole of limb, without motion and without end."[11] Parmenides' belief in one God left a mark on philosophy. His locus for a perfect, permanent, pervasive Being inspired Plato's work and revived an interest in discursive paths to the truth. He treated *mythos* (words used to construct a story) and *logos* (words used to construct an argument or explain the truth) as one and the same, once again resurrecting the position that narratives carried moral or true messages.

While Parmenides sought permanence in one transcendent Being as his guide to understanding truth, Heraclitus (Herakleitos of Ephesus) saw change as the foundation of existence and believed *logos* was the force behind coherence.[12] He defined *logos* as words that "gather-together-an-entity in its unity." *Logos* (naming) establishes stable images in a world of flux; it concretizes entities. Words bring things into existence. Only in the *logos* can the entity be unified because only the *logos* pervades all things.[13]

Heraclitus complained that humans did not recognize the *logos* in all things and instead accepted illusions such as security and wealth in the place of the true *logos*. Fascinated by the lucidity of the primordial vision of Heraclitus, a leading philosopher of the last century, Martin Heidegger (see chapter 9) wrote, "By recalling the beginnings of history, when Being unveiled itself in the thinking of the Greeks, it can be shown that the Greeks from the very beginning experienced the Being of beings as the presence of the present."[14] Heraclitus' radical subjectivity provided an antithesis to the naturalists because if what they were observing was always in a state of flux, their observations were always subject to correction, or being outdated. To put it another way, if all matter is always changing, then it must constantly be reexplained: "You can't put your foot in the same river twice." Fixed principles are difficult to come by, and in such a situation rhetoric becomes more important because it can bring things together and make sense of them.

Heraclitus' argument that change, whether continuous or discontinuous, is reality also provided a dialectic with Parmenides, who believed permanence is reality and change is illusion. Thus, among the mystics, disagreements were common. Furthermore, the struggle between various mystical and scientific schools proved to many that the truth may not yet have been found and if found was at best relative.

The turmoil in the philosophical community was matched in the political arena. Debate flourished in political and legal forums since definitive evidence for important questions often did not exist or was open to various interpretations. A new rhetoric was born to deal with such contingencies since cases for public positions had to be made.

Several fragments of the writings of influential pre-Socratics provide an insight not only into this need for rhetoric but into the relativism that ultimately freed Greek thought from the naturalist net woven by Thales. Anaximander of Miletus, for example, could not explain chaos until he developed his notion of the indefinite,[15] that in turn undermined certainty. One basis of Anaximander's theory was that the origin of humans is "unintelligible, inarticulate." That is, he made sense of the world by claiming that how we got here is an unanswerable question. This skeptical view became a major strain of pre-Socratic thought and is certainly evident in the thinking of leading Sophists.

It led the poet Xenophanes, who rejected the anthropomorphic concept of the gods, to conclude that one could not know the truth but could only build resemblances of it. Heraclitus' student Empedocles built a rhetorical theory with an emphasis on delivery skills.[16] Parmenides' student, Zeno of Elea, developed a dialectic that provided the Sophists with a *logos* of the relative. Many of his students became experts at *reductio ad absurdum*. For example, Zeno proved that *logically* it was impossible for an arrow to reach its target because the arrow had to pass a point halfway to the target first. Since there was always another halfway point between the arrow and its target, it could never reach the target because it had to pass another halfway point first. Zeno thereby revealed the inadequacy of logical language. Plato later complained about Zeno's ability to reduce any argument to nothingness.[17]

The Sophists

Not surprisingly, by Plato's time, humans were capable of using language not only to construct their universe but to attack the constructions of others. Language had gained both a creative and a destructive dimension. The Sophists developed these dimensions more fully during their ascendancy, starting in the age of Pericles.[18] Badly needed, because governmental and jurisprudential reforms called for democratic argument, these *metics* (cunning residents, but not citizens, who lived and taught in

Greece in the age of Pericles.

Athens) dominated the arts, politics, and education as Athens converted from an agrarian to a trade-centered economy.[19] The Thracian Protagoras of Abdera, the first Sophist to establish himself in Athens, arrived in 443 BC and became an advisor to Pericles.[20] Protagoras encouraged the development of democracy in Athens.

The Sophists were united in the need to develop virtue *(areté)* in their young charges: the practical knowledge of how to function in domestic, political, and social life in an oral society. They were less united on other subjects because of their commitment to skepticism, which contributed to a more pluralistic and tolerant society than would exist at any other time in Greece.[21] Their love of display helped reinforce the notion that rhetoric was an art.

Protagoras

It was an art that could serve in the search for the proper way to conduct civil affairs. Protagoras' (c. 485–411 BC) reaction to objective naturalism and to the division between Parmenides and Heraclitus provides a case in point. As a *metic* and a diplomat,[22] Protagoras sought to reestablish human existence at the center of philosophical inquiry, arguing that the *subject* determines thoughts and perceptions.[23] According to Protagoras' *On the Way to Truth*, only relative truth exists because humans are incapable of knowing absolute truth. Yet, they have no choice but to become "the measure of all things."[24] Education helps in the measurement process because it teaches us about probabilities and alternatives. That humans are the measure of all things became a starting point in his system of civic education, which included political science *(politike techné)* and sought ways to create consensual agreement in society.[25] Protagoras was one of the first scholars to establish criteria for measuring how well speakers had constructed their version of reality using words, a talent absolutely essential in a subjective world.[26] He also taught such successful playwrights as Euripides,[27] whose plays explore Sophistic notions of truth while reinforcing the mythology of ancient Greece.

Protagoras may have been the first among the philosopher-teachers of the time to concentrate on turning his pupils into civic leaders, "men of the city" who could convince others of the better probabilities *(eikos)* in a world with only limited amounts of objective truth.[28] *Eikos* appeals to the audience's perception of the way things are, which may not be how they actually are. He also developed theories of *peritrope*, turning an opponent's argument against him or her, and *antilogoi*, engaging in a direct rebuttal or clash of arguments.

By arguing that most questions have at least two sides, Protagoras became the father of debate and a chief proponent of dialectical disputation.[29] He envisioned debate as the "prudent" way to conduct business and philosophy. When a matter is debated, it is more likely to be examined carefully. Debate allows for an attack on established beliefs, thereby either strengthening them or reforming them in such a way that society benefits. Aristotle among the Greeks and Cicero among the Romans, as we shall see, reinforced and refined this tradition.

Protagoras also believed that there could be no theory without art, and no practice without theory.[30] Criticism of public address informs the theory of rhetoric, while theory helps to define and guide the art of public speaking. He believed that refined rhetoric could change perceptions so that humans would embrace the good, the just, and the beautiful.

In *Concerning the Gods*, Protagoras argued that life is too short and the gods too obscure for humans to know if they exist for sure. Like many of the Sophists, Protagoras did not believe in resignation to the divine will of the mythic gods;[31] instead he proposed that humans take control of their destinies and use rhetoric to that end. That is why "learning," according to Protagoras in his fragment B3, "must begin in youth. . . . Teaching needs endowment and practice." Despite his call for civic virtue, Protagoras' agnostic approach to the gods led to his banishment from Athens. Even the fact that he had been a trusted advisor of Pericles could not save him.[32] Protagoras escaped by sea only to die when the ship he boarded sank.

Lesser Sophists

Democritus followed Protagoras' lead by claiming that "either truth does not exist or it is hidden from us."[33] Rhetoric, he argued, is essential to survival in a world without definitive truth. Athenian esteem for rhetoric is dramatized by the fact that Antiphon (480–411 BC), perhaps the first psychologist and one of the few Sophists who was a native of Athens, opened a cure-by-words consultantship in the city. He also developed a theory of congruence, which argued that audiences will not believe a speaker who contradicts what they *believe* to be true.[34] To help his students learn how to debate various kinds of cases, Antiphon composed several fictional speeches in his *Tetrologies* that set out two sides in a series of cases moving from circumstantial (indirect) evidence to material (direct) evidence. In each case, evidence is examined from the contrasting points of view of each side; they form a thesis and an antithesis.

Antiphon may have taught the great historian Thucydides. Examples of this tradition of two-sided debate derived from Protagoras and Antiphon abound in Thucydides' famous *History of the Peloponnesian War*, including the debate over whether to invade Syracuse and the debate over whether to annihilate the men of Mytilene. In the case of Syracuse, the sophistical Alcibiades convinces the assembly to invade, but the next day they decide to temper Alcibiades' judgment by requiring two older generals to run the invasion with him. The compromising among the three leads to disaster. In the case of Mytilene, the assembly votes to punish the island by sending a ship to kill all of Mytilene's men, but the next day, after a speech by Diodotus opposing the killing, the assembly sends a second ship to overtake the first one and provide a more lenient penalty. The second ship arrives in the nick of time.

Perhaps the most interesting teaching of Antiphon appears in fragment B44b, in column 2, which reveals the impact of skepticism and tolerance in the Sophistic community. Antiphon, a leading politician of his time, writes, "We are all by nature born the same in every way." This may have been the first utterance in Western civilization that all humans are created equal, a thesis reborn, as we shall see, in the works of John Locke in 1690 and in the Declaration of Independence in 1776.[35] Antiphon recognizes that nothing is worse for humankind than anarchy; thus, consensual rules must be worked out among humans.[36] Antiphon's radical thesis cost him his life since it inspired his taking part in an attempted coup by a group of 400 citizens, for which he was condemned to death in 411 BC.[37]

Aspasia of Miletus.

Aspasia of Miletus (c. 470–410 BC) was from the same city as Thales, Anaximander, and Anaximenes. She in fact studied with Anaxagoras. When the city declined, she moved to Athens where she held her own in a male-dominated society while teaching and practicing rhetoric.[38] She participated in dialogues with Socrates, advised Pericles on politics, and befriended Protagoras. She is rumored to have had a hand in the famous funeral oration delivered by Pericles during the war with Sparta.[39]

Aspasia's experience reveals that Athenian society created a tremendous need for rhetoric; of the arts, only rhetoric provided the sense-making systematic practice *(praxis)* essential to survive and/or compete in a world riddled with uncertainties. Because of the Sophists' success, rhetoric became a major subject of philosophical disputation, textbook writing, and lecturing. The Sophists so dominated Greek culture that rhetoric became the master discipline of their Athenian curriculum. It would remain prominent throughout the Mediterranean world beyond the end of the Second Sophistic in Rome.[40]

Gorgias

The dominance of the Sophists in Athenian society is demonstrated by the career and teaching of Gorgias of Leontini (485–380 BC) on the island of Sicily. He provides the best example of a practicing Sophist who came to dominate his adopted city. In fact, the Athenians were said to have built a statue of him at Delphi in gratitude for his introducing the study of rhetoric to Athens in 427 BC and in honor of his speaking ability. A year after Pericles' death, Gorgias supported the call for an invasion of Syracuse on Sicily, hoping to dislodge the Spartans who had formed an alliance with the Syracusans.

Gorgias foreshadowed several major uses of rhetoric in a world based on probabilities, including rhetoric's impact on politics and how it transcended fiction *(mythos)* and nonfiction *(logos)*. For example, to bring to life his defense of Helen, whose affair with Paris, the son of Priam, King of Troy, caused the Greeks to launch a thousand ships starting the war between Troy and Greece, Gorgias quoted the speeches of Paris that enticed Helen away from her husband. Gorgias' address was no mere display, although it certainly entertained its audience; it advanced a theory of rhetoric and demonstrated a model for speeches of defense, called *apologias.* Gorgias claimed rhetoric to be "a powerful lord who by means of the finest and most invisible body affects the most divine works." Speech, unlike writing, is invisible to the audience; they hear it but do not see it. Thus, it has magical powers that writing does not possess. Words borrowed from songs *(epoidai)* can charm an audience and have a narcotic effect.[41] Thus, speech can cause euphoria, as do some drugs, but it can also heal, as do other drugs. Speech can also work as a magic incantation that bestows pleasure and takes away pain.

In this *Encomium of Helen*, Gorgias went on to divide *logos* into persuasion and poetry. Poetry is "speech having meter," and those who hear it respond emotionally, developing, for example, pity, longing, and even "shuddering."[42] Gorgias clearly understood the superiority of rhetoric over the more narrow sciences. Even in the unflattering Platonic dialogue that bears his name, Gorgias has this to say when responding to Socrates' puzzlement about the "almost superhuman importance" that Gorgias attributes to "the scope of rhetoric":

> Ah, if only you knew all, Socrates, and realized that rhetoric includes practically all other faculties under her control. And I will give you good proof of this. I have often, along with my brother and with other physicians, visited one of their patients who refused to drink his medicine or submit to the surgeon's knife or cautery, and when the doctor was unable to persuade them, I did so, by no other art but rhetoric. And I claim too that, if a rhetorician and a doctor visited any city you like to name and they had to contend in argument before the Assembly or any other gathering as to which of the two should be chosen as doctor, the doctor would be nowhere, but the man who could speak would be chosen, if he so wished.[43]

Few Sophists were better paid or more admired than Gorgias, a great speaker in his own right. As the ambassador of his home city, Gorgias revealed that Sicilians had a tremendous respect for rhetoric and speech writing. The tradition can be traced to Corax and Tisias, a teacher and his student, who helped Syracusans in 467 BC after they replaced the tyrant Thrasybulus with a democracy in which citizens were forced to defend their land claims without the benefit of counsel.[44] Two lawyers from Acragas, Corax (Korax, meaning raven) and Tisias (meaning eggs) were the first speechwriters *(logographers).*[45] The intelligence of the two is represented in a story that is probably apocryphal yet gives us a feeling for the appreciation of rhetoric in ancient Sicily.

When Corax sued his pupil Tisias for the tuition he owed Corax for his training, Tisias argued that if he lost the case, it proved he wasn't well trained and therefore should not pay the tuition. If he won the case, then he didn't need to pay the tuition. Corax countered that if Tisias won the case it proved he was well trained and, therefore, owed Corax the tuition. If Tisias lost the case, he still would owe Corax for his training. The judge, recognizing an inescapable dilemma, threw the case out of court with the line, "Bad raven, bad eggs." Apocryphal or not, the story demonstrates that the Greeks had a wonderful understanding of rhetorical devices long before they began to codify them into textbooks. Whoever Corax and Tisias were, they left behind notes that became one of the first textbooks in the Greek language. And by the way, Syracuse remained a democracy for the next sixty-two years.

Gorgias represented this tradition and the training of his most influential teacher, Empedocles, who believed that our souls pervade our bodies. Empedocles' theory is partially responsible for the sculptures of the time giving more attention to the shape of the body, moving from the rather flat and draped figures of the previous century to the rounded, more natural naked figures of the golden age of Athens. This theory of the soul pervading the body inspired Gorgias to call for more attention to body movement in speaking situations. If the soul permeated the body, then audience members would become more fully immersed in a speech if the speaker aroused the soul in all parts of the body. Aristotle claimed that Empedocles, not Corax or Tisias, was the first to teach the art of rhetoric.

Gorgias impressed the assembly and Greeks in general, even winning the Olympics on three occasions with his orations. Public speaking was an Olympic event at the time. He was a very influential teacher not only because he was very good, but because he lived nearly a century.[46] The brightest students in Athens, much to Socrates' dismay, became Gorgias' pupils. He promised them fame, power, and influence if they would learn the art of rhetoric. Most importantly, he taught them that by exercising their rhetorical talents they would learn about their own potential for leadership and become "men in the city."

In the process of teaching and practicing, he also advanced the art of rhetoric in several significant ways. For example, he borrowed literary devices from poetry and used them in rhetorical contexts.[47] Metaphors, internal rhymes, analogies, and rhythm were in the province of poetry in Gorgias' time. He believed they could be used to enliven speeches, which had been limited to plain and simple language. Thus, he made speeches more fascinating for his audiences.[48]

Gorgias is also considered the father of ceremonial *(epideictic)* speaking,[49] later converted into a genre by Aristotle. Ceremonial speaking has been important in every culture because it functions to celebrate the good and chastise the bad. It is a way to create a civil religion by honoring the deeds of heroes, condemning the evil acts of enemies, and celebrating the days of national pride—thereby healing and strengthening the body politic. The eulogy at the funeral, the commencement address at graduation, and the after-dinner speech at the political fund-raiser can be traced to Gorgias' development of the speech that celebrates values in the contemporary society.

One rationale for Gorgias' love of rhetoric can be found in his statement: "Being does not exist; if it did exist, it would not be cognizable; and if it were cognizable, the cognition would not be communicable."[50] That Gorgias was probably ridiculing Parmenides in no way diminishes the significance of the statement. It certainly echoes the thinking of other pre-Socratics, especially Anaximander, Antiphon, and Heraclitus. Gorgias believed there was "no permanent criterion"[51] for anything; thus rhetoric was essential to survival and making sense out of the chaotic world. Since we can know no truth for sure, since no fixed stars exist to guide us, everything is a matter of speculation. Thus, we must create illusions to cope with our condition and that requires rhetorical talent. If many citizens are trained in rhetoric, there will be competing illusions in the culture, which means that training everyone in society to learn rhetoric is essential so that audiences have access to a multitude of illusions and can select the strongest. Gorgias' object then is not to find the truth, because it is not communicable; his object, like that of Protagoras, is *to build the better illusion*. Gorgias claimed that speakers needed to know when it was appropriate to use rational arguments and when it was appropriate to overwhelm the imagination with stylized images. Rhetoric is crucial to the process because it can move beyond logic to provide imagery, emotion, and authority that enhance the believability of illusions.

Gorgias' theories of rhythm, "fitting timing" *(kairos)*,[52] animation (from Empedocles), and coordination with the cosmic order *(kosmos*, from Pythagoras) evolve from this foundation. *Kairos* teaches a speaker to seize the proper moment and to meet the expectations of the audience.[53] The god *Kairos* brought opportunity; it was up to the mortal to seize it.[54] Animation helps speakers develop a sense of delivery that matches action with mean-

Kairos, Francesco Salviati.

ing. *Kosmos* helps speakers proportion their speeches so that introductions and conclusions are suitable for the length of the speech and arguments are placed in the proper order and kept approximately the same length. A long digression would destroy the *kosmos* of a speech, as would a short introduction for a long speech.

Gorgias established the Sophistic tradition that can be traced through to the *Rhetorica ad Alexandrum*, one of the very first textbooks on persuasion. He also influenced his pupil Isocrates, who was perhaps the most esteemed teacher of rhetoric in ancient Greece. Gorgias argued that rhetors and philosophers should unite to preserve their place in the curriculum.[55] Isocrates reflected Gorgias' belief that rhetoric was hegemonic, that is, a unifying force among humans.[56]

The Sophists were the first to make absolutely clear that rhetoric is essential for survival and success. Like Odysseus, the Sophists believed that speakers needed to possess cunning.[57] The Sophists were often referred to as *metics* not only because they traveled around to teach, but because *metics* is derived from the word *metis*, which means cunning intelligence. Their appreciation for the art of rhetoric has never been surpassed; perhaps no group has had more influence on its own society. Most of the playwrights and politicians were products of Sophist teachers if not Sophists themselves. No wonder this era also produced great diversity of thinking.

Isocrates

The Sophist Isocrates (436–338 BC) expanded the province of rhetoric by arguing that it could enhance civic pride and lead people to their higher destiny.[58] Isocrates was born of a wealthy flute maker who paid for his son's education. He studied with Protagoras, Prodicus of Cheos,[59] and Gorgias.[60] Isocrates soon discovered that his gentle nature and stage fright would prevent a career in politics, so he became a speechwriter and then in 392 BC a prominent teacher. Essentially, Isocrates was a pragmatist warning in his *Nicocles* that airy philosophy will not help much in governing. His formula for success was to find students with natural speaking talent, which Isocrates believed was a gift of the gods that must be used for good in order to honor them. Once Isocrates found such students, he developed their god-given talent with heavy doses of practice, theory, and imitation of great speakers, while inculcating the students with a strong sense of civic duty. He saw piety as a very important virtue to be displayed by speakers. A side benefit of such displays was that they would work to heal public corruption.[61]

Isocrates believed that demagogues and sycophants had corrupted Athenian society. He called for a return to older values and a system in which the elites of society wisely guide it toward a better future by uniting all Greeks against less cultured countries. In other words, he endorsed a conservative moralism that catered to the elite. When a student became a politician, he would then display civic virtue in his speeches, mainly by praising or blaming the behavior of the state and its leaders. Obviously this formulation elevates speaker credibility.

Isocrates tried to persuade his fellow Sophists that rhetorical invention was intimately involved with all parts of the speech. He believed the word choice or style (lexis) of speakers would reflect on their character; in fact, he held that the presence of the speaker through delivery makes the speech more persuasive than if it were read by the audience. He used the body metaphor to explain that a speech must have a head (introduction), torso (substantial argument), and feet (conclusion). Furthermore, calling up appropriate emotions required conjuring images that would evoke emotions. This view gained ascendance when Cicero, the Roman senator, consul, and orator, defended it in *De Oratore* (see chapter 5).[62]

Isocrates also had success with his theory of periodic style in which he tried to match meaning and rhythm. Ancient Greek is a sing-song language that allows for the memorization of long passages in an oral society. Thus, rhyming was inherent to it; Isocrates sought to match the rhyming with intricate meanings, not only improving the language but advancing the art of poetry.

He also inspired Aristotle, who in his *Rhetoric* references Isocrates more than any other thinker. From Isocrates, Aristotle derived his theories that humans are different from animals because humans speak, that *ethos* (trust in the speaker) is the most important element in persuasion, and that rhetoric is an art, not a science. Isocrates put it this way:

> Because there has been implanted in us the power to persuade each other and to make clear to each other whatever we desire, not only have we escaped the life of wild beasts, but we have come together and founded cities and made laws and invented arts. . . . [G]enerally speaking, there is no institution devised by man which the power of speech has not helped us to establish.[63]

In *Antidosis*, he defends himself against imaginary accusations of sophistry. In the course of this defense, Isocrates reinforces his innovative threefold approach to public speaking, which holds that *practice and knowledge of theory* should refine *natural talent*.[64] "The man who wishes to persuade people will not be negligent as to the matter of character. . . . [H]e will apply himself above all to establish a most honorable name among his fellow citizens."[65] This was to be accomplished through learning three important concepts. The first is *therapeai*—just as it sounds, it has a therapeutic function to heal or cure. However, it goes beyond healing or curing the individual; it has a medicinal effect on the whole community. The second is *douleia*, which means service to the state. The third is *melete*, which means to attend to or to practice caregiving. These values lay a foundation for character and are reflected in Aristotle's notion of *ethos*, which we shall investigate in the next chapter.

In his *Demonicus*, Isocrates wrote about the benefits of imitation; he argued that young students should memorize the speeches of great orators and then try to imitate their best characteristics. He generalizes to learning about civic virtue in the same way. Imitate the character of good rulers, and you will become a good ruler. Remember, however, that good rulers are also good speakers. Understanding civic virtue gives one the ability to make good decisions; rhetoric allows one to justify these decisions. Through such action and rhetoric, a ruler displays knowledge and civic virtue that is then emulated by the citizens. To illustrate the importance of displaying virtue through eloquent speech, Isocrates told the story of General Timotheus, who won many victories for Athens but was later falsely charged with treason. Though Timotheus was a virtuous person, he was inept at persuasion and lost his case. The truth does not speak for itself and is not in itself persuasive.

Isocrates' teachings are summarized in the *Antidosis* and the *Panegyricus*, which inspired many of his followers. He hoped his fellow citizens would use the power of rhetoric to end the feuding between the city-states of Greece and to form a Pan-Hel-lenic Union.[66] He favored hegemonic alliance-building over dissention. In fact, in his dotage, he wrote a letter to King Philip of Macedon urging him to lead the Greek states against the Persians. His advice was rejected by Philip, but not by Philip's son Alexander, who, during his reign (336–323 BC) twenty years later, followed the plan of Isocrates. Philip had taken possession of the wealthy and cultured Greek city-states, including Athens, from his almost barbarous mountain kingdom of Macedon, despite repeated warnings by the orator Demosthenes to the people of Athens. When Philip was assassinated, Alexander spread Hellenism across the known world, easily absorb-ing the rich culture he inherited. Ironically, Alexander, his legendary teacher Aristotle, and his father's enemy Demosthenes would all die in one short year-and-a-half period around 323 BC. But these events came after even more severe attacks on the Sophists during the golden age of Athens prior to the conquest of Philip.

SOCRATES AND PLATO

Socrates (469–399 BC) and his chief publicist and student Plato (427–347 BC) attempted to repudiate the Sophists and their teachings. To understand fully the devel-opment of the art of rhetoric, it is essential that we examine this attack and Aristotle's response to it; for it is that response that becomes the *Rhetoric*, the most important work in the history of our field.

Socrates, who served in the war against Sparta, lived through the defeat of Athens only to be condemned to death for impiety, "corrupting" the youth of his city and vio-lating a ban on his teaching. The government in Athens would not tolerate Socrates' attack on their form of government and refused to allow him to teach. At age 70 in 399 BC he drank hemlock and died surrounded by his admirers. In the *Apology*, his speech of defense at his trial, Socrates said, "I always address the individual." In other dialogues, his notion of dialectic is explored more fully. It argues that the torment of questioning produces the truth much in the same way the labor pains of the mother produces a child. Socrates saw himself as a midwife in this dialectical process.[67] In the process of seeking the truth, Socrates gave the world some of its most famous apho-risms such as "Wisdom begins in wonder"; "he is richest who is content with the least"; and "our youth now love luxury," a thought that echoes into our own time.

While the Sophists flourished in their own day, some of their writing was lost when the library at Alexandria, Egypt, burned (see chapter 5); it contained the most important texts of antiquity. Furthermore, the Sophists had not taken the time to refute the lengthy writings of Plato that eventually tarnished their luster and greatly influenced such early Christian apologists as Augustine. Plato's famous Academy in Athens was to educate Aristotle and to last nearly 900 years. While his Academy could not compare to the glamour of the Sophists' schools, it outlasted them and thereby got the last word.

Like Parmenides, Plato constructed a "truth" found in another world. This place beyond physical reality, where perfect forms exist permanently, he called the "*noume-nal* world." The ideas and objects of the world that we experience through our senses are imperfect imitations of *noumenal* forms, but they have sufficient resemblance to give an impression of reality. Reeling from the influence of the Sophists and deter-

Death of Socrates, Jacques Louis David.

mined to return philosophy to a truth-based footing, Plato developed an elaborate scaffolding that *bridged Heraclitus' notion of change and Parmenides' notion of permanence.* The world in which our bodies are trapped is the world of change, shadow, and illusion; the world from which our souls came and to which they will return is the world of permanence. Using this description, Plato propagated Socrates' "noble rhetoric" that taught that it is better to suffer pain than to inflict it, and better to be a reflective philosopher who knows him- or herself than to be a "man in the city."[68] Only through philosophical dialogue, introspection, and recollection will people find their way back to the truth of the *noumenal* world, which is indelibly etched into our souls.

Plato dealt with the contingent position of humans by suggesting that our condition is not relevant to the individual's highest aspirations—the attainment of true knowledge from the *noumenal* world—and in fact distracts us from that quest. Plato sought to develop the souls of his students so they could return to the perfect, transcendent world. It is a very persuasive model because it plays to our nature as *anamalia metaphysica*, creatures who have a longing for the permanent and the spiritual. It deals with the contingent not by confronting it, or mastering it the way Gorgias did, but by transcending it.[69]

The synthesis of Parmenides' permanence and Heraclitus' change led Plato to argue that universal ideas, which are in a *noumenal* place, are permanent forms in which the transitory material world participates only imperfectly, somewhat like reflectors. Universal ideas embody rational thought; they are stable, permanent, and valid. Sense perceptions are mired in material experience, individual variables, transience, and appearance. Universal ideas are spaceless, matterless, and permanent, and all particulars merely reflect them imperfectly: the material chair of our world is a flawed imitation of the ideal chair in the *noumenal* world. On the one hand, while the material chair in this world can help your soul recall the perfect chair in the *noumenal* world, it can never emulate it perfectly. On the other hand, the universal idea has generative powers because it reveals the perfect potential for the form.[70] In this way, universal ideas are the *formal causes* that allow things to come into existence in this world. They inspire the artist and the craftsman to try to imitate them. Recalling the perfect chair from the *noumenal* world, a carpenter tries to construct one to match it in this world. Universal ideas are also the *energia* or life force of the entity, and therefore are more real than the entity. It is the form of the oak that determines changes from season to season and year to year. Ultimately, universal ideas are the *telos* or final cause, for they determine the purpose or "towards which" of the entity. It is the latent form of the oak tree that determines its ultimate shape. For all these reasons, Plato argued that the idea is more real than the material, which decays and changes.

These perfect forms allow artists to see where they align their creations with perfection and where they are defective. Thus, Plato's normative theory of criticism has positive and negative corrective functions. If it reflects perfection, a work of art can break through our common thoughts and worldviews. It can also reveal what we don't have and/or what we are missing in our lives.

According to Plato, one of the great tensions in life is the battle between reason, which carries the soul back to the ideal, and the senses, which distract the soul and lead it to the phenomenal and material. For him, pure reason, often in dialogue, is the key to understanding; rhetoric is too involved with the "real" world and too often plays to the senses and the material, thereby confusing and corrupting the soul. He did, however, posit a "noble" rhetoric, which we will examine later in this chapter.

Plato's bias for the *noumenal* world explains his prejudice against the Sophists. Since he believed in an absolute truth, he established dichotomies that the Sophists rejected: inquiry is preferred to persuasion; reason is preferred to emotion; one-on-one communication is preferred to mass persuasion. These bipolarities forced philosophers to choose between rhetoric and dialectic instead of wedding them as Isocrates did. Isocrates believed that rhetoric has a role to play in the inquiry process and that reason is surely a part of every speech that makes an argument. But Plato would brook no such integration. The object of the ideal teacher is to call the truth out of the soul of the pupil without the aid of rhetorical strategies. Plato believed the truth is in and of itself persuasive and needs no ornamentation, watering down, emotional appeals, or appeals to credibility.

Communication and the Dialogues of Plato

Plato's "noble rhetoric" is dialectical, aimed at leading the soul back to the emanating good/God. This theme is manifest in Plato's most important dialogues. In the *Meno*, the discussion begins with Socrates and Meno attempting to define virtue. Meno believes that virtue is relative; each audience decides on its own definition. Socrates protests that virtue must have some common characteristics and those would constitute a stable definition. Meno does not agree, so Socrates shifts the discussion to such specific virtues as justice, hoping that a more inductive approach might provide a useful definition. Socrates invites Meno to join the search. He convinces Meno of several crucial assumptions: (1) they are both ignorant and so they must seek the truth outside of themselves; (2) they are capable of learning something they do not already know; (3) how we learn determines what we learn.

Socrates then argues that the best way to learn is to *recollect* the truth from the *noumenal* world where the soul learned the truth while disembodied. Recollection is accompanied by recognition, an intuitive realization that the standard for judgment is correct. The standard for virtue is in the *noumenal* world, which the soul has experienced before coming into the world of the senses. We should note that in the *Theaetetus*, Plato differentiates memory from recollection. Memory is like soft wax on which an experience leaves an impression. The purer the wax, the more accurate the impression. While memory is the "mother of muses," recollection is superior because it does not rely on our experiences, rather it takes us to the *noumenal* world. He compares it to walking into an aviary and being able to name all the different real birds, as opposed to those we might recite from memory.

Socrates demonstrates this doctrine using Meno's slave, who under questioning from Socrates produces the Pythagorean theorem, which was previously unknown to him. Socrates seals the persuasion by asking, "What do you think, Meno? In answering, did the slave boy express any knowledge that was not his own?" Meno responds, "No, they were all his own." Socrates crows, "[T]hese true beliefs were in him, weren't they?"[71] Thus, Socrates argues that we come to knowledge by recollecting what is already in our souls. This *a priori* knowledge is more reliable than knowledge gained through the senses, since they can be fooled. If one can recollect geometry, surely one can recollect virtue. Thus, Socrates' epistemology, how we learn what we know, is based on recollection of perfect knowledge from the *noumenal* world.

In the *Euthydemos*, Plato tried to show the difference between a truly philosophical argument and one that is a trick. Two Sophists banter two young brothers into confusion over the question of whether one can be a philosopher and a politician at the same time. Socrates rebukes the Sophists and with the proper questions straightens one of the poor youths out. He ostensibly proves that wisdom is the only good; ignorance is the only evil—themes repeated in the dialogue named for *Protagoras*. Philosophy and political rhetoric are so different that someone who participates in both will do well in neither. The reflective and thoughtful philosopher will fail as a politician because the voters will believe the philosopher is indecisive and not a person of action. The politician will fail as a philosopher because speeches to large audiences and shortcuts in logic have no place in the philosophical community.

Plato's *Sophist* follows the same theme by trying to demonstrate that true rhetors use their power to clear the soul of the illusions of this world, while sophists use rhetoric to confuse the soul with more illusions. True rhetors educate the citizens of their country and give them good reasons upon which they can base their decisions. The Sophist merely flatters and excites them to act without a firm basis in reason.[72]

Part of Plato's bias against the Sophists resided in his belief that thought is superior to language. Because speech is more physical, more corporeal, it is less likely to be able to reach the nonmaterial world of perfect ideas. Thought, however, is immaterial and, therefore, a better vehicle for reaching the ideal. In other works, particularly his *Seventh Epistle*, Plato argued against writing, claiming that the practice of writing words down instead of speaking them out loud will lead to diminished memory and exclude the corrective function of oral give-and-take. This argument is not unlike that of educators who claim that giving calculators to students undercuts their ability to perform mathematical functions on their own.

In the process of his argument, Plato developed a reductionist theory of language, a way by which language can be reduced to basic essence. By looking behind various ideas and how they are woven together, a rhetorical theorist can determine if ideas are properly related. To guide this hermeneutics, or interpretation of truth, Plato recommended *diaeresis*, division and categorization according to kinds, much like a biologist's lists of phylum, class, order, family, genus, and species.[73] This excessively dialectic approach to knowledge would win over many a medieval and Renaissance philosopher, including the influential Peter Ramus (see chapter 7).

The *Laws* is another dialogue in which the Sophists are attacked because of the way they empower audiences and then deceive them in order to get their way.[74] Plato prefers a hierarchical society in which every member has a useful role to play. Unfortunately, that means that his public audience is slotted into well-defined positions and not allowed to defy the philosopher king. The function of rhetoric in such a society is to convince the public to support the laws of the land. Only those with expertise would be allowed to speak in Plato's community. That expertise would come from dialectic; rhetoric would be confined to an explanatory role or one that assured loyalty to the state and its order. Perhaps the best face that can be put on Plato's theory of rhetoric in the *Laws* is that it is to be used to induce consent of the governed by the governors.[75] However, it is clear that Plato endorsed the use of threats and other forms of coercion.[76]

The *Gorgias* contains the most stinging attack on the Sophists and the dialogue containing the most spirited debate with Socrates. Here the question is: Isn't rhetoric corrupt when it is part of the art of getting what one wants by fair means or foul? Gorgias and his pupil, Polus, gather with Socrates at the home of an influential politician named Callicles. Gorgias begins the debate by arguing that power and influence come with the ability to impress an audience. Socrates replies that "rhetoric is the art of persuading an ignorant multitude about the justice or injustice of a matter, without imparting any real instruction."[77] In dialectic the victor is clear because everything is reasoned to its conclusion. But in rhetoric, the situation is clouded where several speak in turns without adequate follow-up, give-and-take, and purity of language. Rhetoric is further corrupted by its reliance on the authority of the speaker and emotional appeals to induce belief but not necessarily truth.

Gorgias replies that justice is a sufficient practical knowledge of human affairs to know what is conventionally moral in any given case, and rhetoric is the art of persuading people to bring about the greatest good. Thus, justice and rhetoric are compatible. So are healing and rhetoric as when one persuades a child to take medicine. Socrates answers that rhetoric can also bring about the greatest evil. Furthermore, rhetoric "produces persuasion in the soul," and is therefore powerful, but it merely supplies probabilities not knowledge.

At this point (464b–481b), Polus steps in to defend the Sophists' position. He argues that the greatest good is power. Socrates admires Polus' frankness but contends that rhetoric is not of much use in the world because it is not a *techné;* it does not rest on universal principles that can be taught. For example, justice corrects legislation, gymnastics tones the body, and medicine heals it. Rhetoric, however, is either inspired by the gods or it is a knack, like cooking (464b–466a). In either case, says Socrates, it is not a genuine academic discipline. Sophistry flatters and rhetoric imitates the truth, just as cooking flatters the stomach and cosmetics hide the flaws of the face. By making the worse appear to be the better, rhetoric allows the guilty to go free and does a great deal of damage in the world.

Polus contends that rhetoric can be used to defend the innocent in court. Socrates refuses to accept this point, responding that defending the innocent doesn't matter because it is noble to suffer an injustice; such suffering expands the soul. However, it is ignoble to inflict injustice; therefore, the evil that rhetoric does is relevant. It corrupts the soul. If we eliminate all the good that rhetoric does, some will suffer, but this is not a vice because it does no harm to the soul. If, however, we allow rhetoric to be taught in the name of doing good, it will be used for evil as well. Since doing wrong is a greater evil than suffering at the hands of the wrongdoer, rhetoric should be abolished.

Polus surrenders to this attack and turns his seat over to Callicles, their host who urges Socrates to abandon philosophy.[78] Socrates, perhaps ironically, compares Callicles to a touchstone for testing gold. He has intelligence, goodwill, and candor.[79] Socrates claims that if he can convince Callicles, then Socrates knows that he has spoken the truth. To this point, Socrates has admitted that rhetoric has limited uses. These include (1) confessing to a crime before a judge, (2) confessing the crimes of one's friends and family before a judge, and (3) defending one's enemies before a judge in this life so that they will be properly punished in the afterlife. This last use of rhetoric is what baits Callicles into the dialogue. He resists Socrates' theory about an eternal soul that will be judged in another life.

Socrates then collapses his concerns into the most important question of the dialogue: What role does rhetoric play in making life meaningful?

> We are arguing about the way of human life, and what question can be more serious than this to a man who has any sense at all; whether he should follow after the way of life to which you exhort me, and truly fulfill what you call the manly part of speaking in the assembly, and cultivating rhetoric, and engaging in public affairs, after your manner; or whether he should pursue the life of philosophy.

Callicles' response is scathing and no doubt offensive to idealists and academics:

> The philosopher creeps into the corner for the rest of his life, and talks in a whisper with three or four admiring youths, but never speaks out like a freeman in a satisfactory manner.

And so the debate is finally framed around the issue of how one is to live one's life and the role rhetoric will play in it: Will you become a contemplative philosopher skilled at dialectic or a "man in the city" skilled at political speaking? Each vocation requires a different kind of discourse. The philosopher needs to master dialectic; the orator must possess rhetorical skill. Socrates claims that rhetorical skill blinds the orator to what dialectic can reveal; political rhetoric convinces the mob that the shadow of a donkey is a horse. It does not make sense of the world; it clouds our vision.

Callicles responds that he must develop his talents fully to know who he is, and that means becoming a man in the city, a participant in civic debate.[80] To do this one must master rhetoric rather than merely engage in pandering to an audience. Socrates agrees that there is a noble rhetoric that makes the citizens of the state better people. However, Callicles' version of the noble rhetoric is too political. To illustrate this point, Socrates attacks those who most Greeks considered to be statesmen: Cimon, Themistoclies, Miltiades, and shockingly even Pericles. Socrates claims that only his rhetoric is noble, and therefore, he is the only real statesman in Athens.

Callicles is exasperated by Socrates' arrogant claim and rejects his reasoning. Abandoning dialectic, Socrates pleads with Callicles in long speeches in an effort to convince him that the philosophical vision makes more sense. Callicles will have none of it. He accuses Socrates of contradicting himself by engaging in mob oratory and says, "The truth, Socrates, which you . . . follow is this: Luxury and intemperance and license, when they have sufficient backing, are virtue and happiness." After Callicles walks out of his party, Socrates makes one last plea to those who remain: The afterworld in which one will be judged is based on one's true nature, not the appearance one leaves with the public. Rhetoric is concerned with appearance in the city; philosophy is concerned with knowledge in the afterworld. Thus, only philosophy can bring you to your true nature and to the true world.

Despite the fact that Socrates abandoned dialectic, employed Sophistic tricks, and appealed to the emotions, his thesis has not only survived, it has at times flourished. It was solidly reinforced in the artful dialogue the *Phaedrus*, where the noble rhetoric mentioned in the last part of the *Gorgias* is fully explored. The *Phaedrus* begins with three speeches. The first is a speech by the Sophist Lysias, a famous speechwriter who has beguiled the young Phaedrus.[81] On the way home from this presentation, Phaedrus meets Socrates, who is dangling his foot in the Ilissus River. When prompted by Socrates, Phaedrus reads the speech of Lysias[82] to Socrates, who finds it offensive and then demonstrates that Lysias was speaking from ignorance. Socrates admonishes the youth not to believe anything just because he admires the language used or the source. In other words, don't believe in an idea because the words are highly stylized, impressive, and entertaining, or because the speaker is a great performer. Believe it instead because it is true.

Socrates then gives a speech on the same subject, love; the rather naive and clueless Phaedrus is once again impressed. The speech does have deeper implications in that Socrates actually talks about speech construction in this monologue, trying to demonstrate the interrelationships between the quality of the form of a work of art, in this case a speech, and its moral content. He claims that the speech needs to possess an order that appeals to the soul of the listener to call out its lessons. But Socrates admits that this speech, too, is a fraud because he has been false to the knowledge he has. Like the seducer, he has wooed Phaedrus with clever and artful words and his own credibility but has not shared the truth with him.

Socrates then gives the final set speech of the dialogue, which argues that true love *(Eros)*, a metaphor for the noble rhetoric, is a *complete* sharing between equals of the knowledge of the *noumenal* world. This speech is true to knowledge. There is no Callicles present to point out the use of metaphors—a Sophistic device. Instead, an admiring Phaedrus listens as an ideal rhetoric is explored. The goal of the noble rhetoric is to perfect humans by revealing their *noumenal* nature, their ability to associate with perfection through the rational facility of the soul. Socrates argues that a glimpse of beauty can inspire the soul, which allows it to grow wings and fly upward toward the *noumenal* world.

In the rest of the dialogue, Socrates sets out his definition of a philosophical or noble rhetoric. It begins with adaptation to an audience. Beginning at line 272, the speaker is urged to learn "what type of man is susceptible to what kind of discourse." The speaker "tell[s] himself, 'that is the man, that character now actually before me is the one I heard about in school, and in order to persuade him of something I have to apply these arguments in this fashion.'" Speakers must define and divide their topics dialectically. They should know the truth and, therefore, be a philosopher before they speak: "Come out, children of my soul and convince Phaedrus, who is the father of similar beauties, that he will never be able to speak about anything unless he becomes a philosopher."[83] You must then organize the speech with a head, body, and conclusion. You must be true to knowledge and bring the other's soul to it. You must only adorn the speech enough to adapt to the soul of the listener. In love, as in noble rhetoric, both parties are rewarded, both concentrate on the spiritual, and both conceive something new. Every person is simultaneously a lover/speaker (active) and a beloved/listener (passive). These are the conditions that constitute both love and noble rhetoric. Thus, Plato's rhetorical theory is limited to dialogic, dialectical confrontation committed to an open and equal search for the truth.[84]

Influenced by the Neoplatonic school at Alexandria, early Christian thinkers, including Augustine, were avowed Platonists. There is among some philosophers and others the feeling that dealing with pragmatic existence, being a "man in the city," is ignoble. The theme was extended by such important thinkers as Søren Kierkegaard and Martin Heidegger, as we shall see in chapter 9 of this book. We need to note that the enduring quality of Plato's position results from its rhetorical formulation, not from the fact that philosophers embrace it as obviously true. Plato's *noumenal* world might have been no more than an idealization of the material world, or so Aristotle apparently thought when he reduced Plato's forms to categories. Plato's conceptualization condemned the Sophists' rhetoric as a corrupter of the soul, one that blinds humans to the emanating good and deceives them into thinking shadows are reality. Plato substituted a dialectical discourse, wholly concerned with returning the soul to its *noumenal* vision. Because he believed reason alone is sufficient to find the truth, Plato privileged dialectic. Rhetoric is not, as his dialogue the *Meno* makes clear, wisdom. More often than not, it is used to defeat wisdom.

The positive influence of Plato can be seen in the works of many rhetorical theorists. In the last century, Karl Wallace (1925–1973) called for a "rhetoric of good reasons," where speakers not only give reasons for a given proposition but discuss its downside.[85] Wallace believed that values lie behind all arguments and that responsible speakers make clear the values to which they are appealing. Both sides of the question should be examined before a conclusion is recommended.

Richard Weaver (1910–1963) advanced an idealism that he hoped would show that dialectic can inform rhetoric.[86] Like Plato in his *Phaedrus*, Weaver demonstrated that there are "noble" as well as "ignoble" speakers. In *Ideas Have Consequences*, he argued that language can improve our lot on earth only if we purify the language we use and we understand values before we speak.[87] To do that, dialectic must come first and rhetoric second; that is, *inquiry must precede advocacy*. Furthermore, we need to assess how words or phrases become "ultimate terms"—"God terms" and "devil terms" that change our view of the world. For most Americans *work* is a God term; work is good of and by itself. It is better to work than to be *unemployed*, a devil term. By loading the words with values, we reinforce the capitalist system. But if you stop and think about it, work in and of itself is really not necessarily good. It is more likely that the rewards the work produces will determine whether or not it is good. Is it creative? Does it better humankind? Is the money it generates used for good? Or is work mind numbing, corrupting, or polluting?

In *The Ethics of Rhetoric*, Weaver showed that some "language is sermonic" and that the highest order of appeal is based on definition or the nature of the thing. Such appeals show the audience what is permanent, that is, what transcends the world of flux. He gives the example of Lincoln's definition of what it is to be human and claims that such speakers are "conservatives in the legitimate sense of the word."[88] The lowest level of arguments are those that appeal to circumstance because circumstances are most likely to change.[89]

Weaver's Platonic approach helps us see how language works in rhetorical ways to shape our values and helps us guard against what he calls in "tyrannizing images" such as the work ethic. On a more positive note, he showed that rhetoric also keeps order in society and prevents a kind of barbarian anarchy from taking over. He did this by demonstrating that the "sources of argument" often reveal the ethical base of the arguer.[90] Thus, he was true to the Platonic ideal.

CONCLUSION

The golden age of Athens was marked by tensions that helped generate the first rhetorical theories. The naturalists, led by Thales, sought to replace the mythologists; the mystics, led by Parmenides, attacked the naturalists. In this turbulent era marked by considerable government reform, the Sophists emerged as the supreme teachers who eventually dominated Athenian society and the development of rhetoric. Finally, reformers like Isocrates and radical new thinkers like Plato revived the question of ethics and truth to form a new theory of the ideal rhetoric.

This debate reveals that, generally speaking, the more relative and skeptical a philosophy is, the more likely it is to embrace the need for rhetoric. The more democratic a society is, the more likely it is to employ rhetoric to achieve its ends. The flowering of Athenian culture produced not only great playwrights, but also speaker-leaders such as Pericles, Alcibiades, Gorgias, Demosthenes, Hippias,[91] and Lysias.

The unending debate over what constitutes the proper study of rhetoric helped give birth to one of the most important contributions of Greece to the ancient world: the *paideia* or cultural heritage of Hellenism converted into a curriculum. The Greeks believed that a well-rounded person should master logic, grammar, rhetoric, arithmetic, geometry, astronomy and music. The Sophists helped integrate this curriculum by showing its crosscurrents and the relevance of rhetoric as a capstone discipline. After the Sophists, rhetorical curricula developed the *progymnasmata*,[92] a series of exercises that helped young men evolve into eloquent orators. This "rounded education" was spread through the Western world by Alexander's conquests.[93]

Thus, Greek culture produced divisions among those who taught scientific observations, those who taught the art of illusion building, those who taught rule-bound exercises, and those who believed the truth was self-persuasive and did not need the aid of rhetoric. Each of these philosophies had its flaws; in the wrong hands, each could be used for evil purposes. The high-minded Platonist can become the dogmatic fascist; the amoral Sophist can become the cynical manipulator of audiences. Demagoguery is possible on all sides.

That is why Aristotle is so important. He would synthesize the best of these theories and explain their uses in the world of human problems and endeavors. He believed that his teacher Plato made a mistake when he saw the exchange between dialectic and rhetoric as a one-way street. Plato refused to admit to the possibility that rhetoric can inform dialectic—that, in fact, rhetorical moments often occur in dialectic. Witness Socrates' extensive use of rhetorical tactics in the dialogues. This obvious flaw in Plato's system inspired his pupil Aristotle to remedy it. The next chapter turns to that remedy.

Study Questions

1. Which of the schools discussed in this chapter best represents your philosophy? What are its implications for a system of rhetoric? Using it, how do you obtain the truth?

2. What is the relationship between the political development of Greek city-states, particularly Athens, and the development of rhetorical theory? Is there an analogy with contemporary America?

3. Compare and contrast the philosophical positions of Parmenides and Heraclitus. With whom do you most identify and why?

4. The Sophists were characterized by skepticism, tolerance, and a belief that the truth was at best relative. Can you think of modern-day equivalents?

5. How does Protagoras' view of the truth contribute to a rhetorical theory that is useful in governing the city-state?

6. What is Gorgias' definition of rhetoric? What are its uses?

7. Compare and contrast the rhetorical theories of Gorgias and Isocrates.

8. Attack or defend Plato's theory of a *noumenal* world using contemporary examples from film, painting, or public address.

9. What is it that Socrates and Plato want us ultimately to attain? Is there a role that rhetoric can play in that quest?

10. Are the dialogues of Plato rhetorical? Using the definition of the noble rhetoric as set out in the *Phaedrus*, provide a contemporary example of it.

11. What is the difference between a science, an art, and a knack? How would you categorize public speaking? Give examples of contemporary politicians you would compare to Gorgias, Polus, Callicles, and Socrates.

12. What is the *paideia*? Do we have one in this country?

Notes

1 The court then became known as the Heliaea and met in the Agora, along with the less important courts, known as *stoas.*

2 Members of the Areopagus held their seats for life. Rome followed this model for its senate.

3 This term may have been corrupted over time. Thales is the father of science, but in his day science and philosophy were very closely linked. The same is true of *techné* and art. *Techné* means a discipline with rules that can be taught. Later its meaning was expanded to include art, which generally relies on generative principles instead of rules.

4 Simon Hornblower and Anthony Spawforth, *The Oxford Classical Dictionary* (New York: Oxford U. Press, 1996), p. 86.

5 See, for example, *Poetry, Language, and Thought,* Albert Hofstadter, trans. (New York: Harper and Row, 1971); *What Is Called Thinking?* Fred D. Wieck and J. Glenn Gray, trans. (New York: Harper and Row, 1968), particularly p. 10.

6 The persistence of this idea in our own time is made clear in Dilip P. Gaonkar, "The Idea of Rhetoric in the Rhetoric of Science," *The Southern Communication Journal,* 58 (1993): 258–62.

7 His grandfather had been the dictator of Sicyon.

8 It met in the Bouleuterion to consider legislation; hence the nickname Boulé. Also, the Greek word for deliberation was *bouleuesthai.*

9 There is some debate over the actual evolution of the term rhetoric. For example, Edward Schiappa in his *Protagoras and Logos: A Study in Greek Philosophy and Rhetoric* (Columbia: U. of South Carolina Press, 1991), pp. 40–54, 199 claims that the word *rhetorike* was first used by Plato, and therefore, it was not until his time that rhetoric was recognized as a true discipline for study. Richard Enos, on the other hand, argues in his *Greek Rhetoric Before Aristotle* (Long Grove, IL: Waveland Press, 1993) that rhetoric was probably a discipline by the fifth century BC; it was part of *logos* studies.

10 Drew A. Hyland, *The Origins of Philosophy: The Rise in Myths and Presocratics* (New York: Putnam, 1973), p. 193.

11 See H. Diels and W. Kranz, *Die Fragmente der Vorsokratiker,* 2, 10th ed. (Berlin, 1960), fragment 8.3–4.

12 See G. S. Kirk and J. E. Raven, *The Presocratic Philosophers* (Cambridge: Harvard U. Press, 1971), pp. 186–89; Hyland, p. 156; Robert S. Brumbaugh, *The Philosophers of Greece* (New York: Peter Smith, 1964), p. 45.

13 See Diels and Kranz, fragments 12, 49a, 82, 83, 91, 102. For more fragments see C. J. DeVogel, *Greek Philosophy: A Collection of Texts,* 1, 4th ed. (Leiden, Netherlands: Humanities Press, 1969). See also Hyland, pp. 158–59.

14 Walter Kaufmann, *Existentialism from Dostoyevsky to Sartre* (New York: Random House, 1966), p. 215.

15 Kirk and Raven, p. 105. See also, Hyland, pp. 33–42.

16 See Enos, pp. 60–65.

17 Hyland, pp. 207–8; Kirk and Raven, p. 321.

18 See John Poulakos, *Sophistical Rhetoric in Classical Greece* (Columbia: U. of South Carolina Press, 1995). The collected fragments of the Sophists' works that remain extant amount to only about twenty pages and few are contextualized.

19 James L. Jarrett, *The Educational Theories of the Sophists* (New York: Columbia U. Teachers College Press, 1969); Friedrich Solmsen, *Intellectual Experiments of the Greek Enlightenment* (Princeton: Princeton U. Press, 1975); Mario Untersteiner, *The Sophists,* Kathleen Freeman, trans. (New York: Philosophical Library, 1964); Harold Barrett, *The Sophists* (Novato, CA: Chandler & Sharp Publishers, 1987).

20 Protagoras provided a balance to the rationalist teachings of Anaxagoras whom Pericles followed.

21 See H. I. Marrou, *A History of Education in Antiquity* (Madison: U. of Wisconsin Press, 1948); see also John Poulakos, "Hegel's Reception of the Sophists," *Western Journal of Speech Communication,* 54 (Spring, 1990): 161–68.

22 For example, he wrote the constitution for the Athenian colony of Thurii.

23 G. B. Kerferd, *The Sophistic Movement* (Cambridge: Cambridge U. Press, 1981), p. 7. For a full treatment of Protagoras and his influence see Schiappa.

24 E. Rohde, *Psyche: The Cult of Souls and the Belief in Immortality Among the Greeks* (New York: Books for Libraries Press, 1920), p. 438.

25 At the beginning of Plato's *Protagoras* (312 D), a student refers to the great teacher as "a master of making one a clever speaker."

[26] See Schiappa, pp. 119, 125, 148–51.

[27] Euripides was also a student of the Sophist Prodicus of Ceos. He wrote such important dramas as *Medea, Hecuba,* and *The Trojan Women.* Aristophanes, a comic playwright, made fun of Euripides in the play *The Frogs.* Because of the ridicule he had to endure in Athens for his tragedies, Euripides moved to the court of King Archelaus of Macedonia. There he wrote *The Bacchae* and died in 406 BC.

[28] It is precisely this notion that Plato has Socrates attack in the dialogue *Gorgias.*

[29] He wrote several books on the subject of dialectical disputation including *Antilogies* and a *Method of Argument.* The influence on the playwright Euripides is evident in many of his works including *Antiope* (189 N) where he declared, "On every subject, it would be possible to set up a debate of double arguments, providing one was skilled in speaking."

[30] Bromley Smith, "The Father of Debate: Protagoras of Abdera," *Quarterly Journal of Speech,* 4 (1918): 197.

[31] In *On the Gods,* he wrote, "About the gods, I am not able to know whether they exist or do not exist" (fragment B 4).

[32] Protagoras served as ambassador to Thurii in Sicily for Pericles. See Untersteiner, p. 5.

[33] H. Diels, fragments 117 and A112.

[34] It is contained in his work *On Truth,* discovered in 1915 but another fragment written on papyrus turned up in 1984.

[35] In fact, the similarities between Antiphon and Locke do not end there. Antiphon envisioned humans at liberty in nature and shackled by laws in society. (See his *First Tetralogy.*) These laws required mutual consent. But loyalty to the justice system often means performing in ways that are contrary to one's nature. This theme is well represented in Plato's *Gorgias* by Callicles (see below in this chapter). In the same way that Locke echoes Antiphon, Thomas Hobbes echoes the more obscure Sophist Thrasymachus, who believed that humans always operate in their own self-interest and thus must be checked. Hobbes' influence on our Constitution comes through Madison and Hamilton, among others.

[36] See his *On Concord,* fragment B 44.

[37] Some scholars argue that there were two Antiphons, the political orator and activist, and the teacher. It is odd that of all of the famous Sophists, Antiphon is the only one not mentioned in Plato's dialogues. For more on Antiphon, see Scott Consigny, *Sophist and Artist* (Columbia: U. of South Carolina Press, 2001) and Michael Gargin, *Antiphon the Athenian: Oratory, Law and Justice in the Age of the Sophists* (Austin: U. of Texas Press, 2002).

[38] She is mentioned in Plato's Menexenus and by Quintilian in his *Institutes of Oratory* in V.xi.27–29. See also Madeleine Henry, *Prisoner of History: Aspasia of Miletus and Her Biographical Tradition* (New York: Oxford U. Press, 1995).

[39] Unfortunately, none of Aspasia's writings remain. Her life and thought must be re-created through the eyes of others. She is chronicled by Plutrach in *Twelve Lives.* Philostratus links her to Gorgias' methods. See A. Cheree Carlson, "Aspasia of Miletus: How One Woman Disappeared from the History of Rhetoric," *Women's Studies in Communication,* 17 (1994): 26–44.

[40] See Charles Sears Baldwin, *Medieval Rhetoric and Poetic* (New York: Macmillan Co., 1928), pp. 23–38. George Kennedy in *The Art of Persuasion in Greece,* Werner Jaeger in *Paedeia* (especially in volumes I and III), and Nancy Struever in the first chapter of *The Language of History in the Renaissance* explore the Sophists' contributions to rhetorical theory. See also Kerferd; Hyland, p. 187; Laszlo Versenyi, *Socratic Humanism* (New Haven: Yale U. Press, 1963), p. 111.

[41] After his *Helen,* he composed the *Palamedes* about the Trojan unjustly accused of high crimes. In this second *apologia,* Gorgias firmly establishes the genre for future generations.

[42] *Encomium* at 9.

[43] I do not mean to imply that Plato's portrait of Gorgias is accurate. He is held up to ridicule in the dialogue. But this passage pays Gorgias his due and captures the spirit of his love for rhetoric. It makes the mistake, however, having Gorgias deny that geometry and arithmetic are forms of rhetoric, which he probably would not have done.

[44] Years earlier, Gelon and Theron had saved Sicily from invading Carthagenians and established their family as rulers. The end of the line came with Thrasybulus, who succeeded to the throne around 467 BC. When he was overthrown, the island was overrun with lawsuits about who owned what land.

[45] Tisias, which may be a nickname for Corax, may have been a teacher of Gorgias and may have come with him on his first ambassadorship to Athens. Tisias is mentioned in Plato's *Phaedrus* at 266 D.

[46] Untersteiner, p. 92.

[47] See Kennedy, pp. 33, 64. Gorgias was particularly fond of antithesis, isocolon, parison, and homoeoteleuton. Dionysius of Lalicarnassas believed that Gorgias' use of "word-play," "parallelisms," and "antithesis" were "excessive." See Dionysius' *On Thucydides,* Stephen Usher, trans. (1974), p. 24.

[48] Plato, *Gorgias,* W. C. Helmbold, trans. (New York: Bobbs-Merrill, 1952), pp. 450e to 451a. See 451d–e where he points out that rhetoric was productive of the greatest human good. See also his *Encomium of Helen;* William K. C. Guthrie, *The Sophists* (Cambridge: Harvard U. Press, 1971), pp. 192, 272; Jacqueline de Romilly, *Magic and Rhetoric in Ancient Greece* (Cambridge: Harvard U. Press, 1975), pp. 3–22.

[49] See Theodore Chalon Burgess, "Epideictic Literature," *Studies in Classical Philology,* vol. III (Chicago: U. of Chicago Press, 1902), p. 102.

[50] Gorgias, *On the Nonexistent.* See C. Bakewell, *Source Book in Ancient Philosophy* (New York: Gordian, 1909), p. 67. Kennedy writes that "both Protagoras and Gorgias denied that absolute truth can be known," p. 31.

[51] Guthrie, pp. 196–98; L. Versenyi, *Socratic Humanism* (New Haven: Yale U. Press, 1993), pp. 22, 37–38, 47.

[52] It meant adaptation to or taking advantage of an opportunity through fitting response and proper timing. The word *kairos* is one of many words for different types of time derived from the sons of Zeus: *kairos* refers to opportunity that is appropriate for seizing (see Kennedy, p. 66); *kronos* (also *chronos,* the root for chronology) refers to linear time, seconds, minutes, hours, days in a row. Gorgias' development of these notions had an impact on many rhetors, including Isocrates. See Michael Cahn, "Reading Rhetoric Rhetorically: Isocrates and the Marketing of Insight," *Rhetorica,* 8 (1988): 129; see also Barrett, p. 18.

[53] For more definitions of *kairos,* see William H. Race, "The Word *Kairos* in Greek Drama," *Transactions of the American Philological Society,* 111 (1981): 197–213. The pre-Socratic healer Hippocrates referred to *kairos* and the role it played in medicine: "Time is that in which there are opportune moments, and an 'opportune moment' is that in which there is not much time. Healing goes on in time, when the moment is opportune." In *The Presocratics,* Philip Wheelwright, ed. (New York: Odyssey Press, 1996), p. 272, Plato used the term *kairos* to mean propriety in timing in the dialogue named the *Gorgias.* It was later expanded into the more sophisticated notion of *decorum* developed by Cicero and Quintilian, which we will investigate in chapter 5. It also influenced Longinus' conception of the "power of forming great conceptions" by joining rhetoric and poetic.

[54] In the Fourth Century BC, the sculptor Lysippus represents *Kairos* in bronze with a long forelock of hair blowing forward off an otherwise bald head; it is by this forelock that one grabs the god of opportunity before he passes you by. This god is athletic, young, and quick—he has wings on his feet and back; he is often pictured standing on a ball because opportunity comes from many different directions. In Rome, *Kairos* evolves into the goddess *Occasio,* from which "occasion" is derived.

[55] This thought is from Gorgias' *Encomium of Helen.* For a full examination of Gorgias' *Encomium of Helen* see Edward Schiappa, "Gorgias's *Helen* Revisited," *Quarterly Journal of Speech,* 81 (1995): 310–24. Schiappa does a wonderful job examining the many interpretations that have been put on this work.

[56] We will return to this term when we take up Marxist (chapter 10) and feminist theory (chapter 13). Both argue that hegemonic strategies of persuasion tend to maintain current power structures. Gorgias would not have disagreed.

[57] Marcel Detienne and Jean-Pierre Vernant, *Cunning Intelligence in Greek Culture and Society* (Sussex: Harvester, 1991).

[58] See, for example, his letter *To Nicocles.*

[59] Prodicus also taught Thucydides and Euripides among others. He was a Sophist concerned with propriety of expression and precise meaning. Like Gorgias, he was an ambassador from another city.

[60] William L. Benoit, "Isocrates on Rhetorical Education," *Communication Education,* 33 (1984): 109.

[61] See Kenneth R. Chase, "Constructing Ethics through Rhetoric: Isocrates and Piety," *Quarterly Journal of Speech,* 95 (2009): 251.

[62] Robert N. Gaines, "Isocrates, Ep. 6.8," *Hermes* (1990): 165–70.

[63] Isocrates, *Antidosis,* in *Isocrates,* George Norlin, trans., vol. I (Cambridge: Harvard U. Press, 1962), pp. 327, 329.

[64] See Benoit, 109–11.

[65] Isocrates, *Antidosis,* p. 327.

[66] See, for example, his *Panathenaicus.* This idea was a major theme of Gorgias; see his *Olympian Speech.*

[67] See the *Theaetetus.*

[68] Socrates attributed the phrase "Know thyself" to the Oracle at Delphi.

[69] Plato's long prolific life was dedicated to laying out and defending his views. In 387 BC when he was 40, Plato opened the Academy after having run a school for children of the rich. In the 40 years remaining in his life he taught, revised what he had written earlier, and wrote a great deal more. His most fascinating writing on rhetoric was done from 398 to 387 BC before the Academy opened its doors. This period is marked by Plato's anti-Sophistic, ethical dialogues including the *Apology, Crito, Meno, Euthydemos, Gorgias,* and *Ion.*

[70] This notion is very important to Aristotle's *De anima* where he explores the complicated relationship between actuality and potentiality.

[71] *Meno* at 85B8–C5.

[72] Richard Weaver is perhaps the most influential Platonic rhetorical theorist. His work focuses on the role dialectic plays in informing rhetoric. See, for example, Richard Weaver, "Ultimate Terms in Contemporary Rhetoric," reprinted in *Language Is Sermonic,* Richard L. Johannesen, Rennard Strickland, and Ralph T. Eubanks, eds. (Baton Rouge: Louisiana State U. Press, 1970).

[73] This same system of abstraction would, of course, affect many philosophers to follow. While John Locke, for example, believed we are born with a tabula rasa or a blank slate, a position Plato opposed, Locke nonetheless adopted abstraction as a means of understanding.

[74] The *Laws* at 908d, 933a.

[75] See Ellen M. Wood and Neal Wood, *Class Ideology and Ancient Political Theory: Socrates, Plato, and Aristotle in Social Context,* (New York: Oxford U. Press, 1978), pp. 191–92.

[76] The *Laws* at 711c, 721b–e.

[77] The quotations used here are from the translation of the *Gorgias* by W. C. Helmbold (New York: Bobbs-Merrill, 1952).

[78] *Gorgias,* 486 A4–7.

[79] These preview the divisions of Aristotle's *ethos,* sagacity, goodwill, and virtue. See *Gorgias* at 487 A2–3.

[80] See *Gorgias,* 485 C–D and 527 E, for example. Kenneth Burke explores this theory in his definition of the "Good Life" in *Attitudes Toward History* (Boston: Beacon Press, 1937/59), pp. 256–60. The "good life" includes the maximum opportunity to be passionate, and physical. Callicles also can be seen as a precursor to F. Nietzsche's superman (*obermench*).

[81] Lysias was a well-known Sophist who studied under Protagoras. He wrote many speeches for his legal clients to present in court. He was called a logographer (*logographoi*).

[82] Phaedrus has borrowed the speech from Lysias to memorize it.

[83] The quotations used in this section are from the translation of the *Phaedrus* by R. Hackforth in *The Collected Dialogues of Plato,* Edith Hamilton and Huntington Cairns, eds. (Princeton: Princeton U. Press, 1971), pp. 475–525.

[84] There is a myth at the end of the dialogue that creates a context for Plato's condemnation of the evil effects of writing.

[85] Karl R. Wallace, "The Substance of Rhetoric: Good Reasons," *Quarterly Journal of Speech,* 49 (1963): 239–49.

[86] See Richard Weaver, *The Ethics of Rhetoric* (Chicago: Henry Regnery Company, 1953).

[87] Richard Weaver, *Ideas Have Consequences* (Chicago: U. of Chicago Press, 1948).

[88] Weaver, *The Ethics,* p. 112.

[89] Ibid.

[90] Not surprisingly, Weaver finds the "argument from circumstance" the least ethical because it is the most expedient; it resists normative Platonic bases (*The Ethics of Rhetoric,* p. 57).

[91] Hippias developed a famous system for memorizing speeches and served as an ambassador.

[92] See the *Rhetorica ad Alexandrum,* the fourth-century BC text composed by teachers in Athens that refers to the *Progymnasmata.* See also the *Progymnasmata* composed by Hermogenes of Tarsus, which remained in the Byzantine world until George Trebizond (see chapter 7) brought it to Italy in 1416. Hermogenes wrote in the second century AD and brought Sophistic theories to the Second Sophistic.

[93] Anaximenes of Lampsacus (c. 380–320 BC) wrote a text on rhetoric and dedicated it to Alexander, one of the first *Rhetorica ad Alexandrum*s.

Aristotle's *Rhetoric*

Born in 384 BC to a well-to-do family in Stagira, a small town in northern Greece, Aristotle would influence not only history but also science and the liberal arts. He would become the teacher of the man who conquered the known world. He would write definitive books that would endure for over two millennia on subjects ranging from biology to political science. He would write the first lexicon of philosophical terms. Most important for our purposes, he would recognize that rhetoric is a distinct art that is crucial for human survival. While many in Athens thought that its golden age under Pericles was the high point of civilization, those alive in Aristotle's time were to see a new leader unite the Greeks and bring them fame beyond their wildest dreams. Aristotle was a *metic*, a foreigner in Athens who was not allowed to own property. Nonetheless, Aristotle functioned as a major transitionary figure in Western civilization.

He finished his education as a favorite pupil of Plato at his Academy;[1] in fact, Aristotle's inspiration for writing his text on rhetoric may have come from Plato's call for a philosophical rhetoric in the *Phaedrus*. When Plato died in 347 BC, Aristotle joined a group of students who served Hermeias, a ruler in Asia Minor who had once himself been a pupil of Plato. Four years later, Philip II, King of Macedonia, hired Aristotle as a mentor for his son Alexander.[2] He studied with Aristotle from 343 to 340 BC; four years later Alexander became ruler of Macedon and Greece upon the assassination of his father. In 334 BC Aristotle founded the Lyceum, his own school, in Athens at the heart of the city, a mile from the Acropolis. When Alexander died in 323 BC, Aristotle was charged with impiety, the same crime for which Socrates was condemned to death in 399 BC. This charge was brought because of Aristotle's friendship with Alexander, who had not been popular with the aristocracy in Athens. This great philosopher and teacher was forced to flee to Chalcis where he died within a year's time.

Throughout his life, Aristotle was a keen observer of human activity, and his observations are reflected in his books. More important, those books led to a major shift in philosophical thinking. While Plato urged humans to seek the truth in the *nou-*

menal world, an idealized heaven open only to our souls, Aristotle turned human consciousness toward this world and developed a system of categories based on his observations. His categorical approach was to dominate the sciences and philosophy through the modern era.

Aristotle's study of rhetoric led him to believe that Plato's view of the world was impractical if humans were to survive and prosper. Like Isocrates, Aristotle knew rhetoric was an essential art with disciplinary integrity that could be taught. For twelve years at the Lyceum, he taught his students that the world is thrust upon us constantly and we must often make decisions before we are ready for them. We must learn to deal with the contingent nature of the world if we are going to survive, let alone succeed. His *Rhetoric* emphasizes the unsure nature of life; it situates rhetoric in the pragmatic world of probability. To appreciate his theory, however, we need to see how it was complemented by his other works. They provide a context for my interpretation of the *Rhetoric*.

We can begin with his *Politics*, which examines humans as speaking animals who attempt to use rhetoric under different forms of government:

> [T]he human being alone of the animals possesses *logos*. . . . For it is the unique property of human beings in distinction to other animals that they alone have perception of good and bad and right and wrong and other such things, and it is partnership in these things that makes a household and a *polis*.[3]

Aristotle argued that different forms of government are necessary for different situations and that a form of government can make the difference between suffering and living well. Like rhetoric, politics must be adjusted to the given situation. The ultimate goal of government is the happiness of its citizens. Furthermore, he showed that different forms of government require a different kind of character in their leaders.[4] This character is to be generated by rhetorical skill. Finally, of course, public speaking is crucial to each form of government whether it is a monarchy in which a king needs to generate the respect of his followers or a democracy in which citizens contend with one another in an open forum.[5]

To help his readers determine right and wrong, and to educate the citizen to serve in the *polis*, Aristotle wrote the *Nicomachean Ethics*. It lays out an understanding of virtue and vice that provides a foundation for the development of the strategic use of *ethos*, the persuasive force of the credibility of the speaker. The doctrine of *to kalon* defines what is "honorable, fine, or noble." These virtues are then incorporated into Aristotle's advice on epideictic speaking (praising and blaming) in the *Rhetoric*. Just as important, Book Six of the *Ethics* explains his conception of prudence, which was very influential on Cicero, whose work dominated not only the Roman era but the Middle Ages and the Renaissance. Prudence requires knowing the lessons of history. Such an education inculcates a sense of tradition, while balancing action with reflection.

In his *Organon*,[6] which consists of (1) Categories *(Categoriae)*, (2) On Interpretation *(De interpretation)*, (3) Prior Analytics *(Analytica prioria)*, (4) Posterior Analytics *(Analytica posteria)*, (5) Topics *(Topica)*, and (6) Sophistical Refutations *(De sophisticis elenchis)*, Aristotle creates his system of logic. In the more probability-based *topoi* (places for arguments) and *enthymemes* (syllogisms based on probability) of the *Rhetoric*, he adapts that logic to the contingent nature of the human condition. The *Topics* deals with knowledge obtained through dialectical processes such as those evident in the dialogues of Plato. It establishes a systematic approach to inquiry that generates the arguments and evidence needed to make a case for any given action or theory. At the end of this book, Aristotle noted that the use of dialectic in society would require rhetorical skill because "reference to another party is involved." When we engage others, whether it be to inform or to argue, we must adjust to deal with their level of understanding; hence, some audience adaptation is always necessary even in the case of logical disputation.

The *Analytics* deals with scientific knowledge, which requires the manipulation of true premises in order to deduce the truth about the physical world. The book recognizes that rational form can be imposed on false premises to give them the appearance of truth, but its focus is clearly on true statements from which other true conclusions can be drawn. We know that the molecular composition of water is two hydrogen atoms and one oxygen atom; therefore, we can conclude that water is a source of oxygen. The *Rhetoric* provides a counterpart to such reasoning by dealing with knowledge and persuasion that result from probable premises or appeals to character and emotion when a decision is necessary and true premises are not available. Since we can't know for sure whether we will win a war, those in favor of the war must persuade us using probable premises—we have superior forces; we have right on our side; our allies will join us in this fight; we must put an end to terrorist attacks—therefore, we should enter this war. None of these premises can be argued with certainty; they must be supported with evidence and their probability established with the audience.

On the way to defining the six elements of tragedy (plot, character, thought, diction, music, and spectacle), the *Poetics* also provides useful concepts for rhetoric. For example, it explores ways to bring a scene alive before an audience,[7] a talent useful in forensic speaking.[8] Character *(ethos)*, the second element, is revealed in the choices one makes. Most interestingly, in chapter 19 Aristotle claims that *dianoia* (the connecting process that determines the course of events in the story) is the province of rhetorical theory because rhetoric is more concerned with proper timing, appropriateness, and the contingent nature of humans. In other words, the invention of a plot for a play is a rational process that necessarily involves thinking rhetorically.[9]

The *Poetics* also develops the notion of catharsis *(katharsis)* by which emotions are released and the soul is cleansed. In the *Poetics*, Aristotle focuses on the use of emotions for a consummatory art form: the play is an end in itself; the emotions are drained and expurgated. In the *Rhetoric*, Aristotle's discussion is far more complicated because the emotions are used to motivate an audience to do something *after* the speech is ended. As we shall see, they are used instrumentally in rhetorical situations.

The *Poetics* defines humans in terms of their ability to imitate others, *mimesis*.[10] Just as actors imitate characters and action, so must speakers conjure images of reality and create personas.

In conjunction with the *Poetics* and the *Rhetoric*, Aristotle wrote a short treatise on *Memory and Recollection*, wherein he differentiates between the two. He notes that animals have memories, but they do not have recollection, which is a gift given only to humans. Memory *(mneme)* allows us to memorize parts in a play or a whole speech. Memory is triggered by current experiences, which it then compares with past experiences. Like his teacher Plato, he compares these experiences to stamps in the wax; we compare the imprints to see if they match. Memory can work with imagination to create new concepts and it can help invoke the *pathé* by recalling various experiences that trigger different emotions. However, the memory can fooled and can misremember past events, shaping them to current needs.

Recollection *(anamenesis)* can correct false or imprecise memories. It recalls what has been learned without the need of a prompting experience. Recollections helps with building arguments on recalled truths. For Aristotle, recollection is a discipline, a *techné* in its own right.

De anima, Aristotle's book on psychology, makes clear that human souls are unique because they can override instinct, move from an initial actuality to a potentiality to a new actuality, and make decisions. In his *Physics* and *Metaphysics*, Aristotle claimed there are four causes that brought things into being: (1) the *material cause* is the substance from which the thing is made; words are the material cause of a speech just as marble is the material cause of a sculpture; (2) the *efficient cause* is the activity of the creator; the speaker is the efficient cause of the speech just as the sculptor is the efficient cause of the statue; (3) the *formal cause* is the form imposed on the matter; the speaker organizes words using a certain pattern just as the sculptor imposes his vision of the body on the statue; (4) the *final cause* is *telos* or end goal; the speaker seeks to persuade an audience to take some action; the sculptor seeks to create beauty that will call us to spirituality.

In these works on nature, Aristotle establishes his theory of essence and accidents (attributes), which was resuscitated by Thomas Aquinas (see chapter 6). Basically Aristotle argues that the substance of being is the essence of objects, their realistic core that determines "what a thing is and what it is to be."[11] Their attributes are not essential. They are accidental properties that do not affect the essential core, but do help us refine definition.[12] Thus, there are biological essences that make something a man and there are accidents, such as the color of the skin and the hair, that are not essential to making a thing a man but do help to differentiate one man from another. This theory is the basis of Aristotelian realism as opposed to Plato's idealism. Aristotle's realism is anchored in matter and objectivity. Plato's idealism rests on form and perfection. The two theories battle one another for the rest of time.

Luckily, from this tension between realism and idealism, we can develop a system of criticism that compares what is actual to what is potential. For example, when sculptors try to create a statue from a block of marble, they have a potential form in mind that could emerge in reality once the sculpting is complete. A critic can compare the actual statue to the potential—what is achieved to what is possible—and issue a judgment.[13] The same can be said for a speech. The critic can compare the actual speech as delivered to the potential speech, the best one possible for the situation, and an assessment can be made. But how do we determine what that potential is? Aristotle provides the answer in his *Rhetoric*.

Aristotle's *Rhetoric* was constructed from 342 to 330 BC and significantly advances the theories that preceded it.[14] My goal here is to outline his major contributions and to illustrate them with case studies because Aristotle's work is a major synthesis point in the history of rhetoric. He brought together what preceded him and provided a sturdy foundation for all that followed. His book is used as a text to this day even in legal seminars.

As we attempt this survey, we need to be aware that while Aristotle was writing about speaking in a democratic forum, his culture was different than ours in significant ways. Women were allowed neither to vote nor to participate in debate. Slavery was common. Obviously, media were primitive. Nonetheless, what he has to say is remarkably useful to the persuasive process in the contemporary world and is consistently verified by modern empirical studies in communication theory.

Throughout the *Rhetoric*, and in his other works for that matter, Aristotle worked as an empiricist who examined what worked and what failed, and categorized what he learned into principles that could generate an artifact. His emphasis on categorization in his scientific works so impressed the scholarly community that it remains influential to this day. Unfortunately, when dealing with an art form, categorization can often turn generative principles and useful questions into rules that are too inflexible to provide useful guidance in every situation. Therefore, it is important to remember that *Aristotle's advice on how to create a speech should be seen as series of powerful, generic questions that need to be adapted to specific situations.* They were never meant to be rules that work in every case.

The *Rhetoric* begins with a list of the uses of the art that clearly repudiate Plato's arguments against rhetoric. First, Aristotle believed that rhetoric allows truth and justice to triumph over falsehood and injustice. Second, rhetoric is instructive; it helps us to make things known: "Even if our speaker had the most accurate scientific information, still there are persons whom he could not readily persuade. *True instruction, by method of logic is here impossible.*"[15] Third, Aristotle also wrote about "the power of saying whatever is appropriate to the occasion." The tradition of appropriateness was carried on by Aristotle's pupil Theophrastus[16] and became an important component of Cicero's definition of *decorum* (see chapter 5).[17] Fourth, rhetoric, like dialectic, can defend either side of a question and is therefore useful in disputation. Finally, rhetoric is as important to self-defense as physical prowess.

Since we must cope with an encroaching world, rhetoric should play an important role in each citizen's civil education. Aristotle based his theory of rhetoric on the premise that probable truth, not certainty, determines the answers to most important questions. "True opinion" is only that for which the reasons can be given; that is, evidence and proofs help speakers build their truths, but in most cases it is something for which we must argue. That is why Aristotle contended, "Rhetoric is the counterpart of dialectic." If dialectic discovers the truth, it still needs rhetoric to present it to various audiences. Since most important questions are decided by probability, dialectic—which requires true premises—is inadequate to answer these questions. Rhetoric when properly conceived does deal with these various questions because it is the "art of finding in any given case the available means of persuasion." For example, questions of whether or not to marry, whether or not to have children, and whether or not to end a life raise certain risks that could be addressed by logic but generally are more effectively resolved using rhetorical strategies. The types of persuasion available may be *enthymemes*, which are syllogisms (discussed later in this chapter) based on probable premises,[18] and can be formed from *topoi* (commonly accepted lines of argument); appeals to credibility, which provide authority for claims; manipulations of the state of mind of the audience; or word choice, organization, and delivery. Whatever the strategies ("proofs" as Aristotle called them), they are more useful than logic when it comes to persuading people to decide important questions that require the consideration of probable premises instead of ones that are certain.

Clearly, Aristotle understood that rhetoric is essential to the discovery of self and truth because of its role in decision making and its ability to deal with probabilities outside the realm of logic. The trick in learning this art is to avoid the pitfalls of the Sophists—putting too much emphasis on the emotions, style, and delivery or speaking without knowing what you are talking about—and to avoid being naive about the truth's ability to sell itself. As with most things, Aristotle directed his students down a middle path.

If rhetoric is the counterpart of dialectic, it is also the counterpart of literature including poetry and drama. In the *Rhetoric* and *Poetics*, Aristotle investigated the power of speech to rationalize and approximate, to persuade and fascinate.[19] In order to do so one must establish probable truth in the mind of the hearer. For example, in the *Rhetoric* Aristotle wrote that the prosecutor must establish the probability of guilt; in the *Poetics*, the author must never make up a story using "improbable incidents."[20] On the one hand, Aristotle understood, as did Gorgias, that rhetoric could give force to literature by giving messages to poetry and appropriate speeches and dialogues to plays. *Poesis* needs rhetoric's sense-making function; that is, transforming random events into a coherent story that is plausible to an audience. On the other hand, rhetoric needs devices of fascination found in *poesis* in order to hold the attention of its audience and to clarify ideas.

Thus, in the first two chapters of the *Rhetoric*, Aristotle establishes a teachable discipline. He defines it, differentiates it from other disciplines, and demonstrates its crucial role in our world. The remainder of the *Rhetoric* advises on how to determine which strategies will work in a given situation. When read as a set of questions to ask in each rhetorical situation, the *Rhetoric* can be remarkably revealing. Aristotle's work is enduring because it presents rhetoric as an "art"—a set of generative principles that produce a specific speech that adapts a particular message to a particular audience, speaker, and situation. The changing nature of the audience, the malleability of messages, the invisibility of speeches, and the diversity of speakers prevent rhetoric from being reduced to a science. Because it relies on adaptation, it is one of the most difficult arts to master.

More than any other art, rhetoric bases its generative principles on a close and definitive analysis of its audience; that is where the potential strategies can be found. Thus, rhetoric, much more than such arts as literature, music, or painting, is inevitably tied to the moment and to the contingent nature of humans. Van Gogh painted many pictures that he could never sell in his lifetime, but he was appreciated as a great artist in the next century. Orators will not be considered rhetorical artists unless they succeed in the immediate present, no matter how literate their speeches may be. Speakers do not gain credibility with an audience by being ethical; they gain credibility by *being ethical in ways that the particular audience admires*. Speakers do not arouse an audience to anger unless they understand *what causes anger in the particular audience*. Speakers do not create eloquence with elevated word choice and proper grammar; it is done by *meeting the expectations of the audience in terms of language level and occasion*.

Aristotle carefully cautioned his students not to study his various "proofs" in isolation. While he had to isolate them to define them and analyze them, he wanted to make sure that his students understood that they were related. If we trust *(ethos)* a speaker—believe that he or she possesses a sound character—we are more likely to accept his or her arguments *(logos)*. If the speaker can create dramatic imagery (style), we are more likely to be moved *(pathos)* by his or her appeals. In fact, character *(ethos)*, state of mind *(pathos)*, and appeals to reason *(logos)* constitute the three major strategies of invention, the discovery of persuasive "proofs" that help an audience make a judgment. The three work together to make a complete persuasive appeal. We shall see that while character is centered in the speaker, it must appeal to the virtues a specific audience holds dear. While speakers create appeals to reason and emotion, they must do so with a specific audience in mind, or their rhetoric will fall on deaf ears.

After presenting his definition of rhetoric and his discussion of its uses, Aristotle divided the strategies he would examine into two major categories: *inartistic* and *artistic*. He then disposed of inartistic strategies quickly by pointing out they were not created by the speaker; instead, they were incorporated into speeches where needed. These included such items as laws, oaths, contracts, and so forth. The same is true today. Speakers often need to cite amendments to the Constitution, contracts drawn up by various parties, or confessions of criminals on trial in order to make a case. The question to ask is what materials do we need to cite or show to make the best possible case?

Anyone watching a contemporary trial can see how far we have come from Aristotle's time. Such inartistic proofs as videotaped re-creations, computer-analyzed blood samples, and PowerPoint presentations that put events into a narrative sequence are incorporated into the cases of both sides. The multimedia age has expanded the category of inartistic proofs incredibly. Yet, the basic question remains the same, what inartistic proofs are essential to the persuasive effort?

The remainder of the *Rhetoric* concerns the artistic strategies available to the speaker. These are created by the speaker to develop and enhance the speech, and they are the focus of the remainder of this chapter.

ETHOS: TO BE "WORTHY OF BELIEF"

Aristotle argued that credibility is the most potent form of persuasion.[21] By that he meant that if the speaker is believable and trusted, audiences are much more likely to be persuaded by what that speaker has to say. If the speaker is neither believable nor trustworthy, it will make little difference what the speaker says, because the audience will probably reject it. The genius of Aristotle's conception of *ethos* is that it is audience based. A speaker may be honest and trustworthy, but if the audience fails to perceive it, those qualities don't count for much in a persuasive situation. How then do speakers develop credibility for an audience in any given situation?

Aristotle set out several categories to examine as the speaker attempts to build credibility. First, because of past decisions, most speakers have a *prior reputation* with most audiences. While Aristotle did not specifically list this constituent of *ethos*, he clearly implies it in his analysis of decision making,[22] and we are certainly aware of it today. When former President Clinton came to speak at the 2012 Democratic Convention, he brought with him certain benefits and baggage before he uttered a single word. He presided over a long peacetime economic boom, and after his presidency, on the one hand, he gave time and energy to address issues of global importance. On the other hand, however, for some audiences, he was a draft dodger who contrived not to serve his country, sold access to the Lincoln bedroom for campaign contributions, and was a womanizer. Thus, Clinton's persuasive force was enhanced or limited by his prior reputation.

In the speech itself, a speaker has several other artistic strategies available to use. They include *sagacity, goodwill,* and *character,* which reflect Plato's discussion of knowledge, goodwill, and candor in the last third of the *Gorgias.* Sagacity (wisdom) concerns how speakers demonstrate that they know what they are talking about or how they demonstrate expertise. Aristotle believed that intelligence is the product of *nous,* that part of our mind that apprehends sense data. From it we get our sense impressions of the world—whether it is hot or cold, what color the rose is, how certain chemicals react, and so forth. *Nous* is at the primary level of knowing.[23]

A second component of intelligence is *dianoia,* that part of our mind that connects things with their attributes and links events in a sensible way. We know that bees sting, that cats meow, and that snow is cold. *Dianoia* helps makes sense out of the world and keeps it coherent.

Nous and *dianoia* are the roots of knowledge, but we are also capable of learning scientific knowledge *(episteme),* which is objective and based on principles produced by demonstration. Physics and mathematics are examples of *episteme. Techné* is knowledge of artistic principles such as those that constitute music, sculpture, and rhetoric. *Sophia,* or theoretical wisdom, is also part of intelligence and can be acquired from the study of philosophy. Speculation on how the soul functions to move a body from one state to another is an example of *sophia.* Finally, and importantly, comes *phronesis* or practical wisdom, which is taught through ethics, history, and political science. All of these categories of knowledge provide the speaker with a vast reservoir of information that can be used to impress an audience, and they were taught directly to Aristotle by his mentor Plato.[24]

The use of evidence, the recall of important events, a strong sense of organization, and even proper word choice can affect how the audience perceives the speaker in terms of expertise on a given subject. The appearance of a lack of knowledge can have devastating effects on a speaker. As a presidential candidate, George W. Bush on occasion mispronounced words and employed questionable grammar, which hurt his credibility. However, as president in his speech to a joint session of Congress on September 20, 2001, his credibility was enhanced when he was able to speak fluently about such countries as Uzbekistan. The appearance of expertise is important. In the Republican presidential campaign leading up to the primaries of 2012, Newt Gingrich's ability to spout facts and construct compelling rebuttals in debates led to a rise in his credibility and poll numbers. When Governor Rick Perry of Texas could not name all three of the cabinet departments he claimed he would eliminate, his credibility and poll numbers plummeted.

Goodwill *(eunoia)* means demonstrating that you have the audience's best interests at heart. Aristotle compares it to friendship, "wishing for someone things you believe to be good, for his sake and not for your own, and being ready to do these things to the extent possible."[25] This is particularly difficult for politicians, who are often suspected of wanting to win the election to gain political power rather than to work for the good of their constituents. They try to overcome audience cynicism by promising to protect audience members' interests. These interests can be divided between survival needs (such as food, shelter, and clothing) and growth needs (such as education, tolerance, and freedom). This particular category provides speakers with myriad choices that are useful in enhancing the impression that they care about the audience.

In the era of poll data, politicians have become particularly adept at finding which issues concern voters most. These issues are then linked to voters' survival or growth needs to produce persuasive units within speeches. Cutting taxes, for example, gives voters more money with which to feed their families or to pursue happiness in different ways. Lowering tuition at state universities makes the dream of higher education available to more citizens.

Character, Aristotle's version of the Sophists' *areté*, is the third constituent of his notion of *ethos*. On this subject, the *Rhetoric*

Aristotle.

reveals the complex nature of his thinking as it weaves the notion of moral excellence into the matrix of credibility. Justice, courage, self-control, magnificence, magnanimity, liberality, common sense, and wisdom are explored as ways to produce and preserve what society values. The deeds that result are noble; their opposites are ignoble. Accordingly, a person who performs such deeds is noble or ignoble.

It is from these standards that Aristotle constructed his notion of virtue and vice in the *Rhetoric*. Vices are caused by excesses and deficiencies. Virtues are at the "mean," a kind of reasonable middle ground between our excesses and deficiencies. Let's take the example of courage. A person with an excess of courage is called rash—the commander who constantly endangers troops by charging into battle without proper support. A person with a deficiency of courage is called a coward—the soldier who refuses to enter battle even with proper support and equipment. Persons with courage are somewhere in between; they are prudent enough not to be rash or cowardly. We can represent Aristotle's conceptualization using various virtues and their attendant vices this way along several continuums:

Vice (excess)	Virtue	Vice (deficiency)
foolhardy	courageous	cowardly
spendthrift	magnanimous	stingy
gluttonous	self-controlled	austere
lustful	loving	indifferent

In the *Ethics*, Aristotle explained:

> Virtue, then, is a state of character concerned with choice, lying in a mean. That is, the mean relative to us, this being determined by a rational principle, and by that principle by which the man of practical wisdom would determine it. Now it is a mean lying between two vices that which depends on excess and that which depends on defect.[26]

This model is more complicated in the *Rhetoric* because Aristotle observes that different audiences may have different conceptions of what it is to be virtuous. For example, the Veterans of Foreign Wars may think it was courageous for a pilot to have participated in bombing runs over Iraq, while an audience of pacifists might believe it was foolhardy or even a crime. Thus, speakers not only need to know what virtues are and how they are constructed, they also need to know what particular audiences think of those virtues.

Having defined the constituents of *ethos*, Aristotle then reunited them to show how they must all be present if a speech is to be effective. Speakers who have a good reputation and possess wisdom, goodwill, and virtue are particularly persuasive.[27] It is subtleties such as these that make Aristotle's *Rhetoric* so valuable to the study of persuasion in our society. In almost every case, he advanced the knowledge of the art that had been accumulated up to his time. It is no different with *pathos*.

PATHOS: FRAME OF MIND

In Book II of the *Rhetoric*, Aristotle explored the relationship between *pathos* and the human psyche in an effort to promote the effective use of rhetoric in public forums. His object was to help the orator determine how to "put hearers . . . into the right *frame of mind*" with regard to certain issues and the speaker's persuasive intent.[28] This is necessary for a number of reasons. First, wicked persons will use the emotions to "pervert" the legal process.[29] These emotions must be allayed before the good person can present a case. Second, Aristotle understood that the human condition is contingent; humans must often make decisions without conclusive evidence. These decisions are made when humans are in one state of mind or another, and these states of mind affect decision making.[30] If, as Aristotle supposed, the end of rhetoric is proper judgment and the end of proper judgment is truth, then those seeking to guide their listeners need to know how appeals to emotions work in rhetorical situations not only to defend the truth but to attune the audience to it.

Aristotle's understanding of the *pathé* (individual states of mind such anger and fear) is based on his observation that a change in one's state of mind is a product of certain conditions orienting a person to the world.[31] To this end, Aristotle provided a model of *pathos* that has several complexities. First, emotions do not exist in isolation; they work in concert with other feelings. For example, experiencing fear may cause one to become angry with those who caused the fear. Or one who is angry may evoke fear in another. Aristotle believed that the "souls" of listeners can be moved or move along various continuums from central positions where emotions are at "rest" to the extremities where they are felt intensely. But how is intensity achieved? That question leads us to the third complication in Aristotle's model.

Aristotle contended that intensity is a function of *proximity;* the intensity of emotions can be described in terms of the nearness or remoteness of the objects that trigger emotions, including the personal relationships that stimulate them. For example, the closer what we fear is in time and space, the more intensely we experience that fear; the more remote the cause of the fear, the less intense is the experience of fear. We have very little fear of bears roaming the woods in Alaska as long as we are not in the woods in Alaska, but if the bear is in our home, our fear is greatly intensified. Aristotle specifically linked the images created to perceptions of proximity: "it is, therefore, the expectation associated with a mental picture of the nearness of what keeps us safe and the absence or remoteness of what is terrible."[32] Generally speaking, a slight received from someone close to us, such as a relative, is more painful and more intensely felt than a slight received from someone who is remote, such as a stranger. Intensity then is a measure of the "pain and pleasure" that attach to each emotion.[33] A speaker can "move" the listener to more or less intensely felt states of mind by bringing the causes of emotions closer or removing them from the listener's temporal/spatial field of perception. This may require only a recounting of facts, or a simple narrative, but it may also require a carefully crafted appeal to the imagination. In the latter case, mastery of word choice and image construction would be crucial. In chapter 12 we shall see how twentieth-century theorists use this advice in achieving "presence" and "immediacy" for their arguments.

This model of *pathos* demonstrates that Aristotle's theory of rhetoric is interactive not only between speaker and listener but among the other rhetorical "proofs" or strategies, such as image building through style. It provides a practical way by which the orator can intensify or dissipate the various *pathé*. Understanding this system helps critics understand how a speaker interacts with listeners to bring them to a state of mind compatible with the speaker's aims while at the same time transforming them into a more cohesive group.

To explore this theory, we can begin with Aristotle's claim that a jury whose frame of mind is "angry or hostile" will think very differently than one whose frame of mind is "friendly or placable." The strength with which these emotions are felt (their intensity) influences the jury's judgment and their cohesiveness.[34] If we think of the jury as individuals with emotions, we can see the importance of Aristotle's conception. A jury whose members do not share a state of mind is less likely to reach a consensus than one that does. Thus, lawyers must understand how to evoke the *pathé* if they are to unite the jury emotionally in a way that is compatible with the verdict sought. For example, it makes a great deal of difference if the jury feels *sympathy* for the accused than if the jury is *hostile* toward the accused.

Aristotle set out a threefold process for examining the *pathé;* it is first organized around anger:

> Take, for example, the emotion of anger: here we must discover (1) what the state of mind of angry people is, (2) who the people are with whom they usually get angry, and (3) on what grounds they get angry with them. It is not enough to know one or even two of these points; unless we know all three, we shall be unable to arouse anger in any one.[35]

These three questions enable Aristotle to conduct a systematic investigation of individual *pathé,* of the interrelationships among the *pathé,* and the use of the *pathé* in "moving the soul" of the listener. The scope and depth of Aristotle's analysis can be appreciated by following his specific investigation of anger. Anger is an emotion that is most potent when directed at human beings as opposed to other entities. We get madder at people than we do at objects. If you have seen someone smash a tennis racquet or bend a golf club, you can imagine the damage they might do if they were angry with another person. Aristotle understood that personal relations intensify anger, which is the impulse to seek "a conspicuous revenge for a conspicuous slight" received from someone close to us in some way—a relative, a friend, a colleague. When we are slighted, the *pain* involved remains as a *privation* until the slight is redressed. It also prompts *pleasure* in two forms: (1) it is pleasant to seek revenge because one feels one can attain a goal, or relieve a privation; and (2) pleasure results from the images called to mind while plotting the revenge.[36] "It is also attended by a certain pleasure because the thoughts dwell upon the act of vengeance, and the images then called up cause pleasure, like the images called up in dreams."[37]

This "expectation of revenge," with its attendant pleasure, suggests an important temporal dimension associated with the experience of anger. Aristotle wrote: "the angry man is aiming at what he can attain, and the belief that you will attain your aim is pleasant."[38] The pleasure of anger emerges as people imagine how *in the future* their anger can be appeased. Their imagination takes them to another place, another time, and another role. The more people focus on the future consequences of their anger, the more their sense of time and space is changed. The more vivid the image of the act of revenge, the more the listener "lives" in the future. This temporal dimension also works to evoke the past. For example, using language to detail a vivid image of the slight that caused the anger moves the listener to relive that past moment: "Lance continuously insulted you in front of your whole family at Christmas dinner. How can you live with that?"

Aristotle explained that as the future recedes into the present and the past, and as one's expectations are fulfilled, relaxed, or forgotten, anger loses its intensity and its ability to move the listener. It dissipates as the object of anger becomes remote: "when time has passed . . . anger is no longer fresh, for time puts an end to anger"[39] and converts it to calm. Because orators seek to transform anger into calm as often as they seek to transform calm into anger, they need to understand how to move their hearers away from the pleasures of future revenge and away from the circumstances that provoked the anger as much as they need to understand how to intensify hurtful experiences.

If intensity is a function of temporality, it is also a function of personal relationships. As Aristotle discussed the various kinds of slight (contempt, spite, and insolence), he explained the ways in which we relate to others. People become angry with others who slight them in front of their kin or friends or before five other classes of people: "(1) our rivals, (2) those whom we admire, (3) those whom we wish to admire us, (4) those for whom we feel reverence, (5) those who feel reverence for us."[40] In other words, if David Letterman is insulted by Madonna, but no one else hears it, the sting of the insult is much less than if Madonna insulted Letterman on his television program. Worse yet, if Madonna is related to Letterman, the sting is more intense. Notice that in each of the five cases, the particular group bears a particular proximity to a person in terms of social rank and intimacy; generally that proximity determines the intensity of the slight.

Aristotle examined these relationships and their attendant attitudes among the young, the wealthy, and the powerful.[41] These groups consider others to be unimportant; they thwart the wishes of others, and/or shame them. By these attitudes and actions, they commit slights. Those slighted feel anger, with its attendant pains and pleasures, and they feel it more intensely if they are slighted in the presence of intimates. Their state of mind is transformed, particularly if the pain of the slight (a deprivation of honor) and the pleasure of revenge (imagining getting even) are heightened by appeals to the imagination. In this way, a speaker can motivate others to seek revenge against those who are perceived to have caused the slight initially: the young, the wealthy, and the powerful.

To this point, we have seen that the intensification of emotions is a function of *temporal and spatial proximity*, and that *imagination* has a crucial role to play in the interaction between the speaker and the listener in terms of achieving the various states of mind. Consequently, when it is advisable that the audience should be frightened, the orator must make them feel that they really are in danger of something; that it has happened to others who are stronger than they are; and that it is happening, or has happened, to people like themselves, at the hands of unexpected people, in an unexpected form, and at an unexpected time.[42]

Such a perception is enhanced by the imagination that is evoked by *careful word choice*, or style. During his discussion of pleasure, for example, Aristotle said, "There will always be in the mind of a man who remembers or expects something, an image or picture of what he remembers or expects. If this is so, it is clear that memory and expectation also, being accompanied by sensations, may be accompanied by pleasure."[43] The role style plays in stimulating recollections and images is dealt with at various stages of Aristotle's analysis.

Aristotle believed that the *pathé* were capable of creating unity in an audience. This becomes evident when the *Rhetoric* explores how each emotion forms a continuum with its opposite. The continuums also provide an integrated approach to *pathos*, which overcomes the more isolated three-step analysis of each *pathos*. This interrelating of the *pathé* began when Aristotle concluded his three-step examination of anger and analyzed its opposite, calm. From the first sentence, he made clear that he was not only offering another analysis but also advancing his entire psychological theory:

> We may lay it down that Pleasure is a movement, a movement by which the soul as a whole is consciously brought into its normal state of being; and that Pain is the opposite. . . . It must therefore be pleasant as a rule to move towards a natural state of being.[44]

Aristotle claimed that the soul moves or is moved along several continuums bordered by opposite emotions; the orator's goal is to bring listeners into conformance by moving them to the same state of mind. Thus, the orator must master the continuums and learn how to move the soul of listeners along them.

Each *pathé* has its counterpart that serves as a polar opposite; these include anger/calm, friendship/enmity, fear/confidence, shame/shamelessness, kindness/cruelty, pity/indignation, and envy/emulation. The soul moves between two poles: either toward a settled (least affected) position, or to the opposite pole. Aristotle put it this way, "In general, the things that make us calm may be inferred by seeing what the opposites are of those that make us angry."[45] Frustration creates anger; its opposite, success, creates the opposite of anger, that is, calm. A child trying to open a box will become frustrated, and then cry. When the child opens the box, the child will calm down, the frustration having been removed.

We have already examined how emotions are evoked, interrelated, and intensified. Aristotle reconceptualized this information into strategies by which the orator "moves" the soul of the listener from one point on each continuum to another. The points along the continuums are measures of intensity. For example, in the middle of the continuum between fear and confidence, the listener's soul is at rest; neither emotion is held with any intensity. As the soul moves or is moved toward one polarity or the other, the emotion is experienced with more and more intensity. In turn, as the soul moves or is moved toward the center or the opposite polarity, the experienced emotion is dissipated. Thus, the orator's task is to use the conditions of intensity "to stir," "to move," "to excite," or "to rouse" the soul of the hearer along a continuum until it is in a range compatible with the aim of the speaker.[46]

Aristotle's explanation of how ineffective orators often defeat their own purpose is also explained in terms of his theory of continuums. Inept speakers may produce no emotional movement or, worse, stimulate one that is contrary to their purpose. In this case listeners may not have been roused from their indifference, or inappropriate emotions may not have been dissipated, or reaction to the speaker may have been so hostile as to unite the audience against him or her. Aristotle claimed that in such cases the soul of the listener has not been moved into the proper range along the continuum.

An orator can also prove ineffective if the soul of the listener moves *beyond* the proper range. In such cases, the listener may overreact or become incapacitated. A sermon by Jonathan Edwards provides a strong illustration. He was so frightening from the pulpit during a sermon in Northampton, Massachusetts, in 1730 that he drove his uncle to suicide. Undoubtedly, Edwards sought to put the fear of God in the assembled congregation. His object was to bring the congregation together into a collective emotional catharsis that would lead to salvation. However, for his uncle, the causes of fear were brought too near; the emotional restructuring went beyond the intended range, and the old man went home and slit his throat.[47]

When a speaker uses inappropriate appeals, the audience members are either moved beyond the range compatible with the aim, as in Edwards' uncle's case, or not close enough to the range, as in the case of a speech that fails to touch the audience. One of the keys to these cases of misunderstanding is expectation. In many rhetorical situations, listeners expect a certain network of emotions to be evoked. For example, an audience listening to a eulogy at a funeral expects to hear words that will allow mourning. This requires the invocation of pity and other appropriate emotions through identification with the deceased's kin. The eulogizer's task is to bring the listeners together in a state of mind that is compatible with the occasion. Because it is usually inappropriate on such occasions, lightheartedness would evoke sections of the emotional web inimical to expectations; it might even evoke hostility toward the speaker.

Contrarily, an orator may want to use the *pathé* to change the expectations of the audience. In such a case, his or her task is more difficult because the audience cannot merely be adapted to, it must be turned from its current expectations and the states of mind that go with them to new expectations. Pericles in his "Funeral Oration" moves his listeners from mourning to pride in an effort to establish war aims that are honorable. Lincoln in his Gettysburg Address moves his listeners from grief to a rededication to confidence in the ideals of the Declaration of Independence. Again demonstrating his integrated approach throughout Book II and Book III of the *Rhetoric*, Aristotle tries to solve the problem of dealing with the expectations of the audience by relating his conception of the *pathé* to style, *logos*, the various ages of humans, and the impact of fate on the soul.[48]

LOGOS: THE ENTHYMEME AND THE EXAMPLE

The strategic use of reason to enhance believability is common in public and private persuasion. Its importance is dramatically illustrated when you read Rule 401 of the U.S. Federal Rules of Evidence. The rule points out that "relevant" evidence "means any evidence having any tendency to make the existence of any fact that is of consequence to the determination of the action more probable or less probable than it would be without evidence." Evidence, clearly an inartistic proof in Aristotle's view, takes on many forms: story, sign, effect, hearsay, testimonial, material, physical. In each case, the evidence becomes the nucleus of the argument that is spun around it. The evidence is used to support a conclusion; the bridge between the evidence and the conclusion is usually a general premise that the audience accepts without debate.

Aristotle explored two kinds of arguments in the *Rhetoric:* deductive arguments, which he called *enthymemes*, and inductive arguments built around telling examples, which can be drawn from actual or fictitious events. Inductive arguments move from specific cases to general conclusions by comparing things in the same category. For example, you may meet a blond woman who is very bright, and then another and another. Eventually, based on these inductive examples you have experienced, you might draw the conclusion that all blond women are bright, particularly if you never meet one who is not. The strength of induction lies in its ability to satisfy the audience's need for a *sufficient number of examples to make the conclusion seem valid*. President Reagan was superb at this tactic. He often provided his audience with a litany of statistics and/or examples to prove his point. Then he usually punctuated his inductive proof with a revealing vignette. For example, after a long detailed attack on the government's welfare system, Reagan would conclude by talking about the "welfare queen" who drew many checks from the government using twelve different names and claiming a total of forty-nine dependent children. She drove a Rolls Royce. This single example did more to turn audiences against the welfare system than did all the statistics. However, the statistics served as backing for the telling example and demonstrated that Reagan had expertise *(ethos)* on this topic.

An *enthymeme* is a syllogism based on *probable* premises that are acceptable to the audience. In his other works on logic, Aristotle defined deductive syllogisms as categorical, hypothetical, and disjunctive. He expected students of persuasion to be well versed in these forms of logic before they attempted to construct *enthymemes*. The categorical syllogism draws a true conclusion from two true premises if a valid placement of categories is achieved. Here is an example:

All women are mortal.
Angelina Jolie is a woman.
Therefore, Angelina Jolie is mortal.

The first category established is "women," and it is placed inside the second category, "mortality." Most of us believe this statement (premise) to be true. In the second premise, the smallest category, "Angelina Jolie," is placed into the first category, "women." Most of us believe this second premise to be true. Thus, the conclusion, that Angelina Jolie is mortal follows validly because since she is in the category of women, she must also be in the category of mortality if the major premise is true.

The hypothetical deductive syllogism works a little differently but is just as common. Here is an example:

If Brad Pitt is in Chicago, he is not in Los Angeles.
Brad Pitt is in Chicago.
Therefore, he is not in Los Angeles.

The use of the word "if" is the tip-off that this is a hypothetical syllogism. The first phrase balances the second and because of the laws of contradiction, only one of the phrases can be true. The third premise, "Brad Pitt is in Chicago," must affirm the first phrase of the first sentence for the syllogism to be valid. Obviously, if the third premise said, "Brad Pitt is not in Chicago," it would not prove that he was in Los Angeles. He could be in New York. Thus, if the statements are true, this would be a valid syllogism and the conclusion would follow.

The disjunctive deductive syllogism is very similar. It uses an "either/or" construction to govern the initial premise with the laws of contradiction. Here is an example:

Either I will marry, or I will become a priest.
I will not marry.
Therefore, I will become a priest.

The disjunctive syllogism must begin with a true premise that is based on a true alternative. However, unlike the hypothetical syllogism, the second premise of the disjunctive can affirm or deny either side of the first sentence. If it does and it is true, then a valid conclusion can be drawn. Notice that a true conclusion could be deduced using any of these second premises: "I will become a priest," "I will not become a priest," "I will marry," or "I will not marry." This extra freedom within the disjunctive syllogism has made it one of the most popular, even though we often see it used invalidly to force decisions on the unwary. For example, during the Afghan War some people claimed, "Either you are on the side of Al-Qaeda or you are on the side of the United States." Yet this premise was not necessarily true. It was possible for someone to condemn both sides in that conflict and transcend the premise.

Building on these forms of argument, Aristotle fashioned a new *logos* around the *enthymeme* in his *Rhetoric*. It is a *syllogism based on probability wherein the audience usually supplies a suppressed premise*. Unlike the inductive example, the *enthymeme* attempts to apply a general rule to a specific case. According to Aristotle, *enthymemes* are governed by four general lines of argument that are common to all speeches: (1) what is possible and impossible, (2) what is past fact, (3) what is future fact, and (4) what is the size, greater or smaller. Each of these questions can be used to generate an argument. (1) Since it is not *possible* to be in two places at the same time, and since several people saw Joe at Harry's Deli at the time of the murder, he could not have killed Alan, who was stabbed in his home. (2) Since Meryl Streep has been nominated for the Academy Award in the past, it is likely she will be nominated again. (3) Since an election is coming in the future, we had better nominate a candidate. (4) Since Texas is larger than California, and California is larger than Mississippi, then Texas must be larger than Mississippi.

Enthymemes are commonly accepted by the public and often produce conclusions that become maxims, or truisms. Maxims concern what is to be chosen or avoided in human action: "A stitch in time saves nine"; "haste makes waste"; "don't judge a book by its cover"; "clothes make the man"; "never a borrower nor a lender be." Speakers use maxims to allow audiences to identify with them in terms of shared common wisdom. Notice, however, that common maxims often contradict one another. That is because they are built on persuasive rather than logical force.

Common signs can also provide premises for *enthymemes*. Based on many inductive examples, signs argue *from effect to cause;* that is, the effect, smoke, is seen as a *sign* of the cause, fire. Signs are of two types, fallible and infallible. For example, the argument from sign, "where there is smoke there is fire," is fallible because sometimes smoke is caused by things other than fire, for example, dry ice or smoke machines. The argument from sign, "a frozen pond is a sign of cold weather," is infallible because a pond can freeze only when it is cold. For his example of an infallible sign, Aristotle claims that lactation is a sign that a woman has given birth recently.[49]

Finally, more specific *enthymemes* can be built from *probabilities* that are more specific to the case at hand. These lines of argument can be deduced either from specialized topics, such as medicine, biology, or the law, or from common topics understood by audiences in general.[50] To help in the construction of *enthymemes*, the *Rhetoric* provides 28 *topoi*, or common lines of argument that generate material for speeches. Not all of them are relevant to our time, but many hold up remarkably well. Included here is a sampling with the number they are assigned in the *Rhetoric*, Book II, chapter 23:

1. *Argument from opposites:* If A is the opposite of B, then the opposite of what is true of A must be true of B. (Since heaven is the opposite of hell, if heaven is wonderful, then hell is awful. If heaven is pleasant, hell must be painful.)

2. *Argument from inflection:* If something is true of one form of a word, it may also be true of another form of that word. (Since noble is the root for nobility, then nobility, it might be inferred, is noble.) (Since human is the root for humane, it is human to be humane.)

4. *Argument from more or less:* If a thing or characteristic is found where it is least likely to be, there is a better chance of finding it where it is expected. (If seals can

exist in polluted water, think how much more likely it is that they can exist in clean water.) If an action is taken in unusual circumstances, there is a good chance of it happening in more normal circumstances. (If a man strikes his father, he is even more likely to strike his neighbor.) (If God protects even sparrows, think how much more likely it is that God will protect you.) This *enthymeme* is often referred to as *a fortiori*.

6. *Argument from opponent's utterances:* Your opponent's words can be used against him or her, or for your side of an argument. (When he ran for governor of Massachusetts, Mitt Romney supported universal health care. When he changed his position in presidential primaries years later, his earlier statements were used against him.) This tactic is also known as "turning the tables" on your opponent.

7. *Argument from definition:* An accepted definition is offered and then applied to the specific case. (Murder is defined as the premeditated taking of a human life, with the opportunity and motive to commit the crime. Jared Loughner, the gunman in Tucson, Arizona, who killed six people and severely wounded Congresswoman Gabby Giffords, had the opportunity and the motive to commit the crime. He pled guilty to murder and was sentenced to life in prison.)

8. *Argument from ambiguous terms:* Because of the many meanings of some terms, we can pick the meaning most suitable to our purposes. (Sure I told him I loved him, but I didn't mean in a lustful way; I meant as a friend.) (They told me he was cold; I thought they meant he was unfeeling, but they meant he was dead.)

9. *Argument from division:* The speaker divides the question up in such a way as to cast aside what he or she believes is irrelevant and to focus on what is relevant. (In reaching a settlement in the war, we have three courses of action. We could withdraw all of our troops, but we would lose face in the world and endanger our allies. We could send in more troops, but we are already at 500,000 and it is doing no good. Therefore, we should accept my course of action, to increase aerial bombing while withdrawing our troops from the battlefield.) This is also known as the "method of residues."

12. *Argument from parts to the whole:* What is true of the parts will be true of the whole. (Since none of the juices used to make this punch were alcoholic, the punch is not alcoholic.) But like the other *topoi*, this one can be used fallaciously. (Since all of the member states are democracies, the European Union must be a democracy.) In the EU case, the argument falls victim to the fallacy of composition since the governance of the EU may not reflect its members.

14. *Argument from crisscross circumstances:* This is an attempt to create a dilemma from which your opponent cannot escape. (If you express your thoughts, you will be stoned. If you do not express your thoughts, many souls will be lost. You are damned if you do and damned if you don't.) But most dilemmas can be turned back on those who propose them. (If I express my thoughts, I will save souls. After that, if I am stoned, I will go to heaven.)

19. *Argument from attributed motives:* The obvious motive may not support our case, so we infer another motive is at work that better suits our aim. (Alvin didn't give you that gift out of the goodness of his heart. He got you that gift because he wants a

raise. Therefore, you should not be nice to Alvin.) (America did not enter the Iraq war to free the country from a dictator. It entered the war to protect its supply of oil. Therefore, it was an unjust war.)

21. *Argument from incredible occurrences:* The story told or the event is so incredible it could not have been made up. (Man is incapable of inventing the idea of God because the idea of God is so unbelievable. Therefore, there must be a God.)

24. *Argument from cause to effect:* The cause invariably leads to the effect. (Where there is fire, there is smoke.) (Where there is pneumonia, there is a fever.) This is the reverse of an *argument from sign*, which moves from the effect (smoke) to the cause (fire).

28. *Argument from the meaning of names:* In ancient Greece, names had a more direct relationship to the identification of a person. Someone might be called Peter because he is like a rock. So a play on the person's name would carry more weight than such a tactic today. However, plays on a name remain common in contemporary rhetoric. In 2008, comics joked about Hillary Clinton, implying that if Hillary were elected, her husband would be part of a copresidency. Online gossips played on Barack Hussein Obama's middle name to imply he had Muslim loyalties.

After listing these *topoi*, Aristotle explored nine sham *enthymemes* (fallacies) to be used in refutation.[51] These are spurious arguments that every speaker should be equipped to refute. The common fallacies listed are:

1. Equivocating, use of deceptive language, or playing with terms: "I promise to achieve peace with honor." (What does "honor" mean?)

2. Attributing the characteristics of the parts to the whole (fallacy of composition): "Every member of the group is a coward; therefore, the group as a whole will act in a cowardly manner." (It is not necessarily true.)

3. Constructing or predicting the awfulness of a situation that has not yet happened: "If you marry Ichabod, you will never be happy."

4. Using fallible signs: "They sure spend a lot of time together. They must be having sex."

5. Arguing from accidental occurrences: "The hurricane is a curse from God."

6. Taking something out of context: "Jesus must have favored public floggings because he chased the money changers from the Temple using a whip made of rope."

7. Attributing a present condition to a previous act (also known as *post hoc ergo propter hoc* or false cause): "The stock market collapsed because earlier in the week, Mars came too close to the earth."

8. Omitting relevant circumstances of time and manner: Historian one: "Julius Caesar murdered many people in conquering Gaul." Historian two provides important missing details: "Caesar attacked tribal soldiers only because they refused his offer of amnesty and alliance and attacked him."

9. Taking a particular probability as universally true: "That carrot-topped Holly has a terrible temper. I think all redheads are hotheads."

Aristotle advised that refutation could be accomplished in four ways: (1) by attacking an opponent's premise as untrue or unsupported, (2) by substituting a new premise that is more refined or more relevant, (3) by presenting a contrary premise that opposes the one your opponent embraces, or (4) by arguing from precedent by showing that what has happened in the past will happen in the future.

Enthymemes can be very effective while also being ethically suspect. For example, in his presentation to the UN Security Council, Secretary of State Colin Powell argued that aerial surveillance of trucks and facilities indicated that Iraq had developed weapons of mass destruction. Enemies of Iraq filled in the missing premise that these weapons justified going to war. But those opposed to war rejected the call and asked for more direct evidence of weapons of mass destruction. During her 2008 primary campaign, Senator Hillary Clinton ran an advertisement in which she is shown answering the phone at 3:00 AM in the White House. The narrator asks who the audience would most trust to answer a crisis call as president. The implication of the *enthymeme* was that Senator Clinton was more able to handle a crisis than her rival, Barack Obama. During the 2012 presidential campaign, advertisements claimed that because Mitt Romney, as CEO of Bain Capital, had supported companies that outsourced jobs to foreign countries, once he became president, he would initiate policies that send jobs overseas. Speakers need to make sure that *enthymemes* are adjusted to audiences and do not imply unintended or untrue premises.

STYLE AND DELIVERY *(LEXIS)*

Style is word choice that is clear and appropriate. The two major hallmarks of good style are clarity and appropriateness because truth cannot be separated from the words used to express it. More specifically, Aristotle recommended avoiding various vices (frigidities) of style by keeping it pure; that is, specific words should be employed instead of vague ones. Connectives should be appropriately placed; compound words should be avoided if simple words will do. A speaker should be incisive rather than ambiguous.

Aristotle also recommended the use of a natural style that contained only a few of the colorful devices of poetry of which Gorgias was so fond (see chapter 3). A speaker must use language that is appropriate and not "diverge too far from custom toward the extreme of excess." The orator must not appear to be harsh or contriving in his or her message; thus, the use of current terms, everyday language, is an important component of style. Aristotle endorsed the use of self-deprecatory remarks to project a sense of humility or humor.

Yet, as we have seen particularly in regard to appeals to emotions, speakers need to be able to develop vivid and lively imagery to make events seem real for the audience. Aristotle's favorite device was the metaphor, which "above all else gives clearness, charm, and distinction to style." Metaphors should sound good, be easily understood, bring variety and novelty to the speech, and avoid being far-fetched.

A metaphor functions in several ways. On the surface, it simply compares something from one category to something from another category to clarify meaning. For example, if I tell you that the human mind *is* a computer (assuming you are familiar with computers and not with the mind), you will understand more about the human mind. It has a memory that stores information; it has programs that direct its actions. Just as a computer with a Pentium chip operates more quickly than a 286 computer, a mind with a high IQ operates more quickly than one with a low IQ. The complication comes when we realize that metaphors are persuasive. If I convince you that your mind operates like a computer, then you may conceive it as a computer in all respects and ignore its emotional and spiritual qualities. Or you may come to believe that your mind is incapable of original thinking and depends solely on programming. To avoid such problems, Aristotle recommended that metaphors be proportional in terms of what is being compared. The precise comparison needs to be laid out so that inadvertent comparisons are not made by the listeners.

Metaphors are one of the ways by which a speaker can make the speech impressive. Aristotle listed several other strategies. For example, a speaker could substitute a description of the mere name of a thing, for example, referring to Paris as "the city of light," or referring to the Gulf War as "the mother of all wars." A speaker can also substitute plurals for singular forms, as in "the Lady MacBeths of this world." A speaker can tell an audience what something is not in place of what it is, as in "Philadelphia is no New York" or Richard Nixon's famous line, "Your president is not a crook."

In using these devices, the speaker should strive for a sense of liveliness *(asteia)* and actualization *(energia)*. Along with metaphors, similes contribute to liveliness; they are softened metaphors relying on the words "like" or "as" to make the comparisons: "Your mind is *like* a computer." Hyperbole also can enliven a speech since it is a gross exaggeration that makes a point in an ironic manner: "That horse is faster than lightning." Antithesis, one of Aristotle's favorite figures, enhances credibility with its reversal of phrasing: "Don't talk to me because you love me; love me because you talk to me." Most important, imagery through style sets the picture of things in action for an audience, or captures an idea in a striking and fascinating way. As I shall show in

To showcase public speeches, religious ceremonies, and plays, the Greeks built large amphitheaters that were semicircular in design. The theater at Epidaurus was constructed around 330 BC.

the next chapter, the Romans built on Aristotle's codification of figures of speech to create many more.

Aristotle also spent some time on rhythmical qualities in spoken prose. Here the link between style and delivery is clearest. The speaker needs to choose words that will please the ear. This was particularly true in ancient Greece because the language had a sing-song quality of rhyming to help with memory. Thus, restraint was the order of the day. Speakers needed to be rhythmical without being metrical; that is, a certain amount of phrasing to a beat could be pleasant, but it should not punctuate every line. The following line from Lincoln's second inaugural address is a beautiful example of how rhythm in the English language can sustain a thought and hold attention:

> With malice toward none, with charity for all, with firmness in the right as God gives us to see the right, *let us strive on to finish the work we are in*, to bind up the nation's wounds, to care for him who shall have borne the battle and for his widow and his orphan, to do all which may achieve and cherish a just and lasting peace among ourselves and with all nations.

Notice that the array of prepositional phrases that lead into and out of the main thought, which I have italicized, help the speaker sustain a rhythm appropriate to the message. Aristotle called this the *periodic* style because of its compact nature. It could be varied with the rambling or *loose* style that is more fluent and less marked by rhythmic phrasing. It could be reinforced using antithetical structure, which was a favorite of President John Kennedy. Here's just one of many that appeared in his inaugural address: "Let us never negotiate out of fear, but let us never fear to negotiate." Note that the repetition of words and the balance between the two phrases creates a powerful internal rhythm. It is for these reasons that Aristotle concluded that "the way a thing is said does affect its intelligibility."[52]

In Book III, chapter 1 of the *Rhetoric*, Aristotle linked delivery to the "correct management of the voice to express the various emotions." He then focused his attention on "volume of sound, modulation of pitch, and rhythm." That is, speakers can achieve vocal variety and hold attention by speaking louder or softer, at a higher or lower pitch, and more or less rhythmically. Aristotle's student, Theophrastus, followed Aristotle's lead by dividing the techniques of delivery into those relevant to the voice and those relevant to gesture. Later it would be the Romans who more fully developed style, delivery, and even memory in rhetorical theory, as we shall see in the next chapter.

ORGANIZATION *(TAXIS)* AND FORM

The second major subject of Book III is organization of speeches. Aristotle sets out four parts essential to any speech. The *proem*, or introduction, gains attention, allays hostility, obtains goodwill, and previews the ideas to be discussed. The *narration* can be interspersed throughout the body of the speech or condensed right after the proem. It outlines the case to be made, discusses the evolution of the problem at hand, explains the importance of the problem, and attempts to make the subject matter of the speech relevant to the audience. The *argument* sets out the pros and cons with regard to the selected subject. The *epilogue* or conclusion has four elements: (1) leaving the audience with a favorable impression of the speaker and an unfavorable opinion of his or her opponent, (2) magnifying or minimizing leading facts or arguments, (3) exciting the required emotions in the audience, and (4) recapitulating the main arguments of the case being made. As with style and delivery, the Romans would have much to add to Aristotle's brief outline of the standard speech, but they would not improve on his very thorough notion of form or genre.

Observing the needs and practices of Athens, Aristotle explained the *forms* of public address. They included the *forensic*[53] for legal battles, the *epideictic* for ceremonial events, and the *deliberative* for legislative arenas. Essentially the *Rhetoric* provides three genres of public address, each uniquely defined in terms of the role of the audience, the subject matter, the ends, and the time factor involved.[54]

A deliberative speech usually advises an audience that will act legislatively concerning ways and means, national defense, and such matters with regard to creating a more expedient situation in the future. Political or advisory speeches attempt to exhort or dissuade an audience with an eye toward what would be expedient or useful for the state and produce happiness among its people. Speakers engaging in this kind of discourse need to be aware of various forms of government, political philosophy, and the foundations of happiness for the citizens of the state. Aristotle provided this information in a summary in the *Rhetoric* and more fully in his *Politics*. The speaker also needs a specific knowledge of ways and means (taxing and spending), war and peace, national defense, exports and imports, and the legislative process, according to Aristotle. In deliberative speeches, orators must be able to advise about which action serves the greater good, including the acquisition of good things and the removal of harms. Goodness includes happiness (contentment) and justice. The State of the Union address by the president of the United States is a typical deliberative address as are speeches on the floor of the Senate, at the local city council meeting, or during a school board session.

An epideictic (ceremonial) speech is for an audience of observers interested in the praise or blame of a subject with an eye toward reinforcing current values.[55] Many of these speeches were used to memorialize events, heroes, and shrines, as they are to this day. The word epideictic is drawn from *epi-deixis*, meaning a "showing forth" or display. Thus, epideictic speakers may display virtues in their own lives or display virtues and/or vices through the praise or blame of others. In order to achieve the goal of an epideictic speech, which is to honor or dishonor its subject, the speaker must obtain a thorough knowledge of virtues and vices, which are summarized in the *Rhetoric* and developed more thoroughly in the *Ethics*. Aristotle claimed that what is noble is desirable in and of itself and wins praise for its good. That which is virtuous provides benefits on all occasions and preserves the good. The ignoble and vices are the opposite. In an epideictic address, a speaker magnifies or minimizes nobility, ignobility, virtue, and/or vice. A eulogy or a commencement address is a typical epideictic speech, and Aristotle surveyed the great funeral orations from Pericles' time to his own to carve out this genre.[56]

Celeste Condit deepens Aristotle's epideictic form by showing that it has a "tendency to serve three functional pairs—definition/understanding, display/entertainment, and shaping and sharing of community."[57] The speaker defines things for the audience so that its members can understand them. The speaker displays eloquence so that the audience can fulfill its role as a judge. The speaker shapes the virtues being endorsed so that they can be shared with the audience. Whether it is First Lady Barbara Bush speaking at Wellesley College or J. K. Rowling speaking at Harvard or Steve Jobs speaking at Stanford, it is not difficult to find outstanding commencement addresses that "show forth" personal virtues or try to persuade graduating seniors embrace them.[58]

A forensic speech is for an audience who will assess the accusation and defense to determine guilt or innocence regarding past acts. The aim of the speech is justice or injustice. Forensic speakers need to be knowledgeable in subjects such as crime and its incentives, the state of mind of someone who commits crimes, and what kind of persons are likely to be wronged or invite crime. Thus, speakers on behalf of themselves or others need to know why wrongdoing occurs; that is, whether it is the product of chance, nature, compulsion, habit, calculation, anger, or longing. Aristotle divided the causes of human action into involuntary and voluntary. The involuntary, which are more excusable in court, include acts committed because of chance, nature, and compulsion. The voluntary, which are less excusable, include habit, reason (calculation), passion, and desire. This division is reflected in Aristotle's advice that speakers understand both the particular laws of the state and the universal laws of nature. Because motive is such an important question in criminal cases, forensic speakers also need to understand the pleasure principle: that humans avoid the painful and seek the pleasurable, which motivates criminal activity. A speech to a jury in defense of a client is a typical forensic speech.

We can construct a grid based on the information found in the *Rhetoric* to guide the speaker through each of the genres.

Type	Elements	Time	End or Aim	Audience
Deliberative (political)	Exhortation & Dissuasion	Future	Expediency & Inexpediency	Legislative
Epideictic (ceremonial)	Praise & Blame	Present	Honor & Dishonor	Observers
Forensic (legal)	Accusation & Defense	Past	Justice & Injustice	Judge or Jury

One way in which we have sophisticated Aristotle's generic theory of public speaking is through understanding that more specific speech forms can be derived from the general ones above. For example, the *apologia*, a speech of defense or explanation first developed by Gorgias (see chapter 3), has been transformed into a more nuanced form over time. In the contemporary era, we know that *apologias* engage in denial, bolstering, differentiation, and/or transcendence.[59] The fact is that *apologias* often take on an epideictic cast when speakers compare themselves to heroes or a forensic cast when speakers condemn the actions of others or try to plea for their own innocence. A recent dramatic example was the forensic speech of Amanda Knox in Perugia, Italy, pleading with an Italian court to overturn her conviction for murder.

Apologias can also be preemptive in nature. That is, a speaker may wish to rebut arguments that might be made in the future. From his camps in Gaul, Julius Caesar wrote letters to the Senate in Rome explaining his actions to preempt objections from his rivals.[60] In defense of his decision in the infamous Supreme Court case of *Bush v. Gore* (December 13, 2000), which resulted in George W. Bush becoming president, Chief Justice William Rehnquist wrote a preemptive *apologia* in the form of a concurring opinion. Early in his campaign for the presidential nomination in 2012, Mitt Romney appeared before a group of supporters to explain why his Mormonism would not interfere with carrying out the duties of being president.

Aristotle himself adds sophistication to his categories when he demonstrates that a speaker can *camouflage an element of one form of speech inside another*. For example, a priest giving a sermon may condemn sinful acts (forensic), praise or blame various virtues and vices (epideictic), and then call for a conversion to Christianity (deliberative). A car salesperson may urge you to buy his/her product (deliberative), while pointing out the flaws of the competitor's product (epideictic). Thus, a speaker in developing discourse needs to make sure that each category of persuasive speaking has been examined to determine if all of the available means of persuasion have been generated in the given case.

Aristotle also listed the special needs of each genre. For example, epideictic speakers have a special need for mastery of amplification, elaborate style, and comparison of thoughts. Forensic speakers need to know about motives and the mental state of criminals. Deliberative speakers need to know what makes the public content. Aristotle segmented the genres by the time frame of the address, a reflection of the way humans reason. The deliberative mind makes decisions that look to the future, such as the next date, the next meal, the next trip. The epideictic mind enjoys the quality of the present, such as the bouquet of the wine, the engineering of the car, the honesty of the conversation. The forensic mind ponders past decisions. Should I have said that? Would I marry him again?

Aristotle's analysis of the forms of public address generates a very sophisticated system of practical knowledge rooted in the deceptively simple advice that speakers must state their case and then prove it.[61] We can demonstrate the sophistication of Aristotle's system by studying effective speakers in our history. Congressman and Senator Daniel Webster, who twice served as secretary of state, is considered the most effective member of the triumvirate that included Henry Clay and John C. Calhoun during America's golden age of oratory. Webster was a prominent speaker until his death in 1852.

Genre, Style, and Webster

Webster's use of form is subtle. His arguments before the Supreme Court, ostensibly forensic speeches, are known to have influenced Justice Marshall's decisions on deliberative matters and reflected Webster's own political positions.[62] During the debate over the Missouri Compromise, he spent a good deal of time explaining the "injustices" done to the New England states. In his deliberative replies to Senator Hayne, Webster praised the Union, an epideictic moment in the midst of a deliberative case for disposition of public lands. During the 1850 Compromise debates, Webster had praise for some senators and states, and blame for others. In fact, one would be hard pressed to find a *deliberative* effort by Webster that did not contain forensic and epideictic aspects.

Furthermore, an analysis of Webster's major ceremonial addresses demonstrates an effective fusion of deliberative and forensic elements with epideictic form.[63] This sophisticated integration allowed Webster to advance the National Republican agenda in the sheep's clothing of praising American civic virtues. For example, "The First Settlement of New England" was delivered in 1820 to celebrate the bicentennial of the landing of the Pilgrims. Webster's firm belief that history, tradition, and generational loyalty are the mystical cords that bind a people into a nation is clearly evident.

> We have come to this Rock, to record here our homage for our Pilgrim Fathers; our sympathy in their sufferings; our gratitude for their labors; our admiration of their virtues; our veneration for their piety; and our attachment to those principles of civil and religious liberty with which they encountered the dangers of the ocean, the storms of heaven, the violence of savages, disease, exile, and famine, to enjoy and establish.[64]

In form, this passage reveals the periodic cadence that typified Webster's style. In substance, this perspective on what citizens owe their ancestors framed the obligation that Webster's audience owed to future generations.

Having reinforced transcendent values and a sense of linkage with the past, Webster endorsed a new course for the nation by fusing deliberative argument with epideictic form. The subject was slavery:

> If there be, within the extent of our knowledge or influence, any participation in this [slave] traffic, let us pledge ourselves here, upon the Rock of Plymouth, to extirpate and destroy it. It is not fit that the land of the Pilgrims should bear the shame longer. I hear the sound of the hammer, I see the smoke of the furnace, where the manacles and fetters are still forged for human limbs. I see the visages of those, who by stealth, and at midnight, labor in this work of hell, foul and dark, as may become the artificers of such instruments of misery and torture. Let that spot be purified, or let it cease to be of New England.

The appeal to the audience's senses of smell, hearing, touch, and sight reinforces Webster's condemnation of slavery and suggests a deliberative end, abolition. He thereby concealed deliberative and forensic arguments in the epideictic form by reinforcing the basic value of New England's Puritan founders. John Adams was effusive in his praise of the address in calling Webster "the most consummate orator of modern times."[65]

On June 17, 1825, in his "First Bunker Hill Address" (also known as "Laying the Cornerstone of the Bunker Hill Monument"), Webster argued for national defense, individual liberty, union, preservation of the Constitution, and independence; he also speculated about South American revolutions. The Marquis de Lafayette, America's most noted foreign ally in the Revolution, and two hundred veterans of the battle sat on the stage near Webster. This situation allowed him to place the moment into the context of the American heritage and then use it to reinforce the most important values in civic life: "We consecrate our work to the spirit of national independence, and we wish that the light of peace may rest upon it forever."

Events of a mystical nature would soon give Webster a chance to reinforce his version of civil religion. The deaths of both John Adams (the last Federalist president) and Thomas Jefferson (the first Democratic-Republican president) on July 4, 1826, exactly 50 years after they signed the Declaration of Independence, created an event so mystical and so replete with national heroes that it required the epideictic form to meet expectations of the audience. Webster knew that obvious deliberative and forensic elements might demean the occasion.[66]

On the day of the eulogy, August 2, 1826, Webster sat on the stage with Governor Lincoln, Major Josiah Quincy, Harvard's President Kirkland, and John Quincy Adams, whose father would receive most of Webster's accolades.[67] Webster's challenge was to address both the occasion (the deaths of two national heroes) and the audience.

Aristotle specifically recommended appeals to honor and dishonor for the epideictic address.[68] His discussion of the other virtues indicated that they are to support the strategies surrounding honor or dishonor in order to make the claims believable. One method of achieving believability is to ascribe to the subject those "qualities an audience esteems."[69] Aristotle also offered recommendations for arrangement in epideictic speaking. The speech should begin with a preview of the ideas to be presented. He suggested that themes be integrated into the text to ensure continuity. Consistent with this advice was the recommendation that the narration be intermittent throughout the speech, and that eulogy and

Daniel Webster served in the House, the Senate, and twice as Secretary of State.

argument be interwoven.[70] Aristotle was concerned with both an organizational structure appropriate to the occasion and a structure that demonstrates some sense of proportion. He realized how easy it would be for a speaker to exclude the audience while eulogizing the dead (a past event) or while vilifying an opponent or a nasty deed. So he advised the speaker to bring the audience into the occasion.

Webster's eulogy effectively meets Aristotle's criteria.[71] The introduction describes the extraordinary coincidence that has brought the audience together. From the first sentence, Webster brings the event into Faneuil Hall by calling attention to the room itself. He connects the mourning in the hall to his sense of history: "The tears which flow, and the honors that are paid, when the founders of the republic die, give hope that the republic itself may be immortal." Death reinforces life. This sublime contrast is soon matched by another when Webster tells his audience that Adams and Jefferson "took their flight together to the world of spirits" in the midst of national rejoicing over the fiftieth anniversary of independence.

Webster had created a pattern that would guide him through the speech. The audience would be involved in the "account of the lives" by references to the occasion. The occasion would be explored by references to the parallel lives of the two patriots. Also foreshadowed in the introduction is a wonderful metaphor concerning the universe; it surfaces several more times in the speech and is brought to culmination near the end. The stars in the sky, and then later the planets and their orbits, provide a unifying image for the address: "These suns, as they rose slowly and steadily, amidst clouds and storms, in their ascendant, so they have rushed from their meridian to sink suddenly in the west." Webster certainly heeds Aristotle's call for enhanced style in the epideictic address.

The first section after the introduction is devoted to John Adams' life to the year 1776. The next section explores Jefferson's life to the same year. The praise for both men centered on their particular accomplishments as evidence of honor. Jefferson's role as leader-statesman, philosopher, and founder is compared to Adams' political commitments and service on the Massachusetts Supreme Court. Other accomplishments are used to demonstrate virtues attendant upon honor. These biographies were written in a plain, declarative style that allowed them to speak for themselves and to provide a much-needed contrast to the florid introduction.

Webster had little difficulty imputing courage and sacrifice to the two patriots in the early sections of the speech and then reestablishing these virtues toward the conclusion. In between he maintained continuity with three striking metaphors. One involved the turbulent ocean and the mariner bringing his ship safely home. The metaphor had great appeal to Americans because the great bulk of the population lived in such ports as Boston (where the speech was delivered), New York, Philadelphia, and Charleston.

Another metaphor concerned the growth cycle and helped unify various elements in the speech. In its simplest form, the metaphor was a reference to the past, the present, and the future. In this speech, it concerned the seed, the sapling, and the tree. The seed was the accomplishments of the two patriots; the sapling was the present and the audience's understanding of virtue; and the tree, which reaches to heaven, was the future, guiding the living and providing a lasting tribute to the dead patriots. Webster showed great skill in making the virtues he attributed to his subjects believable. At one point, he combined the lives of Adams and Jefferson in a forty-five-minute review of the writing and debate over the Declaration of Independence. Although no record of the debates existed, Webster contended that Adams' debating skill was crucial to the passage of the Declaration: "John Adams had no equal." How to reinforce Adams' rhetorical contribution was the task at hand. First, Webster cited Jefferson's praise for Adams as a "colossus . . . not elegant, not always fluent" but capable of "thought and expression, which moved us from our seats." Second, Webster heaped praise on Adams and described his eloquence: "It was bold, manly, energetic." These passages undoubtedly created an expectation in the audience that Webster then fulfilled with his famous "ghost speech." Webster uttered the speech in the plain, bold, manly style he attributed to Adams. The opening of the "ghost speech" is rhythmic and powerful: "Sink or swim, live or die, survive or perish, I give my hand and my heart to this vote." The hail of rhetorical questions that followed held attention as Webster became Adams. The extended metaphor at the end rises from the declarative desert that precedes it. Then comes the last line: "It is my living sentiment, and by the blessing of God it shall be my dying sentiment, Independence, *now, and independence forever.*"[72] The impersonation of Adams worked because it was explosive, in marked contrast to the exposition of Jefferson's contributions.

Within the epideictic form, Webster satisfied the needs of this particular rhetorical situation with proportion and grace. He treated the subjects separately and then united them: "Both had been presidents, both had lived to great age, both were early patriots, and both were distinguished and ever honored." Webster learned well Aristotle's lesson concerning praising a person for a course of action the orator would have others follow. When Webster finally translated the patriots' "principles" into a course of action, the deliberative advice seemed natural to the discourse: "Be it remembered . . . that liberty must, at all hazards, be supported." In the last paragraph, Webster argued that America was a model for the world, that it embodied a new approach to government, that its citizens must preserve its institutions, and that all must be guided by God. Only Webster's references to the occasion and the forefathers maintained an epideictic veneer over a deliberative message concerned with the ways to achieve and preserve happiness, with the good in society, with forms of government, and with duties of citizens.

Webster's speech was an enormous success. Richard Rush wrote to Webster: "The speech . . . made my hair rise. . . . Nothing of Livy's ever moved me so much."[73] From that time, Webster was often referred to as the "Godlike Daniel." Within a year, the state legislature elected Webster to the United States Senate.

This analysis reveals several important strategies. First, the overlap between genres occurs in two theoretically distinct ways: (1) a masking process where purposes proper to one genre are developed in a speech ostensibly belonging to another genre, and (2) a borrowing process in which the purposes of one genre are served by using the devices from another. The latter case is exemplified in the above analysis where Webster in the body of the address uses deliberative and forensic elements to reinforce the epideictic *telos* or end.

Second, there seems always to be a *controlling* or dominant form. Generally, audiences that gather to hear a speech are often called upon to serve in a loose sense as jurors, observers, or deliberators, but they may also serve a secondary function at the same time with or without the encouragement of the speaker. For example, those gathered as observers of Webster's "Eulogy" could think as jurors or policy makers at various points in the address. Thus, *audience role* stands out as one of the major constituents by which we can identify the controlling form.

Setting is also useful: that a speech is given in court, or in Congress, or in celebration of a holiday helps the critic determine the dominant form shaping the discourse. Again we should note that while one setting may dominate, another might be called to mind. Webster's conversion of Faneuil Hall into the Congress for the "ghost speech" is a case in point.

Aristotle used *time* as another determinant of controlling form. If one intended to issue a judgment about the past, the forensic form was useful. Speaking to the future necessitated deliberative utterance, and endorsing values for the present was epideictic. Here again while one time period may be emphasized, and thereby help us identify the controlling form, secondary time periods often appear. Webster's vindication of Jefferson's past was part of an overall strategy to reinforce present values so that future policies would be improved.

The notion of form examined here is useful in explaining why Webster was so successful. He adapted epideictic rhetoric to fit the audience, subject, time, and setting. He understood that Aristotle's three genres cast three different lights on the persuasive situation. Each light revealed different "available means of persuasion" that Webster employed, which explains why his public address was complex, effective, and enduring.

CONCLUSION

Aristotle's *Rhetoric* is the most important work in our field for many reasons: it describes the role dialectic can play in informing a speech; it brings Platonic form out of the *noumenal* world into this one to frame the various persuasive genres; it underlines the importance of storytelling in its advice on the use of narrative, particularly in forensic and epideictic speeches. It develops *ethos* and *pathos* into powerful and complex engines of persuasion, and invents a persuasive form of logic with the *enthymeme*. The fact is that Aristotle's approach—asking the right questions of each rhetorical situation—provides the basis for the five canons that would be codified in the Roman's *Rhetorica ad Herennium:* invention (inclusive of *ethos, pathos,* and *logos*), delivery, organization (inclusive of the forms of public address), memory, and style. Most of the theory that comes after him extends what Aristotle had to say; in very few cases are wholly new conceptualizations developed.

By the time of Caesar, Aristotle's works had been edited, published, and filed at libraries in Athens, Pergamum, Alexandria, Ephesus, and Rome. The Greek texts were readily available in the Byzantine Empire. His, however, were not as popular as the Roman works that followed. While Boethius (see chapter 6) would translate Aristotle's *Categories* and *On Interpretation* in the Middle Ages, the entire *Organon*, Aristotle's works on logic, would not be translated into Latin until the 1100s. In the mid-1200s, the *Rhetoric* and *Politics* were translated by William of Moerbeke from the Greek to Latin and brought into the curriculum at the University of Paris and then other universities.[74] The return of Aristotelian logic was a great boon to scholastics, as we will learn in chapter 6, but they did not equally embrace his rhetorical theories. The *Rhetoric* did not gain ascendance until the sixteenth century. The vacuum was filled mainly by the works of Cicero and Quintilian and the *Rhetorica ad Herennium*, to which we now turn.

Study Questions

1. What is the most significant way in which Aristotle differs from his teacher Plato?

2. How do Aristotle's works on logic and politics help to contextualize and make sense of his rhetorical theory?

3. What skills outlined in the *Poetics* are useful to the public speaker?

4. Do the major uses of rhetoric listed by Aristotle correspond to the ways you use rhetoric?

5. Using the major constituents of *ethos* as a guide, analyze a contemporary speech to assess its credibility.

6. What is an *enthymeme?* Compare and contrast it with a logical syllogism.

7. Diagram Aristotle's theory of *pathos* inclusive of its continuums and notions of temporality. Examine a television commercial and determine upon which of the *pathé* it plays.

8. What are the constituents of a forensic speech, an epideictic speech, and a deliberative speech? Provide a contemporary example of each form.

9. What is the most important advice that Aristotle gives on delivery of speeches?

10. How does Aristotle define metaphor? Why is metaphor important to the style of a speech?

11. Is Aristotle's advice on style more Platonic than his other advice?

12. In what ways is rhetoric the counterpart of dialectic?

13. In what ways is rhetoric the counterpart of literature?

14. Illustrate the *topoi* in the text by constructing an *enthymeme* for each one. Comb a newspaper for examples of the sham *enthymemes* that appear.

Notes

1. Most believe he entered Plato's Academy at age 18, although others have claimed it was not until he was 30.

2. Philip's father used Aristotle's father as his personal physician, thus establishing a tie between the two.

3. Aristotle, *Rhetoric*, W. Rhys Roberts, trans. (New York: Random House, 1954), 1253a. My reference numbers to Aristotle's texts use the universal Becker pages. That is, Aristotle's writings have been numbered so that scholars using different translations can find the same sentences. *Politics*, Benjamin Jowett, trans., in Richard McKeon, ed., *The Basic Works of Aristotle* (New York: Random House, 1966), pp. 1127–324.

4. *Politics* at 1279b. Machiavelli, whom we shall study in the Renaissance section of this book, picked this theme up and expanded it in his work, *The Prince*.

5. The Greek term for freedom of speech was *parrhesia*, a frank, candid speech.

6. *Organon* means instrument for investigation.

7. Aristotle, *Poetics*, W. Rhys Roberts, trans. (New York: Modern Library Random House, 1954), 1455a22.

8. Unless otherwise noted, universal numbers refer to the *Rhetoric*, in this case at 1441b24.

9. Aristotle says the plots of the most effective plays run "a single revolution of the sun." This penchant for compactness increases tension and forces the author to remove extraneous material. While it runs a bit longer than one day, Shakespeare's *Romeo and Juliet* is a model of compact plotting.

10. See particularly the first three chapters of the *Poetics*.

11. See his *Metaphysics* in section Z.4 and following. (Aristotle's book was originally called *After the Physics* probably to distinguish his order of publication. Later translators changed the title. In this section, he defines substance as "the what is was to be" or "the what it is," which so confused Latin translators that they changed the definition to "essence." See also 1032b14.)

12. Ever the lover of categories, Aristotle created nine for the different kinds of accidental properties he developed.

13. Aristotle's notions of actuality and potentiality can be found in *De anima* and also in the *Metaphysics* at 1049b to 1051.

14. See, for example, Michael J. Hyde and Craig R. Smith, "Heidegger and Aristotle on Emotion: Questions of Time and Space," in *The Critical Turn: Rhetoric and Philosophy in Contemporary Discourse*, Ian Angus and Lenore Langsdorf, eds. (Carbondale: Southern Illinois U. Press, 1992), pp. 68–99. See also, Craig R. Smith, "A Reinterpretation of Aristotle's Notion of Rhetorical Form," *Western Speech Communication Journal* (1979): 14–25.

15. 1355a16.

16. See James J. Murphy, *Rhetoric in the Middle Ages: A History of Rhetorical Theory from St. Augustine to the Renaissance* (Berkeley: U. of California Press, 1974), p. 18. Theophrastus wrote books *On Enthymemes, On Epicheiremes, On Humor, On Style, On Amplification, On Delivery*, and many more while trying to maintain Aristotle's school.

17. See Aristotle, *Poetics,* 1450b4–8.

18. Aristotle writes at 1355a6: "now every kind of syllogism falls within the province of Dialectic, and must be examined under Dialectic as a whole, or under some branch of it. Consequently, the person with the clearest insight into the nature of syllogisms, who knows from what premises and in what modes they may be construed, will also be the most expert in regard to *enthymemes*, once he has mastered their special province [of things contingent and uncertain such as human actions and their consequences], and has learnt the differences between *enthymemes* and logical syllogisms." What Aristotle is saying here is important. He believes that one who is facile in the use of syllogisms can more easily master *enthymemes* that have a similar form but are based on probabilities. He concludes, "Consequently one who is skilled in discerning the truth can do well in weighing probabilities." A fully stated *enthymeme* is an *epicheireme*.

19. See particularly 1410b30–1412b5.

20. *Poetics*, 1460a27–28.

21. 1356a10ff.

22. The reason for the de-emphasis of prior reputation in Aristotle is that he is trying to lay out ways to create credibility in the speech itself rather than "account for preexisting opinions" (1356a7–12). The

Roman theorists Cicero and Quintilian criticize Aristotle for not specifically identifying the antecedent *ethos*. It weighs heavily in their rhetorics and in that of Machiavelli.

[23] This position was highly influential and will resurface in the work of John Locke.

[24] See Martin Heidegger, *Plato's Sophist*, Richard Rojcewicz and André Schuwer, trans. (Bloomington: Indiana U. Press, 1997).

[25] 1380b34–1381a1. Aristotle notes that this may involve the emotions. For example, sympathy is a *pathé* that also demonstrates goodwill. Aristotle defines a *pathé* as a single state or frame of mind, such as confidence or sympathy.

[26] *Ethics*, 1107a.

[27] See 1378a15–16.

[28] 1377b24.

[29] 1354a24–25.

[30] 1378a20.

[31] Michael J. Hyde, "Emotion and Human Communication: A Rhetorical, Scientific, and Philosophical Picture," *Communication Quarterly*, 32 (1984): 122, 128, 130 (note 6); and Hyde and Smith, "Aristotle and Heidegger on Emotion." These essays reveal that Aristotle recognizes that emotions function primordially as vehicles for the active sensibility of human beings: an emotion is an act of consciousness that serves to orient a person toward the world in a certain way.

[32] 1378b8–9; see also 1370b33.

[33] 1378a21.

[34] 1377b31–1378a5.

[35] 1378a22–28.

[36] 1378b8–9. Research published by the University of Zurich proved that contemplating revenge stimulates the dorsal striatum in the brain, which is normally activated in anticipation of pleasure, such as good food or sex. See Marilyn Elias, "Revenge May Be All in Anticipation," *Los Angeles Times* (October 18, 2010). http://articles.latimes.com/2010/oct/18/health/la-he-revenge-20101018 (accessed July 11, 2012).

[37] 1383a17–18.

[38] 1378b3–5.

[39] 1380b5.

[40] 1379b24–26.

[41] Aristotle completes a similar analysis of how we exist with others when discussing other emotions. For example, when discussing "Friendship and Enmity" he writes, "Your friend is the sort of man who shares your pleasure in what is good and your pain in what is unpleasant, for your sake and for no other reason," 1381a4–6. Here again how one relates to others is conditioned by emotions.

[42] 1383a7–12.

[43] 1370a28–30.

[44] 1369b33 to 1370a4.

[45] 1380a31.

[46] See, for example, 1378b20–21, 1379a21–27, 1383a7–12, 1386a30, 1386b8, and 1388b28. As Bate writes, "[Aristotle] was quite in accord with the general Greek confidence in the power of art as *psychagogia*, the leading out of the soul." Walter J. Bate, *Criticism: The Major Texts* (New York: Harcourt, Brace, 1952), p. 13.

[47] Neuroanatomical studies explain the phenomenon this way: the amygdala, a small, almond shaped structure in the lower brain, scrutinizes sense-data and attaches an emotional weight that is normally put in context by the cortex. Dr. Joseph LeDoux argues that "overly emotional reactions stem from the amygdala responding too strongly to information sent by the senses before receiving the big picture from the cortex." In Margie Patlak, "Emotional Impact," *Los Angeles Times* (June 24, 1991): B3.

[48] See, for example, 1408b16–18, 1418a11–13, 1388b31–1390b10, and 1390b11–1391b4. Aristotle's discussion of style may prove an exception to his integrated theory since it is not mentioned until the end of Book II. This oversight opened the door to the Roman integration of style into the other proofs, particularly, as we shall see, in the works of Cicero.

[49] 1357b15–16.

[50] In chapter 12 we explore how Stephen Toulmin built on this bifurcation in his theory of field variant and field invariant argumentative forms.

[51] These have their parallels in his book on *Sophistical Refutations*.

[52] 1404a8.

[53] This was called *dikanikon* in Greek because it concerned *dike*, the Greek word for justice.

[54] For a modern application of genre theory, see H. W. Simons & A. A. Aghazarian, eds., *Form, Genre, and the Study of Political Discourse* (Columbia: U. of South Carolina Press, 1986); Karlyn K. Campbell and Kathleen H. Jamieson, eds., *Form and Genre: Shaping Rhetorical Action* (Falls Church, VA: Speech Communication Association, 1990).

[55] For a survey of these, see Donovan J. Ochs, *Consolatory Rhetoric: Grief, Symbol, and Ritual in the Greco-Roman Era* (Columbia: U. of South Carolina Press, 1993), chapter 3.

[56] Praise and blame were fundamental principles in the archaic Greek community and often show up in the *Iliad* of Homer. Aeneas was a master of the poetics of praise and blame. The laws in Sparta were built on praise of the noble and blame of the base. See Marcel Detienne, *Les maîtres de vérité en Grèce archaïque*, 3rd ed. (Paris, 1993), pp. 18–27.

[57] Celeste Condit, "The Functions of Epideictic: The Boston Massacre Orations as Exemplar," *Communication Quarterly*, 33 (1985): 289.

[58] In her 1990 commencement address at Wellesley College, Barbara Bush overcame hostility toward her in her opening remarks and then undercut the feminism of her critics by reasserting traditional family values. In 2005 Steve Jobs provided lessons of importance he learned once his cancer was diagnosed. His speech is even more poignant because of his recent passing. J. K. Rowling describes her troubled past and rise to fame as the author of the Harry Potter series in her 2008 commencement address. All of these speeches are available on YouTube as of this writing.

[59] B. L. Ware and W. A. Linkugel, "They Spoke in Defense of Themselves: On the General Criticism of Apologia," *Quarterly Journal of Speech*, 59 (1973): 273–83.

[60] These letters were eventually collected into the book, *Caesar's Commentaries on the Gallic Wars*.

[61] See Book III, chapter 13.

[62] See Claude Fuess, *Daniel Webster* (Boston: Little, Brown, and Co., 1930), vol. 1, pp. 231–35.

[63] Craig R. Smith, *Daniel Webster and the Oratory of Civil Religion* (Columbia: U. of Missouri Press, 2005) pp. 56–58, 94–96.

[64] This address entitled "The First Settlement of New England" can be found in *The Papers of Daniel Webster: Speeches and Formal Writings*, 2 vols., Charles M. Wiltse and Alan R. Bertolzheimer, eds. (Hanover, NH: U. Press of New England, 1986–88). All of the quotations from Webster's speeches in this section of text are taken from the Wiltse volumes.

[65] Smith, *Daniel Webster and the Oratory*, p. 63.

[66] See letter from Joseph Story to Daniel Webster, July 11, 1826, *The Papers of Daniel Webster, Correspondence*, vol. 2, Charles M. Wiltse and others, eds. (Hanover, NH: Dartmouth U. Press, 1974–85), pp. 126–27.

[67] Much has been written about the difficult relationship between Adams and Jefferson. They rubbed each other the wrong way during debates on the Declaration of Independence, during debates over the ratification of the Constitution and the Bill of Rights, during Washington's and Adams' administrations. Their "feud" was known to the public. For example, during 1789 they exchanged cool letters regarding the Publicola affair in which Jefferson had endorsed Paine's *Rights of Man* and a writer using the pseudonym Publicola had attacked them. Adams denied being Publicola and told Jefferson to stop slandering him. Jefferson indicates in his notes that Publicola may have been John Quincy Adams. If true, John Adams' denials were disingenuous.

[68] 1358b28.

[69] 1367a31.

[70] 1414b25–29, 1416b15–16, 1418b33–34.

[71] Of the three forms, Aristotle claimed that the epideictic "is the most literary, since it is meant to be read," 1415b28–29, 1414a12–16. Aristotle's claim found support in Webster's practice of not publishing his speeches until he had revised them and in the success his published speeches enjoyed.

[72] For years later, Webster would paraphrase this line and use it to conclude the most famous speech ever given in the U.S. Senate. The occasion was a debate with Robert Hayne of South Carolina. Webster ended his speech, "Liberty *and* Union, now and forever, one and inseparable!"

[73] Wiltse et al., *Papers of Daniel Webster, Correspondence*, vol. 2, p. 129.

[74] Another copy of the *Rhetoric* was translated in Toledo, Spain, in 1246.

The Roman Rhetorical System

Following the death of Alexander the Great, the Greek Empire was divided into regions, each ruled by a different general. Soon ethnic strife led to subdivisions among these principalities. As the Hellenistic Empire slid into decline, other powers around the Mediterranean Sea grew in influence. Chief among these were the Romans of central Italy and the Carthaginians of North Africa. Carthage had begun as a Phoenician colony near what is now Tunis; its natural harbor and its ability to develop mineral mines in Spain helped it become a powerful nation. Soon Rome and Carthage were at each others' throats, fighting to rule the Mediterranean area. The strife continued through three armed confrontations called the Punic Wars, until the Romans prevailed, destroyed Carthage, and built an empire that rivaled Alexander's. The center of civilization shifted from Athens to Rome and Alexandria. Though Athens retained its reputation in educational circles, many teachers moved to Rome and Alexandria where they were joined by others from around the Empire.

Roman rhetorical theorists, aided by teachers from Greece, synthesized the Isocratean and Aristotelian traditions. Education was intended to arm an individual with strategies essential for a meaningful existence in this world, particularly if one chose a public life. Students learned rhetorical skills for surviving in a hostile world, for building a sense of self, and for making sense of the world. Roman theorists believed that speakers who were adept at rhetoric were capable of defending and presenting the truth. In fact, they helped to cultivate public morals and codes of valuation through epideictic speaking. These speeches reconstituted a public that would temper the rule of the emperors when they went astray during the imperial period, which was often. The new generation of Sophists used rhetoric to reinforce a standard to which emperors and others could be held.

ROMAN NATION BUILDING

Like the Greeks, the Romans used the rhetoric of mythology to build a sense of nationhood. The stories of the founding of Rome provide examples of how this *mythos* worked and how it imitated the Greek model. Virgil's *Aeneid*, written during the reign of Caesar Augustus around the time of the birth of Christ, had tremendous impact. Augustus commissioned the work, which, even after eleven years, was not completed. It begins, "I sing of warfare and the man." It supported the belief that while Greece was a place of art (Virgil particularly cites rhetoric), Rome was a place destined to govern an empire:

> Remember, Roman, thy art is to rule
> O'er other peoples, found their peace in law,
> Put down the proud and spare the humble ones.[1]

Virgil's Rome was founded by Aeneas, the warrior-hero who traveled from Troy after that city fell to the Greeks. Aeneas, the son of Venus, escaped the burning city of Troy carrying his father on his back and holding his young son's hand. Before arriving in what would become Rome, he stopped in Carthage, fell in love with its queen, Dido, then deserted her to follow his destiny. She then took her own life. The story is Virgil's way of foreshadowing the defeat of Carthage in the Punic Wars. Aeneas visited the underworld, developed a strong sense of justice, married Lavinia, and inherited the throne of Latinum. He led his people in conquest, and when he was killed in battle, he ascended into the famed Elysian Fields.

As they built their mythology, Romans not only disparaged Carthage and borrowed Aeneas, they made the Greek gods their own by renaming them: Zeus became Jupiter, Ares became Mars, Dionysus became Bacchus, Poseidon became Neptune, Aphrodite became Venus, Hera became Juno, Hephaestus became Vulcan, Artemis became Diana, and Kronos became Saturn. Ovid, another leading poet in Augustus' time, rewrote the stories of Greek mythology into his 12,000 line *Metamorphoses*. These myths influence us to this day. For example, Jupiter's favorite bird was the eagle and his favorite tree was the oak, both of which are standard symbols of the United States. Jupiter's goatskin cloak was called *Aegis*, which to this day means protection as in, "She is under the aegis of the court."

Though the second story of Rome's founding is more ancient, it was incorporated by Virgil into his own. Virgil claims that Aeneas' son founded Alba Longus, and that he produced the virgin Rhea Silva who became a high priestess and was then raped by Mars. She gave birth to twins, Romulus and Remus, who were set adrift on a raft by her jealous king. The twin babies were suckled by a she-wolf in the Velabro, a marshy field in Rome.[2] They were discovered by a shepherd, Faustolo, who raised the boys to manhood. They grew up to found Rome on seven hills. Remus, who built his settlement on Aventine Hill, was the envy of his brother Romulus. At this juncture, the story resembles the tale of Cain and Abel: Romulus, who gave his name to the city, killed Remus, who dared to jump over a wall that Romulus had built. The story was meant to warn Rome's enemies never to breach its walls.

Mythology aside, history tells us that while Etruscan civilization can be traced back to at least 800 BC, it was absorbed by the Romans a few centuries later. The Roman Republic did not emerge until about 550 BC when certain kings believed a council similar to a senate would help them keep order. The monarchy was finally brought down in 509 BC; Lucius Junious Brutus led a group of men who forced the ruler Tarquin to resign when the matron Lucretia committed suicide after being raped

Romulus and Remus as infants taking milk from the she-wolf.

by Tarquin's son. In 508 BC the Senate deposed Servius, who had become a dictator in Tarquin's place, and created a republic with two consuls who ruled jointly for one year. A peace treaty of Latin tribes was signed in 493 BC. In Rome, an assembly of the lower class, the Plebeian Assembly, was formed in 471 BC. It elected tribunes who could veto the action of the Senate, the body representing the patricians composed of aristocrats from the founding families.

Subsequently, Rome began a long period of expansion. It defeated Sabine, Alba, Latinum, Rutuli, Volscia, and Veii and merged with Etruria. By 338 BC all of the Latin tribes were subjugated to Rome. As it grew in influence so did the Senate. Soon political groups formed around major leaders. The original Senate had 100 members, but was eventually expanded to 300 members drawn mainly from the patrician class, at the top of the hierarchical society. Beneath them were the *equites* (equals, merchants), then came the plebs (common citizens), then the slaves. Senators were selected by the Censors, until Sulla reformed the system to allow entry through a Quaestorship, an official accountant for consuls and governors. Tribunes of the plebs were considered members of the Senate, though patrician members of the Senate spoke before all others were allowed to address the body, which normally met in the *Curia hostilia* in an area in the heart of Rome called the Forum. The Forum was a collection of public buildings and temples. The Senate advised the magistrates on such matters as the treasury, taxation, foreign affairs, and the appointment of governors for the regions of the empire. Legislation, as we shall see, was reserved for the assemblies. In 123 BC in an important reform, Rome acceded to the wishes of Caius Gracchus (see below) and expanded the Senate to 600 members. This opened the Senate to more knights *(equites)*, one of whom was Cicero, the most important rhetorical theorist in Roman history.

Consuls were on the top rung of the Roman power hierarchy known as the *cursus honorum*. Two were elected each year by the Centuriate Assembly. They began service on the first of the year, the one receiving the most votes being senior. Consuls carried out the wishes of the assemblies. By the end of the Roman Republic, both consuls could be plebs, but they both could not be patricians. This was the result of the constant discontent of the plebs, which played a major role in reforming the republic and increasing the need for public address. For example, in 493 BC the plebs resisted a call for military volunteers for a new war.[3] The Senate then conceded to the plebs the right to have two tribunes to represent them in the Senate.

One of the most important reforms occurred in 451 BC when the Senate approved a new legal code, known as the Twelve Tables of Appius Claudius. This code is often cited as Rome's greatest contribution to Western civilization. It created a court system that required skill in argumentation, one that would welcome the Greek theories of forensic speaking. The courts, *judicia publica*, were divided by crime: one for treason, one for bribery, one for murder, and so forth. In 445 BC patricians were allowed to marry plebs and the number of tribunes was increased. Aediles, four Roman city officials, were elected by the patrician's Popular Assembly, but two of them had to be plebs.

Assemblies of various ranks became audiences for speakers over time. Very often the Rostra in front of the Senate House *(Curia)* was used as a platform for speakers. The front of the Rostra held the prow of a ship to symbolize Roman superiority over the Mediterranean Sea. These gatherings included the patricians' Popular Assembly developed from the 35 tribes of Rome; it could be called into session by the consuls or praetors (important magistrates in the city). In 300 BC the priesthood was opened to plebs, and in 287 BC the Tribunal or Plebeian Assembly was given law-making powers; this assembly was called into session by its tribunes. Centurial Assemblies were formed from the armed forces and converted to assemblies based on economic status. They were allowed to select magistrates, to initiate legislation, and to veto decrees of the Senate on specific matters.[4]

When the Greek cities pledged allegiance to Rome in 270 BC, it stood on the brink of dominating the Mediterranean. One obstacle remained—Carthage. The second and most important Punic War, in which the Carthaginians were led by the able general Hannibal, was the most costly. Hannibal descended from a noble line in Carthage and spent most of his life in what is now Spain. He expanded Carthage's hold on Spain, allowing it to become rich from the silver and gold mined there. In a bold gamble, Hannibal brought his army, replete with elephants, through Spain and over the Italian Alps, surprising the Romans. He occupied Roman territory for many years but never conquered the city of Rome itself. Retrenching in Campagna near what is now Naples, the Carthaginian army became dissolute and corrupt. Seizing this opportunity, the Roman general Scipio led an expedition into North Africa and onto the plain outside of Carthage itself, a city surrounded by seven forty-foot walls on its inland side and by the Mediterranean Sea on the other.[5] Hannibal was forced to return to Carthage to defend it. He made the mistake of meeting Scipio's forces in an open battle on the plain of Zama, where he was defeated in 202 BC. Rome stood alone astride the known world.

An epic agrarian reform movement that lasted from 145 to 78 BC threatened this stability. The importance of public address to the Romans during this crisis was demonstrated by the early success of Tiberius Gracchus, and later by his brother Caius. The mother of these brothers had made sure they were trained in rhetoric, most notably by the rhetor Diophanes of Mitylene, around 140 BC. In 134 BC Tiberius was elected one of the ten tribunes representing the plebs after he returned from success on the battlefield. He had saved 20,000 trapped soldiers by negotiating with the hostile Numantines. Taking a cue from Caius Laielius, he immediately proposed a major land redistribution scheme that pleased his followers: twenty acres each to the poor and an upper limit of 667 acres for anyone else. His rhetorical talent is evident in this passage from his speech in support of the proposal:

> The beasts of the field and the birds of the air have their holes and their hiding places; but the men who fight and die for Italy enjoy *only* the light and the air. Our generals urge their soldiers to fight for the graves and shrines of *their* ancestors. The appeal is idle and false. *You* cannot point to a paternal altar. *You* have no ancestral tomb. *You* fight and die to give wealth and luxury to others. *You* are called the masters of the world, but there is not a foot of ground that you can call your own.[6]

This speech opened the old wound of the poor fighting wars to protect the rich and revealed the importance of ancestry and mythology to the Romans. This heritage would grow in importance as public speakers used it to craft appeals to bolster their credibility. Tiberius used these themes to get the Tribunal Assembly to vote out the tribune who opposed his land reform, and then to pass the bill.

Tiberius was a gentle and composed speaker who gained credibility from his efforts on the battlefield. When he warned the citizens of Rome that the Senate was becoming hostile to his proposals, many were so moved that they camped outside of his house in tents to protect him. His success was short-lived, however. During a debate over a measure for Tiberius' impeachment, senators marched out of the *Curia*, where they had broken up chairs, and went to the Temple of Fides, where Tiberius and his followers were assembled. The senators surrounded him, pulled pieces of furniture from under their togas, and beat him to death as the awestruck crowd watched. His body was thrown into the Tiber River, which flows through Rome on its way to the sea.

Less than a decade later, Caius Gracchus, nine years the junior of his brother, assumed the mantle of leadership among the plebs when he was elected a tribune in 124 BC. Like his older brother, he believed in radical reform but thought it should start with the Senate instead of distribution of the land. When he called for the election of 300 new senators, a civil war ensued. The reform was carried out in 123 BC but the Gracchi forces were defeated in the war. Caius was captured but committed suicide before he could be killed by the Senate party. His head was cut off, filled with lead, and auctioned off for the price of gold; his body was dumped into the Tiber. His home was plundered, and 3,000 of his followers were killed.

Over the next few decades, the Senate slowly repealed some of the reforms he had implemented. By 104 BC, only 2,000 citizens owned land. Popular Senate leaders or victorious generals backed by the army became the new consuls. Marius, Julius Caesar's uncle, was elected consul seven times and named "First Man of Rome." His protégé, Sulla, took over in 88 BC after a brilliant military career. Sulla, like others who followed him to the throne, soon slipped into the role of dictator, stripping the tribunes of their power, though he did make access to the Senate easier through a quaestorship.[7]

After Sulla, a new group of speaker-orator-warriors emerged that included Pompey, Cato the Younger, and Caesar, who would restore the tribunes and their venue for deliberative oratory. Cicero wrote that Caesar had a "chaste style" and asked a friend in a letter, "Do you know any man who, even if he has concentrated on the art of oratory . . . can speak better than Caesar?"[8] Caesar was born in 100 BC and gained attention in his first case in 77 BC when he prosecuted Dolabella for extortion. Caesar was only twenty-three but already an accomplished orator. However, his military success would overshadow his rhetorical accomplishments. From his time on, potential Caesars were trained in both oratorical and military tactics. Suetonius tells us that Gaius Caligula, for example, paid a great deal of attention to oratorical training, as did Nero, though the latter preferred poetry to rhetoric.

Stoic and Epicurean Style

Major philosophical schools of the time produced their versions of rhetorical theory. In Athens, the Epicurean school was established by Epicurus, who wrote on rhetoric, though none of his texts have survived. He was born in 342 BC on the Greek island of Samos. According to accounts of his works, Epicurus believed the gods did not interfere with human life, having realized long before that peaceful and infinite bliss was the perfect state of existence. Epicurus suggested that one should establish avoidance of pain and the refinement of pleasure as the objectives in life. He also would have us rely on our own feelings and intuitions to find the truth, instead of on gods and religion. His school revived the theory of atoms, based on the work of Leucippus and his pupil Democritus, to explain why there was chaos in the universe. An infinite number of particles in an infinite number of shapes unpredictably combined, uncombined, collided, and recombined to produce all of the objects in the universe. Nothing exists that is not made of atoms; they are the seeds of things. Aside from them is only the void. Once people understood this theory, they would be free of the gods and free of superstition.

The work of Philodemus of Gadara (c. 110–35 BC), a leading Greek Epicurean, contained two books on persuasion written after he came to Rome to teach; the most important book was entitled *On Rhetoric.*[9] He believed that rhetoricians were incapable of developing arguments in substantive fields of study such as mathematics or chemistry. He did, however, recognize the usefulness of rhetoric to *prepare* orators for the invention of arguments by making them *aware of the rhetorical situation prior to the discovery of arguments* and then aiding orators in *adapting* those arguments to their audiences. He believed that rhetoric was analogous to medicine in that it could heal the body politic, but he believed it should not be substituted for philosophy that produced universal truths.[10]

The most prominent propagator of Epicureanism, however, was Lucretius, who lived from 99 to 55 BC. He applied Epicurean philosophy to real-life situations. It was for him a poetic way to the truth and therefore an enlightened life here on earth. His poem *On the Nature of Things (De rerum natura)* was written in Latin hexameters and in the tradition of the Greek pre-Socratic naturalists. That is to say, he examined the world, not some abstract alternate universe or ethereal God, to find the truth, which led him to reject the idealism of Plato and embrace the pleasures of the material world. He focused on beauty and learned to contemplate it properly. He revived Leucippus' and Democritus' theory that everything was composed of atoms and that their infinite ways of combining and detaching explained how objects came in and out of being. He speculated that human speech evolved from cries and gestures into sounds from the tongue that eventually formed words.

The Stoics were followers of Zeno, a pupil of the pre-Socratic Parmenides, who argued that God was an impersonal, pantheistic force. As we have seen, Parmenides was one of the first Greeks to espouse monotheism; his God was perfect and nothing else was worth human time or effort. According to Parmenides, humans possessed creative spirit by which they could reunite with God. Though mainly upper-class citizens, Stoics attempted to live with just enough means to keep their mind active and to keep the material world of pleasure and pain at bay. Their philosophy was eventually enhanced by Epictetus, a slave boy who became a tutor of Emperor Marcus Aurelius, whose own commentaries reflect Stoic teaching. Epictetus advised speakers to use appropriate words and realize that speech was a gift of God. He taught that desire was the root of all pain. Stoics believed in self-control and correct conduct.

The most influential Stoic in the first century AD was Lucius Annaeus Seneca, born in Hispania in 4 BC and soon after transported to Rome where he was educated. Eventually he became a lawyer and quaestor, a kind of high-ranking clerk. However, Emperor Claudius exiled him to Corsica, where he spent eight years from 41 to 49 AD before returning to Rome to become a close advisor to Nero.

Seneca believed that the soul was a god hiding in our bodies. He did not condemn wealth but held that it must come of its own accord and not become an obsession. The happy life is one that diminishes desire and excess. To ensure contact with this inner spirit, one should focus on this first cause. If one were in touch with one's spirit, one could generate the proper response to deal with any circumstance, and that response is based on a fundamental understanding of attitude.

A much smaller group than the Stoics and Epicureans were the Skeptics. They were the doubters of the day and could trace their lineage back to Diogenes, the philosopher who searched for one honest person. They doubted all presentations, which led them to be passive nonparticipants in the world of politics. An off-shoot of skepticism is cynicism, the belief that most acts are from bad motives or self-interest. The Cynics tended to be from the lower class, perhaps motivated by their poor conditions. The teachers who were Cynics tended to be itinerant and often vagrant.

Other philosophies produced variations on these themes and reignited the dispute between philosophers and rhetors over the role rhetoric should play in society. Dionysius of Halicarnassus, who taught after the assassination of Caesar, believed that imitating the great orators of Athens was the key to successful speaking. This paradigmatic approach characterizes many Roman theories of rhetoric. Like Philodemus, Dionysius reflected Isocrates' view that orators need ethical guidance.

Cicero

In this same period, Marcus Tullius Cicero (106–43 BC) emerged both as a leading politician and a rhetorical theorist. Born the eldest son of a wealthy landowner in Arpinum near Rome, he had an excellent education, which included military training in 90–89 BC and philosophical study with Greek rhetors. Cicero's impressive speaking abilities made him a leader among the plebs and equites. His first law case occurred in 81 BC. However, he believed he could have been less nervous and more forceful. He used Sulla's reign of terror as an excuse to travel to Rhodes to study rhetoric with Apollonius Molon and to Greece in 79 BC to study rhetoric and Stoicism. On his return, his successes in court continued, particularly the defense of Roscius, and in 75 BC got him elected quaestor, a kind of executive secretary who handled fiscal matters, province income, and the like.[11] Cicero soon married into wealth and was rich enough to qualify for the Senate, which took a "campaign fund" of a minimum of one million sesterces. His wife, Terentia, bore him two children, Tulia and Marcus. Senators were elected to replace those who died, resigned, or were found guilty of crimes. The polling took place in the Campus Mars between Capitoline Hill and the Tiber River, and Cicero took first place.

Cicero.

His reputation as a lawyer soared in 70 BC with his prosecution of Verres, the governor of Sicily. This corrupt official was defended by the redoubtable Hortensius, who was at the time a senator and the best lawyer in Rome. However, Cicero overwhelmed the jury with evidence of corruption. When Cicero finished his summation, Verres was so terrified he went into exile.[12] Cicero was then known as the greatest orator in Rome and was selected to be an Aedile (city official) in 69 BC. At one point, Caesar dedicated his book *On Analogy* to Cicero, whom he praised for discovering all of the treasures of oratory.

Nonetheless, Cicero sided with Caesar's rival Pompey. Cicero defended the military adventures of Pompey in a successful speech to the Plebeian Assembly, which endeared him to Pompey, a consul-to-be. Pompey had not only defeated Mithridades, king of Pontus, but added to Rome's holdings in the Middle East. On his way back to Rome, he mopped up the last of Spartacus' slave rebels, who had been defeated in an earlier battle with Crassus. With the support of Pompey, Cicero was elected praetor, one of only eight high judges in Rome.[13] His crowning achievement came in the summer of 64 BC when he was elected consul at age 42, the youngest elected to that date, to begin service in January of 63 BC. He received a majority in each of the Centuries (which made up the Century Assembly) casting votes. Reaching the highest rung on the ladder of power only encouraged Cicero to be bolder. When elections were to be held for his successor, he delivered a speech favoring Lucius Murena, who was opposed by Senator Lucius Catiline. When Murena won the consulship and Catiline lost, Cicero discovered that Catiline, who had killed a cousin of Cicero earlier, was planning a coup at the behest of Crassus. In his last months as consul, Cicero intercepted the messages of the conspirators to one another and to the Gauls to come join in the coup.

In a series of speeches of blame, dishonor, and accusation, Cicero accused Catiline of sexual abnormality, theft, adultery, and conspiracy.[14] Throughout, Cicero identified himself with "father Rome" and called on Jove to come forth and protect the nation. During Cicero's first attack, one by one the senators sitting near Catiline rose and moved to the other side of the room, until he was left sitting alone. Cicero allowed Catiline to leave the Senate because he wanted him defeated in battle rather than in a court of law, where bribes might be possible. That night Catiline fled to Etruria with his 20,000 troops. Cicero continued his attacks until the Senate agreed to destroy Catiline and his army, a task accomplished by Marc Antony's father. Using the advice of

Cicero denouncing Catiline, sitting by himself.

Cicero, Antony's father trapped Catiline near Pisa where he was hacked to death. Catiline's coconspirators in Rome were arrested and strangled. Cicero was then unanimously voted *Pater Patria*, father of the country. He moved into a mansion on Aventine Hill and continued to prosper as a lawyer and senator.

The First Triumvirate, a dictatorship that included Caesar, Pompey, and Crassus, was not supported by Cicero because he saw it as a threat to the republic. Cicero soon discovered that Caesar, as Pontifex Maximus (high priest), had allowed the patrician Clodius to become a pleb so he could run for tribune and advance Caesar's agenda. In the Senate, Cicero attacked the arrangement but lost the debate, which led to his exile in 58 BC. When he returned to the Italian peninsula in 57 BC, he was greeted by large crowds at Brundisium and cheered all the way to Rome. He wisely gave a speech in the Senate supporting the triumvirate. It fell apart when Crassus was executed in the Middle East after losing a battle to the Parthians in 53 BC. Cicero decided it would be best to leave Rome. As governor of Cilicia in 51–50 BC, he routed bandits from its Amanus Mountains.

Civil war between Caesar and Pompey broke out in 49 BC when Caesar defied the Senate and Pompey, and crossed the Rubicon River with the troops. The war ended when Caesar defeated Pompey in Thrace in 48 BC.[15] Pompey fled to Egypt with Caesar in pursuit; to befriend Caesar, the young Egyptian King Ptolemy had Pompey beheaded. Caesar, however, fell in love with Ptolemy's sister Cleopatra and removed her brother from the throne, fathered her son, and made her queen of Egypt.

In the years that followed, Cicero produced many books and speeches in which he showed his admiration for the Greek *paideia*.[16] Caesar favored Marc Antony, making him consul of Rome. In a carefully staged moment during the festival of Lupercalia, Antony offered a laurel crown to Caesar, who three times refused. None of this playacting fooled Cicero. He hated Antony and had nothing but disdain for Cleopatra, whom Caesar housed on the west of the Tiber in a mansion with a large garden.[17] When Caesar was assassinated in 44 BC,[18] Cicero supported the adopted heir to the crown, Octavian.[19] Cicero's last great speeches were called the *Philippicae* (after Demosthenes' *Philippics* warning about the tyrant Philip taking over Athens).[20] In fourteen speeches, many of which packed the Forum, Cicero attacked the ambitious Marc Antony, claiming the man was guilty of embezzlement, lechery, drunkenness, and unnatural sex. Cicero called for the restoration of the republic and the power of the Senate, but it was a lost cause. Octavian cut a deal with Marc Antony to form a triumvirate with Lepidus. Then Marc Antony and Octavian each composed a list of enemies. Cicero's name appeared on Antony's list and the triumvirate put a price on Cicero's head. Cicero, age sixty-three, tried to flee, but found it impossible. Eventually he was found on his litter waiting for execution. His head was severed from his body and fell into the sand. Back in Rome, his tongue was nailed to a pike to symbolize the silencing of this powerful orator. (Some claim his hands were nailed to the Rostra.)

Before we examine the rhetorical theory of this great practitioner of the art, we need to review the first major Roman text, the *Rhetorica ad Herennium*, which was published early in Cicero's lifetime. For many years, this work was mistakenly believed to be a product of his pen, which helps to explain its importance during the next 1,500 years.[21]

RHETORICA AD HERENNIUM

This first major Roman rhetoric text was named for Gaius Herennius and was written in about 90 BC, probably by an older contemporary of Cicero named Cornificius. While the Romans certainly practiced oratory and were privileged to Greek theories, their own studies evidently did not begin until 161 BC. Suetonius reports, on page one of his book *On Rhetoricians*, that censors had noted in 92 BC that "there be men who have introduced a new kind of training, and that our young men frequent their schools; that these men have assumed the title of Latin rhetoricians, and that young men spend whole days with them in idleness." Soon they would have a text. The *Rhetorica* converts the Greek notion of epideictic speaking into demonstrative *(demonstrativum)* speaking.[22] Speakers were to display the emotions, narratives, and ideas that they wanted their audiences to perceive or accept. Performing in the demonstrative genre would require a certain dynamism that energized the speech. This most often was achieved with vivid images that were a product of careful stylistic crafting.

The *Rhetorica* divides existing rhetorical theory into five canons: (1) invention *(inventio)*, including *ethos, pathos,* and *logos,* used to make the speech believable; (2) organization *(dispositio)*, used to arrange arguments and other elements of the speech; (3) style *(elocutio)*, used for the selection of words and construction of sentences appropriate for the speaker, audience, message, and occasion; (4) memory *(memoria)*, to hold ideas in the head; and (5) delivery *(pronuntiatio,* later *actio)*, the proper use of voice, gesture, and movement.

One of the most important contributions of the book was that it made concepts apparently unknown in Rome readily available, particularly *ethos, pathos,* and *logos.*[23] The *Rhetorica* uses imitation of models or paradigms to teach its lessons. Students were often forced to memorize a speech after translating it; later students might be required to paraphrase the speech in order develop their language skills. *Imitatio* became an important part of the Roman curriculum and was further developed by Cicero and Quintilian. The *Rhetorica* also makes a contribution with its development of memory through such strategies as parallel structure and mnemonic (from Mnemosyne, the Greek goddess of memory) devices. Organizing a speech in parallel fashion makes it easier to memorize. Many schoolchildren memorize their lessons using mnemonic devices. For example, the phrase, "My Very Elegant Mother Just Served Us Nine Pickles," can cue recall of the names of the planets. The first letter of each word is the first letter of one of the planets, and they are in the order of distance from the sun: Mercury, Venus, Earth, Mars, Jupiter, Saturn, Uranus, Neptune, Pluto (now considered a dwarf planet).[24] Thus, memory becomes "the treasure-house of ideas . . . the guardian of all parts of rhetoric."[25]

Aside from converting Greek theory into Latin, the most important contribution of the *Rhetorica* is its detailed study of organization. It begins by accepting the three kinds of speeches laid out by Aristotle, the demonstrative (epideictic), deliberative, and judicial (forensic), and then develops a sophisticated theory of organization. The *Rhetorica* develops arrangement into the following sections:

1. The *exordium* serves to make hearers attentive, receptive, and well-disposed.

2. The *narration* states the case, or tells the story.

3. The *division* states facts stipulated by both sides, enumerates points to be made, and offers a brief preview of what is to come.

4. The *confirmation* establishes the case and is the most important and developed part of most speeches. (It is examined in detail in the next section of this chapter because of its importance to rhetorical theory, particularly forensic speaking.)

5. The *refutation* points out flaws in opponents' arguments.

6. The *conclusion* sums up, amplifies, and makes a final appeal to emotions (peroration).

The Stasis System

In the section on the confirmation, the *Rhetorica* develops a *stasis* system for the invention of arguments and the organization of forensic speeches, whether they are given in the courts or on the floor of the Senate. Although the system was first developed, as far as we know, by Hermagoras of Temnos in 150 BC, either his text had been lost or it was not as influential as the *Rhetorica*. Here is an adapted and abbreviated translation of the system with illustrations.[26]

I. Questions of Conjecture: What happened and why?

    A. Did the alleged act occur? Evidence of violence, lost goods, testimony, and so forth, is used to establish the fact that a crime occurred. In many trials this issue is stipulated, that is, agreed to on both sides. A crime did occur. In the famous Scopes trial on teaching evolution, no one disputed that in his Tennessee classroom, Scopes taught evolutionary doctrine from Darwin. There were other issues that led to contentions, or major arguments of the case. However, whether a crime actually occurred can be the major bone of contention in a law case. In the impeachment trial of President Clinton before the House of Representatives, the president's team argued that no act was committed that fell under the high crimes and misdemeanors section of the Constitution pertaining to the executive branch. Republicans argued that the president's illicit affair and his misleading of a grand jury were high crimes and misdemeanors.

    B. Did the accused have a motive to commit the crime? Evidence in the case of motive often tends to be more subjective and in some cases based on impressions of character witnesses. Of course, this issue is more hotly debated in most trials. Scopes sought to strike down a Tennessee law and so had a motive to violate it.

    C. Did the accused have the character of one capable of committing the crime? In the O. J. Simpson criminal case, the defense tried to portray their man as a loving father, beloved athlete, and innocent dupe of the real murderer in an effort to show that Simpson did not have the character of a killer. The prosecution played tapes demonstrating he was a wife beater and, therefore, capable of being a killer. In post-trial comments, it was interesting to note that jurors did not buy the link between wife beating and murder. That is to say, they did not believe that wife beaters necessarily had a character capable of murder. Thus, the defense prevailed on this important issue in the criminal trial. However, in the civil trial that followed a year later, the tables were turned. As one juror said, "The bottom line as far as I was concerned . . . was the testimony regarding his beating his ex-wife. We had two witnesses who testified that they had seen it."[27]

II. Questions of Definition: Can the act be defined as a crime? In many trials, this can become a hotly debated issue. For example, many Americans believe that having an abortion is tantamount to murder, while many others do not believe it is a crime. The debate over this issue depends on when one believes life becomes viable. As another example, if a mother picks her child up from school but does not have custody of the child, is she guilty of the crime of kidnapping?

Treason, often defined as aiding and abetting the enemy, can be difficult to define. During the Civil War, Northern newspaper editors were thrown in jail for running editorials critical of President Lincoln's war policy. Were they really guilty of treason, or were they simply exercising their First Amendment rights?

During his trial on negligent manslaughter, Dr. Conrad Murray's lawyers argued that Murray's sympathy for Michael Jackson's pleas for sleeping medicine did not amount to a crime. Definition is a crucial issue in forensic proceedings.

III. Questions of Quality: What is the quality of the act that lies behind the crime?

A. Was the act justified and therefore not punishable? While admitting that the accused committed the act in question, those accused of certain actions may argue that what was done was justified. For example, a woman who suffers constant battering from her husband may decide to take action to prevent further attacks; if her action results in the death of her husband, she could make a claim of self-defense. In the spectacular Menendez brothers' trial in Los Angeles, Lyle and Eric Menendez claimed their lives were in danger, and they had no choice but to shoot their parents in self-defense.[28] Obviously, the prosecution must overcome these kinds of arguments if they are to gain a conviction.

This is roughly akin to the "lesser harm doctrine," in which defendants argue that they commit a crime to prevent a greater harm.

B. Were there mitigating circumstances that excuse the act even though it was wrong?

1. Is the accused a victim of temporary or permanent insanity? The defense admits that a killing took place, but because the accused could not tell the difference between right and wrong at the time of the crime, the accused seeks rehabilitation rather than incarceration. The accused was on drugs or drunk at the time of the crime and thus was not in a rational mental state. In a case of road rage, a woman driving an expensive car cut a man off on a busy Los Angeles street while he was on his way to a very important appointment. Catching up to the woman at the next light, the man leapt from the car and began telling the woman off. Her pet poodle Fifi began barking at the man incessantly. So he grabbed the poodle and tossed it into oncoming traffic, which resulted in the poodle's death. Onlookers held the man in custody until the police arrived. The man was accused of violating California's cruelty to animals statute, but the defense claimed his capacity to tell right from wrong had been diminished by his anger. He also may have suffered temporary insanity. The jury did not agree; he was sentenced to four years in jail.

2. Was the crime an accident rather than premeditated? A teenager playing with a gun shoots his best friend. A senior citizen loses control of her car while driving and kills a pedestrian in a farmers' market. If arguments that these deaths were the result of an accident are successful, the defense is usually able to have the charges reduced in some way, perhaps to involuntary manslaughter.

3. Is the accused a product of societal pressure or governmental neglect? Often parents, peers, recording artists, movies, the government, and/or the society as a whole are blamed for the crime or for shaping the accused into a criminal. In cases of drug crimes in large American cities, defendants often claim they are not responsible for their actions because they live in a culture that is fraught with fatherless families, that traps ethnic minorities in ghettoes, and that provides no means of income other than selling drugs or stealing. Therefore, children who are products of inner-city ghettoes should be measured by a different standard of justice than those who have had more opportunities.

C. Even though the act was wrong, did events justify it? Perhaps there is no better example of this argument than the speech in Shakespeare's *Julius Caesar* in which Brutus justifies the assassination of the title character. Brutus was one of several conspirators who stabbed Caesar as he arrived for a session of the Roman Senate. Brutus was then chosen to explain the act to the Roman mob. He claimed that because he loved his country more than he loved Caesar, he had to slay him. Caesar had become ambitious and tyrannical, thereby threatening the foundations of the republic. Preserving the republic, a clear benefit, provoked the necessary evil of assassination.

In our own country, civil rights demonstrators often defied existing laws prohibiting minorities from sitting in the front of buses or at lunch counters. Although they were guilty of violating the laws at that time, the benefits they provided to society justified their actions.

D. Was the criminal act justified because the person attacked deserved to be punished? In this argument, which is similar to the one above, the accused takes the law into his or her own hands, not for some benefit to society or others, but because the victim deserved to be punished. In California, a woman walked into court with a concealed gun, and killed a man who was on trial for sexually molesting her son. She declared no remorse for killing the man who committed so heinous a crime. The crime against her son was used as an extenuating circumstance when she was brought to trial for premeditated murder.

E. Does the accused deserve leniency? If all else fails, the accused can argue that the punishment for the crime should be reduced or suspended. The plea for leniency can be based on a previous good record if the crime is a first offense. It can be based on the fact that the accused was unfamiliar with the law, though the courts have generally held that ignorance of the law is no excuse. It is the duty of a citizen to learn the law.

IV. Questions of Jurisdiction: Does this court have jurisdiction over the alleged crime? A whole other series of arguments can be built around the question of proper jurisdiction. When Serge Prokofiev was put on trial by Soviet Premier

Joseph Stalin for creating music that violated the Communists' standards of taste, he turned his chair to the wall and refused to recognize the court. A political court was not the proper place for the consideration of artistic merit. After the Civil War, the Supreme Court reversed the wartime conviction of a civilian because he had been tried in a military court in violation of the rules of habeas corpus. The accused in many cases seeks a change of venue to avoid the selection of a prejudicial jury in the locale where the crime was committed.

V. Questions of Procedure: Has the case been brought in a proper manner? The relevance of this issue to American jurisprudence was significantly heightened in 1961 when in *Mapp v. Ohio* the Supreme Court of Chief Justice Earl Warren ruled that the states had to adhere to the federal rules of procedure in criminal cases. Because local enforcement officers in Ohio had conducted a search that violated those rules, the evidence they obtained had to be thrown out and the conviction they had gained was overturned. *Mapp* was followed by a series of rulings in which the stricter federal rules of procedure for police and agents were imposed on the states. *Miranda* forced local officials to read arrestees their rights. *Gideon* required the states to provide a public defender for the indigent. *Pointer* made sure those charged with a crime had a right to confront witnesses. There are now multiple safeguards to protect the rights of the accused providing defense lawyers with the opportunity to find procedural errors on which to base an appeal.

The stasis system establishes a catalogue of the questions any speaker needs to ask to create a speech of defense or prosecution. It demonstrates that the burden of proof in criminal cases is enormous, and that the range of arguments available to each side is extensive.

Finally, the *Rhetorica* codifies styles along a continuum that moves from the grand to the plain. Each has its function and any speech may contain more than one style. The *grand* is used to move the audience and is therefore more sublime, copious, dignified, and ornate than the others. The *middle* is used to please the audience, and is therefore sweet, with a little vigor. The *plain* is used to prove and therefore is often rhythmless, free, and without much oratorical furniture. To fill in this continuum, the *Rhetorica* explores various tropes (turnings of words and phrases from proper meanings) and figures (arranging words to hold attention) (which we will examine in greater detail later in this chapter).[29] They are used to define the character of style that makes a speech distinctive yet appropriate to the occasion.

The *Rhetorica ad Herennium* is an important document historically because it shows that the Romans were adept at developing rhetorical theory. It is also important because of the contributions it makes to the sophistication of rhetorical theory, particularly with regard to organization, memory, and the three types of style. The *Rhetorica* was a dominant textbook in Europe for the next 1,500 years, serving as a primer for students who then moved on to the more sophisticated work of Cicero and Quintilian.

CICERO AND QUINTILIAN

Cicero, and later Marcus Fabius Quintilian (AD 35–95), enhanced the Roman codification of Greek theory by developing the relationship between the art of persuasion and effective service to the nation—civic virtue. In his *De republica*, Cicero adapted Greek notions of forensic speaking to the Roman environment, making the case that rhetoric allowed justice to succeed. One of his first improvements was to create a stronger linkage between style and invention. He saw that the choice of words and sentence structures brought clarity to ideas: "Every speech consists of matter and words, and the words cannot fall into place if you remove the matter, nor can the matter have clarity if you withdraw the words."[30] For Cicero and later Quintilian, the study of rhetoric developed latent talent, and talent built character.[31] Character was a crucial ingredient of virtue; and virtue led to heroic acts for the state.

Cicero on Forensic Speaking

Cicero was particularly taken with Aristotle's claim that a good argument was the product of invention and judgment, a position that would be reflected in Cicero's own books. Cicero wrote the *Topica* to help lawyers generate arguments. Aristotle, as we saw in chapter 4, set out twenty-eight *topoi* or lines of arguments, and nine sham enthymemes to unveil fallacies. Cicero was more concise when he wrote:

> Every rule necessary for the finding of arguments is now concluded; so that when you have proceeded from definition, from division, from the name, from conjugates, from genus, from species, from similarity, from difference, from contraries, from adjuncts, from consequents, from antecedents, from things incompatible with one another, from causes, from effects, from a comparison of things greater or less or equal—there is no topic of argument whatever remaining to be discovered.[32]

Thus, Cicero reduced Aristotle's twenty-eight *topoi* to sixteen categories on a checklist for creating arguments for a speech. He also believed that lawyers needed to manage testimony carefully and to expand the standard external inartistic proofs to include laws, contracts, witnesses, tortures, oaths, prophecies, divinations, and oracles, proofs peculiar to Roman culture.

Like other Romans, Cicero also listed various fallacies of which lawyers and others needed to be aware. Some examples include:

1. *Ambiguity* occurs when, during the course of an argument, one word is used in two different senses. "Because he was a just man, he was just a man." In this case, the term "just" is used in two senses ("just" meaning "fair," and "just" meaning "merely"), so the argument is fallacious.

2. *Ad antiquitam* is the fallacy of claiming something is true or good simply because it is old. "Social Security has been with us since 1935 and therefore has proven its worth."

3. *Ad baculum* is the fallacy, often used by children and parents, which contains a threat to win the argument. "If you don't let me go out tonight, I'll just die." "If you don't do the dishes, you'll be grounded."

4. *Ad crumenam* claims that those with money are more likely to be correct than those who are poor. "She's a rich woman; she must know what she is talking about."

5. *Ad hominem* is an attack on the person in order to undercut the truth of his or her statements. "Would you take the word of a drunk on this matter?" It ignores the fact that bad people can make true statements.

6. *Ad ignorantiam* is an appeal to ignorance that is far more common than most people think. "My claim is true because you have failed to prove that it is false." "I am innocent because no one has proven me guilty." "You're guilty because no one has proven you innocent." "There is no evidence indicating that anyone helped James Earl Ray shoot Martin Luther King Jr. Therefore, he must have acted alone."

7. *Ad misericordiam* substitutes an appeal for pity for a legitimate argument. "This poor, sick woman could not be guilty of a crime."

8. *Ad nauseum* uses repetition to assert the truth in the belief that if something is said enough times people will believe that it is true. Hitler used the strategy often in propagating his "big lies" about race and history. In the 2012 presidential election, Barack Obama's citizenship was questioned over and over despite the fact that he presented evidence of being born in Hawaii.

9. *Ad numeram* asserts that something is true simply because many people believe it is true. "Seventy thousand Frenchmen can't be wrong." "A majority of voters oppose affirmative action; therefore, it must be wrong."

10. *Petitio principii* is begging the question. Here the conclusion of an argument is already assumed in its premises. This fallacy is also known as circular reasoning. The simplest form of this fallacy is the tautology: "Harry is right, because Harry is right." "Is this terrific or is this terrific?" The more complicated route involves several iterations: "Plato is right because he relies on his pupil Aristotle, who is right. Aristotle is right because he relies on Socrates, who is always right. And Socrates is right because he learned so much from his pupil Plato."

11. *Composition* assumes that the whole has the same property as its parts. "Thus, since every state in the United States has a governor, the United States must have a governor." "Since every person in this army is strong, the army must be strong." In this second example, you can see that composition is often combined with ambiguity; strong is used in two different senses.

12. *Division* assumes that each of the parts contains the qualities of the whole. "Because the army is strong, every person in the army is strong." Again, this fallacy is often linked to ambiguity.

13. *Post hoc, ergo propter hoc*, false cause, is the fallacy of assuming that because one event follows another, the first event causes the second or the second results from it. "Every time my cat lies down, my mother calls."

14. *Plurium interrogationum* is the trick of demanding a simple answer to a complex question. "Have you stopped using racial epithets? Yes or no." Either way you answer this question leaves the impression that you are or were a racist.

15. *Straw man* attacks a fabricated or weak argument of an opponent and then declares victory without attacking stronger arguments that are on the opposing side. "We went to war in Iraq to maintain low prices for oil. But oil prices are high. Therefore, the war was a failure." Not everyone would agree that the United States went to war solely to maintain low prices on oil. The removal of Hussein and the establishment of a republic are arguments in favor of the war.

16. *Guilt by association* implies that an argument is bad because bad people support it. When the California initiative on affirmative action (proposition 209) was endorsed by David Duke, the former Klansman from Louisiana, the opposition to the initiative argued that voting for it made you a racist. If David Duke likes chocolate ice cream, does eating chocolate ice cream make you a racist?

17. *Tu quoque* literally means "thou also" but refers to the fallacy of two wrongs making a right. Richard Nixon was fond of arguing that dirty tricks of other administrations were far worse than the crimes he was accused of committing. The commission of even worse crimes does not alter or excuse the original crime.

Cicero and the other notable Romans understood these fallacies and often seized on them when speakers used them in the Senate or from the Rostra. Like the stasis system, they were part of an orator's arsenal of strategies. Cicero's speeches against Catiline were legendary, as was his understanding of the stasis system used to construct his case. Like other Romans, Cicero relied on the system to develop his own stock questions for the invention of arguments. Cicero's *De inventione* summarized the stasis system this way:

> Every subject which contains in itself a controversy to be resolved by speech and debate involves a question about a fact, or about a definition, or about the nature of an act, or about the legal processes. . . . When the dispute is about a fact, the issue is said to be conjectural, because the plea is supported by conjectures or inferences. When the issue is about a definition, it is called the definitional issue, because the force of the term must be defined in words. When, however, the nature of the act is examined, the issue is said to be qualitative, because the controversy concerns the value of the act and its class or quality. But when the case depends on the circumstances that the right person does not bring the suit, or that he brings it against the wrong person, or before the wrong tribunal, or at a wrong time . . . the issue is called translative because the action seems to require a transfer to another court or alteration in the form of pleading. There will always be one of these issues applicable to every kind of case; for where none applies, there can be no controversy.[33]

Cicero's *stasis* system provides a way to invent lines of argument for the speech that concerns guilt or innocence, whether it be a summation to a jury or a sermon to a wayward congregation. His system is so similar to that developed in the *Rhetorica ad Herennium* that there is no need to review it here; it is one of the many reasons he was thought to be the author of that work. If you have the courage to march through his *De inventione*, you will find a long series of subquestions under each of these major considerations.[34] It reflects the Roman penchant for categorization and codification, a tendency that resulted in a rich system of paradigmatic invention. It is also the product of the fact that senators were appointed for life; so one way to remove them from office was to accuse them of a crime. Cicero, like most other prominent senators, had to defend himself before the Senate on many occasions; hence his preoccupation with legal rhetoric.

After his exploration of *stasis*, Cicero demonstrated that he was adept at developing arguments around such specialized forms as the dilemma.[35] He used these specialized forms to give structure to loose, weak, or otherwise undistinguished arguments. Because of his experience in the courtroom, he knew that matters of law are contingent, that is, based on probability. Thus, form, style, and substance had to be blended to create a reality that the jury would accept.

The Good Speaker and Public Virtue

Public address was not limited to jurisprudence. In *De oratore*, a dialogue in the style of Plato set in 91 BC is carried on among Lucius Licinius Crassus,[36] a noted lawyer and politician; Antonius, who was consul at the time; and several students, who also act as attendants.[37] Crassus' father-in-law Scaevola joins the group in Book I and then leaves with the entrance of Catulus and Strabo, who create the foils for the dialogue in Book II. Throughout, Crassus expresses his love for style in speeches while Antonius prefers argumentation.

Through this dialogue, Cicero claimed that "[i]n every free nation, and most of all in communities which have attained the enjoyment of peace and tranquility, [the art of rhetoric] has always flourished above the rest and remained ever supreme."[38] Rhetoric's functions—to teach, to please, and to move—became the *officia oratoris* of Cicero.[39] Satisfying an audience was important when speaking in the Roman Forum, whether the orator was addressing epideictic, forensic, or deliberative issues.[40] The Forum, and particularly at its Rostra, was a raucous place where civic leaders, particularly senators, would shout approval and disapproval of the colorful orators. Speakers were known to hire professional applauders and to invite their friends to cheer speeches and shout down opponents. As the lower classes gained political clout, rhetors had to adjust to the new members of the audience. Crassus was one of the first to turn his attention from the patricians to the general audience in the Forum. Large crowds filled it to hear popular orators, and political leaders became more adept at audience adaptation.

Although this situation required an increasing use of *pathos* and stylistic devices, the creation of a public image that pleased and impressed the crowds was most important. Cicero saw this clearly when he wrote in *De oratore*, "Men take a decision oftener through feeling than through fact or law. . . . They are moved by evidences of character in the speaker and in his client. . . . Orators must have a scent for an audience, for what people are feeling, thinking, waiting for, wishing."[41] More than that, "genuine orators" were hard to find because the art required that a speaker had "investigated and heard and read and discussed and handled and debated the whole of the contents of the life of mankind."[42]

Quintilian built on this theme by making clear that since the time of Cato the Elder, orator-leaders had advised speakers to become "a good man, skilled in speaking" *(vir bonus dicendi peritus)*.[43] The Romans enhanced this concept by wedding Aristotle's notion of character based on making good decisions with Isocrates' call for an understanding of civic virtue. For example, in *De oratore* Cicero claimed that "the wise control of the complete orator is that which chiefly upholds not only his own dignity, but the safety of countless individuals and the entire state."[44] Such factors would elicit admiration from the public.

Cicero added several important terms to the mix. *Auctoritas* developed the moral authority of the speaker in the speech.[45] What we refer to as magnitude or integrity, Cicero called *gravitas*, or substance. Possessing this quality would require a history of doing good deeds, giving good advice, or making good decisions, as it did in Athenian society. The Romans expanded the concept to include one's relatives and associations.[46] These intricate patterns of family relations affected how one was perceived. In this regard, for example, Cicero's career was held back because his family was only of the *equite* class, as opposed to the upper class represented by the Caesars and Sullas. Cicero's friendship with Pompey and his rhetorical abilities helped him overcome the disadvantages of his background, allowing him to advance.

Cicero solidified this notion of *gravitas* by adding a person's family history as represented in the monuments of a special place or time.[47] Like the Greeks, the Romans produced a large group of patriots and a rich body of legend in their quest for nationhood, as we have seen. They valorized these legends and their actual history in countless monuments, coins, sacred places, and numerous allusions and narratives in literature.[48] Cicero recommended incorporating this national lore into a speech if it would enhance the case being made. For example, when accepting the nomination of his party in 2012, President Obama appealed to "a nation that triumphed over fascism and depression; a nation where the most innovative businesses turned out the world's best products, and everyone shared in the pride and success."

Finally, Cicero retrieved Aristotle's notion of judgment as the ultimate quality of the good man *(vir bonus)*. Aristotle believed the prudent ruler was levelheaded, would take into account all possibilities, and would act on them in a practical way that balanced courage with sensible compromise. Cicero advanced this concept, arguing that leaders need to be receptive to multiple explanations of causes of events and to demonstrate moderation and self-control.[49] Cicero decried the separation of philosophy from rhetoric:

> Socrates, himself a master rhetorician, separated philosophy and rhetoric, and, as an unfortunate consequence, we must now learn to think with the guidance of the philosophers and to speak with the rhetoricians. . . . Those who declaim against rhetoric do not realize that eloquence, properly understood, encompasses nearly all knowledge, especially knowledge of human behavior.[50]

He wrote further that "if we bestow fluency of speech on persons devoid of . . . virtues, we shall not have made orators of them but shall have put weapons into the hands of madmen."[51] Since the goal of education was to produce men who could perform practical affairs, oratory was essential to education, as that education was essential to sound oratorical practice.[52] Only in this way can one achieve supreme wisdom *(summaque prudentia)*,[53] which alone could lead to the blending of change *within the context of historical advancement*.[54] To hammer home this point, Cicero contrasted judgment with rashness *(temeritas)*, a term that implies a lack of forethought or impulsive action.[55] Thus, the prudent orator "can by his eloquence either arouse or calm, within the souls of men, whatever passion the circumstances and occasion may demand."[56] This *oratio* was the true art of eloquence, which extended the notion of propriety to questions of ethical conduct, thereby specifically linking it to character: one's credibility is the sum of one's conduct.[57] This linkage holds particular relevance for rhetoric as an art form. Language choice is volitional and creative; the choice of words reveals a sense of self. As the French scientific writer Georges Louis Buffon (1707–1788) would claim, "Style is the man himself."[58]

Cicero's early success as a lawyer led to his later career in the Senate. He believed the development of a *vir bonus* persona accounted for his effectiveness. A study of

The Roman Forum.

Cicero's letters demonstrates how pervasive this notion was for him.[59] Through them he explained how political opportunities emerged under a republican government; in the process, he confessed his belief that letters are the way by which a man establishes his public character.[60] Although he did not admire the Greek Sophists, Cicero, like them, was certainly an advocate of the active life *(vita activa)* over the contemplative, but letters provided a way by which his rhetoric could assert calm judgments into the hectic Roman world.

In 48 BC, Cicero developed eight rhetorical-political propositions regarding the obligations of the citizen-leader in times of turmoil. These were to help answer such sticky questions as, should a citizen stay in a country when it is taken over by a tyrant? The question was generated by the civil war between Caesar and Pompey. Like Protagoras, Cicero found solid arguments on both sides of the propositions he explored. They indicate that he understood the contingent nature of life in the polis long before his execution was ordered by Marc Antony. The consideration of these propositions also asserts various values.

Values are deeply held beliefs that influence our worldviews and behaviors. Values are rhetorical because they persuade individuals to protect the society to which they belong and often to attack societies with different values. The same values that help a society survive also make it more or less warlike.[61] When two societies have different values, they may be driven to war by the rhetoric they generate. Quintilian believed that the Peloponnesian War between Athens and Sparta fit this model. Unless a society is willing to tolerate a debate over its values, it will be forced into conflict with other societies that have different values.

The relationship between rhetoric and values is multiple. Rhetoric helps shape values both in the individual and in society through mythmaking and public discourse. Daniel Webster, for example, greatly enhanced the value of national unity with his reply to Senator Hayne in 1830. Abraham Lincoln provided a renaissance for the values of the Declaration of Independence with his Gettysburg Address. Rhetoric, in turn, uses the values of a society to advance other goals—sometimes for good, sometimes for evil. During the war in Vietnam, Lyndon Johnson and Richard Nixon argued that freedom of expression of dissenters should be curtailed because they were giving comfort to the nation's enemies in North Vietnam. Jesse Jackson argued that to enhance educational opportunities for minorities, we must propagate affirmative action programs at the expense of white majorities. President George H. W. Bush argued that to preserve freedom, we had to go to war in the Gulf region. Finally, rhetoric can open values to reexamination. For example, should national security be a higher value than individual freedom (an issue brought to the forefront of many minds after the incidents of 9-11-2001)? What limits should be placed on the use of force in foreign policy? Are preemptive strikes justified against sovereign nations? What are the moral and legal implications of using drones to fight terrorists?

Cicero on Delivery and Humor

These momentous issues did not keep Cicero from commenting on other canons of rhetoric. For example, he had a strongly held opinion about the delivery of a speech. He linked it to the emotion that the speaker wished to convey: "For nature has assigned to every emotion a particular look and tone of voice and bearing of its own;

and the whole of a person's frame and every look on his face and utterance of his voice are like the strings of a harp, and sound accordingly as they are struck by each successive emotion."[62] He went on to associate anger with shrill, hasty, and abrupt clauses; sorrow with wavering, halting, and mournful speech; fear with despondent, low, and hesitating phrases; joy with a gushing, smooth, and gay style. Each of these also needed to be accompanied by the proper gesture to emphasize what was being conveyed. He concluded, "But for effectiveness and distinction in delivery the greatest share undoubtedly belongs to the voice."[63]

Cicero's advice on humor seems as fresh today as it must have during his lifetime. Book II of *De oratore* begins the discussion of humor in chapter 58. Cicero carefully divided his topic into five subheadings: humor's nature, its sources, whether it is appropriate to the speaker, the limits of the license the speaker can take, and a classification of things that are funny. Cicero claimed that the nature of humor is unrestrained, by which he meant an audience *cannot help but laugh* if the words are strung together in the right way. He claimed that the sources of humor included obnoxious or ill-mannered behavior and that which is ugly. The matter of appropriateness goes to the heart of what a speaker should joke about in a given venue. For example, on the last night of the Republican Convention of 2012, actor Clint Eastwood came to the podium with a chair and pretended that President Obama was sitting in it. He then put words in the president's mouth that implied profanity. Many in the viewing public thought this was distasteful.

The limits of humor include making fun of those who are weak, destitute, or infirm. One should not joke about serious criminal activity because it reflects badly on the speaker's values. Mocking the helpless can make the speaker seem cruel or arrogant. Those things subject to ridicule include flaws in those who are not respected or those who are perceived to be unethical or guilty of crimes for which they have not been punished. Thus, when President Obama violated the War Powers Act during America's attack on Libya in 2011 by not seeking congressional approval for his actions in a timely manner, he was fair game for comedians on that issue.

Humor can also be generated by looking at current events and other facts. Jay Leno of *Tonight Show* fame is the master of using the day's newspaper stories to make jokes about contemporary matters. Humor can be generated by puns and plays on names. For example, Gilda Radner created a character on *Saturday Night Live* named Emily Latella. Ms. Latella got things mixed in her citizen-response editorials on "Weekend Update." One night she began her editorial by complaining, "What is all this talk about violins on television," obviously playing on the word "violence."

Taking words literally ("I am shocked." "Well, then, pull out the plug."), using humorous quotations ("Rumors of my death are greatly exaggerated."), and sarcasm were all part of Cicero's arsenal of humor. He also recommended the use of apt epithets to disparage an opponent. An English parliamentarian once said of his opponent, "He is like a mackerel laying on the beach in moonlight: he shines while he stinks." Cicero also included mimicry in his bag of tricks. When all the pundits had predicted that President Truman would lose the 1948 election, he got even at a celebratory banquet by imitating the news broadcaster H. V. Kaltenbourn predicting Truman's defeat.

Caricature of an opponent can also prove effective. Senator Daniel Webster once attacked President Polk by saying that his mind was like a drop of water on a hot skillet; it skittled all over the place. Speakers can achieve the same effect with understate-ment, a kind of irony. "John Kennedy was a fine president except for the little snit he got in with the Russians over nuclear weapons in Cuba." Since the "little snit" almost led to nuclear war, the remark is a massive understatement and therefore humorous. Cicero also recommended surprise, indecency, and making faces, which could be used in a humorous manner if the speaker were judicious. Cicero was the complete theorist and he was the best example of his own theory. Few Romans were better or more accomplished speakers than Cicero himself.

Quintilian and the Teaching of Rhetoric

Quintilian stressed the importance of the teacher in educating citizen-orators about values.[64] He was born in Calagurris (Calahorra), Spain, of Roman parents and had first come to Rome as a young apprentice to the lawyer Domitius Afer. Quintilian could be confident of his teaching ability; he had taught with such success when he returned to Spain that the regional governor Galba took him to Rome when Galba became emperor following the suicide of Nero in AD 68. However, these were turbulent times: the Brits and the Jews revolted, and civil war embroiled Rome. Galba fell from power and things did not settle down until General Vespasian was recalled from Judea, where he was putting down the Jewish revolt, and was made emperor. He began the Flavian dynasty. Vespasian and his son Titus, who succeeded him to the throne, patronized Quintilian's school, giving him a special chair in rhetoric. Quintilian came out of the classroom at one point to defend Titus' queen, Bernice, a Jew he had fallen for in Jerusalem. When Titus' brother, the cruel and anti-Christian Domitian became emperor, Quintilian was pulled from retirement to teach the emperor's grandnephews. Domitian was poisoned in AD 96, and Quintilian may have died in the same year.

One gets a sense of how good a teacher Quintilian was by reading how ideas excited him. For example, when explaining the organization of the speech, he writes:

> The gift of arrangement is to oratory what generalship is to war. The skilled com-mander will know how to distribute his forces for battle, what troops he should keep back to garrison forts and guard cities, to secure supplies, or to guard commu-nications, and what disposition to make by land and sea. But to possess this gift, our orator will require all the resources of nature, learning, and industrious study.

Quintilian was awarded imperial subsidies for his school, where he trained Pliny the Younger (who became an orator, quaestor, tribune, praetor, and finally consul in AD 100, a few years after Quintilian is believed to have died), among others. Buoyed by his influence in imperial circles, Quintilian argued that even philosophy was sub-sumed under the discipline of rhetoric because orators, while they "cannot have knowledge of all causes" are "able to speak on all."[65] Philosophers have merely "usurped" what orators have abandoned.[66]

By the time of his death, Quintilian had devised a rigorous course of study in his *Institutes*, which he began writing in AD 88. His curriculum, which influenced such major thinkers as Erasmus, Juan Luis Vives, Martin Luther, and Lorenzo Valla, began with imitation of great speakers, and we have some of the exercises, speeches, and debates that students were to memorize. Quintilian immersed his students in the grand style of great speakers. These exercises developed his students' vocabulary, their pronunciation, and their sense of rhythm.[67] Students were then required to paraphrase what they had memorized or to develop new arguments on the same theme. The next phase of their education included the composition of five different kinds of narrative: praise of a famous man; denunciation of a wicked man; comparison of two characters; a declamation on commonplace virtues, vices, and offenses; and a comparison of value propositions, such as city life is better than country life. Eventually his lectures would be written into *Institutio oratoria (Institutes of Oratory)*, which in twelve books provides an extensive compendium of Roman theory. The book was particularly popular because by the time of Quintilian's death, students had stopped learning by following mentors into government and were instead assembled in classrooms. The more dictatorial and exclusive the imperial system became, the less room there was for hands-on experience.

The first book outlines the task of teaching rhetoric; the second deals with "rudiments of schools of rhetoric and with problems concerned with" the definition of rhetoric as a discipline. The next five books deal with invention and organization of speeches and reflect the theory of

Quintilian.

Cicero and the *Rhetorica ad Herennium.* The next covers style, memory, and delivery. Style must not be independent of subject matter, nor must it become so caught up with display that it becomes grotesque. Instead a healthy style is built on a vocabulary improved by reading and dignity. He extended the notion of *decorum* with his concept of *visio* derived from what the Greeks called *phantasia*, the ability to bring to the mind's eye *(oculis mentum)* those objects that stimulate the emotions.[68] Words should be carefully crafted to help the listener visualize the causes of the emotion that the speaker wishes to call up.

Quintilian claimed that memory is a gift of nature that is improved with practice, and it is quite useful, not only for making one's speeches appear spontaneous, but for remembering the arguments of one's opponents. He recommended composing a speech in such a way that each part is associated with a part of one's home. Thus, remembering a speech is as easy as walking through a house. "Some place is chosen of the largest possible extent, and characterized by the utmost possible variety, such as a spacious house divided into a number of rooms. Everything of note therein is carefully committed to the memory, in order that the thought may be enabled to run through all the details without hindrance."[69] In this section, Quintilian also recounts the tale of Simonides who in 477 BC remembered all of the guests at a tragic banquet. The house in which they were eating collapsed, killing all inside; luckily Simonides had associated each member of the banquet with his place and could identify all of the bodies. After Simonides, many poets and rhetors began to use locations as a way of remembering arguments and story lines. The speaker might mentally walk through his or her house while delivering a speech, having associated each point in the speech with a different place in the house; for example, the introduction might be on the front door, the narrative might be in the hallway, and so forth. Thus, *loci* became part of the rhetorical and poetic lexicon.[70]

While his treatment of delivery is traditional, Quintilian does spend some time advising on how to use one's eyes and hands to emphasize points. The final book discussed the character of the orator. Just as Isocrates had turned on his fellow Sophists to protest their lack of virtue, so too, Quintilian criticized his fellow orators and teachers for failing to inculcate their students with proper values. He also called for an end to showy style and a return to the direct masculine style of the republic. To this end, he recommended that words be carefully selected and that sentences and arguments be properly put together.

The prominence of Greek teachers, the great conveyors in the Roman Empire of liberal education that included public speaking, attests to the effectiveness of this system.[71] Through the end of the Roman Republic in 31 BC, and later during the Second Sophistic (a time of great display in ceremonial speeches), rhetoric retained its high place in the curriculum. Centuries later, even Jerome[72] in his *Expositio evangelica*, a book on writing sermons, endorsed the use of style to make the scriptures more appealing.[73]

ROMAN THEORY OF STYLE

While the expansion of Greek notions of character, public virtue, and education were important in Roman rhetorical theory, the most impressive Roman contribution may well have been the advances made with regard to style. The need for proper words to impress an audience inspired Quintilian's belief that rhetoric is a teachable art that helps the "good man" speak well,[74] and/or leads society to its destiny.[75] Rhetoric has the ability to fashion a speech into a "distinctive style" that not only enhances the message but also enriches the reputation of the orator. To this end, Quintilian taught his students to be lucid, to avoid far-fetched or unusual words, and to enhance the plausibility of their narratives, especially in legal cases.

Cicero considered style the most difficult subject to master.[76] In *De oratore*, the speaker's ability to choose words properly is linked to how audiences perceive character.[77] This was a major advance on Aristotle's theory. In reaction to the Sophists, he had severed style from invention.[78] Cicero reopened the passageways between style and *ethos*. He showed that amplification can "win credence in the course of speaking by arousing emotion."[79] He and Quintilian advised that "vivid description" lends believability to a story, brings the causes of emotion closer, and enhances a legal case or an argument.[80] The artistic arrangement of words is not an afterthought; it alters the meaning of the message and causes speakers to rework their entire thesis. In short, style has more inventive powers than Aristotle had acknowledged.

Quintilian took Aristotle's instruction on emotion a step further by arguing that judges and other audiences for speakers need to be engaged emotionally to make the proper decisions. While reason can lay out a case, emotion is required to achieve commitment to a cause and mete out a proper sentence in court: "For it is in its power over the emotions that the life and soul of oratory is to be found."[81] This emotional engagement can be achieved by lively, realistic images, the creation of which are the province of style. That is why Quintilian is as thorough on the subject of *decorum* as Cicero.

Cicero, and after him Quintilian and Longinus (see below), demonstrated how fruitful the joining of *inventio* (the finding of arguments) and *elocutio* (putting them into proper language) can be. They vastly expanded the less detailed notions of "appropriateness" and "fitness of function" developed by the Greek Sophists,[82] because they understood the infinite variety of choices humans have of words and sentence structures. The lesson is an important one for our own time. Psycholinguists estimate that it would take one person to the tenth power centuries to utter all the twenty-word sentences one could construct in the English language. The Roman manner of managing the myriad choices in their language provides a useful model for our own.

Decorum

The Roman rhetorical system centered on the term *decorum*, which meant propriety in terms of meeting and creating expectations. Cicero's notion of *decorum* sent the speaker to find figures of thought and figures of speech, including tropes, which would fashion the rhetorical situation.[83] He explored 97 figures to be used for embellishment. They are the building blocks for Cicero's definition of *decorum*. He called them the flowers of language and the gems of thought.[84] Over a century later, Quintilian defined a trope as "the artistic alteration of a word or phrase from its proper meaning to another."[85] The most common tropes are metaphor and simile. He defined a figure as a way of "amplifying force and charm to the matter" of a speech.[86] Figures or "schemes" are usually reorderings of words to achieve a certain effect; they include alliteration, repetition, and polysyndeton (see below).

How does one build *decorum* through figures? The answer resides in an understanding of *ornatus*, or *ornamenta verborum*, meaning beautiful order to achieve distinction. Internal *ornatus* emerges from the body of the speech; external *ornatus* clothes that body and transforms it into something more appealing. *Ornatus'* meaning evolved during the Roman epoch. In the republican period, while the Senate held sway over Rome, the term generally referred to functional adornment, the material of fashioning a speech to *create and meet expectations*.[87] "It is necessary to choose the style of oratory best calculated to hold the attention of the audience, and not merely to give them pleasure but also to do so without giving them too much of it."[88] When adornment is proper, it is inseparable from the thought it expresses.[89] Cicero supported this contention by comparing the perfect speech to the perfect body or perfect sailing ship: each part is essential, nothing is useless. In *De oratore*, he added that rhythm results from dividing words into phrases that can be uttered in a single breath while maintaining a continuous flow. In another book, *Orator*, he dealt with rhythm's origin, nature, cause, and use, claiming that rhythm is not merely beautiful but is also useful.[90] In this, it is similar to the movements of athletes where muscle action is both functional and artistically pleasing.

Both *decorum* and its subdivision *ornatus* represent a powerful conjoining of rhetoric and poetics into a highly structured system aimed at "fashioning" or transforming the speech.[91] Quintilian claimed, "Here is the dwelling place of prose; here is the point to which the audience looks forward; here is the orator's whole merit."[92]

During the imperial period, which began under Caesar Augustus, *decorum* emphasized adaptation to the expectations of the audience. This practice was also common during the Second Sophistic, beginning about AD 35, because speakers became more concerned with rhetoric as beautiful than with rhetoric as powerful.[93] To help speakers fashion a speech acceptable to the audience, the Romans developed a series of commonplaces for discovering appropriate figures. While the *Rhetorica ad Herennium* listed sixty-four figures of thought and speech (including tropes), and Cicero listed ninety-seven; many more were developed by the end of the Second Sophistic. The rhetors of Byzantium considered figures to be fundamental in education. They could take up a fourth of a typical rhetorical textbook, and they were often used in the construction of arguments. By the reign of Elizabeth I, while Shakespeare's plays were being performed at the Old Globe, two hundred figures were known to have been taught to students of the English language. In the twentieth century, Chaim Perelman and Lucie Olbrechts-Tyteca recommended using figures to bring arguments to the forefront for audiences (see chapter 12).

MAJOR FIGURES

The following figures are some of the most commonly used in the English language. Contemporary speakers should learn them for the same reasons Roman orators did—to help meet or create audience expectations when fashioning a speech. They are pervasive. You will find examples not only in political speeches, but in newspaper editorials, advertising, and sports writing. (When it exists, I have provided the Latin equivalent to the term from the *Rhetorica ad Herennium*.)

1. *Metaphor (translatio):* A trope by which one thing is described in terms of another. A word is used in a sense different from what was intended. Normally, a comparison is made from one category to another. For example, General Electric claims they make appliances that serve in the "heart of the home." The heart is a metaphor for the kitchen, revealing its crucial function in any household. Some politicians attempt to explain how they would protect social security funds by putting them in a "lock box." Metaphors can advance arguments as well as entertain their audiences.

2. *Simile (imago):* A metaphor that is weakened or softened by the use of the words "like" or "as." "The kitchen is *like* the heart of a home." "My plan would work *like* a lock box."

3. *Personification (conformatio):* A figure of thought by which human qualities are given to nonhuman entities. "The chasm yawned before us." "The cloud stretched its fluffy arm toward the plane."

4. *Allegories (permutatio):* A trope that develops metaphors or analogies into stories that deliver a message. They are often used to paint a larger picture. "I admire the

man in the arena whose face is marred by dust and sweat and blood, who strives valiantly, who errs and comes short again and again because there is not effort without error and shortcoming, but who does actually strive to do the deeds. . . ."[94]

5. *Synecdoche (intellectio):* A trope that substitutes a part to represent the whole, or that substitutes the whole to represent only a part. "She was in love with a handsome blond." The part, "blond," represents the whole man. "I'll give you a copper for that salt." Here the whole material, "copper," is named rather than a part fashioned from it, a penny.

6. *Irony:* A trope that posits an unexpected meaning. "It is ironic that a rich man dies penniless." "It is ironic that Reagan, the man who hated the evil empire, should befriend its leader, Gorbachev." Often a contrary meaning is implied. Sarcasm is an example of irony. After a dull lecture, a student might say, "Boy, that was a sizzling presentation." The *Rhetorica* confines irony to understatement *(diminutio).*

7. *Hyperbole (superlatio):* A trope that is a massive exaggeration. "He was so thin he could enter the room without opening the door; he could stand in the shower without getting wet."

8. *Aposiopesis (praecisio):* A figure of speech whereby speakers are so moved by their own words that they break off speaking for moment. When he finally became the speaker of the House of Representatives, John Boehner broke off his acceptance speech several times while he cried. Sophists did it on purpose to convey sincerity. It happens naturally during eulogies, acceptance speeches, and farewells when speakers are overcome by emotion.

9. *Balance:* A figure of speech in which two clauses or phrases of matching rhythm and length are brought together for effect. My mother used to say, "If I can stand and cook it, you can sit and eat it." Senator Marco Rubio at the Republican Convention of 2012 gave us another example when praising his father: "He stood behind the bar in the back of the room, so one day I could stand behind a podium in the front of a room." At the Democratic Convention that followed, Vice President Joe Biden developed a balance of his own, speaking about his relationship with the president: "I learned the enormity of his heart; he learned the depth of my loyalty."

10. *Antithesis (contentio):* A sophisticated balance in which the two phrases or clauses oppose one another. "Ask not what your country can do for you; ask what you can do for your country." "A coward dies often; a brave man dies once."

11. *Oxymoron:* Placing two words together that normally have opposite meaning or context. "A wise fool." "A liberal Republican." "An independent dog." Shakespeare has Romeo build a whole speech around oxymorons near the beginning of *Romeo and Juliet* to show that Romeo is not really in love with Rosalind. He speaks about "cold fire" and "feathers of lead."

12. *Apophasis:* A figure whereby speakers deny what they are actually doing. "I'm not about to mention my opponent's drinking problem." "I won't even allude to her fooling around behind her husband's back."

13. *Rhetorical questions (erotema):* These are questions uttered by speakers for which they expect no response. They are often used to organize thought or to force the audience to draw a conclusion. "Have we at long last endured enough of this

president? How much longer must we suffer?" When the speaker asks a questions and then answers it, it is known at *ratiocinatio.* "Are we better off than we were four years ago? Certainly not."

14. *Epanaphora (repetitio):* A figure of speech repetition for emphasis. "I have a dream" was used seven times in the conclusion of Martin Luther King Jr.'s famous speech at the Lincoln Memorial in August of 1963. Ann Romney, the wife of the Republican nominee, created rhythm in her address to the convention in 2012 with her refrain, "I want to talk about . . ."

15. *Asyndeton (dissolutum):* A figure of speech using multiple words but eliminating the connectives for emphasis. Aristotle gave an example near the end of the *Rhetoric:* "I spoke, you heard, you know, decide." Julius Caesar's words after his victory in Pontus are even more famous: "I came, I saw, I conquered" *(Vini, vidi, vici).* Asyndetons are a useful way of issuing a complaint: "Here at Mossback State University, we are poor, downtrodden, abused, overworked, undernourished. I will have no more of it."

16. *Polysyndeton:* The opposite of asyndeton. Here more connectives than are needed are added to impress the audience. "We are poor and downtrodden and abused and overworked and undernourished."

17. *Onomatopoeia (nominatio):* A trope by which words imitate sounds. "The cannon boomed; the bird screeched."

18. *Homeoteleuton (similiter desinens):* An internal rhyme, a figure of speech in which words that end with the same sounds are used for effect. "His affliction was addiction." "The best attitude is gratitude." "Whatcha doin', Marshall McLuhan?" "See ya later, alligator."

19. *Alliteration:* A figure in which the first sound of several words is the same. "Lassie licked the luscious lady, who laid down and laughed." Perhaps no political figure gained more fame from the use of alliteration than President Nixon's vice president, Spiro T. Agnew. Agnew was a virtual unknown when he became vice president, but soon, through the use of alliteration, became one of the most quoted vice presidents in history. In 1970, in the midst of protests over the war in Vietnam, Agnew told an audience in San Diego that "we have more than our share of nattering nabobs of negativism." Those who would negotiate a weak peace treaty in Vietnam were dubbed "pusillanimous pussyfooters" or "vicars of vacillation." His press critics became "the hopeless, hysterical hypochondriacs of history."

20. *Anastrophe (conversio):* A figure of speech by which normal word order is inverted. "Throw mama from the train, a kiss." This figure was used to develop the character of Yoda in the *Star Wars Trilogy.* He often inverted sentences for effect, "A Jedi, you are." "Happy, you will never be." This was also a favorite device of Shakespeare. In *Measure for Measure,* Isabella says, "To speak so indirectly, I am loath." In *King Lear,* Lear says, "Through tatter'd clothes, small vices do appear."

21. *Apostrophe (exclamatio):* A figure of speech by which one addresses someone or something that is absent. "Hear me, O great spirit." "O freedom, hear my call." "Our Father, who art in heaven." In his 2012 acceptance of the nomination, President Obama said, "But know this, America: Our problems can be solved."

22. *Euphemism:* A figure of speech by which we substitute a more pleasant phrase for an obnoxious one. There is a whole list of euphemisms for sexual intercourse including "made love," "slept together," "made the beast with two backs," and "boinked." We also avoid the use of the word death with such phrases as "passed away," "ate the big enchilada," and "checked out."

23. *Paromologia:* A tactic in debate where a speaker concedes minor points to solidify his or her position on major points. For example, in 2012, Prime Minister David Cameron of Great Britain traveled to Scotland to try to convince the Scots that voting for independence was a bad idea. He conceded that Scotland and England could rule themselves but argued that by remaining united, they would be better off: "Of course, Scotland could govern itself. So could England. My point is that we do it so much better together."

24. *Triplets:* This figure arranges phrases into the magical number three, holy in Western civilization from the trinity. First Lady Michelle Obama used several in her very successful address to the Democratic Convention in 2012. One instance reads, "We were so young, so in love, and so in debt." A more complicated example comes at the beginning of Marc Antony's famous speech in Shakespeare's *Julius Caesar:* "Friends, Romans, countrymen, lend me your ears." Not only are three introductory words used, but the effect is amplified by the fact that "friends" is one syllable, "Romans" is two syllables, and "countrymen" is three syllables. Thus, the phrase is a triplet squared, if you will.

Ornatus uses rhythm and figures to shade, turn, and elicit meaning in such a way as to arouse the proper *decorum.* "*Ornatus* is precisely what brings about the intensification of our basic linguistic orientation in reality because it represents the complete mastery of linguistic possibilities."[95] This relationship between *ornatus* and *decorum* renders intelligible the continuum from the plain to the grand style.[96] On the one end is the "Asiatic" speaker who seeks to "impress and secure the attention of an audience . . . by fluency, by florid and copious diction and imagery, or by epigrammatic conciseness."[97] Quintilian argued that the grand style created an "impression of grace and charm [using] rhetorical figures."[98] On the other end, we find the "Attic" orator, who speaks plainly and cleanly, especially in the forensic mode. The continuum from plain to grand is clearly laid out in Book IV of the *Rhetorica ad Herennium.*[99] Cicero had a similar vision:

> Metaphors are used in the plain style to make the meaning clear, not for entertainment. . . . [The orator] will avoid elaborate, contrived symmetry and repetition as well as the more powerful figures of speech. . . . Moderate vocal variety and slight gesticulation are typical of an orator speaking in the plain style. . . . The middle style is more robust. . . . Ornamentation is appropriate. Metaphor, metonymy, catachresis, allegory may all be used effectively. The orator using this style will present his arguments in detail and in depth. The [grand] style is described by the words full, ample, stately, and ornate. . . . Eloquence of this sort sways and moves an audience. Anyone who speaks only in this mode should be despised, since clarity and precision of the plain style and the charm of the middle style must be used to prepare an audience. . . . That man is eloquent who can speak about ordinary subjects in a simple way, great subjects grandly, and topics between these extremes moderately.[100]

Each of these styles had a corrupted counterpart: (1) the meager for the plain, which means it is too thin to maintain interest; (2) the slack for the middle, which means it did not receive enough care to hold together; (3) the swollen for the grand, which means that it is so overloaded with tropes and figures that meaning is lost.

Throughout most of his works, particularly Book III of *De oratore*, Cicero warned against overindulgence in stylistic devices.[101] *Ornatus* in rhetoric was similar to *ornatus* in other arts: If the adornment did not serve a function, it was superfluous. The flying buttress that reinforces the wall of a cathedral is beautiful yet functional; it would meet Cicero's standard. The metaphor that holds attention and supports an idea, yet retains its beauty, is the rhetorical analog. Quintilian agreed and implored students to choose "words that express thoughts best."[102] However, reflecting the preference for display in the Second Sophistic of the imperial period, he quickly added that words must make a speech worthy of admiration and productive of pleasure.[103]

Commonplaces and figures dominate *decorum* to this day. Mastery of *decorum* and *ornatus* gave power to Jesus' rhetoric in the King James version of the Bible and to Lincoln in his many memorable speeches. They surface in political slogans and advertising campaigns. The interplay between *ornatus, decorum*, and *inventio* allowed Cicero and others to develop other stylistic tactics such as elaboration (expansion of an idea or argument), illumination (clarifying an idea or argument with an illustration), and paradox (catching attention with a striking contrast). The next step was to take style to an even higher, more artistic level.

The Second Sophistic

We have seen that during the time of Plato, Athens was dominated by Sophists, many of whom were both rhetorical theorists and superb practitioners of the art of public speaking. In his book on forty leading speakers, Philostratus coined the term "Second Sophistic" to reflect favorably on the declamations of the time. The Second Sophistic during the height of imperial Rome reached a peak in the Greek city-states around AD 100. The famous speakers were cultural conservatives and pagans. They were often granted immunities and given honorary chairs by such emperors as Vespasian, Nerva, and Trajan. Vespasian established chairs of Greek and Latin rhetoric. Trajan provided scholarships in rhetoric for 5,000 young men. One of the most learned emperors, Marcus Aurelius created an Imperial Chair of Rhetoric that paid 10,000 drachmae.

Some of the more prominent speakers of this period include Cornelius Fronto (95–166), who used the grand style to great effect. He was also a teacher of Marcus Aurelius and one who condemned the Christians. Aelius Aristides (c. 117–181) revived the "Attic" style of Cicero and Pericles.[104] His epideictics "To Rome" and "Panathenaicus" won him praise for their historical detail. More importantly, these ceremonial speeches revealed an important tactic used by these prominent speakers to form a sense of imperial morals. They praised what they found to be worthy in other cultures or leaders, hoping their rulers would embrace the same values. The Greek stoic Dio Chrysostom (c. 40–110) used stories about the heroes and gods of Rome to the same effect.[105] Emperor Domitian eventually exiled Chrysostom when it became clear that his oration on the Parthian King was really an attack on the practices of Domitian. Pliny the Younger *(Secundus)* (61–112), trained by Quintilian, became a consul on the strength of his intricate speeches that were full of balances. His "Panegyricus" is the only speech we have remaining from his opus; it celebrated his rise to consul, and praised Trajan and condemned Domitian in true epideictic fashion.

In more recent times, we have seen political leaders combine beauty and power in rhetoric in order to advance their own careers. Huey Long served as governor of Louisiana and then senator. He became a virtual dictator of the state before his assassination in 1935. One explanation for his rise to fame was his incredible rhetorical talent. Here is a passage from a speech he gave on the campaign trail in 1928 while running for governor. It begins with a reference to a part of the mythology of Louisiana but quickly and beautifully moves to the present condition of the state.

> And it is here, under this oak where Evangeline waited for her lover, Gabriel, who never came. This oak is an immortal spot, made so by Longfellow's poem, but Evangeline is not the only one who has waited here in disappointment. Where are the schools that you have waited for your children to have, that have never come? Where are the roads and the highways that you send your money to build, that are no nearer now than ever before? Where are the institutions to care for the sick and disabled? Evangeline wept bitter tears in her disappointment, but it lasted through only one lifetime. Your tears in this country, around this oak, have lasted for generations. Give me the chance to dry the eyes of those who still weep here![106]

The passage moves from the sadness of Evangeline to the tears of those present. The pathos is overwhelming and carries into Long's promise to dry the eyes of those crying before him. This had to be one of the most sublime moments on his campaign trail.

On the Sublime

The Second Sophistic provided a laboratory for ceremonial speech and particularly for the grand style. Teachers revived the series of exercises developed by the original Sophists, known as the *progymnasmata* (see chapter 3). However, they became so calcified that some teachers sought more original ways to help their students and clients develop eloquence. That would lead to the writing of *On the Sublime*, thought to be by Cassius Dionysius Longinus (AD 213 to 273), a citizen of Athens who studied Plato and became a teacher of philosophy and rhetoric. His references to Genesis and Moses in a Roman work are quite rare and may indicate that the author was a Hellenic Jew, who admired Philo of Alexandria (see next chapter). *On the Sublime*, known as *Peri hupsous*, was a Platonic approach to rhetoric in that it sought to take audiences to the *noumenal* world, the spiritual world for Christians. The object of the speaker was to display the divine, model virtue, and/or prepare the soul for this mystical world. Ideally, the speech would lift the soul from the body, creating an ecstatic state. Although we are no longer sure about this attribution (sometimes referred to as Pseudo-Longinus), we do know that the work gives us evidence that the theory of *decorum* was alive and well during the Second Sophistic, a time when display and ceremonial speech reigned supreme. Chapter III of *On the Sublime* emphasizes the importance of expectation in the audience, and the author lists the specific means of achieving *decorum* starting in chapter XVI. The book argued that devices that enhance imagination *(phantasia)* make the real more real, and the true more true for the audience.[107]

But the book seeks more than that. The author wants to teach students "not to persuade the audience but rather to transport them out of themselves." This requires forming "great conceptions" that stimulate the human soul; the orator must "inspire the passions" with "the due formation of figures, . . . noble diction," and "dignified and elevated compositions." The author claimed that sublime prose would cause the orator to be revered in "each succeeding age." He went on to link style to persona: "Sublimity is the echo of a great soul."[108] To heighten this effect, the speaker needs to find a poetic link, which can be achieved by combining figures, by majesty of expression, and by the use of elevation,[109] elaboration, and amplification. Elevation, for example, results from great thoughts, vibrant emotions, combinations of figures, elegant word choice, and dignified word order. The sublime stresses the spiritual over the material, and delicacy and grace over the crude and simple. It would reach its most refined manifestation in the Romantic movement of the eighteenth and nineteenth centuries.

What we have then is a system of style that transforms the stage of a play or the platform of a speaker into a world that the audience has never seen. It takes them to another time and place. Cicero, Quintilian, and Longinus enriched the three purposes of oratory—to move, to teach, to please—by seeking the style appropriate to each occasion.[110]

Decorum in Shakespeare

Kenneth Burke (see chapter 11) once remarked, "The rhetorical devices can become obtrusive, sheer decoration . . . but . . . even the most ostentatious of them arose out of great functional urgency."[111] Burke described the ways by which these commonplaces not only meet expectations but "carve out" an audience.

He claimed that identification between audience and speeches is enhanced by the use of these devices[112] and that dramatic symbolism constructs new "reality."[113] He was fascinated by the power Shakespeare achieved through *ornatus:* "Having chosen the plays of Shakespeare for my speculation about form, I was greatly impressed by the wealth of evidence indicating the playwright's constant concern with devices for pointing arrows of an audience's expectations."[114]

In other words, an analysis of any Shakespearean play would be superficial without a proper understanding of how *decorum* and *ornatus* were used to create expectations, advance the plot, and reinforce characterization.[115] In the following analysis, the Roman system reveals how language creates expectations. Stylistic analysis bridges the gap between fictive and nonfictive

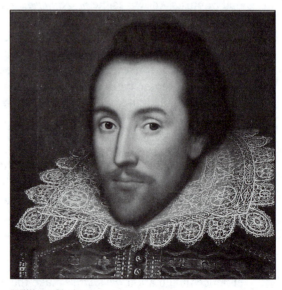

William Shakespeare.

works. It acquaints us with some of the most artistic and appropriate uses of *ornatus* by the leading literary figure in the English language.

Figures of speech and thought abound in many of the speeches in the plays of Shakespeare. Some of the most memorable metaphors, personifications, and analogies can be found in the use of objects in the universe to enhance the depth of the love Romeo and Juliet feel for one another. He compares her to the sun and it is so radiant it makes the moon jealous. She says this of him: "and cut him out in little stars/ And he will make the face of heaven so fine/ That all the world will be in love with night" (Act III, Scene ii, lines 22–24).

Examined here is a short, relatively unnoted speech by Escalus, prince of Verona in *Romeo and Juliet* (Act I, scene 1).[116] This text reveals that even in minor speeches, Shakespeare skillfully uses language to create expectations:

> Rebellious subjects, enemies to peace
> Profaners of this neighbor-stained steel—
> Will they not hear? What, ho! you men, you beasts,
> That quench the fire of your pernicious rage
> With purple fountains issuing from your veins!
> On pain of torture, from those bloody hands
> Throw your mistemp'red weapons to the ground
> And hear the sentence of your moved prince.
> Three civil brawls, bred of an airy word
> By thee, old Capulet, and Montague,
> Have thrice disturbed the quiet of our streets
> And made Verona's ancient citizens
> Cast by their grave beseeming ornaments
> To wield old partisans, in hands of old,
> Cank'red with peace, to part your cank'red hate.
> If ever you disturb our streets again,
> Your lives shall pay the forfeit of the peace.
> For this time all the rest depart away.
> You, Capulet, shall go along with me;
> And, Montague, come you this afternoon,
> To know our farther pleasure in this case,
> To old Freetown, our common judgment place.
> Once more, on pain of death, all men depart.

Before looking at the *ornatus* and *decorum* in the speech, we need to examine its context. The setting is the town square in Verona. Two distinguished families, the Montagues and Capulets, are involved in an ancient feud. From the opening remarks, we gather that the streets of Verona have been a battlefield for years, with family and friends waging their own private war. Prince Escalus has had to step in with warnings (before the play began) to try to put an end to the bloodshed.

The play begins with yet another riot full of fury and running with blood.[117] Outraged, Prince Escalus rides into the scene and provides the first instance where we see what expectation means. By employing partial sentences in an emphatic rhythm at the beginning of the speech, Shakespeare indicates that royalty is speaking. These sentences label the prince's subjects as a god would name his creations. He says, "Rebellious subjects, enemies to peace," and "you men, you beasts." Both phrases are limited asyndetons—a series of words or phrases with conjunctions omitted to add emphasis—that cut through the yelling of the mob and establish a regal presence.

Very early in the speech, Shakespeare signifies the nobility of the leaders of the mob through the colorful metaphor, "With purple fountains issuing from your veins!" Purple invokes images of royal blood drawn from the two families. Notice that when a phrase can serve more than one purpose, Shakespeare often takes advantage. The blood reference reinforces the *decorum* of the scene. The phrases, "purple fountains" and "bloody hands" are carefully placed metaphors that paint a vivid picture for the audience while summarizing the events they have just witnessed.

In fact, the blood image pervades the prince's speech thereby sustaining its sense of *decorum.* In the second line, he refers to "Profaners of neighbor-stained steel," the stains being dried blood, of course. Even the line, "To part your cank'red hate," elicits a vision of open wounds that can be traced into the past. Later in the play, references to "rust" remind the audience of dried, rust-like bloodshed in a time-worn feud.

The metaphors in Prince Escalus' speech serve a second purpose. They focus attention on the wrongs being done by these two families. This step foreshadows the tragic end of the play: because of this feud, many lives, including Romeo's and Juliet's, will be lost. For example, the prince says, "Throw your mistemp'red weapons to the ground." The double entendre compares poorly forged steel to steel being used for an evil purpose. At the same time, the invocation of the word "temper" within "mistempered" evokes the fury of the fight and the anger of the prince. In this way, the language of the speech subliminally enhances the expectation of the audience.

The prince then indicts the cause of the feud by the use of the metaphor, "Bred of an airy word." Reinforcing one of Shakespeare's favorite themes, the prince reveals that all of this very real death is based on nothing but a word between contesting parties. The elegance and power of the phrase arise from its hyperbolic and synecdochal nature. "Word" is an exaggeration for many words and phrases—fighting words, slanders no doubt. Furthermore, an "airy word" filled with breath alone has bred something capable of killing solid flesh. In fact, the subtlety of the phrase may lie in its oxymoronic nature; the airy word has bred not life, but death.

Prince Escalus also points to proper expectations of the scene by making clear how the crisis has been reached. Both families have brought these "civil brawls" (another oxymoron that plays on the double meaning of "civil") to the quiet streets of Verona without regard for the good citizens of the city. He uses the metaphorical phrase, "Cast by their grave beseeming ornaments" to indicate how cheaply the lives of friends have been treated and how easily the garb of citizens can be abandoned in a reckless moment. All of this is the fault of the Montagues and the Capulets, who use their friends as if they were mere pawns in a chess game.

The pronoun placement and rhythm of the speech also have an impact on the audience. Shakespeare's use of the pronoun "you" supports the *decorum* by changing the rhythm of the speech. He places "you's" in the speech to identify persons at fault for a crime. For example, "you men, you beasts" is used in the beginning of the speech. In the middle of the speech, however, the "you's" are implied, as befits royalty. Three-quarters of the way through the speech, the "you's" reappear, awakening the audience to the reemergence of personhood. At the end of the speech, they are implied again as the prince lays down the law in royal terms. This tactic sustains rhythm in the speech as a whole while supporting the meaning of specific phrases.

Another syntactic change occurs when the prince shifts from the grand to the plain style. In the first half of the speech, the prince uses metaphors to characterize what has taken place, show what is happening, and reveal how he feels about it. Suddenly, a contrast is provided when Shakespeare alters the prince's style to be as clear and succinct as possible. "And hear the sentence of your moved prince. . . . If ever you disturb our streets again, your lives shall pay the forfeit of the peace. . . . Once more, on pain of death, all men depart." The Capulets and Montagues, as well as the audience, are to understand without question that the prince has been provoked and will impose the death penalty if the peace is lost. The prince sustains this serious tone when he declares that each family will meet with him at a different time, "To know our farther pleasure in this case." The use of the royal "our" and "farther pleasure" enhance the nobility of this otherwise plain sentence.

A condition has now been established that if met will result in tragedy. Thus, when fighting breaks out again, the audience becomes concerned. When the fighting results in Romeo killing Tybalt, a Montague killing a Capulet, Romeo must flee for his life. That event continues a whole set of incidents that lead to the tragic death of Romeo and Juliet. In other words, these few lines are crucial not only to set the scene but to establish the plot. If the audience fails to understand them, the plot will fail. Hence, the change in style when the conditions of the prince are handed down is crucial.

In this way, style functions to create the expectation of the moment in a play while preparing the audience for what is to come. It is a masterful example of the proper use of *decorum* and *ornatus*.

Conclusion

The Roman epoch is marked by several influential rhetorical works and theorists. The *Rhetorica ad Herennium* opens the epoch demonstrating that the Romans were not shy about borrowing from the Greeks and codifying their work. Nor were they afraid to expand on Greek notions of organization. *On the Sublime* three centuries later shows that the Romans greatly sophisticated the Greek notion of style and became fascinated with how speeches of display could achieve the spiritual. In between these two books came the works of Cicero, who often practiced what he preached, and *De institutione* of Quintilian, who demonstrated the impact a good teacher can have.

Studying Athens, we saw that democracy tended to encourage the use of rhetoric, which in turn led to the proliferation of works on public speaking. In Rome the evolution of the republic helped to create the need for public speaking. During the Republican era, invention was stressed over mere adaptation and entertainment, especially in forensic speeches. *Decorum* was used not only to meet expectations but to create them. Cicero is the great symbol of the Republican era. As judge, lawyer, senator, and consul, he demonstrated that rhetoric is essential in rising above class and informing the political process. This experience led Cicero to write many important books on rhetoric that laid out the themes he believed to be most important. Orators need to be properly trained, which includes an education in all sorts of subjects, particularly history and philosophy. Orators need to develop character in order to impress and identify with their followers; character is composed of factors ranging from one's family to one's bearing and word choice. Orators need to take great care with style to be sure it creates a sense of propriety by using functional adornment sparingly.

Once the functions of republicanism withered in the age of the Caesars, style became more important than substance—meeting expectations was more important than creating them. Quintilian understood that, in the Imperial era, orators needed to take care that they did not offend the powers that be; instead they needed to impress them while reinforcing virtue in demonstrative speeches. Like Cicero, but in much more detail, he laid out the education of the citizen-orator. He developed the notion of the good man and how training in rhetoric could help him speak well, by which he meant guiding the people toward moral right.[118] He further refined the notion of Roman style, demonstrating that *decorum* and *ornatus* work in tandem to create a beautiful yet purposeful speech. His own success as a teacher and his love of rhetoric allowed him to declare at the end of his career that rhetoric was the most important of all disciplines. At least for the next few centuries he was right.

Study Questions

1. How did the formation of the Roman Republic influence the development of rhetorical theory?

2. What is the contribution of Philodemus to rhetorical theory?

3. How does Cicero's public career complement his rhetorical theory? Can you name a contemporary parallel example?

4. While Aristotle's approach to rhetorical theory was empirical, that is, based on observation, the Roman approach is paradigmatic, that is, based on models or touchstones of rhetoric. What evidence can you bring to defend or attack this thesis?

5. What is the historical contribution of the *Rhetorica ad Herennium* to rhetorical theory? Outline the five cannons of rhetoric.

6. Using the *stasis* system, outline the arguments that could be generated in a contemporary or historic trial.

7. How is the continuum from the grand to the plain style useful in contemporary oratory or advertising? What are the role of figures of speech and thought in determining style?

8. In your contemporary society, what would constitute a good person speaking well? Provide examples.

9. Using the list of figures provided in this chapter, illustrate each with an example from current media. (Hint: advertising and sports writing tend to use them most.)

10. Define *decorum* and *ornatus*. What is the relationship between them?

11. What does the word "sublime" mean? How do you achieve it using stylistic devices?

Notes

[1] Virgil worked on the *Aeneid* for ten years, but never finished it. He died returning from a trip to Greece.

[2] The place is marked by the church of St. Giorgio today.

[3] It is from the word *pleb* that the modern plebiscite, to put to a popular vote, is derived.

[4] These became the Centuriate.

[5] The sophisticated city of Carthage contained an amphitheater for public speaking. In 1943, Winston Churchill traveled to Carthage to rouse British troops fighting Nazi forces. He spoke in the ancient amphitheater because the acoustics were so perfect, he did not need a microphone.

[6] As quoted in Will Durant, *Caesar and Christ: A History of Roman Civilization and of Christianity from the Beginnings to AD 325* (New York: Simon and Schuster, 1944), p. 114.

[7] While Sulla was off on a mission, Marius came back to power, which led to a civil war. Marius had many of Sulla's followers killed, then Marius died. Sulla returned to power in 83 BC and had over 6,000 of Marius' followers killed while Sulla delivered a speech in the Senate.

[8] Suetonius, *The Twelve Caesars*, Robert Graves, trans. (New York: Penguin Books, 1989), p. 38.

[9] R. N. Gaines, "Philodemus on the Three Activities of Rhetorical Invention," *Rhetorica*, 3 (1985): 155–63.

[10] He also wrote *On Methods of Inference* which teaches how to create inductive arguments and arguments from sign.

[11] Marc Antony served as a quaestor to Julius Caesar. Quaestors were also allowed to serve as, or with, provincial governors.

[12] Cicero's remarks are referred to as the Verrine Orations.

[13] Until 243 BC there was only one praetor in all of Rome. The position was just under that of consul.

[14] Cicero's slave Tiro became his secretary and invented shorthand. So we have fairly accurate versions of Cicero's speeches and other works.

[15] Cicero left Italy during this war to join Pompey, then changed his mind and returned to Rome. This disaffection was duly noted by Marc Antony and would have dire consequences for Cicero.

[16] See, for example, Cicero, *De oratore*, E. W. Sutton and H. Rockham, trans. (Cambridge: Harvard U. Press, 1959), III.xxxiv.137ff.

[17] The villa was taken over by the Farnesi family and can be visited today. Cleopatra's garden is now the Botanical Garden of Rome.

[18] Caesar had made the mistake of pardoning Brutus and Cassius, who had sided with Pompey. After the assassination of Caesar, Marc Antony and Octavian defeated Brutus and Cassius at Philippi in 42 BC and established the Second Triumvirate, which included the aging Lepidus.

[19] Cicero had divorced his wife in 45 BC. In Rome at the time all you had to do to obtain a divorce was to ask your wife to leave the house. Cicero then married his wealthy teenage ward; her dowry allowed him to pay off his debts. He divorced her a month later.

[20] We believe that Cicero delivered 106 major speeches in the Senate of which 58 have survived.

[21] Cicero's *De oratore* was generally unavailable until 1422 when it was rediscovered by humanists.

[22] *Rhetorica ad Herennium*, Harry Caplan, trans. (Cambridge: Harvard U. Press, 2004).

[23] Aristotle's *Rhetoric* was published some years later in Rome.

[24] To this day, scientists have yet to crack the mystery of how the memory works. We know that the structures of the basal ganglia help with learned skills. The hippocampus provides conscious memory of facts and events. Associative learning, such as salivating when food is mentioned, is controlled by the cerebellum. And emotional memories are handled by the amygdala.

[25] *Rhetorica ad Herennium*, p. 205.

[26] Most of this information can be found in Book II of *Rhetorica ad Herennium*. Other references can be found under Hermagoras and *constitutio* in Caplan's index. Cicero treats the same topics in his *De inventione,* H. M. Hubbell, trans. (Cambridge: Harvard U. Press, 1959) in Book II under forensic speeches *(genus iudicale);* see also, *De oratore,* Book II.xxiv–xxvi. Quintilian deals with this subject most specifically in Book III, chapter iv (entire) in *Institutio oratoria* (hereafter *Institutes*) H. E. Butler, trans. (Cambridge: Harvard U. Press, 1920–22/1980).

[27] "What They Said," *Los Angeles Times* (February 11, 1997): A18.

[28] While successful in gaining a hung jury in their first trial, the brothers were convicted in their second.

[29] The *ad Herennium* develops four forms of thought, (1) contrast for embellishment, (2) negation for proof, (3) abridgement for clarity, and (4) parallel for vividness.

[30] Cicero, *De oratore*, III.v.19–20.

[31] In fact, Cicero subtitles his *De oratore*, "The Making of an Orator."

[32] Cicero, *Topica,* 18.71.

[33] Cicero, *De inventione*, I.viii.10. This early work by Cicero became enormously popular as a text in the medieval period, but Cicero himself believed it to be rather primitive compared to his other writings. See William W. Fortenbaugh, "Cicero, *On Invention* 1.51–77 Hypothetical Syllogistic and the Early Peripatetics," *Rhetorica*, 16 (1988): 25.

[34] *De inventione* claims that rhetoric is the practice of political persuasion based on a set of rules (See Book I, Chapter V). The book became very popular in medieval schools often paired with the *Rhetorica ad Herennium*.

[35] Christopher P. Craig, *Form as Argument in Cicero's Speeches* (Atlanta: Scholars Press, 1993). In particular see Craig's analysis of Cicero's *Pro roscio amerino*.

[36] This Crassus lived from 140 to 91 BC and should not be confused with the general who defeated Spartacus and was eventually killed by the Parthians.

[37] *De oratore* was completed in 55 BC during the time Cicero withdrew from public service because of the assumption of power by the First Triumvirate. The Antonius of this dialogue is the grandfather of Marc Antony.

[38] Cicero, *De oratore*, I.viii.30. At I.iv.16, he wrote, ". . . the truth is that this oratory is a greater thing, and has its sources in more arts and branches of study, than people suppose."

[39] Cicero differentiated between public speaking and conversational speech *(sermo)*. The latter is to be used with philosophical groups or in social settings. See G. Remer, "Political Oratory and Conversation," *Political Theory,* 27 (1999): 39–65.

[40] See Richard Leo Enos and Jeanne L. McClaran, "Audience and Image in Ciceronian Rome: Creation and Constraints of the *Vir bonus* Personality," *Central States Speech Journal,* 29 (1978): 98–106. During Cicero's time Pompey built a large forum in the Largo Argentina area in Rome. It contained a Senate house, and that is where Caesar was assassinated after he had defeated Pompey and became dictator. When Octavian became Caesar Augustus, he built a new, much larger forum along the Sacred Way. Today it runs north of the Coliseum to Capitoline Hill.

[41] Cicero, *De oratore,* III.xlii.178, xliii.182, xlv.190.

[42] Ibid., xxiv.54–55.

[43] See Quintilian, *Institutes,* XII.i.1, 44. See also I.preface.9. Cato the Elder built the first basilica in 184 BC.

[44] Cicero, *De oratore,* I.viii.34. For a full discussion see I.ii–iv, viii, which are devoted to this topic.

[45] Cicero's conception of civic virtue has been investigated by S. Botein, "Cicero as a Role Model for Early American Lawyers: A Case Study in Classical 'Influence,'" *Classical Journal,* 73 (1978): 313–21; L. K. Kerber, "Salvaging the Classical Tradition" in L. Kerber, *Federalist in Dissent: Imagery and Ideology in Jeffersonian America* (Ithaca: Cornell U. Press, 1970), pp. 95–134.

[46] As we shall see in chapter 7, Machiavelli picks up on this notion and expands it further in the Renaissance.

[47] See Ann Vasaly, *Representations: Images of the Ancient World in Ciceronian Rhetoric* (Berkeley: U. of California Press, 1993), chapter 1. Cicero may have inspired Kenneth Burke's notions of concretization and localization in his discussion of substantial identification in his *Rhetoric of Motives.* See chapter 11.

[48] See Vasaly, chapter 1. Livy's *Histories* and Virgil's *Aeneid* are filled with Roman legends and links to Roman forbears and the gods.

[49] Cicero's thought on the need for the orator to be erudite pervades *De oratore,* see especially I.xxxix.176ff, I.xlvi.201ff. His comments on the moderate and prudent judgment also pervade his work, see especially I.xv.67 on moderation and self-control, II.lxxv.347 on judgment, II.lxxiv.342 on wise management, and II.lxxxiv.342 on temperance. Quintilian concurs in, for example, VI.iv.10, "Moderation, and sometimes even long suffering, is the better policy." See also, VI.v.3, where Quintilian claims "There is no great difference . . . between judgment and sagacity."

[50] Cicero, *De oratore,* III.xiv.55 & 70.

[51] Ibid., 55.

[52] Ibid., see especially III.xv.55–xxii.82. Throughout *De oratore,* Cicero claims that to accomplish this end one must have a solid education. See II.xiii.55ff, II.xviii.76, II.xii.92–94. This position influenced many important medieval and Renaissance thinkers, not the least of whom was Machiavelli.

[53] Ibid., xiv.55; see also III.xvi.60. See also Quintilian, *Institutes,* II.xx.5–6.

[54] Ibid., xv.55–xxii.82. See also Quintilian, *Institutes,* XII.i.3. At XII.i.19 *prudentissimos* is translated as "sensible."

[55] See also the *Rhetorica ad Herennium,* IV.xxv.35, "temeritas est cum inconsiderata dolorum perpessione gladiatoria periculorum susceptio."

[56] Cicero, *De oratore,* I.xiv.202.

[57] See Cicero, *Orator,* H. M. Hubbell, trans. (Cambridge: Harvard U. Press, 1962), at p. 70 and *De officiis,* H. G. Edinger, trans. (Indianapolis: Library of Liberal Arts, 1974), at I.144. Or see the Loeb edition of the *De officiis* by Walter Miller.

[58] John Bartlett, *Familiar Quotations,* Emily Morison Beck, ed. (Boston: Little, Brown and Co., 1980), p. 349.

[59] As we shall see in chapter 7, the humanist Petrarch discovered 800 letters written by Cicero and another 100 written to him.

[60] Robert Hariman, "Political Style in Cicero's Letters to Atticus," *Rhetorica,* 7 (1989): 145–58.

[61] In his lectures on the Sophists, Hegel points out that the Peloponnesian War caused philosophers to withdraw from the world. That made the mob even less responsible. G. W. F. Hegel, *Introduction to the Lectures on the History of Philosophy*, T. M. Knox and A. V. Miller, trans. (Oxford: Clarendon Press, 1985), pp. 113–14.

[62] Cicero, *De oratore*, III.lvii.215–16.

[63] Ibid., lix.224.

[64] See Quintilian, *Institutes*, II.ii.1–iii.12.

[65] Ibid., xxi.15. Prior to that at II.xxi.5, he quotes Cicero to the same effect, that is, that orators require "a knowledge of all important subjects and arts."

[66] Ibid., xxi.12–13.

[67] *Institutes*, II.vii.3-4.

[68] *Institutes*, 6.2.29. Recall that Aristotle makes the same point when he talks about bring a given emotion (*pathé*) closer to the audience in time and space.

[69] Ibid., XI.ii.11–17.

[70] We saw a similar concept in Aristotle. However, instead of physically associating *loci* as places of invention, Aristotle recommended using commonplaces to store standard forms of arguments such as his 28 *topoi*. And we will see the concept again when we examine the rhetorical theory of Chaim Perelman and Lucie Olbrechts-Tyteca in chapter 12.

[71] See G. W. Bowersock, *Greek Sophists in the Roman Empire* (Oxford: Oxford U. Press, 1969), pp. 2, 8, 11, 13, 30, 43–58, 109.

[72] The official Church translator of the New Testament into Latin, *The Vulgate*.

[73] See Paul Piper, "C. De Arte Rhetorica," in *Die Schriften Notkers und seiner Schule*, 1 (Freibur I.B. und Tubingen, 1882), p. 681.

[74] See Quintilian, *Institutes*, VI.i.2–18, XII.i.1–28.

[75] Ibid, II.xvi–xvii.

[76] See Cicero, *Brutus* (Oxford: Clarendon Press, 1966), pp. 25–26. See also Cicero, *De oratore,* III.xxxv.142–43; *De inventione* I.2.5–7, 9; *Brutus* 69, 151, 291. Aristotle makes a similar point in the *Rhetoric* at I.i.2. The importance of *decorum* can be seen in other Roman theorists. See, for example, Susan Lundy and Wayne Thompson, "Pliny, a Neglected Roman Rhetorician," *Quarterly Journal of Speech,* 66 (1980): 414.

[77] See Cicero, *Orator,* H. H. Hubble, trans., 70 and *De officiis*, I.xl.144.

[78] See Richard Leo Enos, *Greek Rhetoric Before Aristotle* (Long Grove, IL: Waveland Press, 1993).

[79] Cicero, *De partitione oratoria*, H. Rackham, trans. (Cambridge: Harvard U. Press, 1942), xv.53.

[80] Beth Innocenti, "Towards a Theory of Vivid Description as Practiced in Cicero's *Verrine* Orations," *Rhetorica*, 12 (1994): 355–82.

[81] Quintilian, *Institutes*, VI.ii.7.

[82] For example, see Quintilian, *Institutes*, I.vi (entire), II.xxiii.8–11, XI.i.82–83. See also, Charles Seltman, *Approach to Greek Art* (London: Dutton, 1949), p. 29.

[83] Cicero was so taken with the term that he developed four divisions of it by which persons could organize their lives with propriety. See Cicero, *De officiis* I.

[84] Cicero, *De oratore*, III.xxiv.96–97.

[85] Quintilian, *Institutes*, VIII.vi.1.

[86] Ibid., IX.i.2.

[87] Ibid., VIII.ii & iii; and XII.x.3–9. See also Doreen Innes, "Cicero on Tropes," *Rhetorica*, 6 (1988): 307–25; Elaine Fantham, *Comparative Studies on Republican Latin Imagery*, Phoenix Suppl. 10 (Toronto: U. of Toronto Press, 1972)

[88] Quintilian, *Institutes,* III.xxiv.97–98.

[89] Cicero, *De oratore*, II.vi.24. In *The Arts of Poetry* Horace concurred, "if a speaker's words are out of gear with his fortunes, all Rome, horse and foot, will guffaw," in Allan H. Gilbert, *Literary Criticism: Plato to Dryden* (Detroit: Wayne State U. Press, 1962), p. 131. Horace may have been borrowing from Cicero's line, ". . . in actions as well as words, in the expression of the face, in gesture and gait," in *Orator*, p. 74. See also Cicero's *Lucullus*, 125, where he says that order is naturally wonderful and that style brings order to discourse, and *De natura decorum*, II.58, IV.417; and Raymond Di Lorenzo, "The Critique of Socrates in Cicero's *De oratore:* Ornatus and the Nature of Wisdom," *Philosophy and Rhetoric,* 22 (1978): 251–54.

[90] The development of rhythm in nonpoetic discourse can be traced to Thrasymachus.

[91] For example, Thomas Gibbons' *Rhetoric* (London: Oliver and Bartholomew, 1967) lists over 288 tropes and figures.

[92] Quintilian, *Institutes,* IX.iv.62.

[93] See John Graham, "Ut Pictura Poesis," in *Dictionary of the History of Ideas,* IV (New York: Scribner, 1973), p. 466. See also Elaine Fantham, *Comparative Studies. . . .*

[94] This allegory was developed by Theodore Roosevelt and paraphrased by Richard Nixon in his resignation statement to his staff.

[95] Hanna-Barbara Gerl, "On the Philosophical Dimension of Rhetoric: The Theory of *Ornatus* in Leonardo Bruni," *Philosophy and Rhetoric,* 11 (1978): 178–90. See also Elaine Fantham, *"Varietas and satietas: De oratore 3.96–103 and the limits of ornatus," Rhetorica,* 6 (1988): 276.

[96] See *Rhetorica ad Herennium,* IV, Cicero's *De oratore,* Book III, and most of *Orator* which is devoted to elocutio for the most part. This notion of plain to grand style was still being detailed in the 1700s by such critics as Samuel Johnson. See Rene Wellek, *A History of Modern Criticism: 1750–1850,* vol. I (New Haven: Yale U. Press, 1955) pp. 90–93. See also Celica Milovanovic-Barham, "The Levels of Style in Augustine of Hippo and Gregory of Nazianus," *Rhetorica,* 11 (1993): 1–25.

[97] John C. Rolfe, *Cicero and His Influence* (New York: Cooper Square, 1963), p. 33.

[98] Quintilian, *Institutes,* II.xiii.11.

[99] The *Rhetorica* became the basic text throughout the medieval period, falling from grace only with the development of texts in more modern vernacular. Cicero's *De oratore* and Quintilian's *Institutes* were used for more advanced students.

[100] Cicero, *Orator,* pp. 82–100. I have condensed and simplified some passages for the sake of brevity here. The last thought reads, "Is erit igitur eloquens . . . qui poterit parva summisse, modica temperate; magna graviter dicere."

[101] See also Bruce M. Psaty, "Cicero's Literal Metaphor and Propriety," *Central States Speech Journal,* 29 (1978): 109–12.

[102] The whole of VIII.ii, of *Institutes,* serves to reinforce the notion that ornament is inappropriate without propriety. See also Horace, *Ars poetica* (London, 1928), pp. 1–23, 68–118, 153–178, 311–18.

[103] See the emerging volumes of *Historical Lexicon of Rhetoric,* G. Ueding and W. Jens, eds. (Tubingen: U. of Tubingen Press, 1990, 1994, and 1996); Craig R. Smith and Paul Prince, "Language Choice, Expectation, and the Roman Notion of Style," *Communication Education,* 39 (1990): 63–74. While much of what the Romans said about rhythm, archaic language, and neologisms is indigenous to their culture, some of their advice provides a useful guide for our own development of style. Rhythm is the third division of *ornatus* discussed by Cicero in *De oratore.*

[104] See Joseph W. Day, *The Glory of Athens: The Popular Tradition as Reflected in the Panathenaicus of Aelius Aristides* (Chicago: Ares Publishers, 1980), p. xiii.

[105] J. W. Cohoon, *Dio Chrysostom,* vol. 1 (Cambridge: Harvard U. Press, 1932), p. ix.

[106] Huey Long, *Everyman a King* (Baton Rouge: LSU Press, 1933), p. 99.

[107] See Barbara Eakins and R. Gene Eakins, "Comparison: Proof or Ornament," *Central States Speech Journal,* 26 (1975): 99–106; Edward Doughtie, "Simplicity and Complexity in Elizabethan Air," *Rice University Studies,* 51 (1965): 4; Nancy Struever, *The Language of History in the Renaissance* (Princeton: Princeton U. Press, 1970), pp. 114, 164, 179–83; Gerl, "Philosophical Dimensions of Rhetoric," pp. 178–90.

[108] Longinus, "On the Sublime," *The Great Critics,* James Harry Smith and Ed Winfield Parks, eds. (New York: W. W. Norton, 1959), pp. 71–79.

[109] From the Greek *hypsos.*

[110] See particularly Cicero's *Orator,* which spends a good deal of time clarifying his notion of style using the "to prove, to please, to move" division.

[111] Kenneth Burke, *A Grammar of Motives and Rhetoric of Motives* (Cleveland: Meridian, 1961), pp. 589–90; see also pages 56–60, 582–83, and Michael Leff, "Burke's Ciceronianism," *The Legacy of Kenneth Burke,* Herbert Simons and Trevor Melia, eds. (Madison: U. of Wisconsin Press, 1989).

[112] Burke, p. 611. See also Ronald H. Carpenter, "A Stylistic Basis of Burkean Identification," *Today's Speech* (1972): 19–24.

[113] See Kenneth Burke, *Attitudes Toward History* (Boston: Beacon Press, 1961), p. 262 and all of chapter 6; Burke, *Permanence and Change: An Anatomy of Purpose* (Indianapolis: Bobbs-Merrill, 1965), pp. 17, 35; and Burke, *Counter-Statement* (Berkeley: U. of California Press, 1968), pp. 31, 152–57.

[114] Kenneth Burke, "Colloquy: I. The Party Line," *Quarterly Journal of Speech,* 62 (1982): 62. See Kenneth Burke, "Shakespearean Persuasion," *Antioch Review,* 24 (1964): 19–36. We should note that Shakespeare was a contemporary of those who would translate the new English Bible for King James, which, in part because of its use of beautiful language, became a standard of excellent style in Western civilization.

[115] See Sister Mariam Joseph, *Rhetoric in Shakespeare's Time* (New York: Harcourt, Brace, World, 1962). For a concise history of these notions after the Second Sophistic, see Graham, pp. 469–70; G. W. Bowersock, *Greek Sophists in the Roman Empire* (Oxford: Oxford U. Press, 1969), pp. 43–58, 109; Struever, pp. 114, 164. Though he tends to float above the particulars of Shakespeare's style, Mark Van Doren is capable of insightful criticism when he descends for a close look at figures. At one point, he writes, "The unity of any play is not alone a matter of images, though the coherence of its metaphors may be amazing." See *Shakespeare* (Garden City, NY: Doubleday Anchor, 1953), p. xiii. Other examples may be found on pages 77, 89, 146, 234, 274, and 282.

[116] In the movie version starring Leonardo di Caprio, the speech is given by Captain Prince of the police force.

[117] Several stagings of this play, including that of the Royal Shakespeare Company for the Time-Life Educational Series, include the wounding of an infant.

[118] George Kennedy, *Quintilian* (New York: Twayne Publishers, 1969), p. 58.

PART II

Rhetoric in Medieval and Renaissance Europe

St. Peter's Basilica in the Vatican.

The Fall of Rome and the Rise of Christianity

As the empire began its long decline, rhetorical theory faced new challenges to its evolution and survival. Christian leaders who believed they had the truth returned to the Platonic ideal, arguing that the truth is persuasive in and of itself and needs no help from rhetoric. The study of invention in rhetorical theory ebbed with the conversion of Rome to the empire of the Caesars. As Tacitus makes clear in his *Dialogue on Oratory*, once democratic procedures were eliminated, rhetoric decayed.[1] Specifically, while rhetoric was needed for ceremonial occasions and for self-defense in the courts of the empire, its deliberative function began to atrophy once the Emperor Tiberius eliminated the assemblies.[2] However, over the next 400 years, rhetoric found a new outlet in preaching; this period is known as the *patristic* era in which sermons revealed the return of rhetorical invention culminating in Augustine's revival of classical rhetorical theory.

The first stage of our story centers on the transformation of the pagan Roman Empire into one that would welcome Christian oratory. The Roman Peace *(Pax Romana)* began after Julius Caesar's heir Gaius Octavius defeated the combined forces of Marc Antony and Cleopatra at Actium in a huge sea battle. Octavius became Caesar Augustus and quickly exercised his new power by stripping the Senate of a great deal of its authority.[3] He even banned the publication of the Senate proceedings. Since he had studied rhetoric from his boyhood, Augustus understood what a powerful weapon it could be against a ruler.[4] He made sure no one would rise out of the Senate to challenge his authority.

The imperial regime reinforced its power around the Mediterranean more militantly after the death of Augustus in AD 14. His successor Tiberius Caesar reduced the need for forensic speaking by relying on the word of informants, often pronouncing a sentence the minute he heard a report.[5] Some of the accused stayed home and/or committed suicide rather than attempt to defend themselves during this reign of terror.

In a fateful decision, Tiberius persecuted various religious sects thought to be subversive to the interests of Rome. He particularly despised Egyptian and Jewish cults, exiling Jewish military men to the far reaches of the empire. Tiberius' successor, Caligula, delivered a eulogy to Tiberius and then continued his practices. Also trained in oratory, Caligula regularly held public speaking contests that played a large role in the Second Sophistic, named for the rise in speeches of display. Losers in these contests were often forced to lick their chalked names off the slate of contestants.[6]

Once Christianity became a force to be reckoned with, its leaders were also persecuted, particularly by Nero, the last of the Julian dynasty. He martyred Peter and Paul of the new Christian movement in AD 67. The martyrdom of these founders of Christianity served to make them saints in the eyes of their followers. The Christian church was developing its own sense of narrative history and *mythos*. Just as important, Paul, a Hellenized Jew and Roman citizen educated in Tarsus, had shown that rhetoric was important to the propagation of the faith. Gentile Christians, as opposed to Jewish converts, tended to appreciate the Greek tradition of rhetoric more than their counterparts, and this kept it alive.

Several factors helped the Christians survive. The Jewish desire for self-rule led to almost constant military rebukes before, during, and after Jesus' lifetime. When, after being named *persona non grata* by the Senate, Nero committed suicide in AD 68, the Jews rose up against Rome and the Christians fled into the hills around Pella to avoid the conflict. In AD 70 Titus, the son of the new Emperor Vespasian, completed the slaughter of Jewish leaders and the destruction of their temple in Jerusalem. The Jews living during the great Jewish diaspora in the Holy Land were killed, exiled, or made slaves and the Christians emerged from their hiding places and filled the religious void.

Another factor in the surprising success of the Christians was that a whole brigade of Christian apologists emerged to defend their faith against pagans. Orators, such as Justin Martyr (AD 100–162)[7] (who was martyred in Rome), Melito, Tatian (who was a pupil of Justin), Athenagoras (who made the case for Christianity to two emperors), and Theophilus of Antioch, assured Christianity's survival especially at a time when most cities were disorganized socially.[8] The great Christian teachers and theorists aided the efforts of these orators.

The most sophisticated city in the empire, Alexandria, with its fine library, was the center of learning. Here, the Jewish scholar Philo (20 BC–AD 50) refined the art of hermeneutics (biblical interpretation) while trying to wed Jewish and Platonic theology. Philo believed that humans were created in the image of the divine *logos*, the basis of a noble rhetoric. Like Plato, Philo believed that God was the cause of all good things and could do no evil or punish people. God employed angels for that purpose. In Philo's view, the other fallen angels were responsible for evil because they played on human desire and ignorance. Satan coordinated these corrupting influences, which was the basis of an ignoble rhetoric of desire. Christian leaders in Alexandria appropriated Philo's theory. For example, after studying in Alexandria, Origen (c. 185–c. 255) opened a school in Caesarea in Palestine. He also wedded Christian theology with Platonic philosophy in an effort to woo separatist Christian Gnostics back to the true faith. He theorized that God transcends reason and essence as pure spirit. *Logos* as the word of God serves as the mediator between God and humans; it thus inspires the work of the "holy fathers," and allows for biblical interpretation, the art of hermeneutics.[9]

Clement of Alexandria (c. 150–c. 219) believed the ancient Greek philosophers had functioned to prepare the way for Christianity. This position rationalized the study of the Greeks by Christian theologians and opened the door for Augustine's retrieval of other pre-Christian pagans two centuries later (see below). Clement argued that the light of the true word *(logos)* had inspired the Greeks to discover many truths. He regularly referenced the theory of knowledge found in Plato's *Republic*.

A third factor in the success of the Christians was the fact that civil wars among potential leaders of the empire distracted them from attacking the Christians. For example, despite the pleas of church fathers, Diocletian (ruled 284–305) and his co-emperor Maximinianus launched major persecutions to stop the Christianization of the Roman Empire.[10] However, these attacks on Christians proved unpopular and combined with other factors to force Diocletian and Maximinianus to resign. Constantius I became the ruler in the West. The new ruler in the East was Galerius (ruled 305–310), who continued to persecute the Christians until the waning hours of his administration when he gave Christianity equal status with other religions in an attempt to gain the Christians' support.[11] When Constantius died in 306, Galerius recognized Severus as emperor in the West, but Maxentius, the son of Maximinianus, claimed the throne and defeated Galerius and captured Severus. The Christian-hating Licinius tried to intervene when he became the new emperor in the West. In the ensuing civil war of 312, the Christians supported Constantius' son Constantine, who

Battle at the Milvian Bridge.

Constantine.

eventually emerged as the victor. He defeated Max-entius at the battle of the Milvian Bridge, where Maxentius drowned.

Constantine's vision of the cross with the words *hoc vince* (by this conquer) convinced him to issue the Edict of Milan granting tolerance for Christians. Not long afterward, he made Christianity the official religion of the empire, taking for himself the traditional title of *pontifex maximus*, head of the state religion or pontiff, a title once held by Julius Caesar.

However, after this amazing turn of events, heresies (departures from church doctrine) began to plague the Christian movement. The most powerful of these was led by Arias of Alexandria (250–336), a very effective speaker, who argued that Jesus was inferior to God and, therefore, not fully divine. At the behest of other church leaders, Constantine convened and presided over the conference at Nicaea (325) that endorsed the creed that became the bedrock of the Western notion of Christ's divinity.[12] Despite much support in Egypt, Arianism lost the support of the emperor who finally sided with the powerful Bishop Athanasius, who was then empowered to decide which books would be included in the official Bible of the church. Using his pulpit and power, Athanasius attacked heresy until his death in 373.

Constantine did not completely consolidate power until 324, when he defeated the army of Licinius on the Bosphorus across from the Greek colony at Byzantium. He then built a new city in commemoration of his victory and called it Nova Roma; its seven hills reminded him of the seven hills of Rome. When Nova Roma was completed in 330, he dedicated the city and designated it as the Eastern capital of the empire, which eventually became known as Constantinople. Eusebius of Caesarea (c. 265–c. 340) became the church's leading historian and responded to the attacks of the Neoplatonist Porphyry (see below) by arguing that Plato had borrowed his truths from the Old Testament.[13] Eusebius became an advisor to the Emperor Constantine. Constantine's mother Helen traveled to the Holy Land to give thanks and commissioned the building of the Church of the Nativity over the spot where Jesus was supposedly born. Later claiming that she found the true cross from the crucifixion, she replaced Hadrian's temple to Venus with the Church of the Holy Sepulchre. Constantine was baptized into the church on his deathbed in 337.

Christian victories continued when the public practice of paganism was abolished in 342. That did a great deal to support Christianity in the empire,[14] and it suffered only a brief setback under Julian "the Apostate," a nephew of Constantine and a Neoplatonist, who ruled from 360 to 363 and tried to reestablish paganism as the official religion of the empire. Julian's death in battle was attributed to his anti-Christian stance. Many believed that God had punished him. The church reached its zenith when orthodoxy was reestablished in the West and when Theodosius, who had vanquished the Goths, outlawed all other religions in the East.[15]

In the meantime, church leaders emerged who embraced classical rhetoric particularly in the face of heretical attacks. Let me focus on just four to make my point. They came from the same area; they studied with same teachers of rhetoric; and they became major leaders in theocracy of the Byzantine Empire. The region from which these men came was Cappadocia, now in the middle of Turkey. The city of Mazaca had been converted to Caesarea (not to be confused with several other cities by the same name in the Middle East). Caesarea was made the capital of Cappadocia, which also included the major cities of Nyssa and Antioch.

The first of the four is Basil of Nyssa (330–379), who recommended the study of Greek orators and used rhetoric to defend the Nicene Creed of Christian faith from his pulpit.[16] With his brother Gregory, he had studied rhetoric under the pagan Libanius of Antioch, who was a very famous orator in his own right. The brothers became Cappadocian priests; the Cappadocians became known for their attempt at marrying Christian and Greek philosophy, their defense of monasticism, and their support for the notion of the Holy Trinity, that God is three entities in one with Jesus and the Holy Spirit. Basil gathered followers such as Gregory of Nazianzus (see below) in Pontus to study theology and develop a consistent church catechism. There he declared that rhetoric should be clear and does not need to be polished with "euphony" or "sophistic vanities."[17] Around 365 he joined his brother back in Cappadocia to fight the Arian heresy using his skills as a debater. Because of this success, Basil was named the successor to Eusebius in Caesarea and began his administration of the church in 370, eventually becoming Basil the Great.

Basil's brother Gregory of Nyssa (335–395) made the case for God being an infinite entity whose essence *(ousia)* cannot be comprehended by humans. Since God cannot be understood, belief in God is a matter of faith not reason, and the belief is achieved by overcoming ignorance and embracing divine illumination. Thus, it is better to bring people to God through rhetoric, which can induce faith, than through reason, which is

Byzantine Empire, AD 300–400.

limited to dealing with truths in this world. Gregory taught rhetoric but became disillusioned with his students. So he turned to the priesthood and advocated using rhetoric and dialectic to reveal the mysteries of the church and explain them to others.[18]

His friend, Gregory of Nazianzus (also Nazianzen, 329–390), another Cappadocian, adapted sophistic epideictic to Christian preaching and defended the doctrine of the "Holy Trinity" until his death in 390.[19] The son of wealthy parents, Gregory was able to study rhetoric and philosophy not only close to home in Caesarea but also in Athens and Alexandria. In fact, on the way to Athens he had a religious experience when his ship was attacked by a storm. In Athens he befriended Basil and stayed there to teach rhetoric for a time. Then he returned to Nazianzus in Cappadocia in 361, where he was ordained and became a minister to the poor and sick. Ironically, one of his classmates from his days in Athens became the Emperor Julian, who, as we have seen, tried to restore the pagan faith. Gregory strongly opposed this effort, speaking against the emperor on many occasions. When the emperor was killed doing battle with the Persians, Gregory was among those who attributed the event to the hand of God. The new Emperor Jovian was pro-Christian, which allowed Gregory to turn his attention to combating the Arian heretics. While he was preaching in Anastasia, Arians burst into Gregory's church service and he was wounded in the ensuing mêlée. However, when Theodosius came to power and denounced the Arians in 380, he turned to Gregory and asked him to become Archbishop of Constantinople. Having the emperor's ear helped Gregory make his theology influential in the early church.[20] However, in the end, attacks by rivals forced Gregory to resign from his post and head home to retirement and a life of contemplation.

Born in Antioch, John Chrysostom (c. 347–407) proved that public speaking skills were essential to the dissemination of the word of God. Chrysostom, a name given him after his death, means "golden tongued." He was taught rhetoric by Libanius and then continued studies at the School of Antioch in theology. After memorizing the Bible, he was ordained first as a deacon and then as a priest. His homilies on the Bible proved very popular in Antioch. He then moved to Constantinople where he founded a number of hospitals for the poor and continued to be a popular preacher. In 398, he was named Archbishop of Constantinople. His humble ways and calls for reform in the church made him popular with the masses, but unpopular with church leaders, aristocrats, and government leaders. He railed against resurgent paganism and defended monastic life. He became even more controversial when he welcomed refugee priests trying to escape the iron rule of Archbishop Theophilus in Alexandria. These activities led to John being exiled in 403. However, the people of Constantinople protested by destroying parts of Hagia Sophia, the Church of Holy Wisdom built by Constantine II. And so the emperor recalled John to the city. However, when a statue of the empress was erected, John compared her to Herodias, the wife of Herod Antipas and the mother of Salome by her first husband, and believed by some to be the leader of a cult of witches. Thus, John was again banished from the city. He died shortly thereafter but was known as the greatest orator of his time.[21]

Thus, practicing leaders of the church were educated in rhetorical theory and for the most part supported it in the curriculum. Unfortunately, there were dissenters regarding its usefulness despite the success of Christian defenders and preachers. Cyprian (c. 200–258), who once taught rhetoric in Carthage, renounced oratory as a pagan practice. Reflecting the view of Socrates in the *Gorgias*, this former teacher of speech, and a convert to the church, said rhetoric was a tool of the ambitious. He became Bishop of Carthage, and his doctrine of divine grace greatly influenced Augustine. Arnobius the Elder, who became a Christian around 300, taught rhetoric in Sicca, Numidia. He contended that rhetoric was a "heathen" tool incapable of finding the truth.[22]

Arnobius' pupil, Lactantius Firmianus (c. 240–c. 320), converted from paganism and became known as the Christian Cicero, even though he wrote that oratory "trained young men not to virtue but altogether to cunning and wickedness." He warned that pre-Christian pagan writing was "sweets which contain poison" and reiterated Plato's claim that God's truth needs no ornamentation.[23] The Emperor Diocletian summoned Lactantius to teach rhetoric in Nicomedia, and later he taught Emperor Constantine's son, who himself became an emperor years after his teacher died. Lactantius was an ardent foe of the Epicureans because of their love of pleasure and earthly beauty. In 313 while advising Constantine, he wrote that God loved his human creations and like any father could become angry with his children if they strayed from loyalty to him.

A century later, Jerome (c. 347–c. 420) emerged as a major force in Christian thinking. He was fond of Cicero's works partly because of his training in Rome and his study of rhetoric. After his conversion, he sought converts in the Eastern empire and then withdrew into the desert to study and write. He was later ordained a priest in Antioch and then in 382 returned to Rome where he won the confidence of the pope and began to write the *Vulgate*, the Latin version of the Bible, which was officially adopted by the Catholic Church in the 1500s. To finish this massive undertaking, Jerome moved to Palestine where he founded two monasteries in Bethlehem, one for priests and one for nuns, and resided there for the rest of his life. In his works, he warned that rhetorical ornamentation was sinful; he called on preachers to produce lamentation rather than applause among their listeners.[24] He referred to rhetoric as a weapon of the pagans and called on Christians to rely on divine revelation for the truth.[25] In a famous dream, Jerome arrives at heaven's gates only to be accused of being an advocate of Cicero instead of Christ. Awaking from the dream, Jerome pledged never to read pagan works again.

During this time, the church shared a new threat with Rome, "barbarian" tribes,[26] who were encouraged by divisions among the empire's leaders. When Emperor Gratian was assassinated in 383, five years of turmoil was finally ended when Theodosius took power in 388. The Visigoths, who had embraced Arianism, attacked the territories of Theodosius, so he bribed them to go to Italy and mount attacks there. He also had around 7,000 civilians killed in the Hippodrome in Constantinople to stamp out heresy. In 391 he made Christianity the official religion of the empire, abolishing paganism. He empowered the Christian patriarch of Alexandria, Theophilos, to close the pagan temples there. In his zeal, the patriarch allowed the temples to be sacked, resulting in the destruction of the libraries in the Mouseion and Serapeum,[27] a tragedy that recalled the accidental burning of the Great Library of Alexandria during Julius Caesar's invasion of the city. When Theodosius died in 395, the Roman Empire was divided between the East and the West, which would eventually result in a division in the church between Roman Catholic and Greek Orthodox.

In the meantime, the barbarian invasions continued. England was divided between the Picts and Britons; what is now Denmark and its surrounding area was controlled by the Angles, Jutes, and Saxons; Gaul was divided into the kingdoms of the Franks, Burgundians, and Ostrogoths. The Spanish land mass was divided between the Sueves in the western parts and the Visigoths in the eastern half. It wouldn't be long before the Huns, holed up in what is now Russia, would force another wave of barbarian atrocities on Europe. In defense, the Christians stepped up their conversion of the barbarians. Rhetoric, as restored by Augustine (see below), was very instrumental in the propagation of the faith. St. Patrick began the process in Ireland even before the sack of Rome; Gregory the Great (see below) sent another Augustine to Britain to convert the Saxons. Several centuries later, the job was finished by Charlemagne, using war, gifts, and persuasion.[28]

In 409 the emperor in Rome was finding it so difficult to find recruits for the army that he allowed slaves to serve.[29] These ragtag groups were no match for Alaric, the king of the Visigoths. However, rather than kill the Romans, Alaric sacked their city in 410. It was the first violation of the city in 800 years. Augustine, then Bishop of Hippo, and Jerome, the gospel translator, were shocked. In response to the crisis, Augustine wrote his famous book *City of God*, in which he argued that Rome was the city of materialism that had been punished by God, and Christians should turn their attention to Heaven, the city of God. After the sack of Rome, the bishop of that city, Innocent I, who was pope from 402 to 417, gained more influence because the emperor had fled to Ravenna. Luckily for the church and what was left of the Western empire, Alaric caught a fever and died. Pope Innocent, not the emperor, directed Rome's reconstruction.

In 430 Pope Celestine consolidated the power of the pontiff and clarified the title of pope by declaring the "Apostolic Succession"—that the pope's power derives from Peter, who was declared the first pope by Jesus himself.[30] Next came the powerful rule of Pope Leo the Great (440–461). Emperor Valentinian III gave Leo jurisdiction over all bishops in the Western church, further consolidating the power of the pope. It was Leo who would negotiate with the threatening Huns (451) and Vandals (455), not the emperor. However another wave of barbarians finally did Rome in. On September 4, 476, the last emperor, Romulus Augustus, surrendered Rome to Odoacer, a German tribal general.

Meanwhile, the dominance of the church in the East was further strengthened by the building of great protective walls and Justinian's long reign (527–565); he was one of several emperors who took a hand in the operation of the church. He brought a sense of order to canon law since he had developed the codes of Roman law in 529. The church was now so much a part of the empire that it could afford to engage in controversies surrounding dogma that flared up in Alexandria, Rome, Antioch, and Constantinople. Its position was solidified when Justinian defeated the Vandals in 533, who then faded into oblivion. He sent General Belisarius to free Rome from the yoke of the German tribes. Belisarius succeeded in 541, making Justinian the first emperor to rule over a united Roman empire in over a century. Justinian rebuilt Hagia Sophia into the large domed church that is now a museum. In Justinian's time, the dome, at 107 feet high, covered four acres; built over other domes, it was the largest in the world. Justinian died at the age of 83 in 565, and the Roman Empire again divided between Roman (West) and Byzantium (East).

During this time, the success of the church in dealing with the barbarians was spectacular. For example, Clovis, the ruler of the Franks, was baptized into Christianity in 493 after his victory over the Alamans. His Carolingian line provides yet another example of the church's effectiveness at conversion. Clovis, as the new Constantine, was victorious over the Visigoths in 507, creating a new capital in Paris where he built the Church of the Holy Apostles. Another Carolingian, Charles Martel, held off the Islamic invasion with his victory at Poitiers in 732. In league with the papacy, Martel provided safe passage for Boniface to begin his conversion of northern and British tribes. Martel's son Pippin was eventually anointed king by the pope, after Pippin defeated the Merovingians for control of the Frankish tribes and the land mass of Gaul. Boniface attended the event to bless the new ruler. Pippin then sent Boniface to complete the conversion of the Franks. Boniface was eventually hacked to death by pirates and thereby became a martyr of the church, assuring his sainthood.

But why were these preachers so successful? Why by 600 were there over 300 monasteries and convents in Gaul and Italy alone? What did they say to convince barbarians to become Christians? First, the Christian notion of "divine right of kings," that is, one rules by God's will, was a strong incentive for tribal leaders to convert to Christianity. Being chosen to rule by God certainly added to their credibility and their subjects followed their lead. Second, the priests that came to these rulers offered them education and became their advisors, acts that made conversion easier to achieve. Third, Christian preachers obtained official permission to convert tribal sites to churches. After all, the church of Saint Clement, who succeeded Peter as pope, was built over a temple to Mithra, the pagan god. Fourth, church ceremonies were colorful and church architecture could be awe inspiring. These factors overwhelmed the drab paganism of the barbarians. Fifth, the preachers offered a panoply of saints, some of whom were admirably courageous martyrs, to replace the pagan gods and goddesses. Sixth, the preachers supplied a unified, universal catechism of rules and sacraments that were not difficult to obtain. These led to salvation and the promise of a place in Heaven, which many found irresistible. The preachers' influence often went beyond conversion to Christianity; for example, in 860, Bishop Cyril not only converted Moravia to Christianity, he created the Slavic language.

While his priests were converting barbarians, Pope Gregory the Great (590–604) was building on Leo the Great's legacy. Gregory was elected pope by acclamation against his will. Those who selected him were impressed by his sincerity, evidenced by his turning many Roman homes into monasteries. His noble Roman birth gave him access to administrative positions in the empire. As pope he defended the city, negotiated with the menacing Lombards, commissioned liturgical music, outlined the first *ars dictaminis* (art of formal letter writing, often "dictamen" in English),[31] practiced it with great skill, and reformed the calendar. As the ruler of Rome, he was able to extend the influence of the church. He told his bishops not to destroy the pagan temples, but, following the common practice, to convert them to churches. For example, the great Pantheon built by Caesar Augustus's best friend, Marcus Agrippa, and expanded with Hadrian's famous dome, became the church of St. Mary and the Martyrs during the papacy of Boniface IV around 609.

Perhaps no clearer sign of the church's power existed than on Christmas Day, 800, when Charlemagne was crowned by Pope Leo III before the altar of St. Peter's basilica in Rome.[32] The emperor would return to his courts in Tours and Aachen, where he would continue to promote a minor renaissance in scholarship inclusive of rhetoric. However, before we can examine that moment, I need to return to the story of the evolution of rhetoric during this Christian ascendancy.

THE AUGUSTINIAN TURN

As we have seen, the early Christians were not without their rivals nor were they immune to internal divisions. These theological disputes often required sophisticated rhetorical skills because the issues at hand were not a matter of material verification. One of the earliest dissenters from the standard church line was Marcion, who was born about AD 85. He was admired for promoting Christianity in Rome when it was terribly dangerous to do so. However, when he advanced his theory that Jesus was not the son of the Jewish God but the son of a great God of beneficence, he was condemned as a heretic. Marcion defended himself using arguments built on the Gospel of St. Luke.

Other Christians were attracted to Gnosticism, the belief that wisdom was the true source of salvation.[33] Their "heresy" argued that Jesus never materialized but was always a transcendent spirit, the *logos*. They gained a large following and were influential in promoting rhetorical skills in order to defend their theological positions. Polycarp tried to incorporate the Gospel of John into the church's liturgy because John had, in response to the Gnostics, famously claimed that Jesus was the *word made flesh*. At the same time, Polycarp spent a great deal of his time attacking the Gnostics because they viewed Jesus as the nonmaterial wisdom or reason of God.[34] Irenaeus (c. 125–202), one of the early church fathers from Lyon and a disciple of Polycarp, believed that *logos* was the voice of God.

For some, Gnosticism evolved into Manichaeanism. Founded in AD 300 by Mani, Manichaeanism equated God with light and Satan with its absence, darkness. Mani had a revelation in AD 242 while a youth, and began to preach in Persia. Shapur I, a King of Persia, banished Mani, who returned to his birthplace in Baghdad. He saw himself as the natural extension of Zoroaster, Jesus, and Buddha; his religion became popular despite his being persecuted across the Middle East and Asia. The teachings of Zoroaster, also a prophet of Persia, but who lived before 500 BC, were used to provide a foundation for Manichaeanism; beneath the supreme God, the universe was a battleground between good and evil spirits. For a time, Augustine would embrace Manichaeanism on his path of conversion to Christianity.[35]

Contending with the Christian apologists were many other philosophical schools. The credibility of the Neoplatonic School at Alexandria was extensive in part because the current cosmology had emphasized the One as the cause of celestial motion by a process of "emanation," and Plato had argued that his notion of ultimate good was the emanating force behind all perfect forms.[36] Further, the Ptolemies were Greeks and descendants of one of the generals Alexander left in charge of his empire after he died. Egypt was their prize possession and Cleopatra one of their most famous offspring. Members of the ruling class maintained the various schools at Alexandria in the Greek tradition and admired such Greek thinkers as Socrates and Plato.

Ammonius Saccas (175–250), who founded the Neoplatonic School at Alexandria, taught important future scholars such as Origen (see above). Saccas' followers, such as Plotinus (205–269) and his student Porphyry (234–305), retrieved Plato's incorporeal notions of form as a defense against the mystical philosophies and religions that were sweeping the empire as it began its decline. Plotinus, who sought to open the pathways between the "visible and invisible,"[37] brought his Platonic sensibilities to bear on questions of the sublime and beauty when he taught in Rome and won the favor of the Emperor Gallienus.

Porphyry, who collected Plotinus' writings, wrote *Against the Christians* from his teaching position in Athens.[38] He later wrote his own commentaries of some of Plato's dialogues. Another important Neoplatonist, Iamblichus (c. 245–c. 325), a student of Porphyry, taught in Syria and revived pagan mysteries and Pythagorean doctrines. He was also the teacher of Julian the Apostate (see above), who provided the strongest resistance to Christianity since Nero. Iamblichus wrote about the soul and the gods in non-Christian terms. He strengthened the Neoplatonists with a new curriculum that included the systematic study of Plato's dialogues.

Martianus Capella, a contemporary of Augustine and a North African as well, revealed the influence of Neoplatonism in his *On the Marriage of Mercury and Philology*, probably composed between 410 and 427.[39] The book contains a rather dry chapter on rhetoric, which is derived from Cicero; however, it endorsed an enduring medieval curriculum composed of the trivium (grammar, dialectic, and rhetoric) and the quadrivium (geometry, arithmetic, astronomy, and harmony). The allegorical description of rhetoric comes in Book V:

> Helmeted and crowned with royal majesty, she held ready for defense or attack weapons gleamed with the flash of lightning. Beneath her armor the vesture draped Romanwise about her shoulders glittered with various light of all figures, all schemes; and she was cinctured with precious colors for jewels. . . . For as a queen in control of things she has shown the power to move men whither she pleased, or whence, or to bow them to tears, to incite them to rage, to transform mien and feeling as well of cities as of embattled armies and hosts of people.[40]

By Capella's time it was common to refer to the uses of figures as "coloring" a speech. Capella's book was used in the training of mystics and was revived during the Carolingian Renaissance after 800 under the rule of Charlemagne.

Capella's pagan revival produced a strong reaction among Christian leaders. As we have seen, some conceived of rhetoric as serving a solely discursive function: bringing the word to the masses, explaining the scripture to the faithful, converting the heathen.[41] Ambrose (340–397), whose father had been prefect of Gaul, became a powerful Christian orator during this period and was made bishop of Milan in 374. Ambrose embraced the view of Eusebius that a church centered in Rome could wed Christianity to the empire. In 382 the Western Emperor Gratian brought Ambrose to Rome—reinforcing the strong link between church and state. Ambrose then wrote his *Duty of the Clergy (De officiis ministrorum)* based on Cicero's *De officiis*, which had been and would remain a standard text on civil practices. In its time, *Duty of the Clergy* engendered a growing ethical and Stoic movement in the church. Working hard to establish a method of allegorical interpretation, which undoubtedly influenced Augustine, Ambrose also had tremendous influence over Theodosius, emperor in the East, arguing that the emperor was *in*, not *over* the church. When Theodosius had thousands of heretics burned in the hippodrome (see below), Ambrose rushed to the palace and condemned the emperor to his face. The emperor recanted his sin. By some accounts, Theodosius actually died in Ambrose's arms; in any case, Ambrose's funeral oration for the emperor was greatly admired.

The lessons of Ambrose's life and writing were not lost on his most famous pupil, Augustine, particularly the notion of using Cicero's ethical system to build a Christian *ethos.* Although his mother Monica was a Christian, Augustine did not hear the call of Christ during his youth.[42] At first Augustine followed more closely in the footsteps of his pagan father, Patricius, who converted to Christianity only on his deathbed. Augustine enjoyed a pleasurable life in Thagaste (also Tagaste), a Berber community of the Roman Empire. His early training in rhetoric was conducted in Carthage where he took a mistress and fathered a son, Adeodatus. Augustine described himself as a "word merchant" *(venditor verborum).*

Cicero's *Hortensius* seems to have awakened a spiritual hunger in Augustine when he was nineteen, and he became entranced with Manichaeanism. To make a living, he took up the study of law while teaching rhetoric from ages twenty to thirty. In 374 he briefly returned to Thagaste to teach Latin literature and grammar, but in the same year he opened his own school in Carthage where the pay and students were better. By 383 Augustine found Carthage to be deficient in meeting his needs; he moved to Rome to open a school of rhetoric there. Augustine must have been both a genius and a great teacher because his stay in Rome was cut short in 384 when he was offered the municipal chair of rhetoric in Milan where he met Ambrose, his most important mentor. The chair in rhetoric was given to Augustine by Symmachus, a pagan who admired Augustine's speaking skills. By that time, Milan had become the residence of the Western emperor. During this time, Ambrose's sermons, along with the pleading of his mother, led Augustine to begin reading commentaries on Plato and Paul in his quest for truth.

Soon afterward, he heard an account of the life and conversion of Victorinus, which greatly moved him. Victorinus was a teaching Sophist from North Africa who converted to Christianity in his old age.[43] The priest Pontitianus told Augustine another story, the story of St. Anthony of Egypt, which convinced Augustine that it was time to clean up his life. One hot afternoon in the summer of 386 as he pondered his moral condition at his home with a friend, Augustine was overcome by emotion and began to weep uncontrollably. He ran into his garden and crouched under a fig tree "giving full vent to my tears." His mental anguish forced out the cry, "O Lord, how long? How long, O Lord! Will you stay angry forever?" Then he heard the voice of a child over the garden wall: "Take, read, take, read." He immediately opened the New Testament to the letter of Paul to the Romans, read it, and was converted. He retired from his professorship and began to contemplate and write including *De Manichaeis*, a denunciation of his former religion. The book became a text for those wishing to enter disputations with other religious figures.

Augustine was baptized into the church in 387 by Ambrose in Milan, on the condition that he give up his lover. So he sent her away and, with his son, went to a rural monastery to study theology. Eventually, he decided to return to his homeland, but before he could embark, his mother died in Italy, happy her son had converted to her faith.

He returned to Thagaste in 388, where he became a monk. He was ordained in 391 and established a monastery in Hippo near Carthage, where he lived, taught, and wrote. However, he was brought out of his isolation when the townspeople nominated him to be their priest; soon after, he was elevated to bishop. During his tenure, Augustine turned his immeasurable talents to advancing the church and argued that since it was a Christian's duty to spread the word of Jesus, it was also a Christian's duty to learn to speak well.[44] The seeds of Puritanism and intolerance born of his Manichaeanism were planted in some of Augustine's Christian teachings; he believed that "true education begins with physical abuse" *(per molestias eru dito).* In Augustine's time, it was not unusual to smack a student on the back of his head if he was not paying attention, or to rap his knuckles if he gave the wrong answer. On occasion Augustine

St. Augustine, Philippe de Champaigne. Note the illumination of truth, *veritas,* in the highest point of the painting.

demonstrated his own skills at rhetoric. For example, in 404 he debated an infamous Manichaean named Felix. Augustine was so overpowering that Felix converted to Christianity on the spot.

Augustine's writings reveal that he had several influences in addition to Ambrose for his double conversion: from Sophist to Platonist and then from Manichaean to Christian. From Plato, for example, he borrowed the notion of the soul; from St. Paul, he borrowed divine providence,[45] a concept that was later converted to predestination by some Protestant sects. I have already mentioned the impact of the story of Victorinus, but still more distant figures played an important part in shaping Augustine's rhetorical theory, which is prominently featured in his *De doctrina christiana (On Christian Education).* The book was completed only four years before his death, which occurred on August 24, 430, from a fever while Hippo was under siege by Vandals.[46]

The Influence of Cicero

As we have seen, Augustine admitted that it was Cicero's *Hortensius* that opened him not only to spirituality but to the study of language. Augustine was familiar with Jerome's teachings. Jerome's claim that Virgil, Cicero, Horace, and Plautus demonstrated better word choice than the writers of the Bible reinforced Augustine's admiration for pagan prose and poetry.[47] Jerome would work with Augustine to suppress heresy, but Augustine proved more liberal and tolerant than his more conservative friend. In any case, Augustine's love for Cicero and for language motivated his brilliant rescue of rhetoric from its condemnation as a product of paganism.

Augustine's task was difficult because Cicero believed in putting one's country before one's religion. Rhetoric rode on the back of civic politics to gain ascendance over philosophy in imperial Rome. Thus, rhetoric meant adjusting ever-changing subject matter to various audiences through invention and stylistic adaptation. In the patristic era, however, nationhood was not high in the pantheon of values. In fact, nationalism was subjugated to the will of the church, which served as a safe haven in the insecure, deadly Dark Ages that followed the sack of Rome in 410.

The spiritual revival provided a more unified public with which to work. Rhetoric would help those issuing the call of conscience to make their interpretations of scripture clearer and/or more attractive to their audiences. As we shall see, interpretation was very important to Augustine because it could correct the misjudgment human minds make about what they sense.[48] Thus, Augustine's reconstruction of Cicero involved designing rhetoric for religious, rather than civil, uses. He then illustrated Cicero's methods and tactics with passages from the Bible.

Augustine's most comprehensive statement on rhetorical theory appears in Book IV of *De doctrina christiana*, which is full of references to Cicero. *De doctrina*'s application of classical rhetorical terms to Christian sermonizing would not be duplicated until Alexander of Ashby wrote *On the Mode of Preaching (De artificios modo predicandi)* around 1220. What is borrowed from Cicero is quite clear. The necessity of practice and imitation was stressed in order to become an accomplished speaker. Augustine strongly endorsed the Roman teaching technique of *imitatio*, the teaching of eloquence through the reading, hearing, and speaking of paradigmatic models. Instead of recommending classical orators, he substituted church fathers. As he wrote, "[T]he rules of eloquence are found fully exemplified in the speech and discourses of the eloquent."[49] In this way students improved their pronunciation, expanded their vocabularies, and got a feel for words and oral composition.

For Augustine, eloquence was a *reflection* of the divine message; the interaction between subject matter and style is not a two-way street as it was for Cicero.[50] Augustine's next move was subtle: "[L]et us examine these kinds of style in the writings of those men who through their reading of the Scriptures have attained knowledge of the divine and saving truths."[51] Here he subordinated the pleasing style, which seeks glory for the speaker, to teaching and moving to reflect divine truth.[52] The priest was to obtain the divine message, translate it, and then stylize it for a specific audience. Paul is portrayed as a man whose eloquence is inspired by divine truth. He represents the model for Christian apologists, the defenders of the faith. However, once Christianity came to dominate the Roman Empire, spreading the faith was more important than defending it. Thus, Augustine abandoned the deliberative, epideictic, and forensic forms for a single genre, preaching, which is aimed at securing the "eternal welfare" of humans.[53] Eventually, this single form would become the *artes praedicandi* ("the art of preaching"; see last section of this chapter) of the Middle Ages, a rather rule-bound system.[54]

Augustine also called for a joining of hermeneutics (particularly allegorical interpretation) and rhetoric to help deal with the obscurity of Christian scripture for mass audiences.[55] He had sharpened his understanding of hermeneutics under the tutelage of Ambrose, who regularly helped Augustine understand difficult biblical passages by explaining what the figurative language meant.[56] Augustine attempted to lay open *(aperi-ret)* the text by removing its mystical veil. His examination of style shows how the technique worked. Quoting Cicero's *Orator* Augustine wrote, "An orator ought to speak in such a way as to instruct, to please, and to persuade. . . . It is necessary, therefore, that the sacred orator, when urging that something be done, should not only teach in order to instruct, and please in order to hold [attention], but also move in order to win." In *De doctrina* he borrowed the notion of three kinds of style (plain, *genus submissum;* middle, *genus moderatum;* and grand, *genus sublime)* from Cicero and converted them to three levels of style to be used to adapt the message for various purposes that would attract audiences. Cicero's grand style was used by Augustine to fascinate and please—to make the student or the audience obey the priest's suggestions and to convert those who resisted the faith. The middle style played on the will and was used to persuade, condemn, or praise. The plain or subdued style was used to instruct and prove. For example, if the audience needed to know something before it could be persuaded, then the plain style was used to instruct before the middle style was used to persuade, and the grand was used to convince.

A second major alteration in the classical tradition occurred when Augustine argued that the message was more important than the speaker and that the speaker was more important than the audience. At the opening of Book IV of *De doctrina*, he claimed, "There are two things upon which every treatment of the Scripture depends: the means of discovering what the thought may be, and the means of expressing what the thought is." Later in the book he wrote, "[T]here is a certain eloquence suitable to men especially worthy of the highest authority, and who are clearly inspired. With such eloquence our authors have spoken. No other is fitting to them, nor is theirs to others."[57] Augustine's theory is critical to what follows in the medieval period, for he has taken the first step to *linking style to position and authority:* "Wherefore, let us claim that our canonical writers and doctors possessed eloquence too as well as wisdom—eloquence of such a kind as was fitting to men of their character."[58] In other words, there is a correlation between language level, education, and ethos.

This assessment led Augustine to conclude that some people were incapable of understanding various kinds of subject matter: "There are some matters, which in their true force are not intelligible . . . no matter how great the eloquence, nor how extended nor how clear the speaker's explanation. Such matters should be put before a popular assembly either rarely . . . or not at all."[59] His reference to feedback from the audience reinforces this point: "But an assembly eager to learn generally shows by some movement whether it has understood, and until it does show this, the matter in hand ought to be presented in many different forms."[60] Thus, Augustine created a new relationship among style, message, speaker, and audience—one, which when corrupted by medieval scholastics (discussed below), would link various kinds of discourse to various audiences.

The Influence of Plato

If the message is the most important part of the communication triangle, then obtaining or discovering the message becomes the most important task of the orator. In fact, near the opening of *De doctrina*, Augustine distinguishes between the method of *discovery* of the divine truth, and the method of *delivering* or expressing the message.

Like many of the church leaders who preceded him, Augustine drew heavily on Plato in this regard. Augustine argued that the truth is otherworldly, comes only through divine revelation, and no preacher should speak without it. In his *Confessions*, Augustine claimed that the Neoplatonists taught him "to seek for a truth which was incorporeal."[61] That made him susceptible to the Christian notion of soul and converted him from his material ways. Augustine's transformation of Neoplatonic teachings changed the history and development of rhetorical theory.[62]

Augustine wrote that his mind turned to the spiritual and "his will was converted from its desire of world honors, wealth, and sense pleasures, to the love of humble Christian virtue, chastity, comparative poverty, and detachment from the world."[63] His zealous nature forced him, particularly in *De doctrina*, to subordinate Plato's truth to God's. This was not an easy task since in his earlier work, *City of God*, he had enhanced Plato's position by tracing his intellectual lineage from Pythagoras and Thales through Anaximenes, Anaxagoras, Archelaus, and Socrates. In *City of God*, Augustine used Platonism to condemn the sense-bound Epicureans and Stoics (see chapter 5), who placed supreme good under the control of the body; therefore, they placed their faith in personhood instead of God. Thus, according to Augustine, they came down on the side of the City of Babylon instead of the City of Jerusalem, a dialectic that reflected Augustine's Manichaean roots. Babylon became a metaphor for the earthly state (Rome), while Jerusalem became a metaphor for the church (Catholicism). In Babylon, they loved the material; in Jerusalem, they loved the spiritual. Augustine argued that Alaric's sack of Rome in 410 was God's punishment.[64] By the time he wrote *De doctrina*, the Neoplatonists, whom Augustine often engaged in debate, were to him no more than rhetoricians who lived for applause. Like actors, they placed the audience and their own egos before God and the truth.

To establish his new order, Augustine relied on the preaching and epistles of Paul to condemn the Neoplatonists for not understanding the importance of Jesus dwelling among us. Augustine's understanding of Plato was filtered through Paul and other Christian thinkers such as Clement and Origen.[65] Rhetoric was to be used to dispel the illusions of this world and clarify the meaning of God.[66] This tenet in Augustine's theory is reflected later in the work of Francis Bacon, who sought to dispel the "idols" of culture, and in the work of John Locke, who sought to bring the meaning of signs into conformance with sensed experience (see chapter 8).

Although Augustine believed in the importance of signs and in the accuracy of language, he also believed absolute meaning existed only in God. The ability to destroy illusions depends on the ability to see divinely inspired truth. To ready oneself for such inspiration, one needs to read and understand scripture, which requires an understanding of the art of biblical interpretation (hermeneutics). Such interpretation is a rhetorical process through which the reader/interpreter constructs a proper understanding of scripture for him/herself and eventually for the congregation. Interpretation is also to be guided by the tradition, mystery, and authority of the church.

After this preparation, which includes prayer and meditation, it is possible for the preacher to receive the truth from God. Augustine believed that the truth (as idea from God) is immutable and gives us standards by which we can assess the ideas of the world. Having glimpsed inspired beauty for example, we can judge whether one symphony is more beautiful than another. In other words, a belief in universal *truth* establishes universal standards that are not altered on the basis of such attributes as taste, race, or belief. Truth is beyond human reason—beyond human categories—but is objectively obtainable through intuition, which is the apperception of the truth by the mind that is prepared to receive it. This truth, according to Augustine, comes in the form of an idea, which becomes a source for themes for sermons.[67] Every *thing* is a sign of something God wishes us to discover. A material thing such as a mountain can be a sign of God's creation. This natural sign can be converted to a "conventional sign" in the process of naming or labeling—that is, signifying something. The natural sign, mountain, becomes the conventional sign "mountain" when we name it. This theory of signs becomes Augustine's "meta-rhetoric. In *De trinitate*, Augustine struggled to explain the link between the Word of God and words of humans:

> If anyone can understand how a word *(verbum)* can be, not only before it is spoken aloud but even before the images of its sounds are turned over in thought—this is the word that belongs to no language, that is, to none of what are called the languages of the nations, of which ours is Latin; if anyone, I say, can understand this, he can already see through this mirror and in this enigma some likeness of that Word of which it is said, "In the beginning was the Word." It is the thought *(cogitatio)* formed from the thing we know that is the word which we utter in the heart.[68]

So how does the preacher bridge the gap between the immutable ideas of God and the adaptation of them for the purpose of teaching an audience?

The solution for Augustine was to explore semiotics, the nature of signs and signification in language. The idea becomes thought, which is then symbolized in the brain. The symbolized thought is then converted into signs (literal and figurative use of words), which are written or spoken. This process requires those who would preach to master grammar, logic, and rhetoric. By placing rhetoric in his chain of interpretation, Augustine justified the teaching of it. Note that while rhetoric does not produce the truth, it is essential to preparing one to interpret scripture and crucial in the translation process from God to the preacher and from the preacher to the congregation.

Once transmitted, the sermon must be decoded by the receiver. The goal is an exact replication of the original thought. The process of decoding relies on recollection (again Platonic), which requires a good education in language arts. That is to say, the audience members need to be versed in grammar, logic, and rhetoric if they are to obtain (translate) the word of God. Once again the teaching of rhetoric was important to Augustine's goal. The decoded message modifies the understanding of receivers and alters their will. That in turn changes behavior and should lead to stronger belief or conversion. This model of the communication process has held up for years and is influential even today. It might be represented this way:

GOD (Ideal Truth)
Divinely illuminated Idea is symbolized in mind of the sender ⟶
the sender translates the Idea into signs ⟶
the signs are transmitted as the sermon ⟶
the receiver captures the signs ⟶
the signs are decoded into the Idea in mind of the receiver ⟶
the Idea changes the understanding of the receiver ⟶
the Idea influences the will ⟶
which results in enhanced belief or conversion.

Book I of *De doctrina* claims that the preacher must find and interpret meaning in scripture and then teach it to others. The teacher must make sure that the signs, those signifiers that cause the pupil to think of something beyond the sign itself, are accurate. As we have seen, Augustine's semiotic theory divides signs into "natural" *(signa naturalia)* and "conventional" *(signa data)*. Natural signs unintentionally make us aware of things beyond themselves: the bending of trees reveals the influence of wind; the radiating heat of a furnace reveals that something is burning inside. Animate beings use conventional signs to express their ideas, intentions, and feelings to other beings. The cat meows to indicate to its master that it is hungry.

Conventional signs are divided between those that are literal and those that are figurative. The literal sign conveys denotative meaning; it labels: the rose is red; it defines: cats have four legs, fur, and tails. The figurative sign conveys a meaning different from its denotation in order to advance understanding: she is as pretty as a rose; she is as clever as a cat. Misunderstanding results when the audience does not understand a sign or the sign is ambiguous or vague. In such a case one thing is incorrectly taken for another, or a false quality is attributed to something.

Like philosophers before and after him, Augustine realized that there is not a direct correlation between signs and what they signify. Many signs are ambiguous or vague, and this fact of language leads to miscommunication. This is particularly true of such abstract concepts as love, justice, and beauty. Thus, those who interpret scripture, preach, or teach need to be well versed in language and need to adapt signs to their audience's understanding. In this regard, figurative signs are more troublesome than literal ones because figurative signs are often culture-bound. Thus, when one preaches to a different culture, members of that culture may have difficulty understanding a preacher who uses figurative language. Augustine noted that signs are inherently correct, but they are validated only by common consent. Preachers need to take care to select signs appropriate for the listening audience.

Truth guides eloquence when one has been properly trained in the language arts. It allows the preacher to bring the message of God to the people in a way they can comprehend. In turn, education readies them to receive the word. Therefore, education in *language arts* is crucial to Christian preaching and learning. Yet, as we know, education became less available as civilization slid into the Dark Ages.[69] Thus, Augustine's dream of an educated populace open to conversion also faded. Conversion would have to be based on other factors—fear, ignorance, inspiration—as preachers sought to extend and reinforce the faith.

Another Platonic influence on Augustine's theory manifests itself in the dividing of humans into two classes. Just as the mind either pursues the material or the abstract, so too there are two kinds of persons: those who pursue materialism and those who seek the spiritual.[70] This Platonic division lies behind Augustine's dedication of Book II of *De doctrina* to intellectual cleansing. For example, he explained the appropriateness of *correctio* (admonition) for certain classes but not for others in a move that links kinds of discourse to kinds of audiences.[71] His dialogue *De magistro* (*On the Teacher*, 389) noted that because words do not always match the things to which they refer, one must transcend language by using recollection and illumination to refine interpretation.[72] In short, God guides one's use of words and provides prelinguistic thought.

Augustine's conception of the human mind mirrored Plato's arrangement of ideas: the lower the idea in the hierarchy the more likely it is to be an objective, material form; the higher the idea, the more likely it is to be an abstract form. Rocks, trees, and chairs are at the lower end, while love, truth, and beauty are at the higher end. Augustine extended this doctrine by arguing that the mind has lower and higher capacities that reflect the ability to conceive of objects at the lower end and abstract qualities at the higher end. This view carries over to the subject of speaking; speeches about objects are less important than speeches about abstract concepts, such as the soul and faith.

To summarize, Augustine believed that immutable truth is the product of divine illumination and recollection by one who has prepared oneself to receive it.[73] Rhetoric is used to translate this truth and adapt it to an audience. In terms of the speaker, this means that *ethos* flows from the reception and translation of truth and is to be used only in the service of God's word.[74] In terms of the audience, this means rhetoric can ready a congregation for the coming of the "Word" but it cannot provide the illumination itself; the receiver must be ready for it, and like that of the preacher, the preparation includes prayer, meditation, fasting, biblical study, church tradition, and language development.

The Influence of Jesus

Augustine's conception of style and audience may also have been the result of a close reading of Jesus' teaching methods. Augustine used biblical and early Christian writings as his examples in the teaching of rhetorical theory. He also wrote an extensive commentary of the gospel according to St. John and gave hundreds of sermons that explored the nuances of the New Testament. Thus, Augustine was familiar with Jesus' rhetoric in two ways: first, as a new convert to the church and a learned Christian scholar, and second, as a rhetorical theorist who admired Jesus' technique and used it to illustrate his own teaching of the principles of preaching. At numerous junctures, Augustine told his readers that they must speak as if they were the living Christ *(imitatio Christi)* and they were to live in the image of Christ *(imagines Christi)*. Augustine envisioned Christ in an intimate way; for example, "Our Lord God Himself wished to be called our neighbor."[75] Or, "The greatest reward is that we enjoy Him."[76] Like Jesus, Augustine believed in extemporaneous preaching.[77] Like Jesus, Augustine practiced obscurantism; he sought to make what one saw "through a glass darkly" into something clear. He sought to make his message inviting by mystifying it in an attractive style.[78] As he concluded *De doctrina*, Augustine praised teachers who embodied scripture the way Christ did.[79] And in doing so, he was a precursor to the existential definition of "commitment" (see chapter 9) in that he argued that *ethos* is living in accord with what you preach.[80] Finally, because Augustine performed close textual readings and hermeneutical analyses of Paul's letter, as is evident in Book IV of *De doctrina*, we can safely assume he did the same with Jesus' preaching. Thus, Augustine must have possessed an intimate knowledge of the teaching methods of Jesus, since Augustine was a teacher of teachers himself.

Four audiences are implied by Jesus' teachings: (1) those with faith, such as the apostles, who do not need parables to understand Jesus' message; (2) those who are educated but do not share Jesus' vision, such as Jewish leaders; Jesus believed dialectical discourse was better suited to dealing with this group; (3) the multitudes, for whom he spoke in parables; and (4) children, who are so pure that they need no preaching, but are instead an audience that proves divine grace exists.

Jesus' implied divisions of audience was perhaps a prologue to Augustine's argument that style needs to be suited to subject matter and to the medieval belief that discourse needs to be adjusted to the audience. Jesus' divisions of audience inspired the patristic tendency to use demonstration with believers, argumentation (dialectic) with the educated but heathen, and rhetoric with the masses.[81] In this way, Jesus may be responsible in part for the turn made in the medieval period to debase rhetoric and subjugate it to demonstration and dialectic. We have already reviewed Augustine's role in this change. He subordinated rhetoric to a translational, presentational, persuasive, and explanatory role. It is now time to turn to later medieval thinkers to see how they contributed to suppression of rhetorical theory.

THE MEDIEVAL PERIOD

Wedding his version of Platonism and Ciceronian theory with scripture, Augustine advanced a rhetorical theory to be used for teaching and converting while at the same time refuting the Neoplatonists. Augustine's theories significantly influenced such philosophers as Anselm, Hugh of St. Victor, Abelard, and Francis Bacon. I would argue that Augustine is the father of *scholasticism* and *humanism*, each having Augustinian foundations.[82] The scholastics were forward-looking philosophers who believed logic, mainly strict syllogistic demonstration, could provide the answers they were seeking.[83] For example, William of Sherwood and Peter of Spain attempted to reduce language to clear, unambiguous terms, a goal reflected later in the works of several philosophers, notably Francis Bacon and John Locke. The scholastics tended to be Neoplatonic and thus placed rhetoric beneath logic and reduced its importance. For example, in Alcinous' *Didaskalicon*, rhetoric was considered a "lesser mystery" and logic a "greater mystery."

The humanists had more faith in the past and in human imagination; like Augustine, they retrieved the scholars of antiquity to reinforce the current art forms they hoped to advance. As we shall see, they included such thinkers as Dante, Valla, and Vico. The humanists would reclaim ancient scholars who had a great appreciation for rhetoric.

Medieval scholastics who followed Augustine connected the various means of discovering truths with alternative modes of discourse employable in the persuasion of different classes of humans; that is, their "classes of men"—sometimes political divisions, sometimes defined by levels of intelligence—led to a corresponding hierarchy of discourse. Hugh of St. Victor (an Augustinian) and Thomas Aquinas (an Aristotelian rationalist) demonstrate the pervasiveness of this view across philosophy and time because they categorized their audience members the same way.[84] Rhetoric became identified with the ignorant; truth with logical demonstration to the learned. Many medieval rhetorical scholars focused on tropology, the analysis of biblical tropes and figures, and limited invention to the *stasis* system. Scholastic writers on rhetoric such as Cassiodorus, Martianus Capella, Sulpitius Victor, Boethius, and Isidore of Seville mainly imitated the Roman rules of rhetoric.[85]

Boethius (c. 480–524), whose father had been a consul of Rome, studied at the famous and long-lasting Academy started by Plato. He eventually became Master of Office in Rome and translated Aristotle's *Organon*, which he then combined with Cicero's *Topica*. This combination was sustained until the thirteenth century when new translations were made of Aristotle's works on logic. Because of Boethius' knowledge and use of the Greek skills at managing the state, he became the right-hand man of Theodoric, King of the Ostrogoths. Although he was imprisoned in Pavia and executed in 524 because of his defense of the Senate, the *Topics of Boethius (Topica Boettii)* enjoyed major popularity during the Middle Ages; it placed invention of arguments through topics under dialectic; rhetoric could sway an audience but only dialectic could decide an issue definitively. Dialectic is based on questioning and responses; rhetoric is steady communication. Dialectic proceeds with true syllogism; rhetoric uses enthymemes. Dialectic overcomes an opponent; rhetoric persuades judges. His study of Aristotle's work was important in keeping Aristotle's vision of logic, psychology, and physics alive for later scholars. In fact, Boethius' definition of a person is based on his study of Aristotle's doctrine of substance—a rational mind is found in the nature of individual substance. It was readily embraced by Aquinas.

Boethius' pupil, Cassiodorus Senator (c. 477–c. 565), mimics Cicero and Quintilian when he says rhetoric ought to be concerned with "the science of speaking well in civil questions" as opposed to dialectic, which "separates the truth from the false."[86] Cassiodorus' *Institutes* included rhetoric among the several liberal arts, which, as we have seen, were composed of the trivium on discourse (grammar, dialectic, and rhetoric) and the quadrivium on science (arithmetic, geometry, music, and astronomy). The *Institutes* was to provide a summary of what had been written before on each topic. Cassiodorus wrote a *Commentary on the Psalms* that argues that the Bible should be the basis of the curriculum. He was a devoted follower of Augustine's teachings. At the behest of Boethius, he became a speech writer for Emperor Theodoric; after Boethius' fall from grace, Cassiodorus took over as Master of Offices. When he retired, he took his library to an abbey at Vivarium where he began the practice of copying manuscripts to preserve knowledge. The practice quickly spread to other abbeys and monasteries and is responsible for the preservation of many important works from the classical period.

Sulpitius Victor limited rhetoric to civil questions and then divided it into questions of thesis and hypothesis. However, once it was limited to civil questions, rhetoric became a victim of a second subordination by these early scholars. Isidore, the Archbishop of Seville (c. 565–636), Saint Bede (673–735), an encyclopedist, and John Scotus (c. 810–c. 870), a scholastic, proved typical when they followed Boethius' lead and argued that rhetoric was inferior to logic.[87] Isidore's *Origines* set out a curriculum requiring one to study the seven liberal arts before one was permitted to study theology. Bede's *Book on Figures and Tropes* made him the first Englishman to write a rhetorical text. He used examples from scripture to demonstrate the various figures he defined. Scotus, an Irish-born scholar who taught in the Palatine School of Emperor Charles the Bold, relied heavily on Gregory of Nyssa and followed the Platonic line as refined by Augustine. True authority is "the truth found by the power of reason and handed on in writing by the Fathers for the use of posterity."[88] Thus, hermeneutics, the interpretive function of rhetoric that was so important to Augustine, is incorporated into dialectic by Scotus. By the time of Thierry of Chartres and Hugh of St. Victor (discussed below) rhetoric was conceived as only one of the eight divisions of logic![89]

The Rise of Islam

While Christian scholars believed they had the truth on their side and dominated thinking in Europe, a new religion emerged in the Saudi peninsula, which would eventually threaten Christian hegemony in Europe. It became the first challenge to Christianity in the postimperial period and would eventually play a role in the Renaissance that would follow centuries later.

The leader of this new religion was a powerful speaker named Muhammad (Mohammed), who had been orphaned and raised by his uncles. At 25 he married a wealthy woman, which allowed him to study at will. At the age of 40 he entered a cave in Mount Hira outside of Mecca and began to meditate and fast. His followers believe that the archangel Gabriel came to Muhammad with the Word of God. When he returned to preach in Mecca, he was at first spurned and then persecuted. He taught that Muslims were descended from Ibrahim's (Abraham's) illegitimate son Ishmael (Ismail), by the slave Hagar. When his wife died and he lost protection in 622, Muhammad and his followers fled to Yathrib, which is now Medina (City of the Prophet.) This event, known as the Hijrah (Hegira), allowed Muhammad to form a government, complete with a foreign secretary, secretary of defense, and head of the legislature. This was the beginning of the Muslim tradition of unifying church and state. Under Muhammad's leadership, Medina defeated Mecca in a civil war and

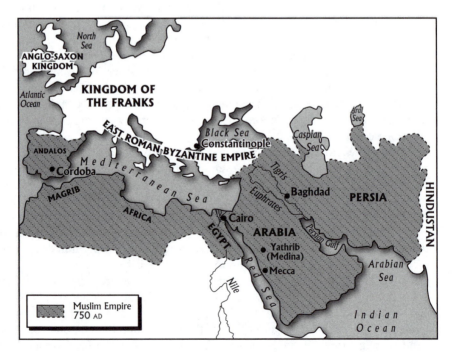

Muslim Empire, AD 750.

Muhammad's followers soon took control over the entire peninsula. Muhammad passed his word on to his followers who captured it in 114 *suras* (chapters), known as the Qur'an (Koran), the first prose work in the Arab language; it established the five pillars of Islam; "Islam" means submission to Allah.[90]

Muhammad's followers believe he is the messenger who brings the words of Allah to His people; these words provide enlightenment for the path to paradise.[91] In chapter 4, the Qur'an claims to be Allah's "speech." As to the speech of humans, the Qur'an advises that it be sound because you are judged by your words.[92] In fact, the "tone" of your voice can reveal your intentions.[93]

While the terms rhetoric and persuasion are not found in the Qur'an, it does contain advice regarding proper speech and argumentation. Argumentation is recognized as a form of self-defense,[94] and the term *ayat* means evidence, proofs, or lessons. Specifically, the book argues that "goodly words" take root like a good tree, and that evil words must be uprooted like a bad tree.[95] This uprooting can be seen as a form of refutation as can the calls in the Qur'an to remove the false, sinful, and incorrect in speech.[96]

Importantly, the five pillars can be seen as goals for an Islamic rhetoric. The first is acceptance of faith, which requires each member to live in harmony with nature and to obey and bear witness to the one God and accept Muhammad as his prophet: the Qur'an claims "there is no god but Allah." Those who submit to his will are known as Muslims. The name for their religion is Islam. According to the Qur'an, the transcendent Allah may grant will, knowledge, hearing, sight, and speech to humans. Allah, by divine will, chose not to know everything, thereby giving humans free will and freeing them from predestination. As in the book of Genesis, he also used language in his creation of the world.

The second pillar requires prayers five times a day, absolutions, and purification. These prayers are often in the form of rhetorical supplications. The third pillar requires alms giving as an expression of devotion and donations *(zakat)*. The fourth pillar requires fasting, particularly during the holy month of *Ramadan*. The fifth pillar requires that once in one's lifetime a pilgrimage *(hajj)* be made during the holy twelfth month of Islam to see the black stone of Kaaba.[97] Some scholars argue that a sixth pillar of Islam is the notion of the *jihad*, which refers to a struggle for the faith. *Jihad* is often taken to mean a holy war in the name of Allah. The Qur'an states, "O you who believe, fight the unbelievers who are near to you." Some Islamic scholars interpret this to mean that each community must provide a troop of fighters for either expansion or defense of the faith. Rhetoric was often used to motivate these fighters. However, *jihad* can mean a struggle to learn the rudiments of the religion, a struggle to become enlightened, or a struggle to lead a purer life.

Muhammad accepted Jesus[98] as a prophet and venerated Adam, Noah, Abraham, Moses, Jacob, and Job from the Old Testament. The Qur'an includes the six days of creation. However, Muhammad claimed that his preaching was corrective on both the Old and New Testaments. Instead of God punishing Adam and Eve by exiling them from the Garden of Eden, Islam teaches that God gave the world to Adam and Eve as a gift, thereby emphasizing nature and setting humans above angels in His hierarchy. While Jesus was right to argue that intent in one's heart and mind is more important than the effect of one's acts, thereby liberalizing Jewish laws, Muhammad believed that Jesus' followers went too far and that more rigor was needed among Muhammad's religious followers.

In 632 Muhammad died and his followers believe that he was transported in a dream to Jerusalem, where he ascended into heaven from the Temple Mount, which by 691 became the Dome of the Rock. He was succeeded by the four "rightly guided" caliphs who were his companions. Over time Muhammad's successors shifted the capital of the Islamic empire from Baghdad to Damascus and several other cities. They maintained the practice of removing icons from places of worship, a practice that spread to the Christians known as iconoclasts, because they destroyed statues (icons) to saints and the Virgin Mary. The Iconoclastic movement began in the Byzantine Empire, which bordered the Islamic states. As this Eastern empire was crumbling outside of the walls of Constantinople, Emperor Leo III came to Hagia Sophia and declared that God was opposed to Christians praying to icons and idols, as such behavior violated the First Commandment. Leo argued that Muslim victories were the result of their not having icons in their mosques. Iconoclasm spread like wildfire and was endorsed by Leo's son and successor, Constantine V, who became the most destructive iconoclast of all. The movement did not die out until 843.

By 732, the Islamic Empire stretched from India to Spain. In that year, Charles the Hammer (Martel) defeated the Muslim army at Poitiers, stopping its advance. Pope Gregory II (739–40) asked Martel for protection from further Islamic threats.

While Europe languished in the Dark Ages, Muslims created a learning center in Cairo that preserved classical texts, advanced theories of mathematics and astronomy, and created new theories of architecture. Another major Islamic center arose in Córdoba (in southern Spain) where another magnificent library was created. Baghdad was the third major center of activity. Smaller but important centers could be found in Toledo and Lisbon by 1100. Al-Bukhari (810–870) and others wrote consensual interpretations of the Qur'an. The writer al-Jahiz (776–868) of Basra developed stories with moralistic threads concerning an Islamic ethos; these often focused on the difference between love and friendship or endorsed sincerity while condemning pride, lying, and jealousy. There is a whole book dedicated to the difference between *Levity and Seriousness*. Following the ecological theme of Islam, he wrote a large *Book of Animals*. In Andalusia, Ibn Tufayl (c. 1105–1185) wrote about a boy who finds himself on a deserted island and must teach himself to reason to survive. He advances through many stages of enlightenment, each taking seven years. (Seven being a sacred number for Jews and Muslims alike because of the seven days of God's creation.) The boy learns that the spirit takes material form, but ultimately leads him back to Allah.

Islam used poetry and storytelling as a means of reinforcing values instead of relying on more direct means of persuasion. These methods of interpreting verse, often to overcome conflicts with discovered scientific fact, contributed to divergent leadership and subsects within Islam. The resulting divisions did not stop the spread of Islam. By 1053 there were only five Christian bishops left in North Africa, whereas at the time of Augustine's death there had been more than 500.

The Crusades resulted in crucial cruel clashes between Islamic and Christian cultures. While the First Crusade succeeded in "liberating" Jerusalem in 1099, and the second in 1146 reinforced some Christian positions, Saladin, a Kurdish warrior, reconquered Jerusalem in 1187. Soon after, the Mongol conquest of the thirteenth century changed Islam. The Mongols seized Persia and in 1258 took Baghdad, annihilating the Islamic population. However, the Mongols eventually converted to Islam, built great and elegant mosques, and transformed Islam into the Ottoman Empire. However, like the Christian theology, the Islamic one divided among various practices, prophets, and caliphs. "Followers of the way" were loyal to Abu Bakr, an Islamic leader after Muhammad. They compose the majority strain of Islam known as Sunni Muslims. The main body of the Ottoman Empire headquartered in Istanbul adopted the rule-bound, down-to-earth Sunni sect. The second largest strain, the Shiite Muslims, followed a cousin of one of the original four, Ali ibn Abi Talib, who Shiites believe should have been the legitimate heir to Muhammad. They commemorate the death of Husayn, the son of Ali, and the grandson of Muhammad. The Safavids, a Shia sect that first came to prominence in the Kurdish area, focused on bringing Islam to rural areas and developed centers of worship, not unlike Christian monasteries. Safavids became the Sufi Muslims, who endorse a mystical interpretation of the Qur'an. As their movement spread, Ismail declared himself their leader in Tabriz in 1501; he became the Shah in 1510 when he took over the revived Persian state. His expansionist tendency was checked with his defeat by a Sunni army in 1514. Egypt, which had resisted the Mongol takeover, developed its own version of Islam, as did several of the principalities across North Africa. Many of the sects, particularly the Sunni and the Shia, remain rivals to this day and over time have engaged in bloody clashes.

These disruptions did not prevent the further spread of Islam during the Renaissance. The victory over one of the last crusading armies at Varna in 1444 firmly established Ottoman control of Anatolia, now Turkey. Then the Eastern Byzantine Empire, with its capital at Constantinople, fell to Ottoman troops in 1453; they dubbed the city Istanbul, which had been the nickname for the road to Constantinople for centuries. After a campaign in the Adriatic, the Ottoman ruler Mehmet made a bargain with Venice, which paid tribute to him in exchange for trading rights.

However, these victories were counterbalanced by the expulsion of the Moors from Spain in 1492 by Ferdinand of Aragon and Isabella of Castile, who together had formed the joint Kingdom of Spain.[99] Nevertheless, the Ottoman Empire defeated a Persian army in 1514 and expanded into Yemen, Nubia, and the Sahara. It moved north into Eastern Europe, winning the battle of Mohacs in Hungary in 1526, and put Vienna under siege for two weeks in 1529. The Ottoman ruler took Cyprus from Venice in a series of bloody Pyrrhic battles that caused the West to coalesce around Venice. Led by Pope Pius V and Phillip II of Spain, a Holy League was formed that defeated the massive Ottoman fleet in the battle of Lepanto in 1571, finally checking Ottoman ambitions.[100] Since the Venetian galleys were the most instrumental in carrying artillery for the Christian forces, Venice was given much credit for the victory, though the fleet was commanded by Don John, the ruler of Austria, bastard son of the Holy Roman Emperor Charles V and, therefore, half-brother of King Phillip II of Spain.

Before that happened, however, Islam gave the world many learned men, not the least of which was Averröes (1126–1198), who wrote commentaries on the works of Aristotle, which convinced Thomas Aquinas (see below) that there was a difference between faith and reason. Averröes' writing, particularly his *Decisive Treatise*, was influential among Jewish and Christian leaders as well as among Muslims. Born in Córdoba, he spent time in Morocco as the favorite of one of the caliphs there. However, he fell out of favor when his philosophy contradicted some of the teachings of the Qur'an.

The prejudice against rhetoric as a tool for persuasion of the masses only (see above) was not limited to Christian scholars. Averröes claimed that there was a hierarchy of audiences, which he probably based on Aristotle's distinction of venues and kinds of syllogisms.[101] First came a particular class of respondents who are brought to assent through demonstration.[102] The subjects in this class are the brightest humans, who, unlike others, are capable of reconciling the various truths made available to them. The Qur'an provided truths upon which demonstrations could be built.[103] Second came the dialectical class, "who devote themselves to theoretical study" and are less able to apprehend pure truth. Finally came the rhetorical class about which Averröes said: "They ought to forbid demonstrative books to those who are not capable of understanding them."[104] He was eventually driven from his pulpit for saying such things.

Alcuin and Notker

While Averröes and his Jewish and Christian associates adhered to the common belief that rhetoric was for the uneducated, Alcuin (also known as Albinus, 730–804) proved the exception to this trend. He traveled from a monastery in York, England, where he had become a noted scholar and follower of the historian the Venerable Bede (see earlier in this chapter), to Rome in 781. The next year he was invited to head St. Martin's School for Charlemagne in Aachen on the Rhine River. He told Charlemagne:

> [I] must provide devout preachers for the new people, men who are honourable in
> their ways, well trained in the knowledge of holy faith, imbued with the teaching of
> the gospel, and in their preaching of the word of God close to the followers of the
> example of the holy apostles. . . . [P]eoples newly converted to the faith should be
> fed on softer teachings, like the milk that is given in infancy, lest by taking sterner
> teaching of the fragile mind should vomit out what it took in.[105]

He attempted to create a Christian Athens and spent most of the rest of his life in service of his emperor, who had come to power in 771.

Born in 742, Charlemagne was the oldest son of Pippin the Short, a direct descendent of Charles Martel, the man who stopped the Moors from invading Europe in 732. In 774, Charlemagne formed an alliance with the pope and captured Aquitaine. He was crowned Holy Roman Emperor by the pope on Christmas day, 800. In 804, Charlemagne added Saxony to his territories and eventually defeated the Danes. He never learned to write, but he could speak Frankish, Latin, and some Greek.

Charlemagne was fond of bringing noted scholars to his court at Aachen, near Cologne. None were more influential than Alcuin, who arrived in 782. He quickly set about to organize the palace school, build a library to match the one he left behind in York, and teach the most talented sons in the empire, rich or poor, noble or not. All of Charlemagne's family attended. Alcuin retired to the abbey of St. Martin in Tours in 796, only a few miles from his patron. He died in 804.

Alcuin served as a teaching theologian, an administrator of the empire, and a writer of, among other works, *Disputation on Rhetoric (Disputatio de rhetorica)*, completed in 794. This treatise is highly derivative of Cicero, but its dialogic form, which we first saw in the *Dialogues* of Plato, caused a mini-renaissance in rhetorical theory. The dialogue takes place between the king, who seeks to learn, and the teacher, who answers his questions. Even in retirement at the monastery, Alcuin continued to build

Realm of Charlemagne, AD 800.

the library of Charlemagne's Palatine School and to write handbooks on subjects ranging from logic to astronomy.

Although Charlemagne's governmental structure collapsed soon after his death, the Carolingian Renaissance in Europe continued for two centuries. One of the people who made that possible was Rabanus Maurus (776–856), a pupil of Alcuin who wrote an influential text on the duties of priests *(De institutione clericorum)*. Mixing his personal experience with what he learned from Alcuin about Cicero and Augustine, Rabanus devised a pragmatic program which included sermonizing[106] and speaking on civic matters.

This trend continued with Notker Labeo (950–1022) in his *New Rhetoric (Nova rhetorica)*, which focused on finding the arguments that would prove crucial to the rhetorical situation. These he called the "substance of the controversy," or the material of the speech. They were born out of the exigencies of the controversy, those things that created a need for speech. They could run from heroic deeds in need of praise to evil actions in need of condemnation to legislative matters requiring persuasion. Once the argumentative body was formed, rhetoric was employed again to clothe it. Like the Roman's *decorum*, Notker's fashioning "transforms" the material of the speech into something that is adapted to an audience and stylized to hold its attention. Thus, Notker attempted to reestablish a linkage between style and argument while at the same time making rhetorical terms available in the vernacular, an almost unheard-of practice at the time.

Hugh of St. Victor (1096–1141)

The dominant worldview of communication that persisted in Europe can be found in Hugh's *Didascalicon*, which demonstrates how the conception of audience came to dictate theory:[107]

> There are many persons whose nature has left them so poor in ability that they can hardly grasp with their intellect even easy things. . . . There is another sort of man

whom nature has enriched with the full measure of ability and to whom she shows an easy way to come to truth.[108]

Hugh matched types of discourse to levels of intelligence. His *Didascalicon* was so influential it has been called a "critical history of the arts in the middle ages."[109] It contained three books on the liberal arts of the trivium, three books on theology, and one book on meditation. More important, the work had a significant influence on Thomas Aquinas, who would also bury rhetoric under a religious philosophy, a philosophy sculpted with the syllogistic scalpel of Aristotle.[110]

Hugh was an Augustinian monk who ran the school at St. Victor outside of Paris. His dogmatic belief in Christian truth and the power of demonstration limited his need for rhetorical invention. Like many other medieval scholars, he accepted the Augustinian view that the mind was capable of lower objective conceptions and higher abstract conceptions. The poorer the mind, the more likely it was to be concerned with material things and survival. Rhetoric tended to be involved with these questions, whereas pure reason brought the mind to faith. Said Hugh, "Scripture . . . is the source par excellence . . . and theology . . . is the peak of philosophy and the perfection of truth."[111] He then worked out the implications of this view: "Grammar is the knowledge of how to speak without error; dialectic is clear-sighted argument which separates the true from the false; rhetoric is the discipline of persuading to every suitable thing."[112] If one were discoursing with other scholars, the subject matter, that is, truth or faith, would release you from the need for rhetoric.[113] This view held so much sway that Moses Maimonides (Moshe ben Maimon, 1135–1204), the encyclopedist Thierry of Chartres (c. 1100–c. 1150),[114] his pupil John of Salisbury (c. 1115–1180), and Peter Abelard (1079–1142) reduced discourse to "demonstration, dialectic, and sophistry [rhetoric]." This hierarchy of demonstration, dialectic, and rhetoric reflected the Scholastics' annoyance with Peripatetic Sophists and dialecticians from Italy who roamed Europe ridiculing the rules of logic.[115]

Salisbury developed his skill at dialectic under the tutelage of Abelard, who had mastered Aristotle's system of logic. Salisbury eventually became an aide to Thomas à Becket, the Archbishop of Canterbury, and later was appointed Bishop of Chartres. He relied on Augustine and Ambrose in his writing and embraced their hierarchical view of the mind. He also relied on Quintilian in his teaching.

Maimonides was the most respectful of Aristotle's notion of demonstration and dialectic as logic.[116] Maimonides had brought the culture of Muslim Andalusia to Egypt, along with his commentaries on Aristotle's logic. Maimonides was a great Jewish philosopher whose *Guide of the Perplexed*[117] (1190) and *Treatise on the Art of Logic* (1151) were aimed at establishing Aristotelian rationalism among his people to use in "speech about God." In this way he, too, was a forerunner to Thomas Aquinas who, like other Scholastics in the Augustinian tradition, employed Aristotle's rationalism to support a Platonic hierarchy of ideas. Aristotle's rhetoric was subjugated to the status of a handbook for the teaching of the weak minded; in fact, the Latin translation of Aristotle's *Rhetoric*, which Aquinas recommended, was read for its discussion of ethics, not rhetorical theory.

Aquinas (1225–1274)

Thomas Aquinas was born into influential nobility and was well educated as a youth at the monastery of Monte Cassino in Italy. By 1239, he was studying the works of Aristotle in Naples and thinking about becoming a Dominican monk. His brothers violently objected to this decision because the Benedictines, who were devoted to scholarship and liturgical worship, were the more prestigious order. (They would place twenty-four of their own on the throne of St. Peter by the middle of the fourteenth century.) To no avail, his brothers held him prisoner for fifteen months. Aquinas dishonored his family, at least according to them, by becoming a Dominican monk; the order was devoted more to preaching than to scholarship. He then studied under Albert the Great, an Aristotelian, in Paris and followed him to Cologne, Germany, where Aquinas became familiar with Aristotle's distinction between the "substance" of matter and its "accidents." The accidents of a thing are what it gives to the senses; its smell, taste, feel, sound, and color. But these can fool our perception if we don't look beneath its accidents and find the real substance of the thing. Aquinas would use Aristotle's theory to explain how a host at a Catholic mass could in substance be the body of Christ while its accidents made it seem to be merely bread.

He came back to Paris in 1252 to become a teacher at its famous university. Thus, he is one of many scholars associated with the rise of the University of Paris as a center of learning. We have already seen that during Charlemagne's time, the Palatine School at Aachen created a small renaissance. The Palatine School was one of the many incentives that brought scholars to France. Aside from schools at monasteries, there were palace schools and cathedral schools that taught the trivium and the quadrivium. Some also developed advanced degrees in medicine, theology, and law. The latter two subjects were important to the preservation of rhetoric since both required an intimate understanding of the art. For example, doctors of law who taught at these schools included rhetoric in their curriculum, proving themselves wiser than current law schools.

Universities eventually emerged from collections of colleges or schools; Bologna claims to have been the first in 1088. However, the city along the Seine was also found to be an attractive location; the school at St. Victor gained notoriety for this reason. The Cathedral School of Notre Dame soon became the most important congregating place for professors and students. From its various colleges and schools, the University of Paris officially emerged in 1215, one of the first modern universities in the world.[118] Students paid a fee, which allowed them to attend lectures by professors on the readings the students were assigned. They were later tested on these readings. Incoming freshmen were usually around fourteen and stayed at the university for seven or eight years to finish degrees that focused on the seven liberal arts—rhetoric, grammar, dialectic, mathematics, geometry, astronomy, and music. A master's degree required at least one more year of study; a doctorate could take a decade more.

Starting in 1257, Aquinas began studying theology at the University of Paris under Bonaventure, among others. In 1259 he left to teach at various universities in Italy and finally returned to the Dominican order in Rome. There he met William of Moerbeke, a leading translator of Aristotle; together they wrote a series of commentaries on Aristotle's works that became highly influential for centuries. His *Summa contra gentiles* was written during this time. He returned to the University of Paris in 1268 and there defended Aristotelianism against attacks by Augustinians and others. He relied on the works of Avicenna and Averröes, which got him in trouble with the powers that be. By this time, he was so rotund that the monks had to cut a semicircle out of his desk top so he could reach his pens.

A precursor to John Locke (see chapter 8), Aquinas argued that all knowledge began with sensation; our senses give us basic information, the building blocks of knowledge. However, we must always be careful to reveal the underlying substance of a phenomenon. He advocated an ascetic life to control and sharpen the senses and hence our sensed experiences. In 1272 he returned to Naples to start a new center and teach. The Dominican college, San Domenico Maggiore, housed Aquinas and his lecture hall. Aquinas' memory was said to be phenomenal; he was able to dictate four books at a time to his various scribes, waddling from one room to the next remembering where he had left off. As he was writing his *Summa theologica* (the sum of all knowledge in twenty-one volumes), he had a religious experience that strengthened his faith and caused him to stop writing. He died two years later and was canonized in 1323, an event that marked the triumph of his theology (free will) over Augustine's (predestination) in the church.

In his commentary on Aristotle's *Ethics*, Aquinas said that "truth is the end of speculation" and that "right reason" could lead to the truth.[119] For Aquinas, reason and revelation were parallel roads to the truth; revelation was not, as Augustine had taught, superior to reason. What role does rhetoric play in the process? A very limited one according to Aquinas:

> [S]peech alone is not sufficient . . . [good] habit is needed. . . . We see that persuasive speech can challenge and move liberal youths who are not slaves of vice and passion and who have noble habits inasmuch as they are disposed to truly virtuous operations. . . . But many men cannot be induced to virtue by speech because they do not heed to a sense of shame.[120]

Aquinas' *Summa contra gentiles* shows how Aristotelianism became wedded to the hierarchical modes of discourse.

> For happiness is the intellect's perfect operation. . . . Seeing that man's ultimate happiness does not consist in that knowledge of God where He is known by all or many in a vague kind of opinion, nor again in that knowledge of God whereby He is known in science through demonstration; nor in that knowledge whereby He is known through faith.[121]

Hierarchical truth, like hierarchical notions of audience, extended to discourse.[122] Aquinas believed rhetoric to be a lesser and lower category to logic. "[S]acred scripture . . . has no superior science over it . . . it argues on the basis of those truths held by revelation which an opponent admits. . . . [I]t appeals to received authoritative texts. . . . If, however, an opponent believes nothing that has been divinely revealed," then one must drop down to argumentation to refute the charges.[123] Discourse limited to evidence and arguments, then, is used against the educated infidel but not against those who have seen the divinely inspired truth. This position was directly descended from early church fathers who had to defend their faith against other philosophical schools. Paul's defense of Christianity before the philosophers on Mars Hill in Athens provides a good example of this form of defense.

While Paul seemed comfortable with rhetorical appeals, especially the use of the enthymeme, Aquinas was not:

> [O]ne who has no taste for the noble good . . . does not accept anything that is proposed in a speech inducing virtue. Hence it is impossible . . . for anyone to change a man by speech from what he holds by inveterate habit.[124]

Aquinas concluded that even reining in the passions of humans is beyond the power of rhetoric: "the man who lives according to his passions will not willingly listen to the words of an admonisher nor will he understand it in such a way as to judge the advice to be good." He thereby expunged *pathos* from the rhetorical province, further denuding it of inventive power.[125] Thus, even an Aristotelian who broke with the Augustinian tradition by endorsing free will was suspicious of rhetoric.

As the works of Aristotle began to emerge in new translations, they faced censorship from the church because in some cases they could be interpreted to contradict church doctrine.[126] For example, Aristotle's *On the Soul (De anima)* argued that the soul was to the body as form is to matter, which was unacceptable to the church. Aristotle's focus on the eternity of this world could be taken to be a denial of another world, a problem that did not arise in Plato's thinking. Seemingly, Aristotle had no place for divine illumination in his theory, which was crucial first to Plato and then to Augustine. However, scholastics at the University of Paris, particularly Aquinas, were able to explain away these difficulties and eventually succeeded in making Aristotelian logic and methods of inquiry the dominant form of thinking in philosophy. Because it was controlled by scholastics, the university became the hub of the movement that believed reason could lead to the truth.

Bacon (c. 1214–1292)

Roger Bacon, a Franciscan brother, was educated at Oxford and continued his studies in Paris in 1240, where he lectured on Aristotle's *Metaphysics*. In 1247 he returned to England and began to study other disciplines. The result was an encyclopedic work on moral philosophy, *Opus maius (Major Work)*, which relied heavily on Augustine and called for educational reform. Bacon believed that Aristotle's *Physics* and *Organon* were too categorical and rationalistic. Breaking with Aquinas, Bacon preferred a purer empiricism that built truth from observation and united religion and science. In fact, in his book *Opus tertium*, he argued that conclusions drawn by logic needed the support of sensed data. Bacon's scientific experimentation eventually led to his imprisonment.

Just as Averröes discriminated among humans by creating classes based on their "paths of assent" (varying means of becoming convinced of the truth) and just as Hugh of St. Victor and Aquinas claimed that levels of knowledge were the criteria by which classes of thinkers were identified, Bacon disparaged the importance of the investigative and inventive powers of rhetoric for discovering the locus of truth. Instead, he used an empirical approach to inform science.[127] Bacon's bias for science and education eroded his respect for the public:

> I could . . . set forth the simple and crude methods suited to the common run of unbelievers, but that is not worthwhile. For the vulgar is too imperfect, and therefore the argument of faith that the vulgar must have is crude and confused and unworthy of men. I wish therefore, to go higher and give an argument of which wise men must judge. For in every nation there are some wise men who are assiduous and apt to wisdom, who are open to arguments, so that once they have been informed, persuasion through them of the vulgar is made easier.[128]

However, Bacon shifts from Aquinas and mainline medieval thinkers on the uses of demonstration, dialectic, and rhetoric, and the process begins the revival of rhetoric. He confines demonstration to scientific discourse and dialectic and rhetoric to moral discourse: "In moral matters [rhetorical argument] so surpasses all demonstration that . . . one rhetorical argument has more strength than a thousand demonstrations."[129] A rhetorical argument can "sway the mind" but a demonstration is merely a presentation to be believed or rejected without persuasive power of its own. Opinion leaders, scientists, scholars, and theologians would rely on the most appropriate discourse, whether it be dialectic, rhetoric, or demonstration, to pursue, discuss, and present their discoveries.[130] He noted that rhetorical arguments were not known to the "run of arts students . . . because the books of Aristotle [on that subject had] only recently been translated."[131] Furthermore, the treatment of this topic by "Cicero is inadequate."[132] So Bacon recommended a close reading of Aristotle and Augustine on rhetoric for those who would sway humans to the good. He even spent time exploring how the three styles of rhetoric—the grand, middle, and plain, established by the Romans—could be used to draw people to God.[133] "[I]t is necessary that the orator take a teaching and color it, first one way, then another, according to the diversity of his hearers in terms of dignity, office, fortune, age, constitution, morals, knowledge, and all the other things pertaining to personal differences."[134]

Despite Bacon's plea, rhetoric shifted its emphasis in terms of theory development to *ars dictaminis (dictamen)*, the art of letter writing for the church,[135] a *decorum* for missives to popes, cardinals, bishops, priests, and monks, which competed with such other forms of medieval discourse as preaching *(ars praedicandi)* and poetry *(ars poetriae)*.

By Bacon's time, Oxford was a leading university in Europe. At the end of the thirteenth century, John Duns Scotus, another Franciscan, taught there and carried on the quest for proof of God's existence in nature. William of Ockham could be found on the campus in the early 1300s. However, he moved to the University of Paris, where he developed his famous "razor": the simplest explanation of phenomenon is usually the best. One should make as few assumptions as possible and eliminate irrelevant variables. In 1323, Ockham was charged with heresy because of his empirical approach to religion; however, King Ludwig of Bavaria afforded him protection. In Bavaria, Ockham laid the groundwork for a new theory of epistemology: we come to know things through various faculties of the mind. As we shall see, this theory would be expanded by Francis Bacon and John Locke a few centuries later.

Letter Writing

In a world where we are texting more and talking less, letter writing should become more important. No doubt students are aware of the importance of letters of recommendation from their professors and letters of application to graduate school. So as we examine the development of this art, I hope you'll see that it is more relevant than one might expect.

We can start with Julius Victor, a Roman rhetor, who wrote *Ars rhetorica* in the fourth century. It contained an appendix on letter writing called *De epistolis* (on epistles), which divided letters into two categories, official versus familiar. He further divides letters into those going to superiors, where he does not recommend humor, those going to equals, where he recommends being courteous, and those going to persons of lower rank, where he recommends being proud. He writes that letters should be like conversations. His terse comments on the practice of letter writing had been incorporated in the church by Augustine's time. Cassiodorus, the advisor to King Theodoric, left twelve books of letters behind; they are written in the Ciceronian four-part mode following his advice for organizing a speech. And as we have seen, Pope Gregory the Great was a famous practitioner of the art in the sixth century and became a model for teachers. The first manuals solely devoted to the art of letter writing were created in the fifth century for clerks who served the church and royalty. By the eleventh century, the art had become sophisticated. A difference arose between the French form, which stressed grammar and the grand style, and the Italian form, which called for a plain style to get business done.

Around 1050, the Benedictine Monk Alberic of the abbey at Monte Casino[136] wrote down the prescription for letters in his *Breviarium de dictamine*, a fairly precise praxis heavily reliant on the *Rhetorica ad Herennium* and Cicero's system of *dispositio* in his *De Inventione*.[137] Those who followed Alberic often divided letter writers into three camps: the humble, the middling, and the exalted. They then adjusted the rhetoric of letters to the communication dyad at play. For example, a humble priest to another humble priest; or a humble priest to middling monsignor; or a middling monsignor to an exalted archbishop and so forth.[138] Of these theorists, probably the most representative and most important was Hugh of Bologna.

Written around 1124, his *Rationes dictandi prosaice (Writing the Reason for the Decision)* sets out six pairs of relationships, from popes to friends. His formulation consists of four parts drawn from Cicero:

1. The salutation establishes the relationship and provides the proper title and greeting for the addressee. The *intitulatio* is the name of the sender and his titles; the *inscriptio* is the name, title, and attributes of the receiver.

2. The next part of the letter provides evidence of goodwill and is built out of the Roman *exordium*, which asks for goodwill on the part of the recipient and puts the recipient into the right frame of mind. This section could be broken down further by stating your achievements, praising the accomplishments of the recipient, and/or referring to friendly relations.

3. The narration should be an orderly and clear telling of your story, according to Hugh. The narration could be broken in the past (how my church came into being), the present (the church's windows have been blown out in a storm), and the future (if the windows are replaced, my flock will continue to have a place to pray).

4. The conclusion finally gets to the request (petition), which could consist of one of nine different types: supplicatory, didactic, menacing, exhortative, hortatory, admonitory, advisory, reproving, or direct.

Obviously, some of these are top-down letters, warning priests or subjects to behave, and others are bottom-up letters, begging for help. Hugh warned that if you could, you should communicate orally, because oral messages are easier to amend than written ones, and it is harder to turn someone down in person than it is to reject a written request. One could do worse than to rely on Hugh when composing e-mails in our current time.

His system became an often imitated model, for example in the *Rationes dictandi* of the Bolognese. In this popular formulation, the salutation was separated from introduction, which now gave more time to develop goodwill. The salutation prescribed the name of the recipient, who was subscribed at the end, and in both cases encapsulated in appropriate titles and adjectives. Thus, a letter from a priest to his bishop might begin "Your eminence" and end "Your holiness in Christ." It was also recommended that the recipient be "circumscribed" via appropriate mentions in the letter. Next, the sender should establish goodwill by evidencing humility, by flattering the receiver, by playing to the relationship with the receiver, and/or by relating to the circumstance at hand.[139] Once the receiver is in the proper state of mind, an "orderly account of the matter at hand" (narrative) is appropriate. Then the writer can safely move to the "petition" or request. And finally, the letter can move to its conclusion, which should be proportional to the whole of the letter. It should affirm the utility of the letter and play to the interest of the receiver.[140] In our time, fund-raising letters and letters of application to graduate school or for jobs follow the same format, or could be much improved if they did.

In the Middle Ages, *dictamen* became more flattering and baroque over time. French systems of letter writing are believed to have come out of Orleans and took on a humanistic cast. These systems were encapsulated in classes of readers and soon reduced to tropologies for the fashioning of petitions and other letters.[141] The job of rhetoric was to provide the tropes and figures that would illustrate and adorn the divine message and the scriptures. For this and other reasons, rhetoric was retained in the trivium with grammar and logic but would come limping into the Renaissance badly in need of resuscitation. The humanists would be the first to continue Bacon's revival of the art of rhetoric. For example, Petrarch (see chapter 7) discovered some of Cicero's letters and his theory of letter writing, which led to a refining of the style used in the medieval period. He also found a manuscript of Cicero's speech *Pro Archia* in a monastery in Lie'ge, Belgium. Lorenzo Valla (see chapter 7), a rival of Petrarch, also sought to purify liturgical letter writing that would become the subject of satire for Erasmus (see chapter 7), who advanced *dictamen* with new *topoi* and fuller generic considerations.[142]

Public Speaking in the Middle Ages

The controversy over the uses of rhetoric did not eliminate the practice of public address in the medieval era.[143] Obviously, a great many sermons were given, and after the Council of Tours of 813, many were delivered in the native tongue of the listeners. This endorsement of state languages would stir nationalistic desires that eventually undermined the authority of the church and contributed to the literature of the Renaissance.

Before that happened, the church itself continued to produce many public speakers of note. In 1095 Pope Urban II used rhetoric to promote a Crusade to liberate the Holy Land from the Sarazins and incidentally to expand the temporal power of the pope.[144] Peter the Hermit traveled on a mule and effectively echoed Pope Urban II's call. Though the pope had hoped to rally nobles to his cause and rid Europe of warring knights, Peter massed a citizens' army at Cologne that marched down the Rhine, plundered towns along the way for supplies, and destroyed Jewish quarters in many cities. Peter, who hailed from Amiens in France, swept his followers along with charismatic sermons. By the time the mob reached Hungary, they believed that Peter was a living saint. In advance of the nobles and knights, Peter's gang arrived in Constantinople in 1096, much to the horror of Byzantine Emperor Alexius I. He quickly sent them off to battle in Anatolia against the "infidels of Islam." Peter fired up his troops, who broke into two contingents.

The French took Nicaea, plundered it, and killed some of its women and children along with its defenders. The Germans took a Turkish castle nearby, which provoked a response from Sultan Arslan, who not only retook the castle but captured many of the Germans. He then turned his sights on the French and wiped most of them out. Peter survived all of this and retreated to Constantinople, where he awaited the arrival of the official Crusaders. His *ethos* remained strong enough for him to be selected as a negotiator with the Turks of Antioch. They rebuffed Peter, who quickly claimed to the Crusaders that he had a vision of where to find the lance that pierced Jesus' side. When a lance was found in the place Peter designated, it inspired the outnumbered Crusaders to victory over the Turks, and Peter's place in history was assured.

The mystic Bernard of Clairvaux was the chief speaker on behalf of the Second Crusade of 1146 that cost the nobility greatly in terms of money and lives.[145] This failure did not discourage Bernard, who immediately began propagandizing for another Crusade; civil war in France prevented the venture. However, Bernard's natural eloquence allowed him to end many small schisms in the church and to do battle with the redoubtable Peter Abelard (1079–1142), an early advocate of rationalism. Eventually, Bernard agreed to be chief prosecutor at Abelard's trial for heresy. He carried the day, and Abelard suffered imprisonment for his apostasy. By the end of his life, Bernard had raised the funds and labor for ninety-three Cistercian monasteries. His devotion to the Virgin Mary transformed the church. Soon almost every cathedral built after him was named for Mary, most notably Notre Dame in Paris.

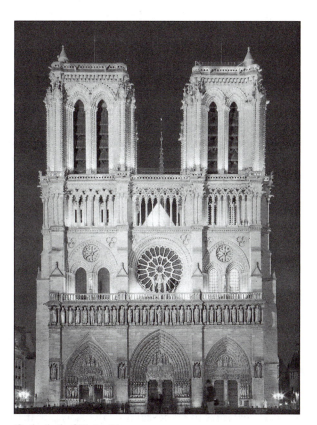

In the early 1200s, Anthony of Padua gave fiery but rational sermons that drew up to 30,000 people in an era marked by insecurity.[146] Shops would close, and women were known to wait in lines overnight when he came to speak in a town. Pope Gregory IX called Anthony "the Ark of the Testament." Religious

Cathedral of Notre Dame.

mystics such as Catherine die Iacopo di Benincasa (1347–1380), better known as Catherine of Siena, translated her mysticism into commentaries that are influential to this day in theological circles. And Joan of Arc was said to give inspirational speeches to her troops when she went into battle in 1430–31 on behalf of the Dauphine of France against the English.[147]

Out of these practices grew the art of preaching *(ars praedicandi)*. It is odd that long gaps would exist between the time Augustine provided his advice on preaching and the development of new manuals that would codify the practice and extend the theory. It was not until the 1200s that a "thematic" approach was provided and then an explosion of treatises appeared.[148] These treatises often reflected the divisions of audiences that we saw earlier based on their ability to comprehend material. And as he did with dictamen, Pope Gregory the Great provided a model for these treatises with his commentary of 591, *Pastoral Care (Cura pastoralis)*, a book on administering the church that includes the role of preaching. Gregory reminds his readers that the first pastors where inspired by the Holy Spirit, literally they were *in-spiritu*. His book is long on the substance of preaching and very short on the theory of preaching, on how to do it.

Preachers were starting down the "how to" road by the time Abbot Guibert (1053–1124) of Nogent laid out four ways to interpret scripture in *A Book About the Way a Sermon Ought to Be Given*. These included learning the history of the scripture, examining any allegorical and/or tropological features, and then determining its spiritual nature. If one were interpreting scripture on the crucifixion, one might put it into its historical perspective during the rule of Rome, then examine how it serves as an allegory for the forgiveness of human sin, then unpack any figures used in the description (Matthew, Mark, Luke, and John use different language and figures in their telling of the story), and finally relate the spiritual aspect of the crucifixion, for example, its transcendent nature. Guibert, like many of the other writers, expected preachers to have followed Augustine's way to the truth by completing extensive training in theology, including church tradition and mastery of scripture, and by meditating, fasting, and praying.

Following Guibert, in 1200 the Cistercian brother Alain de Lille wrote *On the Preacher's Art (De arte praedicatoria)*, which advanced the theory of preaching further. He expands Augustine's steps to the truth by including confession, prayer, receiving grace, analyzing scripture, overcoming doubt, interpreting scripture, and, only then, preaching. De Lille presents forty-seven topics for consideration for sermons such as "On Contempt of Self," "Against Gluttony," and "Perseverance." He refers to a great many church fathers and often quotes from them and scripture. He argues that if students for the priesthood understand examples, they will assimilate them; these students can then pass them on to their flock.

But the most valuable sections of the book are the preface and section one. There de Lille argues that preaching must rely on reason and authority and it must be understood as public address. It is not prophecy or doctrine; it is instruction in faith and morality. Preachers have an obligation to admonish their audiences to follow the virtuous path down here in this world and also to take their audiences to heavenly things. He explores these descending (worldly) virtues and the ascending heavenly things. De Lille sets the stage for the formal pattern of preaching with the following: begin by quoting scripture to establish a theme, then make a proposition that flows from the theme, then use the scripture to divide and/or study the proposition, then apply the scripture to current situations to amplify the proposition, and then call the flock to God by returning to the opening theme. Consistent with his intellectual approach, which would be a hallmark of early Puritan preaching, he rejects display and drama in the sermon. Instead, he endorses the use of humility to win over an audience.

Twenty years after the appearance of de Lille's book, hundreds of treatises were being written on preaching. Part of the reason resides in the rise of universities at Bologna, Paris, and eventually Oxford. In fact, young men could not obtain a theology degree unless they demonstrated that they could preach. Since the universities were turning out the preachers, they needed handbooks on preaching for their students.

Thomas of Salisbury's *Summa de arte praedicandi* is typical of this turn. His main contribution relates to developing a dialectic within the sermon between a theme and an antitheme as a method of invention and persuasion. He spends his time on such topics as prologues, narration, parabolas, similitude, falsehoods of preaching, memory, style, and delivery. He explores his subject matter by connecting with both the Roman sections of the oration and the five canons of Roman rhetorical theory. He concludes the first part of his text by arguing that preaching should announce and instruct on virtues and vices.

In the second part of his text, Thomas follows de Lille's model by suggesting that the preacher set out a theme derived from scripture and pursue it in the sermon, perhaps in narrative form. Like Augustine, Thomas argues that God's words, not the words of the preacher, should be preeminent. However, preachers must understand that they will need to be both direct and subtle if they are to achieve their end. Talented preachers can render their audiences attentive, docile (that is, passive listeners), and well disposed. In terms of organization, Thomas suggests opening with a prayer for divine guidance. He then changes the prologue to a pro-theme. Only then does he introduce the quotation of scripture that is to serve the theme. At this juncture, the audience needs a preview of what is to come (the Roman division). Then the theme is developed following that organizational structure, with sub-themes included and developed with scripture and supported by authority. The conclusion summarizes and makes the main theme clear.

The arts of letter writing and preaching kept rhetoric in the curriculum of the universities and readied it for its reblossoming in the Renaissance. For example, Robert of Basevorn wrote on the *Forms of Preaching* in 1322 and provided a full compendium of advice drawn together in one book. One of the more interesting sections of his book talks about frightening the audience with some terrifying tale or example, a tactic used by many evangelical preachers in America during the Great Awakening preceding the American revolution. By 1372 theorists such as Jean de Chalons had expanded the organization of the sermon to fourteen parts, running from the statement of the theme to the conclusion with stops along the way on such topics as dilation of material and digressions.

By this time, trade routes were open to the East; cities were becoming wealthy. The contact with the Islamic world spurred by several Crusades had brought new knowledge to the West, especially in terms of mathematics, astronomy, and other sciences. The Arabic mathematical system produced new efficiencies in the marketplace.

Mechanical clocks began to spring up in town centers, giving people an earthly sense of time. Medieval schoolmen enhanced the use of capitalization, punctuation, outlining, and alphabetization to improve reading and writing skills. However, the fourteenth-century Renaissance was cut short by the bubonic plague, which by 1350 had wiped out one-third of the population of Europe.

CONCLUSION

The story of rhetoric from the fall of Rome to the end of the Dark Ages is a long one. The journey begins with the ascension of the Catholic Church in the Roman Empire; Christianity becomes Rome's official religion and banishes paganism. The journey continues with Augustine who, in retrieving rhetorical theory from such pagans as Cicero and Plato, synthesized it for use in a "higher purpose." That purpose was preaching to save the souls of Christians, as opposed to Cicero's use of rhetoric to build civic virtue. Augustine separated truth from rhetoric when he claimed that truth came from divine intuition, for which one must be prepared through Bible study, meditation, prayer, fasting, the sacraments, and church authority. Divine illumination lies beyond corporeal (physical) sightings through the eyes of the body, beyond the imaginative thinking in pictures, and even beyond the purely mental and imageless consciousness of thought. Only the intelligence inspired by spiritual light in the soul can enable humans to see eternal truths.

Augustine provided one of the first semiotic studies of language; he closely examined how ideas, when converted to signs, convey meaning to others. Augustine's understanding of audience, at least partially influenced by his close reading of the New Testament, led him to adjust style to audience. Many medieval scholastics went a giant step farther when they argued that different types of discourse should be used with different types of audiences: demonstration for scholars of the same faith, dialectic for the intelligent of other faiths, and rhetoric for the masses. While those who participated in government, such as Alcuin and Roger Bacon, resisted this trend, it dominated the thinking of leading philosophers such as Hugh of St. Victor, Averröes, and Aquinas.

It was not a far step from the scholastic subjugation of rhetoric to the Ramist position (which we will examine in the next chapter) that invention and arrangement were provinces of logic, and rhetoric should concern only delivery *(actio)* and style *(elocutio)*. The tragedy of this sublimation of rhetoric is that it removed the art from its relation to the contingent nature of humanity. Religion would provide for the flock; theology would provide for the shepherds. Generally speaking, the church argued that other than preaching, there was no need for an authentic, serious rhetoric for its congregations in such a world. The danger of this position is that the church did not have all of the truth, and there was significant division among church authorities on many theological issues.

Furthermore, the suppression of scientific advances and independent thought, and the persecution of those who disagreed with the church, reveal the lengths to which those who embrace a dogmatic worldview will go. It is not surprising then that when rhetoric, like other arts, was restored during the Renaissance, it became a powerful tool in the hands of those opposed to one universal church.

Study Questions

1. What is the importance of early Christian apologists to the development of rhetorical theory in the patristic period?

2. Why did some early church leaders condemn rhetoric?

3. What role did popes play in the ascendancy of Christianity and in the crumbling Roman Empire?

4. How did the Neoplatonic School at Alexandria contribute to the development of rhetorical theory under Augustine?

5. Who else influenced Augustine's theory of rhetoric?

6. What is the relationship between the truth and rhetoric according to Augustine? What role can rhetoric play in the discovery of intuitive truth?

7. In what significant ways does Augustine's rhetorical theory differ from Cicero's?

8. Using Augustine's chain of interpretation from idea to decoded sign, explain how an idea can lead to a conversion experience.

9. Augustine implies that style should be adjusted to audience and subject matter. How did those who followed Augustine justify using one form of discourse over another for various audiences?

10. What is the relevance of each of the following to the development of rhetorical theory? Boethius, Cassiodorus, Alcuin, Notker, Roger Bacon.

11. In what ways did the following undermine the integrity of rhetoric as an academic discipline? Hugh of St. Victor, Thomas Aquinas, Averröes.

12. Using the theory of *dictamen*, compose a letter to your instructor asking for a favor.

Notes

[1] Sir William Peterson, trans. (Cambridge: Harvard U. Press, 1946), p. 127. See also P. A. Duhamel, "The Function of Rhetoric as Effective Expression," *Journal of the History of Ideas*, 10 (1949): 344–56.

[2] The point has been made by Lawrence W. Rosenfield, "Central Park and the Celebration of Civic Virtue," in *American Rhetoric: Context and Criticism* (Carbondale: Southern Illinois U. Press, 1989), pp. 237, 249–55. Tiberius, like the other Caesars, had studied rhetoric. He was so confident in his talents that at age nine he was able to deliver the eulogy at his father's funeral.

[3] When known as Gaius Octavius, the adopted nephew of Julius Caesar, Augustus had joined with Marc Antony and Marcus Lepidus to defeat the assassins of Caesar at Philippi. After the death of Lepidus, he ruled with Antony until Cleopatra encouraged Antony to enter into a civil war with Augustus. He defeated Antony at Actium and ruled for another forty-four years as Caesar Augustus, for whom the eighth month of the year is named.

[4] Suetonius, *The Twelve Caesars*, Robert Graves, trans. (Baltimore: Penguin Books, 1957), p. 100. Evidently, Augustus was an accomplished speaker who preferred to read from a text lest he forget his exact words.

[5] Ibid., p. 144.

[6] Other emperors, including Titus and Domitian, were fond of these contests and also were well trained in rhetoric themselves. Suetonius, pp. 293, 302.

[7] Justin was a Platonist who identified with Socrates and may have influenced the work of Augustine. During his life, Justin attacked Simon Magus and Marcion for their heresies.

[8] It should be noted that in the early church women enjoyed higher status than they did in Greco-Roman culture in general. This welcoming environment may account for the number of women who converted to Christianity in its early days; they surpassed the number of male converts. There were also plagues

that might lead people to be more open to spirituality. For example, during the reign of Marcus Aurelius, the empire endured a 15-year epidemic that probably killed one-quarter of the population.

⁹ Origen was always looking for layers of meaning. See his *On First Principles*.

¹⁰ The system of co-emperors was created to govern the vast empire that had reached its peak under Trajan in the early second century.

¹¹ Galerius was appointed Eastern emperor by Diocletian in 293.

¹² The Nicaean Creed is the profession of faith of the early Catholic Church. It remains part of the service to this day. The settling of Arian heresy in favor of the West eventually led to the great schism in the church in 1054. The Eastern position was affirmed when Constantine's son Constantius came down on the side of the Arians, who believed that Jesus was a separate and lesser god than God, as opposed to the mainline position that Jesus was one with God.

¹³ Augustine would be more subtle in the development of this thesis. It prevailed in the writings of church leaders for centuries until it was finally refuted by Thomas Aquinas.

¹⁴ See, for example, Lactantius, *Divine Institutes (Institutiones divinae),* Sister Mary Francis McDonald, trans. (Washington, DC: Catholic U. Press, 1964), III.i; Arnobius, *Against the Heathen* (Whitefish, MT: Kessinger Publishing, 2010), V.i.58.

¹⁵ In fact, in 393 he condemned the Olympic games as a pagan spectacle. They had existed since 776 BC and would not reappear until 1896.

¹⁶ We have some of his sermons focusing on the six days of creation and imploring young men to become priests. Basil, the Greek version of Saint Nicholas, brings gifts to children on January 1st.

¹⁷ A. S. Pease, "The Attitude of Jerome Toward Pagan Literature," *Transactions and Proceedings of the American Philological Association,* 50 (1919): 150–67.

¹⁸ Gregory of Nyssa in his *De hominis opificio* argued that ideal humans in the heavenly world had no sex. Humans in this world were created from the ideal in the divine *Logos*. His theory was influential and reasserted in the Middle Ages by such leading thinkers as John Scotus. Cappadocia was the former Caesarea where Gregory and his brother were born. As bishops they were assigned to Nyssa.

¹⁹ We have 44 orations written by Gregory of Nazianzus.

²⁰ Gregory led the Ecumenical Council of 381. Emperor Constantine VII brought Gregory's remains to Constantinople in 950, but they were later removed to Rome by Crusaders. Pope Benedict XVI returned his bones to Constantinople in 2008.

²¹ We have many of John's sermons on the stories in the Bible, and sixty-four of his policy speeches dealing with everything from public affairs to education. However, we should note that starting in Antioch, many of his sermons were aimed at Jews who were trying to convert Christians back to Judaism. As in Alexandria, these anti-Semitic rants in Constantinople resulted in the persecution of the Jews. Crusaders took John's bones from Constantinople in 1204. Pope John Paul II returned his bones to Istanbul in 2004.

²² Arnobius.

²³ Lactantius.

²⁴ Jerome, *Selected Letters*, F. A. Wright, trans. (Cambridge: Harvard U. Press, 1954), LII.8.

²⁵ G. L. Ellspermann, *The Attitude of the Early Christian Latin Writers Toward Pagan Literature and Learning*, Catholic University of America Patristic Studies, v. 82 (Washington, DC: Catholic U. Press, 1949), pp. 159–60.

²⁶ The word "barbarian" is derived from the fact that the citizens of the Byzantine Empire only heard "bar bar" when the invaders tried to speak to them.

²⁷ The Mouseion and Serapeum were buildings that housed libraries, study halls, and research centers for science and the liberal arts.

²⁸ See Richard Fletcher, *The Barbarian Conversion: From Paganism to Christianity* (New York: Henry Holt, 1998).

²⁹ At one point over 50 percent of the population of Rome were slaves. See R. H. Barrow, *Slavery in the Roman Empire* (New York: Barnes and Noble, 1996), pp. 20–21.

³⁰ The first person to declare himself pope or father was Siricus, the Bishop of Rome, in 384. It was only in 1869 that Pope Pius IX declared that the pope was "infallible" on church matters—when the pope speaks *ex cathedra*, that is for the church.

³¹ It was based on the *Epistolimaioi characteres*, which outlined over 40 types of bureaucratic letters.

³² Leo III had come under attack from hostile forces in Italy. He fled Rome and crossed the Alps seeking Charlemagne's protection.

³³ Carl Jung (see chapter 10), the twentieth-century psychologist who studied with Freud, wrote a book on Gnosticism that provided a foundation for some of his thinking on the collective unconscious. He compared Gnosticism to Buddhist teaching since both advocate an awakening through inner enlightenment.

[34] Iranaeus, *Against Heresies, Book I,* The Gnostic Society Library, http://www.gnosis.org/library/advh1.htm (accessed July 12, 2012). This book is also included in *Ante-Nicene Fathers,* vol. I, Alexander Roberts, ed. (Peabody, MA: Hendrickson Publishers, 1994).

[35] That Gnosticism through Manichaeanism affected Augustine can hardly be denied. This passage from the Gnostic *Gospel of Truth* provides a case in point:

> If one has knowledge [*gnosis*], he is from above. If he is called to hear, he answers, and he turns to him who is calling him and ascends to him. And he knows in what manner he is called. Having knowledge, he does the will of the one who called him, he wishes to be pleasing to him. . . . He who is to have knowledge in this manner knows where he comes from and where he is going. He knows as one who has become drunk has turned away from his drunkenness and has returned to himself, has set right what are his own.

> James M. Robinson, ed., *The Nag Hammadi Library in English* (New York: Harper Collins, 1990), p. 2.

[36] This notion strongly reflects Plato's *Timaeus.*

[37] Plotinus was an admirer of Parmenides and often referred to "the One" as the grounding of all existence.

[38] Augustine's attack on Porphyry is sharpest in Book X of the *City of God.* Porphyry attempted to prove that the Book of Daniel had been written much later than the church claimed.

[39] See Michael Leff, "St. Augustine and Martianus Capella: Continuity and Change in Fifth Century Latin Rhetorical Theory," *Communication Quarterly,* 24 (1976): 2–9. The book, though highly derivative, became popular in the Middle Ages; it endorsed the trivium and the quadrivium, which came to dominate the medieval curriculum.

[40] Capella, *De nuptiis V.* 425, Charles Sears Baldwin, trans., *Medieval Rhetoric and Poetic* (New York: Macmillan, 1928), pp. 93–94.

[41] See Harry Caplan, "Classical Rhetoric and the Medieval Theory of Preaching," in *Historical Studies of Rhetoric and Rhetoricians,* Raymond F. Howes, ed. (Ithaca: Cornell U. Press, 1961).

[42] Ambrose, Monica, and Augustine were canonized as saints by the Catholic Church. He should not be confused with Augustine of Canterbury, from which the Anglican office of Archbishop of Canterbury is claimed to be directly descended. Augustine of Canterbury had been sent to England in 596 and 601 from Rome by Pope Gregory the Great (590–604).

[43] Augustine, *Confessions,* William Watts, trans. (Cambridge: Harvard U. Press, 1912), VIII.v.

[44] See Matthew, 18:20.

[45] This theory is spelled out in Augustine's *De ordine.*

[46] The first three books of *De doctrina christiana* were written in 396.

[47] See Letter 22, *Letters of St. Jerome,* Charles C. Mierow, trans. (London, 1963), 1:134–79. See also Brenda Deen Schildgen, "Petrarch's Defense of Secular Letters, the Latin Fathers, and Ancient Roman Rhetoric," *Rhetorica,* 11 (1993): 124.

[48] In a wonderful phrase that may have inspired Descartes, Augustine wrote *"Si fallor, sum":* Because I can be deceived, I exist. In *De libero arbitrio,* II.iii.7.

[49] *De doctrina,* IV.iii.4.

[50] Ibid., 10.

[51] Ibid., IV.xxi.45.

[52] See Adolf Primmer, "The Function of the *genera dicendi* in *De doctrina christiana* 4," in Duane W. H. Arnold and Pamela Bright, eds. *De doctrina christiana: A Classic of Western Culture* (Notre Dame, IN: U. of Notre Dame Press, 1995), pp. 47–67.

[53] Ibid., 35.

[54] See, for example, the writing of Honorius of Autun or Wibald of Corbai in the twelfth century.

[55] See, for example, the book he wrote in 419 called *De trinitate,* XV.ix.16.

[56] See *Confessions,* VI.iv.

[57] *De doctrina,* IV.vi.9.

[58] Ibid., IV.vii.21.

[59] Ibid., IV.ix.23.

[60] Ibid., IV.x.25.

[61] *Confessions,* VII ix.20.

[62] Peter Brown, *Augustine of Hippo* (Berkeley: U. of California Press, 1967), p. 95.

[63] As quoted in Vernon J. Bourke, *Augustine's Quest for Wisdom: Life and Philosophy of the Bishop of Hippo* (Milwaukee, WI: Bruce Publishing Co., 1945), p. 40.

64 *De doctrina*, VIII.vii. Chapter iii of Book XIX also reveals the strong influence of Platonic thinking when Augustine discusses how the primary needs of the body are harnessed by virtue and intelligence. In chapter xi of Book VIII, he compares the opening of Genesis to the opening of Plato's *Timaeus*.

65 I do not mean to neglect Augustine's praise of Paul's use of *ornatus*. See, for example, chapters xi through xiv of Book IV of *De doctrina*.

66 James J. Murphy, "Saint Augustine and the Debate about Christian Rhetoric," *Quarterly Journal of Speech*, 46 (1960): 409.

67 The idea for Augustine was not subjective. It had an objective essence. See Frederick Copleston, *A History of Philosophy*, vol. II, part i (New York: Doubleday/Image Books, 1962), p. 75.

68 *De trinitate* XV.x.19ff. Stephen McKenna, trans. (Washington, DC: Catholic U. of America Press, 1963).

69 The slide into the Dark Ages can be seen in the attitude of the church toward scientific data. It is interesting to note that Parmenides, Plato, and Aristotle among others believed that the earth was round. However, from the fourth to the fourteenth century the church suppressed such belief. The church's position was the earth was a flat disk with Jerusalem at the center.

70 Bourke, p. 249. This class conception provides the basis for Augustine's *City of God*. See also William Wiethoff, "The Obscurantist Design in Saint Augustine's Rhetoric," *Communication Studies*, 31 (1980): 128–36.

71 See St. Augustine, *Sermo ratio*, ii.2 and iii.3 as cited in Frederick Copleston, *A History of Philosophy: Medieval Philosophy*, vol. V, part ii (New York: Doubleday/Image Books 1962), p. 86; *De vera relig.*, pp. 24, 45 as cited in Copleston, p. 64.

72 He also reinforced his theory of "divine illumination" in this work arguing that Christ is the "Interior Teacher" who transmits knowledge from the teacher to the student.

73 Augustine relies on Plato's dialogue in the *Meno*, which we reviewed in chapter 3.

74 See *Confessions*, VII.ix. The *Confessions* were written from 397–401. Augustine claimed that Plato would have understood this more clearly had he lived after Christ.

75 See *De doctrina*, I.xxx.33.

76 Ibid., I.xxxii.35.

77 Brown, p. 252.

78 Wiethoff, pp. 132–33.

79 *De doctrina*, IV.xxvii.59.

80 Ibid., IV.lix–lxiii.

81 There is some debate in the academic community concerning the influence of Augustine on those who followed. I rely on several sources to support my claims here: Wiethoff, p. 128; James J. Murphy, *Rhetoric in the Middle Ages: A History of Rhetorical Theory from Saint Augustine to the Renaissance* (Berkeley: U. of California Press, 1974), p. 47.

82 My division between Scholastics and humanists is supported by Ernesto Grassi in *Rhetoric as Philosophy: The Humanist Tradition* (University Park: Pennsylvania State U. Press, 1980), p. 72.

83 There is perhaps no better book on this subject than Walter Ong's *Ramus: Method, and the Day of Dialogue; from the Art of Discourse to the Art of Reason* (Cambridge: Harvard U. Press, 1958).

84 See Copleston, vol. II, pp. 53, 58, 75, 117. A similar turn occurs in Islamic philosophy; see "On the Harmony of Religion and Philosophy," George F. Hourani, trans., in *Medieval Political Philosophy*, Ralph Lerner and Muhsin Mahdi, eds. (New York: The Free Press, 1967), pp. 16, 17.

85 See Leff, "St. Augustine and Martianus Capella"; Leff, "Boethius and the History of Medieval Rhetoric," *Central States Speech Journal*, 25 (1974): 134–41; Murphy, *Rhetoric in the Middle Ages;* Charles Sears Baldwin, *Medieval Rhetoric and Poetic* (Glouster, MA: Peter Smith, 1959). Murphy, Leff, and others continue to examine the 1,500-odd manuscripts on rhetoric from this period. The scholar Alcuin's (730–804) methods were a little more original than the others in that he incorporated the Roman principles set out in the *Rhetorica ad Herennium* and Cicero's *De inventione* in his dialogue on values.

86 *Institutiones divinarum et saecularium litterarum*, II. Praef. 4. as translated by Leslie W. Jones, "An Introduction to Divine and Human Readings," *Columbia University Records of Civilization*, XL (1946). Alcuin and other early medieval rhetors take the same tack. See Alcuin's *Disputatio de rhetorica et de virtutibus* 3, Karl Halm, ed. (Leipzig 1863), p. 526.

87 Isidore of Seville was also a noted encyclopedist and meteorologist.

88 As cited in Copleston, vol. V, p. 138.

89 See Dominicus Gaundissalinus, *De divisione philosophiae*, L. Baur, ed. (BGPM, Band iv, Heft 2–3, Munster, 1903), pp. 63–69.

90 Albert Hourani, *A History of the Arab Peoples* (New York: Warner Books, 1992), pp. 51–62.

[91] Suras 4:10–12; 9; 6:104.

[92] Ibid., 38:21: 3.

[93] Ibid., 47:31.

[94] Ibid., 69:31.

[95] Ibid., 14:26–28.

[96] Ibid., 88:12; 56:26.

[97] This stone is said to be traceable back to Adam and is circled seven times by pilgrims.

[98] Jesus is "Issa" in the Qur'an.

[99] Ironically, the parents of the couple had tried to prevent them from getting married. But they carried on a secret liaison that led to marriage.

[100] The Gulf of Lepanto is not far from the scene of another famous sea battle, the battle of Actium, in which the navy of Octavian defeated the fleet of Antony and Cleopatra in 31 BC.

[101] Averröes' commentaries on the works of Aristotle were enormously influential in the centuries that followed, particularly his commentary on the *Poetics* since prior to this time most scholars, following the lead of Porphyry and Plotinus, relied on Plato for inspiration.

[102] Lerner and Mahdi, p. 165ff.

[103] Ibid., pp. 166–67.

[104] Ibid., p. 165ff.

[105] Fletcher, p. 221.

[106] Thirteen sections of the third book of his *The Training of the Clergy* focus on sermonizing. These sections are based on Pope Gregory the Great's *Pastoral Care* (see below) and Augustine's *De doctrina* (see above).

[107] Jerome Taylor, *The Didascalicon of Hugh of St. Victor* (New York: Columbia U. Press, 1961), pp. 3–15.

[108] Ibid., p. 43.

[109] Ibid., p. 5 and footnote 10.

[110] Ibid., pp. 16–17, 29, 81–83, 143–45.

[111] Ibid., p. 35.

[112] Ibid., p. 82.

[113] As we shall see later in this book, Friedrich Nietzsche would attack this Christian tenet by claiming that Christian truth actually enslaved mankind by inhibiting the "will to power."

[114] Thierry wrote the *Heptateuchon* covering the seven liberal arts. His focus on rhetoric is purely Ciceronian.

[115] Ibid., p. 195. See also Zabarella's *De natura logicae*, Campanella's *Philosohia rationalis*, and B. Varchi's *Della poetica in generale*. In Babylon Rabbi Saadia Goan (882–942), the head of a rabbinical school, had translated the Bible into Arabic. He wrote two treatises on argumentation that proved influential in Jewish scholarship. His work focused on interpretations of the law and disputation in court. He was a leader of the opposition to the Karaites sect, which he believed threatened the rabbinical tradition.

[116] See, for example, Maimonides, *Guide to the Perplexed* in Lerner and Mahdi, p. 195.

[117] The *Guide* was written in Arabic due to the fact that Maimonides was born in Moorish-controlled Spain. The work was translated into Hebrew and Latin after his death.

[118] The Universities of Bologna and Oxford contend for this title. Oxford enrolled about 1,500 students by 1300. Cambridge developed soon after. Regardless, Paris was far more influential. Many scholars, Roger and Francis Bacon among them, came to Paris to refine their learning and then returned to Oxford to spread the word.

[119] See *Thomas Aquinas: Commentary on the Ethics*, in Lerner and Mahdi, p. 277.

[120] Ibid., p. 287.

[121] In James Bruce Ross and Mary Martin McLaughlin, *The Portable Medieval Reader* (New York: Viking, 1963), p. 663. Aquinas, *On Being and Essence*, Armand A. Maurer, trans. (Toronto: Pontifical Institute of Medieval Studies, 1949), p. 49 describes the gradation of perfection among men. His discussion of the hierarchy of men can be found in his political theory; see his "Commentary on the Politics," Book I, Lesson One, in Lerner and Mahdi, pp. 305–12, and Book III, Lessons Three and Four, in Lerner and Mahdi, pp. 320–28.

[122] See Thomas Aquinas, *Summa Theologiae*, Thomas Gilby, ed. (New York: McGraw-Hill, 1964), pp. 62, 65. Anselm of Besate, the peripatetic Augustinian, followed suit in his *Rhetorimachia* arguing that rhetoric was the art of imitating the appearance of truth. He relied heavily on classical works to deduce his theory.

[123] Ibid., pp. 29–31. See also Nicholas of Cusa, *De docta ignorantia*, P. Rotta, ed. (Bari, Italy: National Library, 1913).

[124] In Lerner and Mahdi, p. 287–88.

[125] Ibid., p. 288. This is odd since Aquinas' analysis of emotion seems heavily reliant on Aristotle's from the *Rhetoric* that was reemerging in the thirteenth century.

[126] The most damning attack came in Etienne Tempier's *Condemnation of 219 Propositions,* in Lerner and Mahdi, pp. 335–54. At least 15 of the propositions were supported by Aquinas.

[127] See Copleston's discussion of John Scotus and St. Bonaventure, pp. 137–38 and 320–22; and Lerner's discussion of Ibn Tufayl, pp. 135, 137.

[128] Roger Bacon, *Opus Maius,* in Lerner and Mahdi, p. 370.

[129] Ibid., p. 381.

[130] Ibid., p. 379.

[131] Ibid., p. 379.

[132] Ibid., p. 380.

[133] Ibid., p. 383. This is contained in his favorable commentary on Book IV of Augustine's *De doctrina.*

[134] Ibid., p. 388.

[135] Sidney Hill Jr., "Dictamen: That Bastard of Literature and Law," *Central States Speech Journal,* 24 (1973): 17–24.

[136] This was the longest operating Benedictine monastery in Europe.

[137] He also wrote on ornamentation for discourse in his *Flowers of Rhetoric (*also known as *Dictaminum radii).*

[138] Writing between 1111–18, Adalbertus Samaritanus, for example, sets out 34 examples of salutations alone.

[139] This new section was called the *Captatio benevolentiae.*

[140] See, for example, John Bliese, "The Study of Rhetoric in the Twelfth Century," *Quarterly Journal of Speech,* 63 (December 1977): 344; George Kennedy, *Classical Rhetoric and Its Christian and Secular Tradition from Ancient to Modern Times* (Chapel Hill: U. of North Carolina Press, 1980), p. 186. Dictamen would be expanded to other areas in the Renaissance as it was explored by Erasmus and Melanchthon among others. It was also known as or often related to *ars epistolandi, ars dictandi,* and *ars arengandi.* See Emil J. Polak, *Medieval and Renaissance Letter Treatises and Form Letters: A Census of Manuscripts Found in Eastern Europe and the Former U.S.S.R.,* Davis Medieval Texts and Studies 8 (Leiden: E. J. Brill, 1993). Traditionally, the theory of dictamen broke the letter into six parts: *salutatio, captatio benevolentiae, narratio, divisio, petitio,* and *conclusio.*

[141] See for example, Ross and McLaughlin, p. 534; Chaim Perelman and L. Olbrechts-Tyteca, *The New Rhetoric* (Notre Dame, IN: U. of Notre Dame Press, 1969), p. 164; Murphy, *Rhetoric in Middle Ages,* p. 136. The tropologists included Donatus, Prician, Alexander of Villedieu, and Evard of Bethune. No doubt part of the problem was the loss of Aristotle's *Rhetoric* until new Arab translations reached the West at the end of the epoch. Professor C. Joachim Classen proves an exception in "St. Paul's Epistles and Ancient Greek and Roman Rhetoric," *Rhetorica,* 10 (1992): 334.

[142] Erasmus' attack on *dictamen* as practiced around 1521 was directly related to his other calls for reforms in the Catholic Church.

[143] For an analysis of the state and nature of public address during this period see John Bliese, "Deliberative Oratory in the Middle Ages: The Missing Millennium in the Study of Public Address," *The Southern Communication Journal,* 59 (1994): 273–83.

[144] Jerusalem was taken by Christian forces in 1099. When the Crusades failed, and the Turks began their expansion, faith in a Christian God was weakened.

[145] He was a founding member of the Cistercian monks and was put in charge of the third monastery erected in their name. But soon a holy vision beckoned him to begin preaching. His eloquence was immediately effective. His sermon on the Song of Songs became particularly famous. He is said to have restored the speech of one of his relatives who had been stricken dumb. Erasmus praised Bernard's natural eloquence in his *Art of Preaching.* Bernard's *Degrees of Humility and Pride* was a popular analysis of character that was widely read in his day. He was also a founder of the Knights Templars, a religious military order that became enormously wealthy. Bernard's talent as papal legate was well appreciated since he brought many church schisms to an end.

[146] He was a native of Lisbon, who became first an Augustinian monk and then a Franciscan. From his first major sermon at an ordination service, he claimed to be inspired by the Holy Spirit who put the words in his mouth. He converted many heretics and did battle with others. His extant sermons can be found in *Les Sermons de St. Antoine de Padoue pour L'année Liturgique,* Abbé Paul Bayart, trans. (Paris, n.d.).

[147] He became Charles VII. Captured by the English, Joan was accused of witchcraft and burned at the stake in Rouen.

[148] Murphy, *Rhetoric in the Middle Ages,* p. 275. Murphy claims that over 300 treatises survive from this period.

The Renaissance of Rhetoric

When the mystery of the bubonic plague was solved, commerce freed Europe from the dying grasp of the Dark Ages by providing the security and funding necessary for the arts and sciences to flourish. The creation of paintings, sculptures, music, poetry, rhetoric, invention, and discovery engendered a questioning of the need for a domineering church and its version of the "truth." The religious scholars who had subjugated rhetoric to other forms of discourse suddenly needed rhetoric to sustain Catholic theology in the face of heresy, rising nationalism, scientific breakthroughs, and religious reforms. The development of vernacular, local languages reinforced a sense of individual community. Just as the city-states of Greece had nurtured rhetoric, so too, Paris, Oxford, Milan, Turin, Rome, Venice, Alexandria, Naples, and Florence served as incubators for the renaissance of rhetoric and a resurgence of independent city-states. To demonstrate the rebirth of rhetorical principles, it will be necessary at times to follow its course geographically as well as chronologically. I focus on Italy first and then survey theorists in other countries. After that, I take up the impact of the Protestant revolt, religious intolerance, the Catholic response, and the development of rhetoric during the English and Spanish renaissances. In this way we can determine how various forces propelled rhetorical theory toward the modern era.

VENICE, THE FLOURISHING CITY-STATE

By AD 1000 Venice controlled the upper Adriatic Sea, and by 1100 it had taken over the eastern coast of Italy and the western coast of what is now Croatia and Albania. The doges (chief magistrates) grew rich on trade from the East that came by way of the Silk Road out of China. Marco Polo followed that trail, and his stories about the Far East increased the hunger for silk from China and spices from India. Crusaders in the Holy Land discovered the riches of Muslim caliphs.[1] After the Fourth Crusade (1204), Venice took control of Cypress, Crete, and Salonika and brought home four bronze horses from Constantinople to adorn the Basilica of St. Mark, whose body they had earlier stolen from Egypt so they would have a prestigious patron saint

189

of their own. The Venetian ducat became the coin of choice in Europe.[2] In 1348, like the rest of Europe, Venice was devastated by the bubonic plague, which retarded development. However, by 1400 Venice was strong enough to acquire more land as a buffer against invading foes. Venice, after all, had been founded in marshes, where its residents built shelters safe from the marauding barbarians. In 1405 Venice took Padua and other inland areas, eventually controlling Verona, Vicenza, and Padua.

In defiance of the pope, Venice cut a deal with the Turks and built a huge fleet to carry on trade throughout the Middle East. It became a power that the rest of Europe needed. Subsequently, the explorations of Portugal, under the leadership of Henry the Navigator, and of Spain, under Isabella and Ferdinand, reinforced the financial and scientific revolution in Europe. Isabella and Ferdinand merged their kingdoms in Spain with a wedding in the same year that Constantinople fell to the Ottoman Empire, 1453. That collapse heightened the exit of Greek scholars from Byzantium to Italy.

Venice was ruled by 1,500 patricians who elected 300 senators from their number. These senators elected a Council of Ten and a doge, who by secret ballot elected a Council of Three who ran the city. While Venice had a pyramid court system, with eleven lower courts and two courts of appeal, there was no appeal of sentencing by the anonymous Council of Three, who often relied on hearsay and spies to inform their judgments. After 1604, those convicted were ushered across the new "bridge of sighs" along the Grand Canal to their cells or to their deaths, depending on the sentence.

Venice could be a tolerant city by the standards of the time. It built a hall for German Protestants who came to work in the city. Jews became leading merchants and bankers; however, they were required to wear yellow in public and forced to rent rather than own property. When Venice was stripped of her inland territories (see below), the Jews were herded into a neighborhood dominated by a large foundry known as the Ghetto to make room for Venetians returning to the city from outer

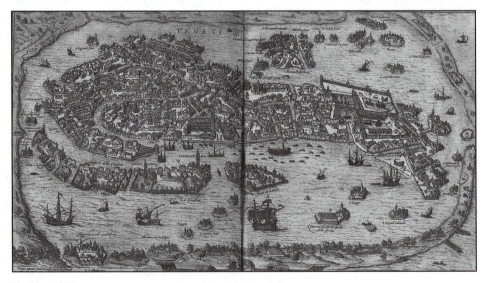

Venice, 1610.

areas. "Ghetto" remains to this day the name of a specific geographic location where minorities live in crowded conditions.

However, the Venetians continued to be quite tolerant of the Jewish population. For example, Judah Messer Leon (c. 1425–1498), who was born and educated in Venice, eventually established a Yeshiva (school) in Ancona on the Italian coast. However, his life proved peripatetic. Having become a rabbi, he studied medicine and law, and soon began to teach and practice in various major cities of Italy. Between 1456 and 1473, he worked in Padua and then Bologna, frequenting the universities in both cities. In 1473 he moved to Mantua, where he published a major work on rhetoric, which followed his other books on logic and grammar. In 1475, he was expelled from the intolerant Mantua and eventually made his way to Naples, where he came under the protection of Ferdinand I. Notes written by his son David indicate that Leon died in 1498.

Leon's *The Book of the Honeycomb's Flow* begins by trying to define what true eloquence is. Though Leon was clearly familiar with Averröes and considered himself a scholastic, he also embraced a humanistic appreciation of the ancients. He provided a thorough commentary on Aristotle, Cicero, and Quintilian, but instead of illustrating his points with Greek or Roman orators, he relied on the speakers of the Old Testament. In this way, his book on rhetoric is a rhetorical analysis of Hebrew scripture. Rhetoric is linked to the prophets of old, such as Moses, Isaiah, and Ezekiel. They provide the "lips of the righteous," who are not only persuasive but speakers of the truth, which they convey because of their rhetorical prowess. From them we learn that the path to justice is often rhetorical and that speech flows from their mouths like honey—golden, shining, and smooth.

While prosperous, Venice was quick to take advantage of new technologies. When Gutenberg developed his press in 1456 in Mainz, Germany, word quickly spread throughout Europe. When he printed 200 Bibles, there were only 30,000 books in all of Europe.[3] By 1500 there were almost nine million. The continent was dotted with publishers. For example, by 1498, Aldus Manutius, a publisher who arrived in Venice in 1489, gathered intellectuals from around the civilized world, and soon many presses along the canals of Venice printed their work.[4] Ermolao Barbaro's translation of Aristotle and Manutius' *Rudimenta grammaticae linguae Latinae* were two of the most popular new publications. Founded in 1500, the New Academy of Venice became a publishing house of Greek texts, a symptom of the intensification of humanism across Italy. Turin, for example, prospered due to its central location. Along with his wife, Beatrice d'Este, Ludovico Il Moro created a Renaissance center in Milan. Ludovico of the Sforza clan housed Leonardo da Vinci in Milan, where he painted his famous *Last Supper* in 1498. It is not surprising then that bubbling beneath the church-induced consensus that rhetoric was a lesser art of discourse was the belief that rhetoric was in fact the most artistic of communication studies. The dynamic tension between those who would relegate rhetoric to mass appeal and those who would retrieve it for humanistic study led to a rethinking of rhetorical theory that eventually resulted in new advances and retrievals of ancient strategies. Fueled by the rediscovery of Cicero's speeches and his *Orator, Topica,* and *De oratore,* Aristotle's *Rhetoric,* and speeches of the Greek Attic orators, the province of rhetoric became a major topic of debate in the Renaissance.[5]

In the meantime, things went less well for Venice. When it attacked the Papal States, the warrior Pope Julius II formed the League of Cambrai with France, Spain, and Austria, and defeated Venice in 1509. Much of its inland empire was taken away. However, its artists continued to flourish and to change the way people looked at the religious world. One of the most important contributions of the Renaissance was to enliven and reify the life of Christ and his contemporaries by painting them as real people instead of flat, lifeless caricatures. The great Venetian painter Tintoretto (1518–1594) was one of the leaders of this movement. He painted the circumcision and baptism of Jesus, *Jesus in the House of Martha*, the *Marriage at Cana*, *Christ at the Sea of Galilee*, *Woman Taken in Adultery*, *Christ Washing the Apostles' Feet*, the *Raising of Lazarus*, the *Last Supper* (different from da Vinci's depiction), and many more. Like many other painters, Tintoretto provided the public with important images that were themselves rhetorical, a persuasive force that enhanced faith in the common man and woman who could identify with a Jesus and Mary who looked just like them.

Venice fought its last major sea battle at Lepanto in 1571, where it led an armada that defeated the Ottoman fleet, ending the advance of the Turks. The plague of 1575–76 combined with the cost of war and led to the further decline of Venice as a power; more than 50,000 people died from the plague. However, the city where Bellini, Titian, Tintoretto, Carpattio, and countless other great artists dwelt was still powerful enough in 1606 to expel the Jesuits in the name of tolerance and scientific advance. Monteverdi would invent the opera there and argue that speech should be master of music. Soon Venice would have more than a dozen opera houses. However, by that time its political power had lapsed.

FLORENCE, THE HUMANISTS, AND THE PRACTICE OF RHETORIC

The renaissance in rhetoric was seeded in Florence when Dante (1265–1321), Petrarch (1304–1374), and Boccaccio (1313–1375) wrote stories of contemporary humans in the vernacular of Tuscany.[6] Dante Alighieri was a true Renaissance model who mastered the works of Aquinas during his schooling, as befitting a child from the lesser nobility of Florence. At only nine years of age, Dante fell in love with Beatrice Portinari, the daughter of the Tuscan ambassador to France; she became the bride of a Florentine banker and then died at the age of twenty-three in 1290. By that time, Dante had taken a wife, Gemmain Donati. However, it was Beatrice who inspired the character who arbitrates beauty in his epic poem, *The Divine Comedy;* she leads him out of the underworld to a new vision of God that becomes his Platonic ideal.[7]

Dante attended the University of Bologna, the oldest university in Italy, and came under the influence of the Florentine humanist Brunetto Latini (1220–1294), a Ciceronian and Aristotelian.[8] Dante studied Aristotle, Cicero, Augustine, and Aquinas. As a member of the prominent Guelf gentry, Dante was active in politics. He even traveled to Rome to plea for help from the pope's allies. The Guelf's archrival party was the Ghibelline, which endorsed nationalism as embodied in a feudal aristocracy and preferred allegiance to the holy Roman emperor over the pope. The dominance of the Guelfs allowed Dante to advance as a civil servant even when the Guelf party itself divided between the Blacks and the Whites. Siding with the Whites, who were less favorable to the machinations of the pope than were the Blacks, Dante continued to advance, becoming a member of the council of Florence. However, politics proved to be volatile in Florence. When Charles of Valois, the brother of the king of France, secretly supported the Blacks, they seized control of Florence, and Dante was banished from Florence for life. He left his wife and child behind.

This event was partially responsible for his strong endorsement of monarchy *(De monarchia)*, which was eventually put on the Catholic *Index* of forbidden books in 1554. He had no use for the shifting political winds of republics. Over the next years, he served many a noble household as a counselor and teacher. He wrote a book on grammar that claimed we learn by "imitation" and that language is humanistic and ever evolving. He warned writers to take care with word choice given that humans are blessed with so many linguistic possibilities. As a semioticist, he believed that signs have the capacity to signify thoughts. He explored the various Italian vernaculars, or local languages. He was fascinated with various idioms and locutions, because, as one who knew the story of the Tower of Babel (see chapter 2), he was interested in language development. His *De vulgari eloqentia* was completed a decade before his more famous *The Divine Comedy.*

After wandering through many prominent Italian cities, he spent his last two years in Ravenna where he went on one last diplomatic mission to Venice, wrote his *Divine Comedy*, contracted malaria, and died. The full title of this sometimes romantic, sometimes satirical poetic epic reveals its rhetorical nature: *The Divine Comedy of Dante Alighieri, Florentine by Citizenship, Not by Morals.* In the Tuscan poetic vernacular, the 100 cantos in this epic lay out a plan for protection of city-states under a benign but strong ruler in opposition to the hypocrisy of the pope. In support of this thesis, Dante re-creates Beatrice as the divine illumination of Augustinian purity and integrates the philosophy of Aquinas. The balance between the intuitive and the demonstrative is important, since without illumination, "how deceiving are syllogistic reasonings that bring your wings to flight so low, to earthly things!" Dante realized that people depend on one another for survival and hence good government.[9] Chaotic political units distract humans from their spiritual quest. For this reason, Dante consigns both the politicians and the popes of his time to his "inferno."

If Dante's "inferno" demonstrates the wrong turns taken by republicans and church fathers, his "paradise" reveals the benefits of empire. He uses "purgatory" to represent the disorganization of Italy, hoping it will soon choose paradise (a united empire) over hell (a collection of avaricious city-states).[10] He places his classic heroes, Hector, Homer, Socrates, Plato, Cicero, and Caesar, in Limbo (the circle of the unbaptized) on the edge of hell, where they can never know God's glory. The *Comedy*'s satirical narrative clearly argues that the temporal intervention of the church was blocking the state's ability to organize Italy into a cohesive unit. It encourages the church to return to its spiritual mission. Dante decried the link between the bishops and the militia of the politicians.

As far as invention was concerned, Dante has Virgil give us his theory in Canto 18, starting at line 56: "Nobody knows where the first ideas come from. They are in you, as the need to make honey is in the bee." God is *logos*, but it gets confused by the inadequate communication of humans. Virgil leads Dante deep into the rings of the inferno finally arriving at the City of Dis, the Roman name for Hades. Virgil cannot enter the city, but Dante can move through it because of his virtue. When Dante emerges on the other side, Beatrice becomes his guide to the lower heavens. From there, Dante proceeds to God finally leaving Beatrice behind. He establishes the ultimate goal of humanists: coming into the presence of God. And once you are in the presence of God, no other beauty can affect you. Nothing can compare.

Francesco Petrarch (1304–1374) was a priest and humanist who greatly admired Augustine's *Confessions* and recommended them to his readers.[11] In Petrarch's dialogues *De contemptu mundi*, Augustine served as his voice. More important, his defense of such writers as Virgil, Cicero, and Seneca was drawn from Augustine, and his letter-writing method was borrowed from Cicero.[12] This is not surprising since Petrarch, the good humanist that he was, had personally unearthed Cicero's lost *Pro Archia* (a speech for the poet, Archias), two of his other speeches, and 800 of his letters including some to Atticus, Brutus, and Quintus. Petrarch believed that the classics could be helpful in developing a sense of rhetorical style, but he warned against accepting their content as a guide to morals. He wrote:

> What good will it do if you immerse yourself wholly in the Ciceronian springs and know well the writings either of the Greeks or of the Romans? You will indeed be able to speak ornately, charmingly, sweetly, and sublimely; you certainly will not be able to speak seriously, austerely, judiciously, and, most importantly, uniformly.[13]

Heeding his own advice allowed him to become a leading diplomat.[14]

Four of Petrarch's characteristics proved typical of those who contributed to the renaissance of rhetoric: he wrote in the vernacular, he was a skeptic, he was a humanist, and he despised the corruption in the church. Petrarch had witnessed the "Babylonian Captivity" of the pope when the papacy was moved to Avignon. In one attack he spoke of the pope's palace in Avignon as "hell on earth . . . the sewer of the world."[15] Such calls for reform spread heresy across Italy.[16] It may also have affected the election, at the age of thirty-nine, of Pope Gregory XI, a humanist who was devoted to the study of Cicero. Nicholas V (reigned 1447–1454), often considered the first Renaissance pope, followed Gregory's lead by acquiring many important manuscripts for the Vatican Library, many from the fall of Constantinople during his reign, and inviting Greek and other scholars to Rome to study them. He even commissioned a new version of the Bible, which went uncompleted when he died. However, Popes Callistus III (1455–1458), Pius II (1458–1464), and Paul II (1564–1571) continued the tradition of welcoming scholars who had fled Constantinople. Upwards of a thousand arrived during their reigns.

Lorenzo Valla (1407–1457), a humanist who served as chancellor of Florence for a time and as apostolic secretary to Pope Nicholas V, resuscitated Quintilian by writing a book on rhetoric, *Elegantiae linguae latinae*. In Lodi, Bishop Landriani discovered the complete text of Cicero's *De oratore* in a church cellar. These rediscoveries not only led to a correction of extant versions of these texts, they also led to a reinvigoration of rhetorical theory.

Giovanni Boccaccio moved beyond the religiosity and intolerance of his teacher Petrarch by praising Muslim thought and writing the ribald *Decameron*, in which monks and priests are ridiculed. He helped lift the spirits of Europe after the devastation of the bubonic plague. The bubonic plague arrived in 1347 carried by rats infested with fleas that hitchhiked onto the Tartar caravans cutting through central Asia. From there the vermin made their way first to Sicily and then other ports aboard trading vessels. By 1348 Florence fared worse than the rest of Europe; half of the Florentines had died from the plague. The *Decameron* is the story of seven praying women and three wandering men who flee the plague and take refuge in the countryside, where each morning a new theme is chosen by one of the "kings" or "queens" for the day for stories to be composed by evening. Each story is humorous, even ribald, but each also has a sharp rhetorical point. The work inspired Chaucer's *Canterbury Tales*, published in 1387.

The Rise of Florence

These humanists flourished in the rising city of Florence, which established itself by taking in the wool of Britain, the Netherlands, and other sheep-raising areas and converting it to cloth, often dyed with brilliant colors. Her station was improved immensely when Florence became the center of capital for Europe. Her currency, the florin, first struck in 1252, soon rivaled the Venetian ducat as the standard for all other currencies. The families of bankers and merchants encouraged artists and guilds and reformed their government.

Giovanni di Bicci de Medici got the banking family established in 1397.[17] He dabbled in the wool trade but focused on banking as a member of that guild. However, he had to overcome the Albizzi family, who hated the Medici family. The Medici became the bankers of the pope, but the Albizzis countered by expelling Cosimo de Medici and his brothers from the city in 1433. However, a financial collapse and a military defeat by Milan embarrassed the Albizzis, and Cosimo and his family were invited back to form a government. The Medici ran Florence for the next sixty years (1434–1494). During that time, they built great libraries, encouraged public speaking, and patronized the arts like no family before them. Tourists to this day are familiar with the beauty of the city of flowers, with its romantic bridges across the Arno River.

Political boss, humanist, and banker, Cosimo de Medici (1389–1464) led this renaissance by creating a cultural center in his "new Athens."[18] The University of Florence, known as the Studio Fiorentino, was founded in 1321, when the University of Bologna was condemned by the pope. By the time of the Medici, the Studio was training humanists such as Poggio Bracciolini, who would later discover rhetorical texts and Lucretius' poem *On the Nature of Things*, which had advanced Epicureanism during the Roman epoch (see chapter 5). In 1415, after the pope he served was dethroned near the end of the Great Schism (1378–1417),[19] Poggio found seven of Cicero's orations in monasteries in Gaul and the German provinces. In 1416 he found a complete text of Quintilian's *De institutione oratoria* at St. Gall, a remote monastery where monks had copied the works of the ancients throughout the Middle Ages. Poggio stayed for fifty-four days to copy the text. But his most sensational find was the manuscript of Lucretius' *On the Nature of Things*, which led to a revival of Epicureanism and atomism.[20] He went on to become chancellor of Florence and the papal secretary to Martin V, where Poggio translated some of Cicero's works including *On the Laws (De legibus)* and a speech about Lucullus. He may have inspired the discovery in 1421 of manuscripts of Cicero's five major works by Bishop Gerardo Landriani in the cathedral of Lodi.

In 1439, the prestige of Florence became clear for all to see when Pope Eugenius IV asked Cosimo to host the convocation seeking to reunite the Roman and Byzantine Catholic Churches. While the bargain that was struck failed to hold, the convocation introduced Florence to many Greek scholars, most of whom were experts in rhetorical theory. After hearing lectures on Plato by Plethon, Cosimo instituted a Platonic Academy that was hugely influential on Renaissance artists, particularly Michelangelo. Within four years of Cosimo's death, his great project of translating the dialogues of Plato into new Latin versions was complete. Like Venice, Florence took in many of the scholars who fled Byzantium when it fell to the Turks in 1453.

Trebizond (1395–1486)

The same phenomenon was occurring in Rome. A great admirer of Aristotle's psychological approach to rhetoric, George of Trebizond left his native Crete to become a teacher in Mantua, Venice, and finally Rome, where he was given a chair of rhetoric at the university when Pope Eugenius IV reinvigorated it. Trebizond wrote commentaries on Aristotle's *Rhetoric* and on the writings of Cicero and Hermogenes. As we have seen, Hermogenes' work was unknown in the West to that time but had developed fifty-nine "schemes" of thought and language.[21] As an Aristotelian, Trebizond was a strong critic of Plato. However, Trebizond's haughty manner offended many of his contemporaries. Finally, his disputes with Poggio and Valla led to his expulsion from Rome, and he took refuge in the Kingdom of Naples where he continued to translate works from Greek to Latin. Trebizond eventually became influential once again in papal circles when one of his pupils became Pope Paul II, and Trebizond served as papal secretary. However, never able to mind his tongue, Trebizond praised the Sultan of Constantinople after a trip to the East. He was expelled from the papal court once again and eventually died in poverty.

His comprehensive study of rhetoric, *Rhetoricorum libri quinque (Five Books on Rhetoric)*, endorsed an amoral theory of "civil science," a concept that was a forerunner to Machiavelli's empirical methods of examining leadership. The text was flawed but influential and divided into six parts. The work includes (1) an extensive retrieval of Hermogenes' *stasis* system, (2) an endorsement of Cicero's view of civic virtue, (3) an expansion of Aristotle's *topoi* to thirty-five commonplaces, (4) a revival of the three forms of public speaking with more commonplaces for each one, (5) the definition of eighty-seven figures, and (6) a review of what had been said in the past about delivery, memory, and style. Juan Luis Vives (discussed in the section on the Spanish Renaissance below), the teacher of Mary Tudor, credits Trebizond in his own work on rhetoric.

Meanwhile, back in Florence, Cosimo de Medici commissioned work to start on Florence's great cathedral that would be capped by Brunelleschi's famous dome, the first in Italy since the Pantheon had been expanded during the height of the Roman Empire. With Jan van Eyck's discovery in Ghent around 1432 that pigment could be mixed with linseed or nut oil to produce much more detail in painting than tempera (egg-based paints), artists were inspired to an altogether new and realistic painting. Cosimo's contemporary, Donatello (1386–1466), became the first of many Florentine sculptors to shock the world with his revealing conceptions of the perfect human body. He liberated the human form from its sterile and saintly medieval wrapping. That Donatello was a known homosexual reveals the tolerance of Florence during this time and its desire to return to Athenian values. Like Cicero in Rome, Cosimo was named *Pater Patria* in Florence.

In 1464 he was succeeded by his son Piero, who had served as ambassador to Paris, Venice, and Milan, where he maintained an alliance with Francesco Sforza. However, it was Piero's son, Lorenzo (1449–1492), who would take Florence to new heights. He came to power at age twenty and survived an assassination attempt in the cathedral that resulted in the death of his brother.[22] He saved the city from a ruinous war by personally negotiating a settlement with the king of Naples, which allowed Lorenzo to continue the family's patronage of such artists as Ghir-

Donatello.

landaio and his famous pupil Michelangelo Buonarroti (1475–1564), who became a teacher in Lorenzo's new school for artists.[23] Michelangelo sustained the Florentine renaissance with his magnificent sculptures, buildings, paintings, and poems.[24] In his writings, Michelangelo claimed he was resurrecting Augustine's dream of merging Neoplatonism with Christian ideals.[25] The publication of humanistic works under Lorenzo, known as "the Magnificent," helped fill the Laurentian library that he had commissioned Michelangelo to design. Lorenzo commissioned Fra Angelico to paint frescos in the monasteries of Florence. Fra Filippo Lippi painted beautiful works for the Medici palace. Lorenzo also allowed printing presses into the city and then had his own poetry published in the local tongue. By 1488, the presses printed the first complete version of Homer's works. The University of Florence developed a specialization in Greek studies, which drew students from all across Europe. Lorenzo also revived the University of Pisa, since he controlled that city too.

Savonarola (1452–1498)

The artistic and humanistic renaissance in Florence was a precursor to the same kind of activity all across Europe. The financial and personal security of the citizens of the city-states led to new calls for nationhood, freethinking, riots, and a rebirth of public address, some of which would shake the foundations of the church. In Florence, the spirit of independence would lead to the fall of the Medici. The year 1492 saw Columbus sail out of the harbor at Genoa toward a new world;[26] it saw Ferdinand and Isabella unite Spain and reinstitute the Inquisition; and it saw the forty-three-year-old Lorenzo de Medici, *Il Magnifico*, take ill and die. His son Piero II took over the family at the young age of twenty-two, ill-equipped to handle the challenge he was about to face.

In 1481, when Girolamo Savonarola, a Dominican friar, failed as a preacher in his native city of Ferrara and several others, he moved to Florence. At first he was considered ill-mannered, plain spoken, tactless, and coarse. Nonetheless he was made a lector at the church of San Marco and lived in its monastery. He gave sermons at the more important church of San Lorenzo. More and more people came to hear him, in a case of content overcoming rather mundane delivery. Like an Old Testament Jeremiah, he began to make prophetic judgments against Florence as if it had become

Sodom. Savonarola was appalled that in its attempt to imitate Athens, Florence tolerated discreet homosexual activity. He claimed that Plato and his pupil Aristotle were burning in hell because of their paganism. He was particularly appalled by the works of the deceased Donatello and the young Michelangelo.

Soon he was allowed to preach in the city's main cathedral and drew even larger crowds. "It is not I who preach, but God who speaks through me," he often proclaimed. He called on Florence to bring its laws in conformance with the law of God. If his hearers did not repent, "the sword of God" would slay them. "Repent, O Florence, while there is still time. Clothe thyself in the white garments of purification." He became known as a speaker of *parrhesia*, what the Greeks called words of unvarnished, hard-to-take truth.[27]

Savonarola's credibility rose when he correctly predicted the deaths of Pope Innocent VIII and the king of Naples. Savonarola also built a following of born-again youths. He called for a new puritanism and presaged some of Martin Luther's arguments by nineteen years:

> You Christians should always have the Gospel with you, I do not mean the book, but the spirit, for if you do not possess the spirit of grace and yet carry the whole book, of what advantage is it to you? . . . The true books of Christ are the Apostles and the saints, and true reading consists in imitating their lives. . . . [L]ook today at the prelates. They are tied to earthly vanities. They love them. The cure of souls is no longer their chief concern.[28]

Foreshadowing Luther's use of invective, Savonarola referred to the new Pope Alexander VI of the Spanish Borgia family as a "devil" presiding over a "harlot" church. Even Pico della Mirandola, who had not been afraid to discuss Muslim and Jewish theology, and Michelangelo, whose libertine ways were well-known, became followers of the Dominican priest. In fact, it was Mirandola who had talked Lorenzo de Medici into arranging the appointment of Savonarola as the prior of the Dominican order at the Church of San Marco in 1490.

When Lorenzo de Medici died in 1492 as Savonarola had predicted, his credibility became so great he was able to rally the citizens of the city to invite the French to seize control and depose the Medici family. In November 1494 Piero de Medici II was forced to flee Florence; he was soon followed by Michelangelo when the artist heard that the puritanical monk had condemned the artist's realistic paintings and sculptures. French King Charles VIII made Savonarola head of the new Florentine Republic. After praising Charles VIII as the savior of Florence, Savonarola demanded that his version of the new constitution be ratified. A puritan government was formed.

Savonarola declared himself dictator of Florence and led a children's crusade to collect all "vanities," including important manuscripts of the pagan ancients along with more contemporary paintings by men who would become masters, into a pile to be burned. The bonfires in the main square have taken on mythic proportions. Even the great painter Botticelli is said to have thrown his paintings of nudes into the fire. But Savonarola's reign was suddenly weakened when he was excommunicated by Pope Alexander VI and condemned for heresy.[29] Savonarola's rule was further undermined by the return of the plague and failed crops. Savonarola hid in the Medici library when he learned that the Florentine senate *(Signoria)* had turned on him. He was found and hanged in the main square with several of his followers on May 23, 1498; then his body was taken down and burned where the "vanities" had been incinerated.[30]

Machiavelli (1469–1527) as Rhetor

Christine de Pisan (c. 1364–1430),[31] Johannes Susenbrotus (1485–1543),[32] and Bishop Francesco Patrizi of Siena (1413–1494),[33] among others, engaged in the debate about the future of the rhetorical discipline. However, no one was more important to the renaissance of rhetoric than the Florentine Niccolò Machiavelli, who wrote about the power of rhetoric with a new realism in *The Art of War*, *The Prince*, and *Discourses on the First Ten Books of Titus Livius*.[34] Machiavelli was neither a humanist nor a scholastic. Like some of the thinkers we have already examined, Machiavelli provided a counterpoint to those who preceded him. Instead of seeking the perfection of the classical era as did the humanists or reasoning his way to God like the scholastics, Machiavelli provided pragmatic advice on how to obtain and retain power in this world. Rhetoric plays a large role in this process. Like the Sophists and Aristotle, whom he greatly admired, Machiavelli separated his thoughts on rhetoric from those on ethics, famously claiming that "the ends justify the means."[35] Machiavelli taught that guile and strength can be converted to cruelty, which can be used for good *(bene)* to keep citizens in line. Writing

Niccolò Machiavelli.

in the Florentine vernacular, he advanced a situational theory of virtue that includes the ability to seize opportunities (*kairos* to the Sophists) and to innovate, which often required rhetorical skills. Like Odysseus of Greece, Machiavelli's hero combines various virtues. He is as strong as the lion and as cagy as the fox, while also verbally adept. Machiavelli illustrated his theory of combined virtue by pointing out that while the lion is courageous, it often steps into traps. And while the fox is smart enough to avoid the traps, it needs the strength of the lion to survive.

Machiavelli used his powers of observation to examine practices in governance. Specifically, he focused on the rise, fall, and rise again of the Borgias and the Medici, his first patrons. Using King Ferdinand of Spain as his model prince, Machiavelli argued that rulers need to establish and/or reinforce leadership, religion, and patriotism. *The Prince* outlined tactics, many of which were rhetorical, for achieving these goals.[36]

He began his more important observations watching the French invasion of Florence, when they put Savonarola in power (see above). When Savonarola was executed, Florence again became a republic; Machiavelli served as second chancellor while the Medici remained in exile. In 1502 he traveled to Urbino and met Cesare Borgia (1475–1507). As the son of Pope Alexander VI, Borgia sought to unite the Italian city-states by force, even putting Florence under siege. In 1506, Machiavelli created a militia for Florence, leading it with his black hair brushed back to reveal his large forehead. After the demise of Alexander VI in 1503 and his son Cesare in 1507, the Borgias' dream of a united Italy went up in smoke. By 1508 Machiavelli was leading his own militia, laying a successful siege of Pisa, and returning in glory to Florence while the Medici continued in exile. However, Pope Julius II appointed Cardinal Giovanni de Medici as his legate in Bologna, which the pope had captured. The pope then chased the French from Italy, but his Medici cardinal was captured by the French as they retreated. In the meantime, Machiavelli continued to advise the rulers of the Florentine Republic. However, when the Spanish army, part of the pope's Holy League, defeated the Florentines, the Medici under the leadership of Cardinal Giovanni, who had negotiated his own release from the French, were put back in charge. Machiavelli hoped the Medici could succeed where the Borgias had failed. Reinterpreting Livy's history of Rome in his *Discourses*, Machiavelli urged the Medici to return to the virtues of the Roman Republic.[37] He argued that republics were better able to adapt to changing times and challenges than other forms of government because republics were more adaptable and leaders were freer to speak out. But the Medici spurned his advice and sent him into exile in 1513 to Percussina where he wrote *The Prince* and other works. Giovanni de Medici became Pope Leo X in the same year and had to deal with Martin Luther four years later (see below).[38]

Machiavelli's low opinion of human nature,[39] particularly when it came to military men, led him to conclude that rulers had a right to maintain control by deception: *The end justified the means*, and one of the most potent means was rhetoric. For those views, Machiavelli is sometimes condemned as a manipulator. However, that opinion seems too narrow when one realizes that his theory of rhetoric was a throwback to Aristotle and Cicero. For example, Machiavelli sought to reestablish Cicero's sense of *virtu*, the ability to rule pragmatically, prudently, and effectively using public address.

Machiavelli also endorsed the use of family heritage and associates to build an elaborate scheme for enhancing a ruler's credibility. These sources of political reputation contribute to a *persona*—a projection of the speaker's psyche—that impresses his or her constituency. While much of this kind of ego-verification is perceptual and even mythological, it works to this day. Individuals attempt to establish their personas by referring to family trees, fraternal organizations, and astrology. "I'm a direct descendant of Betsy Ross." "I'm a Libra; what's your sign?"

Machiavelli designated three categories for building credibility. The first, *ancestors and good parentage*, was derived from Cicero's *gravitas* (see chapter 5). Machiavelli claimed that a prince's subjects believed that good heritage resulted in good children. Roman leaders like the Gracchi brothers obtained some of their credibility from being descendants of the great savior of Rome, General Scipio. A modern example of this phenomenon is the election of generations of Kennedys, Rockefellers, Roosevelts, Tafts, and Bushes in the United States by voters who admire the original political progenitors of these families. They have an advantage over other candidates because their parents served either with distinction or with some sort of notoriety. To the contrary, the descendants of a public figure whose name has been sullied can suffer from an unfair loss of credibility. The offspring of such notorious leaders as Benedict Arnold and Aaron Burr provide examples.

Machiavelli's second category was *associations*. Based on the belief that good people attract one another, you can judge persons by the company they keep. Clubs, fraternities, and so on are formed to reinforce mutual tastes, values, and affections. On the contrary, improper associations can ruin a public image. For many citizens, former President John Kennedy's association with mob boss Sam Giancana through Frank Sinatra remains a blot on his record. In 2008, Senator John McCain's friendship with a lobbyist was criticized as was Barack Obama's association with a minister critical of the United States.

Deeds of the speaker comprise the third category. Like Aristotle's *ethos*, demonstrating that one is in the habit of doing good is important. These deeds can be great achievements, demonstrations of loyalty, and/or the ability to recognize talent in others. Once the prince has achieved a good reputation, Machiavelli advises him to maintain it by showing strength instead of weakness and power instead of prudence.[40] In chapter 17 of *The Prince*, Machiavelli famously advised that "it is much better to be feared than loved."

Machiavelli also wrote with sophistication about the virtues of the public and how they were easily corrupted to serve the purposes of a prince. He broke virtues into two categories: *primary virtues*, which are intangible and therefore difficult to convey in speaking situations, and *secondary virtues*, which are more tangible and therefore easier to relate to the public. The latter are to be used to create the impression of the former. Secondary virtues such as generosity, purity, and seriousness reveal or indicate such primary virtues as religion, compassion, and sincerity. In chapter 18 of *The Prince*, Machiavelli specifically advises what the ruler needs to do to achieve the proper persona.[41] Each primary virtue is named, paired with a secondary virtue that reinforces it, and exemplified with a specific action to enhance credibility. Here are some examples:

1. To convey the primary virtue of being religious, use the secondary virtue of generosity, which can be tangibly shown by making public donations. ("I am dedicating this unused public land for a monastery.")

2. To convey the primary virtue of compassion, use the secondary virtue of sensitivity by saying that you empathize with others. (President Clinton was famous for his empathetic line, "I feel your pain.")

3. To demonstrate faith, be pure in your actions and speech by advocating virtues. (Any number of politicians over the last few years have claimed that they "believe in family values.")

4. To demonstrate sincerity, remain strong and serious in stature and visage. (Observe the behavior of public officials at state funerals.)

5. To demonstrate prudence, ponder and reflect when questions are asked of you. ("Let me think about that for a moment.")

Concluding this strategy, Machiavelli wrote that the goal is for "Everyone to see who you appear to be, and few to sense who you really are."[42]

The role of perception leads to a discussion of the need for "vicious appearances." The ruler should never appear arrogant, devious, frivolous, weak, unfaithful, or wanton because people hold such attitudes in contempt. These are universal vices. However, certain extensions of these vices are sometimes useful when trying to control a constituency. Cruelty (an extension of arrogance) evokes fear, which is more effective than love when it comes to ruling.[43] Lenience (an acceptable form of weakness) evokes gratitude, especially when postponing a criminal sentence is involved.

In order for these categories to generate effective persuasive appeals, the speaker/ruler must understand the times and customs of his constituents. According to Machiavelli, people have and always will have the same passions, and they will produce the same results if existing conditions are properly evaluated.[44] Thus, one must map out political relationships and discover the personal traits of the constituency. Machiavelli encouraged a version of audience analysis on which speakers could rely; he believed that in every constituency there are common traits that can be corrupted for some purposes or uncorrupted for others. That is, leaders often need to convert common traits to corrupted ones and vice versa. Rhetoric is crucial to the process. Here are some examples.

Common Trait	Corrupted Trait
Discontented	Ungrateful-greedy
(simple complaints)	(active rioting)

The best one can hope for among the public is discontent. People will always find something to complain about, but they won't take action unless this trait becomes corrupted into the ungrateful-greedy state. If the people become extremely dissatisfied because they can't get what they want, they may become active. Obviously, a ruler in power, an incumbent, would prefer the more passive, discontented state in order to retain office. Someone seeking power would try to achieve the corrupted trait in order to force the incumbent out. In the 2012 presidential campaign, President Obama tried to keep a lid on public discontent about the economy in the face of Tea Party and Occupy Wall Street activists, while the Republicans sought to provoke the corrupted trait by arguing that unemployment and taxes were too high. They had learned from Ronald Reagan's example in the 1980 presidential debates when he asked the public, "Are you better off today than you were four years ago?" This question posed by Reagan in his debate with President Carter was partially responsible for Reagan's election that year.

Common Trait	Corrupted Trait
Shortsighted	Fickle
(crisis-oriented)	(change leaders)

Machiavelli argued that in the best of situations constituents are merely crisis-oriented; the latest problem holds their attention until it is solved. The corrupted trait is fickleness, in which the constituency votes or moves to change leadership based on the latest crisis. Despite the fact that President George H. W. Bush won one of the quickest wars in our history, in 1992 he was thrown out of office because the fickle nature of the electorate focused on the economy. In 2006, the public became disenchanted with the war in Iraq and put Democrats in charge of the House and Senate. In 2010, they returned the Republicans to power in the House because the economy was still faltering after two years of unified Democratic rule.

Common Trait	Corrupted Trait
Complaisant	Cowardly
(inactive)	(surrender)

Machiavelli argued that at best the public is lazy; it won't take any action. At worst, it is cowardly and may give up the city rather than fight. Perhaps England's policy of appeasement toward Hitler best represents the cowardly state in the modern era. Neville Chamberlain, to his undying shame, openly advocated the policy of "appeasement" before the British Parliament, both before and after he allowed Czechoslovakia to be occupied by Hitler in 1938. Chamberlain remained popular with his constituency until Hitler invaded Poland in 1939. His party then turned Chamberlain out of office and replaced him with Winston Churchill, an arch foe of the policy of appeasement.

Machiavelli, like Aristotle, believed an audience can be moved from one frame of mind to another. Cleverly, he suggested addressing the audience as if it were in the desired frame of mind to get them to assume that mood. For example, speakers would treat the public as if they were greedy or angry when they wanted the public to support a war: "I know that all of you are angry at Iran for its development of nuclear weapons." Machiavelli thus became one of the first rhetorical theorists to explore the power of suggestion by invoking the self-fulfilling wish.

Machiavelli has similar advice when it comes to appealing to the future or the past. On the one hand, the wise ruler realizes that human appetites are insatiable because nature drives people to want more than they can possess. People look toward the future, toward their dreams and wants. On the other hand, a politician can excite dissatisfaction by reminding people that the past was better than the present. In America, speakers often remind their audiences of a simpler time in the country when there was less crime, less regulation, and more opportunity. In this case, the audience is driven to nostalgia for a better time in the past. In the 1996 presidential election, the two major candidates exemplified these strategies. After praising the times in which he was raised in Kansas, Senator Dole asked to be a "bridge to that past"; after examining what his reforms could accomplish, President Clinton claimed to be a "bridge to the future." In 2012, President Obama and Mitt Romney looked to the future since the status quo was mired in wars, high unemployment, and lackluster economic growth.

In concluding his advice on the manipulation of constituencies, Machiavelli argues that it is better that a leader be feared than loved since citizens have less trouble ousting someone they like than someone they fear. Given this reading of Machiavelli, it is not hard to see why his name is associated with adaptation, cruelty, and manipulation. However, his theory of rhetoric is one of the most original and complete of its day. It includes some advice on virtuous leadership, which Machiavelli found to be sorely lacking in Italy. Harkening back to Cicero's notion of prudence, Machiavelli described *virtu* as flexible and useful in persuasion. However, he endorsed the audacious side of *virtu* more often than he endorsed the prudent side.[45] In the tradition of

Europe, c. AD 1500.

the time—remember Martin Luther wrote his *Ninety-Five Theses* in 1517—Machiavelli also questioned the values of Christianity in a politically brutal world:

> [M]en were stronger in [ancient Rome], which I believe to be attributable to the difference of education, founded upon the difference of their religion and ours. For, as our religion teaches us the truth and the true way of life, it causes us to attach less value to the honors and possessions of this world; whilst the Pagans, esteeming those things as the highest good, were more energetic and ferocious in their actions. . . . Our religion, moreover, places the supreme happiness in humility, lowliness, and a contempt for worldly objects, whilst the other, on the contrary, places the supreme good in grandeur of soul, strength of body, and all such other qualities as render men formidable.[46]

Machiavelli criticized the church for not uniting Italy under its power and restoring tradition. As this debate over values flourished, it reinforced the revival of rhetoric.

REFORMATION THEORISTS

Machiavelli was perhaps the most controversial of those debating the role of rhetoric in education and public affairs. But other scholars followed his lead. The most important were Rudolph Agricola, Philipp Melanchthon, Erasmus, and Petrus (Peter) Ramus, because these teachers were well connected to the political, educational, and religious powers of the day. During this time, nation-states were replacing city-states and provinces. By the time Martin Luther (see below) posted his *Ninety-Five Theses* in 1517, new empires had emerged from Spanish, Portuguese, French, and Ottoman (Turkish) holdings. The pope negotiated an agreement between Spain and Portugal to divide the New World and parts of the old. Because of its alliance with Genoa, Spain was able to borrow Christopher Columbus from his home city and begin explorations that would lead to a vast empire that ran from what is now Mexico down through Chile. That conquest inflicted terrible losses on the Aztecs and Incas, among other indigenous peoples.[47] Vasco da Gama journeyed around Africa in 1498, which eventually led to a vast Portuguese Empire that stretched from Brazil to Goa in India and the islands beyond. As we have seen, France consolidated its holdings and often expanded into the Italian provinces. While England sat safe in its island nation, the Ottoman Empire expanded from Istanbul into Greece, the Balkans, and finally Egypt in 1522. These consolidations of power and expansionist tendencies put Venice, Florence, Genoa, and the papal states at risk. Naples and Sicily fell to Spain. When King Carlos of Spain was elected Holy Roman Emperor Charles V in 1520, Spanish ascendency reached its peak by adding the German provinces and the Netherlands to its realm. When they weren't at war, these leaders commissioned a Baroque architecture that reasserted Catholicism in the face of the Protestant Reformation, which itself endorsed a more ascetic, plain architectural style in concert with its purification of the church. At the same time, rhetorical theory was being revived at various places by several important thinkers.

Agricola (1444–1485) and Melanchthon (1497–1560)

Rudolph Agricola and Philipp Melanchthon endorsed the interconnections of hermeneutics (interpretation and translation), argumentation, and rhetoric while reinforcing Cicero's threefold purpose of rhetoric: moving, pleasing, and informing.[48] They also argued that inquiry in the form of dialectic should precede advocacy in the form of speech. In other words, speakers should research their topics, interrogating them thoroughly before setting about to compose a speech. Such exercises include defining a topic, locating and discussing its causes, establishing criteria for any solutions to be proposed, and finally finding a solution to the problem at hand.

Agricola died at the age of forty-one; his works were all published after his death. As one who trained to be a lawyer and a scholastic, he believed no one should speak without being informed; therefore, inquiry took precedence over rhetoric in Agricola's works. Inquiry was the engine of invention for the speaker. In fact, his list of *topoi* is a synthesis of Boethius' *De differentiis topicis* and Cicero's *Topica*.[49] Agricola's work on textual analysis happily coincided with the new interest in Aristotle's *Rhetoric*. His *De inventione dialectica,* which was promoted by Erasmus (see below), treated language in its everyday uses and thereby moved argumentation closer to rhetoric, although Agricola continued to limit rhetoric to style and delivery. While holding the position of chair of rhetoric at Louvain, he separated the *topoi (loci* or *places)* from rhetoric, confining them to dialectic, a move Ramus (see below) would complete.[50]

Another influential voice was that of Melanchthon, who was educated in Heidelberg and Tubingen, where work on rhetoric continues to this day. In Wittenberg in 1519, he issued his *De rhetorica libri tres (Three Books on Rhetoric),*[51] which relies on hermeneutics to instruct readers about how to develop commentaries, and how to use tropology to adapt texts to various audiences. Melanchthon believed that hermeneu-

Philipp Melanchthon.

tics was a rhetorical process because translating and understanding the Bible required the interpreter to re-create context and persuade the reader that the interpretation was correct. Hermeneutics, the act of interpreting divine scripture, was where humans and God met because the scripture was inspired by God and translated by humans. Melanchthon's work on the letters of Paul and the gospel of Matthew continued the trend begun by Leon with the Old Testament, which linked rhetoric to religious interpretation, thereby elevating rhetoric's importance in the academic community in the Renaissance and Reformation.

In the midst of Luther's revolt from the church (see below), Melanchthon, who had collaborated with Luther at Wittenberg, supported his friend using traditional church fathers, such as Paul, Origen, and John Chrysostom to illustrate his text. Harkening back to a technique of Augustine, Melanchthon became the earliest Christian theorist in the Renaissance era to use the Bible to illustrate his lessons on style, arrangement, and argumentation; the latter added to his *Institutiones rhetoricae* of 1521.[52] While texts on preaching certainly used Biblical references, until Melanchthon and Leon, texts on rhetorical theory and handbooks on persuasion normally did not. For example, there is no illustrative use of the Bible in the works of Agricola. This technique was Melanchthon's contribution to the rise of rhetoric in the Renaissance and the Reformation.

From Wittenberg in 1520 he published *Loci communes*, a Protestant catechism that increased his popularity in countries that embraced the Reformation. He also had influence in Catholic countries, such as Spain, where his work was supported by Garcia Matamoros. His writing expanded the art of *dictamen* (the rhetoric of letter writing) by moving it toward an argument-based system. Showing his humanist side, Melanchthon also continued Augustine's work on redeeming the classicists. He wrote a commentary on Aristotle's *De anima* (*On the Soul*) and argued that Plato and Paul were right to reassert that a vision of good was planted in the human soul. Reasoning to that vision strengthened conscience. Like Plato, he believed that the vision of good in the soul could be reached by dialectical questioning and that it was the ultimate premise on which all truth was built.

Melanchthon could practice what he preached. In 1530 he took on the difficult task of composing the famous *Augsburg Confession*, which was approved by Luther, signed by seven Germanic princes, and presented to the emperor as an article of Protestant faith. By 1531, when Melanchthon issued his final rhetoric text, he had developed four forms for orations: judicial, deliberative, demonstrative, and dialectical.[53] He also discovered that tropes could be developed into arguments. An analogy, for example, is a figurative comparison that argues that two entities or concepts have similar traits: oil is like water because oil is normally found in a liquid state, but hardens at lower temperatures.

Erasmus (1465–1536)

The resurrection of the classicists and the religious debate during the Renaissance did a great deal to restore rhetoric as an art form. One of the most important rhetorical theorists who stayed in the Catholic Church was Desiderius Erasmus. Although he came to regret the decision because of the limits it placed on his writing, Erasmus was ordained into the priesthood in 1492. In 1494 he moved to Paris, where he became a lecturer at the College de Montaigu, one of several making up the University of Paris.

His first influential work was his collection of *Adages* published in 1500; the book advanced Christian virtues using fables and made Erasmus into the first humanist to make a decent living off of his writings. In 1508 a new, more popular version was published under the direction of the great Venetian publisher, Aldus Manutius. Erasmus' most famous work, *In Praise of Folly*, was published in 1511; it won him such acclaim that he was invited to visit and stay in the home of Sir Thomas More (another Catholic loyal to his church) in England. Eleven years later during the Protestant revolt, Erasmus published his *Colloquies*, dialogues that continued his enlightened themes regarding freedom, religion, and creativity.

Erasmus.

It was about this time that Erasmus criticized his friend Luther (see below) for his dogmatism and strident rhetoric. Erasmus preferred a more speculative approach to life and an internal reform of the church. He also preferred Aquinas' free will to Augustine's predestination, which provided another bone of contention with Luther. Nonetheless, Luther relied on Erasmus' scholarly version of the New Testament in Latin in 1522 and his translation, in 1534, of the Old Testament into German. Erasmus went around St. Jerome's *Vulgate* back to the original Greek manuscripts to make his transcriptions. In this way, he was able to correct some of the *Vulgate*'s errors. Erasmus' most important work for rhetorical theory was *De copia rerum et verborum (On Fullness of Expression)*, which drew heavily on Quintilian, set out a list of useful commonplaces, and quickly became a standard textbook throughout northern Europe. It suggested that rhetoric could enrich content as well as expression.[54] The book's reliance on humanistic instead of theological truths caused Erasmus to be condemned. Pope Paul IV, the former Cardinal Giovanni Carafa, put Erasmus' books on the *Index* of forbidden readings. Erasmus fled to Switzerland, where at age seventy he died a pauper living under a friend's roof in Basel.

Most of the humanist rhetors endorsed exercises in *suasoriae* (oratory) and *controversiae* (debate) keeping them in the curriculum well into the sixteenth century.[55] These were the natural extensions of the Greek *paideia* and the Roman *progymnasmata*. Humanists like Majoragius (1514–1555) and Nizzolius (1498–1576) even returned to the doctrines of the Sophists to argue that all philosophy is subsumed by rhetoric.[56] Nizzolius, who wrote extensively on Cicero, went so far as to argue that logic made the false appear true, thus turning the ancient attack on Sophists back on the scholastics.[57]

Ramus (1515–1572)

Reacting to these challenges to the scholastics was the influential Peter Ramus.[58] He provided the culmination of the scholastic attack on rhetoric when he stole invention and arrangement for his bifurcated version of logic, which he had derived from Agricola.[59] Ramus interpreted Agricola to divide invention (including inquiry and definition) from judgment (syllogism, arrangement, and method). Ironically, Ramus' theory replaced Agricola's in many schools because it was easier to teach.[60] While he did contribute to the French vernacular and believed poetry had a role in logic, he defined an oration as a syllogism amplified by figures. Ramus explained his distaste for rhetoric this way:

> When I came to Paris, I fell among the subtleties of the sophists, and they taught me the liberal arts through questions and disputings, without showing me any other advantage of use. When I had graduated . . . I decided that these disputes had brought me nothing but loss of time. Dismayed by this thought, led by some good angel, I chanced on Xenophon and then on Plato, and learned to know the Socratic philosophy.[61]

Ramus wrote more than fifty works, including the first analysis of the dialectical system of logic in French. Like a modern dean, he insisted that no academic disciplines should occupy the same space or share the same precepts.[62] Ever bifurcating his subject matter into his beloved "dichotomies,"[63] Ramus split his theory into a concern for hermeneutics (interpretation of texts) and composition of original texts. In the latter category, he reduced rhetoric's role to that of (1) embellishment through expression, including the tropes and figures, and (2) voice and gesture. For embellishment, Ramus provided tropes for "clothing" the speech. Ramus claimed there were only four primary tropes: metaphor, metonymy, synecdoche, and irony. Figures of diction concerned rhythm and repetition, and figures of the sentence included exclamation, apostrophe, and personification. As Walter Ong has made clear, even Ramus' version of style was crimped:

> [T]he Ramist plain style . . . is the verbal counterpart of the coming visualist universe of "objects," voiceless and by that very fact depersonalized, which would soon recommend to the Royal Society, . . . as near the "mathematical" as possible.[64]

On top of that, Ramus reduced memory to a product of arrangement and order, thus converting even memory to a province of dialectic.

Worse yet, he attacked Aristotle's notion of practical reasoning and collapsed all categories of argumentation into analytics.[65] He delighted in ridiculing Cicero and Quintilian by arguing that they had confused dialectic and rhetoric.[66] For this he was censured by a commission established by King Francis I. Ramus' influential friends interceded when the new King Henry II came to power in 1547; they saved Ramus' career, and he became a prominent if arrogant professor at the University of Paris in 1551, where the king made him regius professor. Soon Ramus was attracting huge audiences to his lectures. He refined his earlier writing into *Dialectique* in 1555.

In 1557 he was granted a powerful copyright to license his past and future works. In 1561, he became controversial again when he revealed that he was a Protestant Huguenot. Nonetheless, in 1565, he was promoted to dean of all professors. From 1568 to 1570, he served on the Cultural Commission to Swiss and Germanic provinces, where he was able to propagate his theories. This proved to be his undoing. Although, in deference to her deceased husband Henry II, Queen Marie de Medici and her son King Charles IX had explicitly excluded Ramus from her order to kill a group of Huguenot leaders, he was thrown from

Petrus Ramus.

his window at his lodgings during the purge of Huguenots on St. Bartholomew's Day in 1572.[67] He survived on the street below but was stabbed to death and his body was thrown into the Seine River.

The Calvinists embraced the martyred Ramus and his theories; they sought a purer language to enlighten the understanding and move the soul to conversion.[68] English Calvinists, known as Puritans, spread Ramus' theory in their country and became ascendant under the iron rule of Oliver Cromwell; one of his followers, the poet John Milton, translated Ramus' logic into the English vernacular.[69] Ramus' influence was then passed through Cambridge University to Ireland, where the first provosts of the new Trinity College in Dublin were Puritans, and to America where it came to dominate the early Harvard curriculum, particularly for preachers who needed to achieve conversions among their flock.[70]

THE PROTESTANT REVOLT

While Melanchthon used scholarship to propagate Protestantism in Northern Europe, Martin Luther and Ulrich von Hutten advanced it in more militant ways. Together, they created a new genre of vituperation in their attacks on the Catholic Church. Von Hutten referred to Rome as a "gigantic bloodsucking worm."[71] Luther labeled papal bulls (decrees) as *dreck* (dung); he referred to monks as fleas.[72] When Pope Leo X finally banned Luther's writings in June of 1520, Luther reacted by burning the papal bull and renouncing his penalty that December.

Initially Luther (an Augustinian monk and later lecturer at the University of Wittenberg) took a higher road by standing on the shoulders of those who had gone before him, including Savonarola, John Wyclif, John Hus, and some mystics.[73] In Prague, Hus (1369–1415) had built on the reforms of Wyclif by arguing against the sale of indulgences to fund the pope's war with the king of Naples.[74] Like the Iconoclasts, he opposed praying to statues. He claimed that kingdoms should oversee church property and temporal possessions. More important, he advanced the controversial proposition that transubstantiation of bread into Christ's body and wine into his blood did not take place during the mass. That is, the transformation of bread and wine was purely symbolic. To defend himself against charges of heresy, Hus was granted safe passage by his emperor to the papal court meeting in Constance, near the Rhine, to hear the case against Pope John XXIII in 1410. Nonetheless, Hus was arrested, condemned, and imprisoned in a Dominican monastery. After five years and in ill health, Hus was excommunicated in the cathedral of Constance and taken away in chains. He was burned at the stake a little more than a century before Luther's rebellion.[75] The distraction did not deter the council from forcing the pope to step down; his name was stricken from the list of popes.

A fellow heretic of Hus, Jerome of Prague, nailed his reforms to the gates of the city of Constance. During his trial he took the same position Luther would at Worms: he would apologize only for what could be refuted by scripture directly.[76] After Hus' fate, Jerome recanted but later reasserted Hus' doctrine, for which he too was burned at the same stake. Johannes Eckhart (1260–1328), the German mystic, had posited the thesis that all humans have souls that can put them in touch with God.[77] It is not a far leap from that position to arguing that every person could be his/her own priest, a stance Luther would endorse. Clearly, major tenets of Luther's philosophy as well as his rhetorical strategies had been rehearsed by those who went before him.

Luther (1483–1543) and Protestant Preaching

Martin Luther had an easier time than his predecessors because the printing press spread his attacks across Europe, Germanic princes rallied to his defense, and scientific discovery had eroded church dogma. For example, in 1514, three years before Luther tacked his *Ninety-Five Theses* to a church door, Nicolaus Copernicus argued that the earth circled the sun; the earth was not the center of the universe. Although this notion was too radical for even Luther to accept and he referred to Copernicus as an "upstart astrologer," the new science would certainly strengthen Luther's hand. It would also be strengthened by growing nationalism. He would gain the support of princes who wished to be free of the church and the Holy Roman Emperor.

As an Augustinian monk from the priory at Wittenberg, Luther was trained in the Pauline tradition, provided with commentaries on all of Augustine's works, and steeped in Aristotelian rhetoric, ethics, and logic.[78] He also admired Cicero, not only for his rhetorical theory, but also for his morals. Luther believed that rhetoric and the other arts were servants of God.

Luther's ascetic life made him a keen observer of the luxuries of the Vatican when he visited Rome in 1510 at the age of 31. Though it required a long trek, the visit to the Vatican was a reward for his excellence in teaching. However, Luther was soon affronted by what he saw. Pope Julius II's French hounds were fed on gold plates, and their food was much better than that served to the monks of Luther's austere order. He witnessed other scandalous behavior at the pope's dinner table, including nude children rising out of the pudding being served. When he visited the Sistine Chapel, he found Michelangelo painting the forty-by-fourteen-yard ceiling with nude figures. When Luther visited the catacombs of St. Callixtus, he discovered that the pope was selling indulgences (forgiveness for sins) there and in other places to fund his wars. Luther also saw that the warrior pope was skilled at making alliances and more concerned about the temporal world than the spiritual realm.

Luther was traumatized by his visit to Rome. When he returned to Wittenberg, Saxony, he spent hour upon hour in the confessional. His superiors feared that he was having a breakdown. Six years later on October 31, 1517, Luther began his revolt by tacking his *Ninety-Five Theses* to the front door of Castle Church. This practice was not unusual; theologians regularly put up such documents to invite debate on the nearby campus. In fact, in September 1517, Luther had posted theses attacking the scholastics' reliance on Aristotelianism.[79] What was unusual in Luther's October posting was its timing *(kairos)*. His posting took place on All Hallow's Eve, as pilgrims and the prayerful were coming to town to attend services for the following holy day of obligation, All Saints' Day. When the university refused to sponsor a public debate on his theses, Luther's friends disseminated them. Soon they had bled across the continent; printing presses from Valencia to Copenhagen and from London to Krakow provided outlets for Luther's Reformation. The pope was not amused.

Luther also demonstrated his understanding of audience when he published his attack on the selling of indulgences, *Disputatio pro declaratione virtutis indulgentiarum*, in the vernacular. Now everyone who could read German would know about the abuses of the church. By this time there was much to condemn. When Luther was a child, Pope Innocent VIII (1484–1492) had sanctioned the selling of indulgences even for those who had already died and might be suffering in purgatory. After returning from Rome, Luther was enraged when Tetzel came through his province to sell the indulgences that Pope Leo X (1513–1521) had authorized.[80] Luther's fame was enhanced when Tetzel responded to Luther with a set of antitheses in December of 1517. Luther became a target of the church; the religious community would have to take sides. Sheltered

Martin Luther.

by Frederick the Wise, ruler of Saxony, Luther seized the moment by publishing *Indulgence and Grace*, a treatise advancing his attack on simony, the selling of spiritual items and church offices.

In the new year of 1518, Luther seemed to undergo a change of heart. He tried appeasing Pope Leo X with a disingenuous letter that he would come to regret:

> What shall I do? I cannot recall my theses and yet I see that great hatred is kindled against me by their popularity. . . . I cast myself and all my possessions at your feet; raise me up or slay me, summon me hither or thither, approve me or reprove me as you please. I shall recognize your words as the words of Christ.[81]

It was not to be. When Leo asked Luther to desist in his attacks, the rebellious monk refused. From July 4 to 14, 1519, Luther engaged the theologian Johann von Eck in a lengthy disputation in Leipzig. Luther renounced the pope and the church councils, and endorsed the teachings of John Hus, the heretic of Prague.[82] Speaking for the Catholic Church, Eck argued that since Jesus had created it, the church was perfect and therefore in no need of reform. Most on the scene believed that Luther had been defeated in this confrontation, but they underestimated his continued influence with the middle class. In the first place, the debate recognized Luther as the chief spokesperson of dissenters; in the second, it established a tradition in which rhetoric would play an important role: the debating of religious tenets.

In 1520, again in the vernacular, Luther published *The Appeal to the Christian Nobility of the German Nation*, which declared a "priesthood of all believers."[83] The document not only played on antipapal sentiment among the people and their princes, it encouraged nationalism and individualism. Luther wrote to Georg Spalatin, a reformist who gained the confidence of the elector (prince) of Saxony, that "a revolution is about to take place. . . . The word of God can never be advanced without a whirlwind."[84] Leo X issued *Exsurge Domine* on June 15, 1520, condemning forty-one separate statements by Luther. Luther burned the pope's bull in public and then tossed a book by Eck into the fire.

Many princes sprang to Luther's defense[85] and then protected him after he made his famous statement before the Diet at Worms in April of 1521 under interrogation by Eck: "Here I stand; I can do no other. God help me. Amen."[86] Allies of the pope, including the former King Carlos of Catholic Spain, who had become Holy Roman Emperor Charles V in 1520, and Henry VIII of England, condemned Luther for his refusal to recant his teachings. Luther was now an international cause célèbre.

By 1525 so many peasants believed Luther's rhetoric to be a call for revolt that they took to the streets. However, Luther was no democrat; after all, he had been protected by one prince and many others had supported him. Luther wrote *Against the Murdering, Thieving Hordes of Peasants*, reviving his vitriolic style and offending peasant leaders. When their revolt was crushed, these peasants turned to other Protestant leaders and religions. The Germanic states fell into chaos and would not be united until 1870.

As he continued his reformation into the 1530s, Luther elevated the importance of rhetoric in many ways. With the help of Melanchthon, Luther translated first the New Testament and then the entire Bible into German, thus allowing "every man to become his own priest." His version sold over 100,000 copies. Furthermore, Luther made the sermon the centerpiece of the Protestant service, as opposed to the Catholic mass that featured communion at its center. Sermons became public speaking events, as Luther urged preachers not to write out their sermons but to memorize them or to deliver them extemporaneously, as Jesus and his disciples had done. When the gospels were revived in live sermons, according to Luther, they most resembled what they had been like in Jesus' time.[87]

Together with Melanchthon, Luther reformed and revived the flagging German universities. He sought to replace the teaching of pagans with an emphasis on the teachings of Jesus as explained by St. Paul. Though he endorsed the study of rhetoric, he had nothing but disdain for the person of Aristotle, whom Luther saw as a "damned, conceited, rascally heathen."[88] He wrote curricular plans and textbooks, including one on rhetoric. By mid-century, Lutherans controlled the universities at Wittenberg, Marburg, Tubingen, Leipzig, Konigsberg, and Jena, and rhetoric was a strong part of the curriculum.[89]

The Spread of Protestantism

The revolt against the Catholic Church swept into Switzerland when a priest named Ulrich Zwingli (1484–1531) led a "liberal" reform movement that endorsed the authority of the Bible over the authority of the church. Zwingli had been ordained as a priest in the Catholic Church in 1506. He was a humanist who had great respect for Erasmus (see above), who was 20 years his senior, but came to believe that the discipline necessary for faith could only be achieved outside the Catholic Church. In 1519, he began his own reformation two years after Luther's. Zwingli condemned fasting, celibacy for priests, the sale of indulgences, and the use of mercenary soldiers by the pope, since many of them came from Switzerland. Rising in political circles in Zurich, he was able to have the mass abandoned altogether in 1525 and replaced by a simple communion service.

Zwingli's reconceptualization of the Eucharist provides an excellent example of the kind of theological question that requires rhetorical resolution. He believed that the communion of the mass commemorated the last supper of Christ but did not embody Christ himself. Luther's position, dubbed consubstantiation, was a middle position between Zwingli's and the Catholic one; Luther retained the notion of a miraculous moment in the communion without admitting to an actual change of substance in the bread and wine. Zwingli succeeded in converting Zurich to his reform. He then debated Luther in Marburg, which opened a bitter division between them. Luther referred to Zwingli as "My Judas."[90] Zwingli referred to Luther's work as "lies, slander, sycophancy, and suspicion."[91] In 1531, Zwingli was killed during a battle with Catholics in the Swiss civil war.

While Zwingli attracted a German Swiss following, John Calvin (Jean Cauvin, 1509–1564) began his ministry among the French but was exiled to Switzerland in 1534 for his beliefs. In Geneva he created the Presbyterian church. In a direct challenge to humanists, he preached:

> Read Demosthenes or Cicero, read Plato, Aristotle, or any others of that class; I grant you that you will be attracted, delighted, moved and enraptured by them in a surprising manner; but if, after reading them, you turn to the perusal of the holy

volume, whether you are willing or unwilling, it will affect you so powerfully, it will so penetrate your heart, and impress itself so strongly on your mind, that, compared with its energetic influence, the beauties of rhetoricians and philosophers will almost certainly disappear.[92]

He published his highly influential *Institutes of the Christian Religion* (1536) that became a favorite of the English Puritans. And despite Calvin's warning about Cicero, he read from Cicero's works every year.

Calvin's success is partly due to his rhetorical training while in law school; he was as convincing as Augustine and certainly built on his ideas. For example, Calvin was thoroughly grounded in Augustine's notion of predestination and extended its application to his "chosen few." He also inspired the conformity and cruelty of the Puritans by punishing blasphemy, adultery, and idolatry with death; fornication was punished by drowning. There were reports that a child was beheaded for striking its parents.[93] Since the sin of one was the sin of all, Puritan communities were intolerant of diversity, let alone libertine activity.

Geneva was to become Calvin's City of God, which inspired the sermonizing of Jonathan Winthrop on board the *Arabella* as it sailed to Massachusetts Bay Colony. Winthrop's Puritans were driven from England by the rise of Bishop Laud and by the Anglican resurgence of 1629, and Winthrop sought a "shining city upon a hill" for a new home.[94] For Puritans, the New Zion was the ideal to which they aspired; the Old World was the reality they sought to escape. They would perfect the chosen in order to rectify relations with an omnipotent God. All of these goals were set into a Covenant theology first established by Calvin. In this way he exerted a major influence on the development of American values and rhetorical practice that would evolve into a civil religion (see chapter 10).

RELIGIOUS INTOLERANCE

Competition between religions ushered in a new age of intolerance. Etienne Dolet was burned at the stake for publishing classical works that had been put on the *Index*. The writer Bonaventure Desperiers committed suicide rather than suffer the same fate. In Geneva starting in 1542, Calvin carried on a pogrom against his enemies and sinners, including his stepson. Once the Catholics of Switzerland defeated Zwingli, they burned his body on a pyre. Historian Will Durant writes this about the reformers:

> The intolerant dogmatism of the Reformers, their violence of speech, their sectarian fragmentation and animosities, their destruction of religious art, their predestinarian theology, their indifference to secular learning, their renewed emphasis on demons and hell, their concentration on personal salvation in a life beyond the grave—all these shared in alienating the humanists from the Reformation.[95]

However, the new freedom to debate could not be crushed entirely by the dogmatism of the reformist theologians. As religious debates raged across Europe, as deliberative forums became more common, as courtiers desired to present themselves not as medieval knights but as gentlemen, and as artists like Shakespeare dazzled audiences with their brilliant use of rhetoric, theorists found ways of restoring rhetoric to prominence.

Perhaps no figure better represents the confluence of these threads than the brilliant Dominican monk Giordano Bruno (1548–1600). He was an astronomer and philosopher who advanced the skill of recall with a system that he dubbed "artificial memory." In Rome and Venice and before the royal courts in London, Paris, and Prague, he dazzled many an audience with his ability to recollect obscure facts. He extended the work of Ramon Llull (1232–1316), who had replaced the Greco-Roman system of placing the parts of a speech in various parts of one's house. Llull invented a system of concentric wheels that allowed him to dial up pieces of his memory. In his book *On the Shadows of Ideas*, Bruno used the wheels to organize syllables for various words. He moved the system into the realm of invention when the wheels brought new ideas into association with older ones. Bruno also isolated sense experiences into "first principles," which John Locke (see chapter 8) would call "primary ideas." As would Locke, Bruno worked these "principles" into ladders of abstraction. (I see rose, crimson, and blood, which I abstract into the higher principle of "reds." I see reds, blues, and greens, which I abstract into the higher principle

Giordano Bruno.

of "colors.") Bruno was also a critic of the Catholic Church and condemned as a heretic because he extended Copernicus' theory to argue that the sun was a star around which the earth revolved. He was imprisoned in 1592 and tried by the Inquisition that was particularly offended by his belief that God pervaded nature (Pantheism). He was burned to death on the Campo de Fiori (Field of Flowers) in Rome on Ash Wednesday 1600; his remains were scattered in the Tiber River, a short distance away. Today a statue of Bruno in the center of the Campo commemorates the event.

Scientific breakthroughs, like those of Bruno, crumbled the walls of dogma, even in Italy. By 1610 Galileo had invented the telescope and could verify the theory of Copernicus and observe the moons around Jupiter. He wrote to church fathers to convince them to accept it.[96] Almost as revolutionary was his refutation of Aristotle's theory that bodies fell at a speed proportional to their weight. This led secular Aristotelian scholars to persecute Galileo, though many clerics supported his position. Galileo tried to protect himself by writing his theories into dialogues; ideas that were defended and attacked by various characters, much like Platonic dialogues. This rhetorical tactic was common among scientists and philosophers who did not want to claim directly that they were presenting ideas that the church condemned. In fact, Galileo was sheltered by a nephew of the pope until the Aristotelians planted false data in Galileo's papal file, and he wrote a dialogue that they claimed made fun of the pope. When the church condemned some of Galileo's interpretations, several cardinals refused to sign the judgment. With so many competing nation-states and such a rebirth in discovery, the church could not contain Galileo's ideas. Nor could it prevent the Medici family from protecting the astronomer while they remained in power in Florence. At age 70 he was finally hauled before the Inquisition in Rome, while residing at the Medici palace there. After his hearing, Galileo was put under house arrest, albeit just outside Florence until his death in 1642.

THE COUNTER-REFORMATION

The restoration of rhetoric advanced as the Catholic Church was buffeted by theological attacks and political misfortune during and after the Renaissance. The rivalry among the Catholic rulers undercut their loyalty to the pope. In 1520 Henry VIII, Francis I, and King Carlos of Spain all sought the crown of the Holy Roman Empire. Carlos won the bidding war and became the emperor, Charles V, but that led to more tension. In 1523 Charles and Francis went to war over control of Italy. On his twenty-fifth birthday, Charles' forces won the battle of Pavia, capturing Francis. In 1527 German and Spanish mercenaries sacked Rome when the Medici pope shifted allegiance from Charles V, whom he had crowned, to Francis I. Charles was also hampered by the revolt of Martin Luther, who was protected by Germanic princes even though they were supposedly loyal to Charles.[97] The infighting of Christians and their monarchs continued for many years, sapping the strength of the Christian forces and inviting the Ottoman (Turkish) Empire to expand in areas around the Mediterranean Sea and in Eastern Europe. By 1529, the Ottoman army was at the gates of Vienna. It was saved, but a peace treaty was not signed until 1533. In the meantime, Pope Paul III (1534–1549) called the Council of Trent in 1545. Eighteen years later, it issued a finding that led to many reforms in the Catholic Church; it established a stricter doctrine that led to a renewed asceticism and rejection of that which is worldly. Under Pius V (1566–1572), the catechism of the church was standardized and a common missal was adopted.

In 1547, one year after Luther's death, some believed peace might come when Charles V won the battle of Muhlberg on the Elbe River and consolidated his hold over the German provinces. He had beaten the Schmalkaldic League of Protestant princes. A few year later, Charles V's son, Philip II of Spain, then married the new queen of England, Mary Tudor, further strengthening the grip of the Hapsburgs on Europe. At the same time, the Ottoman Turks were diverted by a war with Persia in 1555, which had its roots in the division between the Sunni Ottomans and the Shia Persians. However, in the same year, Charles was defeated in a series of battles that led to the Peace of Augsburg, which formally recognized all established religions in Europe. Charles' nephew Maxmilian was elected Holy Roman emperor to replace Charles when he abdicated.

Further setbacks plagued the Hapsburg Empire when Philip II pulled Spain out of the Holy Roman Empire resentful that he had not been elected Holy Roman Emperor. His wife, Queen Mary, died of cancer, and Protestants reasserted themselves in England by bringing her half-sister Elizabeth to the throne. Rome responded when Pius V became pope in 1566. He excommunicated Elizabeth I in 1569 and supported the intrigues of Mary Queen of Scots, a Catholic. He eventually formed the Holy League with Spain and Venice when Cyprus fell into Ottoman hands. The pope formalized the league in a great celebration in St. Peter's Basilica in Rome on May 25, 1571, and a few months later it won a tremendous sea victory over the Turks at Lepanto. Even though the Holy League soon fell apart, the persecution of Protestants continued. As we have seen, Queen Marie de Medici of France and her son King Charles IX launched a holocaust on St. Bartholomew's Day in 1572 that raged for three days and resulted in the death of 20,000 Huguenots, among them the scholar Peter Ramus. Then in 1588, the Spanish Armada of Philip II was defeated in the English Channel by the Protestant forces of Queen Elizabeth I.

Throughout this period, the Catholic Church engaged in theological debate, using its best minds to combat heresy. Erasmus consistently rebutted the arguments of Luther, while Jesuits fanned out across Europe to seek and destroy the arguments of his followers. The Jesuits were founded by Ignatius Loyola (1491–1558) and were recognized as an order in 1540. In fact, 35 craters on the moon are named for Jesuits. Loyola was learned in Cicero, Quintilian, Erasmus, and, of course, Aquinas and Augustine.[98] Among his followers, rhetorical training was a must. Their goal was propagation of the faith. Their first college flourished in Padua, encouraging them to establish their most famous one in Rome in 1551. In the process they developed such leading rhetors as Cypriano Soares, who wrote *De arte rhetorica*, which went into more than 100 editions.

Nicolas Caussin (1580–1651) built on Soares' work while serving as confessor to Louis XIII of France. Caussin's tome, *De eloquentia sacra et humana*, expands on Soares' call for a more emotional approach to preaching by retrieving Aristotle's notion of *pathos*.

Claude Buffier (1661–1737) wrote a text on memory in 1705 that was popular on the Continent and in the British Isles. His text on style, *Traité de l'eloquence*, in 1728 was derived from the standard classical scholarship of Aristotle and the Romans.[99] Buffier believed that effective speakers had a natural "ability" to speak eloquently once they understood their subject matter. Rules and practice can refine this talent but cannot produce it where it does not exist. In other words, Buffier very much believed in the Isocratean model of natural ability, practice, and rhetorical theory combining to produce effective speakers.

These Jesuits undoubtedly influenced Charles Rollin (1661–1741) to write his treatise on eloquence or "belles-lettres." Rollin was a prominent educator who had enormous respect for the study of language. He created a curriculum in Paris to compete with the Jesuit exercises. He endorsed imitation through memory, and debates on various propositions. All of these exercises were to produce a student who could speak French and Latin in highly stylized but tasteful ways. In part because it was derived from Quintilian, his text was very popular on the Continent and particularly influential on the Scottish writers on rhetoric, as we shall see in the next chapter.

THE ENGLISH RENAISSANCE

The tension between the kings of England and their nobles led to the rise of a parliamentary system that required polished public speaking. The Parliament evolved from a council of priests, nobles, ministers, and landholders who advised the king. The first reference to the word "parliament" occurred in 1081 after William of Normandy had conquered England. In 1265, when Simon de Montfort seized power and imprisoned Henry III, Simon, the king's brother-in-law, called a parliament for advice. Simon was killed in the ensuing civil war at the Battle of Evesham, but his idea took hold. Henry III's son Edward I regularly called parliaments into session. By 1332, Parliament was divided into a House of Lords and a House of Commons. By 1377 the Commons had its own "Speaker" who represented the wishes of the Commons to the king. By the time of Henry VIII, Parliament was well established but only called into session at the request of the king, for example, to support his reformation of the church.

The Renaissance in England was closely tied to the movement for reformation in the church and the rebirth of rhetorical theory. In the fourteenth century, John Wyclif, an Oxford scholar, urged the Catholic Church to give up its temporal powers and possessions.[100] He harkened back to Augustine's doctrine of predestination, which (as we have seen) became the foundation of Calvin's puritanical sect that appealed to many in England in the early 1600s. The son of the king, John of Gaunt, employed Wyclif to defend the proposition that the crown had the right to confiscate church property. By 1351 the Statute of Provisors weakened papal control over the revenues raised by English parishes. Wyclif went a step further by arguing for the independence of the church in England from Rome and condemning the selling of pardons, a theme, as we have seen, that Luther took up over a century later. These "radical" views eventually lost Wyclif the favor of the crown. However, before that eventuality, Wyclif translated the *Vulgate* of St. Jerome into English, claiming it should be the only guide to faith. This, along with the writings of Chaucer in the vernacular, contributed to the development and democratization of the English language.[101] In fact, when Caxton brought his printing press to England in 1476, he printed documents only in the vernacular, thus stimulating the English language and that country's sense of nationalism.

Wyclif was followed by William Tyndale, who took refuge in Germany because of persecution by Catholics. There he studied with Luther and published an English translation of the Bible in 1526 over the objections of the Catholic Church. Three thousand copies were published in Worms, where Luther had taken his stand against the church. This highly influential book was translated from the Greek and Latin; it was considered a literary masterpiece dotted with such memorable phrases as "filthy lucre," "salt of the earth," and "sign of the times." It was a major improvement on Wyclif's Bible. It later inspired Shakespeare and transformed middle English to a much more literate language.[102] Sir Thomas More, King Henry VIII's chancellor, who later lost his head for not approving of Henry's break with Rome, condemned Tyndale as a "hell hound." The Bishop of London sponsored a burning of a mound of copies of Tyndale's Bible at the end of 1526 on the steps of St. Paul's Cathedral. In 1535 Tyndale was kidnapped in Antwerp and condemned in the Netherlands the next year. He was tied to a stake and, because he was a noted scholar, strangled before his body was burned.[103] But by that time, his Bible had sold 50,000 copies. At least three-quarters of the language in the King James Bible of 1611, the most popular ever, was derived from Tyndale's translation. Among Protestants, the King James Bible replaced the Geneva Bible of the Calvinists as the most popular in England.

In 1521 the pope had named Henry VIII Defender of the Faith because of his condemnation of the Reformation in general and Luther in particular. When Henry was the young Duke of York, he received an education that gives us a look inside the renaissance curriculum of princes. He was tutored by John Rede, a rhetor and poet of some renown. Rede was replaced by John Skelton, a poet laureate at Oxford and also a master of rhetorical theory, particularly Cicero's. He prided himself on continuing to improve on Chaucer's effort to create a vernacular for the English. Skelton was so valuable to the royal family that he was eventually appointed Prince Harry's chaplain, teaching him to speak well or be silent. Eventually, the young Thomas More, who was studying with Erasmus, brought his Latin-speaking mentor to meet Henry at Eltham, where he resided with his sisters. After this visit, Erasmus retreated to Oxford, where he discovered the English renaissance and came to prefer it to the one in Italy.

When Henry was ten, his older brother Arthur, Prince of Wales, suddenly died, and eventually Henry took Arthur's widow, Catherine of Aragon, as his wife. She was the daughter of Ferdinand and Isabella, who had united Spain. Henry seemed happily married to Catherine of Aragon. In fact, when Henry went off to war in 1513, it was Catherine who ran the government and succeeded in the war against James IV of Scotland. However, Catherine's only son died in his sixth week of life; her daughter Mary, born in 1516, was a disappointment to a king who wanted a son, though Henry later gave her the title of Princess of Wales, the only woman to hold the title in English history. Catherine miscarried again in 1517.

The marriage to Catherine lasted another decade. Then Henry fell in love with Anne Boleyn and asked for a divorce from Catherine. The divorce trial in London in 1529 was sensational, especially when Catherine gave an emotional speech recounting her twenty years of marriage to Henry. The case was appealed to Rome. However, the pope was in a difficult position. Catherine was not only the daughter of the king and queen of Spain, she was the aunt of the Holy Roman Emperor, Charles V, upon whom the pope relied for protection. So the pope refused to approve of Henry's divorce from Catherine.

In response, Henry established himself as head of the Anglican church with an Act of Supremacy that

Henry VIII.

ended all connection with Rome. He strengthened the crown's control of the press but at the same time required all churches to make a copy of the Bible available to their parishioners. He closed the monasteries of the Catholic Church and confiscated their properties. In 1539 Parliament supported Henry by passing the Six Articles that defined the Anglican church as a Catholic body separate from a temporal pope. Though Henry had a daughter by Anne named Elizabeth, Anne failed to give him a son. He soon accused her of being unfaithful, and she was beheaded, having been queen only a thousand days. Henry's wife Jane Seymour did give him a son, Edward, who ruled for a short time under a regency after his father died. He was crowned at Westminster Abbey in 1547. His regents, the most powerful of which was his grandfather, developed a mass in the vernacular and a *Book of Common Prayer* in an attempt to strengthen the Anglican church. These moves led to several revolts in the kingdom. A few years later, the sickly Edward died before he could assume full powers over England. His older half-sister Mary became queen and was initially welcomed to London with a great outpouring of support, especially among the Catholic population. As we have seen, she married Philip of Spain and ruled successfully until conspiracies forced her to undertake brutal measures of suppression. After burning several Anglican bishops at the stake, she became known as "Bloody Mary." She was soon brought down by cancer. Her half-sister Elizabeth, the daughter of Anne Boleyn, became one of England's longest reigning monarchs. The civil unrest that surrounded the successions to the throne was accompanied by a revolution in rhetorical theory.

As in other countries, humanism played an initial role in the Renaissance of rhetorical theory in England. For example, the *Progymnasmata*, originally written by Apthonius of Antioch in AD 375, was published in Venice in 1508 and quickly found its way to England. The book explored declamation and various tricks of invention. This approach was imitated by many, including Richard Rainolde, who wrote *Foundacion of Rhetorike* in 1563.

Reflecting the influence of Melanchthon, Leonard Cox wrote the first book on rhetoric in the English language, *The Arte or Crafte of Rhetoryke* (1530).[104] Cox's textbook proved more comprehensive and influential even though it ignored memory and combined style and delivery. He divided the logical genre between simple and compound themes such as definition, cause, and effect. Cox added the "logical" form of public speaking to the standard list of deliberative, forensic, and epideictic. The logical form took up philosophical questions such as: Is justice supposed to be virtuous? or, Can all ethics be written into law?

After studying and teaching at Oxford, Richard Sherry published his *Treatise on Schemes and Tropes* (1550), which was also strongly influenced by Melanchthon. It was an attempt to develop a sense of grammar and elocution, by which Sherry meant proper "expression" in young students. In 1555 he published *Figures of Grammar and Rhetoric*, a revised edition of his first treatise, which acknowledged his debt to Agricola and Cicero. The book reinforced his definition of rhetoric as "wisdom speaking eloquently," by which he meant the truth by itself is not enough. True ideas need to be properly phrased and dressed to be understood and accepted.

More important was the humanist and anti-Catholic, Thomas Wilson (1523–1581), who had an active life as a diplomat and a member of the Privy Council, a formal body of advisors to the monarchy, during the reign of Elizabeth I. He was thrown in prison by Pope Paul IV, but eventually was freed and made secretary of state by his queen. His *The Rule of Reason* was the first book on logic written in English; it reworked the topics set out by Agricola, who had created his list by combining those of Boethius and Cicero. Like Aristotle, Wilson conceived of the topics as "A place . . . the resting corner of an argument . . . none other thing, but the storehouse of reason and the fountaine of all wisedom."[105]

Wilson's *The Arte of Rhetorique* (1553) brought all five classical canons into the English language for the first time, although he privileged invention, arrangement, and style over memory and delivery, which again reflects the influence of Melanchthon on English rhetors. Writing in the English vernacular, Wilson grouped teaching, delighting with words, and persuading under the province of rhetoric.[106] He retrieved the civic ideals of Quintilian and extended the stasis system of Cicero to preaching.[107] On organization, he repeated Cicero's divisions (exordium, narration, confirmation, confutation, and peroration) but did suggest that the speaker's strongest arguments be put at the beginning and the end to shield the weaker arguments placed in between from attack. Wilson claimed that "rules were made by wisemen, and not wisemen by rules." Then in the conclusion, the speaker needed to employ amplification for effect. Echoing *On the Sublime*, Wilson called for grand conceptions that "set the Judges on fire, and heate them earnestly against the wicked offender." Wilson also expanded deliberative oratory to such interpersonal communication as dealing with neighbors. Wilson's text dominated English rhetorical theory until Thomas Hobbes provided commentaries and translations of Aristotle's *Rhetoric* in 1637 (see below).

Wilson's text on rhetoric is grounded in an apocalyptic worldview that endorses a division between good and evil; that dialectic also reflects the influence of Ramus, a contemporary of Wilson. Wilson remained wedded in part to the medieval notion of classes and discourse, often assigning rhetoric teachers the task of making lower classes (which he referred to as "beasts") more articulate by bringing them to the "kynges English." Like the medieval scholastics we studied earlier, Wilson assigned different rhetorical talents to different classes of human beings. He endorsed three types of style, the "mighty," the "small," and the "low," for adaptation to the class structure of England. Worse, he allowed no integration of such styles. Once a speaker chose a level, that style should pervade the entire address.[108]

Wilson believed that every discipline could be reduced to a method.[109] His discussion of memory is the longest of any of the Tudor scholars since he analyzed its relationship with method, organization, and logic. Delivery was divided into voice and gesture, just as Ramus had suggested.[110] Nonetheless, his book did endorse the teaching of the art of rhetoric that led in part to its renaissance in England. The introduction of rhetorical studies to England caused a debate over the proper uses of rhetoric in the courts. In 1600, William Fulbecke wrote *A Directive or Preparative to the Study of Law*, which reviewed and refuted arguments made by Wilson and others in support of rhetoric.

Henry Peacham and George Puttenham argued for and practiced rhetoric as tropology. Henry Peacham's influence on Shakespeare's use of tropes and figures was significant. He published *Garden of Eloquence* in 1577. Puttenham claimed that art was a "certain order of rules prescribed by reason, and gathered by experience."[111] He was caught up in the beauty of the "artificial," that which humans created. The virtue of figurative language was its novelty and sense of liveliness. He believed that language brings art to perfection through practice, including those "artes of Grammar, *Logicke,* and *Rhetorick.*"[112] The figures of rhetoric were superior to the figures of poetry, and poets should consider themselves orators if they were to achieve the pinnacle of their art.[113] Like Horace and Cicero before him, Puttenham believed that style was the image of the speaker (*mentis imago,* or character). That is why in chapter V of Book III, *The Art of English Poesie,* he claimed that style projects one's persona.

The neoclassical period in England revived Horace in poetry and literature, and Cicero and Quintilian in rhetoric, and as we have seen, Tyndale's Bible had improved the language.[114] It was during this period that the King James version of the Bible was written. No wonder its use of language is so striking and its text became so popular. Soon Thomas Hobbes set about to undermine Descartes' (see chapter 8) claims by arguing: because I dream, I may not exist. While establishing a basis for skepticism, he also endorsed Cicero's view that rhetorical training was crucial for counseling, teaching, pleasing, and delighting.[115] In 1635 Hobbes cobbled together a Latin version of Theodore Goulston's 1619 Latin translation of Aristotle's *Rhetoric.* Hobbes then wrote a compendium in English, which he completed in 1637. He is far better known for his *Leviathan,* which warned that humans' first concern was self-preservation. Thus, to overcome self-interest, they must concede certain rights to the state to achieve social order and protection. The quest for this security required the people to place their governmental rules above the laws of nature and the church. Like Machiavelli, Hobbes argued that the public often needed to be motivated by fear.

The belletristic scholars such as Joseph Addison (1672–17199) and Dennis Diderot (1713–1784), who followed in the mid-seventeenth to late-eighteenth centuries, advocated the theories of Aristotle, Cicero, and Quintilian. Then, swept away in the desire to create sublime prose and to imitate nature, they retrieved Longinus' transporting theory of the sublime with English examples. In the next century, Edmund Burke, John Lawson, and Alexander Gerard developed the notion of taste, inclusive of a sense of proportion, symmetry, and appropriateness, which we will review in the next chapter.[116] This led to the further application of the principles of rhetoric to writing, particularly criticism. These writers realized that good criticism was argumentative and persuasive.

THE SPANISH RENAISSANCE

The Renaissance came more slowly to Spain, where the Catholic Church exercised its authority with incredible cruelty, especially under Ferdinand and Isabella who revived the Inquisition in 1480 to ferret out the heretics and convert the Jews and Muslims.[117] Muslim mosques and shrines and Jewish synagogues were transformed into Catholic Churches. Pope Sixtus IV appointed Tomás de Torquemada to be the Grand Inquisitor of Spain at the request of Ferdinand and Isabella in 1483. Many Jews had already converted to Christianity by this time, and many more would convert rather than lose their property or their lives over the next half-century. But around 100,000 fled Spain and began life anew in other lands. The most striking example came at the ruins in Thessaloniki, Greece, where the Jews revived the city. Many Jews and Muslims also fled to Istanbul, where they were welcomed by the enlightened Sultan Bayezid. The Inquisition in Spain became so violent that Pope Sixtus condemned it. Five thousand Jews were publicly punished and another 500 were burned at the stake. The Spanish monarchs vowed to expel Muslims from their land and succeeded in 1492, when a civil war among Muslims broke out in Granada, the last stronghold of Islam in Spain. King Ferdinand and Queen Isabella then incorporated great reserves of Muslim knowledge from Toledo, Córdoba, and Granada. They Christianized these communities but retained their Muslim architects and tile makers.

The persecution of these minorities retarded the development of new ways of thinking and caused an exodus of major scholars from Spain. However, Ferdinand's acquisition of territories in the New World and conquest of Sicily and Naples brought many riches to his kingdom. It is one of the reasons that Machiavelli uses Ferdinand as his model prince.[118] This renaissance in Spain led to a revival of rhetoric there. Gregorio Mayans y Siscar's (1699–1782) *Rhetorica*, which was published in Valencia in 1757, was the culmination of work begun by such scholars as Juan Luis Vives (1492–1540), Alfonso Garcia Matamoros (?–1572), Pedro Juan Nuñez (1522–1602), Bartolomé Jiménez Paton (1569–1640), Baltasar Gracian (1601–1658), and Francisco Sanchez de las Brozas (1523–1600?).[119] Being a Jesuit, Mayans' goal was to write a Christian rhetoric that was more accessible and clear than Augustine's *De doctrina christiana*.[120] Thus, it should come as no surprise that Mayans' *Rhetorica* is highly Ciceronian in its orientation and probably derived from Soares' work.

One of Mayans' forerunners, Vives, who was from Valencia in Spain, was important not only for his writing on rhetoric and his new translation of Augustine's *City of God* but also for tutoring Mary, the daughter of Catherine of Aragon and King Henry VIII. As we have seen, she would become a controversial queen by attempting to restore Catholicism in England. That was heady stuff for Vives whose parents had converted during the Inquisition;

Juan Luis Vives.

in fact, his sister was burned at the stake for being a practicing Jew. Vives was influenced by his friend Erasmus and was something of progressive. He favored admitting women into Jesuit schools, which were fast becoming the best in Europe.

Vives wrote his letter on deliberative speaking in Oxford in 1523, where he also revealed the influence of scholastics on his work by arguing that invention was the province of dialectic, not rhetoric. In a later work, *De tradendis disciplinis* (1531), he recanted a bit when he wrote that rhetoric is of the greatest influence and weight. . . . It is necessary for all positions in life. For . . . the emotions of the mind are enflamed by the sparks of speech. So, too, reason is impelled and moved by speech. Hence it comes to pass that, in the whole kingdom of the activities of man, speech holds in its possession a mighty strength which it continually manifests.[121]

He came to believe that rhetoric was "the living flow of the soul."[122] His theories soften the Ramian influence in the work of Thomas Wilson.

When Mary came to the throne at age thirty-seven in 1553 for her five-year reign, she remembered the religious and rhetorical lessons of her teacher Juan Vives and used them to justify the slaughter of the enemies of the Catholic Church who plotted against her only a year into her short reign.[123] Ironically, because of his humanism, Vives was forced to seek asylum in Bruges, Belgium, in fear of the Inquisition. Remembering what had happened to Ramus undoubtedly influenced his self-imposed exile. While in Bruges, he wrote *De ratione dicendi*, in which he revives decorum, the art of meeting or creating expectations in an audience. He set out ten genres of speeches that the humanist teaching should master. These include description, history, narration, fables, poetic fictions, precepts of the arts, paraphrasing, epitome, commentary, and translation.

CONCLUSION

It would be difficult to underestimate the influence of Christianity on both the development and the retardation of rhetorical theory. As we have seen, Augustine retrieved Cicero from his condemnation at the hands of those who argued that Christians should not read pagan authors. In so doing, Augustine paved the way for Cicero's works to dominate the next 1,200 years. At the same time, since the church governed philosophy during this time and believed it possessed the "truth," there was little need for an art form that dealt with probabilities. Certain truth could be argued within the realm of the faithful using demonstration, and scholastic infidels and heretics could be dealt with using dialectic. Rhetoric was stripped of its epistemic functions and reduced to presentational skills. This line of thinking reached its zenith in the work of Peter Ramus at the University of Paris.

But the Dark Ages with its medieval church could not sustain itself against the onslaught of new knowledge, art, and commerce. The Crusades encouraged new trade routes, new wealth, and a round of humanism that discovered new versions of lost texts. As the infidels pushed west, Greek scholars were forced to flee to the Italian city-states where they helped with the humanist revival.

The Renaissance came with the rise of cities, a new sense of security, patrons, the printing press, and the use of the vernacular. There was no unified political center as shifting alliances and wars gave rise to Machiavelli's retrieval of an Aristotelian view of speaker, audience, and message. New creative views of the art of rhetoric flourished alongside creative conceptions of the other arts.

The Protestant Reformation destroyed any hope of maintaining a world of certitude in philosophical matters. Along with the political debate, now came theological debate, which in turn upset the political balance. Probably no figure in history better symbolizes this mix than Luther. He used rhetorical skill, the vernacular, and the new printing press to spread his message. His sense of timing told him the church was ripe for reform; his knowledge of rhetoric gave power to his message; and his political skill protected him from the fate that befell such predecessors as Wyclif and Hus. However, the frequent verbal and physical conflicts between Catholic and Protestant forces led to many wars, culminating in the horrific Thirty Years War (1618–1648) which annihilated one-third of the population in Germany, Bohemia, and the Netherlands. The famine and disease were accompanied by economic ruin. The madness was finally stopped by the Peace of Westphalia, a series of treaties among the various participants in this war.

As we leave the Renaissance and Reformation, we find rhetoric very nearly where it was in Augustine's time, restored to its former glory by men of the church. In the next chapter, we will see this conception refined by new theories of how the mind operates.

Study Questions

1. If you were a priest during the Middle Ages, to what use would you put rhetoric? What role did humanists play in its revival?

2. Compare a contemporary city to Renaissance Florence, Italy, to show how the concentration of wealth can enhance the growth of the arts in general and rhetoric in particular.

3. What were the main features of Machiavelli's theory of rhetoric? Of what use is his notion of corrupted traits to an orator today?

4. Unlike Machiavelli, Peter Ramus had a very narrow conception of rhetoric's province. What was it and why did he hold it?

5. What role did Rudolph Agricola and Philipp Melanchthon play in the development of rhetorical theory?

6. What was the impact of Luther's revolt on rhetorical theory?

7. How did Erasmus' approach to religion differ from Luther's?

8. What is the link between the English Reformation and the flowering of rhetorical theory there? Provide a description of the contributions of at least two English rhetoricians who were concerned with style in language.

9. What evidence do we have of a major involvement in rhetoric on the part of Catholic scholars during the Counter-Reformation?

10. What is "taste" in the English view? How does it relate to rhetorical theory?

11. Argue for or against the thesis that the renaissance in rhetoric was as active in Spain as it was in England.

Notes

[1] The First Crusade ended in success with the capture of Jerusalem in 1099, but the Second Crusade of 1146 was an abject failure. The Third Crusade of 1190 was a response to the fall of Jerusalem to Saladin in 1187. Christian forces were led by the newly crowned king of England, Richard the Lion Hearted, who spoke only French.

[2] The ducat was first struck in 1280.

[3] Gutenberg printed only 200 Bibles before the church took control of his press.

[4] See Martin Lowry, *The World of Aldus Manutius: Business and Scholarship in Renaissance Venice* (Ithaca: Cornell U. Press, 1979). The Aldine press published twenty-four Greek authors including a five-volume edition of the works of Aristotle. The printing press was spreading rapidly at this time. Queen Isabella of Spain was quite taken with it and soon publishers were operating in Valencia, Segovia, and Seville.

[5] Throughout the Middle Ages, brothers at such monasteries as St. Gall and Fulda were busily reproducing the works of the classical writers, particularly Cicero.

[6] We do not have the space to discuss many other notable teachers and thinkers who contributed to the Renaissance. Teachers of rhetoric such as Vittorino da Feltre and his teacher Guarino Guarini were immensely successful and remind one of the earlier Sophists of Greece. Lorenzo Valla taught rhetoric in Pavia and retranslated Jerome's *Vulgate*. He was a cross between a humanist and a heretic, soon taking on the pope on behalf of his sponsor King Alfonse of Naples. Nor do we have time to discuss the contribution of each city. Padua, for example, created a famous university that taught many of those who would become significant contributors to Renaissance art and writing.

[7] In fact, the beauty of Beatrice struck Dante like divine illumination. "If in the fire of love I seem to flame beyond the measure visible on earth," says Beatrice in Canto Five, "I am so because of perfect vision." The influence of Augustine is seen in the many light metaphors in the poem. In response to Beatrice, Dante says, "I see that in your intellect now shines the never-ending light."

[8] Latini believed that poetry was rhetorical in that it stimulated thought patterns and plots. Martin Heidegger (see chapter 9) was inspired by the idea that poetry could be a kind of "authentic" rhetoric. Latini's pupil Dante put it this way: Poetry works "by openly revealing that which is present in it as something hidden and possible, namely its true achievement, the manifestation of conscious statements." See Dante's *Convivio* (Torino: Loescher, 1968), chapter 1, 10.9.

[9] References to Aristotle and Cicero pepper the manuscript.

[10] Virgil is Dante's guide through the underworld, where it becomes clear that the poem is a vast allegory in which Florence is hell, Italy is purgatory, and the Roman Empire is paradise, a paradise that is lost. Virgil leads Dante to the gates of purgatory, preparing him for his eventual ascension. Virgil represents the purifying nature of reason and the law, the ultimate guides to a better society.

[11] Jacques Barzun considers Petrarch to be the first humanist; *From Dawn to Decadence: 1500 to the Present* (New York: Harper Collins, 2000), p. 47. After him, Guarino Guarini (1374–1460) and Gasparino Barzizza (1360–1431) founded full-fledged humanist schools in Italy.

[12] See Brenda Deen Schildgen, "Petrarch's Defense of Secular Letters, the Latin Fathers, and Ancient Roman Rhetoric," *Rhetorica*, 11 (1993): 121.

[13] As quoted in Ronald G. Witt, "In the Footsteps of the Ancients": The Origins of Humanism from Lovato to Bruni, Studies in Medieval and Reformation Thought vol. 74 (Leiden: E. J. Brill, 2000), p. 242.

[14] Petrarch is often called the "founder of the Renaissance" because of humanism. His library encouraged others, like his friend and pupil Boccaccio, to follow his example. William Habberton, Lawrence Roth, and William Spears, *World History and Cultures* (Palo Alto, CA: Laidlaw Brothers, 1966), p. 203.

[15] *Cambridge Medieval History*, vol. VII (New York, 1924), p. 288.

[16] One measure of Petrarch's impact is that his student, Coluccio Salutati (1331–1406), became the first political chancellor of Florence.

[17] The name "Medici" is derived from the fact that the family had been apothecaries, hence medicine givers.

[18] A rough equivalent in France at this time might be Jacques Coeur (1395–1456), who amassed a fortune beginning with trading with Muslims and providing transport for pilgrims to the Holy Land. He became a great land baron and lender.

[19] The Great Schism refers to a time when there were two rival popes, one in Avignon, due to the "Babylonian Captivity," and one in Rome.

[20] See Stephen Greenblatt, *The Swerve: How the World Became Modern* (New York: Norton, 2011). This excellent study of Poggio also covers other humanists and their impact on the Renaissance, the notion of free will, and hence modernism. Greenblatt points out that *About Nature* (also known as *On the Nature of Things*) was put on the Catholic Church's index of forbidden books and not removed until 1966.

[21] Hermogenes of Tarsus deduced his theories of style in part from his study of Demosthenes' speeches. He urged speakers to find a balance between purity and grandeur. He also developed his theory around several innovative notions including asperity, wherein the speaker criticizes the audience; vehemence, wherein the speaker criticizes an opponent using short, vigorous sentences; and florescence, wherein a

brilliant style includes long phrases composed in graceful cadences. He believed that beauty was generated by balances, anaphora, parison, antistrophe, epanastrophe, and hyperbaton. See H. Rabe, ed., *Hermogenis Opera* (Leipzig: Teubur, 1913), pp. 213–413.

22 Pope Sixtus IV, the former Francesco Della Rovere, was no friend of the Medici and promised the Pazzi family of Florence military support if they rose up against the Medici. The Pazzis attempted the assassination to begin the uprising. The Pazzis and their followers were annihilated, their severed heads hoisted on pikes only hours after the assassination attempt.

23 Lorenzo felt genuine affection for Michelangelo, who became a regular at the Medici dinner table. He lived in the Medici palace for four years.

24 Donatello, a homosexual, came under criticism for his sensitive nudes. Cosimo defended Donatello on the grounds that he was resurrecting the perfection of the Greeks. Michelangelo was bisexual and also criticized for his realistic nudes, which the Medici also defended.

25 Herbert Christian Merillat, *Sculpture West and East* (New York: Dodd, Mead & Company, 1973), p. 54.

26 Columbus would soon be followed by the Florentine Amerigo Vespucci, who succeeded in getting the new continents named for himself. Vespucci explored what is now Brazil.

27 We will encounter this concept again in chapter 13 when we examine the theory of Michel Foucault.

28 Quoted in Piero Misciattelli, *Savonarola* (New York: D. Appleton and Co., 1930), pp. 60–61.

29 Being of Spanish descent, Alexander was an ally of King Ferdinand.

30 Michelangelo did not return to his hometown until 1506; the Medici did not regain control until 1512, when they defeated the forces of the republic.

31 A humanist, Pisan exposed the way in which women were treated. She was born in Venice and became a recognized poet, novelist, and teacher in her own time. She admired Greco-Roman thinking. The year before she died, she wrote an epideictic book in praise of Joan of Arc.

32 As a devout Catholic humanist born in Germany, Susenbrotus was educated in Vienna. He wrote a noted text on figures of speech in 1541, which was adopted in English schools and mostly studied by William Shakespeare. His book catalogues over 130 tropes and figures of speech. Susenbrotus also wrote a book on grammar.

33 Patrizi was a humanist who became involved in papal politics. He is not to be confused with other Francesco Patrizis who preceded and succeeded him.

34 His play *Mandragola* is also well known.

35 As we shall see in chapter 10, Karl Marx would borrow this quotation from Machiavelli.

36 See Robert Hariman, *Political Style: The Artistry of Power* (Chicago: U. of Chicago Press, 1995).

37 See chapter 2 and following of Machiavelli's *The Prince* in *The Complete Works of Machiavelli*, Sergio Bertelli, ed. (Milan: Feltrenilli Editori, 1964). However, in chapter 3, he advises the prince to adapt to and maintain the laws and traditions of a conquered state rather than disrupting it and provoking an uprising. Here he echoes the advice of Aristotle from his *Politics*. Aristotle advised the tyrant to feign religion so the people would think him pious. Machiavelli repeated that advice in chapter 18 of *The Prince* and Book I, chapters 11–15 of *The Discourses* (in Bertelli).

38 Machiavelli did not fall from complete grace with the Medici. His play, *Mandragola*, was performed for Pope Leo in 1519.

39 See particularly chapter 17 of *The Prince*.

40 Chapters 15–21 of *The Prince*.

41 In the same chapter in *The Prince* and in chapter 11 of *The Discourses*, Machiavelli accused the Catholic Church of using religion to instill fear in soldiers to command their loyalty. When these remarks were discovered and the subversive nature of Machiavelli's thought understood, the Counter-Reformation of the Catholic Church condemned his books. In 1559, they were put on the Papal Index of forbidden writings, though when first published after his death, both books came out under the Papal Imprimatur in 1532.

42 *The Prince*, p. 18.

43 Machiavelli echoed Caligula's famous statement: "Let them hate me, so long as they fear me." See Suetonius, p. 169.

44 *The Discourses*, in Bertelli, 3.43.

45 See Victoria Kahn, *Machiavellian Rhetoric: From the Counter-Reformation to Milton* (Princeton: Princeton U. Press, 1994); Eugene Garver, *Machiavelli and the History of Prudence* (Madison: U. of Wisconsin Press, 1987); J. G. A. Pocock, *The Machiavellian Moment: Florentine Political Thought and the Atlantic Republican Tradition* (Princeton: Princeton U. Press, 1975).

[46] *Discourses*, in Bertelli, 2.2.

[47] Aside from vast stores of gold and silver, the invaders brought the tomato from Peru, maize from Mexico, and tobacco from English colonies. Orange and lemon trees and rice came from China along the Arab byways and on Portuguese ships.

[48] See Peter Mack, *Renaissance Argument: Valla and Agricola in the Traditions of Rhetoric and Dialectic*, (Leiden: E. J. Brill, 1993).

[49] Ibid. See also Marc Cogan, "Rudolphus Agricola and the Semantic Revolutions of the History of Invention," *Rhetorica*, 2 (1984).

[50] Lisa Jardine, "Distinctive Discipline: Rudolph Agricola's Influence on Methodical Thinking in the Humanities," in *Rudolphus Agricola Phrisius (1444–1485)*, F. Akkerman and A. J. Vanderjagt, eds. (Leiden: E. J. Brill, 1988), pp. 38–57.

[51] Melanchthon became known as the "Preceptor of Germany." See Judith Rice Henderson, "Erasmian Ciceronians: Reformation Teachers of Letter Writing," *Rhetorica*, 10 (1992): 273–302; Kees Meerhoff, "The Significance of Philip Melanchthon's Rhetoric in the Renaissance," in *The Significance of Rhetoric in the Renaissance*, Peter Mack, ed. (London: Macmillan, 1992).

[52] He published his *Elementorum rhetorices libri duo* in 1531. Eberhard the German, in his books on poetry, used Christian homilies to illustrate rhetorical figures. See William M. Purcell, "Eberhard the German and the Labyrinth of Learning: Grammar, Poesy, Rhetoric, and Pedagogy in *Laborintus*," *Rhetorica*, 11 (1993): 95–118.

[53] See Henderson, p. 287. Melanchthon endorsed the *progymnasmata*, in fact translating Aphthonious' version in 1525.

[54] One of his books was entitled *Forms of Familiar Conversations, Useful Not Only for Polishing a Boy's Speech But for Building His Character*. See *Collected Works of Erasmus*, vol. 24, Craig R. Thompson, ed. (Toronto: U. of Toronto Press, 1978), *Literary and Educational Writings 2: De copia / De ratione studii*, 295–301. See also Mario Nizolio's *De principiis* of 1553.

[55] Such prominent philosophers and teachers as Aquinas and Bonaventure (1221–1274) believed in the retention of the exercises. The tactic paid off when Bonaventure was finally allowed to study theology at the University of Paris along with Aquinas in 1257 by order of the pope.

[56] Majoragius, *Aristotelis Stagyritae de art rhetorica libri tres cum M. Antonii Maioragii commentariis*, Book I (Venice, 1591); M. Nizolius, *De veris principiis et vera ratione philosophandi* iii, 3 (Parma, 1553).

[57] Henry Hallam, *Introduction to the Literature of Europe in the 15th, 16th, and 17th Centuries*, vol. I (New York: Harper, 1854/1880), p. 119.

[58] Also known as Pierre de las Ramée.

[59] Walter J. Ong, *Ramus: Method, and the Decay of Dialogue* (New York: Farrar, Straus & Giroux, 1974), p. 4. Ong explains that Ramism provided the "connecting link between Puritanism and scholasticism." See also Cogan, p. 187.

[60] In his turn, Ramus' work was replaced by more modern writers such as Fenelon, whose *Dialogues on Eloquence* were published in 1679.

[61] In Will Durant, *The Reformation: A History of European Civilization from Wyclif to Calvin: 1300–1564* (New York: Simon and Schuster, 1957), p. 883.

[62] See *Peter Ramus' Attack on Cicero: Text and Translation of Ramus' Brutinae Questiones*, Carole Newlands, trans. (Davis, CA: Hermagoras Press, 1992).

[63] His best work on this subject is *Dialectical Partitions* published in 1543. His famous "dichotomies" were probably borrowed from the mathematician Hermogenes of Tarsus, whom one of Ramus' teachers had lectured about in Paris in 1529.

[64] Ong, *Ramus* (Harvard edition), p. 213. One is reminded of the attempt of Bertrand Russell and Alfred North Whitehead to develop a mathematical language out of logical positivism.

[65] See Peter Ramus, *Dialectic* (Paris: 1576 edition), pp. 3–4. "Indeed these two names, Dialectic and Logic, generally mean the very same thing . . . one and the same doctrine of reasoning well about anything what so ever."

[66] He translated a copy of Quintilian's *Institutio oratoria* just so he could attack it.

[67] The word "defenestration," meaning to throw someone from a window, comes from the Latin "*de fenestra.*"

[68] Calvin had written his *Institutes* as a textbook in Latin and French in 1534. It was revised as Calvinism expanded from its base in Geneva.

[69] See Tamara A. Goeglein, "'Wherein hath Ramus been so offensious?': Poetic Examples in the English Ramist Logic Manuals (1574–1672)," *Rhetorica*, 14 (1996): 73–101; John C. Adams, "Ramus, Illustrations, and the Puritan Movement," *Journal of Medieval and Renaissance Studies*, 17 (1987): 195–97.

[70] Professor Michael Wigglesworth would supplant Ramus with Aristotle a few generations later and prove influential in the teaching of preachers in America.

[71] Durant, p. 351.

[72] Ibid., p. 418.

[73] Luther had planned on becoming a lawyer, which may account for his litigious nature. Upon conversion, however, he joined the Monastery of the Emerites of St. Augustine.

[74] Julius II (1443–1513, pope from 1503) expanded the papal holdings and funded works by Bramanti, Raphael, and Michelangelo. Julius was particularly successful in his war with Venice wherein he reclaimed Ravenna, Remini, and Faenza for himself and his allies, the League of Cambrai. In 1510 he formed the Holy League against the French.

[75] Luther later claimed that all church reformers were Hussites at heart.

[76] Durant, p. 166.

[77] He rejected the scholastic movement and was censored by Pope John XXII.

[78] See Neil R. Lerous, "Luther's *Am Neujahrstage:* Style as Argument," *Rhetorica*, 12 (1994): 1–42.

[79] Later in his "Letter to the German Nobility," Luther requested that Aristotle's "Physics, Metaphysics, The Soul, and Ethics . . . be entirely removed from the curriculum. . . . But I would gladly allow Aristotle's books on Logic, Rhetoric, and Poetics to be kept." Preserved Smith, *Life and Letters of Martin Luther* (New York: Barnes and Noble, 1911/1968), pp. 84–85.

[80] The continuing influence of the Medici is evidenced by the fact that Cardinal de Medici was elected Pope Clement VII in 1523. However, the Medici were exiled from Florence in 1527 when the republican forces succeeded in taking control. The Medici came back with a vengeance in 1530.

[81] Smith, p. 45–46.

[82] "It should be granted that Hus and Jerome of Prague were wrongly burned," ibid, p. 84; see also pp. 71–72.

[83] He also articulated the "every man a priest" doctrine in this work, which is sometimes called *Open Letter to the Christian Nobility.*

[84] Smith, p. 72.

[85] In fact, the term "protestant" dates from April 19, 1529, when Luther's position was endorsed by a group of German princes at the Diet of Spires.

[86] Smith, p. 118.

[87] See C. F. Evans, *Explorations in Theology* (London: SCM, 1977), p. 80. This need for an authentic reconstruction of the gospels explains Luther's endorsement of hermeneutics.

[88] Martin Luther, *Selections from His Writings*, ed. John Dillenberger (New York: Anchor Books, 1962), p. 470.

[89] Durant, p. 787.

[90] Smith, p. 241.

[91] Ibid., p. 242.

[92] Calvin, *Institutes*, I.viii.i.

[93] Philip Schaff, *The Swiss Reformation* (Edinburgh, 1893), p. 491.

[94] The phrase about the city comes from the Sermon on the Mount in Matthew's Gospel.

[95] Durant, p. 425.

[96] Jean Dietz Moss, in *Novelties in the Heavens: Rhetoric and Science in the Copernican Controversy* (Chicago: U. of Chicago Press, 1993), examines this debate closely.

[97] Martin Luther died in 1546; he was followed to the grave in 1547 by Henry VIII and Francis I. Charles V died in 1558. He was succeeded by Phillip II, the titular ruler of Spain, who married his cousin Queen Mary I of England. However, their marriage and her reign were cut short when she died of cancer in 1558.

[98] Marjorie O'Rourke Boyle, *Loyola's Acts: The Rhetoric of the Self* (Berkeley: U. of California Press, 1997), pp. 2, 8, 9.

[99] However, his method was Cartesian, in that it attempted to use his method to explore eloquence, and Lockean, in that it based its method in empirical experience. Dominique Bouhours (1628–1702) followed his fellow Jesuit's lead on this method of producing rhetorical theory. These writers overlap with those in the next chapter; however, they are placed here because of their Jesuit links. The next chapter focuses on a new epistemological influence.

[100] See Wyclif, *Tractatus de civili dominio* (London, 1351).

[101] *The Canterbury Tales,* twenty-four in number, by Chaucer were written in 1387.

[102] The next major advance in the development of the English language would be Ben Johnson's dictionary of correct usage.

[103] Tyndal's Bible is considered superior because he translated from the original Greek and Hebrew, unlike Wyclif who translated only from Jerome's *Vulgate.*

[104] Cox's *The Arte or Crafte of Rhetoryke* is highly dependent on Melanchthon's writing on invention.

[105] Thomas Wilson, *The Rule of Reason; Conteining the Art of Logike* (London, 1551, 1567), p. 37, 61.

[106] G. H. Mair, ed. *Wilson's Arte of Rhetoric* (Oxford: Clarendon Press, 1909), p. 2. Wilson's work was followed by more works on rhetoric in the vernacular, the most prominent of which were authored by Dudley Fenner, Abraham Fraunce, Charles Butler, and Thomas Farnaby.

[107] See Wayne A. Rebhorn, "Baldesar Castiglione, Thomas Wilson, and the Courtly Body of Renaissance Rhetoric," *Rhetorica*, 11 (1993): 261–74.

[108] Russell H. Wagner, "Thomas Wilson's *Arte of Rhetorique,*" *Speech Monographs*, 27 (1960): 27.

[109] See, for example, Abraham Fraunce, *The Lawiers Logike* (London, 1588) or William Kempe, *The Education of Children* (London, 1588).

[110] Much more under the influence of Ramus was Gabriel Harvey (1550–1631). His *Rhetor* (London, 1575) and *Ciceronianus* (1576) are based on his lectures at Cambridge.

[111] George Puttenham, *The Arte of English Poesie*, Gladys D. Willcock and Alice Walker, eds. (Cambridge: Cambridge U. Press, 1936), p. 5.

[112] Ibid., p. 305.

[113] Ibid., p. 196.

[114] See for example John Lawson's *Lectures Concerning Oratory* published in 1758 in London; or John Ward's *Systems of Oratory* of 1759 in London.

[115] Stuart Hampshire, *The Age of Reason* (New York: George Braziller, 1957), pp. 42–49.

[116] It was Lawson who noted that speakers should use ridicule with delicacy because it is "often more hurtful to the person who wieldeth it, than to him against whom it is directed." In *Lectures Concerning Oratory* (originally published in 1758), E. N. Clauson and Karl R. Wallace, eds. (Carbondale: Southern Illinois U. Press, 1972), p. 148. Burke's theory of taste is set out in *A Philosophical Enquiry into the Origin of Our Ideas of the Sublime and Beautiful* (London, 1757).

[117] The Inquisition had been a tool of the church since the 1100s. Isabella authorized her first Inquisition in 1478, and it began in 1480. A later pope allowed the practice in Rome in 1542 to counteract the Protestant reformation. The Roman Inquisition became more violent than the Spanish one and lasted until 1727.

[118] See chapter 21 of *The Prince*.

[119] He was also known as El Brocense, a professor of rhetoric at the University of Salamanca. His writings were later edited by Mayans.

[120] See Don Paul Abbott, "Mayans' *Rhetorica* and the Search for a Spanish Rhetoric," *Rhetorica*, 11 (1993): 162–63.

[121] Foster Watson, trans. *On Education: A Translation of the "De Tradendis Disciplinis"* (Cambridge: Cambridge U. Press, 1913), p. 180.

[122] Ibid., p. 152.

[123] After the death of Edward, Mary had begun her reign as a favorite of the crowds, especially in London. But soon plots against her, particularly those favoring Lady Jane Grey, forced her to act against Protestants. She was encouraged in this endeavor by her future husband, King Philip of Spain.

PART III

Rhetoric in
the Age of Reason

John Locke.

8

Epistemology and
the Modern Rhetorics

The desire of being believed, the desire of persuading, of leading and directing other people, seems to be one of the strongest of all our natural desires. It is, perhaps, the instinct on which is founded the faculty of speech, the characteristic faculty of human nature.

—Adam Smith[1]

Adam Smith, the author of *Wealth of Nations* (1776), believed that speech was an inherent part of being human. During his lifetime, more than ever before, scholars linked speech more closely to the process of gaining knowledge. They believed that rhetoric could function to kindle the flame of education. This chapter will examine the relationship between rhetoric and epistemology by focusing on the faculties of the mind and how humans come to know what they know.

The Renaissance and the Reformation broke through the dogma of the church to create new needs for persuasion and theories of rhetoric. At first the need was met by humanists, who brought classical scholarship to the forefront. Preachers as well as other speakers studied Aristotle, Cicero, Quintilian, the Sophists, and the *Rhetorica ad Herennium* to learn anew how to make powerful speeches on behalf of new religions, in defense of old religions, and for political gains. Freed from church censorship in many areas, science created new ways of thinking and new theories about how humans gained knowledge. This branch of philosophy was called epistemology, and its development in the 1600s and 1700s had a tremendous impact on rhetorical theory, particularly in Great Britain during the Scottish Enlightenment.

The purpose of this chapter is to measure the impact on rhetorical theory of this turn toward the workings of the mind—*how it learns and how it knows*. Let us be clear that almost every philosopher and rhetorician we have studied has a theory of epistemology. The Greek naturalists believed that we learn by observing what surrounds us in nature. Plato, quite the opposite, believed that we learn by examining our soul, which takes us back to the *noumenal* world where perfect knowledge exists. Aristotle used his powers of observation to build his categories of generative principles for persuasion. Augustine, following Plato's lead, believed that inspiration comes from divine truth that informs the mind once it has been prepared to receive it. Epistemology is a defining characteristic that frames the overarching differences among these approaches to rhetoric.

None of these scholars featured the epistemic faculties of the mind in as much detail as the theorists we are about to examine. This innovative turn began as rhetorical theorists used new psychological theories to rethink their discipline in the 1700s. The role of psychology in rhetoric is situated in its audience-based nature. Empedocles' assertion that the psyche pervaded the body led his pupil Gorgias to develop a fulsome theory of delivery. Aristotle's writing on "states of mind" was much more extensive in the *Rhetoric* than it was in his book on psychology, *De anima*. Once the world was again free to investigate the human mind, rhetorical theorists used this information to build new rhetorics. Before we can examine these new rhetorical theories, it is important that we examine the foundation upon which they were constructed. Major new philosophical positions emerged from the Renaissance; they recast the way philosophers talked about the human mind. One of the themes of this new philosophy was doubt. The questioning that began with the early Greeks was converted to a systematic attack on all premises, including the belief that we exist.

CARTESIAN DUALITY AND HUMANISTIC UNITY

Descartes (1596–1650)

René Descartes was one of the most profound thinkers in the history of the world, and he laid the groundwork for much of what would be written in the name of epistemology. His object was to introduce the deductive methods of mathematics into philosophy by using them to question existence. The result was a method of systematically interrogating all hypotheses back to first assumptions, a result, no doubt, of his Jesuit training. He believed that reason, as opposed to imagination or the senses, should supply us with the evidence we use to make claims about existence in the world. The key to Descartes' major discovery was that he could conceptualize himself as not having a body but could not conceive of himself as not having a mind: "I think, therefore, I am" became his great intuitive thesis.[2] The fact that I can question my own existence proves that I have a mind.

Born of a French nobleman, Descartes was educated by Jesuits, who discovered his talent for mathematics. He would become one of the most famous mathematicians of his century, eventually inventing an algebra that served as the basis for calculus. After college, Descartes went into seclusion for two years; he practiced meditation and dialectical techniques based on geometry. He then decided to join the army and to study the world. On the night of November 10, 1619, he had a vision of an "angel of truth" who told him that mathematics was the proper method for the study of natural phenomena. After six years of travel, he settled first in Paris and then in Holland, where he studied the works of Copernicus, Galileo, and others and wrote his most important works. Twenty years later in 1649, just after the horrible Thirty Years War had ended, he accepted an invitation from Queen Christiana to come to Sweden. He died in Stockholm the next year.[3] The writings he had withheld for fear of censorship and condemnation were then published.

Descartes' revolutionary approach to thinking was manifest in many ways. For example, philosophers of the Middle Ages theorized that if you added all of the motion in the world together at any time, it would be a constant. Descartes broke with this theory by positing a new one that allowed for different amounts of motion at different times. He explained that motion was relative: an object moves in relation to another object. Sir Isaac Newton

René Descartes.

would use this theory in formulating the discipline of physics with his *Principia mathematica*, particularly in developing his theory of gravity, which sought to explain the tides and pull of mass.

Ever the skeptic, Descartes preferred dialectic to rhetoric in his quest for the truth. In 1637 at age forty-one, he published *Descours de la Methode (Discourse on Method)*. In it, he raised a significant problem: if one could prove the existence of only one's own mind, how was one to deal with others? How do we know that other people exist? Descartes saw others as complex machines; other people are always objects to us because we cannot get into their heads to know what they are thinking or that they *are* thinking. They might even be projections of our mind. Influenced by the scientific discoveries of his time, particularly William Harvey's theory of blood circulation, Descartes converted Aristotle's theory of the energizing soul to a mechanical model without metaphysical influence. (Aristotle had argued in *De anima* that it was the soul's *energia* that moved the body. The soul of the tree determined how its branches would grow; the souls of humans determined where they moved.) But Descartes argued that only our minds prevent us from being automatons, like the animals. The mind allows us to be spiritual, although it is somehow attached to a body. This bifurcation led to the famous "dualism" of mind and body in Descartes' theory; his investigations segregated the mind from the body and relegated the body to the status of an object, something that could be projected by the mind.

The mind is the receptacle for intuited truths; it also conducts deductive reasoning. Descartes claimed that intuition is the product of "an unclouded and attentive mind"; intuition comes to us without doubt. While the senses cannot be trusted because they can be fooled, geometric deduction can provide certitude and correct the errors of the senses. In *Discourse on Method*, he laid out the rules he would have our minds follow if we are to find intuitive and deductive truth. He called this method "systematic doubt." It became a major force in epistemological studies. Because it questioned so much, it led to a relativity that would enhance the use of rhetoric in speculative philosophy.[4] Rhetoric was needed to overcome doubt or at least allow humans to cope in a skeptical world.

Vico (1668–1744)

Giambattista Vico believed that Descartes' system was too narrow. He was particularly unhappy with the Cartesian tendency to dissect thought using geometric formulations instead of having philosophy aid in the creative process. Invention should be given priority over skepticism. There were more ways to learn than through mental intuition, mathematical manipulation, and logical deduction. In reaction to the Cartesian dualism between mind and body, Vico tried to restore a more unified theory of mental and physical operations, a more holistic view of humans in which the mind and body interacted and were integrated. Aristotle's conception of rhetorical theory was crucial to humankind because it showed that emotions (body) could affect judgment (mind). Moreover, rhetoric was better equipped to deal with everyday probability than was the mathematical *méthodologie* of Descartes. As the Royal Professor of Eloquence at the University of Naples from 1698 to 1741 and member of the Palatine Academy, Vico suggested that a "humanistic imagination" was essential to the task of interpretation. That is, without imagination, it would be impossible to make sense of the world and to develop various hypotheses for science to test. Imagination transformed society and created culture.[5] The imagination could be developed by examining myths and fables, which Vico saw as openings to the origins of civilization. And there, one could find the *parola*, words that interpret reality. The ancient poets spoke in this *parola*, which consisted of the stories of the gods and heroes of previous ages. Out of *parola* came *favola*, true fables, and *allegoria*, true allegories. The humanist's task was to return to this pure time and language, which was an imitation of nature.

His humanistic notion of a universal imagination emerged in 1730 and was composed of the myths and stories that can be reduced to an "imaginative metaphysics" through the proper use of rhetorical analysis. Long before Carl Jung's (see chapter 10) theory of the collective unconscious, Vico was suggesting a collective human knowledge inclusive of the narratives built into various cultures. This collective knowledge not only saves us the time of rethinking and rediscovering important lessons, it can generate new theories for the advancement of humankind. Vico believed there was a universal history of society into which writers could tap. The epistemic nature of this theory is captured in Vico's claim that "when man understands he extends his mind and takes things in, but

Giambattista Vico.

when he does not understand he makes the things out of himself and becomes them by transforming himself into them."[6]

Rather than impediments to reason, Vico saw rhetoric and natural religion as major foundations of society. In fact his *Art of Rhetoric (Institutiones oratoriae)* equates rhetoric with humanity. His *New Science (Scienza nuova)*, of which he published a new edition just before his death, revealed his antirationalist bias in favor of humanism and poetic wisdom. Vico spent a good deal of time in his *New Science* speculating on how language had developed. In his chapter on "Poetic Logic," he talked about how verbs were formed before all the other parts of speech had been discovered. The first verbs were commands, such as God's imperative, "Let there be light."

Ingenuity and imagination help writers and speakers access and extend myths. Common topics help them with invention of ideas, while criticism helps them develop precision. In his view, humans are more rhetorical than rational and more religious than scientific. A plea to his young students in his *On Humanistic Education* made clear his philosophical stance on education: "If you have dedicated yourself to philosophy, listen then to Plato as he considers the immortality of spirit, the eternal and inexhaustible power of divine ideas, of Genii, of God, who is the Supreme Good, and of love free from passion."[7]

Vico's theory of metaphor reflected a humanistic bias toward hermeneutics. He saw metaphor as the original structure, to take one thing for another, to see one thing as another. It is the first way we learn, according Vico. Metaphor is ingrained in language but also makes things known by invoking comparisons. Thus, metaphors are "humanistic" because they tell us something about how language has developed. "Playing it by ear," "that tears it," "kernel of truth," and "dog-eared page," represent metaphors that have become so much a part of the language that we don't even notice that they are metaphorical. Other metaphors are "constructivistic" because they can build new meaning by making striking comparisons: outer space as "the new frontier"; the rotation of the earth as a spinning top. Under metaphor, he refined definitions of metonymy (naming a thing by one of its characteristics), synecdoche (naming a thing by substituting a part for the whole or the whole for a part), and irony (literal meaning is used to express its opposite). (See chapter 5 for examples.) Along with these tropes, Vico believed that figures of thought, if properly fashioned by careful word choice, could fascinate the mind and thereby hold attention or move the soul. In short, he saw tropes and figures ultimately as *mental procedures* and only on the surface as ornaments of speech. Thus, amplification could stir emotions, move an audience, and/or increase the impact of an argument.[8]

Vico claimed that argument was useful in judicial rhetoric because it held the combatants to a common social frame. In court, argumentation should use facts that are based on motive, character, and evidence. When assessing these facts, each side has three choices: refuting the charges, denying the facts, or disputing the application of the law, inclusive of the definition of the crime. An effective lawyer will bring the facts and law into conformance using Vico's revisions of the *stasis* system.

Regardless of the accuracy of this etymology of language, it is important to realize that Vico provided a leavening influence on the dense rational philosophies of his day. He would have his reader reach back through the age of humans, to the age of heroes, and then back to the age of the gods. In this way, he deserves no small credit for preserving the humanistic tradition of searching for new and old truths as a way of creating one's own world history.[9] In this way, Vico maintained the humanistic tradition just as Descartes extended the scholastic tradition.

EPISTEMOLOGY IN GREAT BRITAIN

As we learned in the previous chapter, Leonard Cox, Richard Sherry, Henry Peacham, and Thomas Wilson had laid the foundation for a new understanding of rhetoric in England. Now the epistemological debate provided another layer of sophistication to English rhetorical theory. In addition, Aristotle's forms of rhetorical theory were driving the plots *(dianoia)* of Elizabethan theatre.[10] Public speaking was becoming more important as the English language developed and as Parliament gained more power.

Bacon (1561–1626)

As the youngest son of the lord keeper of the seal, Francis Bacon received a sound education. He entered Trinity College when he was only twelve, in part because his mother, Lady Anne Cooke, was a classicist. He was admitted to the bar in 1582 and wrote his first book on politics in 1584. He gained favor with Queen Elizabeth after she requested that he be brought in to bolster the prosecution in the trial of her former lover, the Earl of Essex. Throughout this period, he began to examine scientific experiments. When James I became king in 1603, Bacon's influence grew. He became attorney general (1613), lord keeper of the seal (1617) (like his father), and chancellor (1618). Like Machiavelli, Bacon practiced what he preached while serving in various public roles. In fact in his *De augmentis*, he extended two lines of thought from Machiavelli. First, he believed in grounding political theory and persuasion inductively using real world examples. Second, he advised politicians to "shape" themselves "according to the occasion."[11] In 1621 Bacon's rivals convicted him of taking gifts improperly; he was imprisoned, fined, and barred from holding further public office. Nonetheless, his writings on epistemology and language proved influential throughout the next century.

In *The Advancement of Learning*,[12] Francis Bacon began to harvest the fruits of this labor when he assigned rhetoric the function of applying *"reason to imagination for the better moving of the will."*[13] Bacon believed that one of the benefits of a good education was eloquence, and he illustrated his point with many historic examples drawn from his study of language, how it functions, and how it reveals the way we learn things. Experimenting with the "new science" a century before Vico, Bacon rejected the contentiousness of scholasticism and the fantasy of hermeticism.[14] He invented the term "induction" to describe his method in contrast to the prevailing deduction used at the time.

Building on the psychology of Plato, the linguistic theory of Augustine, and the dialectical approach of Ramus, Bacon described five functions of the mind that became the basis of "faculty psychology": understanding, reason, imagination, appetites, and will. Bacon expanded Plato's vision of the will as charioteer of the soul. Improving on Augustine, he tried to purify language by extending its roots into the faculties to trace better representations of the world. He put this theory in place using the dialectical precision of Ramus. Each of the discovered functions is described as a faculty of the mind; they implement different functions in the brain.[15] The relationship between these functions can be complex and necessitate a re-knitting of certain elements that Ramus had unraveled. For example, imagination transcends reason and can draw the thinker, the speaker, and the audience up to a different level of thought. An appeal to the imagination can overwhelm an appeal to reason.[16] In this way, rhetoric serves imagination as logic serves understanding; rhetoric provides the images and style that imagination needs in order to achieve a unifying transcendence that defeats an argument from pure reason. Rhetoric also can evoke the emotions, and "divine grace" employs emotions through the imagination to create illumination beyond pure reason.

Bacon believed that just as the arts and sciences produce one kind of product, speech and arguments produce another. The former *generates new knowledge based on sensed data, while the latter retrieves what we already know.* Bacon went so far as to argue that each of the major kinds of academic knowledge are products of the various components of the mind. For example, history is the product of memory; poetry is the product of imagination; and theology is the product of reason and imagination.[17] The faculties allow humans to perform the following functions:

1. *to inquire and invent:* we seek to discover ideas and how things work; we propose hypotheses and link ideas and objects that are similar to one another.

2. *to examine and judge:* we take ideas and objects apart to analyze them; we assess their worth; we employ standards of scientific and artistic merit.

3. *to recall ideas and maintain custody over them:* we remember ideas and objects; we relive events; we retain knowledge and methodologies of computation and analysis.

4. *to transmit thought in language:* we dress ideas in words to make them comprehensible to others; we make comparisons to make our ideas clearer to others.

Language is composed of the "tokens" and "signs" of communication. Bacon then broke language into its various uses:

> The arts intellectual are four in number . . . to invent that which is sought or propounded; or to judge that which is invented; or to retain that which is judged; or to deliver over that which is retained. So as the arts must be four: art of inquiry or invention; art of examination or judgment; art of custody or memory; and art of elocution or tradition.[18]

Bacon claimed that rhetoric's role is to recall and explain what has been discovered by the other arts. "The invention of speech or argument is not properly an invention: for to invent is to discover" what we don't already know.[19]

Ideally, said Bacon, communication should be divided into three realms, each building on the one before it: (1) the "Organon of Tradition" (by which he meant the study of discourse) containing grammar, vocabulary, and diction, including delivery as voice and articulation; (2) the "Method of Tradition" containing rules for judgment, organization, planning, and logic; and (3) the "Illustration of Tradition" containing rhetoric, which includes arguments based on probability, imaginative proof, *ethos*, and style. This latter realm is introduced with a phrase that revealed the lingering influence of the Middle Ages on Bacon's thinking: "Now we descend to that part which concerneth illustration of tradition."[20] Like the medievals, Bacon believed rhetoric was some-

Francis Bacon.

thing to which we descend. He held this opinion because rhetoric was still seen as decorative flattery and incapable of producing new knowledge. Nonetheless, citing Aristotle, Cicero, and Demosthenes, Bacon argued that eloquence prevails in civic life.[21] He also understood that delivery is crucial to carrying one's message to the public. The movement of the body should conform to the organization of the speech and convey the mood of the speaker. Just as the tongue speaks to the ear, so gestures speak to the eye. A speaker who takes a step just as his or her text moves from the introduction to the body of the speech reinforces the organization of the text with physical movement.

For Bacon, civil knowledge was highly dependent on communication that was composed of "conversation, negotiation and government."[22] Reason is superior to the affections because it is conditioned by the past, present, and future, while the affections are only conditioned by the present. Nonetheless, the affections can be used to persuade people to the good, especially the good that has been arrived at using reason:[23] "We conclude therefore that rhetoric can be no more charged with the colouring of the worst part [of human nature], than logic with sophistry, or morality with vice."[24]

This ideal version of how communication should be compartmentalized was tempered by a warning: we must be careful about the use of language because it has been corrupted by four common idols of culture.[25] They are set out in his book *Novum Organum Scientiarum (New Organon of Science)*. The *idols of the tribe* comprise desires, prejudices, and pride, which have been inculcated by the tribe and blind its members to reality. So today, for example, since the tribe believes it is better to be married than to be single, to be employed instead of out of work, to be us instead of them, so do those who are born into the tribe. These survival prejudices are bred into our passions and intellect, according to Bacon.[26] Speakers often tap into these prejudices to advance their agendas.

The *idols of the den* are more individual. They are fallacies derived from living with a limited view of the experiential world, perhaps inside the family. This idol is built on Plato's metaphor of the cave in his *Republic*, in which humans live with blinders, forcing them to stare at shadows projected on a wall. They believe the shadows are real because they have nothing with which to compare them. Thus, for example, the generations who grew up with rock-and-roll music have no interest in jazz. If we live by the ocean, we see no virtue in living in the mountains. The cavern "corrupts the light of nature" and causes humans to search for knowledge in their small area instead of in the larger common world outside the den.

Once we escape the cave, however, we face other idols that can corrupt our use of language. The *idols of the marketplace* cause people to use language in a popular way rather than in a precise manner. They include "names of things which have no existence" (unicorns) and "names of actual objects" that are "confused [and] badly defined" (mistaking a wolf for dog).[27] Bacon is particularly concerned about semantic fallacies that corrupt the language. Today, many students say they "could care less," when they mean they "could*n't* care less." "Just do it," replaces reasoned decision making. Those who read and watch a good deal of advertising begin to spell badly; "cool" becomes "Kool," "neat" becomes "neet." These idols "lead mankind into vain and innumerable controversies and fallacies."[28] By ending their use, Bacon sought to purify the king's English.

The *idols of the theatre*, which have been inculcated by theology, dogmatism, and logical fallacies, fool us into thinking that fiction is true. Like the drama on the stage, we come to believe the oracle, the psychic, or any other fallacious explanations of the world instead of what our reason would lead us to believe.[29] The influence of violence on television might serve as a modern parallel, or perhaps the teenager or young adult who decides to live life like a character in a video game. Those who follow self-help gurus often find that you really *can't* have it all and that it is *not all* good. Happiness is not as easily achieved as the gurus claim. Bacon believed rhetoric should persuade us that the idols are corrupting influences.

These idols, like Plato's or Augustine's worldly illusions, must be banished from the mind in order to protect proper "human understanding." Bacon's desire to purify the English language was carried on by The Royal Society of London, which became the home to scientific writers by 1660 and called for a simpler style among "scientific" writers that would allow the truth to shine through.[30] Many of the members considered themselves practitioners of the "new science," which was experimental and less reliant on the tools of scholasticism. The members sought to purify scientific discourse and, in due course, most all writing. Many of their recommendations were put in the negative. That is, they were more likely to tell writers what to avoid—amplifications, digression, ornate style—than they were to tell writers what positive steps to take. Thus, the members of The Royal Society, men like Thomas Sprat, Joseph Glanvill, and Samuel Parker, followed in the antirhetorical tradition of Peter Ramus, brought to England by Puritanism. Sprat argued for an efficient style that exhibited perspicuity, a term that George Campbell (see below) would make a hallmark of effective rhetoric.

Locke (1632–1704)

John Locke, who was born six years after Bacon died, was witness to turbulent times. James I had succeeded the childless Elizabeth I, the last of the Tudor line. As James VI of Scotland and the son of Mary, Queen of Scots, James was a Stuart and a Catholic. But he accepted an accommodation with the powers that be to become a fairly successful ruler. In 1611, he appointed forty-seven writers to produce the King James Bible, one of the most beautiful works of literature in history, though, as we have seen in the previous chapter, more than 75 percent of it came from Tyndale's Bible. In 1625, James I was succeeded to the throne by his son Charles I, who was less fortunate and less able. Charles had to deal with rampant "Puritans," who comprised a group of many different sects that sought to further reform and purge the Church of England of its reflections of the Catholicism. He also had to deal with a stronger Parliament that forced him to accept the Petition of Right, which required parliamentary approval for the raising of taxes, forbade the quartering of soldiers in private homes and martial law in times of peace, and required specific charges if someone was arrested. However, under the influence of the Archbishop of Canterbury, Charles began to deprive Puritans of their pulpits. This was the first step on the path to civil war.

John Locke was born in Somerset in 1632, the son of a lawyer who became a justice of the peace. Locke's parents were Puritans, and his father participated in the civil war that brought the king down. Thus, Locke was witness to one of the worst governmental convulsions that England faced. When Puritans took over Parliament under the leadership of Oliver Cromwell, he formed the "New Model Army" and won important battles in 1644 and 1645. After the latter, Charles I fled to Scotland. However, while Locke attended school in London, Charles I was turned over to Cromwell for a price and then beheaded at Whitehall in London. Locke may have witnessed the event. In any case, Locke moved on to Christ Church College at Oxford, where he studied medicine and philosophy, preferring the likes of Descartes to the classical philosophers such as Plato.

While he worked toward his bachelor's degree and master's degree (1658), he saw that Cromwell hardly knew a moment of peace because he was besieged by Scots, Irish rebels, and Catholics. By 1653, Cromwell defeated them all, including an army led by ex-king Charles' son. Cromwell became Lord Protector of England. When he died in 1658, he was succeeded by his son, who lacked Cromwell's skill. Parliament decided to restore the monarchy and brought Charles II of the Stuart line from exile to the throne in 1660. By accepting a weakened monarchy, the king had no choice but to allow Parliament to extend its powers. However, the restoration was a clear repudiation of Puritanism, even naming the martyred Charles I a saint of the Anglican Church. England fell into a more pleasurable rhythm.

During this time, Locke polished his skills as a doctor. In 1667, Locke became the personal physician to the Earl of Shaftesbury, moving into his home and saving his life by having a cyst removed from his liver. Under the grateful patronage of Shaftesbury, Locke began working on his philosophy of government and his theory of epistemology, how humans come to understand things. As a leader in the Whig (republican) movement, Shaftesbury became Lord Chancellor in 1671, which led to an advance in Locke's career. He served on several boards that gave him an understanding of economics, trade, and colonial rule. However, when his mentor lost power, Locke decided to travel in Europe not only to see the sites but to familiarize himself with other forms of government, particularly that of Louis XIV in France.[31]

In 1679, Shaftesbury returned to power and encouraged Locke to publish his *Two Treatises on Government*. They were welcomed by the Whigs and established Locke as a founding member of the liberal movement in England that would eventually flow through John Stuart Mill and Jeremy Bentham. However, at the time, Locke's work was seen as subversive to the monarchy, and when Shaftesbury could no longer protect Locke, he was forced to flee to the Netherlands, where he continued to write and hope for a change in his fortune.

In 1685, Charles was succeeded by his son, James II, a declared Catholic, who granted Catholics toleration. This move set off the Whigs. In Parliament, they called for the replacement of James II. Those who remained loyal to the king were called "Tories," and hence the two-party system was born in England. James II's daughter Mary had married the heroic William of Orange, who had successfully resisted Louis XIV's attempt to take over the Netherlands. Locke had by this point become an advisor to William. In 1688, those disaffected from the king suggested that he be replaced by William and Mary, who became England's rulers in a bloodless coup known as the Glorious Revolution. Locke accompanied Mary to England and witnessed her and her husband's investiture. Thus began the Hanover line that rules to this day in England, having changed its name to Windsor during the First World War since Hanover is a German name. In 1689, Locke wrote the Bill of Rights for the new king and queen.

We can begin our examination of Locke's thinking by noting that he reinforced Bacon's claim that the mind was composed of various functions, the most important of which were the will and the understanding.[32] His *Essay Concerning Human Understanding* of 1689 demonstrates that Locke was also influenced by William of Ockham's study of semantics, which called for a more precise use of language. Centuries earlier, Ockham (1285–1347), who taught at Oxford, concentrated on the senses' influence on memory, imagination, thought, and experience.[33] Locke developed these themes, as this passage from *Human Understanding* makes clear:

> Vague and insignificant forms of speech, and abuse of language, have so long passed for mysteries of science, and hard or misapplied words, with little or no meaning, have by prescription, such a right to be mistaken for deep learning and height of speculation, that it will not be easy to persuade either those who speak or those who hear them that they are but the covers of ignorance, and hindrance of true knowledge.[34]

Locke argued that only experience could provide the materials for reason and knowledge, and experience was the sensing of data in the empirical world. Experience provided primary or "simple" ideas. Thus, Locke, along with his friend Isaac Newton, endorsed empiricism and the scientific method: "External objects furnish the mind with the ideas of sensible qualities, which are all those different perceptions they produce in us; and the mind furnishes the understanding with ideas of its own operations."[35] The mind is at the center of the universe, collecting new data through experience, as opposed to collecting knowledge through the church or other authorities. Humans can become the lords of the signifier if they realize that the mind has the power to perceive through the senses and to make decisions through the will.

Locke saw language as a secondary epistemic function because it can only provide an understanding of what has already been discovered by the senses. When the mind reflects on its own operations, it produces "ideas of reflection." Words come into general use by being made the signs of general ideas, and ideas are generalized by separating them from the circumstances of time and place.[36] In other words, the idea comes into being by removing it from the situation that generates it. We understand the concept of robbery because we are able to lift it from specific situations of theft and generalize it into a universal definition of unjust taking.

Furthermore, we remember or retain knowledge of various ideas and experiences by using "abstraction," a kind of pyramid of categories. For example, if I mention the abstraction "football," you can fill it in with such categories as rules, teams, players, great games, and so forth, depending on the level of the abstraction. If I mention the abstraction "quarterback," you can instantly name a few. The mind could not hold all of its information without the ability to categorize and then to build pyramids of abstraction out of these categories. The category "color" is more of an abstraction than the specific category "blue." The category "blue" contains the more specific ideas "delft, cerulean, navy, aqua, powder, and royal." The doctrine of abstraction is Locke's major contribution to the canon of memory and how it operates.

As he developed his theory of epistemology, Locke broke knowledge into several categories. First, like Descartes, Locke claimed his knowledge of self was *intuitive;* the understanding is "not taught to reason" by syllogisms. That is, since we can never prove in any logically satisfying way that we are not dreaming, we must know that we are awake in some other way. We know that we are awake intuitively; although that fact cannot be refuted, it is nonetheless not the product of logic. The second form of knowledge is *demonstrative* and relies on argumentation. Knowledge of justice is based on demonstrative proof wherein reason works with true premises to produce the truth. This method reflects the thinking of Aquinas, Boethius, and Averröes, so dominant in the medieval period.

The foundational form of knowledge is *sensitive;* that is, we build the first two categories of knowledge above from sensed data we experience directly. Knowledge contains all of the simple ideas discovered on the primary level. Locke's most revolutionary and antireligious contention was that humans are born with a *tabula rasa:* with empty souls. We fill our souls with experiences; these are the sensate simple ideas of knowledge. Rhetoric can get in the way by packing our heads with myths, falsehoods, and other illusions. Association is a better way of learning: ideas become legitimately associated with one another over time so that one idea recalls another. They are then organized into the cognitive system through the process of abstraction, as discussed previously. Addition, subtraction, combination, and arrangement build complex ideas from simple ones. For example, "philanthropy" (*philo* [love], *anthro* [humankind]) can be constructed by adding "transfer" to "wealth" and "sympathy." Philanthropists are people who transfer some of their wealth to others because they have sympathy for a particular cause.

Once his system of language and learning was complete, Locke found a place for rhetoric, which matched the purpose attributed to it by Francis Bacon: *the application of reason to the imagination for the better moving of the will.* To put it another way, rhetoric is the ability to take arguments and evidence, which have been deduced from sensed experience, and use them to create or recall a story or picture that will induce change in the hearer. Locke's definition is idealistic and reflects the theory behind most of the preaching taking place in his time. Preachers brought an understanding of scripture to the imagination of their audiences to move those audiences to conversion experiences, which required action by the will.

Locke claimed that the components of the mind function only on the basis of reflection. We do not reason automatically; we have to think about it first. We do not recall things automatically; the memory must be engaged by reflecting on what we want to remember. This definition of communication has both intrapersonal and interpersonal dimensions. *Internal discourse* is more authentic because it is more likely to be based on direct apprehension of pure ideas. The influence of Plato's notion of recollection by the soul is evident in Locke's thinking. It becomes the basis of his "philosophical discourse."

External discourse is more likely to be corrupted by society, culture, and ordinary language. According to Locke, too much "civil discourse" is based on external form, open to corruption by Bacon's idols, and is, therefore, much less accurate than it should be. The job of communicologists is to cleanse internal discourse and then to use it to purify external discourse. We must, said Locke, prevent words from taking on a life of their own. They must constantly be reaffixed to concepts that are grounded in simple ideas. Locke believed that wit and fancy corrupted language. His antiseptic world would be based on an exact social contract: the public would agree on an exact match of word and idea in a philosophical discourse. It is an unfulfilled dream that has existed in philosophy for centuries.

We might ask Locke: Why should we communicate externally if internal discourse is more authentic? The answer is to prevent solipsism, the myopic belief that one's own mind is always correct and may be the only real mind in existence. On this issue, Locke reflects the speculation of Bacon that we must overcome the idols of the den if we are to educate the mind properly. We must communicate *with others* to clarify our ideas and to be sure we are not tyrannized by the language of the cave, tribe, or marketplace. External communication in Locke's ideal community would serve as a *reality check* and build a consensus around what is true. Remember that Locke, like Bacon, ushered in what Immanuel Kant (see chapter 9) would call the Enlightenment, in which philosophers believed that *science and logic could solve all problems and that mutual agreement among experts could verify truth.* All of them tried to make language match the natural order of science as they built the modern era. Thus, the role of external communication is corrective when it brings us into contact with those who have consensually approved knowledge.

By centering on the human mind, Locke argued that we could free ourselves from the manipulation of others. We could find the sensed data that lie behind our communication, since as individuals we are free to think, experience, and express. Thus, Locke's theory of communication was a foundation for his notion of the social contract, which became a central part of Enlightenment thinking—the logical, scientific, and reformed extension of the scholasticism of the medieval and Renaissance epochs.

Locke's epistemic theory has an important political implication. Since each soul is blank at the outset, *all humans are created equal.* This argument inspired Enlightenment thinkers such as Thomas Jefferson to incorporate its thesis into the Declaration of Independence. Locke expanded this political theory by arguing that in their natural condition humans would exist in a state of freedom. Locke argued that they should concede some of their freedom in order to avoid anarchy and gain peace and protection of our "lives, liberties and estates." Chaos is avoided by forming compacts, the first of which occurs in the family. In fact, Locke believed in family values and the family as the nuclear unit in our natural state. Our ability to enter into agreements also allows humans to create social units in which those who govern do so with the consent of the governed. The compacts that are formed are binding until violated. Jean-Jacques Rousseau expanded this theory in his *Social Contract* of 1762. Locke's example of a broken compact was the behavior of King James II, which released his subjects from their vow of obedience. Because of his bad behavior, James II was deposed as king and replaced, as we have seen, by William of Orange. The new King William III readily accepted Locke's *Declaration of Rights* (1688) as a new compact, which provided England with a bill of rights the following year.

Locke advanced the notions of equality, liberty, and consensual government, which was somewhat revolutionary for his time.[37] In his essay on civil government (1690), he wrote that the end of government is the good of humankind. This contribution to the Enlightenment should not be underestimated, for it would lead to the formation of democratic republics, which would provide a free marketplace of ideas and another renaissance in public speaking and rhetorical theory in America. Locke continued to refine his theories by entering into conversations with the writer John Dryden and the scientist Isaac Newton. He composed his important *Letters Concerning Toleration* between 1689 and 1692. He died in 1704.

Enlightened Women

Female rhetorical theorists of the era tended to turn rhetorical theory from public address to conversation or letter writing.[38] Madeleine de Scudery, for example, wrote three books between 1642 and 1684 on the art of conversation in the salon, a gathering place for intellectual discussion. She illustrates her theory with idealized conversations with Cleopatra, Marianne of Judea, and others. If women imitated these dialogues, they might be able to gain control of the give-and-take of conversation about ideas. In her works, de Scudery included notes on wit and suitable timing to encourage women to exclude no topic from conversation as long as it was handled with taste.

Margaret Cavendish (1623–1674), the Duchess of Newcastle, wrote poems, plays, and essays. Her husband was a writer too, but more known for his military adventures. When he was defeated by Cromwell's Puritans, he and his wife were forced to leave England. She studied Locke and Francis Bacon while a member of the royal court in exile in France. Her *The Worlds Olio* is an encyclopedia of feminine conversational technique. She advised her readers to advance social reforms in conversational settings. In dealing with spouses, she advised sticking to reason and avoiding emotional appeals.

Margaret Fell was so aggressive in pushing her agenda that she was jailed in 1677, mainly for her opinion that women should be allowed to preach in the Quaker church. While in prison, she wrote *Women's Speaking Justified*. Her theory focused on rhetoric as dialogue, prophecy, or counseling. She advanced a hermeneutic theory for reading the Bible: creating the context for the particular reading and then employing divine intuition to interpret the passage. Like Plato and Augustine, she believed that preachers should not preach until they have experienced this divine illumination. She illustrates her theory using such biblical models as Mary Magdalene, Esther, and Deborah.

Mary Astell (1666–1731) was an unusual woman for her time. She was a political activist, a writer, and an educator. Her *A Serious Proposal to the Ladies* included a plan for a college. She was conversant in the major theories of rhetoric because she had studied Thomas Hobbes' translation of Aristotle's *Rhetoric* and read Plato and Cicero. Her theory of rhetoric was written explicitly for women and has an Augustinian cast about it.[39] That is, rhetoric's task is to present truth, not discover it. Sophistry is to be avoided; rationalism is to be embraced. In disputing Locke's theory, she revealed a strong belief in God and spirituality, which was beyond the perceptive powers of the human senses. As an educated woman and a person who espoused an educated class, she also believed rhetoric was more suited to the masses and argumentation was more appropriate to the learned.

Hume (1711–1776)

David Hume's fascination with human nature blossomed in the Scottish school of philosophy. He advanced Locke's notion of association of ideas as a form of invention in *An Enquiry Concerning Human Understanding* (1748). He claimed that even complex ideas associate because they have a natural "attraction" for one another in the human mind. The idea of justice attracts the ideas of equity and fairness. Thus, if an audience understands equity and fairness, a speaker can bring them to a sense of justice that will seem natural to them. More specifically, the chemistry of the attraction takes place in the imagination; therefore, the ability to evoke images through style in language is important to this theory. The actual sensing of a phenomenon, such as coldness or heat, is more vivid than its recollection; therefore, speakers should enliven the recollection among their audiences by choosing language that takes listeners back to actual sensations.

David Hume.

Earlier in his *Treatise on Human Nature* (1739), Hume argued that the imagination can educate or confuse the mind. He proved this argument by using the scientific method of observation to describe how the mind separates "impressions" from "ideas." Impressions are the products of sensed data; ideas are constructions of the imagination or recollections of the memory. This distinction allowed Hume to differentiate between feeling and thinking, a major sophistication of Locke's conception of ideas. The mind operated through "resemblance, contiguity in time or place, and cause and effect" when dealing with simple ideas.[40]

In other words, we group things together that are in some sense identified with one another—cats and lions, television screens and computer monitors. The resemblance or identification tells us something about the two objects that are being compared. We also group things because they are near one another in time or space—the Renaissance and the Reformation were close in time, Serbia and Croatia are Balkan countries close in geographic space. The comparison based on time or space gives us new knowledge about the things being compared. Another way we group things is by cause and effect. Cause and effect allow us to explain how certain things happen. You light kindling and it produces a fire.

These three "qualities" of thinking allow individuals to deal with the impressions and ideas that fill their minds. The problem is that such organizations and rationalizations of ideas are not always consistent with reality. To explain this problem, Hume developed what he called a "uniting" principle that groups ideas in ways that please our imagination.[41] The groupings become complex ideas that may be divided into three operations of the imagination: relations, modes, and substances.[42] Obviously, *relations* compares objects based on how they connect to one another—she is his daughter, he is her student. *Modes* compares objects based on their operating principles—both Neptune and Uranus revolve around the sun. *Substances* compares objects based on their material composition—bronze and steel are both metals.

However, we need to be clear that these qualities are not always logical nor do they always correspond to reality. They are instead the patterns the mind uses to organize and explain ideas. The method of thinking described here is not deductive (moving from general rules to specific examples) but is inductive (moving from specific examples to form general rules) because it gives primacy to sensed impressions in the mind.

Hume reconsidered Cartesian and Lockean principles of perception to demonstrate that belief is not necessarily knowledge. First, he agreed that the strongest form of belief is an idea that has impact because it is associated with a present impression.[43] Like Descartes, Hume believed that only our own individual state of mind provides us with evidence of existence. Second, these are not matters of certitude. They are matters of belief. I believe what I see in the desert is water, but I'm not certain to the hundredth degree. Belief is a result of feeling as well as thinking. How we think is affected by our state of mind, our mood: "An idea assented to *feels* different from a fictitious idea."[44] Third, since language can affect this feeling by creating images, rhetoric is capable of making the fictitious seem real and the real seem fictitious.

Hume made a radical departure from the Enlightenment line of thinking. He claimed that reason is ruled by the passions, and often serves them: "[H]uman actions can never . . . be accounted for by *reason*, but recommend themselves entirely to sentiments and affections of mankind without any dependance on the intellectual faculties."[45] This critique of the mind's operation, when combined with his deconstruction of cause and effect, led to his major contribution to the modern resurrection of rhetoric. He popularized "scepticism," a philosophical approach that severely undermined the influence of theology and caused him to be charged with heresy because of his attack on the Christian belief in miracles.

Unlike the skepticism that is merely a doubting attitude, "scepticism" was a method of investigation that led Hume to argue that it was logically impossible to prove that one event caused another because one could not prove that any single event logically "entails" another. Furthermore, pure observation cannot prove causality because pure observation cannot prove that there is a "necessary connection" between objects. To make his point, Hume used the example of one billiard ball colliding with another. The click of the collision and the reaction of the second ball to the first could be mere coincidences. It just may be that an independent click uncontrolled by the balls occurs in time just when the balls collide. Your observation of the event cannot *prove* otherwise, logically speaking. One cannot disprove the theory that humans create the illusion of causality because of the "constant conjunction" between the clicks and the reactions each time we shoot one ball into another.[46]

While there may be a very high correlation between these events, one cannot eliminate all of the possible variables that could be the actual causes of the clicks. Therefore, it is only possible to prove that the two balls and the click correlate in time and space, a succession of before and after events, which we associate and convert into a "cause." Hume explained that "Contiguity and succession are not sufficient to make us pronounce any two objects to be cause and effect."[47] Attribution of causality, then, is nothing more than a product of the imagination that rationalizes simultaneous occurrences. In this way, Hume undermined both the deductive approach of Descartes and the inductive approach of Locke. "Reason alone can never give rise to an original idea . . . reason . . . can never make us conclude that a cause . . . is absolutely requisite to every beginning of existence."[48]

Not surprisingly, many philosophers disagreed with Hume. Another Scottish philosopher, Thomas Reid (1710–1796), wrote *Inquiry into the Human Mind, on the Principles of Common Sense* in 1764 to argue that mental experiences and operations are universal and can be codified into a set of universal rules that cross cultures. This Lockean doctrine of "common sense" can settle disputes and determine matters of taste for all of civilization, a thesis that was very popular among "modernists." In *Active Powers* (1788), Reid tried to refute Hume on causation, arguing that humans cause free actions and that intuition leads to direct knowledge of causation. He was saying in effect, "Look here, Hume, logic may not be able to prove cause, but we surely know that the bumping of billiard balls *causes* the click. We know it intuitively." He argued that innate principles give rise to immediate convictions that form a pathway to direct knowledge. For this association, he is often referred to as the "father of British realism."[49]

In fairness to Hume, we should be clear that he was not an absolute "sceptic." "This sceptical doubt," wrote Hume, "both with respect to reason and the senses, is a malady which can never be radically cured, but must return upon us every moment, however we may chase it away."[50] On this issue, Hume was influenced by Cicero, who believed that there are limits to skepticism.[51] That is to say, if you embrace skepticism in everyday life, it will paralyze you because you can never answer every doubt. Shakespeare's *Hamlet* can be read as an attack on "scepticism." Hamlet's indecision results in many more deaths than would have occurred had he acted on the strong probability that his uncle murdered his father. By scrutinizing every shred of doubt, Hamlet set tragic events in motion that destroyed him, his family, and his country. *In the practical world, prudence must intervene to settle issues at some point.* In the theoretical world, one could be a relativist or skeptic forever. Hume, however, is remembered most for undercutting causality, vastly expanding what could be questioned in the physical world and thereby creating a need for the explanatory powers of rhetoric.

Faculty Psychology and Rhetoric

The thinking of Bacon, Locke, and Hume was codified in David Hartley's *Observations on Man, His Frame, His Duty, and His Expectations* (1749), which formally listed the following faculties of the mind: will, understanding, memory, imagination ("fancy"), and affections.[52] This conceptualization was highly influential, particularly when integrated with the French belletristic movement with its focus on aesthetics, especially the issue of taste.[53] Many in England focused on this term, especially John Dryden, Joseph Addison, Jonathan Swift, and Edmund Burke. They saw *taste* as a propensity of the mind, which has a certain natural and *instinctive sensibility to beauty*. Adam Smith (remembered primarily for his economic theory of free trade) and Robert Watson advanced this conceptualization in their famous lectures on rhetoric in Edinburgh.[54] Smith is widely credited with advancing the belletristic movement in Great Britain by equating taste with elegance, proportion, symmetry, and delicacy—terms that could be applied as easily to architecture or sculpture as to rhetoric. Smith believed that a speaker's style elicited an impression of character from the audience. Thus, taste in style needs to be adjusted to the audience. However, Smith grounded his theory in the epistemology of Locke and the need for rhetoric in the free marketplace of ideas.

Edmund Burke (1729–1797), known as father of political conservatism, combined taste with prudence in his theory of rhetoric. Prudence is that which allows speakers to prioritize their values and the values of their audiences. Burke wrote at length about how speakers must not let adaptation to an audience create inconsistency in personal values. The heroic speaker is a leader who persuades the audience to follow. For example, in 1775 Burke, one of the great parliamentary speakers, argued for conciliation rather than war with the American colonies. He lectured the electors of Bristol about representation and told them his knowledge of subjects was superior to theirs. They were capable of judging his character but not the issues of the day. When his protégé Charles James Fox goaded Burke over his principles, Burke replied that he would keep his principles over his friends, and never spoke to Fox again, even when Burke was on his deathbed and Fox came to Burke's door, begging to visit.

Edmund Burke.

Another tenet of Burke's theory was that beauty is achieved through purity and that purity is achieved by refining the speech. Burke was one of the first to argue that the art of writing is rewriting. He often polished his speeches excessively before publishing them. The following passage of the speech calling for reconciliation with America demonstrates Burke's literate style and his ability to ridicule Prime Minister Pitt's attempt to form a coalition government:

> He made an administration so checkered and speckled; he put together a piece of joinery so crossly indented and whimsically dovetailed, a cabinet so variously inlaid, such a piece of diversified mosaic, such a tessellated pavement without

cement, here a bit of black stone, there a bit of white; patriots and courtiers, king's friends and republicans, Whigs and Tories, treacherous friends and open enemies—that it was, indeed, a very curious show, but utterly unsafe to touch, and unsure to stand on.[55]

The picture of this odd cabinet is complete, detailed, and satirical.

In his theory, Burke advocated imitating nature to engage the passions, a rather Romantic notion.[56] However, with the reign of terror consuming France at the end of the century, Burke and others in England saw that rhetoric could be used for evil purposes, and it began to fall into disrepute.

Before that, a group of writers sought to reinforce the classical tradition without considering the advances being made during the Enlightenment. John Holmes' *The Art of Rhetoric* (1739), John Lawson's *Lectures Concerning Oratory* (1752), and John Ward's *Systems of Oratory* (1759) were precise regurgitations and distillations of previously published material. They did not advance the art of rhetoric; they maintained it.

Others were concerned with the notion of the sublime and reinforced the belletristic style. Influenced by such French stylists as Gerardus Vossius and Bernard Lami of the seventeenth century, John Baillie's *An Essay on the Sublime* (1747) relied on Locke's and Hume's notions of perception and association to strengthen the construction of beautiful and inspirational images.[57] The faculty psychology from the works of Bacon and Locke was incorporated in the writing of Christian Wolff and came to full flower in the work of John Ogilvie in his *Philosophical and Critical Observations on the Nature, Character, and Various Species of Composition* (1774). This renaissance was joined by the noted scientist Joseph Priestly when, particularly taken with David Hartley's medical approach, he wrote *A Course of Lectures on Oratory and Criticism* in 1762.[58]

Priestly was a Unitarian who sought to provide his dissenting group with a means for gaining liberty. He became an ardent supporter of the American Revolution. The lectures are divided into three sections: one focusing mainly on "recollection" and how it serves invention; a second focusing on organization; and a third on criticism and style. Priestly's admiration of Hartley's faculty psychology can be seen in his division of figures into those that appeal to the passions, those that appeal to the judgment, and those that appeal to the imagination. Samuel Phillips Newman's text, *A Practical System of Rhetoric* (1827), which went through sixty editions, brought this rhetorical theory to America.

Campbell (1719–1796)

The impact of faculty psychology on rhetorical theory is seen most prominently in the work of George Campbell, a cleric interested in advancing the art of speaking. He was given a license to preach in 1746 after having been educated at Kings and Marischal Colleges at the University of Aberdeen. He was so admired at Marischal that he was made a professor of theology there and taught from Cicero, Quintilian, and Longinus. Their theories provided the substance for *Lectures on Systematic Theology and Pulpit Eloquence* published eleven years after Campbell's death. In this work, Campbell provided an elementary approach to delivery, eloquence, and organization of sermons.

Campbell's early fame, however, came when he began to deal with Hume's "scepticism." How do we come to know things? What role does discourse play in this process? Like the *reductio ad absurdum* arguments of Zeno, the challenges of Hume and others were undercutting the Enlightenment's preference for logic. Here is an example:

All statements in this box are false.

If we accept the premise of the statement in the box, then the statement must be true, but if it is true then the statement is false. Thus, the inadequacy of the language of logic is revealed. In addition to warming to the idea of "scepticism," people were becoming more secure in the industrial era. The wonders of invention led to the perception that God was less needed; hence, rational sermons that appealed to the understanding were proving rather dry.

Campbell escaped the challenge of Hume's "scepticism" by relying on old-fashioned Augustinian intuition (which he may have borrowed from Thomas Reid) and natural empirical observation (which he derived from Bacon and Locke). His book, *A Dissertation on Miracles*, not only established his reputation, it refuted Hume's attack on miracles. Campbell argued that if reason is inadequate, then something must lie beyond it that will put us in contact with the truth. For Campbell, human instincts were sources of God's wisdom from which he derived his notion of "moral evidence" as an antidote for "scepticism." Moral evidence could be used to deduce the truth—as could intuitive knowledge—because much of it was divinely inspired and hence beyond reason and the senses. This form of evidence was appealing to the intellectual community of Aberdeen, Scotland, where Campbell was a member of the Philosophical Society.

Having established his credentials, Campbell set about to build a theory of argument that included: (1) *the data of experience*, drawn from Bacon and Locke. This is what our senses bring to our minds: what we feel, hear, smell, see, and taste. (2) *The data of analogy* are provided by argument. We compare known and unknown objects to learn more about the unknown. (3) *The data of testimony* from authority can be based either on expertise or in authoritative intuition. Authorities have more natural experience, have practiced more argumentation, and/or have intuited more knowledge than the rest of us. They have reached a consensus about what is true. Hence, we rely on them for knowledge when our own understanding is deficient. (4) *The data from probability* are based on the calculation of chances. We spend much of our lives making decisions based on incomplete knowledge. We compensate for this lack of assurance by betting on probabilities.

Campbell accepted Locke's position that memory is composed of the captured sensations of the mind; they are stored as abstractions and associations. The faculty of memory has for its initial purpose the task of recalling the instinctively true past. Imagination is the ability to pull ideas from the memory and generalize them to a current problem or situation. Campbell not only believed that rhetoric can express ideas, he believed it can also express emotions and create moods. His most famous book was published in 1776 after twenty-five years of writing.[59] *Philosophy of Rhetoric* referred to the classics but overshadowed them with a reliance on Bacon, Locke, and Hartley. Campbell believed the human psyche can be divided into the understanding, the will, the affections, the memory, and the imagination. These "faculties" lead to others, such as the "sympathetic faculty," which make it possible to create unity of feeling in an audience by focusing their attention on an object of pity and then having them share sympathy for that object. It could be the image of a starving child or the story of genocide in a beleaguered nation in Africa.

Although following some of the teachings of Locke (particularly with regard to the faculties of the mind and the doctrine of association), Campbell was determined to show that rhetoric was useful in the world, particularly to preachers. He wanted to free rhetoric from the confining corruptions attributed to it by Locke and Bacon. For many years Protestant preachers, particularly the Puritans, had used the formulations of faculty psychology to design their sermons around appeals to the understanding. The purpose was to create a "morphology of conversion," a mental map of how members of a congregation were moved to have saving experiences.[60] Campbell reconfigured the use of the faculties in rhetoric to expand its scope for use in the conversion process and beyond. He placed the faculties of the mind into a new logical sequence running from memory, recalling what we have learned, that is, understanding; creating new conceptualizations, that is, the imagination; evoking affections, and affections moving the will. Rhetorical preaching was not only to instruct the understanding but to fill or recall the memory, to capture or stimulate the imagination, to move the passions and, thus, to affect the will to act. Campbell's purpose was to provide a "tolerable sketch of the human mind"[61] that created a more holistic approach to preaching.

Furthermore, language needed to become the model of "perspicuity": lucid, pure, and precise but functionally adorned to the extent needed—and only to that extent—to persuade the present audience. Explanation, arrangement, and narration were sub-skills in his rhetorical canon based mostly on the tradition of Cicero. Argument was drawn from demonstration, syllogism, dialectic, and moral reasoning and was to be used for appeals to the understanding. Style in the form of fables, parables, poetic language, allegories, and the like, was used to spark the imagination. Here is an example from President Obama's acceptance speech at the 2012 Democratic National Convention. Note the various faculties to which it appeals:

> I think about the young sailor I met at Walter Reed hospital, still recovering from a grenade attack that would cause him to have his leg amputated above the knee. Six months ago, I would watch him walk into a White House dinner honoring those who served in Iraq, tall and 20 pounds heavier, dashing in his uniform, with a big grin on his face; sturdy on his new leg. And I remember how a few months after that I would watch him on a bicycle, racing with his fellow wounded warriors on a sparkling spring day, inspiring other heroes who had just begun the hard path he had traveled.

Campbell developed a new definition of rhetoric that was highly influential. The ultimate task of rhetoric is to enlighten (argue to) the understanding, to awaken the memory, to engage (please) the imagination, and to arouse (move) the passions to influence the will to action or belief. The tasks of rhetoric—the heart of Campbell's theory—are divided into the faculties of the mind in the audience.

• Enlightening the understanding means explaining the unknown, removing doubt, creating belief, dispelling ignorance, and vanquishing error. It requires skills of argumentation: "The fitness of the arguments . . . depends on the capacity, education, and attainments of the hearers, which in different orders of men are different, this properly belongs to the consideration which the speaker ought to have of his audience, not as men in general, but as such in particular."[62]

- Awakening the memory and pleasing the imagination requires the creation of lively (striking) and beautiful images. Speakers need to sharpen their narrative and descriptive ability.

- Moving the passions requires the ability to astonish, delight, place into a state of mind, and evoke such emotions as love, pity, and grief. The speaker needs to study the *pathé* but not in isolation because some emotions, such as sympathy, require appeals to character as well as state of mind. Like Aristotle, Campbell understood that one emotion could set off another. Moreover, a comprehension of tropes and figures arouses the emotions by bringing out various associations in the imagination. In this way, a listless mind can be brought to life. Action can then overcome languor.

- Influencing the will, the ultimate goal of the speaker, means guiding the audience to correct decisions.

Rhetoric creates *vivacity* by making the ideas of the imagination more real, more vivid, and more applicable to the current situation. Vivacity is accomplished in several ways according to Campbell, many of which reflect the thinking of Aristotle on *pathos*.

- First, the speaker can use contiguity in place; the closer the object is to the audience in space, the more likely the audience is to be affected by it.

- Second, the speaker can appeal to proximity in time; the more recent the happening, the more likely it is to affect the audience.

- Third, the speaker can employ similarity, showing the audience what something is like.[63] The speaker can give an idea *energy* by inculcating it with power and force. The speaker can give an idea *animation* by personifying it and giving it movement. The speaker can render an idea *probable* and *plausible* by showing that it is likely to occur.

- The ultimate goal of the speaker is to achieve "perspicuity" by avoiding vagueness and ambiguity and by being as efficient as the audience will allow. Nothing unnecessary is said and everything necessary is provided.

There are many examples of the use of this strategy in persuasive speaking. Take the case of feminist politics. It is a difficult concept to explain to a lay audience. In the passage that follows, Gloria Steinem accomplishes this goal with perspicuity in a commencement speech delivered at Tufts University in 1987:

> Politics is not just what goes on in the electoral system, or in Washington. Politics is any power relationship in our daily lives. Anytime one human being is habitually powerful over another, or one group over another, not because of talent or experience, but just because of race, or sex, or class, *that's politics*. So when we look at the fields of your state and mine, and see that one color of human being owns them, and another color works on them as migrant labor, *that's politics*. When we find a hundred of one kind of human being in the typing pool, and a few of another in the boardroom, *that's politics*. When children have only their father's name, *that's politics*. When most men have only one job, while most women have two—one inside the home and one outside it—*that's politics too*. And when students of color are still in smaller proportion than are people of color in the population, or women are a

lesser percentage of dentists and engineers, or men a lesser proportion of physical therapists and nutritionists, *that's politics.*

The senses are called into play as we see the fields of migrant workers. Comparisons are efficient as we move from what we know to what we need to know in Steinem's opinion. The arguments from numbers are direct and easily understood. She accomplished all of this in an efficient manner—an excellent illustration of Campbell's notion of perspicuity.

Campbell's rejection of syllogistic discourse for preaching gave rhetoric a renewed influence and respectability. It was now bound to the most intimate mental processes and returned to the center of the epistemic process. Wrote Campbell: "[the study of rhetoric,] properly conducted, leads directly to an acquaintance with ourselves; it not only traces the operations of the intellect and imagination, but it discloses the lurking springs of action in the heart."[64]

Blair (1718–1800)

Perhaps most popular of the Scottish school was Hugh Blair, a minister in Edinburgh who defended David Hume against the charges of heresy. Despite his defense of Hume, Blair was something of a prude. While he derived his epistemic approach from the faculty psychologists of the day, he was more concerned with establishing standards for his time by extending the qualities of a noble rhetoric to writing as well as speaking. Blair was obsessed with good taste and was dedicated to purification of the English language.

To advance his agenda, Blair became a prolific lecturer and writer. He traveled in a small circle of important friends who regularly tested his ideas in the salons of Edinburgh. They included Adam Smith, Alexander Carlyle, James Boswell, and David Hume. In 1762 King George III named Blair the first Regius Professor of Rhetoric at the University of Edinburgh, a kind of rhetor laureate. Between 1777 and 1794, he published four volumes of his sermons after he had become immensely popular as a preacher. In 1783 he published the notes of forty-seven lectures he gave annually at the university starting in 1759. His book, *Lectures on Rhetoric and Belles Lettres*, was enormously influential, derivative though it was.[65] It went through twenty-six British editions, thirty-seven American editions, and fifty-seven abridgments in thirteen different languages.[66] Part of its success resulted from Blair's reliance on faculty psychology, French aesthetics, and his conversion of preaching to a genre.[67]

Like Campbell, Blair believed that rhetoric reflects the human mind. It is epistemic because it reveals how the mind works. Blair claimed that "style is nothing else, than that sort of expression which our thoughts most readily assume."[68] In fact, he believed that "the peculiarity of thought and expression which belongs to" a human reveals his or her character.[69] God has given us beautiful sentiments and wonderful emotions and has also given us the means to express them.

The important thing for speakers to do is to express their thoughts with taste, the centerpiece of Blair's theory. Taste is "ultimately founded on a certain natural and instinctive sensibility to beauty."[70] Thus, the key to understanding taste is its universal appeal: "Nothing that belongs to human nature is more general than the relish of beauty."[71] Taste treats beauty in an "orderly, proportional, grand, harmonious, new, or sprightly" manner.[72] A tasteful speech is beautiful if it meets these universal standards. It is orderly, for example, if it keeps its audience aware of where it has been, where it is going, and enumerates its major points. It is proportional if its contentions are of equal weight and its introduction and conclusion are of suitable length to the rest of the speech. It is grand if it stirs the audience to spiritual thought. It is harmonious if its metaphors do not clash, and one argument leads to the next. It is new if it is original; that is, it tells the audience something they do not know or presents a familiar idea in a different light. It is sprightly if it is lively, that is, animated.

Blair spends some time in his book on *belles lettres* trying to educate preachers about taste. He believed that appeals to the understanding composed with taste express feelings of sentiment in proper style and encourage correctness of judgment. His lectures focused on acquiring a sense of taste through education, imitation of beauty, and development of style in language. It is produced in a speech through propriety, "fitness and design."[73] Blair rejected the Roman grand, middle, and plain styles in favor of a tasteful style that is based on the Roman notion of *decorum*. This sublime style allows the speaker to move his or her audience to new levels of conviction born of appeals to the imagination and the affections.

Hume convinced Blair that the great spring to action is not logic but *pathos.* Blair believed that every emotion has a corresponding set of objects that can evoke that emotion in an audience. Images of hostile, powerful objects (a wild boar) arouse fear; images of weak, friendly objects (a crippled puppy) evoke sympathy. The orator's job is to place the scene or object before the audience to provoke the proper emotion. Accomplishing this feat requires a talent with word choice that can come only from a strong education and rhetorical training.

Because of the "sympathetic faculty," Blair surmised that there is a "contagion"[74] among the emotions that allows them to be called up by speakers. In order to exercise this faculty, speakers need to coordinate their gestures, their looks, their whole manner to weigh on the sympathies of the audience members. The contagion not only runs from the speaker to the audience, it multiplies in the audience as they observe emotions among themselves: "Sympathy is a very powerful and extensive principle in our nature, which we behold expressed by others."[75] If the speaker weeps, then someone in the audience may weep. If audience members weep, then others in the audience will also begin to cry. The same is true of laughter or fear, anger or pity.

Evoking emotions such as sympathy requires mastery of style, especially the sublime, which requires a grandeur, a sense of elevation, expansion, and transcendence. The sublime can be achieved, according to Blair, in terms of removal of boundaries (freedom), appeals to height and depth (up to the mountaintop, down to the valley of death), and the use of sound (voice modulation) and solemnity (seriousness and reflection). Today, the notion of environmentalism can seem remote and unattractive to an audience until a speaker amplifies it using Blair's categories. For example, preserving open space removes the boundaries surrounding our lives and allows us to roam free in an open wilderness. Cleaning the environment allows us to see the fish in the depths of the sea and the mountains that lie behind our cities. Protecting our forests preserves the sounds of nature, the homes of the animals we love, and the pure water that we drink.

Blair also understood the power of metaphors in amplifications that achieve the sublime state. They give "light and strength to description; to make intellectual ideas . . . visible to the eye by giving them colour and substance, and sensible quali-ties."[76] Blair was particularly fond of the vehement style that has the quality of ardor; it is glowing, heated, and affected. But like Cicero, Blair warned that style must be an expression of character and naturally assumed. It must be congruent with the imagina-tion and the emotions. Style is, therefore, as essential to rhetoric as is argumentation.

These lessons cannot be objectified, according to Blair, because rules cannot pro-vide inventive genius or match style to a speaker's persona. The individual mind must be brought to bear on the specific subject for the specific audience by a speaker who is well trained. Rhetoric is an art, not a science. In trying to advance this art, Blair talked about its usefulness to criticism. Critics are rhetoricians in that they must argue for their critique and reveal to their readers that a book or a speech has been done taste-fully. Critics must understand the development of language and such sophisticated notions as harmony of purpose and structure. They must understand the history of eloquence and rely on its best practitioners for inspiration.[77] Last but not least, they must understand the links between poetry and rhetoric, which requires the study of the great literary lights of the time. Blair's course of study, while comprehensive and difficult, proved rewarding for many of his students.

ELOCUTIONARY THOUGHT

Sheridan (1719–1788) and Austin (1753–1837)

This renaissance in *belles lettres* included at least two important commentaries on delivery. The actor Thomas Sheridan and the reverend Gilbert Austin argued that delivery is the most important canon of rhetoric. Educated at Trinity College and run-ning his own academy, Sheridan published at least eleven books that were concerned with proper pronunciation, reading, and "rhetorical grammar." His book on *British Education*, for example, advocated the Greco-Roman curriculum that, as we have seen, placed rhetoric at the center of all studies. Rhetoric, he claimed, would enrich and refine the English language. And from such an improvement in language use, the quality of all other liberal arts would be improved. He sought to make English the suc-cessor to Latin as THE international language.

In his writing, he often sounded like Henry Higgins, the character from *Pygmalion* and *My Fair Lady*, who tries to teach Eliza Doolittle to speak proper English. Sheri-dan's best book on delivery was *A Course of Lectures on Elocution*, published in 1762, in which he argued that oral communication has qualities that written prose does not. These qualities allow speakers to be more effective than writers in certain situations. Translated into modern examples, in-person sales are more effective than telephone solicitation and telephone solicitation is more effective than letters. Furthermore, Sheridan argued, your accent—the way you pronounce words—affects your perceived credibility. The strong Harvard (upper-class Boston) accent of John Kennedy was said to give him added credibility. The southern accent of Jimmy Carter was said to dimin-ish his effectiveness.

Austin published the long-titled *Chironomia; or A Treatise on Rhetorical Delivery: Comprehending Many Precepts, Both Ancient and Modern, for the Proper Regulation of the Voice, the Countenance, and Gesture. Together with an Investigation of the Elements of Ges-*

ture, and a New Method for the Notation Thereof; Illustrated by Many Figures in 1806. He relied heavily on Roman rhetorical theory and Edmund Burke's writing on taste.[78] Although Sheridan preferred conversational delivery, Austin preferred a choreographed delivery, one that was planned down to every movement of the body and gesture of the hand. He acknowledged his debt to Sheridan and John Walker, whose books *Academic Speaker* and *Elements of Elocution* enjoyed some success. Without crediting him, however, Austin "borrowed" from John Bulwer's *Chirologia and Chironomia* of 1644. Bulwer's work emphasized the hands and fingers, while Austin's covered the voice, face, and entire body. Austin pointed out that uncultivated speakers gesture too much, whereas the refined speaker brings a sense of grace to speeches by understanding that gesture represents meaning. In fact, while Sheridan recommended that orators engage their audiences as if they were in conversation with them, Austin developed a set of marks for classically acting your way through a speech. Within a sphere of onstage action, Austin attempted to advise on every possible gesture and movement, matching them to messages and moods. While Sheridan's natural style prevailed, Austin's mannered delivery could prove effective if well rehearsed and performed before large audiences.

In 1996, Elizabeth Dole, who was the wife of the Republican nominee for president, demonstrated a practical application of Austin's method at the Republican convention. In a speech supporting her husband's candidacy, she wowed the convention and television audience when she left the lectern, walked into the audience of delegates, and moving through them delivered the speech from memory. Dole had rehearsed the speech for six months and carefully orchestrated her every move. Delegates known to her were placed in strategic locations so she could stop where each one was seated, recall a segment of her text that she had associated with that person, and continue speaking, giving the impression of speaking spontaneously. She proved that Austin's method can produce the illusion of spontaneity.

Whately (1787–1863)

Bishop Richard Whately became so entranced with the idea that rhetoric had epistemic functions that he reversed the Ramist position: he made logic the province of rhetoric: "[T]he only province that Rhetoric can claim entirely and exclusively is the art of inventing and arranging arguments."[79] This province is huge since rhetoric would provide the substance of arguments, the material from which they were fashioned. In other words, rhetorical invention should precede logical construction. The long title of Whately's book gives you an idea of what he set out to do: *Elements of Rhetoric Comprising an Analysis of the Laws of Moral Evidence and of Persuasion, with Rules for Argumentative Composition and Elocution.* The book went through seven editions.

Whately was the son of an Anglican priest, and being sickly, the young Whately was often confined to lonely reading in his room. After completing his undergraduate education at Oxford in 1808, he became a tutor in Oriel College of Oxford and then completed a master's degree in 1812 and was ordained as a minister. He taught and preached in Halesworth in Sussex until he was given a doctor of divinity degree in 1825 and returned to Oxford to run St. Alban's Hall. He also served as a professor of political economy. In 1831 he became archbishop of St. Patrick's Cathedral in Dublin, where his elitist Anglicanism rubbed many of the Irish citizens the wrong way. None-

Austin believed delivery was the most important canon of rhetoric and could be choreographed.

theless, when Whately became a Liberal Party member of the House of Lords, he supported Catholic emancipation. Perhaps for this largess, he was buried in St. Patrick's. He wrote many books on the operation and theology of the Anglican Church, promoting reforms.

Like Blair and Campbell, however, Whately's lectures inspired books on logic and rhetoric. His first book, *The Elements of Logic*, was published in 1826 and sold well going into nine editions by mid-century. His more innovative work, *The Elements of Rhetoric*, a handbook published in 1828, bows to Cicero, Aristotle, and Campbell. It is noteworthy because it continued to put rhetoric at the center of rational thought. Rhetoric is "the art of influencing the will" to produce conviction in an audience. Whately differentiated between exhortation (appeals to emotions) and argumentation (appeals to understanding). He believed his system of argumentation should be taught to all Christians so that they could defend their faith and interpret the Bible. He claimed that God had given reason to humans so that they can apply the teachings of the church to new situations. Like Campbell and Blair, Whately treated style in terms of creating a sense of perspicuity and taste. Here he retrieved Aristotle's notion of *energia* to study energizing qualities of words for activating ideas.

This philosophical investigation led Whately to his chief goals: (1) to provide preachers with the ability to address their unlearned flocks about the doctrines of Christianity, and (2) to provide defenders of the faith with the skills of argumentation and a sense for the quality of evidence. Thus, Whately's focus was on oral argumentation for direct confrontations using an extemporaneous and natural delivery.

More important, Whately expanded the Roman notion of *onus probandi*, the burden of proof, so essential in legal rhetoric.[80] In the Anglo-American system of jurisprudence the burden of proof lies with the prosecution because the *presumption* is that a person is innocent until proven guilty. However, once the prosecution establishes a *prima facie* case (one that on the face of the matter appears to prove guilt) the burden of proof shifts to the defense. If both sides are talented, the burden shifts back and forth until a judge or jury resolves the issue. However, Whately is quick to point out that while the legal system is based on a prescribed and logical view of presumption, in real life, presumption is determined by the audience. Many preachers, he warned, presume that their audiences accept the existence of God as a matter of faith because of the way they were brought up. However, many audience members make no such assumption or hold to it weakly. A minister who ignores that possibility will be less effective than one who understands it and adjusts to it. Whately argued that many people are waiting to be convinced of the existence of God. Thus, preachers, because of the rhetorical nature of the audience, often have a greater burden of proof than they assume is logically necessary.

Under the topic of presumption, Whately also defines what he calls "deference." Deference is given to authorities, sometimes unconsciously, because they have an established reputation. In the courtroom, deference is given to the judge; he or she is presumed to be correct and responsible for keeping order. Whately also notes that those who assume they deserve deference when in fact they do not are called "arrogant."

In contemporary courtrooms, effective lawyers do not presume that the jury will believe that their clients are innocent until proven guilty. Given the rhetorical nature of jurors and the pressure of media coverage, a jury may believe the accused is guilty before the trial starts because they give "deference" to news accounts. Such a condition puts an initial burden of proof on the defense attorney. Alternately, we have witnessed cases where the accused has been proven guilty beyond a reasonable doubt according to most logical standards, yet the jury found the accused innocent because their rhetorical natures allowed them to make a judgment on factors other than logic. Whately concluded there is "no necessary advantage to the side on which the presumption [logically] lies."[81] The precept of burden of proof had a dramatic effect on the United States during its presidential election in 2000. In one of the most important cases contesting the election results in Florida, Judge N. Saunders Sauls ruled that Vice President Al Gore's legal team failed to carry the requisite burden of proof that five grounds of irregularities, including misconduct, fraud, illegal voting, among others, were met in order to overturn the election.[82]

Even in science, as Whately pointed out, presumption is a rhetorical matter:

> Harvey's discovery of the circulation of the blood is said to have lost him most of his practice, and to have been rejected by every physician in Europe above the age of forty. And Jenner's discovery of vaccination had . . . similar results.[83]

In this way, Whately saw links between *ethos, pathos,* and *logos* that had been lost in the medieval codification of classical rhetoric.

Whately also developed a new way to look at proems (openings) of speeches. The "introduction inquisitive" explained to the audience why the subject was of particular interest, significance, or curiosity to them. Thus, for example, one might begin a speech with, "I am here to discuss the hole in the ozone layer over Antarctica. Why do you think it is relevant to you? In this lecture, I shall show you how it affects the health of each and every one of you."

The "introduction paradoxical" focused on the improbable. "I am here today to bear witness to the human spirit, not with logic, but with incredibility. The human spirit is such an incredible thing that it could not have been invented by humans; therefore, it must be a creation of God."

The "introduction corrective" undid a misunderstanding or misrepresentation. "Many of you gathered here today believe that I oppose affirmative action. That is not true. I support the same notion of affirmative action that John F. Kennedy supported: All things being equal, the preference should be given to the underrepresented minority."

The "introduction preparatory" readied the audience for the reasoning to follow, particularly if it was complex or unusual. "Before I explain to you exactly how this crime occurred, I want to make clear that there is no smoking gun, no videotape of the crime, nor a single witness to what occurred. But none of those things are necessary for a conviction in this case because of the scientific evidence we will present. It shall make the case for us."

The "narrative introduction" started with the story or event to be referred to in the body of the speech that followed. "Let me tell you the story of a young woman who was raised by loving parents, the son and daughter of immigrants from Vietnam. That young woman stands before you tonight nominated for United States Senator."

Whately's final contribution to rhetorical theory involved his attack on the elocutionary movement, particularly as articulated and diagramed by Austin. Whately would have none of the artifice of dramatic speaking; instead, he endorsed natural behavior and conversational style to complement his argumentation. "[W]hoever . . . appears to be attending to his own utterance . . . is sure to give offence and to be censured for an affected delivery."[84]

Bain (1818–1903)

The last of the significant Scottish rhetors of this era was Alexander Bain, who studied in Aberdeen and eventually wrote a number of books that brought the scientific method to rhetorical theory.[85] Like Campbell, Blair, and Whately, Bain admired and extended the work on faculty psychology pulled together by Hartley. Bain was one of the first scholars in rhetoric to use the German psychological theories being developed at the time. Bain used this research to correlate Cicero's purposes of rhetoric with psychological acts: informing deals with thought and understanding; moving with rhetoric is a matter of invoking the will; and pleasing arouses the emotions. He then argued that theories of style should be developed around these combinations to produce and explain "effective" speaking. The influence of Locke through Hartley can be seen in Bain's argument that the various tropes and figures should be used to produce associations in the mind of the listener that correlate with the speaker's purpose. For example, speakers wishing to move an audience need to select tropes and figures that allow for contrasts or comparisons compatible with the speaker's aim in order to initiate willingness in the audience. Speakers wishing to please an audience need to create associations using tropes and figures to call up emotions compatible with the speaker's purpose.

Bain held the University of Aberdeen's first chair of logic. His text on composition was enormously influential and produced many fine writers from the British schools. He is equally important to our study because of his use of new psychological terms in his recitation of rhetorical theory. This incorporation of physiological psychology was the beginning of a whole new look at rhetoric that would culminate with the work of Kenneth Burke in the twentieth century (see chapter 11).

CONCLUSION

The scholars we have studied in this chapter broke new ground by adopting the "new science" as a way of "seeing" how humans learn and what role communication plays in that process. Thinkers like Bacon and Locke used their powers of observation to provide reason with solid data from which new conclusions could be drawn. Both embraced a view of the mind that broke its functions down into faculties. The role of rhetoric in such a system was to excite various faculties to aid in the moving of the will. With modern technology, we have continued to explore the faculties of the mind. For example, we know that sympathy is triggered in the ventral medial prefrontal cortex and that reasoning usually resides in the dorsal lateral prefrontal cortex. Anticipation of reward is located in the orbitofrontal cortex, while conflict monitoring is located in the anterior cingulate cortex. These discoveries already have affected the rhetoric of marketing. Advertising reaches out to these brain locations every day of our lives.

Philosophers with a less rational approach, notably David Hume, turned to "scepticism," a questioning of all premises, which threatened the powers that be, particularly in the religious community. The resulting turmoil proved a boon to rhetoric since many of the theorists we have examined in this chapter were deeply Christian. Campbell wrote a refutation of Hume's "scepticism" of miracles, and Whately, who was a bishop, wrote a parody of it. Thus, Campbell moved away from the scholastic position that had rejected rhetoric's epistemic function; he sought to restore it. Recall that many of the early Christian apologists were very much influenced by Plato and tried to wed his thinking with Christian theology. This often resulted in a disdain for rhetoric. Following Augustine, Christian scholastics, such as Thomas Aquinas, endorsed a kind of supreme rationalism at the expense of rhetoric. Thus, traditionally, even with the Jesuits, dialectic was seen as an ally of theology.

In a more secure world where nationalism, scientific advancement, and industrialization were turning humans into the masters of their fates, rationalism was used to undermine certain theological foundations and to focus humans on individual enlightenment. *Cogito, ergo sum* ("I think, therefore I am"), the cry of Descartes, echoed through the ages to free many philosophers from a direct link to theology. Even those who remained devoutly Christian followed the example of Aquinas and argued that Christian truths could be deduced rationally.

Partly in reaction to this "modernism," and partly out of respect for new psychological foundations, Campbell, Blair, and Whately were particularly interested in refining rhetoric for use in the pulpit. Each believed that congregations could be made to understand the word of God and to embrace Christianity anew if only appeals were properly presented. Each used quotations from the Bible to illustrate his theory.[86] More to the point of this book, these three scholars adapted rhetorical theory to new ways of thinking. They sustained a renaissance in rhetoric in the British Isles that had a tremendous impact on rhetorical practices there and in the Americas. They brought rhetoric into the "modern" era where it could undergo further changes making it into an even more sophisticated art form.

Study Questions

1. What is your epistemology? What does it have to do with how you believe and know things?

2. Do you believe there is a duality between the mind and the body? How are the two segregated?

3. How did Vico differ from Descartes? Why was Vico more sympathetic to rhetoric?

4. What was rhetoric's main function according to Francis Bacon? Why does rhetoric rank so low in Bacon's study of discourse ("tradition")?

5. Give a contemporary example of each one of Bacon's "idols."

6. What did Locke's theory owe to Bacon's? Why is Locke called an empiricist? How does "abstraction" work? Why is it important to memory?

7. What are Locke's categories of knowledge? What is the difference between internal and external discourse?

8. How did Hume think the mind worked? What is "scepticism"? Why is it important to rhetorical theory?

9. What is taste? Does it have universal criteria or is it culture bound?

10. How did George Campbell become prominent? What was his theory of argument? Upon what kinds of "data" does it rest?

11. How did Campbell broaden the scope of rhetoric?

12. What did Campbell mean by perspicuity, contiguity, proximity, and similarity?

13. What is Hugh Blair's most important contribution to rhetoric?

14. What was Thomas Sheridan's theory of delivery? Which contemporary speakers exemplify it?

15. What was Gilbert Austin's theory of delivery? Which contemporary speakers exemplify it?

16. How did Whately define the province of rhetoric? What contributions did he make to our understanding of argumentation?

17. Explain Whately's notion of the "burden of proof" using a contemporary trial.

18. Find examples of Whately's proems in contemporary speeches.

Notes

[1] Adam Smith, *The Theory of Moral Sentiments* (1759) VII.iv.25.

[2] *Cogito ergo sum* in Latin; *Je pense donc je suis* in French. The phrase is from Descartes' *Meditations*.

[3] Queen Christiana converted to Catholicism, abdicated from the throne, and moved to Rome where she received a papal welcome through an archway built in her honor. The archway can be visited today at the Populo gathering place below the Borghese Gardens.

[4] No one understood this better than Bernard Lamy (1640–1715), who wrote his *L'Ar de parler* based on Descartes' "rationalism."

[5] See G. Vico, *The New Science*, Thomas Goddard Bergin and Max Harold Fisch, trans. (Ithaca: Cornell U. Press, 1948).

[6] Ibid., p. 130.

[7] Vico, Oration III, *On Human Education (Six Inaugural Orations, 699–1707)*, G. A. Pinton and A. W. Shippee, trans. (Ithaca: Cornell U. Press, 1993), p. 80.

[8] This last function inspired the work of Chaim Perelman and Lucie Olbrechts-Tyteca in their 1958 book, *The New Rhetoric*. (See chapter 12.)

[9] He was particularly influenced by the teaching of Dante (see chapter 7).

[10] See Joel B. Altman, *The Tudor Play of Mind: Rhetorical Inquiry and the Development of Elizabethan Drama* (Berkeley: U. of California Press, 1978).

[11] Francis Bacon, *De augmentis* in *The Works of Francis Bacon* 15 vols., eds. James Spedding, Robert L. Ellis, Douglas D. Heath (London: Longman, 1870), vol. 5, p. 66.

[12] The Latin version was written in 1605; it was published in English in 1623. See Francis Bacon, *Advancement of Learning* in *Great Books of the Western World*, vol. 30, Robert Maynard Hutchins, ed. (Chicago: Encyclopedia Britannica, 1971).

[13] Ibid., p. 66; italics are mine.

[14] Ibid., pp. 23–25.

[15] Ibid., p. 54ff. Bacon interchanged the words "faculties" and "functions."

[16] Bacon describes two types of imagination: reproductive, which recalls images of past experiences, and creative, which combines images into new forms or looks to the future.

[17] Ibid., p. 32.

[18] Ibid., p. 56.

[19] Ibid., p. 58.

[20] Ibid., p. 66.

[21] Ibid., p. 66.

[22] Ibid., p. 82.

[23] Thus, Bacon finds it odd that Aristotle treats the affections in his *Rhetoric* instead of in his *Ethics.* Ibid., p. 78.

[24] Ibid., p. 67.

[25] Bacon, *Novum Organum: Aphorisms Concerning the Interpretation of Nature and the Kingdom of Man,* in Hutchins, see p. 109ff.

[26] Fulton Henry Anderson, *The Philosophy of Francis Bacon* (Chicago: U. of Chicago Press, 1948), p. 99.

[27] Bacon, *Novum organum*, p. 112.

[28] Ibid., p. 110.

[29] J. Max Patrick, *Francis Bacon* (London: Longman, Green & Co., 1961), p. 31.

[30] Bacon inspired Alexander Bain (see last section of this chapter) to write a book on *English Composition and Rhetoric*, which is systematic and empirically based.

[31] Louis was named king at the age of four in 1638 and ruled until 1715, becoming the most powerful monarch in the world.

[32] I do not mean to imply that Locke endorsed rhetoric. In fact, he said rhetoric was "for nothing else but to insinuate wrong ideas, move the Passions, and thereby mislead the Judgment." For an excellent analysis of Locke's view of rhetoric, see Shawn Spano, "John Locke and the Epistemological Foundation of Adam Smith's Rhetoric," *The Southern Communication Journal*, 59 (1993): 17–20.

[33] Not surprisingly Ockham was jailed for his use of *reductio ad absurdum*, which he called his "razor." He became the Zeno of his time, using reason to undercut church dogma. In 1323 Pope John XXII required Ockham to appear before his court in Avignon. He was imprisoned and did not escape until five years later. He was protected by the Duke of Bavaria for the remainder of his life.

[34] From John Locke, "Epistle to the Reader," *An Essay Concerning Human Understanding*, in Isaiah Berlin, *The Age of Enlightenment: The Eighteenth Century Philosophers* (New York: George Braziller, 1957), p. 33.

[35] Berlin, p. 42.

[36] Ibid., p. 70.

[37] See Locke's *Second Treatise on Government* (1689).

[38] See Jane Donawerth, "Conversation and the Boundaries of Public Discourse in Rhetorical Theory by Renaissance Women," *Rhetorica*, 16 (1998): 181–200.

[39] See Mary Astell, *A Serious Proposal to the Ladies, Parts I & II* (London: Rich Wilkin, 1697). See also Patricia Springborg, ed., *Astell: Political Writings* (Cambridge: Cambridge U. Press, 1996).

[40] Berlin, p. 174. Berlin edits the works of Hume in this volume on pages 162–260.

[41] Ibid., p. 173. This notion, as Hume acknowledged, was based on David Hartley's doctrine of association, which we will examine in the next section of this chapter.

[42] Ibid., p. 176.

[43] Ibid., p. 207.

[44] Ibid., p. 208.

[45] His italics. *An Enquiry Concerning the Principles of Morals,* L. A. Selby-Bigge, ed. (Oxford: Oxford U. Press, 1902), p. 293. Later in the book (p. 462), Hume went further and claimed that "reason is, and ought to be, the slave of the passions." By this he meant that we form intuitive impressions first and then use our powers of reason to rationalize these impressions. That is why two people who view the same event, ideology, or person can reach such different conclusions about them. Hume's position is supported by modern psychological research. See, for example, Jonathan Haidt, *The Righteous Mind: Why Good People Are Divided by Politics and Religion* (New York: Pantheon, 2012), pp. 25–30, 48–50, 114–27, 325–26.

[46] "[N]ecessity is something that exists in the mind, not in objects." Ibid., p. 214.

[47] Ibid., p. 200.

[48] Ibid., p. 211.

[49] Ibid., p. 262.

[50] Ibid., p. 229.

[51] See Victoria Kahn, *Rhetoric, Prudence, and Skepticism in the Renaissance* (Ithaca: Cornell U. Press, 1985).

[52] Hartley certified a change in terminology; Bacon's reason and appetites become understanding and affections.

[53] See Barbara Warnick, *The Sixth Canon: Belletristic Rhetorical Theory and Its French Antecedents* (Columbia: U. of South Carolina Press, 1994).

[54] Smith was trying to develop a language for the new middle class. He was particularly concerned with developing a vocabulary of virtue and taste.

[55] Edmund Burke, "Speech on American Taxation," delivered April 19, 1774. http://www.econlib.org/library/LFBooks/Burke/brkSWv1c2.html (accessed July 11, 2012).

56 See Donald G. Bryant, "Edmund Burke on Oratory," *Quarterly Journal of Speech,* 19 (1933): 1–15; David G. Lavasseur, "A Reexamination of Edmund Burke's Rhetorical Art: A Rhetorical Struggle Between Prudence and Heroism," *Quarterly Journal of Speech,* 83 (1997): 332–50.

57 Vincent Bevilacqua, "Philosophical Influences in the Development of English Rhetorical Theory: 1748 to 1783," *Proceedings of the Leeds Philosophical and Literary Society,* 12.6 (1968): 198–208.

58 Priestly believed the orator's chief task was to "inform the judgment" of his listeners. His advice was often employed by those seeking religious liberty.

59 Because it was written over such a long time, the terms sometimes have different meanings in different places in the text.

60 See the discussion of Calvin's impact on preaching in America in chapter 7.

61 *Philosophy of Rhetoric,* Lloyd Bitzer, ed. (Carbondale: Southern Illinois U. Press, 1963), p. xliii.

62 James Golden and E. P. J. Corbett, *The Rhetoric of Blair, Campbell, and Whately* (New York: Holt, Rinehart, and Winston, 1968), p. 206.

63 This concept reflects the writing of Locke and Hume.

64 Bitzer, p. 1. This notion of "springs" was borrowed by Blair when he wrote of the passions as the greatest springs to human action.

65 The great novelist Charlotte Bronte learned Blair's book by heart. Lyndall Gordon, *Charlotte Bronte, A Passionate Life* (New York: W. W. Norton, 1995), p. 45.

66 One of Blair's rivals was Charles Rollin, who wrote *The Method of Teaching and Studying the Belles Lettres.* By 1769, Rollin's book was in its fourth edition indicating the popularity of this subject. But Rollin's influence pales in comparison to Blair's.

67 A reading of his work will show that he relied on Joseph Addison, Edmund Burke, and Francis Bacon to develop his theories of novelty, beauty, propriety, and the like. He also used Cicero, particularly his letters, to illustrate his points.

68 Hugh Blair, *Lectures on Belles Lettres* (London: J. Cranwell, 1838), p. 116. See also p. 251 where he claims that "style and thoughts" are inseparable.

69 Ibid., p. 230.

70 Ibid., pp. 10–11.

71 Ibid., p. 11.

72 Ibid., p. 11.

73 Ibid., p. 57.

74 George Campbell, writing before Blair, referred to it as an "infectious" state. Campbell, in turn, had borrowed his notion of sympathy from Adam Smith.

75 Blair, p. 223.

76 Ibid., p. 181.

77 He particularly mentions Demosthenes and Cicero.

78 Burke held out against the Enlightenment for all sorts of reasons. For example, he believed Enlightenment thinking encouraged the excessive French Revolution. He claimed that French "philosophes" ignored the importance of "public affections."

79 Richard Whately, *The Elements of Rhetoric* (Boston and Cambridge: James Munroe, 1855), p. 40.

80 Michael Sproule, "The Psychological Burden of Proof: On the Development of Richard Whately's Theory of Presumption," *Communication Monographs,* 43 (1976): 115–29. See also Carol Poster, "An Organon for Theology: Whately's *Rhetoric and Logic* in Religious Context," *Rhetorica,* 24 (2006): 37–78.

81 Golden and Corbett, p. 354.

82 *Albert Gore Jr. et al. v. Katherine Harris et al.* No. 00-2808. http://www.law.fsu.edu/library/election/2808/2808.html (accessed July 11, 2012).

83 Golden and Corbett, p. 354.

84 Ibid., p. 378.

85 *The Senses and the Intellect* (1855), *The Emotions and the Will* (1859), *English Composition and Rhetoric* (1866, revised 1886). Bain was a precursor to modern communication theory scholars who use quantitative methodologies to derive new theory.

86 Golden and Corbett point out (pp. 16–17) that "Campbell . . . quotes from the Bible on seventy-six occasions, while Whately alludes to the Scriptures and to his own ecclesiastical writings forty-one times. . . . Blair developed a lecture on pulpit eloquence."

The Existential Revolt against Modernism

One of the major themes of this text is that rhetoric is a response to uncertainty. The modern philosophers, like the scholastics who preceded them, tried to end uncertainty by combining the discoveries of science and psychology with rationalism. Their aim was progress and a consensus among experts as to what the truth is. Their line of thinking could be traced back through the scholastics and Plato to the naturalists of ancient Greece. However, just as with previous truth-based theories, the modernists' philosophy was assailed by lingering doubts. The existentialists argued that reality often evades definitive and adequate explanation; however, such uncertainty gives one freedom of choice. Uncertainty sustains the need for rhetoric both as a discourse that can make the unclear lucid and as a form of communication that can make sense of the world.

Another theme of this text has been that for every major school of thought, another school of thought forms in reaction. The naturalists of ancient Greece developed theories in reaction to the mythologists who had preceded them. In attacking the Sophists, Plato became one of the most influential thinkers in the history of the world; Neoplatonism flourished for centuries. Humanists fought the rigid logical approach of the scholastics. Thus, it should come as no surprise that there have been several revolts against the objectivism and rationalism of "modernist" philosophy. While Hume's "scepticism" certainly put cracks in the modernist facade, his philosophy was not adopted as a means for existing in the pragmatic world. Questioning all knowledge is fine on a theoretical level, but at some point one must get on with one's life and make decisions based on the information at hand.

Perhaps no philosophy is more concerned with everyday existence and decision making than existentialism. Before we can understand its relevance to rhetoric, we need a picture of the positions against which the existentialists were revolting. This chapter begins by exemplifying modernist thinking by reviewing the contributions of Immanuel Kant, Georg W. F. Hegel, and Arthur Schopenhaur. It then examines the thinking of the five most significant existential philosophers in an effort to deduce a rhetorical theory. In the process, we shall examine rhetoric's role in the quest for transcendent spirit and authenticity in decision making, two major goals of existential philosophers.

THE MODERNIST POSITION

Perhaps the best examples of modernist thinkers are Immanuel Kant (1724–1804), Georg Wilhelm Friedrich Hegel (1770–1831), and Arthur Schopenhaur (1788–1860). These three major philosophers believed that you can determine the truth and achieve your highest aim through rational mental processes. The forerunner was Kant, who, using reason, sought to uncover the universal morality that God had provided to humans.[1] Thus, the modern era of rationalism tried to replace the religious era. Enlightenment thinkers sought to overcome the slavery of dogma and religious wars with human reason and individual critiques that were highly skeptical. In fact, perhaps because his father was Scottish, Kant was greatly influenced by Hume's "scepticism"—hence Kant's book on *Religion within the Limits of Reason Alone* (1793), a refutation of Luther's famous phrase, "Justification by faith alone."

Kant received his PhD in 1755 at the University of Königsberg in Prussia, where he lived off the fees students paid him for his lectures as they prepared for their examinations. He eventually became a professor of logic and metaphysics at the university. While his work on metaphysics was enormously influential, his more humanistic works were largely ignored. For example, his *Lectures on Ethics* was not published in English until 1924.[2]

Kant was a deeply religious and popular lecturer who never published a major work until he was forty-six. Yet, he strongly influenced thinkers who followed him by providing a *Critique of Pure Reason* (1781), which argued that ethical systems should be grounded in reason and then establish moral consciousness.[3] Kant claimed that the mind was powerful enough to order its sensed experiences and relate them to time and space; he called this the "Transcendental Aesthetic." The "Transcendental Logic" is what organizes the concepts we perceive; unlike what Locke supposed, the mind is not blank; it contains "categories" that help us organize what we perceive. Both are universal characteristics in humans and are dubbed "transcendental" because they rise above common ways of knowing things.

Kant's publication of a *Critique of Practical Reason* in 1788 supports a moral view of the world that can be obtained by reason. We rationally apprehend and interpret what our intuition produces in the mind. This interpretation is made possible by categories of reason that operate universally in humans. These transcendent qualities of the mind rely on firsthand contact with the world to provide an intuition; that is, an immediate relation to real-world objects. When properly grounded and developed, reason produces a voice of duty that is a universal "categorical imperative." It may manifest itself in at least two major ways. First is the "juridical duty": the human respect for law, which animal instincts cannot provide. Said Kant, "Act only according to that maxim by which you can at the same time will that it should become a universal law."[4] Thus, all moral decisions require the use of reason to determine their universal nature, which can function as a conscience to guide people aright. Second is the "ethical duty": using inner rational constraint. And when forming a government, we must be sure to constrain it also by providing a bill of rights that defines the "ethical duty" of the government to its citizens.[5]

Kant was quick to point out that there is also an ineffable *noumenal* reality beyond the practical world. Like Plato's *noumenal* world (see chapter 3), it contains different and higher truths; unlike Plato, however, Kant did not believe humans were capable of perceiving it. Nonetheless, it provides a metaphysical and religious escape hatch that prevented Kant from being too severely censored by his ruler, Frederick the Great of Prussia.[6] For example, Kant argued that while human intuition will confirm that causality rules the phenomenal world, in the *noumenal* world it is possible that complete freedom exists.

Kant's call for an abstract intellection undermined the blind dogma of some religious thinkers and replaced it with a universal "categorical imperative" that applied to all humans. In this way, he added a positive layer of human dignity and honor to Locke's more utilitarian system of checks in a social contract. Kant wrote, "Let justice be done even if the world should perish."[7] In other words, the higher principle is not survival, it is moral righteousness. Thus, for Kant natural rights flow from respect for the innate dignity of humans. He believed in the reciprocity of the Golden Rule: "Do unto others as you would have them do unto you." He also believed that reason was the only effective faculty for fighting evil in the world.

Kant invented the term "Enlightenment"; he wrote, "Enlightenment is man's emergence from his self-imposed nonage. Nonage is the inability to use one's own understanding without another's guidance."[8] Kant had a mixed view of rhetoric: "Force and elegance of speech, which together constitute rhetoric, belong to fine art; but oratory, being the art of playing for one's own purpose upon the weaknesses of men, no matter how noble the purpose, merits no respect whatever."[9] He saw too many cases in which oratory was used not to honor others but to take advantage of them.

Like Kant, Hegel supported himself by tutoring until he was appointed to a professorship at the University of Jena in his native Germany. Forced to flee Napoleon's army, Hegel moved to Nuremberg where he taught high school and wrote his *Science of Logic* (1812–1816), in which he claimed in the "Introduction" that logic is the reflection of God before the creation of nature. After a brief teaching stint in Heidelberg, the success of the book led to his appointment at the University of Berlin. His reputation brought students from all over Europe to study with him until his death in 1831. He explored what he called the *Zeitgeist*, a universal, unconscious spirit of the time that leads a people forward through history toward their destiny as a nation.[10] The notion of the collective unconscious was a forerunning of the theories of Sigmund Freud and Carl Jung, whom I will examine in chapter 10.

For our purposes, it is important to understand that, of the three philosophers discussed in this section, Hegel was the most influential on Marx (see chapter 10), who in turn has had more influence on world events than any of these philosophers. Hegel believed freedom is the ultimate good and claimed that one can get to it by using reason alone. He applied Aristotle's dialectic approach to demonstrate that history is driven by the *clash of thesis and antithesis*. The result is a new *synthesis* that preserves the best elements of the thesis and antithesis. In fact, Hegel believed that every thesis implies an antithesis. The thesis, "We should go to war," implies the antithesis, "We should not go to war." Relevant evidence and arguments are mounted in favor of and against each thesis and antithesis. In the ensuing attack and response, the false will be revealed and the true will be retained. The surviving residue is a synthesis, which now becomes a new thesis: "Under certain circumstances, we should go to war." A thesis represented as an entrenched group or established institution could be attacked by an antithesis, represented by a reform or revolutionary group. History revealed to Hegel that the result of the clash was never a total victory for either side. Instead, a synthesis emerged, which was an improvement over the thesis and a better embodiment of the national "spirit" of freedom. Many found this optimistic use of dialectic to be attractive, including Karl Marx, who converted it into an engine of progress known as "dialectical materialism."

Hegel's optimistic approach to history was inspired by Comte Henri de Saint-Simon, who believed that civilization had reached its highest, most mature stage.[11] Hegel claimed that in each stage, a larger percentage of the population enjoyed the fruits of freedom. More progress was possible, however, if we learned the lessons of history and allowed each nation to follow its own "spirit of the times" *(Zeitgeist)* to freedom. To accomplish this, Hegel adapted his dialectical method to history. The "Absolute" is revealed not only in nature, as the Romantics argued, but in history that continually moves forward toward a universal good and freedom.

In this way, Hegel tried to show that history is dialectically dynamic; it is not static nor does it repeat itself. It is a rational upward spiral toward freedom for greater and greater numbers of people. This evolutionary notion placed great faith in the reasoning ability of humans to bring order to free societies. It also inspired a new wave of Romantic philosophers and artists who fought for self-determination of national groups. The poet Lord Byron, for example, died in the fight for Greek independence from Ottoman rule. Hegel's philosophy came to dominate most German universities immediately following his death.

Arthur Schopenhaur, a German philosopher, clearly delineated various manifestations of reason in human society.[12] He sought to elevate empathy and compassion over narcissism and evil doing. Evil comes from the human will, which is inbred and often creates uncontrollable motivations. Thus, he rejected Aquinas' notion of free will. Instead, Schopenhaur's study of the will resulted in a dark view of human nature and a rejection of the optimism of Kant and Hegel. Schopenhaur so despised Hegel that he scheduled his own lectures at the University of Berlin in the same time slot as Hegel's. The ploy did not work; Schopenhaur proved so unpopular that he had drop out of teaching. In his major work, he concluded that reason and aesthetics should be emphasized since the appetites can never be entirely satisfied and will lead one into a life of disappointment and pain. The aesthetic realm can temporarily relieve the pains caused by our various desires. This view is not unlike that of some Buddhist sects.

The modernist approach influences us to this day. It is particularly relevant in republican governments that espouse such modernist ideals as the freedom to pursue happiness, checks and balances within the government, rule of law, and respect for the dignity of others. For example, many of these ideals are reflected in the American Constitution. Hobbes and Locke inspired James Madison's negative view of self-interest, hence his system of checks and balances in the Constitution. Jefferson, however, was more optimistic and focused on the natural rights of humans, such as life, liberty, and the pursuit of happiness. He wrote those rights into the Declaration of Independence and demanded that they be added to the new Constitution in the form of the first ten amendments, better known as the Bill of Rights. These same rights were rallying points for those participating in the Arab Spring that began in December 2010. Rulers have been forced from power in Tunisia, Egypt, Libya, and Yemen, while uprisings continued in other nations—one of the most brutal being in Syria in 2012.

EXISTENTIAL OBJECTIONS

While agreeing with the ideals of the modernists, the existentialists found the logical and universal hierarchies of Kant, Schopenhaur, and Hegel suspect. Thus, existentialists were precursors to the "postmodern" movement (see chapter 13). In fact, existentialists believe that reason is inadequate for discovering transcendent truths; they prefer the subjective to the objective, perception to objectivity. One of the most interesting things about existentialism is the number of times it is hyphenated with other terms in order to explain what is being advocated. There are Christian-existentialists and atheistic-existentialists; there are monological-existentialists and interrelational-existentialists. Some literary critics argue that Shakespeare was the first existentialist, while most philosophers claim Søren Kierkegaard (1813–1855) was the father of existentialism. As evidenced by these variations, existentialism is hard to pin down, has multiple definitions, can be fragmented, and contains various strains within its own movement.

At base, *existentialism is a philosophy of existence*. It studies how we exist, why we exist, and suggests authentic ways to live our lives.[13] Instead of starting with objects, as do empiricists and sensualists, it starts with the study of the subject—the who, the person who lives every day. To this mix, the existentialists add certain principles that help further define their revolt against the modern rationalists. Existentialists believe that we are free to choose as opposed to being determined by a preset causation. In fact, we are condemned to freedom; we have no choice but to choose. Furthermore, we are defined by the choices we make and we develop our sense of self in making choices. Thus, freedom leads to a sense of self and to growth, but we are also responsible for the choices we make. Taking responsibility for what we do and what we decide is living an "authentic" existence.

Kierkegaard (1813–1855)

The earliest existential philosopher was born in Copenhagen on May 5, 1813, and therefore became a young contemporary of the influential Hegel. However, after Hegel's death, Søren Kierkegaard attempted to refute Hegel's dialectical certitude and theory of historic progress by arguing, "All essential knowledge relates to existence."[14] His small inheritance allowed him to attend the University of Copenhagen and to devote his life to writing. His call for an authentic Christianity got him branded as a heretic and fanatic. His last major work, *Attack on "Christendom,"* was published in the year of his death; it satirized the state church of Denmark. Although he was ridiculed in his time, his writings eventually proved enormously influential in the twentieth century, particularly following the horrors of the world wars, which badly undermined the optimism of the modernists.

Søren Kierkegaard.

One of the great quests of existentialism is "the transcendent," which has at least two meanings. Earlier we touched on the first—to transcend means to rise above. For example, if you are involved in a dispute in which it is posited that you either favor or oppose health care for every citizen, you can transcend the argument by showing that you are neither for nor against it. Kierkegaard used this rising-above method to transcend Hegel's dialectical scheme, arguing that there was a legitimate position beyond the thesis and antithesis. Kierkegaard endorsed the One (primordial unity) over the dialectical duality of Hegel's logic. Remember that Hegel and Kant believed that material experience is reality; to be an experience, something or some phenomenon has to be separated from something else. Hence, an automatic division or dialectic is inherent in Hegel's system. For Kierkegaard, however, consciousness itself transcends these divisions as a reflection of the One.[15] The One transcends the material of experience; consciousness presides over, and is superior to, the collision between ideality and reality. For Kierkegaard, then, consciousness is a reflection of the One in that consciousness allows the growth of self in the transcendence of experience. That realization is a freeing moment that allows the self to control its own destiny. Like Socrates, Kierkegaard argued that "one must know oneself before knowing anything else."[16] He is considered the father of existentialism at least in part because he made the subject the proper study of philosophy. His path is the path of subjectivity: "One does not become a hero or a lover objectively."[17] The self should not be objectified because, although it always exists in a "mode," it does not always exist in the same "mode." It is not static but is constantly changing as it makes decisions.

A second meaning of transcendence is spirit—that which allows access to God. Kierkegaard believed that the self contains spirit—that in a sense we are all divine. Only when the self raises the question of existence for itself and experiences it as an existing being in the world can it transcend the material categorization of self and find its spiritual nature, which will lead to transcendent spirit, that is, God. George Bedell writes that for Kierkegaard

> the Spirit is, above all else, an infinitely powerful spirit, absolutely transcendent to the world, who breaks open the contained and orderly Greek cosmos. Therefore, Spirit, who in the final analysis is God, is not beauty and truth but energy and power. . . . He does not simply inspire poets or warriors as in the Greek world; he is the very foundation of freedom to be or to choose one's existence.[18]

But how do we find our "self"? How does the "mode" we choose contribute to the search? There are at least two ways to find our self. First, we need to consider self as a subject-actor in an experiential world and examine who or what is making choices—who or what is relating to others. We live every moment of our existence by choosing. Decision making reveals being because being *is* decision making. Kierkegaard wrote that "in making a choice it is not so much a question of choosing the right as of the energy, the earnestness, the pathos with which one chooses."[19] In his *Concluding Unscientific Postscript*, he claimed that it is not *what* a person decides but *how* one decides, because how a person decides defines self.[20] Intent is more important than effect. Our decisions reveal our *ethos;* how we make decisions is determined by *who* we are, inclusive of our values.

The question of values leads to the second means of self-discovery. Since values serve as guides in decision making, we need to know our core values or we will continue to act in the dark, out of ignorance. Such knowledge comes from intense self-examination and reflection. Kierkegaard concluded that the subject acts, perceives, and defines the world; this creative capacity is what gives us a sense of "selfhood."[21] That self becomes "authentic" *when it takes responsibility for the decisions it makes.*

The existential path to authenticity runs through three stages or "modes of life": *the aesthetic*, which Kierkegaard defined as immediate and unreflective; *the ethical*, which he defined as reflective in the sense that we examine values in a rational, proactive, moral way; and *the religious*, which he defined as spiritual or devoted.

The aesthetic stage in life is reactive; for many people, it is all there is and they never rise above it. Such people are not in control of their lives because they are usually reacting to the initiatives of others, thereby surrendering their individuality to the world. Existentialists claim that if you begin to reflect on your life, you will begin to see that the aesthetic life will always let you down; it will eventually disappoint you. This understanding can, as Kierkegaard makes clear, lead to a paralysis of the will, a tremendous sense of indifference to the world and to those who populate it.

One is shaken from this apathy in unique ways. For example, you can fall into depression, what Kierkegaard called "melancholia." While depressed, you might perform some demonic act, being cruel to a beggar, kicking a cat, or uttering a mean remark. When you commit such acts, you should have the revelation that they are not you; that the "you in you" would not act in such a way. Such a discovery creates a sense of "dread" that can break through your indifference to reach an authentic sense of self. It is that effort that leads to the ethical stage. For example, when some alcoholics hit bottom, they vow to change their existence. Gluttons catch a reflection in the mirror that awakens them to the emptiness of their physical existence. Pain lets us know we are alive, and glimpses of our inauthentic existences lead us to seek an authentic sense of our self.

The ethical life is difficult because it requires reflection and a reprioritizing of values, our guides to decision making. Most existentialists spend a good deal of time on the question of guilt because it is closely linked to discovering a sense of self, to discovering the values we hold, and to embracing responsibility. Guilt can arise because we are overwhelmed by the choices we have available and the values upon which we rely to decide. Whatever choice we make, we will decide against something and for something else. Deciding against causes us to feel guilty.

Guilt also occurs when we violate our values. Here the voice of conscience reminds us that we have been offending the guides that we claim to follow. We are drinking or eating to excess—and harming ourselves and others in the process. We must either redefine the values we embrace (a conscious act of choice and re-creation of self) or we must admit to having committed a sin and take responsibility for such action in an effort to improve (a move toward authentic self). In Dostoyevsky's *Crime and Punishment*, Raskolnikoff commits a senseless murder of an elderly woman, surely a demonic act. He wrestles with his conscience, a process that he learns is worse than torture and imprisonment. The important thing to note is that *something feels the guilt, and that something is the authentic soul inside us.* According to existentialists, until we go through such trauma, we remain a mystery to ourselves—incapable of leading authentic lives, let alone transcending to spirit. Thus, while the goal of existentialism is self-affirming and spiritual, the path to that goal is often dark and troubling.

The last stage in Kierkegaard's project of life, the religious, brings us intuitive knowledge of a transcendent God. R. G. Collingwood puts it this way: "[M]an is also the being whose being is to transcend himself. To the extent to which he submits his will to the will of God he overcomes his self-alienation and fulfills the conditions of his inherent rationality."[22] Transcendence is difficult because the *grammar and logic of ordinary mind* (GLOOM) is committed to keeping us in the experiential, material world. Its vocabulary is inadequate for a world outside the universe or inside our souls. For example, what does Kierkegaard mean when he says that the individual is an "existing infinite spirit"?[23] Existing is temporal, real, contingent; existing is also an abstract concept; finally, existence is decisive actualization. It is this actualizing by reflective decision making that Kierkegaard implores us to embrace. It is his version of enlightenment. When the self relates its existence to itself, it exists spiritually: "Spirit's realization as self-consciousness is, then, the initial effort of the self to relate itself to itself."[24] Spirit arises from creating a sense of self. Freedom to discover and experiment with self is crucial to the process. Freedom creates infinite possibilities and frees the self from being locked into necessity, that is, concrete, predetermined, and/or factual limits.[25] Freedom allows the play of the "either/or," and in choosing we develop selfhood.

In Kierkegaard's work we see the first glimpses of what existentialism might contribute to rhetorical theory. A Kierkegaardian would employ rhetoric *to force and make choices that would manifest self-knowledge, providing a more secure presence for the leap to transcendence.* Rhetoric creates self because speakers make choices as they compose and deliver speeches, and they bring choices to their audiences, who also can use them to assert selfhood. The presence of that self is a means to transcendence, and self is revealed in authentic decision making—taking responsibility for what we choose, what we write, and what we say.

The subjective world of Kierkegaard was full of implicit rhetorical theory concerning responsibility.[26] For example, a person breaks with the thoughtless immediacy of the aesthetic life by ending gossip and other useless forms of communication. On the positive side, Kierkegaard specifically called for "edifying discourse," which helps redefine self in an authentic way by accepting free choice and responsibility for existence. Kierkegaard claimed that "edifying discourse" cannot be communicated by lecturing, arguing, or persuading. Kierkegaard's denigration of public or direct rhetoric leads him to endorse an indirect approach. Edifying discourse is glimpsed in art or seen in a telling example; it is seductive and often ambiguous. The reason for this indirection is that direct appeals, according to Kierkegaard, fail to liberate the person addressed from the illusions of the aesthetic stage of life. In *Point of View of the Author*, he wrote:

> [A]n illusion can never be destroyed directly . . . only by indirect means can it be radically removed. . . . A direct attack only strengthens a person in his illusions, and at the same time embitters him. . . . [T]he indirect method . . . arranges everything dialectically for the prospective captive, and then shyly withdraws . . . so as not to witness the admission which he makes to himself alone before God—that he has lived hitherto in an illusion.[27]

How do we *practice* indirect communication for the good of us or another person; that is, how do we use language to help ourselves and others destroy the illusions of the inauthentic life (such as money and power) and embrace an authentic sense of self—a self that is free to choose, a self that accepts responsibility for choice, and a self that uses its freedom creatively to reinforce its individuality?[28]

First, Kierkegaard encouraged the use of ambiguity for his edifying indirect communication. His endorsement of ambiguity arose from his notion of faith. Kierkegaard argued that if God had saved Jesus from the cross, he would have made faith impossible because disbelief would be impossible. Thus, uncertainty is crucial to producing faith, which is not a rational matter. Ambiguity promotes uncertainty. Kierkegaard saw it as a means of teaching others because it arouses attention and it forces choices. If the ambiguity is artfully constructed, it will force us to choose and in choosing we exercise the self.

Kierkegaard's study of *ambiguity* in the life of Jesus provides an example of his theory of edification. On the one hand, Jesus claims that the meek shall inherit the earth. He advises his followers to turn the other cheek if they are struck. On the other hand, Jesus chases the money changers from the Temple with a whip made of rope. He strikes and withers a fig tree. Are we to live by his words or imitate his actions? The ambiguity forces Christians to reexamine their values and make a difficult choice.[29]

Second, Kierkegaard recommended the use of sincere questioning for edifying purposes. Questions are not always sincere. They can be used to attack others, can have an ulterior motive, or can be disguised messages. For example, if, as you come down the stairs to meet your date, and she says, "You're not going to wear that shirt, are you?" She is not asking a question in reality; she is asking you to change your shirt. Kierkegaard defined sincere questioning as an open, authentic inquiry aimed at helping the other person discover a sense of self. Such questions might include: What is your most important value? What was your most important life experience? What do you believe is your best talent?

Third, Kierkegaard recognized that art can provide an indirect glimpse of transcendence. Art can literally be inspirational and often is, in unsuspecting ways. Such indirect communication can strike us in the theater, the concert hall, or the art museum.

In all of these ways, edifying discourse works indirectly to be healing and helps one get in touch with one's soul.

For Kierkegaard and most of the other existentialists, authenticity leads to *commitment*—living the life you recommend. In rhetorical theory, this means practicing what you preach. In philosophy, it means exemplifying what you advise. Socrates did both. He recommended the contemplative life to his pupils and led that life. He was committed to it and, therefore, projected a sense of authenticity. Had he become a politician, he would have demonstrated a lack of commitment to what he preached. Thus, a Kierkegaardian notion of *ethos* would include holding speakers responsible for exemplifying their messages, particularly the values they espouse.

Sartre (1905–1980)

As an atheist, Jean-Paul Sartre would have resented being connected with anything as otherworldly as spirit, but he clearly strengthened the role freedom plays in the authentic life and further eroded confidence in objective reason. Sartre argued in *Being and Nothingness* (1956) that consciousness "is free by virtue of its being aware of its possibilities, of what it lacks, or of its privations."[30] In fact, persons are "condemned" to freedom: we have no choice but to decide. Even when we do not decide, we have made the decision not to act. And such negative decisions can have serious consequences, as when one fails to report a crime, or child abuse, or on-the-job harassment. So how do we make a *responsible* decision? In *Existentialism and Humanism*, Sartre attempted to provide an answer: "And, when we say that man is responsible for himself, we do not mean that he is responsible only for his individuality, but that he is responsible for all men."[31]

Jean-Paul Sartre.

In his investigation of responsibility, Sartre, like Kierkegaard, revealed the importance of the creative use of language. He claimed that if self-persuasion is powerful enough to be used for inauthentic purposes, what he called "bad faith"[32] or "self-deception," then it can also be used creatively to embrace freedom, discover the self, and remake existence.[33] "Man is nothing else but that which he makes himself. . . . You are free, therefore choose—that is to say invent."[34] In this way, a Sartrean might endorse a speaker's use of language to create a sense of self.

Sartre helped popularize existentialism in the post–World War II era by writing clearly on the subject, by representing its themes in novels and plays, and by bringing credibility to the movement, since he had been a member of the French resistance during World War II. His notoriety was enhanced when in 1948 he was condemned by both the Communist Party and the Catholic Church. His lifelong liaison with the novelist and early feminist Simone de Beauvoir, and his habit of discussing his philosophy in the coffee houses on the Left Bank in Paris, did nothing to diminish his fame.

One of Sartre's clearest injunctions is that "existence precedes essence," by which he meant that self comes before anything that masks it. In his novel *Nausea* (1938), Sartre explained that existence has no connection with "assigned essence."[35] Persons are beings prior to being covered over by what others attribute to their class. In this case, the term "essence" refers to the historic fragrances that arise from the qualities a person is assigned by society. These fragrances, to mix a metaphor, blind persons to their being and blind a person to the authentic existence of others. Thus, our job is to get back to our basic existence. Sometimes this means moving from our animal selves in nature, what Sartre calls "being-in-itself" to our human, reflective reasoning selves, which Sartre calls "being-for-itself."[36]

In *Existentialism and Humanism*, Sartre provided a case in point when he railed against the generalizations that have been made about existentialists by Communists, Christians, and others. He concluded, "So it appears that ugliness is being identified with existentialism."[37] That is, the authentic preexisting existential philosophy has been covered over by the historic slanders of its enemies. These slanders have become its "essence," which in this case is an odor that prejudices the public against it.

The operation of racism provides a case in our own time. Elements in a society sometimes attribute characteristics to a race and assume that each member of the race possesses those characteristics. Persons born into that race are sometimes blinded to their own individuality and assume the characteristics attributed to them, bowing to the authority of society or accepting a past not of their own making.[38] Appearing before a Senate committee studying the plight of African Americans in the armed forces, former Secretary of the Army Clifford Alexander said:

> White America continues to paint pictures of black America that determine our opportunities. You see us as less than you are. You think that we are not as smart, not as energetic, not as well suited to supervise you. . . . These are the ways you perceive us, and your perceptions are negative. They are fed by motion pictures, ad agencies, news people, and television.[39]

Alexander believes society has covered African Americans with disfiguring essences that prevent them from reaching their potential. Golfer Tiger Woods has gone so far as to claim that he is not African American, even though his father was. Some African Americans believe that Barack Obama wasn't black enough, even though his father was Kenyan. Both Tiger Woods and Barack Obama have achieved potentials far beyond those of most Americans.

Existentialists seek to break through these undifferentiated perceptions by dispelling the "assigned essences" and allowing the individual being to emerge. While Sartre cautioned against accepting assigned essences, he encouraged his followers to find their own sense of "Being-for-itself" *(Être-pour-soi)* to create an authentic self. Basically, he argued that too often existence is unconscious, and that in arriving at one's authentic self, one becomes conscious of "Being-for-itself," one's true essence for operating in the world in a meaningful and free way.

Why should we undertake such a project? Because the alternative is assigned essence, which is a form of stereotyping. Existentialists believe that stereotyping is wrong for at least two reasons. First, it does not represent persons as they really are; it objectifies them. They would argue that Barack Obama was not "the black candidate," he was instead a candidate that held many views as an individual. Human beings do not exist in static categories; they are always becoming or "on the way" to becoming something.[40] This fluid state presents us with a stream of decisions; life's potential is not bound up in the categories we inherit or those created by logicians; it is free flowing and hence open to creative forces.

Second, stereotyping prevents persons from realizing their potential to create a self. This covering over of being retards development and leads to artificial understandings of self. The man with the potential desire to become a great novelist or poet becomes a frustrated investment banker because he buys into his subculture's characterization of success. In such cases, the individual loses a sense of "mineness" and control over one's activities, one's existence. The danger is that if society determines what we do with our lives, it determines who we are.

Central to this analysis is the notion of an underlying being or an "authentic" self. Philosophers of existence, as we have seen, get at this concept by emphasizing human experience from the perspective of the subject, as opposed to treating humans as objects to be analyzed. Instead of a scientific or analytic approach to the question of self, the existentialists take a phenomenological approach.[41] That is, they examine existence in context and as a whole without imposing the presuppositions of previous philosophical speculation. Situating his study on the realities of existence prompted Sartre's "revolt against both abstract reason and scientific determinism."[42] He was clearly a postmodern thinker.

Earlier we noted that Sartre strengthened the role freedom has to play in the authentic life. We should also note that freedom overwhelms the individual with choices and may cause anxiety. Anxiety in turn leads to a crisis, which, according to Sartre, can have either authentic or inauthentic consequences. The inauthentic person will try to flee the crisis by re-embracing the herd mentality of the world. The authentic person will embrace the crisis, which will lead to two further reactions: The person will be thrown back upon his or her self, which will lead to intense self-examination; or the person will reach out for communion with others, which may lead to a discovery of self-with-others. In both cases, authenticity arises from the realization that absolute freedom means we are "absolutely responsible" not only for our decisions but for the situations in which we find ourselves and who we are.[43]

If we have no choice but to decide, and we dare not let others make our choices for us, what guidelines do we use? Sartre responded that "nothing can be good for us without being good for all."[44] Humans must decide as if they are deciding for all humankind.[45] This advice leads to a tension between freedom and responsibility in the works of Sartre. He faced this dilemma: pure freedom cannot be responsible because of the damage it can do to others, and anything short of freedom is dangerous because of the damage it can do to the development of the self. Sartre's discussion of the immorality of marriage proves enlightening on this point. If a husband is totally free, he will make his wife into a slave, which is evil. If the husband treats his wife as an equal, then neither are totally free, which is damaging to the development of the potential of each. If the husband gives his wife total freedom, he becomes a slave. If the husband is indifferent to the situation, he is inauthentic, because he is no husband at all while "frozen in the ice of his own indifference."[46] Hence, Sartre opposed marriage. He did provide another solution to the problem he posed. There is "no exit" except to transcend the situation by deciding and taking responsibility for one of the awful choices one must make in a marriage.

One of Sartre's early attempts to escape this bind came in personal experience. For him, freedom was essential to authentic existence, and it could be found even in the most desperate situations if one could transcend them. He determined that we are always free to assert our sense of self and that is the most important freedom. In *The Republic of Silence*, he explained:

> We were never more free than during the German occupation. We had lost all our rights, beginning with the right to talk. Every day we were insulted to our faces and had to take it in silence. Under one pretext or another, as workers, Jews, or political prisoners, we were deported *en masse*. . . . And because of all this we were free. Because the Nazi venom seeped into our thoughts, every accurate thought was a conquest. Because an all-powerful police tried to force us to hold our tongues, every word took on the value of a declaration of principles. Because we were hunted down, every one of our gestures had the weight of a solemn commitment. . . . And the choice that each of us made of his life was an authentic choice because it was made face to face with death, because it could always have been expressed in these terms: "Rather death than . . ." And here I am not speaking of the elite among us who were real Resistants, but of all Frenchmen who, at every hour of night and day throughout four years, answered *No*.[47]

Here we learn that even in the face of annihilation, we can save our self. We assert the self by saying "no." The two major characters in the film *Thelma and Louise* dramatize this assertion at the end of the story when they choose to drive over a cliff rather than surrender to the police. This discovery led Sartre to see that nonbeing is a permanent possibility and a reinforcement of authentic being. Nothingness haunts, inspires, and defines being. In such a world, invention is critical; that is, we must not accept what is thrust upon us, instead we must take responsibility for our own personal freedom since we are what we do in the world. This step will result in an authentic sense of selfhood and, for Sartre, the "good of all."[48]

One of the most fascinating characteristics of Sartre's thinking is that it converts the negative to the positive: nothingness helps define being; that we have no exit demonstrates that we have freedom.[49] He used a similar strategy when he advanced his theory of rhetoric. He began by talking about how rhetoric can be used for self-deceit in chapter 2, "Bad Faith," in *Being and Nothingness*.[50] His point is that individuals often try to escape the responsible freedom of Being-for-itself by committing a "lie in the soul." This violation of conscience is maintained through such rhetorical strategies as role playing, diminishing, rationalizing, sublimating, emphasizing, or avoiding certain "facts." Sartre understood that these rhetorical strategies could cover the truth and delude the self.

Since Sartre would have us re-create our self authentically—that is, without deception and stripped of acquired or assigned essences—he provided a basic rationale for intrapersonal communication. We must speak to our self in inventive ways that help free us from controlling and covering essences, categories, assessments, and the like. Furthermore, because what we decide and what we "fashion" is done for all humankind, public persuasion must endorse what is good for all of us.[51]

Heidegger (1889–1976)

Like Kierkegaard, Martin Heidegger believed that we cannot find transcendent "Being" until we affirm the "being" in our self. Once we realize that we are beings-in-the-world (*da-sein*, "there beings," as he called it), we are in a position to see that we reflect transcendent Being. Heidegger's theory is linked to rhetoric in several ways, the most important of which is his claim that *language is the "house of Being"* and can lead us to transcendent truths, even dark ones.[52] For Heidegger, truth was "un-conceal-ment" *(a-letheia)*. Heidegger sought to free the individual first from the "leveling" influence of the "they" (the common mob or herd) and then from the rational conven-tions of Aristotle, Descartes, Hegel, and Kant, because their systems were inimical to the "poetizing thought" of the mystical side of being that leads to the transcendent, "the great poem speaking us into being."[53]

Heidegger, who was born in Germany, became a Jesuit novice and attended the University of Freiburg, where he became a teacher and eventually rector. When he studied with Edmund Husserl (as did Sartre), Heidegger became fascinated with his teacher's philosophy of phenomenology, which claimed to examine the world from a presuppositionless point of view. Husserl's famous motto was "to the things them-selves." By 1927, however, Heidegger found inadequacies in Husserl's theory, particu-larly when it came to interpreting phenomena. In response, Heidegger invented hermeneutic phenomenology to replace it. As we have seen, hermeneutic means a close reading under watchful observation to provide an interpretation that discovers the authentic meaning of a text. Phenomenology attempts to see things in material context—as they are in the whole without being subject to the scalpel of analytic logic or scientific dissection. Phenomenologists argue that we should experience phenom-ena without presuppositions, biases, or predetermined filters. They want us to see the forest as it is, not as what someone has told us a forest should be, and not as the trees into which the scientists would divide the forest. They want us to see trees as they are, not as leaves and bark; a tree is poetic until broken into its scientific parts. In a way, Heidegger provided the best of both worlds with his hermeneutic phenomenology: he ensured close observation by using hermeneutics and he ensured that the larger pic-ture would contextualize phenomena without distortion by using phenomenology. In the process of applying his new methodology, he took many positions inspired by Kierkegaard, whom he often cites.

During his tenure as rector of Freiburg, Heidegger gave an address in 1934 endorsing the platform of the National Socialist (Nazi) Party.[54] Although Heidegger later claimed he was "not a Nazi,"[55] and although he helped Jewish professors escape Nazi Germany, his early and brief support of Hitler left him tarred in the eyes of many and raised the question of responsibility in existential philosophy, a question to which we will return in a few pages.[56] Due to his powerful lecturing ability and the fact that he had a running romantic liaison with Hannah Arendt, who was Jewish, Heidegger was able to rehabilitate himself and regain his popularity by the early 1950s. He then retired into Germany's Black Forest in 1959 and lived a reclusive life. Nonetheless, his writings became enormously influential; in fact, in the 1950s there were more chairs of Heideggerian philosophy in Europe than those named for any other philosopher.

In his landmark work *Being and Time*, Heidegger opposed using the term *spirit (Geist)* because many of the definitions of spirit provided by prior philosophers had "thingified" it. For example, when Hegel referred to history as essentially the history of spirit, he meant an unfolding of a cultural tradition on the road to freedom; but to Hei-degger this was much too material. As Jacques Derrida (see chapter 13), the decon-

structionist, makes clear, "The Hege-
lian determination of spirit remains
ordered, prescribed, ruled by the epoch of the Cartesian *cogito*."[57] Instead, Heidegger believed that spirit
"is what in no way allows itself to be
thingified."[58] Its power "unites and
engages, assigns, obliges."[59] Spirituality is having and demonstrating transcendent truth.[60] Associating with
spirit always expands consciousness
and does so exponentially.

Martin Heidegger.

To what do existentialists refer
when they write about spirit? Spirit
concerns otherworldly goodness and
an inner sense, often associated with
grace. Spirit is a matter of faith and/
or intuition that sets an example; it is
not a matter of reason or objectivity.
It may inspire outward wisdom, as in
the story of Solomon moved by the
"spirit of wisdom," but it is mainly
ethereal, transcendent, incorporeal, invisible, and not measurable by objective standards. Aldous Huxley, the English writer, explained why when he wrote, "[M]an possesses a double nature, a phenomenal ego and an eternal Self, which is the inner man,
the spirit, the spark of divinity within the soul."[61]

To find transcendence, Heidegger said that humans must first understand that
presence is the experience of existence; the I *as it thinks* precedes all other presences
and the experience of all other beings. In this way, Heidegger reflected the thinking of
Descartes. Individuals' thinking is what is most present and that thinking process
comes before any other experience. Individuals have to be conscious before they can
be conscious of something. Heidegger wanted us to examine closely this conscious
state to establish our "being," much in the way that Sartre wanted us to understand
that existence precedes essence.

Heidegger then urged humans to let go of the established ground; thinking must
follow the path that language opens. However, finding the play of Being in language is
not enough. Heidegger claimed humans have to be ready to receive spirit; the person
must stand in "harkening attunement" detached from the distractions of this world.
Only then will the voice of Being, the call of conscience, come to us. Thus, *authentic listening*, another component of existential rhetorical theory, is crucial to attaining existential spirituality. Authentic listening requires being open and tolerant; it requires critical
assessment of the message; it requires quieting our own responses and prejudices.

Once transcendence has been experienced, Heidegger argued that it is possible to
bring that experience to others by using his version of authentic rhetoric: "poetizing"
in constructive and creative ways. By poetizing, Heidegger did not mean writing or
speaking poetry—he meant thinking and speaking in inventive ways that uncover and

reveal the transcendent truth. The inventive process means giving one's self over to the alien, to the dark, and to wandering in the open, exposed. But like Sartre, Heidegger had a warning about self-discovery. The lifetime prisoner who emerges from the cave at night and sees the moon for the first time may think it is the source of all light. However, it is only a reflection of the sun. So, too, the person who first discovers a sense of self-being may fail to realize that it is a reflection of superior Being.

When conjoined with a concerned harkening, authentic discourse allows the emergence of *logos*, the voice of Being.[62] Then a person may choose to move through the threshold of Being into a dialogue of transcendent quality, which would uncover truth. Heidegger left his readers with the promise that transcendence is there if only one works diligently enough to achieve it.[63] Such a rhetoric would sever individuals from the "they," avoid gossip, situate individuals in harkening attunement, and develop ways to bring others to Being by using the making-known and constructive functions of rhetoric. Heidegger recommended three such forms as "authentic": (1) the examination of language to discover the self as already in the world *(Befindlichkeit)*, (2) the use of language to uncover the truth *(Verstehen)*, and (3) meaningful discourse *(Rede)*. Each of these has a corresponding "inauthentic" form: (1) the use of unclear language *(Zeideutigkiet)*, (2) distracting curiosity *(Neugier)*, and (3) idle chatter, gossip, or prattle *(Gerede)*.[64]

Heidegger also saw the dangerous rhetorical nature of technology; it transforms everything it touches into something different. Building a dam on a river converts it from its poetic, natural role to a piece of inventory for the dam. Using a computer, a phone, or a car changes a person, and so does watching a film. Heidegger called this technological framing *Gestell*. He complained that technology calls for more technology to justify itself. The dam requires a ladder so that the salmon can get through to breed. And the poor salmon are converted from natural fish, penetrating the rapids, into ladder-climbing animals incorporated into the technological picture. We have seen how computers have given rise to additional and new technology: high-speed Internet hook-ups, iPods, iPads, and other devices for downloading and storing media, cell phones that serve as both telephone and computer, and so forth. Technology takes over, pulling everyone into its frame. Thus, Heidegger posited a rhetorical theory that moved from inauthentic interpersonal chatter and technological transformation to authentic intrapersonal dialogue with Being and to poetizing the revealed truth for others.

Like Kierkegaard, he believed that art can draw us to Being and/or put us into a state of hearkening attunement. For Heidegger, however, one is incapable of creating such art unless one has achieved transcendence. Heidegger praises those who glimpse Being and then try to express that moment to others in art. He is particularly fond of the paintings of Vincent Van Gogh and the poems of Rainer Rilke and Friedrich Holderlin.

Jaspers (1883–1969) and Buber (1878–1965)

To this point, we have examined six markers on the path to spiritual transcendence: rejection of the herd mentality, creative use of language, examination of self, concerned listening, accepting responsibility for decisions, and freedom to choose. All are influential on the road recommended by Karl Jaspers and Martin Buber, who situated these elements in authentic interpersonal relationships. Rejecting the solipsism of Kierkegaard and the atheism of Sartre, Jaspers (a Catholic) and Buber (a Jewish rabbi) emphasized that dialectical reciprocity can lead to an authentic sense of self and others. Jaspers was a German psychologist who became a philosopher; his writing is dense and supported with a good deal of evidence. Buber was a Jewish theologian whose approach is poetic.

Though younger than either one, Heidegger laid some groundwork for Buber and Jaspers when he pointed out that "the mode of being of language is talk among human beings. It is constitutive of being-with-one-another, that is, constitutive of human sociality."[65] Yet more important to our purposes, he pointed out: "Hearing is constitutive for discourse."[66] While speaking can be monological, hearing requires dialogue. You listen to another, not to nothing, even if the other is your inner voice or the voice of conscience.

Karl Jaspers.

Jaspers and Buber described an authentic dialogic as the rhetoric of response (I-Thou) as distinguished from a monological rhetoric of isolation (I-it).[67] They point out that "I-it" relationships are often necessary to get by in the world. The grocery clerk, the ticket salesperson, or the waiter may not be people with which I can have authentic dialogue, but I do have to deal with them. Such relationships should be held to a minimum. On the contrary, the "I-Thou" dialogic relationship encourages each partner to identify the potential for authentic existence in the other. Said Jaspers, "Self-being is only real in communication with another self-being."[68] It is one of the choices we can make, and for Jaspers, "Self-understanding begins with the individual concrete acts of choice."[69] The formulation prescribed goes through several steps including the discovery of self as recommended by Kierkegaard, the discovery of another authentic person with whom to have free and

Martin Buber.

open dialogue in pursuit of further authentic understandings, and the realization of the transcendent *in* the relationship.

Jaspers and Buber emphasized that *dialectical reciprocity* can help infuse a sense of responsibility. For Buber, communication in I-Thou relationships is characterized as:

1. *Immediate:* it is in the here and now; the give and take are in the present.

2. *Confrontational:* the one-on-one situation forces the participants to face one another and themselves; questions will be direct and often personal.

3. *Risky:* the respondents must be honest and reveal things that are secret, intimate, or damaging.

4. *Exclusive:* only those who have an authentic sense of self are allowed into the dialogue.

5. *Creative:* entering into a dialogue requires skill at wordplay and argumentation; there is no script; the conversation flows.

6. *Responsible:* each participate must care for the other and must divulge information honestly; sharing must be equal and complete.

7. *Unfolding:* each person must be revealed and let the story of self be told.

8. *Confirming:* each person will be acknowledged by the other and affirmed by the experience.[70]

Jaspers saw the desire for conformity as a terrible enemy: "In nonexistential mundane existence, the decisive factor is the leveling will of nonentities."[71] The herd pulls members into the herd mentality. For Jaspers, like Plato, authentic dialogue "involves complete openness, unqualified renunciation of the uses of power and advantage, and concerns the other's self-realization as fully one's own."[72] In such relationships, the subjective "I" has power, acts, and invents creatively. In inauthentic relationships, the "I" and/or "the other" is objective; that is, passive, acted upon, and incapable of creativity.[73]

Dialogue that is open and empathetic is more likely to confirm a sense of self in the other person because it is less distracted than other forms of communication. Public speakers are concerned with their messages; shoppers are concerned with the product and its price. However, people in dialogue are more concerned with issues of self than are people at work or play.[74] Dialogue breaks down presuppositions and causes each person to be preoccupied with the being of the other.[75]

Like Heidegger and Kierkegaard, Buber and Jaspers also see the transcendent as inspirational of art. That is, all of them believe that *true art reflects a glimpse of transcendent spirit*. Buber and Jaspers, however, define the transcendent in an interpersonal way. It is the manifestation of a sense of self, the construction of self through the use of creative language in a dialogue, and a higher sense of self developed in cooperation with another away from the leveling masses and into spiritual transcendence.

THE EXISTENTIAL CHALLENGE

We have explored the reaction of five existentialists to the modernism of Hegel, Schopenhaur, and Kant. These existential philosophers of existence can help us understand how individuals retrieve spirit and achieve transcendence. They demonstrate that freedom allows for the creative use of language that in turn leads to a sense of self and association with the transcendent. They challenge us to reconstruct life in such a way as to make each of us the captain of our destiny. If the existentialists are correct, then creative use of language can serve both individuals and society. It can provide the strategies for the authentic reconstitution of self. It can provide the ambiguity for the indirect seduction of Kierkegaard's "edifying discourse." It can provide such strategies as minimization and rationalization for Sartre's invention of self and the freedom in language that would help those engaged in I-Thou relationships.

That brings us back to the nettlesome question of *responsibility*. What is the existential theory of conscience? Consistently, those who have written about the existential roots of spirituality have faced the argument that existentialism can be used to justify the rhetoric of Osama bin Laden as well as Mother Theresa. There are two problems here. First, the existentialists, like the Platonists before them, are right to point out that sometimes rhetorical transactions promote evil. Murray Edelman cites an interesting case from history:

> *The Pentagon Papers* show that the intelligent, highly educated policy makers of the Kennedy and Johnson Administrations were convinced that military intervention in Vietnam would stop the spread of world communism through a war that would be won quickly at small cost, and that they continued to believe it after several years of counter-evidence—exemplifying a degree of reconstruction of reality few psychotics can ever have matched.[76]

Edelman's example reinforces Sartre's point: our minds are so powerful when it comes to language that we can fool ourselves. For this reason, existentialists are rightly sensitive to the charge that their subjective approach can invite irresponsible action. We know that talent in public speaking does not always serve the good. We must not be afraid to issue ethical judgments that protect the community and ourselves from the irresponsible actions of orators and audiences. To be credible, such ethical assessments must be grounded in philosophies that *hold individuals accountable for the choices they make*. Existentialism provides such a philosophy.

That leads to the second problem with existential notions of responsibility. Since existentialists often seek to transcend worldly questions by focusing on *how* decisions are made instead of *what* they are, their critics often ask: What constitutes the correct/moral use of authenticity? Can't persons who believe they have a clear understanding of self, who have made a leap of faith, and who take responsibility for their actions still commit evil acts? Existentialists answer this challenge by making each of us accountable for our decisions. This call for personal responsibility constitutes a safeguard against irresponsible action.

However, different existentialists provide different measures of responsibility. Jaspers and Buber call for a reality check from another in intimate dialogue. Heidegger calls for attunement to the call of conscience. Sartre calls for making decisions as if you were making them for all humankind. A stronger safety net might be built by combining the various injunctions of the existentialists into an eight-part test useful for our quest. Synthesizing the existentialists we have examined in this chapter, we can deduce the following questions to establish a foundation for authenticity and responsibility in rhetorical transactions:

1. What evidence exists that the speaker has subjected values to scrutiny and has a clear, undeceived understanding of self?

2. What evidence exists that the speaker has taken responsibility for the speech and the action it advocates?

3. What evidence exists that the speaker encourages audience members to make decisions and take responsibility for them?[77]

4. What evidence exists that the speaker has engaged in authentic dialogue as a check against solipsism and as a means of reinforcing a sense of self?

5. What evidence exists that the speaker has reached conclusions by deciding as if he/she were deciding for all of humankind?

6. What evidence exists that the speaker has moved beyond immediate gratification to stages of moral and ethical development?

7. What evidence exists that the speaker heard the call of conscience or was inspired by transcendent spirit?[78]

8. What evidence exists that the speaker is committed to what is recommended? Does the speaker practice what he/she preaches?

If used properly, these means of accountability should help reveal whether a speaker is responsible and hence contributes to authenticity among listeners.

CONCLUSION

Our examination of existential rhetoric has led to a theory of creativity: since the manipulation of language forces choice, it helps us develop a sense of self, which in turn allows us to associate with spirit. If we can associate with spirit, we can use that association to refine our rhetoric, to make it more artistic—a creative art form that calls others to the transcendent level. The philosophers examined in this chapter contribute *the way to spirit;* what rhetoric provides is an *art form by which spirit can be expressed and by which others can be brought to a sense of it.* If, as some believe, spirit is the call of conscience, then rhetoric is a way by which speakers can make that call known to others. From the prophets of old to the moral leaders of the twenty-first century, rhetoric has been used in the service of conscience.

For example, Socrates was enormously influential in small settings where inhibitions were reduced (usually with wine), where he was involved in a one-on-one dialogue, and where those present seemed interested in pursuing and sharing knowledge in an environment of mutual respect. Two other, modern-day examples are Mahatma Gandhi and the Fourteenth Dalai Lama. Gandhi was able to move masses with his gentle speech and his devotion to nonviolence. For many, Gandhi was a living saint who inspired a nation. By fasting, he brought a national civil war to a halt from his sick bed. The Dalai Lama has inspired many people of all nations with his words promoting a middle ground and nonviolence. He said, "I think it is our own responsibility to make this century [the twenty-first century] be [the] century of dialogue." He further stated that "constant war" is outdated. His call for nonviolence invites us to face problems with "determination [and] vision."[79]

Whereas the pursuit of spirit is certainly the province of religion, it is not *solely* the province of religion, as the several approaches of the five existential philosophers suggest. Great rhetoric retrieves spirit: creating with language. Like the palette of the painter or the notes of the musician, words provide the substance of the rhetor's art. Even these comparisons do not give language its due, because it can be more subtle than any hue a painter can produce and has much more variety than any combination of notes available to the composer. Language is the stuff of an ultimate art that is better able than any other to help us reach a sense of spirit through creativity and to hear the call of conscience through its making-known function.

Thus, rhetoric has a large role to play in the existential project. As an art form, it can reveal freedom, force choices, and call others to spirit. It can question, use, and prioritize values, which serve as guides for the self. It can, by quieting itself, establish an attitude of "harkening attunement" to spirit. It can provide the creative dialogue of authentic "I-Thou" relationships. In short, rhetoric provides a *praxis*, a practical operation for existentialism that copes with the provisional nature of knowledge and the uncertainty of everyday existence. Existentialism provides a measure of authenticity that enhances the responsible use of rhetoric. It is hard to imagine a happier marriage of disciplines.

Study Questions

1. In what ways is your education a product of "modernist thinking"?

2. Why did Kant, Hegel, and Schopenhaur put so much faith in reason?

3. In what ways would you define yourself as an existentialist?

4. On what precepts do most existentialists agree?

5. Why is decision making so important to Kierkegaard's theory of existentialism? What did Kierkegaard mean by "edifying discourse"? How often have you used it?

6. What is Sartre's theory of responsibility? Do you agree with Sartre's definition of "bad faith"? What does Sartre mean when he says that existence precedes essence?

7. What is Heidegger's quarrel with the "modernists"? What are its implications for rhetorical theory? What is the role of authentic listening in this theory?

8. Which of the relationships in your life are I-it and which are I-Thou? What is the role of rhetoric in I-Thou relationships?

9. What is an "authentic" existence? What do existentialists mean by commitment?

10. What negative facets of rhetoric do the existentialists point out?

11. In what ways can rhetoric be used to enhance a sense of self, explore authentic relationships, and create art?

12. Take a speech by a contemporary speaker and subject it to the eight-part test for authenticity and responsibility. What is your conclusion?

Notes

[1] Immanuel Kant, *Critique of Pure Reason,* Werner S. Pluhar, trans. (Indianapolis: Hackett Publishing, 1996), p. 193.

[2] Kant also invented the term pragmatism, albeit in German, in his *Critique of Pure Reason.* Compton's encyclopedia ranks Kant with Aristotle and Plato in terms of his importance to philosophy.

[3] See also his *Critique of Judgment* and *Critique of Practical Reason.*

4 Immanuel Kant, *Foundations of the Metaphysics of Morals*, L. W. Beck, trans. (New York: Liberal Arts Press, 1959), p. 39.

5 Note that Kant was writing around the time of the American Revolution (1776–1781) and its adoption of a Constitution (1789) and a Bill of Rights amended into that Constitution in 1791.

6 Frederick was an Enlightenment thinker who created a Renaissance court. Trained in military tactics and a well educated homosexual, he ascended to the crown of his disaffected father in 1740 and united disparate provinces under Prussian rule. He confronted Russia and in 1772 took possession of parts of Poland. However, Frederick did not spend all of his time on the battlefield. He created many beautiful buildings, improved the infrastructure of his kingdom, and loved classical music. He played the flute and composed many sonatas for it, along with four symphonies. He endorsed religious freedom which may have resulted from his lifelong correspondence with the French writer Voltaire. He promoted the Berlin Academy, which became a major haven for Enlightenment philosophers and scientists.

7 Immanuel Kant, *Toward Perpetual Peace and Other Writings on Politics, Peace, and History*, Pauline Kleingold, ed., David L. Colclasure, trans. (New Haven: Yale U. Press, 2006), p. 102.

8 As quoted in Peter Gay, *The Enlightenment: A Comprehensive Anthology* (New York: Simon & Schuster, 1973), p. 384.

9 Immanuel Kant, *The Critique of Judgement: Part I, Critique of Aesthetic Judgement*, James C. Meredith, trans. (Oxford: Clarendon Press, 1952), section 53.

10 *Zeit* literally means "time" and *geist* literally means "spirit," or "ghost." Together, they came to mean the "spirit of the times." Prior to Hegel, the German romantic writer referred to a *Volksgeist or "folk spirit."* Psychologists often explore our personal *zeitgeists*, which can be inspirational. For example, it is no secret that Ronald Reagan admired Franklin D. Roosevelt, who may have been a *zeitgeist* for Reagan's optimistic rhetoric.

11 Egypt was civilization's infancy; the Greco-Roman period, its youth.

12 After a strong cup of coffee, you might want to read Schopenhaur's *The World as Will and Representation* and *On the Four Fold Root of the Principle of Sufficient Reason*. Like many thinkers of his time, Schopenhaur believed that homosexuality was a vice, though uncontrollable except by severe punishment, and that women were meant to obey men.

13 In his *Meditations*, trans. George Long (Mount Vernon, NY: Peter Pauper Press, 1960), p. 170, Aurelius wrote, "These are the properties of the rational soul: it sees itself, analyzes itself, and makes itself such as it chooses."

14 See, for example, his *Philosophical Fragments*, David Swanson, trans. (Princeton: Princeton U. Press, 1844/1971).

15 This notion is not new to us. We saw it in the pre-Socratic speculation of Parmenides.

16 Søren Kierkegaard, *A Kierkegaard Anthology*, Robert Bretall, ed. (New York: Modern Library, 1946), p. 6.

17 Ibid., p. 209.

18 George C. Bedell, *Kierkegaard and Faulkner: Modalities of Existence* (Baton Rouge: Louisiana State U. Press, 1972), pp. 25–26.

19 Søren Kierkegaard, *Either/Or*, vol. 2, Walter Lowrie, trans. (Garden City, NY: Doubleday, 1959), p. 171. See also Raymond E. Anderson, "Kierkegaard's Theory of Communication," *Speech Monographs*, 30 (1963): 1–14.

20 Søren Kierkegaard, *Concluding Unscientific Postscript*, David Swenson and Walter Lowrie, trans. (Princeton: Princeton U. Press, 1946), p. 181.

21 Søren Kierkegaard, *Fear and Trembling, the Sickness Unto Death*, Walter Lowrie, trans. (Garden City, NY: Anchor Books Edition, 1954), pp. 146–47.

22 R. G. Collingwood, *Faith and Reason*, Lionel Rubinoff, ed. (Chicago: Quadrangle Books, 1968), p. 238.

23 Kierkegaard, *Concluding Unscientific Postscript*, p. 75.

24 John W. Elrod, *Being and Existence in Kierkegaard's Pseudonymous Works* (Princeton: Princeton U. Press, 1975), p. 53; Kierkegaard, *Fear and Trembling*, p. 146.

25 Kierkegaard, *Fear and Trembling*, p. 172.

26 Anderson, pp. 1–14.

27 In Bretall, p. 332. See also Kierkegaard's *Training in Christianity*, Walter Lowrie, trans. (Princeton: Princeton U. Press, 1967), pp. 139–43.

28 The emphasis on individuality in Kierkegaard can be overwhelming. He broke off his engagement to Regina Olsen arguing that a person can never really know others and hence they will always be objects that distract a person from becoming one with God.

[29] Abraham Lincoln often used ambiguity to draw audiences into his rhetoric. See David Zarefsky, "Lincoln's 1862 Annual Message: A Paradigm of Rhetorical Leadership," *Rhetoric and Public Affairs,* 3 (2000): 13; Angela Ray, "Learning Leadership: Lincoln at the Lyceum, 1838," *Rhetoric and Public Affairs,* 13 (2010): 349–88.

[30] As quoted in Mitchell Aboulafia, *The Mediating Self: Mead, Sartre, and Self-Determination* (New Haven: Yale U. Press, 1986), p. xvi; see also p. 46.

[31] Jean-Paul Sartre, *Existentialism and Humanism,* Philip Mairet, trans. (London: Methuen, 1965), p. 29.

[32] Sartre may have been influenced by Nietzsche's concept of "bad conscience." See Ernest Jones, *The Life and Work of Sigmund Freud,* vol. 3 (New York: Basic Books, 1957), p. 283.

[33] Walter Kaufmann, *Existentialism from Dostoyevsky to Sartre* (New York: Doubleday, 1968), pp. 255, 266–70.

[34] Ibid., p. 28.

[35] He makes this point more efficiently in *Existentialism and Humanism,* p. 42.

[36] The difference is explored in his novel *Nausea* (1938) when the protagonist of the story, Roquentin, undergoes an existential crisis moving from his animal nature to his human nature. Jean-Paul Sartre, *Nausea,* Lloyd Anderson, trans. (New York: New Directions, 1964).

[37] *Existentialism is Humanism,* p. 24. Sartre is a little confusing here since he does not use the word "essence" in the traditional sense. Remember that Aristotle defined substance as essence, and nonessential characteristics are accidents. But Sartre's essences are Aristotle's accidents. Essences are the nonessential properties that cover over existence.

[38] e.e. cummings hit on this phenomenon when he wrote: "To be nobody-but-yourself—in a world that is doing its best, night and day, to make you everybody else—means to fight the hardest battle which any human can fight." In "A Poet's Advice to Students," *A Miscellany Revised,* George J. Frimage, ed. (New York: October House, 1965), p. 335.

[39] As excerpted in "Whites Only Let African-Americans Nibble at the Edges of Power," *Los Angeles Times* (May 23, 1991): B7.

[40] Karl Jaspers, *Way to Wisdom,* R. Manheim, trans. (New Haven: Yale U. Press, 1970), pp. 129–30.

[41] Phenomenology seeks a return to examination of phenomena in context and in the whole form. It rejects the dissection of phenomena proposed by analytic philosophy and logical positivism. One of its chief advocates, Edmund Husserl, sought to bracket out presuppositions that he believed distorted our vision of phenomena.

[42] George Campbell, *Philosophy of Rhetoric,* Lloyd Bitzer, ed. (Carbondale: Southern Illinois U. Press, 1963), p. 156.

[43] Jean-Paul Sartre, *Being and Nothingness: An Essay on Phenomenological Ontology,* Hazel E. Barnes, trans. (New York: Philosophical Library, 1956), p. 653.

[44] Jean-Paul Sartre, *Existentialism and Human Emotions,* B. Frechtman and Hazel E. Barnes, trans. (New York: Philosophical Library, 1957), p. 17.

[45] Sartre, *Existentialism and Humanism,* p. 29.

[46] I borrow this last phrase from Franklin Roosevelt's condemnation of Herbert Hoover during the 1932 presidential campaign.

[47] Jean-Paul Sartre, *The Republic of Silence,* A. J. Liebling, ed., Ramon Guthrie, trans. (New York: Harcourt, Brace & Co., 1947), pp. 498–99.

[48] A critique of Sartre's position can be found in Heidegger's "Letter on Humanism," in *Phenomenology and Existentialism,* Richard Zaner and Don Ihde, eds. (New York: G. P. Putnam's Sons, 1973), pp. 155–70.

[49] Sartre's play *No Exit* not only argues for this point of view, it reinforces the solipsism of Kierkegaard. The three characters of the play soon determine that "Hell is other people."

[50] Walter Kaufmann translates "Bad Faith" as "Self-deception and Falsehood," in *Existentialism from Dostoyevsky to Sartre.*

[51] See Sartre, *Existentialism and Humanism,* p. 30.

[52] Gerald L. Bruns, *Heidegger's Estrangements: Language, Truth, and Poetry in the Later Writings* (New Haven: Yale U. Press, 1989), p. 158. Heidegger admits to the influence of Hegel's phrase "God is being." See Martin Heidegger and Eugene Fink, *Heraclitus Seminar,* Charles H. Seibert, trans. (Evanston, IL: Northwestern U. Press, 1993), p. 93.

[53] Robert Hopper, "Speech Errors and the Poetics of Conversation," *Test and Performance Quarterly,* 12 (1992): 120–32.

[54] Heidegger was strongly influenced by Plato and brought a military ambiance to the campus not unlike that described in Plato's *Republic.*

55 Martin Heidegger, "'Only a God Can Save Us': *Der Spiegel* Interview of 1966," William J. Richardson, trans., in *Heidegger: The Man and the Thinker*, Thomas Sheehan, ed. (Chicago: U. of Chicago Press, 1981), p. 61.

56 Despite Heidegger's reputation of being a Nazi supporter, Jean-Paul Sartre, who fought in the French resistance, acknowledged the influence of Heidegger's notion of *da-sein* (there-being) on his work *Being and Nothingness*, which was published during the war. After the war, Karl Jaspers, who at one time was a friend of Heidegger and whose wife was Jewish, recommended that his former friend not be allowed to teach.

57 Jacques Derrida, *Of Spirit: Heidegger and the Question*, Geoffrey Bennington and Rachel Bowlby, trans. (Chicago: U. of Chicago Press, 1989) p. 126.

58 Ibid., p. 16.

59 Ibid., p. 65; see also pp. 83–86.

60 Michael Zimmerman, *Eclipse of Self* (Athens: Ohio U. Press, 1981), p. 201.

61 Aldous Huxley, "Introduction," in Swami Prabhavananda and Christopher Isherwood, *The Song of God: Bhagavad-Gita* (New York: Mentor, 1951), p. 13.

62 As Michael Zimmerman writes, "[O]nly when appropriated by the *Logos* can the poet become sufficiently released from representational thinking to give voice to the *Logos*," p. 268; see also Bruns, pp. 118–21, 158.

63 Craig R. Smith, "Martin Heidegger and the Dialogue with Being," *Central States Speech Journal*, 36 (1985): 269.

64 Thomas Langen, *The Meaning of Heidegger* (New York: Columbia U. Press, 1959), pp. 22ff.

65 Martin Heidegger, *Being and Time*, John Macquarrie and Edward Robinson, trans. (New York: Harper and Row, 1962), p. 204; see also Bruns, pp. 20–21. Jaspers befriended Heidegger at a birthday party in 1920 for Heidegger's mentor, Edmund Husserl. Later, Heidegger wrote to Jaspers about the meeting: "Those eight days at your home are continually with me. The sudden, outwardly noneventfulness of those days . . . the unsentimental rough step with which friendship came upon us, the growing certainty of a comradeship-in-arms sure of itself on both 'sides'—all this to me is uncanny in the sense that the world and life are uncanny to the philosopher." As quoted in Rudiger Safranski, *Martin Heidegger: Between Good and Evil*, Ewald Osers, trans. (Cambridge: Harvard U. Press, 1998), p. 120.

66 Heidegger, *Being and Time*, p. 206.

67 The continuum of relationships is explored further in Donald L. Berry's *Mutuality: The Vision of Martin Buber* (Albany: State U. of New York Press, 1985), pp. 54–60, 67.

68 Quoted in Kaufmann, p. 147.

69 Karl Jaspers, *Philosophy*, vol. 2, E. B. Ashton, trans. (Chicago: U. of Chicago Press, 1970), p. 363.

70 Martin Buber, *I and Thou*, (New York: Charles Scribner's Sons, 1954), p. 12.

71 Jaspers, vol. 2, p. 378.

72 Charles F. Wallraff, *Karl Jaspers: An Introduction to His Philosophy* (Princeton: Princeton U. Press, 1970), p. 135.

73 See Jaspers, *Philosophy*, vol. 3, pp. 72–80.

74 Kaufmann, p. 145.

75 Buber, *I and Thou*, p. 12. Jaspers phrases it this way in his *Philosophy*, vol. 1, on pages 52 and 53, "I do not reach the point of communication by my own actions alone, the other's action must match it." And later on page 124, he writes, "The truth begins with two."

76 Murray Edelman, *Political Language* (New York: Academic Press, 1977), p. 25.

77 Michael Hyde and I address this question in "'Rethinking the Public': The Role of Emotion in Being-with-others," *Quarterly Journal of Speech*, 77 (1991): 446–66.

78 Here we can look at the New Testament gospels to see how they parallel the wisdom of spirit in the Old Testament especially in Daniel, Susanna, Solomon, and Isaiah.

79 "Dalai Lama Urges Hope in Seattle Speech, but Avoids Tibet Crisis" (4/12/08). Foxnews.com/story/0,2933,351021,00.html (accessed May 13, 2008).

Identification and Ideology

T he revolutionary thinking of Sigmund Freud and Karl Marx built new paradigms of thought, learning, and economics. This chapter focuses on how these two major thinkers, along with Carl Jung, Jacques Lacan, and Jürgen Habermas, contributed to Kenneth Burke's theory of rhetoric (discussed in chapter 11), the most important of the twentieth century.

Freud radically questioned many of the assumptions of psychology. Carrying on the Delphic injunction to "know thyself," Freud sought to find the ways by which the unconscious influenced the conscious, just as Marx would try to show how "false consciousness" influenced the conscious life of each individual. When Freud began to publicize his written theories in 1896, no other psychiatrist practiced psychotherapy. Psychoanalysis was a brand-new term. In reaction to Freud's first controversial paper, one of his former professors rose from the audience and attacked the premises of the study. Eventually, Freud was vindicated. His redefinition of the human psyche opened the door to a new view of persona and identification, which Burke would incorporate into his work.

Marx fused Hegel's historical dialectic with materialism to illuminate the influence of the forces of production on society. His thinking would inspire many, some of whom would form Communist Parties and create a major rift in Western civilization. Marx's critique of the ideologies in society and the hidden forces that lie behind them inspired Burke to uncover the buried dialectics in the discourse he examined.

Jung and Lacan were both psychiatrists; the former developed psychological concepts such as the archetype and the collective unconscious, while the later contributed to the correlation between language and the unconscious, and the difference between actual and potential consciousness. Habermas developed a social theory that speech acts should have the goal of mutual, rational understanding. He believed that humans have the competence to effect that understanding, and a civil, public sphere should provide the space for such discourse. The public sphere, however, is at risk from mass media, with their hidden ideologies and the power to turn the public sphere into a passive consumer of information. The chapter ends with an illustration of the ways by which hidden ideologies can be reinforced.

SIGMUND FREUD (1856–1939)

If Copernicus removed humans from the center of the universe and Darwin removed them from being God's special creations, Freud established that they were influenced by unknown dark and animalistic forces—"half-tame demons." In fact, he showed that in many if not all humans the irrational was more powerful than the rational, the unconscious more powerful than the conscious.

Freud was born in Freiberg, Moravia, in 1856. After graduating from the University of Vienna, he studied medicine under the famous neurologist Josef Breuer in Vienna from 1873 to 1881. In 1883 he moved to Paris to study with Jean-Martin Charcot, an expert on hysteria. In 1886, he learned hypnosis. After his return to Vienna, he married Martha Bernys, with whom he had six children. In 1897 he began self-analysis in an effort to cure his bouts of depression. He took this gamble after he was unable to defend the hypotheses he had developed using the usual methods of psychology. Soon he discovered that his depression had been caused by guilt arising from jealousy of his father; Freud was suffering from the effects of an "Oedipus Complex."[1] He was his mother's favorite child and had feelings of love for her; jealousy of his father triggered his guilt. This breakthrough led him to many other discoveries. His examination of women suffering from hysteria revealed that most of them had been victims of incestuous violations. By helping them surface the painful memory, Freud discovered that the hysteria could be cured. With regard to the Oedipus Complex and hysteria, Freud concluded that the truth could release his patients from neurosis or psychosis. Thus, being entirely honest with oneself became a cardinal rule in his psychoanalysis.[2]

More important to our purposes, Freud believed words were essential to the discovery of self. He experimented with free association, demonstrating that the "random association" of words is not so random and can provide clues to the unconscious. As we shall see, this theory inspired Kenneth Burke's "cluster analysis" of texts. Freud endorsed Aristotle's theory of catharsis, the release or freeing of emotion by acting out

Sigmund Freud.

problems. Soon Freud was writing his thoughts into scholarly papers and books. In 1900 he wrote *The Interpretation of Dreams*, which argued that our dreams were suppressed wishes and revealed unconscious desires in symbolic forms.[3] The unconscious is perfectly capable of dealing with and retaining contradictory concepts and objects; incompatible ideas can exist side by side. Ideas are uninhibited and the unconscious has no concept of time. It often incorporates ideas and concepts from the past into the present. The unconscious creates a self-contained world that operates on its own rules. Freud claimed that when all else failed, he could return to analysis of a patient's dreams to unlock the keys to abnormal behavior. Since the mind works as a censor protecting us from our desires, bad memories, and youthful experiences, even in our sleep, an outside interpreter of our dreams is essential.

In 1902, despite rampant anti-Semitism in Vienna, he was appointed to a chair in neuropathy and began to recruit students. In 1904 Freud wrote *Psychopathology of Everyday Life* in which he criticized the overuse of hypnosis and called for a return to free association. A second thesis of this book was that the unconscious often interferes with the conscious, causing it to malfunction. In 1905 his very controversial *Theory of Sexuality* argued that sexual urges are influential at a very young age and that all positive feelings of sympathy, friendship, and camaraderie are derived from, or are acceptable rationalized forms of, sexual sources: "Originally it was only sexual objects that we knew."[4]

During World War I, Freud lost two sons and his accumulated wealth. Out of this devastation, he developed two new theories in 1920. One concerned a "death wish," whereby the patient desires to return to the earth or to a state of calm. The second was to have a profound effect on Kenneth Burke; it argued that members of a group identify with their leaders and that leadership is a function of this identification.

In 1930 *Civilization and Its Discontents* took Freud's theories to a grander and more pessimistic scale. *Civilization* was the story of the conflicts between individual desires and wishes, and the strictures of society. The individual, argued Freud, wants to act out aggression, to satisfy sexual urges, and to reach a state of peace. However, the need for order in society blocks the energy generated by aggression and sex, leading inevitably to unhappiness for most humans in the form of pent-up energy and/or guilt. This book extended Freud's theory that people cause their own accidents to punish themselves for their guilt. Nations make mistakes to punish themselves for their collective guilt. In 1933 he and noted physicist Albert Einstein coauthored *Why War?*—just as Hitler came to power in neighboring Germany. Hitler outlawed psychoanalysis. When he succeeded in taking over Austria in 1938, Freud was forced to flee to London.

Freud died the next year at the age of 83. His daughter Anna was among those who defended his work. So were Erich Fromm and Karen Horney, who de-emphasized infantile sexuality in their Freudianism in favor of examining the contemporary pressures of society.

Like Aristotle, Freud based his theories on observation and concluded that humans sought pleasure and avoided pain. Pleasure was the release of energy, whether it be the rush of sex, athletic achievement, or violence. Pain was the deprivation of such a release. This "pleasure principle" explained the need for "gratification," which is problematic because an individual often seeks pleasure at the expense of others. That is why society has created rules to contain either abnormal or criminal behavior resulting from the quest for gratification. The blocking of desire results in pent-up energy, which may be channeled in healthy (normal) directions or unhealthy (abnormal) directions. In the former case, the result might be healthy competition or expressions of creativity; in the latter, the result might be criminal behavior or destructive acts. In either case, the manipulation of energy becomes a powerful motivator among humans and is often at the root of their decision making. This explanation of motivation plays an important role in Kenneth Burke's theory of identification and persuasion, which we will develop in the next chapter.

Freud began his attempt to map the mind with the belief that humans are influenced by three levels of consciousness. The first is the preconscious from which we inherit the ability to feel things instinctively. The fear of falling is evident in infants. Many of us fear spiders or snakes, even though we were never taught that such animals are dangerous. Current psychological research has advanced this theory to argue that when we are born we have an inherent script that is rewritten as we go through life. The second level is the conscious. In a conscious state we are aware of the phenomena around us; in fact, *to be conscious is to be conscious of some thing*. We can access both of these levels of consciousness on our own.

Normally, the third level of consciousness, the unconscious, is not readily accessible to us. We must have help to uncover what is there. Freud claimed that without the help of another (usually a trained psychiatrist), a human cannot reach, let alone control, his or her unconscious. Because the unconscious is not logical, it is usually revealed accidentally in some irrational way. Freud claimed that it surfaces in dreams. These are often difficult to interpret because they are expressions of the id's libidinal energy that the ego's "reality principle" (see discussion in next section) finds unacceptable. The interpreter of dreams sees the actions in the dream as symbolic and then interprets them using the patient's "terministic screen" (point of reference), a phrase that Burke would borrow from Freud.

The unconscious also surfaces in word association games, hypnosis, rituals, and what have come to be called Freudian slips. A man who thinks of his wife as a threat might say, "I'd like you to meet my knife, I mean my wife." In a heated argument I overhead between a gay student and a straight student, the straight student yelled, "Don't fag your winger at me!" Thus, his repressed fear or hatred of homosexuality leapt to the surface. Another method of revealing the unconscious is the Rorschach test, in which people interpret visual representations from ink blots. A woman who hates her sister might see a snake strangling a woman in an inkblot that means nothing to someone else. All these methods indicate that the unconscious is reflected, not seen directly.

The Structure of the Psyche

Like Plato, Freud conceived of the human psyche as having three major parts: the id, the superego, and the ego.[5]

- The *id* is the substructure of drives, the source of sexual energy (libido),[6] and the "pleasure principle." It is amoral and cannot tolerate being frustrated. Should it provide too strong an influence, it can cause criminal and/or abnormal behavior. The objective of the id is satisfaction.

- The *superego* is the moral structure of the psyche and operates on the "reality principle." It offers rewards for good behavior that are based on societal, peer group, and family-derived "models." President Theodore Roosevelt provided a classic case of superego guidance when he said that he never made a decision without considering what his father would have done. Freud claimed that the superego is possessed of "ideologies," which resist change in order to maintain values. The superego seeks perfection. A person can become a helpless victim of a very strict or overdeveloped superego, which can lead to conditions of incapacitation, an overly critical personality, or low self-esteem that in turn require therapy.

- The *ego* seeks reality and self-validation but must do battle with three tough masters: the external world, the superego, and the id. The ego contains the will that must synthesize the desires of the id with the morality of the superego while wrestling with the external world. A "normal" ego seeks the maximum amount of pleasure allowed by the rules of society. The ego rides the horse of desire using the reins of morality. Thus, the ego is nearly always in a state of conflict resolution between the rules of the superego and the desires of the id.

The tripartite psyche is often overwhelmed by its own impulses and by the world. This condition explains the phenomenon known as anxiety—fear without a cause that is known to the victim. Id anxiety results from being overwhelmed by the need for pleasure. Superego anxiety results from being overwhelmed by rules and subsequently guilt. Ego anxiety can result from a lack of recognition or acknowledgement from others. To deal with these and other problems, we have developed strong defense mechanisms that have important rhetorical functions. The following six are the most important.

- *Projection* makes what is internal and unacceptable into something that is external and distant. "I'm not hostile," says the young man using projection, "others are hostile. It is their problem." A woman who can't deal with compliments says, "You know why Irene made that nasty remark to Helen? Irene just can't stand praise. Anytime anyone says anything nice about her, she snaps at them." Projection as a defense mechanism is a classic case of the kettle calling the pot black. If you are observant, you will see how it is used by associates. Georgia tells you that Mike talks too much, and you are surprised because it is Georgia who does all the talking. Alex tells you that Margaret can't keep a secret when in fact Alex has revealed every confidence you have ever shared with him.

- *Denial* of reality is a powerful rhetorical tactic that is often more revealing than the user of the tactic would like. President Nixon's claim that he was not a crook was suspect; if he was not a crook, he didn't need to make such a denial. Cries of "I'm not a racist," or "I'm not an anti-Semite" often reveal inner guilt feelings of being precisely what the protester denies.

- *Isolation* removes a concept from feelings of emotion. For example, love can be intellectualized so that its lustful side is suppressed. The pleasure of food can be intellectualized into a time and place for good conversation. The reason for this rhetorical ploy is that emotions often make us feel uncomfortable, uneasy, guilty, or unclean. They offend the super ego. So we remove the objects of our desires from their emotional attachments, thereby isolating them into something acceptable.

- *Rationalization* is similar to isolation because it explains the unacceptable in accept-able terms; it switches a base motive for a noble one. Take the case of the young man who drinks in order to satisfy his id's craving for a euphoric state. When questioned about his drinking, the young man may rationalize by saying that drinking makes him more sociable or less inhibited or helps to cure his cold. Hamlet demonstrated his ability to rationalize his violent verbal assault on his mother wherein he confronts her with her sins and claims, "I am cruel only to be kind."

- *Repression* uses energy to bury some thought or occurrence that we wish to forget. Normally, this occurrence is prompted by the id through some instinctive behavior that society wants to control.[7] The psyche believes that what it does not know can't hurt it. Some of the most important operations psychiatrists perform are to surface repressed items so that an individual can be free of them and the energy they drain. The young boy who feels unworthy, and therefore constantly fails, discovers that at a very young age his father beat him. If his father did not love him, then he must be a failure. The recollection forces a confrontation with the memory and shows the young man the cause of his low self-esteem.

- *Sublimation* replaces the object of gratification with a higher cultural good. Some professors sublimate their desire to have a family by teaching and publishing books. Their students and their books become their offspring. According to Freud, sublimation can turn a useless or even unhealthy desire into a creative force. Many artists, for example, sublimate lower forms of gratification by creating works of art.

As we saw in the writing of the existentialist Jean-Paul Sartre (see chapter 9), strategies of self-delusion are intra- and interpersonal rhetorical acts. They hide the things we choose—or our unconscious chooses—not to know. In this way, rhetoric functions at the instinctual level and is crucial in determining who we are. Freud provided a deep structure of this self-persuasion and thus laid the groundwork for a major advance in rhetorical theory.

The Theory of Identification

Freud's analyses of identification, alienation, and hatred are important in understanding Burke's theories. As Burke wrote, "If men were not apart from one another, there would be no need for the rhetorician to proclaim their unity."[8] Identification begins in the development of the ego. Most psychoanalysts believe that its invention is a dialectic involving the superego and id in the realm of the unconscious.[9] The superego internalizes the social standards of parents, peers, caste, class, religion, and culture; it censures the ego, which is full of thoughts, wishes, and actions, some of which are supplied by the id. The trichotomy of id, ego, and superego is best thought of as an analytical description of aspects of the mind much the way *ethos, pathos,* and *logos* may be aspects of the same sentence. Since identification is developed and motivated by factors in all three areas, one finds evidence of identification in all phases of ego development. Understanding the psychological roots of the building of self becomes important: "The infant's inner sensations form the core of the self. They appear to remain the central, crystallization point of the 'feeling of self' around which a 'sense of identity' will become established."[10] Freud believed that individual personalities form at a very young age and that identification with others plays a large role in the process. Thus, we all have selves to discover when we mature.

Freud understood that identification, whether it be narcissistic self-love[11] or anaclitic caretaking or caregiving, causes a corresponding alienation. If I identify with the Democrats, I am alienated from the Republicans. If I identify with my father, I am alienated to some extent from my mother. Worse yet, every alienation brings with it a sense of loss and creates boundaries between self and others. Speakers who use the strategies of alienation and division are often aware of these feelings. They understand that identification is motivated by love and that alienation is motivated by hatred. To survive these tensions, they structure various ties—to family, to party, to country—to protect audiences from alien others. This phenomenon leads to in-groups and out-groups that eventually build into gangs, cults, or nations that may go to war when these feelings are intensified by making them sacred or national. The history of religious war is fraught with such Freudian overtones.

Freud gave the world a deeper, richer, and more dangerous understanding of the human psyche than had previously been available. He explained why people engage in irrational acts when they are motivated by various kinds of energy channeled by the reality principle of the superego or the pleasure principle of the id. He showed how people group themselves into pods that survive by alienating themselves from others, which helps explain the irrational behavior of nations. Out of this understanding of human nature, Kenneth Burke would build a sophisticated rhetorical theory.

Carl Jung (1875–1961) and Jacques Lacan (1901–1981)

Freud's work was extended by his most famous pupil, Carl Jung, who broke with Freud in 1913 and then suffered a nervous breakdown when World War I fulfilled his apocalyptic dream. When he recovered, he developed his own theory of symbols.[12] He rejected the empirical objectivism and case studies of Freud and turned to mythology and symbology to unlock the secrets of the mind. He divided symbols into four groups: (1) symbols of origination including but not limited to mothers, females, caves, and past time; (2) symbols of oneness or unity including circles, stones, and hoops; (3) symbols of transcendence including champions, idols, rebirth, ritual, and flight; (4) symbols of spirituality including energy forces, springs, and light.[13] Jung's work and long life allowed him to be a major force in the field of psychology.

In terms of our quest for the roots of Kenneth Burke's theory, it is important to note that Jung draws heavily on archetypal images floating in the "collective unconscious"—the knowledge with which we are all born or into which we can tap. Archetypal images organize, direct, and inform human thought and behavior. These images emerge in the form of myths, symbols, rituals, and instincts of human beings. Archetypal images include the persona, the shadow, the mother, and the wise old woman or man.

Jung argued that each of us projects a "public persona" in order to cope with life, but we are also destined to be an authentic persona. The public persona has a "shadow" that represents our dark side and its suppressed desires. The success of the book, play, movie, and musical versions of *Phantom of the Opera* is due in part to its representation of the dark side in all of us. At some point, we all hear the "music of the night" and arouse our poetic yearnings. Jung's "dark mother" shadow is based on such mythological characters as Medea and Medusa; she is a lusty temptress. Jung's "wise old man" is seen in such contemporary characters as Obi-Wan Kenobi from *Star Wars*. Unlike Freud, Jung placed his emphasis on the effect of these images rather than on identification with them. While we normally only identify with one character, we can feel the effects of many images. These archetypes can trigger repressed thoughts and experiences. They can also blur the distinction between reality and myth.

Freud disagreed with Jung generalizing individualized specific analyses into a public consciousness. Freud believed Jung's popularizing of his theories endangered their proper use in individual cases. Jung's criticism of Freud was that Freud put too much emphasis on sexual urges to explain abnormal behavior.[14] He redefined Freud's libido as a general tension, as opposed to a sexually specific one.

Combining Marx with Jung, the Marxist critic and psychologist Jacques Lacan (1901–1981) adds to our understanding of effective rhetoric by arguing that effective speakers discover what the actual consciousness of an audience is. For example, in America we believe every citizen has the right to vote and one is innocent until proven guilty. However, in other countries there is no tradition of voting, and one is presumed guilty if arrested. According to Lacan, speakers can exploit this "actual consciousness"; that is, they can adapt to it and reinforce it. Or they can use it as a starting point to draw an audience to their "potential consciousness," or higher calling. (He cites Lenin's phrase, "The land to the people," as an example of appealing to "potential consciousness," which led to a redistribution of land.)

Lacan argued that every text has a subtext that is built on the images of other personas; the images match the lost cathexis. For Freud, the lost cathexis was the object of our first attachment, the thing from which we were first divided, normally the breast of the mother. The lost cathexis for Jung was an archetype that we embraced. The replacement cathexis that we find is often our "mirror" image, with which we struggle (Lacan gives the example of Laertes being Hamlet's mirror; a more contemporary example might be Batman's mirror being the Joker).

Karl Marx (1818–1883)

Marx provides a remarkable balance to Freud. If Freud is the therapist for the individual psyche, then Marx is the therapist for the world's psyche. To succeed, Marx was forced to oppose the glorification of the individual, elevating the collective community in its place. In unity there is strength; alone we accomplish very little. He modified the system of Georg W. Friederich Hegel (see chapter 9) in at least two ways to accomplish his goal. To spin out his story of the world, he first substituted "historical materialism" for the national spirit used in Hegel's dialectic. Marx argued that material forces—capital, labor, production, land—are responsible for the twists and turns of history. He grafted the materialism of Ludwig Feuerbach to the trunk of Hegelianism to produce a major new branch of economics, political science, and philosophy. Second, just as Hegel believed his dialectic would move the national spirit to bring democracy and freedom to the middle class, Marx sought to empower the lowest level of workers in a society. But he purged Hegel's theory of all nonmaterial elements.

Marx believed history is "determined" by changes in the relationship of production and consumption, and consumption is often a product of rhetorical pressures imposed by hidden ideologies.[15] These controlling ideologies create a "false conscious-ness" full of illusions that should be destroyed. These illusions are created when words are not properly grounded in the social and productive condition. They are an outgrowth of the material *interests* of those in power and can be revealed as false by comparing them to the material *realities* of the world. For example, many U.S. citizens believe that the capitalistic state is invincible, but this illusion is often shattered when material reality shifts. The housing crisis of 2008 revealed a false con-sciousness created by major lending institutions. When challenged, it was clear that Republican deregulation of

Karl Marx.

banks combined with Democrats' calls for more minority housing conspired to create an environment in which obtaining a mortgage was relatively easy. When the equity bubble burst, many people found themselves with property worth less than their loans. Marx viewed ideology as the mask that has to be removed to reveal the real causes of material conditions in the world.[16] What clearly emerges in Marxist theory is a belief that everything is economically determined and bound up in a class struggle that will inevitably result in the rise of communism.

Karl Marx was born in Trier, Germany, in 1818. He studied law, then philosophy, becoming an expert on and disciple of Hegel, even though Hegel had died five years before Marx came to the University of Berlin in 1836. At twenty-four he became a newspaper editor in Cologne, which sharpened his rhetorical skills. His controversial opinions forced him to move to Paris in 1843, from which he was expelled in 1845. When Paris was rocked by revolution in 1848, Marx watched with excitement from his exile across the border in Belgium.

His collaboration with Friedrich Engels (1820–1895) produced a number of works. Engels could not have been more different than Marx; Engels was from a rich German family and ran its textile businesses in Liverpool and Manchester in England. Marx and Engels' most important work was the "Manifesto of the Communist Party." The London Communist League requested the manifesto, hoping to stir up trouble in Europe. Dra-matically, the manifesto concluded: "Let the ruling classes tremble at a Communist revo-lution. The proletarians have nothing to lose but their chains. They have a world to win.

Working men of all lands, unite!" A few months later, Europe was racked with uprisings. His role in writing the manifesto caused Marx to be expelled from Belgium. He moved back to Cologne, Germany, where he denounced the middle class for deserting an alliance with the working class. At his trial for incitement to treason, Marx gave a brilliant and impassioned speech that won his acquittal. His opinions, however, forced him to move to England in 1849, where his family lived an impoverished life in Soho for a time. These conditions caused the death of three of his children; then Engels came to his rescue. Marx was also helped by Horace Greeley who regularly published Marx's articles in the *New York Tribune*. Marx died in 1883 and is buried in Highgate Cemetery in London.

Das Kapital (Capital), a three-volume work that elaborated on the philosophy of the manifesto, began appearing in 1867. It labeled the oppressive middle class the "bourgeoisie" (the thesis) and the poor working class the "proletariat" (the antithesis). *Das Kapital* tried to justify an agenda that would take "from each according to his ability; [and give] to each according to his needs."[17] Attacks on Marx by philosophical soul mates allowed him to sharpen his critique of society in preparation for the more serious attacks from capitalists and others who would be far more hostile to his message.[18]

In issuing his critique of the social order, Marx argued that notions such as "spirituality" and "ideology" are dangerous because they delude individuals into ignoring the truth that there is only materialism and that matter is trapped in history.[19] History moves inexorably toward its destiny through "class struggles" and the clash of the forces of capital. The emerging synthesis is a result of this "dialectical materialism." Within this system, Marx sought to awaken citizens to the fact that politics is a rationalization for control and political ideology is a rhetorical trick that oppresses and sublimates various individuals. A critique of the texts of ideology reveals there are hidden subtexts and subliminal messages.

Extending the Marxist Critique

Marx tried to demonstrate that society's structure and economic mechanisms drive the rhetoric of those in power. His goal was to demystify ideology and to provoke a dialectic that would force a new synthesis, ending the false consciousness that prevents the advance of civilization. For contemporary Marxists, demystification is achieved by asking certain questions that uncover material realities and those who control them. Depending on which Marxist or neo-Marxist author you read, questions may vary as to intensity and emphasis, but in most cases, the relevance to rhetoric and its role in the Marxist critique is readily apparent. If you seek revolution, you must know who the powers are and how they exert influence. They can be found by asking the following questions.

- First, *Who is allowed to speak?* It is ironic, given how much we value freedom of expression in America, that there are still people who are pushed to the margins of society and have no voice. In the United States, for the most part, students were not empowered prior to the campus revolts triggered by the Free Speech movement at Berkeley in 1964 and the Vietnam War. Even today, U.S. students remain remarkably docile about tuition increases and the structure of their education. Marxists might explain this by pointing out that universities are generally set up in a way that *marginalizes* student rhetoric.

  California, for example, regularly faces budget crises that result in increased tuition. When students complain to university presidents in the state system, the smarter presidents join the students and complain to the board of trustees. The board of trustees claims its hands are tied by the rules that require them to balance the system's budget. When protesters go to the governor, he blames the state legislature. When protesters visit the state legislature, its leaders point out that a proposition passed a few years back committed a certain percentage of the state budget to grades K–12, leaving the state universities out in the cold. Thus, the voters are to blame, not the legislators. In this way, the protesters are frustrated; they lose their voice not because they have no forum, but because the forum to which they need to speak is either a moving target or too large and diffuse to be addressed.

- Since being allowed to speak is different from being able to speak, it is important to ask: *Who has the power to speak?* For example, under the First Amendment of our Constitution, Congress should make no law abridging freedom of speech or of the press. Thus, we are all free to use to our favorite public forum to give a speech. We are all free to publish a newspaper. In either case, however, if we cannot command an audience, our words will fall on deaf ears. So Marxists ask the follow-up question: *Who can afford to speak and who controls the means to get messages to the society?* We listen to politicians, but many of them take money from and represent the interests of political action committees or large donors. It may be the corporate or union political action committees who are really speaking through the politicians. In this case, the politicians provide the cover for those who hold the reins of power.

- The previous question begins to reveal the message manipulation that dominates society. To advance this critique, Marxists examine: *What is being said?* Marxists argue that the text we see is not always what is being said. There may be a text beneath the surface. We need to look for the full text and determine what material forces are being advanced. Take the case of the young man who wears Nike basketball shoes because he believes they help him play better. Marx would argue that the young man is being manipulated by Nike. He has no real choice because advertising has overwhelmed him. He believes the shoes will make him a better basketball player, or at least look like one, because advertising has created a false sense of consciousness in him. Worse yet, he may be unaware that Nike products are made by workers being exploited in sweatshops in countries such as China, Vietnam, Indonesia, and Mexico.[20] The ideology of advertising is pervasive; it cannot be comprehended by most people because they are possessed by the *false consciousness.* The parallel to Freud's unconscious is not accidental. Marxists mean to be the external agents, like psychiatrists, who set the populace free of its illusions.

The one thing that can save this young man, and his society, is the evidence of manipulation found in the full rhetorical text of those in power. For example, the Marxist attack on the church is based on Marx's view that religion is the opiate of the people. Using what Marx called a utopian rhetorical strategy, religion keeps people under the thumb of this world by promising them something better in the next.[21] In this example, prayers are the textual fragments of the dominant underlying religious script that requires contributions of money to the church, participation in rituals, pacifism in the face of government injustices, and membership in a hierarchical order. In the same way, each separate commercial on television is really part of a larger capitalist script that reaffirms our false consciousness by urging us to spend more on items we don't need. The advertisements succeed in part because of another rhetorical strategy: they are embedded in environments that we admire. For example, corporations that support public broadcasting, the arts, and ecological projects mask their real purpose: to make money regardless of the impact on the environment.

- *What lies behind the promises being made?* Yet another ironic feature of the Marxist critique is its suspicion of promises of a better life. Sports cars will attract members of the opposite sex. Whiter teeth will improve your sex life. Politicians use promises to offer privileges and some version of heaven here on earth. The lottery, the welfare state, even the proverbial ivory tower on a campus have all been used to keep people loyal to one illusion or another while suppressing their individualism and creativity. People are content to suffer now as long as there is some hope for a better time in the future.

- *Who actually created the message?* That is, who *paid* for it, who wrote it, who delivered it, and who is the target audience? Marxists urge society not to let the text become aestheticized; just because it appears in a story on the screen doesn't mean there isn't a hidden agenda that reinforces the capitalist message. We watch advertising on television, but don't often realize how large the conglomerates are that are speaking. Time-Warner, for example, not only owns *Time Magazine*, it also owns Home Box Office (HBO), Turner Broadcasting (which includes CNN), Warner Bros. Entertainment, and Global Media Group. Nor is MTV an independent, irreverent David confronting the establishment's Goliath. It is a subsidiary of Viacom, which also owns Nickelodeon, BET (Black Entertainment Networks), and Paramount Pictures. Marxists argue that those who have the power to create the message are those who control the airwaves or those who can afford to get on the airwaves. The rest of us are marginalized by media that are too large and diverse to penetrate.[22]

- *What systemic strategies are in place?* Very often messages, speakers, audiences, and their persuasiveness are determined by systemic structures. For example, teachers on college campuses are divided into a caste system; there are graduate teaching assistants, lecturers, assistant professors, associate professors, and full professors. Some of these teachers are full-time and some are part-time; some are tenured with permanent contracts and some are not. Marx would argue that the persuasive power of teachers would be diminished or enhanced by their status in this matrix, and the matrix would determine their income. In two ways, then, tenure becomes a systemic strategy for keeping control of what teachers say and what they earn. Picking up on this theme, Kenneth Burke refers to the "terms of order" in an institution:

  > The hierarchic principle is not complete in the social realm . . . in the mere arrangement whereby each rank is overlord to its underlings. . . . It is complete only when each rank accepts the principle of gradation itself.[23]

  We are in a continuing struggle for position in the hierarchical structure. We are concerned about our "position" in the family, in the company, in the world. Burke referred to "a system encompassing both rhetoric and community that functions to position human subjects in terms of social, political, and ideological constraints."[24]

- *What communalizing strategies are in place?* It is ironic that Marx, the great advocate of collectivization and communism, nonetheless condemns ideologies that tend to make everyone alike. The rhetoric of these ideologies is often *hegemonic;* it retains control by arguing that individuality and uniqueness are antithetical to the goals of a society.[25] The strategies of this rhetoric are systemic because they can be traced to the division of labor in the culture and to the metaphoric terms that are applied to that division.[26] For example, those without work are condemned as "unemployed" as opposed to those who are "gainfully employed." The linguistic symbols in the language encourage people to move from the former category to the latter, to become one with the employed. Another repressive dialectic exists between those who are "cool" and those who are "not hip," or those who are "out of it." The dialectic then motivates behavior that causes a person to try to become "cool," which, over the last half-century, could lead to smoking, drinking, and drug abuse. Communalizing strategies such as playing on categorical qualities of race, religion, or gender and supporting fads in wearing apparel, drug use, and the like are used to reinforce the collective consciousness at the expense of individualism.

Marx believed that social identification determines consciousness.[27] Advertising and films are superb at this. If your child does not have the latest video game, the desire for which is implanted by hours of advertising, he or she will let you know about it. Bette Davis probably sold more cigarettes than any tobacco company advertisement with her performance in the classic movie *Now Voyager*. When box office sensation Clark Gable removed his dress shirt in *It Happened One Night* (another film classic) and was not wearing an undershirt, sales of undershirts plummeted. In 1997 when Jerry McGuire yelled, "Show me the money," it became the mantra of society in general. Examples of false consciousness and conformity are everywhere, and permeate all age groups, especially preteens and teens. Just examine such phenomena as Hannah Montana or Justin Bieber. Early fame resulted in highly popular concert tours, films, sound tracks, video games, clothing, and accessories—all must-haves by "tweengirls" and "fan boys."

• *What strategies of omission or marginalization are in place?* These strategies operate off the old premise that what you don't know won't hurt you. Many people who complain about the homeless want them removed from view. The city of Santa Barbara, for example, exacerbated the problems of the homeless when it forbade them from sleeping in public parks at night. The homeless disappeared from view, but the undetected places to sleep were often behind trash bins that were located in alleys infested with rats. The condition of the homeless was made even worse, but the citizens of Santa Barbara were no longer offended by the sight of the homeless in the parks at night.

• Finally, Marxists ask, *what dialectical oppositions have been revealed by these questions?* Examination of the American political system, for example, reveals several opposition value clusters: On one hand is the valuing of individual success, which includes such subvalues as freedom, individualism, ambition, competition and hard work; on the other hand is the valuing of caring for others, which includes such subvalues as cooperation, sharing, nurturing, and welfare. In order for the caring value system to survive, we must tax individuals to pay for it. Yet, the tax on individuals limits their ability to succeed, thereby threatening the value of individual success. The balance between these two value clusters is represented in the balance between the two major political parties of this country. Republicans generally identify themselves with the cult of personal success, while Democrats identify themselves with the cult of welfare.

However, individual speakers of either party may create other dialectical tensions to advance their own agendas. On August 17, 1998, President Clinton addressed the nation to explain why he had lied about having sexual relations with a White House intern named Monica Lewinsky. The short address attempted to place certain questions in the public realm, mainly legal matters, and to place other questions in the private realm, mainly moral matters. The president tried to convince the public that the press and government lawyers had every right to investigate legal issues where he claimed he had done nothing wrong, but that they had no business exploring moral issues, where he may have shown bad judgment because "even presidents have private lives." The dialectical tension is established early in the nationally televised address:

> Indeed, I did have a relationship with Ms. Lewinsky that was not appropriate. In fact, it was wrong. It constituted a critical lapse in judgment and a personal failure on my part for which I am solely and completely responsible. *But* I told the grand jury today, and I say to you now, that at no time did I ask anyone to lie, to hide or destroy evidence, or to take any other unlawful action. . . . Now, this matter is between me, the two people I love most—my wife and our daughter—and our God.

Note the use of the axial "but" in the middle of the paragraph to establish the dialectic and to place various issues into one or the other category. By putting moral issues, where he is most culpable, into the private category, Clinton reduces their importance and removes them from public scrutiny.

HABERMAS' REFORM

The Marxist critique has focused on communication in the works of Jürgen Habermas (1929–), who seeks to defend communicative rationalism from what he sees as the destructive forces of electronic mass media, relativism, and irrationalism embodied in the contemporary postmodern movement.[28] In reaction to the horror of Nazism, Habermas turned to the "Critical Theory" of Marxist Theodor Adorno and used it to become a social critic and popular philosopher. Habermas' Marxism is also tempered with the work of Hans Georg Gadamer, who believed that a hermeneutic (close interpretation) of communication is essential to figuring out what presuppositions precede communication and who is privileged and who is marginalized. Gadamer was a modernist who embraced Aristotelian unity as the "decisive condition and basis of all human reason."[29]

Jürgen Habermas.

The result of Habermas' study is a thousand-page tome entitled *The Theory of Communicative Action* (1981), which attempts to move scholarly focus from consciousness to language itself, a move endorsed by such French writers as Ferdinand de Saussure earlier in the century. Like Marx, Habermas seeks to unmask the controlling "ideology" that is causing communicative neuroses. But unlike Marx, Habermas is a humanist who opposes Marxism's mechanistic approach at the expense of reflexivity. To overcome the objections of postmodernists (see chapter 13 of the present book), Habermas attempts to construct "communicative rationality" based on agreement among the rational in society performing in optimum speaking situations.[30] His theory is meant to complete the project of the Enlightenment by creating spaces for mutual understanding, from the interpersonal to the international level. He rejects the correspondence theory of positivists who argue that to be true, a sentence must correspond to the reality it represents. The sentence, "My professor is over six feet tall," can easily be verified using the correspondence theory. The sentence, "We should not allow Iran to develop nuclear weapons," presents a different problem. Positivists would argue it has no meaning, because it does not correspond to reality and needs to be broken down into its "atomic" parts. Habermas would disagree and would verify its truth or lack thereof using his consensus theory of the "public sphere."

He developed this theory in *The Structural Transformation of the Public Sphere* (1962), arguing that it first emerged in the 1700s when the middle class entered the political dialogue. One might well argue that the "public sphere" reemerged at that time since it existed in democratic Athens centuries earlier, as Thucydides makes clear. In any case, the "sphere" operates to allow all participants to question all proposals, allowing all participants to bring any proposal to the table, and allowing all participants to express any attitudes, wishes, and/or needs, as long as they are presented *rationally*. Habermas advocates public spheres to be created in objective, subjective, and even social settings. Each of these settings has different kinds of claims, of which moderators need to be aware if they are to function properly. In objective spheres, moderators should verify truth claims; in subjective spheres, moderators should seek sincerity; and in social spheres, moderators should seek normative standards, that is, what is accepted as ideal.

Because he knows that communication lapses and failures are possible, Habermas tries to safeguard his theory by creating ideal speaking situations in the "public sphere." The object is to "negotiate common definitions of a situation"[31] and to make "argumentation" into "a court of appeal that makes it possible to continue communicative action with other means when disagreement can no longer be headed off by everyday routines and yet is not to be settled by the direct or strategic use of force."[32] The consensus Habermas seeks must be achieved using rational means, including verifiable evidence and valid arguments; all participants must have an equal chance to object to or defend the hypotheses. Such "ideal speech situations" are democratic and in theory eternal. They require speakers who have at their disposal "basic qualifications of speech and symbolic interaction."[33]

These basic qualifications of speech and symbolic interaction are defined when Habermas discusses ideal speech situations. They are limited to the rational, which creates a very cramped view of rhetoric. For example, presuppositions are to be stated, not inferred or implied; truth conditions are to be established for propositional sentences; expression must reveal intention; speech must be performed in a way that precludes deception and conforms to norms.[34] Tropes and figures are discouraged, as are humor and surprise. The result would be lengthy, dry, and unexciting exchanges. These normative standards are difficult to achieve in a political world where values vary greatly, diversity abounds, and desire overcomes reason. Given Habermas' history with fascism's use of irrational appeals, however, his endorsement of a rationalistic theory is not difficult to understand. He requires, as he says in *The Philosophical Discourse of Modernity* (1985), being committed to achieving impartial consensus on disputed claims and morals, using questioners who have equal opportunities to speak and are free of limitations.[35]

In *Between Facts and Norms* (1996), Habermas tries to create a theory of law for democracies. For him, law is a legitimate structure founded on reason that allows the body politic to function properly. This system requires an informed public, which feeds at the trough of the public sphere, a place where ideas and information are exchanged. In the sphere the normative rules are created out of the empirical data gathered in support of opinions. If one overemphasizes the empirical, then rule of law breaks down; every case is an individual case. If one overemphasizes normality, then the rules override reality; no case can change the law. Thus, in Habermas' reconstructed public sphere, there is a constant tension between empiricism and normality. The trick is to achieve informed consensus by embracing such guides as equality, mutual respect, rationality, and nonviolence. These guides for consensus building allow for a determination of what constitutes a legitimate claim. There is no place for coercion in this system, nor for Habermas is there much need for rhetoric, as he defines it, because it is too strategic for his rational sphere. Habermas believes that these guides transcend culture, that universal standards of rational argument exist, positions for which he has been roundly criticized by postmodernists.

Habermas does defend radical social movements that "bring up issues relevant to the entire society to define ways of approaching problems, to propose possible solutions, to supply new information, to interpret values differently, to mobilize good reason, and criticize bad ones."[36] These movements seek recognition for themselves and their issues, and rhetoric is intimately involved in this fight for acknowledgment, that is, entry into the public sphere. "Occupy Wall Street" provides a contemporary case. Many of these demonstrators sought to highlight the vast disparity in wealth between the top 1 percent income level and the other 99 percent. They sought to reveal corrupt bank practices and government malfeasance.

Often it is those outside of government or its normal channels that surface the issues that have been ignored or marginalized. Habermas concedes,

> Only through their controversial presentation in the media do such topics reach the larger public and subsequently gain a place on the "public agenda." Sometimes the support of sensational action, mass protests, and incessant campaigning is required before an issue makes its way . . . into the core of the political system and there receive formal consideration.[37]

The movement for women's suffrage provides a case in point. At the end of the Civil War, when black men were given the vote, the suffrage movement began a campaign to obtain the vote for women. The movement ultimately succeeded in 1920 but only after a prolonged struggle which included suffragists chaining themselves to the fence around the White House, being jailed, and engaging in hunger strikes.

In the tradition of reformed Marxism, Habermas wants to tear down oppressive structures, end illusions, halt irrational rhetoric, and replace them with rational rule by consensus. He does not endorse Marx's call for a dictatorship that would eventually wither away and be replaced by a socialist cooperative. We know that Marxism, because of its lack of incentives and because it used the very strategies it condemned, eventually became a failed ideology in its own right. However, it left behind an attitude that has spawned a critical dialectic useful in discovering the hidden agendas of many a persuader. Thus, contemporary Marxists often focus their attention on the enormous impact of mass media and their insidious ability to mask actual intentions. For this reason many Marxists argue for an ideological turn in rhetorical studies.[38] This in turn seeks to uncover agendas and/or ideologies that are often hidden in a subtext. The following discussion of civil religion examines how patriotic appeals can function to reinforce hidden ideologies.

The Rhetoric of Civil Religion

One of the most powerful ideological tools of speakers has been appeals to "civil religion" to advance their cause.[39] The phrase was first used by Jean-Jacques Rousseau in 1762 in the conclusion of his *Social Contract*. Rousseau hoped humans would use their intellectual powers to rise to their best natures and make that their "civil religion."

In the New World, the ideology of civil religion held that America was a chosen land—Puritan leader John Winthrop's and much later President Ronald Reagan's "shining city set on a hill"—populated with a "chosen people" who are on a mission to be an example for the rest of the world. Politicians often claim that America is a chosen place born of an "errand into the wilderness," whether that errand be to settle the west and bring culture to the indigenous population or to fulfill America's "manifest destiny"[40] or its "rendezvous with destiny."[41] In the former case, the power and danger of these ideographs can be seen in America's destruction of vast numbers of Native Americans and in the latter case, its entry into a war with Mexico in 1846 and with Spain in 1898. The treaty following the Mexican-American War increased the size of the United States by one-fifth. The treaty following the war with Spain brought the Philippines, Puerto Rico, and Cuba under American control.

Speakers often tell their audiences to rely on their Creator ("In God we trust."), their patriotic saints, and their sacred documents, especially the Declaration of Independence and the Constitution in the United States. One of the watershed moments in the use of civil religion came when the second generation of patriots converted the "civic duty" of Washington, Hamilton, Jefferson, and Madison to the patriotic duty of Webster, Clay, Calhoun, and Jackson. In their rhetorical appeals, the latter generation romanticized American history and made its founding documents sacred. Abraham Lincoln continued this trend. In fact, even at the age of twenty-eight, Lincoln said that respect for the law should "become the political religion of the nation."[42] In 1858 in Springfield, Illinois, accepting the Republican nomination for senator and condemning slavery, Lincoln went so far as to paraphrase Jesus when Lincoln claimed that "a house divided against itself cannot stand."[43] As president, he used the Gettysburg Address to elevate the Declaration of Independence to new stature among America's sacred documents, shifted the Civil War's aims, and reconstituted the Northern public in terms of its moral compass. Preachers have often crossed over into the political realm to advance an agenda compatible with their values; preachers fought for the Bill of Rights just after the new Constitution was ratified; they led the abolition movement; and they have been intimately involved in the debate over abortion rights.

In the contemporary era, Robert Bellah (1927–) provided the groundbreaking research on civil religion.[44] He found that sustained patriotic appeals created a set of American political saints and texts. We can deepen our understanding of civil religion as rhetoric by turning to another scholar interested in ideological structures. Michael Calvin McGee's (1943–2002) analysis of constituted publics found that they "shared ideographs,"[45] societal phrases and symbols that not only make sense of the world but bond a people together. An ideograph "is a high-order abstraction representing collective commitment to a particular but equivocal and ill-defined normative goal." McGee envisions ideographs as the rhetorical building blocks of ideology.[46] These "ideographs" function like archetypal metaphors or the warrants in enthymemes. They ground public storytelling and arguments; they are familiar and accessible to large segments of the public. Ideographs are usually pieces of sacred text taken from our civic and/or civil religion. They include "liberty," "freedom of expression," "the right to vote," "family values," "equal protection under the law," "free enterprise," "innocent until proven guilty," "the pursuit of happiness," and "law and order," among others. Thus, ideographs serve as links to an overarching ideology. Speakers attempt to align their causes with these ideographs in order to gain the adherence of a wider group of followers. How can one possibly oppose these iconic terms? Speakers who offend the values that ideographs represent or reject these ideographs without substituting some of their own tend to lose support.

Rhetorical theory has developed several subsets to civil religion. For example, while studying the separatist movement in Quebec, Canada, Maurice Charland found that the rhetoric of civil religion can bring an audience into being by creating a collective identity. He called this subset "constitutive rhetoric"; the speaker brings a constituency into being by "creating a collective identity."[47] The elements of this theory include the notion of identification borrowed from Kenneth Burke in both its substantial (material) and consubstantial (personal, values) forms. (These are explained in detail in chapter 11.) To reach an audience, a speaker projects a persona and/or appeals to a location or some concrete manifestation with which the audience can identify. Identification begins with audience members recognizing they are freely entering a persuasive encounter; Charland calls this moment "interpellation."

A second constituent is transhistorical subject matter, that is, using narrativized themes and events to create common stories. Importantly, these are most effective when they collapse time by bringing distant memorable events into the present time. For the people of Quebec, these could be famous battles in the French and Indian Wars, or the repelling of American attacks during the War of 1812. During the current debate over abortion policy, pro-life speakers often compare *Roe v. Wade*, the decision allowing a woman to decide to have an abortion, to the *Dred Scott* decision of 1857, which certified that slaves were property. They seek a transhistorical link between giving slaves and fetuses personhood.

A third constituent of constitutive rhetoric is the establishment of a circle or border of inclusion for the constituted audience and exclusion for those the speaker wishes to carve away. When Daniel Webster sought to achieve his compromise of 1850 to save the nation from civil war, he included moderates in the North and South and excluded such extremists as abolitionists in the North and slave holders in the South. This carving away is another constituent that Charland borrows from Kenneth Burke.

In these kinds of persuasive efforts, speakers usually tell audience members that they are free to join or not join the movement, thereby giving them the illusion of freedom, when in fact the logical conclusion of the speech is that one must join the movement or reject the arguments and ideographs of the culture.[48] There were many such speeches in Tunisia, Libya, Egypt, and Syria during the Arab Spring of 2011 where "self-determination" and "freedom" became ideographs for the ideology of revolution.

Another subset comes in the form of a more extreme take on civil religion bordering on the Manichaean, named for the ancient religious movement that divided the universe into good or evil, light or dark, wise or ignorant. George W. Bush's use of Manichaean rhetoric served him well for the first six years of his administration. Following the tragedy of September 11, 2001, for example, he tied the "saints" of the "greatest generation" from World War II into his call for vengeance against Al Qaeda. He divided the world into those who were with us or those who were against us, including those who harbored terrorists. In his 2002 State of the Union Address, he referred to Iraq, Iran, and North Korea as an "axis of evil." Often speakers who take on the mantle of Manichaeanism are identified with the prophet Jeremiah, since he invoked the wrath of the God and fire and brimstone of Hell in his lamentations.[49] Speeches of this type are often called Jeremiads.

Another subset is the use of civil religion in political campaigns. For example, in a speech at the Citadel in South Carolina, Republican presidential candidate Mitt Romney argued that "God did not create this country to be a nation of followers. America must lead the world. . . . This must be an American century." Invoking Ronald Reagan, a saint for conservative civil religion, Romney declared, "I believe we are an exceptional nation with a unique destiny." He then honored the "generations that had fought in world wars, that came through the Great Depression and that gained victory in the Cold War."[50]

Invoking civil religion affects rhetorical tactics. Unless carefully crafted, speeches relying on civil religion will fall into false dichotomies because of the uncompromising dialectics the style creates. Civil religion, particularly in its Manichaean form, eliminates the middle by dividing its subjects into good or evil. Sometimes such divisions are not subtle enough to contain reality: "America, love it or leave it." "It is either my way or the highway." The result can damage speakers' credibility and/or argumentation.

The rhetoric of civil religion tends to flourish in the narrative mode. The conflicts it portrays are more dramatic when enfolded into a story line with heroes and villains, good and evil empires (see examples of Ronald Reagan's 1964 speech later in the next chapter). Within this framework, a presidential speech can be enhanced by using persons in the audience to reinforce the values of the story line or who embody the type of heroes that are being praised, such as when the president singles out someone in the gallery during the State of the Union Address.

Yet another characteristic of the rhetoric of civil religion is its reliance on apostrophes, the direct address of another who is not present. Because of the dramatic setting and narrative, it does not seem unnatural for speakers to invoke God or condemn their enemies directly. In fact, such tactics often reinforce the dramatic nature of the moment at hand. Recall Ronald Reagan's famous apostrophe in Berlin: "Mr. Gorbachev, tear down this wall."

CONCLUSION

In this chapter, I have attempted to lay the groundwork for a proper understanding of Kenneth Burke's contributions to rhetorical theory and criticism while at the same time deducing rhetorical strategies from the writings of Freud, Jung, Lacan, Marx, and Habermas. The two giants among these thinkers are Freud and Marx. Freud's revolutionary definition of the psyche argued that deep ontological structures, often irrational, govern behavior, including the desire to identify with another person. He demonstrated that the mind developed rhetorical strategies that alter reality and suppress the truth.

Marx argued that the course of history is rhetorical, guided by the clash of thesis and antithesis. It was his belief that this clash would reveal hidden ideologies, which sustained false consciousness among the people. He provided a critical and skeptical rhetoric to unmask various subtexts.

As we shall now see, Burke relied heavily on the identification theory of Freud and the dialectical theory of Marx to build a new rhetorical theory.

Study Questions

1. Can you think of ways in which words you have used revealed your inner self or the motives of others?

2. What is Freud's theory of psychic energy? What are the results of frustrating that energy? Can you provide examples?

3. What are the levels of consciousness described by Freud? What is the structure of your psyche? Using yourself as an example, detail some of the values that your superego supplies and some of the desires your id supplies.

4. Give examples of the rhetorical nature of projection, denial, isolation, rationalization, repression, and sublimation.

5. What is the difference between anaclitic and narcissistic identification? With which type are you most likely to identify? Why?

6. Do you believe that Freud's theory was improved by the adjustments of Jung?

7. Why was Marx opposed to spirituality and ideology? How can rhetoric help to unmask an ideology?

8. What is the role of rhetoric in maintaining a false consciousness? Can you give an example from contemporary society?

9. Construct a full text from the fragmented advertisements that surround one product.

10. What are systemic strategies? What is meant by communalizing society? Explain why you believe a certain group has been marginalized.

11. What is the Marxist theory of Jürgen Habermas?

Notes

[1] The phrase is based on the story of Oedipus, who kills a man who turns out to be his father and later marries a woman who turns out to be his mother. The play, *Oedipus Rex* ("Oedipus, the King") was written by Sophocles in ancient Greece and tells the story of how fate rules our lives.

[2] This theme is repeated throughout his lectures on psychoanalysis. See *The Complete Introductory Lectures on Psychoanalysis,* James Strachey, trans. (New York: W. W. Norton, 1966).

[3] In early editions of this book, Freud did not mention sexuality in children. But in the 1911 revision, he brought it into line with his other work, which argued that at three to five years of age, children choose love objects.

[4] As cited in Ernest Jones, *The Life and Work of Sigmund Freud*, vol. 2 (New York: Basic Books, 1955), p. 232. Jones was a student and then a close associate of Freud.

[5] He built this theory out of Plato's model of the chariot from the dialogues *The Symposium* and *Phaedrus*. The charioteer represents the controlling will, the white horse represents virtue, and the dark horse represents the appetites.

[6] Id is Latin for "this" or "this thing." The libido, Latin for "lustful desire," is the product of the sexual instinct and has psycho-physical manifestations. Freud described it as "that force by which the sexual instinct is represented in the mind . . . sexual longing, and regards it as analogous to the force of hunger, or the will to power, and other such trends among ego-tendencies." As cited in Jones, p. 282.

[7] Freud was the first to admit that suppression of instinctive behavior was a key to the advancement of society. However, he believed that civilized society had reached a point where things needed to be brought back into balance. The Victorian Era smothered healthy practices with its puritanical system of values.

[8] See Kenneth Burke, *A Grammar of Motives and a Rhetoric of Motives* (Cleveland, OH: Meridian Books/World Publishing, 1961), p. 546.

[9] See, for example C. G. Jung's studies of "primordial images" in the "collective unconscious" in *Man and His Symbols* (New York: Dell, 1978).

[10] M. Mahler, *On Human Symbiosis and the Vicissitudes of Individuation* (New York: International U. Press, 1968), p. 11.

[11] "On Narcissism" was an essay published in 1914 that focused on how self-love can lead to megalomania or hypochondria. Properly understood, however, Freud maintained that self-love is the beginning of all love. That unless one loves oneself, one cannot adequately love others. It is also a root of self-preservation.

[12] From 1906 to 1910, Jung worked very closely with Freud and embraced his theories. Freud even brought Jung along on a trip to America. Freud referred to him as his "crown prince" until Freud became disillusioned by Jung's extramarital affairs and dabbling in paranormal psychology. For his part, Jung believed that Freud was too patronizing to work with. Jung came to head the Zurich circle, while Freud headed the Vienna psychologists. Under the influence of Jung, the Zurich group moved away from Freud's emphasis on sex toward more transcendent concepts. However, the group did retain Freud's emphasis on a "talking cure."

[13] His influence on Burke can be found in *Terms for Order*, S. E. Hyman, ed. (Bloomington: Indiana U. Press, 1964), pp. 147–72.

[14] Initially Freud was also very close to Alfred Adler. But Adler's differences with Freud eventually led to their disaffection also. Adler developed the theory that some people overcompensate for feelings of inferiority, which leads to aggressive behavior. Adler believed aggression is more important than sex in explaining abnormal behavior. He eventually came to believe that Freud's notion of the unconscious was merely a descriptive, theoretical construct.

[15] See William Ebenstein, *Today's Isms*, 4th ed. (Englewood Cliffs, NJ: Prentice-Hall, 1964). My interpretation of Marx is enlightened by classes I took with Ebenstein at the University of California, Santa Barbara, but includes much updating since that time. See, for example, J. Fiske, "British Cultural Studies and Television," in *Channels of Discourse*, R. C. Allen, ed., (Chapel Hill: U. of North Carolina Press, 1987), pp. 254–90.

[16] See, for example, James Arnt Aune, *Rhetoric and Marxism* (Boulder, CO: Westview Press, 1994).

[17] Marx paraphrased social commentator Louis Blanc.

[18] The strength of Marx's ability to defend his position is evident in his refutation of Pierre Proudhon, who believed owning property was theft; Mikhail Bakunin, who believed in communism but not in centralization; and Ferdinand Lassalle, who advanced an "iron law of wages."

[19] My translation of Marxism relies in part on criticism from the work of Fredric Jameson, particularly his *The Political Unconscious: Narrative as a Socially Symbolic Act* (Ithaca: Cornell U. Press, 1981).

[20] A little-known supplier of Nike was located in Vietnam and had been charged with unfair labor practices.

[21] Marx also condemned socialism for attempting to impose a utopia from the top. He believed all utopias were reactionary, except for his Communist dream.

[22] As examples of campaign media use and spending, in the first few months of 2012, Barack Obama's campaign bought nearly $16.4 million worth of online ads. Mitt Romney spent $7.8 million. Obama used MTV to launch his first national TV ad campaign in June 2012. Romney spent $134,000 on a campaign ad that ran on TV in New Hampshire in 2011. See www.cnn.com/2012/06/03/politics/online-campaign-spending/index.html (accessed July 10, 2012).

[23] Burke, *A Grammar of Motives and A Rhetoric of Motives*, p. 663. See also Kenneth Burke, *Rhetoric of Religion: Studies in Logology* (Berkeley: U. of California Press, 1961), pp. 174–83.

[24] Douglas Thomas, "Burke, Nietzsche, Lacan: Three Perspectives on the Rhetoric of Order," *Quarterly Journal of Speech*, 79 (1993): 337.

[25] Perhaps no theorist has done more to explore this theme than the Italian Marxist Antonio Gramsci. He saw the state as the embodiment of a hegemonic power. See A. Gramsci, *Selections from the Prison Notebooks*, Q. Hoare and G. N. Smith, eds. (New York: International Publishers, 1971).

[26] See Aune, *Rhetoric and Marxism*.

[27] See preface of Marx, *Critique of Political Economy* (London, 1859).

[28] His attack on postmodernism is discussed in chapter 13 of this book.

[29] Hans Georg Gadamer, *Reason in the Age of Science* (Cambridge: MIT Press, 1981), pp. 81–82.

[30] Habermas has admitted that this model of the "public sphere" in his early work tended to exclude minorities and other marginalized groups. See his "Further Reflections on the Public Sphere," in *Habermas and the Public Sphere*, Craig Calhoun, ed. (Cambridge: MIT Press, 1992), p. 466–68.

[31] Jürgen Habermas, *The Theory of Communicative Action*, vol. 1, Thomas McCarthy, trans. (Boston: Beacon Press, 1984), p. 95.

[32] Ibid., p. 17–18.

[33] Jürgen Habermas, "Toward a Theory of Communicative Competence," *Inquiry*, 13 (1970): 367.

[34] Jürgen Habermas, *Communication and the Evolution of Society*, Thomas McCarthy, trans. (Boston: Beacon Press, 1976), p. 29.

[35] Jürgen Habermas, *Philosophical Discourse of Modernity* (Cambridge: MIT Press, 1987), pp. 294–95.

[36] Jürgen Habermas, *Between Facts and Norms: Contributions to a Discourse Theory of Law and Democracy*, William Rehg, trans. (Cambridge: MIT Press, 1996), p. 370.

[37] Ibid., 381.

[38] The initiator of this movement is Philip Wander. See his "The Ideological Turn in Modern Criticism," *Central States Speech Journal*, 34 (1983): 1–8; "The Third Persona: An Ideological Turn in Rhetorical Theory," *Central States Speech Journal*, 35 (1984): 197–216.

[39] For further studies on civil religion see, Robert Hariman, *Political Style: The Artistry of Power* (Chicago: U. of Chicago Press, 1995); Roderick Hart, *The Political Pulpit* (West Lafayette, IN: Purdue U. Press, 1977); Roderick Hart and J. L. Pauley, *The Political Pulpit Revisited* (West Lafayette, IN: Purdue U. Press, 2004).

[40] President James K. Polk picked up this phrase from a New York newspaper to justify his imperialist war policy.

[41] This phrase was coined President Franklin D. Roosevelt and repeated by Ronald Reagan, starting with his speech in support of the candidacy of Senator Barry Goldwater in 1964.

[42] R. P. Basler, *The Collected Works of Abraham Lincoln,* vol. 1 (New Brunswick, NJ: Rutgers U. Press, 1953), p. 112.

[43] See Mark 3:25.

[44] Robert Bellah, "Civil Religion in America," *Journal of the American Academy of Arts and Sciences,* 96 (Winter 1967): 1–21.

[45] Michael McGee, "The 'Ideograph': A Link between Rhetoric and Ideology," *Quarterly Journal of Speech,* 66 (1980): 1–16. For a revision of this position see McGee's, "Text, Context, and the Fragmentation of Contemporary Culture," *Western Journal of Speech Communication,* 54 (1990): 274–89. See also McGee, "In Search of 'The People': A Rhetorical Alternative," *The Quarterly Journal of Speech,* 61 (1975): 245–47; "A Materialist's Conception of Rhetoric," *Explorations in Rhetoric: Studies in Honor of Douglas Ehninger,* R. E. McKerrow, ed. (Glenview, IL: Scott Foresman, 1982), pp. 23–48; and McGee and Martha Martin, "Public Knowledge and Ideological Argumentation," *Communication Monographs,* 50 (1983): 47–65.

[46] McGee, "The 'Ideograph'" pp. 7, 15.

[47] Maurice Charland, "Constitutive rhetoric: The case of the *Peuple Québécois,*" *Quarterly Journal of Speech,* 73 (1987): 133–50.

[48] Ibid., pp. 139–41.

[49] See the Book of Jeremiah in the Bible. He is one of the later prophets.

[50] Mitt Romney delivered this major foreign policy address on October 7, 2011.

Kenneth Burke's Expansion of Rhetoric

K enneth Burke was born in Pittsburgh in 1897 and moved to New Jersey with his parents in 1915. He attended Ohio State University for one semester and then Columbia University (in New York City). However, Burke claimed that colleges in those days taught you things to teach and how to teach but did not make you into a writer—so he took up self-education by reading what interested him. Although he did not graduate from Columbia, he met a Freudian named Leon Adler, who became the father of "biographical criticism." The two became good friends. Burke then became editor of the influential "little magazine" known as *The Dial*, published in Greenwich Village where he frequented the coffee houses and provoked stimulating conversations. He married Lilie Batterham in 1919, who eventually bore him three daughters. His Village gatherings became rarer when Burke decided to move to Andover, New Jersey, in 1922, and lead a more ecological life.

This is no small point since Burke would spend some time writing on the dangers technology poses to nature. He lived without an indoor toilet or electricity until 1950, and running water until 1960. With a change of house and a wife—Burke divorced Lilie and married her sister Libbie in 1933—the little town became his home base for the rest of his life. Libbie bore him two sons, and eventually even his grandchildren lived in Andover, from where he wrote music reviews for *The Dial* and later for *The Nation* from 1933 to 1936. His attempts at fiction included a book of short stories (*The White Oxen*, 1924) and a novel (*Toward a Better Life*, 1932), but neither met with critical acclaim, and Burke decided he was more suited to developing the art of criticism. From the Second World War to 1961, he taught at Bennington College, which allowed him to bounce some of his ideas off of students. He fell in love with the process and eventually became an itinerate professor who visited such campuses as Stanford, Pennsylvania State University, UCLA, and UC Santa Barbara, where I was privileged to hear his lectures and meet him. He died in 1993 at the age of ninety-six.

Kenneth Burke fused Freud's psychological insights with the dialectical approach of Marx. Trying to extract the best from this synthesis, Burke established logological and dramatistic methods of analysis and soon became one of the twentieth century's most significant critics. By logological, he meant the "insight into the nature of language itself as" it reveals human motives.[1] By dramatism, he meant that which is propelled by intentional action as opposed to scientism, which is concerned with nonintentional motion.[2] Plants grow in an unintentional way, but humans can decide, for the most part, what actions they are going to take. Thus, the human drama is motivated because intention implies a motive, values, and the ability to speculate.[3]

BURKE'S CONCEPTION OF RHETORIC

Burke saw humans as symbol users. In fact, he claimed that symbols separate us from nature and that symbols allow moralizing.[4] It follows then that he defined rhetoric as "symbolic inducement," the attempt to move others in desired directions through the manipulation of symbols. The use of rhetoric is ontological; that is, it is essential to existence and it reveals how we operate. Because human communication is symbolic—that is, because it represents or stands for something—it is also "dramatistic." The play represents something; it is not itself reality. The drama is the way that humans as symbol users manage society. Thus, Burke's overarching approach is to look at life in general and rhetoric in particular as a tragic and comedic drama complete with plot and actors.

Burke's next step moves us to the center of his rhetorical critique. Actors persuade us to act in certain ways. Thus, it becomes important to understand how they accomplish this persuasion. Burke's key term for his concept of persuasion is "identification," as first developed by Freud.[5] Burke adopted the psychoanalytic continuum running from anaclitic to narcissistic to explain what motivates identification—and the ego's demand for self-verification—within the hierarchies of society. *We identify with those with whom we share traits*.[6] The anaclitic prizes persons "on account of the satisfactions they render to the primal needs in life"; the narcissist adopts "in place of the ego itself, someone as nearly as possible resembling it."[7] Such motives open rhetoric to new areas of development. Burke did not come to his notion of identification quickly. He worked in the vineyards of literary criticism for many years before he advanced his own theory, built on his fusion of Freud and Marx.[8]

STRATEGIES FOR CRITICS

In 1931, Burke published his first major book, *Counter-Statement*. It reflects his revolutionary view—at least for literary critics—that art is less about self-expression than a rhetorical relationship between the author and the audience.[9] The role of the critic is to make a case for his or her criticism and to balance the criticism of others and the argument of the work under investigation. If successful, the critic provides a "counter-statement" to incorrect and/or ideological themes. The book introduces ideas that Burke would develop more fully in later writings. For example, he recognized that division and alienation are the counterparts of unity and communion. Those emphasizing division employ the rhetoric of alienation not only to carve away those who will not support a persuasive effort but to provide an enemy to enhance the identification of the chosen audience.

Counter-Statement is most important because of the way it is built on the Greek notion of *kairos* (fitting timing) and the Roman notion of *decorum* (meeting expectations) by arguing that form arouses and fulfills desires and expectations. Based on this analysis, Burke set out the major forms operating in discourse after dividing them between natural forms (reality) and art forms (symbolic constructs):

Kenneth Burke.

- *Syllogistic progression*, where the speaker starts with a premise and then develops arguments that move the audience step by step toward a conclusion, is common in murder mysteries and summations to juries. It is a deductive approach that takes readers or listeners by the hand and leads them to a logical conclusion.

- *Qualitative progression* is more complex because one quality is established in the mind of the audience so that another can be introduced. In other words, one quality is a prerequisite for another. We do not give money for the homeless (exemplifying the quality of *generosity*) until we feel *sympathy* for the homeless. Thus, the quality of sympathy must be established before the quality of generosity can surface.

- *Repetitive form* is often misunderstood to mean a simple repetition of a theme or phrase. For example, when Martin Luther King Jr. ended his famous 1963 address in Washington, DC, with seven sentences beginning "I have a dream . . . ," he used the simplest kind of repetition. However, Burke had something more complex in mind: A theme is transformed into a principle and that principle is exemplified in new guises each time it is introduced. The principle that it is better to be honest and decent than clever and greedy appears over and over in the character of Forrest Gump, in the movie by the same name. He falls into one piece of good luck after another—he meets presidents; he makes lucky investments—as the principle is advanced throughout the movie. To turn to a rhetorical example: if I am giving a speech on equity, I might first describe it in terms of sporting rules, then in terms of sharing the responsibilities of child-rearing, and then in terms of equal opportunities for jobs. The principle is reiterated continually through different examples.

- *Conventional forms* are standard means of organizing speeches, poems, plays, and novels. The most common is to divide all components into a beginning, middle, and end. Once this form is invoked, the audience will follow and expect a standard conclusion that is proportional to the rest of the work, whether it is a speech or a concerto. Using the past, present, and future to organize thoughts is another conventional form often seen in deliberative speeches advocating a policy. The speaker tells us what we have been through, perhaps discussing the causes of the problem; then tells us where we are, perhaps discussing the effects of the problem; and then suggests a solution to solve the problem in the future.

Also common is the cycle of birth, death, and rebirth. In Disney's *Lion King*, Simba is born, sees his father die, falls from grace, goes into exile, accepts the life of leisure, finally to return as the new savior-king. In the play *War Horse*, which was made into a film, both the young hero and his horse begin in peaceful settings, face challenges, are separated by war, then wounded in that war, before they are reunited in a better world. As Burke made clear, rebirth means reidentification; you emerge redefined and the new identification is usually deeper and less naive than the one formed before a crisis.

• *Minor or incidental forms* occur at the micro level. Tropes and figures, such as metaphors and synecdoches, are common minor forms as are the uses of contradiction and paradox. In filmmaking, minor forms include such techniques as slow motion filming for emphasis, filming through gauze to make a scene more romantic, or using flashbacks to recount the history of a character.

Revealing the influence of Marx, Burke linked these forms to various ideologies. For example, the repetitive form provides comfort to Catholics who are used to repeating phrases and prayers during the mass. For Protestants who employ less ritual, the repetitive form might cause discomfort. Burke noted that forms redefine situations in ideological, psychological, and/or mythological ways. A tragic death becomes a "sacrifice" in the ritual of birth, death, and rebirth, thereby relieving our grief. An ordinary birth becomes a symbol of "regeneration," thereby elevating its importance in our lives. Many forms become archetypal; they become patterns of experience. We expect happy endings; we expect people to pay for their crimes; we expect speakers to return to their openings to signal that they are closing. In this way, Burke traced form to symbolism and symbolism to subliminal expectation.

Burke published *Permanence and Change: An Anatomy of Purpose* in 1935 to urge critics to find ultimate motives in discursive works.[10] In the midst of the Great Depression, Burke believed that society was ill and needed a cure. He provided equipment for critics to use in examining various conditions and creating a poetic attitude as a corrective. His corrective philosophy, as he called it, would shift the critical emphasis from a philosophy or psychology of prose to the prose or poetry itself. Critics need to be interpreters of the work at the simplest level: What does the speech say literally? Only then should they move to evermore complex levels of meaning and motive: What does the speech imply? What does the symbolism connote? Does it establish a symbolic dialectic of values and/or ideas? Critics need to be integrators who demonstrate how a text fits in with other texts that it retrieves. How does the speech play to the socially constructed network into which it is delivered? What collective aspects of meaning are evident?

Locating Motives

At one point in *Permanence and Change*, Burke talks about the difference between eulogistic and dyslogistic uses of language and how they can be used to impute positive or negative motives. When we eulogize something, we place it in a cloak of admiration: the simple act of eating becomes an epicurean adventure. When we dyslogize something, we place it in a cloak of negativity: the simple act of eating becomes gluttony.[11] Later, in his *A Rhetoric of Motives* (1950, see below), Burke uses Aristotle's model of virtue to show that the term, say courage, is eulogistic, while the terms of excess and deficiency, say rashness and cowardice, are dyslogistic. Building on Aristotle, Burke shows that dyslogistic language and eulogistic language establish tonalities of the negative and the positive in terms of motives. If, for example, we say a soldier rushed into battle because he was courageous, it presents a very different picture than if we say the soldier rushed into battle because he was foolhardy.

Examination of these tonalities reveals what motives are being imputed to a subject and what motivates those who use such words. Always trying to get behind the language and into the head of the symbol user, Burke would ask, "Why did you describe the soldier in a eulogistic or dyslogistic way?" "Are you a war monger or a pacifist?" Furthermore, if we look at certain aphorisms, we can see that they often provide contradictory advice, which can also be dyslogistic. For example, we say that "a stitch in time saves nine"; but we also say that "haste makes waste." We say that "clothes make the man"; but we also say, "Don't judge a book by its cover." Thus, over time, eulogistic and dyslogistic sayings have worked their way into our culture. Finally, using what Burke called a *perspective by incongruity*,[12] the critic takes a word or phrase from its customary category and applies it in a different category. "Blue" is a usually seen as a color, but when applied to a mood, it conveys sadness. We can extend this exercise by bringing together two seemingly unrelated authors or ideas and see what results from the pairing. To put it another way, a perspective by incongruity allows us to view an entity from the perspective of another entity, which opposes it, and thereby reveals a side of it we might never have thought of.

Critics need to look for what can be exposed by examining the relationships between objects that have been ignored because of an emphasis on the rational, the logical, or the sensible. What is left out? Who is not seen? Why are they ignored? What contrasts are being made and what kind of dialectic do they imply? These questions help critics shift points of view to open things up or to challenge conventional wisdom. We can suddenly see things in terms of something else. The classic film *The Grapes of Wrath*, based on John Steinbeck's novel, examines the Depression from the point of view of the dispossessed Joad family and reveals the pain inflicted by capitalist greed. When speakers appeal to "family values" as paramount, what does their message imply for single parents and gays? *Permanence and Change* established Burke's questioning attitude, a critic always looking for clues, clusters, and cues. However, Burke does have a concluding recommendation: "Our thesis is a belief that the ultimate metaphor for discussing the universe and man's relations to it must be the poetic or dramatic metaphor."[13]

Interpretation

Burke wrote but did not publish *Auscultation, Creation, and Revision*, or *The Rout of the Esthetes*, or *Literature, Marxism, and Beyond*.[14] This rambling jaunt reveals not only Burke's preference for the aesthetic over the material, it includes several of Burke's breaks with Marxism, after it reaffirms Marx as useful in constructing a rhetoric of demystification. He thereby hopes to move Marxism away from scientism and logical positivism and toward a critical theory of interpretation. He claims that the bourgeois/proletarian split is "faulty" because it overemphasizes differences between two groups instead of seeing their similarities in terms of humanistic and psychological factors. He objects to Marxists finding ideologies under every literary rock because that often reduces important literary works to mere propaganda. In a complex turn of phrase he writes, "It is agreed that criticism analyzes the processes which poetry exemplifies—it is not sufficiently recognized that poetry throws great light upon the processes which criticism exemplifies."[15] And so he asks that the "Marxian method" be reapplied to take a little pressure off the poets.[16] The rest of the themes in this work are better developed in *Permanence and Change* and *Attitudes toward History*.

ATTITUDES TOWARD HISTORY

Burke published *Attitudes toward History* in 1937 to investigate how communication works to overcome the trauma of existence. Burke takes us through three eras in history: (1) the magical, which I reviewed in chapter 2 of this book as the mythic; (2) the religious; and (3) the scientific. Each of these eras provides a different rationalization for the social world and each comes from a different attitude. The magical seeks to constrain the power of nature and finds answers in the mysterious and the mythic. The religious seeks to constrain human forces and finds answers in prayer, the spiritual, and supernatural. The scientific seeks to constrain the forces of technology and finds answers in observation and quantification.

Burke defines attitudes as "incipient acts" that precede action.[17] One can take an attitude toward a task such as doing it "fervently" or "half-heartedly." Burke argued that in the face of anguish, communication adjusts our attitudes. The eulogy helps us mourn death; the myth helps us accept tragedy; the rhetoric of religion helps us cope with injustice in this world. However, in the process of his investigation, Burke establishes yet another dialectic, this time between necessity supported by technology and utilitarianism, and ecology supported by nature and the aesthetic. The rhetoric of necessity looks to the present, the need now. The rhetoric of ecology looks to the future, preservation of that which is sacred in nature. In this way, Burke's thought can be traced back through Walt Whitman and Henry David Thoreau. Three major themes emerge in *Attitudes toward History*. We discuss the Marxist and Freudian themes in this section. The third rhetorical theme is awarded its own section.

Marxist Theme

The first theme is quite simple: private property should not be overlooked as a major motive for action and for the speaker. The rhetoric of property can create a hegemonic state. For example, the government provides tax breaks for home owners but not for renters. Thus, the government provides an inducement to become a home owner, and home ownership is hegemonic. This condition is achieved through rhetoric's "constabulary function," which Burke illustrates using capitalism's hold on its audience. To put it another way, persuasion polices the marketplace to keep all of the players in line. It tells them what is fair and what is not.

Freudian Theme

The second theme is Freudian and much more complex: the guilt, purification, and redemption cycle is a powerful motivator of human action within and between hierarchies in the social drama.[18] To begin his exploration of the guilt cycle, Burke claimed that if we reject traditional hierarchies, as many revolutionaries and reformers do, we will feel guilt. A young woman marries a man outside of her culture. A priest leaves the church to protest its policies on homosexuality. It is difficult to live with the guilt that follows these actions because it alienates us from our former selves while denying the voice of hierarchies in our superego.[19] The culture tells the young woman that she is overturning hundreds of years of decisions made by others who may be wiser than she. The church calls to the priest that he is overturning thousands of years of tradition. These instances of guilt cry out for relief.

One way out of these dilemmas is to purify the rejected model of tradition with some sort of sacrifice or ritual that allows us to feel redemption. The purification can be self-inflicted (for example, fasting, flagellation, meditation, and prayer) or the victimization of others (for example, the sacrifice of the mass, the purification of the hero through trial, or the slaughter of the scapegoat that is seen to bear our guilt).[20] Thus, guilt can be relieved by naming a scapegoat and then sacrificing it. The speaker uses alienation to create the scapegoat and identification to bring his or her audience into the ritual of the kill. Once the sacrifice has been made, audiences emerge having been one in the kill and having achieved a "purified identity."[21] Martin Luther rejected the Catholic Church and provided a purified version of its teachings based on Paul's epistles. Those embracing the new Protestantism could relieve the guilt they felt over leaving the Catholic Church by sacrificing its colorful ritual and system of indulgences for the more straightforward and ascetic "justification by faith alone." In this way, they became redeemed.

Martin Luther King Jr. often used the same approach in his speeches on civil rights. Any guilt felt for abandoning the system of separate but equal treatment or criticizing the United States government was relieved by the sacrifices demonstrators made in the name of higher values. Their redemption came not only through purifying the present system but also from suffering in marches and demonstrations. Note that in each case, the rhetorical effort is effective only to the extent that the purification attempted is *proportional* to the guilt felt. You cannot exculpate the guilt of rejecting your church by giving up eating cookies on Wednesdays. Luther's and King's successes are explainable in part because of the proportional sacrifices they asked of their followers.

Burke presented the dangerous side of this guilt cycle equation in his 1961 book *The Rhetoric of Religion: Studies in Logology.*[22] He again defined humans as symbol users in their very being, which made the study of language crucial to understanding human operations. He shows that language can be exclusive, carving away members of an audience, or inclusive, reinforcing identification in the cult. Theology becomes the locus of his study because it induces humans to perfection (entelechy) using God terms and thereby creates a sense of sin and victimage for those who fail to reach perfection.

He claimed that if speakers can locate one who is acting as the victimizer, usually an aggressor (for example, terrorists or racists), speakers can then constitute an audience of victims. These victims can then be made to seek revenge and become part of the cult of the kill. Burke put it this way:

> Here are the steps
> In the Iron Law of History
> That welds Order and Sacrifice:
> Order leads to Guilt
> (for who can keep commandments!)
> Guilt needs Redemption
> (for who would not be cleansed!)
> Redemption needs a Redeemer
> (which is to say, a Victim!)
> Order
> Through Guilt
> To Victimage
> (hence: Cult of the Kill)[23]

Later in this chapter, we will return to this theme to see how it provides a means of achieving identification with an audience.

RHETORICAL FRAMES

Burke set out a taxonomy or classification of "frames of acceptance" for literary works. These included the epic (heroic tales of individuals overcoming hardship), the tragic (stories where fate defeats the individual), and the comic (stories where chance intervenes).[24] Comic frames allow for chance and luck. Like Freud, Burke believed that humor is often used to relieve fear and that much humor derives from just such incongruities: two things brought together that are not normally seen that way or events that differ from the expected.[25] The frame functions to feature certain items, symbols, or actions. The frame creates expectations. For example, because Romeo's friend Mercutio is a comic figure, his friends believe he is joking when in fact he has been fatally wounded in his fight with Tybalt. The moment is only reframed as tragic when Mercutio actually dies after placing a "curse on both your houses." Think of how a camera frames a scene in such a way as to show different meaning. A close shot of the U.S. Capitol during the inaugural of a president shows it in its gleaming glory. A long shot from a nearby ghetto reveals the hollowness of the American dream.

To return to *Attitudes*, we find that its third theme concerns the comic frame—concerning how we may be victims of fate. Burke writes:

> Human enlightenment can go no further than in picturing people not as *vicious*, but as *mistaken*. When you add that people are *necessarily* mistaken, that all people are exposed to situations in which they must act as fools, that every insight contains its own special kind of blindness, you complete the comic circle, returning again to the lesson of humility that underlies great tragedy. (His italics.)[26]

In *Language as Symbolic Action: Essays on Life, Literature, and Method* (1966), Burke argued that comedy helps us cope with the impossible, the absurd, and even the tragic. Before the humor can work, a "comic frame" needs to be established so that the audience is prepared for the irony to come. People who begin jokes, "Did you hear the one about . . ." establish a "comic frame" that prepares the listener for what is to come. The dark comedy *Fargo* begins with a brutal murder. The comic frame is established when the chief of police (a pregnant woman) arrives at the murder scene and quickly deduces exactly what happened the night before while an amazed deputy looks on. In the films *Knocked Up* and *Juno*, chance produces an unintended pregnancy, which signals a comic frame.

Framing is an important rhetorical strategy that runs the gamut of everyday life situations to presidential politics. We have all established "comic frames" on occasion by winking or using such phrases as the retrospective "I was just kidding," or the prospective "Get this." We also have the ability to change frames with lines like "Now seriously," or "That was inappropriate." Finding the boundaries of those frames is important in the process of audience adaptation. What passes for humor on "shock jock" radio shows often fails at after-dinner speaking occasions.

However, we should be clear that Kenneth Burke's comic frame was meant to be more overarching than these simple examples. He is talking about the intervention of chance into a hero's life. When Romeo loses control over his emotions and seeks to avenge the killing of his friend Mercutio, he chases down Mercutio's killer, Tybalt, does battle with him, and kills him. It dawns on him that by killing Tybalt of the rival gang, he has triggered the prince's warning that anyone caught fighting in the city will be exiled. Realizing his plight, Romeo yells out, "I am fortune's fool."

But we need not travel all the way back to Renaissance Italy to see the comic frame invoked to rationalize action. In 1969, Senator Edward Kennedy drove off a bridge in Chappaquiddick, Massachusetts, and a passenger in his car, Mary Jo Kopechne, who had been an aide to his brother, Robert, was drowned. In his apologia to the public, Kennedy referred to an "awful curse" that hung over the Kennedy family, reminding viewers that his brothers Joe, John, and Robert had all been cut down in their prime perhaps by the intervention of chance.

Ultimately, Burke hopes that the comic frame allows us to see ourselves as actors on the stage of life. Specifically, he synthesizes his previous definitions into one:

> Man is the symbol-using (symbol-making, symbol-misusing) animal inventor of the negative (or moralized by the negative) separated from his natural condition by instruments of his own making goaded by the spirit of hierarchy (or moved by the sense of order) and rotten with perfection.[27]

With such a frame, we become active in creating and correcting our actions.[28] To put it another way, the comic frame allows us to transcend ourselves to better observe what we are doing.

There are many other frames of which we need to be conscious if we are to be aware of the kind of persuasion that is taking place. For example, when people analyze a problem by asking for the bottom line, they are using an economic frame. When they examine a work for its perfection or flaws, they are using an aesthetic frame. When they explore good and evil, they are using a moral frame. When they seek friends and avoid enemies, they are using a political frame. And when they say something like, "If it ain't broke, then don't fix it," they are using a pragmatic frame. The frame thus screens our vision of the situation and thereby has an enormous influence on how we can be persuaded. Effective persuaders select the frame that will best serve their ends.

SYMBOLIC ACTION

Adding to his theory of frames, Burke's *The Philosophy of Literary Form: Studies in Symbolic Action* sees "literature as equipment for living"[29] because it provides readers with symbolic strategies for coping with everyday life. It sharpens our ability to think critically and assess options. Three previous themes are extended in this work. First is agon analysis: what is the dialectic in the work; what fights with what? Second is progressive from *counter-statement;* here Burke examines what follows from what. Third is cluster analysis, which I will examine in detail below. These three modes save us the time of learning through experience because we can learn through literature.

It is not difficult to extrapolate what Burke said in his 1941 volume to rhetoric in the contemporary era. Just as in literature, a rhetorical reader can explore symbolic action and word clusters. Associated clusters, as we shall see in the subliminal symbology example below, reveal motives and create dialectical tensions. Burke argues that dialectics exist in almost all communication and that they are often subliminal. To expose them, a critic must examine the *symbolic action* that takes place in a speech because it may reveal what is going on *ideologically.* Burke retrieved the important consideration of imagery and topology first developed by Gorgias and perfected by the Romans. Applying the Marxist concept of dialectic to imagery, Burke provided a system of analysis that again takes the critic back to motive. The following example illustrates Burke's questioning, dialectical approach from *The Philosophy of Literary Forms* while serving to preview Burke's notion of substantial identification through localization and concretization, which he developed in *A Rhetoric of Motives*, originally published in 1950.

Subliminal Symbology

In October of 1964, Ronald Reagan gave a speech entitled "A Choice, Not an Echo" on national television on behalf of Senator Barry Goldwater, the Republican presidential candidate. The speech not only raised more money than any political speech given on television up to that time, it catapulted Reagan into the limelight in the race for governor of California two years later. The rest is history. At the time of the address, however, Reagan was an over-the-hill actor who was a television personality and the corporate spokesman for the General Electric Company.

The success of this speech can be explained by the effective use of *decorum* to establish dialectical dichotomies that create tensions, alienations, and identifications while reinforcing the message. Using cluster and agon analysis, assessment of dialectical symbology can be divided into three areas: determining the dialectical character of the imagery, determining the ways in which images reinforce ideas, and determining the purpose of the whole body of imagery. By examining Reagan's speech with these probes, we can see if the symbolism of the speech reinforces its ideology and thereby explains its success.[30] In the process, we can uncover Reagan's ultimate motives. One tip-off, or what Burke would call a "cue," is that Reagan never mentions Goldwater in the speech.

Several *image clusters* emerge when we question Reagan's address using the grounding Burke provides. Our first question is: What is the dichotomy established by the imagery in this discourse? Reagan gives us a "cue" when he says, "There is only an up or down," referring to the path of government policy. He identifies "up" with "us," "we," and "individualism" throughout the speech; he equates "down" with "them," "they," and "totalitarianism." By paragraph 19 of the speech, Reagan has identified "private enterprise" with "up" and "big government" with "down." He fills out the dialectic clusters by envisioning private funds as "protecting" while Social Security is pictured as "a bare cupboard." He reinforces the dichotomy between privacy and collectivism by describing "government handouts" using the devil term "temptation." In paragraph 41, the up/down dichotomy is broadened to include more images. "We are faced," Reagan claims, "with the most evil enemy mankind has known in his long climb from the swamp to the stars." He has expanded the simple opening up/down dichotomy to an allegory carrying us up from the lowly swamp to the heavenly stars. At the same time, Reagan has carved away communists, bureaucrats, and those who support

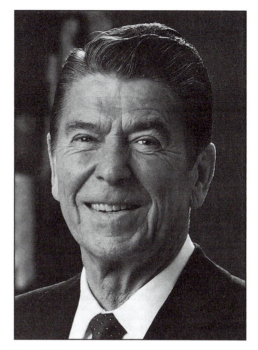

Ronald Reagan.

big government solutions from his coalition. The tensions that follow continue the narrowing process so that identification is enhanced by the imagery of the speech.

Does the dichotomy of clusters contribute to the dramatic intensity Reagan seeks? From the outset, Reagan's drama is a battle to the death. The opening paragraphs concern a "silent war with the most dangerous enemy known to man. . . . If we lose that war . . . [we] lose our freedom." By paragraph 20, the dialectical intensity is less subtle. We are "assailing our allies for so-called vestiges of colonialism while we engage in a conspiracy of silence." The description provides an antithesis with the next sentence: We should be "aiding our allies by sharing our material blessings with those nations which share our fundamental beliefs." Notice that Reagan creates an identification based on materialism *and* ideology. In paragraph 42, these and other images are clustered: on one side are "up, fight, die on feet, Moses, Christ, Concord, Martyrs"; on the other side are "down, surrender, accommodate, slavery, iron-curtain, deal, live on knees, liberals."

What makes this image equation even more effective is that these images are linked to values that supplement the ideological composition of the address. With "up" are such God terms as "courage, simplicity, moral, danger, and risk"; with "down" are such contrasting conceptions as "immoral, safety, and disgrace." The hero with whom Reagan wants us to identify has courage, takes a risk by facing danger, and in his/her simplicity protects the moral order. The forces of evil seek safety and comfort, are disgraced by their cowardice, and thus are alienated from us. Paragraph 43 reduces this structure to its essential message once again: we should "choose the high road." We face either a "rendezvous with destiny" or a "thousand years of darkness." Clearly, the image clusters of the speech are dramatic, concrete, and dialectical and foreshadow Reagan's attack on the "evil empire" a generation later (March 8, 1983) in a speech before the National Association of Evangelicals, an assembly of Protestant ministers.

But how does this imagery reinforce the message? Already, we have seen God-terms clustered around the initial dichotomy. To extend the analysis, we need to determine how the imagery localizes ideas—how it brings them into immediate focus for the particular audience. Reagan's conceptualization of government serves as a case in point. His object is to alienate the audience from its government so the audience will support the conservative candidacy of Goldwater, who is committed to reducing the size of the federal government. The images he uses enhance the audience's alienation from their government by giving it an organic quality.

Reagan begins in paragraph 4: The government is seen "laying its hand"; the government "tends to grow and take on weight"; in paragraph 10, "the government has found its most fertile growing bed." By paragraph 20, the government as swamp-thing will not "reduce itself" and is near to "eternal life." It has become a "big . . . complex . . . permanent structure." It begins to "hold life-and-death power." In paragraphs 34 and 35, the "huge and entrenched" growth has seized and sold cattle. It finally invades and assaults our rights.

This extensively developed image is tied to the original cluster in several ways. First, plant life grows down in the "swamp," and Reagan, leaving nothing to the imagination, pictures governmental ideas as "filtering down" through the muck to the poor citizens stuck in the mire. Second, since it is a large impersonal entity, which is highly threatening, "moral courage" will be required to defeat it. The images serve to "localize" the problems and in so doing provide a mental backdrop for the propositions in Reagan's speech.

The purpose of the imagery as a whole can be found by asking two questions: First, what is the symbolic action of the imagery? Second, what motives are imputed on the basis of this action? Once the symbolic action is established, we need to determine what it implies. Are some actions preferred over others? Through the imagistic action we ostensibly are taught what policies are valid or invalid. Progressive taxes, for example, are called an unfair burden that would pull an individual "down." Proportional taxes are described as steady and stable as opposed to "unsound."

Reagan's message, reinforced by the complex image and value clusters, is very simple. We can choose one of two paths. We can take the easy road, advocated by our enemies and permitted by the "architects of accommodation," down to collectivism; or we can take the high road, filled with risk and reward, up to our destiny. Since Reagan's imagery says symbolically what the speech says ideologically, it reinforces the message of the address and explains its success. However, there is a deeper possible motive that is revealed by this analysis: Reagan wanted to become the spokesperson for the conservative movement, knowing full well by the time of the speech that Goldwater would not win the election. He demonstrates that *decorum*, when supplemented with identification and dialectical tensions, is a powerful tool for the modern speaker.

The Pentad

Burke realized that many speakers are successful because they have the ability to use dramatic techniques in the rhetorical arena. The modern separation of rhetoric and drama into discrete areas of study interferes with the ability of each to inform the other. Thus, to continue the cross-pollination he began in *Counter-Statement* and to set rhetoric into a dramatistic paradigm, Burke articulated his famous pentad in his *Grammar of Motives* published in 1945. The pentad contains five terms: act, agent (actor), agency, scene, and purpose. They are roughly based on five of the standard questions journalists use for any good story: who, what, when, where, and why. Behind each of these questions also lies an ideological approach to the world.

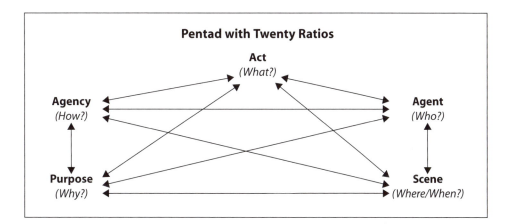

Pentad with Twenty Ratios

Act
(What?)

Agency
(How?)

Agent
(Who?)

Purpose
(Why?)

Scene
(Where/When?)

For Burke, the "who" is the agent or *actor*. It corresponds to the ideology of idealism, for it is the agent who dreams of a better future. For example, when presidents are inaugurated and give their address to the nation, they become actors in a rhetorical event, but also they explain their idealistic dreams for America.

The "what" is the action that is taken, the *act* that makes the drama. It corresponds to the ideology of realism, the "taking form" of something. In the case of the president, the inaugural address celebrates an induction into the presidency. The person "takes the form" of president.

The "when" and "where" is Burke's *scene*, in which he included not only the time and the physical surroundings, but also the "backdrop" of values. It corresponds to the ideology of materialism because the scene, through its inevitable materialistic dialectic, determines outcomes.[31] In the case of inaugurals, the scene includes a local and national audience, television cameras, official Washington, and the moment in time when America is about to embark on a change of administration or reaffirm one readying for a second term. The scene also includes the audience's values as translated into political action and the hierarchies among various classes.

Burke added a "how" to the list of dramatistic questions; it reveals the *agency* by which the act is achieved. It features the ideology of pragmatism, how to get things done. In the case of inaugurals, the agency is rhetoric and all of its attendant strategies inclusive of tropes and figures, appeals to emotion, credibility, logic, delivery, and organization. They provide the means by which a person inaugurates his or her presidency.

The "why" is the *purpose* of the act; it features ends over means, and the philosophy of mysticism. The inaugural is the mystical ritual that confirmed an election to the presidency, which was present in Barack Obama's 2009 inaugural address: "We will harness the sun and the soil . . ."

This simple way of breaking down a speaking situation helps us understand why it was successful or unsuccessful. Filling in the information in the pentad of act, actor, agency, scene, and purpose was only the beginning—a kind of simple interpretation that Burke saw as the homework for the criticism to follow. Burke argued that each of the constituents of his pentad was like the wake of one of five speed boats heading across the water, and that the most interesting analysis occurred where the wakes crossed. Thus, Burke established what he called *ratios* between each of the constituents as a means of opening up the rhetorical situation to further analysis.

Ratio analysis forces out the dominant term in discourse. The ratios help us determine what controls what, or who controls whom. Thus, we might ask, in what ways does the scene control the agent? And, in what ways does the agent control the scene? For example, in Franklin Roosevelt's First Inaugural in 1933, the ratios reveal that the new president is taking control of the scene with his agent-driven discourse. Unless Congress gives him the legislation he wants, the president will use his emergency powers to end the Great Depression as if we had been invaded by a foreign nation. Normally, when the agent is trying to achieve some change, the dominant worldview is pragmatism, which certainly was the key method of Roosevelt's New Deal. In his second inaugural, Lincoln sought to restore the peace of the prewar period but also to create a new scene of tolerance both for emancipated African Americans and for Southern whites willing to pledge allegiance to the Union. The scenes, whether projected or real, dominate the discourse. For Burke, the ratios are "principles of determination," which help explain why things happen the way they do, particularly with regard to symbolic inducement.[32]

For example, the ratio between act and scene asks, what kind of act is proper to the scene? Or what impact did the act have on the scene? Hamlet does not kill Claudius when he finds him in prayer because killing him while he was praying, it was believed at that time in Denmark, would send him straight to heaven—the very last thing Hamlet wanted to do. Thus, the scenic backdrop of values prevented Hamlet from acting at that moment. Scenes invite particular qualities in acts. History can also serve as a scenic backdrop that forces action. For example, in the summer of 1972 several aides suggested to President Nixon that he consider telling the truth about the White House involvement in the Watergate fiasco. They supported their argument by showing Nixon poll data that revealed he was far ahead of his opponent in the upcoming presidential election. Nixon responded that he had been way ahead of other political opponents in the past only to lose on Election Day or to have the election come in so close as to cripple his ability to govern. Citing his races with John Kennedy, Edmund Brown, and Hubert Humphrey, Nixon rejected the argument of his staff and ordered the cover-up. The historical backdrop to the scene helped motivate an act that proved politically fatal.

The ratio between actor, or agent, and scene asks the question: What is the actor capable of in this scene? The range runs from obvious physical limitation (the president cannot levitate during his inaugural) to more subtle judgments about appropriateness to the scene (the formality of the occasion precludes using a lighthearted approach). The ratio also asks: What impact does the actor have on the scene? Does he or she change the values of the audience? Does the actor change the physical nature of the scene?

The ratio between agency and purpose asks: What strategies can an agent use to achieve his or her purpose? Here the list may be very long and may include *ethos, pathos, logos*, style, strategies of identification, or any other rhetorical tactics. Once we have that list we can use it as a benchmark against which the actual performance of the speech can be assessed. In a president's case, we can ask: Does he or she establish the proper emotional tone to accomplish the purpose of appearing presidential? Does he or she sound presidential in terms of style?

The ratio between agent and act asks: What actions are appropriate to this agent? What actions is the agent capable of performing? Can the president take the oath of office given the election results? Can the president deliver an effective speech? Can the president unite the country behind his or her leadership?

The multifaceted two-way ratios should be seen as the points on a five-pointed star or as your fingertips. The lines between the points are the ratios that Burke would use to establish probing questions for the speaking situation, which he hoped would reveal the effectiveness of the work and, most important, reveal the motive of the speaker, by which Burke means the worldview that the speech endorses. *Because the ten links go both ways, a critic using the system should view them as twenty ratios.* For example, the agent-scene ratios ask at least two questions: what can the agent do in this scene? And what effect does the scene have on the agent?

Just as Marx sought to reveal a hidden ideology, Burke seeks to reveal a latent worldview, a philosophy of operation that tells us something about the speaker. Like Aristotle and Machiavelli, Burke argued that speakers can hide their real motives, which include gaining advantage. Those real motives can be found by tracing the various ratios to a center, like the palm of a hand.

In an "addendum" to *A Grammar of Motives*, Burke added "attitude" to his formulation. Attitude concerns the manner in which an act occurs or can concern the attitude of the agent during an act. Thus, firing a gun is a means (agency) to complete an act; but firing the gun in anger is the manner (attitude) in which the act was committed. Attitude becomes a way of getting back to mood. Is the agent pessimistic, optimistic, in love, and so forth? Once the basic attitude is established, the critic can examine various ratios to it. What is the ratio between the agent and the attitude? That becomes an important ratio in many court cases. The attitude of the accused, if properly established, may determine the degree of guilt associated with a crime. For example, many courts impose lengthier sentences if a crime is accompanied with hate speech because such speech reveals a harsher attitude on the part of the perpetrator.

Strategies of Identification

In *A Rhetoric of Motives*, Burke explained why we identify with one another and how we can use the strategies of identification to construct our personas and to seek communion in our society. He advanced Aristotle's notion of *ethos* by providing a means by which a person could develop potentialities that were hitherto unrealized. In Freud's works, ego is synonymous with the "self."[33] Burke recognized that individuals externalize their ego-ideals by *identifying* with the egos of others. In other words, people *project* an image onto others whom they admire. Burke argued that identification is based on these psychological ties. An ego identifies with another and then tries to behave like it and imitate it, eventually absorbing all of its characteristics. The divisions of the psyche, the internalized voices of adults, and the social nature of knowledge evolve as the ego develops. This phenomenon led Burke to speculate that identification is a form of sublimation. The libido is repressed in such a way that the ego needs to reestablish the lost object of identification. In many cases the ego reactivates fantasies of past object identification to rationalize present reality. Such activation exercises the creative process. In creating fantasies and in rationalizing the present, the individual is forced to recall the past, re-create it, and alter the present to "make sense out of it." Once again, rhetorical capacity is at the center of our lives. To cope, we must make sense, and to make sense, we must be rhetorically talented.[34]

Burke understood communication to be a generalized form of love that ranged from sexual love to religious love to ideal platonic love. He recognized in rhetoric the individual's original motive: finding a satisfactory object for one's love. If a speaker can become that object for an audience, he or she necessarily enhances his/her credibility. Burke's conceptualization of the relationship between alienation and identification closely parallels Freud's interpretation of the relationship between a lost love object and identification: identification is compensatory to division. Burke claimed, "[Y]ou persuade a man only insofar as you can talk his language by speech, gesture, tonality, order, image, attitude, idea, *identifying* your ways with his."[35]

Burke thus creates a complex matrix that can be used to generate rhetorical appeals or to explain their effect. Alienation (division) is seen in dialectical tension with identification (unity). For every "them," there is an "us." A speaker can divide an audience from "them" using strategies of alienation: "they" are different in attributes (race), "they" are different in substance (size of house), "they" are different in values (ideology), "they" are different in habits (culture, religion). There is a wonderful musical number in Leonard Bernstein's and Stephen Sondheim's *West Side Story*. On a rooftop, the members of a Puerto Rican gang known as the "Sharks" are meeting with "their women." The men don't like being in America while the women do. Soon the debate is put to music, but what makes the scene so compelling is the dialectic. You have men versus women: love of Puerto Rico and disdain for the United States versus love of America and disdain for Puerto Rico. The dialectic is localized in terms of Manhattan representing America and San Juan representing Puerto Rico. Behind the dialectic is the conflict in values supported by each group. Its compelling and entertaining nature can be explained in terms of Burke's theories.

However, this kind of dialectic can also be quite dangerous. Very sophisticated, and perhaps dangerous, speakers can make "them" the scapegoat, what Burke calls the "vessel" of our unwanted evils or "our troubles."[36] As I have shown earlier in this chapter, using the rhetoric of the "negative," speakers can symbolically or actually call for the sacrificing of the "scapegoats" in order to solve "our problems" or to purge "our guilt," thereby purifying "our cult."[37] Burke emphasized, "the negative helps radically to define elements to be victimized."[38] The negative derives the rules and morals that guide us; in fact, Burke says our quest for perfection has made humans *rotten with perfection*. In Western civilization the Ten Commandments, filled with "thou shall nots," use the negative to achieve the positive. When Judeo-Christians violate these rules, they fall into a negative state and remain guilty until redeemed. Thus, the negative is a way not only to unite an audience but to redeem it.

Burke certainly understands Freud's notion of guilt, which surfaces when we fail to meet self-imposed standards of perfection. What he adds to it is the symbolic nature of language. We are guilty when we are condemned in language, whether it be the language of our conscience or the language of others. Uncomfortable with guilt, we seek redemption—and redemption can be achieved by linguistic cleansing, perhaps in prayer. As we have seen, our guilt can be relieved by victimage, which blames an enemy or puts the sins on a scapegoat. Or our guilt can be relieved by mortification, an inner transformation resulting from some sort of punishment, perhaps fasting.[39]

Once we have participated in the sacrifice (rite of purification by victimage) with the speaker, we are further identified with him or her both in our sin and in our redemption, which Burke called the two great "moments" of dramatism. Burke's essay on the effectiveness of the speaking of Adolf Hitler makes just this point.[40] Hitler had an uncanny knack for the dramatic. He held many of his rallies at night so that the audience was enveloped in light against the surrounding darkness, thereby huddling them into one united mass. He prefaced his speeches with parades, music, and rituals reinforcing this sense of unity and place. Most effective of all was his use of the scapegoat to create what Burke calls the "cult of the kill," in which Hitler blamed the Jews for Germany's problems. This powerful rhetoric of identification and alienation replaced the moral compass of many in Hitler's audiences, which led to the holocaust.

Hitler's rhetoric of alienation was devastating, and yet we find many positive and negative uses of such rhetoric every day. As the chart below indicates, the rhetoric of alienation can be cast in terms of superiority or elitism. In this case, speakers argue that they and their audiences are better than some "others." Many religious groups claim to

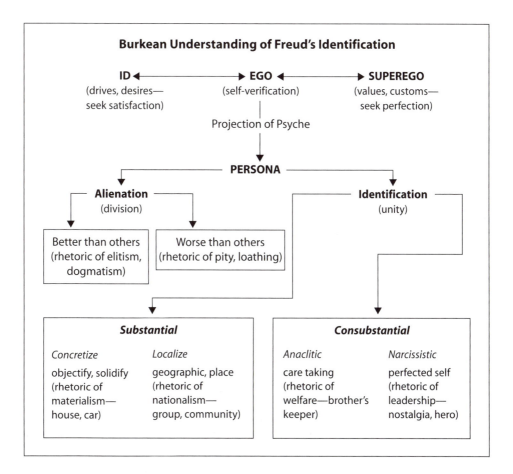

be purer, truer to the prophet's words, and/or more devout than others. The rhetoric of alienation can also be cast in terms of inferiority, prejudice, or pity. For example, when Charles Barron, a former Black Panther, became a member of the New York City Council, he advanced his call for reparations for African Americans in his "inaugural address." At one point he said, "We were raped. We were murdered. We were burned. And you have the nerve to say forget about it? Not in my lifetime!"[41] Barron and "his people" are the victims in his worldview and white oppressors are the enemy.

Victimization can also be used to carve groups away from or alienate them from the in-group. During his primary run for president in 2008 at what he thought was an off-the-record meeting, Barack Obama criticized "bitter" small-town voters who "cling to their guns or religion." During the 2012 presidential campaign, Mitt Romney was secretly recorded answering a question at a fund-raising event. When talking about putting his coalition for victory together, he said he would not appeal to the 47 percent of the population that did not pay income taxes; they "believe they are victims" and deserve government handouts. "My job is not to worry about those people. I'll never convince them they should take personal responsibility and care for their lives." Both Obama's and Romney's comments smacked of exclusivity.

The strategy of identification uses substance to achieve advantage for a speaker. The strategies of substantial identification can include material and geographical location values shared with the speaker. In his acceptance of the 2012 nomination, President Obama said, "Everyone gets a fair shot, and everyone gets a fair share, and everyone plays by the same rules from Main Street to Washington, D.C."

Concretization can also be used positively, as when an environmental group seeking to preserve endangered species identifies itself not with ugly lizards or frightening spiders but with cuddly panda bears. As I mentioned earlier, one of the more famous examples of concretization occurred in Jesse Jackson's address to the 1988 Democratic convention. In his plea for unity, he compared various special interests in the party to patches of a quilt:

> Now, Democrats, we must build such a quilt. Farmers, you seek fair prices and you're right, but you cannot stand alone. Your patch is not big enough. Workers, you fight for fair wages. You are right. But your patch is not big enough. Women, you seek comparable worth and pay equity. You are right. But your patch is not big enough. Women, mothers, you seek Head Start and day care and pre-natal care on the front side of life, rather than jail care and welfare on the back side of life, you're right, but your patch is not big enough.[42]

As Jackson pulls his audience together symbolically, he also does so ideologically. In creating a quilt, he is mending the tattered Democratic party, taking what is divided and making it into something that is united and better than its parts.

Localization can be used positively also, as when America is identified with a "shining city upon a hill" or New York City is converted into Jerusalem. In his 1988 address, Jackson demonstrated his facility with localization when he said:

> Think of Jerusalem—the intersection where many trails met. A small village that became the birthplace for three great religions—Judaism, Christianity, and Islam. Why was this village so blessed? Because it provided a crossroads where different peoples met, different cultures, and different civilizations could meet and find *com-*

mon ground. When people come together, flowers always flourish and the air is rich with the aroma of a new spring. Take New York, the dynamic metropolis. What makes New York so special? It is the invitation of the Statue of Liberty—give me your tired, your poor, your huddled masses who yearn to breathe free. Not restricted to English only. Many people, many cultures, many languages—with one thing in common, they yearn to breathe free.

Consubstantial strategies, that is, those that show the speaker and audience are of the same substance, also enhance identification. Burke argues that "common sensations, concepts, images, ideas, [and] attitudes" can serve as a foundation for shared substance.[43] However, the most powerful identification is achieved using the *anaclitic* strategies and *narcissistic* strategies found in Freud.[44] For example, a narcissistic audience member may identify with a speaker because the audience member idealizes the speaker in terms of what the speaker is in actuality, what the speaker seems to have been, or what the speaker aspires to be. If the audience member is a young black woman who aspires to lead, she may identify with Jesse Jackson in his capacity as a leader in the civil rights movement. In turn, if Jackson wishes to identify with narcissistic members of his audience, he needs to use rhetoric to form an image of being an idealized leader.

Another example of identifying with an idealized speaker can be seen in former Governor Mitt Romney's acceptance speech at the 2012 Republican Convention:

My friends cared more about sports teams we followed than what church we went to. . . . I grew up in Detroit in love with cars and wanted to be a car guy, like my dad. But by the time I was out of school, I realized that I had to go out on my own, that if I stayed around Michigan in the same business, I'd never really know if I was getting a break because of my dad. I wanted to go someplace new and prove myself.

In this passage, Romney identifies with young men, and anyone with a dream of making it on his or her own.

Anaclitic audience members may admire the speaker who takes care of them, the speaker who protects them, or the speaker they can care for or protect.[45] A young man seeking a career in the ministry so that he can take care of others is most likely to identify with a speaker who embodies the same quality. Speakers seeking to evoke such feelings of identification need to demonstrate their caring sides or their need for care. "Help me in this cause. I cannot succeed without your help."

The power of this aspect of *ethos* derives from Burke's ability to trace identification back to motive and motive back to substance. For example, he asserted that "[i]f man is the symbol-using animal, some motives must derive from his animality, some from his symbolicity, and some from mixtures of the two."[46] For members of an audience to identify deeply with a speaker is for them to share a common set of motives. Burke explored how motives translate into attitude, value, or principle when used in persuasive and poetic contexts to transcend a moment, a crisis, or a contrary worldview.

Burke sought to use this new, more powerful rhetoric to make *this* world a better place by adjustment of substance and motive. His insightful analysis of Hitler's rhetoric, especially its use of scapegoating and sacrifice, revealed the dark side of this psychologically dynamic rhetoric and its uses for evil purposes. However, Burke also saw that enlightened uses of rhetoric help untangle us from our baser motives and misprogrammed psyches. Thus, Burke's project was to provide a rhetoric that would set us free from the unhealthy illusions of the social order.

Mediated Identification

Because Burke's approaches to rhetorical theory are based in dramatism, they easily lend themselves to analysis of various media that have gained ascendance in our society. Isolating rhetorical theory to public speaking not only limits its usefulness but misses an opportunity for us to discover persuasion in other forms of communication. In chapter 2's consideration of myth and narrative, I showed that both are useful in helping uncover persuasion in ostensibly informative formats, such as news coverage of political events. "Mediated Identification" will show how Burke's theory is useful in uncovering ideological persuasion in the cinema.

One of the reasons we are pulled into films is because we identify with at least some characters on conscious and unconscious levels. Successful movies have characters that appeal to large segments of the audience by defeating the forces from which we are alienated. Other films create characters for whom we generate sympathy or admiration. Because characters attract audiences, one of the chief tasks of a cinema critic is to determine what kind of identification the filmmaker is achieving. Just as important is the ideology that is being advanced by the identification and symbolic action of the film. The first *Star Wars* trilogy provides a case in point because it is driven by dialectical tensions that arise from character identifications. In fact, the trilogy succeeds as good entertainment and effective propaganda because of its unique combination of identification, alienation, ideology, and dialectic. These factors help to explain its enormous box office appeal and how it generated and continues to generate many more millions in toy departments.

From the title sequence, the audience realizes it is watching the unfolding of a political drama that takes place "a long time ago in a galaxy far, far away . . ." The opening music is commanding in tone, alerting us that a great military struggle is underway. Soon we are faced with glittering technology that overwhelms and dazzles. We have been taken out of our world and placed in another time and space (scene) that fascinates and entertains.

However, we would soon lose perspective and perhaps interest if there were not a good story to tell and strong characters with whom to identify. Luke Skywalker is the white knight, pure of heart and full of spirit. While a bit naive at the outset of the adventure, he grows into a full-fledged Jedi warrior by the end of the trilogy. His concern for Princess Leia, whom he does not know is his sister, and the starfleet shows his anaclitic side and reinforces the identification between him and the audience.

Princess Leia is a strong young woman with a feminist attitude that is geared to the contemporary audience. She doesn't put up with any nonsense from her suitors, and she is as tough in battle as they are. Yet, she has a tender and vulnerable side.

Han Solo is the buccaneer of the group. He ventures into outlaw territory and is much more cynical than Luke. He is the older brother who knows how to get things done. Under his tough exterior, however, we discover a heart of gold. Along with Luke and Leia, he will lead the republican forces against the fascist regime of the evil Emperor. The plot works in part because it recalls the real-world wars between the republicans and fascists in Spain in the mid-1930s, the war with Nazi Germany beginning in 1939, and the Cold War that was going on when *Star Wars* was released.

The chief operative for the empire is one of the most evil creations in the history of film, Lord Darth Vader, a former Jedi who has been converted to the dark side. Vader wears nothing but black from his shiny helmet to his boots. His cape flares behind him as he marches through scene after scene. Having suffered a war wound, he breathes loudly through an apparatus that covers his face in black metal. He possesses supernatural powers. He can strangle troopers who fail him without touching them. Vader demonstrates that when the "Force" is with you, it can be used for good or evil.

Audience members may subconsciously identify with Vader because he represents Jung's shadow persona and the id's desire for power. Others may identify with his narcissism or his being a father figure. These unconscious identifications are not brought to the side of good until Vader is unmasked, both literally and figuratively, at the end of the trilogy. On the conscious level, however, almost all members of the audience are alienated from him. Thus, we are united with those who oppose him and his "master," the evil Emperor.

The supporting cast of characters is equally appealing. They not only entertain, they advance philosophical positions in unique ways. Obi-Wan Kenobi, the Jedi knight who advises young Luke, combines with a completely different-looking Jedi named Yoda to advance the philosophy of the spiritual force. They train young Luke in meditative techniques that allow him to tap the "Force." Both Obi-Wan and Yoda had guarded the Old Republic, which Luke seeks to restore.

R2-D2 and C-3PO are androids who provide comic relief and some technological skill when needed. We identify with them because, for all their wrangling, they are committed not only to taking care of one another but to protecting the heroes of the story whenever they can. C-3PO is the fastidious, ever-worried prude who must put up with R2-D2's curiosity and childlike nature. They make the perfect anaclitic pair.

Chewbacca the Wookie, a kindly Big-Foot, serves Han Solo and represents the virtue of loyalty. Like R2-D2, "Chewie" speaks no English, yet Han understands his growling perfectly. They are dedicated to one another, underscoring two of the most important themes of the *Star Wars* trilogy—friendship and commitment.

There are a host of secondary characters that advance various themes, plot lines, and values. Jabba the Hut, for example, is a giant slug representing gluttony and sloth. The Ewoks of part three, *Return of the Jedi*, couldn't be cuter or more cuddly; they demonstrate the virtues of teamwork as they deal with the empire's troopers.[47] The characters in the famous bar scene in the first part, *Star Wars*, are genetically amazing and humorous at the same time. Clearly, George Lucas understood the importance of filling his films with interesting personas who could cause an audience to identify with them. Furthermore, each of the major characters represents a different ideology and symbolizes a different segment of the story.

Our attention is also held by the dialectical tensions that underlie the script. The most obvious battle is between the forces of good and evil. While both have access to the "Force," a transcendent spiritual power, the forces of good are more likely to succeed with it because they have purer motives and are less distracted by the material pleasures of the universe. Luke and Leia seek to serve their people and restore the Republic. The fascists of this story are diverted by their desires. Vader wants power; his minions want victory; the outlaws want wealth.

A second tension develops when both Luke and Han vie for the hand of Princess Leia. Their rivalry motivates heroic deeds and is eventually resolved in part three, when it is revealed that Leia and Luke are siblings. This discovery frees Leia to pair with Han. Everyone lives happily ever after while the Jedi look on.

A third tension is oedipal, Luke doing battle with his father, Darth Vader. This classic struggle allows the antagonists to advance arguments for their philosophical positions. Luke is educated and advised by the more knowledgeable Obi-Wan and Yoda, who become part of Luke's superego. Luke favors the good, although it is outgunned and appears doomed. Vader is the voice of the dark side, arguing that it is better to win than to be right. This tension results in Vader maiming Luke in part one and then saving his life in part three when he returns to the side of good. The climactic scene puts Luke in the hands of the Emperor, who calls up Luke's anger in an attempt to turn him to the dark side. Luke does not give in and does battle with Vader. When Luke fails and lies wounded, the Emperor engulfs him in a force field causing Luke to cry out in pain for help from his father. Vader rescues his son by lifting the Emperor over his head and throwing him down a great hole in the Death Star. This act severely damages Vader, who asks to be unmasked while lying in Luke's arms. The kindly old knight is revealed and the division between father and son is ended.

A fourth tension runs between technology and intuition. On one side, the trilogy dazzles us with equipment that can perform miracles or be terribly destructive. From laser swords to high-powered floating scooters, we see what technology can do. The TIE fighters do battle with Luke's fighter pilots using Y-wing and X-wing jets. We allow ourselves to be drawn in because we live in an age when technology is admired and is advancing very rapidly. On the other side, the trilogy endorses meditation to reach an intuitive state where one can tap into the "Force." All training and all technology is finally left behind when Luke flies into the heart of the enemy's death star and drops a bomb in precisely the right spot by allowing his intuitive powers to override his rational skill. He "feels" the "Force"; he does not use reason to reach it.[48]

The *Star Wars* films, which began in 1977, have significant dialectical tensions that have been built on characters with whom we can identify. The resolution of these tensions advances philosophical positions that could change the way audience members conduct their lives. In this way, the trilogy is highly rhetorical. It is also mythic in the sense that it plays off cultural narratives, prevalent since Homer's *Iliad* and *Odyssey* through the adventures of the American frontier. The power of the trilogy to develop into mythology was best demonstrated when President Reagan referred to the Soviet Union as the "evil empire" and to his strategic defense initiative as "star wars." And of course, the success of the first trilogy led to the creation of a prequel trilogy.

Redefinition

Insightful as Burke's theories of form, dialectic, cluster analysis, dramatism, and identification can be, they do not exhaust his arsenal of critical approaches. Burke's theory of redefinition provides yet another grounding for rhetorical artistry and another way of tapping into the rich strategies of persuasion so pervasive in our culture. The definition of a conflict often determines its scope, those who are included, those who are excluded, and the eventual outcome. Borrowing from Freud, Burke argued that definitions are "terministic screens" on reality.[49] For example, how you define when life begins probably determines where you stand on the issue of a woman's right to have an abortion. People who believe that life begins at or near conception usually believe that abortion should be illegal. Those who believe life starts much later, say in the third trimester or at birth, usually favor a woman's right to have an abortion in the early stages of pregnancy.

Terministic screens are rhetorical because they reflect, select, and deflect. They reflect the reality that we believe exists. They select by focusing on a part of that reality that interests us. They deflect by marginalizing or ignoring that part of reality that does not interest us. In this way, terministic screens operate as filters. Imagine for a moment that you come across the scene of a traffic accident. Traveling with you is a lawyer, who will operate through a legal terministic screen and probably look for evidence of negligence, and a doctor, who will operate through a medical terministic screen and probably look for ways of saving life. Our screens become projections of ourselves, and they shape the ways in which we see the world and act in it.

Burke's theory of redefinition not only allows us to examine how redefinition is accomplished, it allows us to speculate on why it is done. Very often the motives are political. At the 2012 Republican Convention, Mitt Romney attempted to redefine his opponent in a negative way:

> His policies have not helped create jobs, they have depressed them. . . . His plan to raise taxes on small businesses won't add jobs, it will eliminate them. His assault on coal and gas and oil will send energy and manufacturing jobs to China. His trillion-dollar cuts to our military will eliminate hundreds of thousands of jobs, and put our security at risk. . . . And his trillion-dollar deficits will slow our economy, restrain employment, and cause wages to stall.

Tactics such as those used by Romney exemplify Kathryn Olson's insightful point that "a rhetor using a definition is not merely presenting an undisputed concept, but is advocating adherence to the particular definition and the perspective sponsoring it."[50] She argues that redefinitions can transform or they can transcend. *Transformational redefinitions* change the boundaries of a dispute. For example, those arguing for the legalization of marijuana often claim that if it were legal, money would be saved on law enforcement and the drug could be used for medicinal purposes without prescriptions. In this case, by putting marijuana inside the boundaries of legality, they redefine it by transformation. This is precisely Burke's use of the term: something is changed in the dialectic between matter and social context.

Transcendental redefinition occurs when elements of opposing sides are blended to overcome differences or when a redefinition uses ambiguity to overcome division. In the summer of 1968, when Richard Nixon faced a sharply divided America over the conduct of the war in Vietnam, he spent four long paragraphs in his acceptance of the nomination for president detailing the causes of the war. He then said that while he could not detail his plan for an end to the war because he did not want to undercut negotiations underway in Paris, he could promise "peace with honor." By transcending the dispute, the phrase appeased both hawks and doves in his own party and, to a significant degree, the nation as a whole.

Both transformational and transcendental redefinition can change the participants in the debate and with whom each side is associated. For example, when a speaker says, "This decision is not about the guilt or innocence of my client, it is about the fairness of our justice system," the case at hand is transformed because the system is put on trial rather than the accused. Or when a speaker says, "We not only march here for our civil rights, but the spiritual rights of our people," he or she not only transcends into the spiritual realm but associates with those who have religious interests.[51] Thus, Burke provided a complex matrix for the analysis of redefinitional strategies.[52]

The investigation of transcendental redefinition leads Burke to a fourfold approach to the dialectic in a text. As we have seen, Burke encourages the critic to search out the dialectical tension or give and take in any text, whether it be generated argumentatively or symbolically. A speaker, or a playwright for that matter, has four options in dealing with the polarity. First, the speaker can deny one or the other side of the polarity. As in the debate over the abolition of slavery, this seems to be the strategy of both sides in the abortion debate. There is no possibility of compromise or transcendence to resolve the dispute because each side believes the other side to be clearly and irrevocably wrong.

Second, the speaker can deny that polarity exists at all. In this case, the speaker presents evidence that there is no conflict between the sides—the disagreement is in fact imagined or created by mistake. In the debate over whether we should have a flat tax or a progressive income tax, flat tax proponents sometimes argue that because the more you make, the more you pay under a flat tax, it is also progressive. There is no dialectic because the alleged polarity is based on faulty terminology.

Third, the speaker can incorporate various elements of each side in the debate and use them to craft a compromise that transcends the polarity with "frames of acceptance."[53] Senator Daniel Webster's speech of March 7, 1850, provides a good example of such a strategy of redefinition attempting to prevent a civil war. He offered the South the return of fugitive slaves, the paying off of Texas' debt, and the right for several territories to organize for statehood. He offered the North the admission of California to statehood, the end of the slave trade in Washington, DC, and the preservation of the Union. In fact, Webster was quite clever about dropping down to the pragmatic level where he found consensus and moving to the transcendent level of union when he needed to overcome division.

Fourth, the speaker can transcend the conflict completely by declaring a plague on both sides or urging them to move beyond the confines of the debate to a new space where consensus can be achieved. Some advocates argue that both sides in the debate over gay marriage rights are wrong. There should only be civil unions that could subsequently be blessed in any way the couple chose, thereby avoiding mixing church and state in marriages.

The strategic use of language in these cases often leads to what Burke calls "pontificating thirds," that is, third terms that are added to the two terms of the polarity to effect denial of one side, denial of a polarity, or compromise or transcendence.[54] "Tolerance" is a pontificating third, as is civil union. These phrases serve to create a "higher synthesis" or an "ultimate term" to the extent that they are successful.[55]

We can summarize Burke on the interplay of dialectic and transcendence with some everyday examples.

1. The dialectic poses the following question: "Would you rather be known as the most famous person in the world or the kindest?" The transcendent answer might *incorporate* the terms of the dialectic: "I would rather be famous for being kind."

2. The dialectic presents the following dilemma: "You are either for us or against us." The transcendent answer might *reject the terms* of the dialectic: "I am indifferent to you and your enemies."

3. The dialectic presents the following duality: "You are either a liberal or a conservative, and that is all there is to it." The transcendent answer might be generated by *denying* that polarity exists: "There are conservatives who believe in the bill of

rights as strongly as do liberals. And there are liberals who favor individual competition just like conservatives. The labels just don't stand up any more."

4. The dialectic presents the following conundrum: "To solve the budget crisis, you want to raise taxes but we want to cut spending." The transcendent answer might be generated using a *"pontificating third"*: "Let's rise above partisan bickering and do our civic duty."

CONCLUSION

Essentially, this chapter has been about how Kenneth Burke fused two brilliant theories of human nature with his own understanding of drama to create a potent rhetorical arsenal of theory building and textual criticism. Burke was fascinated with Freud's insights into the human psyche. He saw that in its tripartite nature there were unconscious elements that humans could not predict or control without the help of others. Freud believed that we could discover an authentic sense of self only in psychoanalysis, but that pieces of the unconscious often floated to the surface in dreams, in "Freudian slips," in word associations, and in symbology. These were clues to the psyche, inclusive of the call of conscience in the super-ego, the will to decide in the ego, and the urges in the id. This theory led Burke to his notions of "image clusters" as revealers of deeper motivations.

From Freud he also took the theory of identification in all of its deep-structured complexity to help explain why some speakers, playwrights, and artists are so effective. Burke showed that creators of discourse could be overwhelmingly persuasive if they understood that humans are seeking the object of their lost love. Sometimes audiences incline to the narcissistic, seeing in others the vision of their perfect past, present, or future. Sometimes audiences incline to the anaclitic, seeing in others care needers or caregivers. Effective persuaders also understand what Freud taught about the ability of the human mind to deceive itself with powerful strategies of sublimation, rationalization, projection, and the like.

Burke was also fascinated with Karl Marx's analysis of history. Marx believed that history was a dialectical battle of material forces. He grieved for those who were held down by a false consciousness created by inauthentic ideologies. He believed the truth could set these prisoners free and embraced a rational critique of society to achieve his ends. Burke converted the ideological criticism of Marx into a rhetoric of demystification. Burke used it to reveal the dialectic in persuasive and fictional works, and the motives that lie behind these works. He also realized that humans were not persuaded only rationally, and he was not as sanguine as Marx about the truth setting us free. Surely, Burke's "counter-statement" and his urging of critics to reveal motives were part of his Marxist agenda to end false consciousness, but Burke also saw the potential to create new dramas that made better sense of the world. This was the equipment for living that he gave us. As he aged, he moved closer and closer to the existential notion of inspiration. Those of us lucky enough to have been instructed by Burke found him much more tolerant than Marx because dramatism is open to more possibilities than is pure, rational truth.

Burke's pentadic analysis, his ability to write strikingly insightful assessments of speeches and literary works, and his theories of form, identification, and redefinition did more to advance rhetorical theory than any other thinker in our time. His passing at nearly a hundred years of age marked the end of a life devoted to finding better ways to persuade humans to talk to one another. Burke revealed once more how important rhetoric is to the construction of self and the world. He showed us that rhetoric can do more good than harm if we only realize its artistic potential.

Study Questions

1. Why is Burke's theory called "dramatistic"?

2. What is the difference between syllogistic and qualitative progression? Provide an example of each.

3. Exemplify "perspective by incongruity."

4. Provide rhetorical examples of the redemption or the rebirth cycle.

5. How does symbolic tension work dialectically to reinforce message?

6. Describe the dramatistic pentad. What is the importance of ratios?

7. What is the difference between consubstantial and substantial identification?

8. What is Burke's theory of definition?

9. What is the difference between the comic and tragic frame?

10. Use Burke's theory of redefinition to overcome a contemporary problem between two political parties.

Notes

[1] Kenneth Burke, *The Rhetoric of Religion: Studies in Logology* (Berkeley: U. of California Press, 1961/1970), p. vi.

[2] Ibid., pp. 38–40.

[3] For a look at Burkean theory see James W. Chesebro, ed., *Extensions of the Burkean System* (Tuscaloosa: U. of Alabama Press, 1993).

[4] Kenneth Burke, *Language as Symbolic Action* (Berkeley: U. of California Press, 1966), pp. 3–24.

[5] Burke was influenced in this regard by his friend Leon Adler, a proponent of Freud's methods. Freud, in turn, may have been influenced by Nietzsche. In *Daybreak* (1881) Nietzsche wrote: "To understand another person, that is, *to imitate his feelings in ourselves*, we do indeed often go back to the *reason* for his feeling this or thus and ask for example: *why* is he troubled?—so as then for the same reason to become troubled ourselves; but it is much more usual to omit to do this and instead produce the feeling in ourselves after the *effects* it exerts and displays on the other person by imitating with our own body the expression of his eyes, his voice, his walk, his bearing. . . . Then a similar feeling arises in us in consequence of an ancient association between movement and sensation," as quoted in Ronald Lehrer, *Nietzsche's Presence in Freud's Life and Thought: On the Origins of A Psychology of Dynamic Mental Functioning* (Albany: SUNY Press, 1995), pp. 38–39.

[6] Kenneth Burke, *Permanence and Change: An Anatomy of Purpose* (Indianapolis: Bobbs-Merrill, 1965), pp. 201–4.

[7] Sigmund Freud, *A General Introduction to Psychoanalysis* (New York: Pocket Books, 1952), pp. 433–34. Freud wrote, "Parental love, which is so moving and at bottom so childish, is nothing but the parents' narcissism born again, which, transformed in love-object, unmistakenly reveals its former nature." From "On Narcissism: An Introduction," in James Strachey, trans., *The Standard Edition of the Complete Works of Sigmund Freud*, vol. 14 (New York: Basic Books, 1956), p. 91. For a modern application and revision of Freud's position, see Alice Miller, *The Drama of the Gifted Child: The Search for Self*, R. Ward, trans. (New

York: Basic Books, 1982). She reforms Freud's theory of narcissism so that it is seen more as a continuum with anacliticism than as a separate category.

[8] See Bernard Brock, ed., *Kenneth Burke and Contemporary European Thought* (Tuscaloosa: U. of Alabama Press, 1995).

[9] Kenneth Burke, *Counter-Statement* (Berkeley: U. of California Press, 1931; reissue 1968), see particularly pp. 50–54.

[10] Hidden in the title are references to Parmenides, who you will recall explored what is permanent, and Heraclitus, who believed everything is in a state of change (see chapter 3 of this book.)

[11] Burke referred to these cloaks as "ethical wrappings." *Permanence and Change*, p. 191.

[12] This term was inspired by Burke's reading of Nietzsche, who advocated examining things from odd angles.

[13] *Permanence and Change*, p. 263.

[14] *Auscultation, Creation, and Revision* was eventually published in *Extensions of the Burkean System*, James Chesebro, ed. (Tuscaloosa: U. of Alabama Press, 1993), pp. 42–172.

[15] Ibid., p. 145.

[16] Ibid., p. 166.

[17] Kenneth Burke, *Attitudes toward History*, vol. I (New York: The New Republic, 1937), p. 348; Burke picks this theme up again in *The Grammar of Motives*. It would be interesting to add "attitude" to the pentad and make it a hextad as Burke once suggested in his seminar at UC Santa Barbara. He joked that he had created the pentad because he had five children and had he had one more, he wouldn't have made the mistake of leaving attitude out of his equation.

[18] This mix of Freudian and Marxist themes shows up often in Burke. Note this passage from *Rhetoric of Motives* (Berkeley: U. of California Press, 1968), p. 663: "Out of the seat came the womb, out of the womb came the child, out of the child came the enlightened division of labor, out of the division of labor came the hierarchy, and out of the hierarchy came the new goadings of social property."

[19] Burke develops the analysis of the language of hierarchies in part 3 of *A Rhetoric of Motives*. Anticipating Michel Foucault (see chapter 13 of this book), Burke sees hidden identification inside the levels of the various hierarchies he explores.

[20] See W. H. Rueckert, "Dramatism: Language as the Ultimate Reduction," in *Kenneth Burke and the Dawn of Human Relations*, W. H. Rueckert, ed. (Minneapolis: U. of Minnesota Press, 1963), pp. 128–63.

[21] Burke, *A Grammar of Motives*, p. 406.

[22] Burke, *The Rhetoric of Religion*.

[23] Ibid., pp. 4–5.

[24] Burke also wrote about frames of rejection such as burlesque and ridicule.

[25] Another study of the role of incongruity in humor can be found in J. Morreall, *The Philosophy of Laughter and Humor* (Albany: State U. of New York Press, 1987).

[26] Burke, *Attitudes toward History*, p. 44.

[27] Burke, *Language as Symbolic Action*, p. 16.

[28] Burke, *Attitudes toward History*, p. 171.

[29] Kenneth Burke, *The Philosophy of Literary Form: Studies in Symbolic Action* (New York: Random House, 1961), pp. 64, 293–304.

[30] See Burke, *Counter-Statement*, pp. 107, 112, 135, 146; *A Grammar of Motives and A Rhetoric of Motives*, pp. 608–11; *The Philosophy of Literary Form*, pp. 6–13, 28–31, 108.

[31] For more on how Burke's theory facilitates analysis of the role of materialism in discourse see Celeste M. Condit, "Post-Burke: Transcending the Substance of Dramatism," *Quarterly Journal of Speech*, 78 (1992): 349–55.

[32] Notice that determination reflects the Marxist strain in Burke's thinking.

[33] A. D. Weisman, *The Existential Core of Psychoanalysis: Reality, Sense and Responsibility* (Boston: Little, Brown, and Company, 1965), p. 183. Others who build on Freud's theory and clarify it include Mahler, *On Human Symbiosis . . .* , D. W. Winnicott, "The Theory of Parent-Infant Relationship," *International Journal of Psychoanalysis*, 41 (1960): 585–95, and H. Kohut, *The Analysis of Self* (New York: International U. Press, 1971).

[34] As Burke wrote, "The Freudian psyche is quite a parliament, with conflicting interests expressed in ways variously designed to take the claims of rival factions into account." *A Grammar of Motives and A Rhetoric of Motives*, p. 562.

[35] Ibid., p. 579.

[36] Burke's concern for this problem is demonstrated by the fact that he raises it in *A Grammar of Motives*, *Permanence and Change*, and *The Philosophy of Literary Form*.

[37] Burke relies heavily on Freud's book, *Totem and Taboo*, which explores the sanctions that cause guilt and the need for purgation.

[38] Burke, *Language as Symbolic Action*, p. 18.

[39] See Burke's *The Rhetoric of Religion*.

[40] Kenneth Burke, "The Rhetoric of Hitler's Battle," in *The Philosophy of Literary Form*, pp. 164–89.

[41] Jeffrey Gettleman, "Radical New York Councilman Aims to Shake City Up," *Los Angeles Times* (January 6, 2002): A20.

[42] Quotations from Jackson's speech are taken from a videotaping of the event.

[43] Burke, *A Rhetoric of Motives*, p. 21.

[44] As Weisman wrote, "The idealized person is usually an extension of our own ego image" (p. 191). Miller took the analysis a step further by arguing that the narcissistic wish for an "approval echo, understanding, and for being taken seriously" plays into the hands of the anaclitic, the caregiver (p. 24). Thus, the two may operate in communicative situations as symbiotic extremes on a continuum. Our ego can slide between the self-absorption of the narcissistic projection of self and the care needing/caregiving anaclitic projections of self and identifications.

[45] Sigmund Freud, *A General Selection from the Works of Sigmund Freud*, John Rickman, ed. (New York: Doubleday, 1957), p. 114.

[46] Burke, *Language as Symbolic Action*, p. 7; see also pp. 27–28.

[47] Calling them "troopers" is an important cue, as Burke would call it, that they are evil. The connotation of Nazi "storm troopers" is hard to miss.

[48] This is quite a contrast with the heroics of *Independence Day* where the Americans figure out how to get into the alien spaceship using Yankee ingenuity.

[49] Kenneth Burke, "Terministic Screens," in *The Rhetorical Tradition: Readings from Classical Times to the Present*, Patricia Bizzell and Bruce Herzberg, eds. (Boston: Bedford Books of St. Martin's Press, 1990), pp. 1034–41.

[50] Kathryn Olson, "The Controversy Over President Reagan's Visit to Bitburg: Strategies of Definition and Redefinition," *The Quarterly Journal of Speech*, 75 (1989): 131.

[51] See Thomas, p. 336, 339–40, for his comments on the "supernatural" nature of Burke's theory.

[52] Stephen Julian, "Advancing a Theory of Redefinition: An Examination of Pat Robertson's 1988 Presidential Campaign." Paper presented at the Annual Meeting of the Speech Communication Association, San Antonio, November, 1995.

[53] Kenneth Burke, *Attitudes Toward History*, pp. 3–4.

[54] Burke, *A Grammar of Motives and A Rhetoric of Motives*, p. 405.

[55] Burke, *Philosophy of Literary Form*, p. 52.

PART IV

Rhetoric in the Contemporary World

Occupy Wall Street demonstrator.

Context, Function, and Media

Capitalizing words in an e-mail message means you are shouting. Calling that little spot that shows up in URLs a "period" instead of a "dot" reveals that you are an Internet illiterate. This little combination of signs, :), in an e-mail or text message means, "I was just kidding," or "I'm happy," depending on context. Acronyms and text message shorthand are widely used wherever and however people communicate with each other online. The Internet, like every other new communication technology, has changed the way we communicate right down to the jot, title, backslash, and tilde. Because of the ever-changing nature of technology and the renewed interest in the study of public address, rhetorical theory continues to grow and change in the contemporary era. The goal of this chapter is to examine important technological and juridical theories, some of which build on the past and some of which explore new technologies of communication. For example, while the roots of I. A. Richards' theory can be found in Augustine's writings on signs and symbols, Richards reformulates semiotics into a broadcast model. Other theorists explored in this chapter use the judicial system, or some forum of argumentation, as their model for ideal communication in society. Chaim Perelman, Lucie Olbrechts-Tyteca, and Stephen Toulmin are very open about their debt to Aristotle and to modern jurisprudence. All three try to work out the problem that Aristotle raised: how to find a form of reason that will work in the real world—a place where, all things being equal, the truth will prevail.

Perhaps the most original thinker covered in this chapter, and certainly the boldest, is Marshall McLuhan, who built his theory around modern technology and argued in typical overstatement that "the medium is the message." His radical theory about how form (the medium) overwhelms substance (the message) is as relevant to cyberspace as it is to television to which he first applied it.

This chapter also provides some guides to the twentieth-century explosion in theory that will help students of rhetoric recognize new opportunities for theories offered by changing conditions, particularly in the way we communicate. We begin with a writer who linked rhetoric to semiotics and conclude with one who linked rhetoric to technology.

MEANING IN CONTEXT

Throughout this text we have encountered the concepts of contingency, connotation, and context. To review, contingency refers to the relative and probabilistic nature of our lives. Connotation refers to attributed meanings outside of the meaning given a word by dictionary writers. Context is the situation in which words are uttered. At times the various terms were celebrated as primary clues in the search for meaning. At other times they were relegated to barely a mention or denigrated as deceptive, emotional detours on the road to universal truths. Recent thinkers addressed many of the same concerns, resurrecting old issues and adding new interpretations.

Richards (1893–1979)

Ivorson A. Richards sought to match words (signs) with objects (referents) by pointing out how context, past experience, and cultural interference can corrupt or clarify meaning. His theory of rhetoric begins with Augustine's concern for signs and their epistemic value. Augustine's speculation was the most sophisticated early understanding of semiotics, defined as the study of something being taken as a sign.[1] Richards' semantic triangle echoed Augustine's discussion of semiotics. Richards compared (1) the *word* in the world to (2) the *referent* in the mind and to (3) the *object* in the world to which the word refers. He showed how the mind collects data, puts it in context, compares it to past experience, classifies it, and attaches meaning during the processing of data. Richards' goal (like that of Augustine, Francis Bacon, and John Locke, among others) was to study how misunderstandings occur and to provide remedies for such instances. At the same time, he updated Augustine's model by bringing it down to earth and having it reflect the broadcast model, complete with transmitter (speaker), receiver (audience), and channel (medium).

In *The Meaning of Meaning*, coauthored with C. K. Ogden in 1923, Richards compared radio broadcasts with the "source experience" in which a "selector" (tuner) perceived and encoded sensed data in the mind. This element of the model is drawn from Locke's theory of experience. The source experience (the *reference*) of the selector is the perception of some event, object, or piece of data that is taken into the mind. That experience becomes a message (a *referent*) when it is translated into signs, that is, given *signification*. It is signified (sign - ified) by words.

In an important step, Richards was quick to remind his readers that signs are interpreted in context; that is, words are not isolated. They are affected by the context into which they are uttered and out of which they are drawn. When I use the word Republican, it might evoke notions of individualism, freedom, and tax cutting in the context from which I draw it. But in your context, it might evoke notions of cutting Medicare, protecting states' rights, and/or curtailing deficit spending. Thus, interpretation of signs (hermeneutics) in context plays an important role in communication. (This is a theme we will explore further in the next chapter when we examine postmodern theory.)

Next, the message is transmitted through an environmental channel, where it could face interference (such as competing noise or diversion), to a receiver (the destination mind), who, if the process is effective, decodes the message and "develops" it into a source experience identical to the sender's. At the front end, source encoding uses sense, feeling, tone, and intention. At the back end of the communication process, the destination mind uses indicating (prompting a selection), characterizing (prompting a sorting), realizing (prompting an awakening), valuing (prompting a concern for something), influencing (prompting a change), controlling (managing, directing), and/or purposing (seeking, trying) in its effort to comprehend what is being transmitted.[2] The ideal situation results when the source experience, interpretation, and decoding result in the same message. For example, I see a beautiful white orchid. I want to tell you about it. So I encode it into the available signs in my brain—large, white, waxy, fan-shaped petals that look like an iris—then use those signs to broadcast the image of the orchid to your mind. Your mind then decodes the words, ideally without too much interference in transmission, putting exactly the right interpretation on them because of my cues, and the image of the white orchid appears in your mind.

Transmitting the image of a white orchid is somewhat complicated, but not nearly so complicated as an attempt to transmit one's sentiments regarding love, war, or justice, or Einstein's general theory of relativity. As we all know, accurate transmissions are rare because alignments between senders (speakers) and receivers (audiences) depend heavily on context. When I say to a friend, "I love you," meaning I love you like a brother, he may decode it to mean, "I love you sexually," which can lead to a serious misunderstanding. Based on his observations about context, Richards concluded that *meaning resides in the mind* and that scientific language is more clear in terms of being "symbolic" than rhetorical language because rhetoric is more emotive.[3]

Richards was born and educated in England, most significantly at Oxford, where he fell under the influence of G. E. Moore, a leading English philosopher of his day.[4] After graduating in 1915, Richards studied medicine. The tragedy of World War I prompted him to begin a study of how to improve communication between nations and indigenous peoples. He eventually became a professor of moral philosophy and literary criticism at Oxford. The influences on Richards were varied and help to explain his eventual solution to the problem of misunderstanding. For example, Charles Peirce, the leading semiotician of modern times, argued that the meaning of a word or proposition depends on the effect it has, not necessarily on what was intended. This hypothesis led Richards to examine context and connotation in meaning.

Bertrand Russell, who like Richards was influenced by G. E. Moore, attempted to take semiotics in a different direction when he developed his theory of "logical atomism." Russell's goal was to break meaning into its smallest atoms and then match those components with reality, a process he called "correspondence." He wrote that in a "logically perfect language the words in a proposition would correspond one by one with the components of the corresponding fact."[5] Components include particulars, predicates, and relations. If the elements cannot be verified in reality, he declared them to be meaningless. Accurate images, whether recalled from memory or created by the imagination, must be prototypes of reality. Russell wanted to prevent us from making inferences about the world based on the nature of language; instead he recommended working from reality back to language, much the way Locke did.

In collaboration with Alfred Whitehead, Russell attempted to reduce language to a mathematical logic in *Principia Mathematica* (1910–1913).[6] He believed mathematics could be understood through logic and logic could be symbolized through mathematics. This equation required that logic and mathematics be consistent. However, Kurt

Godel refuted this theory and exposed its paradoxes in his study *On Formally Undecidable Propositions of Principia Mathematica and Related Systems* (1931). Godel's work reawakened philosophers to the relative nature of language, including scientific and logical discourse.

I. A. Richards attempted to avoid the trap that ensnared Russell by substituting the contextual approach for the atomistic. *The Philosophy of Rhetoric* (1936) was based on a series of Richards' lectures, which studied misunderstanding and its remedies. He sought to avoid the "Proper Meaning Superstition" in which we believe that words have precise and fixed meanings. He also sought to avoid the "Proper Usage Superstition" in which we believe that there is a correct use for every word. The antidote was his "Context Theorem of Meaning," which was supposed to prevent improper readings and baseless assumptions about meaning. People need to understand that words do not stand alone, nor does their usage. Words are contextual, and the context is in the mind of the sender (speaker) and the receiver (listener). Unless there is some sort of close match, miscommunication will occur. Thus, *connotative meaning* becomes almost as important as denotative meaning, and audience analysis becomes crucial to deciphering the *context of associations* with words used. For these reasons, Richards' theory is rhetorical at its core. Context creates meaning.

Denotative meaning refers to dictionary definitions of "correct" usage. Connotative meaning refers to the meanings a word has collected over time in the consciousness of a person, group, or culture. It is an associated signification that is often implied by the use of the word. The denotative meaning of "salt" is sodium chloride, often used to season or preserve food, harvested from sea water or underground mines. The connotative meaning of "salt" includes basic goodness or humility, as in "you are the salt of the earth," or spicy language, as in, "That sailor is a little salty with his language." The denotative meaning of "yellow" is the color on the spectrum that resembles the skin of ripe lemons. The connotative meaning includes cowardice, since the liver was thought to produce courage; those with liver disease turned yellow.

Context is particularly important in oral communication since you cannot see the words that are being spoken. If I say, "Let's take that tern," you can't see the spelling of the word "tern," meaning a sea bird. Instead you might hear "turn," which gives a different meaning to the sentence. On a beach where I point to a bird, the context will more likely produce the proper meaning in the mind of the receiver.

Richards hoped this "new rhetoric" would help to prevent conflict and improve communication at all levels, whether intrapersonal, interpersonal, or mass communication. By making sure people understood the slippery nature of meaning, he hoped to force them to pay more attention to the impact of context, perception, and connotation in language. He advised that we be sure we understand what was *meant* before we act on what we *heard*.

Perelman (1912–1984) and Olbrechts-Tyteca (1899–1988)

Chaim Perelman and Lucie Olbrechts-Tyteca sought to resurrect the "practical reasoning" of Aristotle, particularly as described in his *Topics*. This rhetorical argumentation is more useful in the contingent world of probabilities than in the scientific, mathematical, or formal worlds of scholasticism. In his early work and in his later collaboration with Olbrechts-Tyteca,[7] Perelman consistently found that the rules of logic that were valid in the objective world of science were inadequate to the world of politics, philosophy, jurisprudence, and the arts.

Lucie Olbrechts-Tyteca was born in Belgium and educated in liberal arts at the University of Brussels. She later studied the rhetoric used by advocates, including lawyers, judges, and campaigners. A book on figures of speech by Jean Paulhan, who relied on the Florentine humanist Bruno Latini (see chapter 7 of this book), helped her further classify the arguments with which she was dealing.[8] The connection to Latini led her back to Cicero and Aristotle. These humanistic interests led her to collaborate with Perelman starting in 1948. She later wrote a book of her own, *Le comique du discours* (1974).

Born in Warsaw, Poland, Perelman moved with his family to Belgium and did his college work there. He received a law degree in 1934 and a doctorate of philosophy in 1938 from Free University in Brussels. During World War II, he formed the Committee for the Defense of the Jews and was forced to go underground. He fought for the resistance movement against the Nazis. The failure of negotiations, resulting in the war, partially motivated his desire for improved communication. In an essay, "The Rule of Justice," he explained that he sought a way to reach agreement without recourse to violence.[9] In the case of foreign policy and much of the law, formal logical demonstration proved useless. Thus, he used a judicial model to create a "nonformal logic" as a counterpart to formal logical demonstration. This theory of rhetoric had an immediate impact on departments of speech communication in the United States. Beginning at Pennsylvania State University in 1962, Perelman popularized his work by lecturing across the United States, where he was surprised to find a whole discipline devoted to the new rhetoric.[10]

His book with Olbrechts-Tyteca, *The New Rhetoric: A Treatise on Argumentation* (1958), pays homage to the early Greeks and Romans. Perelman and Olbrechts-Tyteca relied heavily on the differences between Aristotle's formal logic ("demonstration") and his more probabilistic approach ("argumentation"). The authors' retrieval of practical argumentation studies the arguments of various advocates in real-life contexts. Sixty-five procedures of practical argumentation are deduced from this empirical study. It draws a clear line between argumentation, which often must rely on probability and gathered evidence, and formal proof, which is based on scientific evidence or definitional premises. In other words, the book looks at argument as an artistic mode of proof addressed to an audience, whether that be a campaign rally, a classroom, or a jury.[11]

Argumentation is often ambiguous and personal, while demonstration is mathematical, impersonal, axiomatic, and certain. Demonstration is defined as a "calculation made in accordance with the rules that have been laid down beforehand."[12] Argumentation is defined as "the study of the discursive techniques that induce or increase the mind's *adherence* to the theses presented for its assent."[13] Speakers try to *transfer* the belief that audiences have in primary premises to the premises the speaker proposes. This requires making the various premises *present for the audience*. Generally, we pay attention to that which is most vivid to us. Hence, style becomes important to the Belgians' theory, not only because tropes and figures can be seen as structures of thought and new ways of arguing, but also because they can *make an argument more vivid and hence more present for an audience*.[14] To put it another way, to feature one argument or premise is to marginalize another.

We now know from scientific study that the human mind does not literally multi-task; instead it toggles from task to task and/or moves along in serial fashion. Since speakers are consistently jockeying for our attention and seeking endorsement for their views, it is important that they understand the techniques of making their arguments *present* for the chosen audience, that is, getting an audience to toggle to their argument instead of someone else's. This can be done by making the argument more fascinating with tropes and/or figures. For example, in his inaugural address, Pope Benedict XVI combined identification with repetition to create presence in his argument: "I do not have to carry alone what in truth I could never carry alone. All the saints of God are there to protect me, to sustain me and to carry me. And your prayers, my dear friends, your indulgence, your love, your faith and your hope accompany me." Perelman in his book *The Realm of Rhetoric* (1982) assigned to rhetoric alone the art of creating presence. Rhetoric calls things in a given symbolic landscape to our attention; it causes us to focus on something we might have otherwise ignored.

The New Rhetoric is divided into three sections. The first seventy pages covers the "framework" for a rhetorical approach to argumentation and lays out a rationale for this approach based on the court model. In this section, Perelman and Olbrechts-Tyteca set out their theory of audiences, which includes a universal and an actual audience. The *universal audience* is the one that philosophers claim they address; it is the standard by which most claims and arguments are assessed. It is educated and has reached a consensus on certain rules of procedure and standards of evidence and argument. The *actual audience* is the one orators carve out in an attempt to gain adherence to their ideas. It is the audience for which speakers must make their arguments present; that often means using stylistic devices such as tropes and figures. A metaphor can bring an argument into the foreground of the actual audience's consciousness, where it is then given careful consideration. If the argument is not encapsulated into a metaphor, it might not be considered at all. When the president tells the world that Iran, Iraq, and North Korea have formed an "axis of evil," many may disagree, but first they are forced to confront the dramatic metaphor.

The actual audience is also the audience for which the speaker may perform a "dissociation of notions," taking what the audience assumes is a unified concept and breaking it into separate parts, entities, or ideas. For example, juries often think of murder as a unified concept; the accused either did or did not commit a murder. However, defense lawyers often seek to dissociate murder into the facts of the crime and the motive for the crime, or the act of killing versus a justification for the killing, such as self-defense or insanity. Like Toulmin (see below), in this instance Perelman and Olbrechts-Tyteca examined the *function* of argument as opposed to its style or form. For example, dissociation creates a different set of questions for the court than the unified concept. Guilt or innocence moves from, "did the criminal commit the murder?" to, "did the criminal have a legitimate reason for committing the act?"

They also provided guidelines for a comparison of the two audiences. The orator must understand to what degree the actual audience embodies the potential universal one. The universal audience is built on consensus about objective fact, while the actual audience seeks knowledge, needs to be informed, and will then align itself with the universal audience, under ideal circumstances.[15] The universal audience sets the standard for conviction (certainty) because it is the idealized version of who should decide the issues at hand. The universal audience is composed of reasonable persons (a standard of appeal often cited in court decisions) who understand what kinds of evidence are irrefutable and what values are universal. The actual audience sets the standard for persuasion in the particular rhetorical situation at hand. To put it another way, the speech to a universal audience should convince the best minds of what is true; the speech to an actual audience should persuade those addressed of what is likely to be true and provide any information they need to reach that conclusion.

One subset of the actual audience is the *composite audience*, which consists of different groups in the same audience or different audiences for the same speech.[16] When a presidential candidate delivers an acceptance of the nomination at the party convention, he or she addresses the delegates, the visitors in the gallery, the news media, the national audience, and various international audiences. This concept is useful in the contemporary world because, with modern technology, it is often the case that world leaders address a local audience and that media then carry their speeches to other audiences around the globe. Thus, construction of the actual audience can be quite complicated.

The second section of *The New Rhetoric* covers the starting points of argument by examining the common grounds and justifications audiences accept when they embrace a position. Various kinds of premises are examined in terms of their ability to generate "adherence" or agreement. These are then used to perform the transfer of belief to new premises that the speaker subsequently introduces. Perelman and Olbrechts-Tyteca labeled the values *loci* that arrange other values into hierarchies.[17] Using "starting points" derived from *loci*, a speaker may transfer the adherence gained from primary premises to secondary ones introduced to persuade the audience to new positions or to reinforce positions already held. The *loci* create "liaisons" between premises and the conclusions the speaker wishes the audience to draw. That is to say, *loci* are part of the process of moving from evidence to claims or from accepted premises to claims. The accepted or common *loci* get the audience from the evidence to the conclusion. The problem for the advocate is to figure out what *loci* the audience favor. The universal audience for any argument would possess all the knowledge necessary to understand it; however, the actual audience may not have the expertise to understand the argument as constructed or accept the *loci* of the speaker. Thus, the speaker may have to educate the audience by edifying them of new *loci* so that the proper liaisons will be there for the speaker to lead his or her audience to the proper conclusion. Recalling Aristotle's *topoi*, common places, and topics, Perelman and Olbrechts-Tyteca examine the most common *loci*, such as quantity (the more years something lasts, the better it is; the more people vote for a candidate, the better the candidate is) in their quest to create "practical reasoning." Once the *loci* of advocacy are established, the speaker can create a "web of arguments" in which to ensnare the audience and gain adherence.

The *loci* can be viewed as starting points for building this web. In a legal case, a lawyer may try to move from legal *loci*, such as definition of a crime, to moral *loci*, such as mercy, and then transfer the associated values to the audience. The *loci* of the *noumenal* world (see Plato) transfer values of perfection and transcendence; the *loci* of the phenomenal world transfer values of materialism, objectivism, and sensuality. The *loci* of nature might transfer values of survival and ecology, while the *loci* of technology might transfer values of progress and efficiency.

However, the *loci* can also be used to achieve a "dissociation of concepts" in which arguers separate certain "appearances" from notions so that they become incongruous with the audience's experience or values.[18] A speaker might separate an unpleasant or incongruous appearance in order to make his or her argument more acceptable to an audience, and a speaker might integrate an unpleasant or incongruous appearance with the argument of his or her adversary to attack the argument. Those in favor of a woman's right to abortion often dissociate the notion of "abortion" from the appearance of killing and associate it with the appearance of free choice; they are "pro-choice." The reverse is true for those who oppose a woman's right to abortion; they are for "the right to life."

The third section of *The New Rhetoric* explores the techniques of rhetorical argumentation, including how tropes and figures (see chapter 5 of this book) can be used to gain the adherence of an audience by bringing the speaker's argument into focus, making it present for the audience. The value of these tropes and figures is determined in a pragmatic way: they are useful to the extent that they persuade an audience. Thus, the use of analogy before an audience of formal logicians would probably prove ineffective because formal logicians view the use of analogy with suspicion. However, the same form of argument is regularly used in campus lectures, around the dinner table, and before the Supreme Court. For example, the Supreme Court often uses metaphors—such as references to the "chilling effect" on free speech or the "pig in the parlor" for zoning regulations, or the "slippery slope" to the loss of civil rights—to render its decisions more persuasive.

Perelman and Olbrechts-Tyteca intimated that philosophy is a province of rhetoric because philosophy cannot live by formal logic alone, and philosophical argument is highly dependent on the audience to which it is addressed. Furthermore, they claimed that philosophers such as René Descartes, G. W. F. Hegel, and Immanuel Kant created false dichotomies, separating humans into faculties and logic into a restricted formalism that often imitates the axioms and theorems of geometry. Worse yet, philosophers such as David Hume and Bertrand Russell embraced either skepticism or a positivism that eliminated value judgments from their systems of formal logic. Instead, philosophers must learn to reason practically and rhetorically: "[I]t is in terms of an audience that an argumentation develops."[19] In his "Reflections on Justice" (1951), Perelman wrote, "Every metaphysician must furnish reasons for the superiority of his system and, so long as his system is not admitted, he can only resort to the processes of rhetorical argumentation."[20] The audience determines the acceptability and the ethical quality of the arguments made.

Speakers and/or speech critics can use the universal audience to help in the selection and/or evaluation of arguments, appeals, tropes, and figures. *The New Rhetoric* instructs that tropes and figures must advance an argument and must not be detected as literary devices if they are to prove effective. It cites *antimetabole* for its example. In this type of figure, a reversal is used for emphasis, for example, "You may be born in the ghetto but the ghetto is not born in you." Not all uses of this device are effective. For example, politicians often claim, "I say what I mean, and I mean what I say." While appealing as a clever manipulation of words and often rhythmically mellifluous, the literary device does not advance any particular understanding.

Perelman and Olbrechts-Tyteca introduced the language of contingency into their system to allow the restoration of the "humanistic tradition" and the development of a new set of *loci* that "supply reasons for preferring one type of behavior to another."[21] For example, both loyalty and truth are values, but in different circumstances one is more important than the other. Loyalty is more important than truth in survival situations; truth is more important than loyalty in legal situations. The *loci* of the universal audience help speakers work out these priorities in any given situation: "each individual, each culture, has thus its own conception of the universal audience."[22] Particular conceptions are based on which values are used to structure other values; that is, certain values have priority and set priorities. Furthermore, their system identifies ways to display "certain elements on which the speaker wishes to center attention in order that they may occupy the foreground of the hearer's consciousness."[23]

When put into effect, these concepts help speakers determine who should constitute their audience. For example, when Daniel Webster rose in the Senate in 1850 to defend compromise legislation, he knew that abolitionists were unalterably opposed to his position, as were hard-line Southern states' rights advocates. So he carved these two groups away from his actual audience by criticizing their inflexibility in sarcastic and metaphorical language. Attempting to convert entrenched opponents to his point

Daniel Webster speaking to the Senate.

of view would have been futile; time was better spent on building a consensus among an actual audience open to persuasion. Webster's success was due at least in part to his strategic understanding of audience construction.

While Perelman and Olbrechts-Tyteca were developing their theory on the European continent, Stephen Toulmin was publishing a treatise that would directly confront the logicians of England. Like the Belgians, he used jurisprudence as the basis for his theory of argumentation and grounded it in "field theory." That is to say, the specific audience addressed and its level of expertise are critical factors in Toulmin's theory of argumentation. All three theorists believe that rhetorical reasoning not only finds truth and error but rationalizes and justifies various claims.

Toulmin (1922–2009)

In the same year that the Belgians published *The New Rhetoric*, Stephen Toulmin was turning the syllogism on its side and exploring the backing for enthymemes (see chapter 4 of this book), also known as rhetorical syllogisms, in his *Uses of Argument* (1958), which was introduced in the United States by Wayne Brockriede and Douglas Ehninger in their text on debate. Toulmin had been educated at Cambridge in England, where he studied science and math. The Second World War interrupted his studies when he went to work for the air ministry, but he finished his doctorate in 1948, out of which came his first book, *An Examination of the Place of Reason in Ethics*. It was roundly ridiculed in philosophical circles and was unattractive to rhetoricians because it equated rhetoric with emotional statements.

Perelman and Olbrechts-Tyteca were interested in bridging the chasm between logic and rhetoric that had been created by Ramus and Descartes. By the late fifties,

Stephen Toulmin.

Toulmin wanted to follow that lead because he believed the philosophy of reasoning had become so isolated it was useless. He introduced his functional theory of argumentation by calling it *generalized jurisprudence:* "Arguments can be compared with lawsuits, and the claims we make and argue for in extra-legal contexts with claims made in the courts, while the cases we present in making good each kind of claim can be compared with each other."[24] In this way, Toulmin mounted a major attack on Cartesian rationalists, argumentative idealists, and mathematical logicians such as Bertrand Russell.

He went on to develop a field theory of argument. Formal arguments and universal tactics are usually field invariant; that is, they are usable in many contexts and across many fields. Lesser forms, specialized methodologies, and content are often field dependent; that is, they are credible only in their own disciplines or they operate from rules and conventions that are indigenous to certain fields.[25] The laws of contradiction and fallacy are generally *field invariant;* they are true in almost any context among reasonable people. Whether you are arguing before a judge or a scientific committee, an object cannot be in two places at the same time, and two objects cannot occupy the same space at the same time. (For another view, see the discussion of quantum theory in chapter 13 of this book.) However, the methods of determining the truth may differ vastly among chemists, children, historians, lawyers, and politicians; thus, their means of arguing and their premises are *field variant*. What works for the courts may not work in the laboratory, and vice versa. For example, while psychiatrists believe in recovered memories as accurate accounts of the past, these memories are not acceptable in a court of law if they were induced under hypnosis. The findings of social scientists (for example, that violence begets violence) carry less weight in courts of law than the findings of physical scientists (for example, DNA identifications).

Toulmin's key discovery was that the *warrant* for most reasoning through dialectic is usually a suppressed premise drawn from the common *topoi* of convention within a given field. The warrant operates much like Perelman's and Olbrechts-Tyteca's *loci* or Aristotle's *topoi*. It provides a bridge from the data to the claim. If the warrant (often the major premise) or the data (often the minor premise) were to need support, then "backing" would be provided from the field for which the argument was made.[26] Thus, sources are acceptable in arguments if they are *credible* within a particular field; evidence can prove an argument only if it is acceptable within that field.[27] This move roots argumentation in rhetoric because these fields reside in audiences who determine the acceptability of evidence and arguments.[28] The system is audience-based and can be schematized this way:

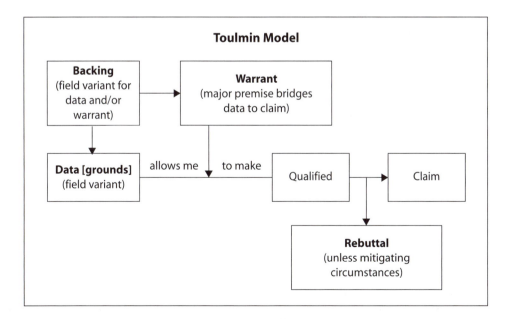

Deconstruction of an argument using this scheme is not difficult. Let's begin with a paragraph and then diagram it.

> The fact that Osama bin Laden had a history of fomenting terrorism indicates that he probably was the mastermind behind the attack on New York City's Twin Towers and the Pentagon in Washington, DC, unless someone else confesses to the crime. Every mastermind terrorist I know favors attacks on large buildings as the means of terrorizing people and demoralizing nations. In any case, records retrieved after his assassination indicate that he sent the terrorists to the United States. Associates of bin Laden that have been captured attest to his involvement in the planning of the attack.

The paragraph can be reformulated into Toulmin's model this way:

Data: The fact that Osama bin Laden had a history of fomenting terrorism indicates that

Claim: he probably *(Qualifier)* was the mastermind

Rebuttal: unless someone else confesses to the crime.

Warrant: Those with a history of fomenting terrorism are more likely to be guilty of terrorist acts than those who do not have such a history.

Backing for Warrant: Every mastermind terrorist I know favors attacks on large buildings as the means of terrorizing people and demoralizing nations.

Backing for Data: Records retrieved after his assassination indicate that he sent the terrorists to the United States. Associates of bin Laden that have been captured attest to his involvement in the planning of the attack.

Notice that these labels are derived not from truth value, or validity, but from the *function each phrase performs in the argument.* One phrase *backs* another one; another phrase allows the speaker to draw a *warranted* conclusion from phrases that function as *data.*

Toulmin's position is a major attack on formal logic, which is field invariant.[29] To Toulmin, formal logic is "static" and stereotypical.[30] Most importantly, he realized that it cannot reflect pragmatic realities, nor does it lay out the *functions* of propositions in real-world ways.[31] That which varies by field, formal logic rejects. As Toulmin made clear, the formal logic of Russell and his followers in science is what Aristotle called "analytics." Toulmin is even critical of scientist Thomas Kuhn, upon whom some postmodernists rely.[32] As we have seen, medieval thinkers such as Aquinas called analytic logic "demonstration." Their rejection of probability, opinion, morals, and function meant that formal logic is unable to consider the most important matters of the subjective, existential realm. What a logical positivist may call meaningless may be the most important question in the world to the person posing it. Thus, the debate between the rhetorical argumentation theorists and the positivist-formalists returns us to Aristotle's important conception of rhetoric as the counterpart of dialectic.

Like Aristotle, Toulmin believed that formal logic is insufficient to deal with the contingencies of the real world. Thus, rhetorical logic—the enthymeme, for instance—must stand in its stead. Toulmin created a system for the analysis of argument based on probable, not necessarily true, premises. He included qualifiers (probably, most, some, many, at the .05 level of significance) and rebuttals (unless, although) in his functional analysis of argument, thereby creating a model much more reflective of the real world than we find in the writings of the formalists and the positivists: "A radical re-ordering of logical theory is needed in order to bring it more nearly into line with critical practice."[33]

Toulmin converted argumentation into a rhetorical process, and in so doing strengthened the rhetorical arsenal upon which we can rely to reconstruct our lives and our world:

> By making explicit the arguments underlying [a human's] conceptual ambitions and dissatisfactions, we bring to light [the] epistemic self-portrait; the particular picture of human beings as active intelligences. . . . The general problem of human understanding is, in fact, to draw an epistemic self-portrait that is both well-founded and trustworthy; which is effective because its theoretical base is realistic, and which is realistic because its practical applications are effective.[34]

Argumentation gives us a way of making a case for ourselves, of defending our decisions, of reaching our decisions.[35] Toulmin gives us a way of checking the functions the argumentative phrases serve.

MEDIATED RHETORIC IN THE CONTEMPORARY ERA

To this point, we have treated rhetoric in relation to its audience and thereby its culture and its philosophical environment. With the exception of printing texts in the vernacular of the audience, and Richards' broadcast model, we have not taken a close look at the relationship between new forms of communication and rhetorical theory. In no century did forms of media evolve so quickly as in the twentieth. This evolution began with the first radio transmission in 1906 and ended with the Internet explosion, digital high-definition television, interactive cable systems available over fiber-optic phone lines, and communication transmissions via satellites. These various media have significantly changed our lives. Telephone, radio, television, Internet, cable, smart phones, and tablets have made the world into what Marshall McLuhan called a "global village." Speakers now address multiple audiences, many of whom are unknown to the speakers. When William Jennings Bryan addressed the Democratic Convention of 1896, he sent attendees into a frenzy and emerged the surprise nominee of the party the next day. Yet, the nation did not hear about those events until they were reported in the newspaper. Today, convention speeches are instantaneously beamed not only to the nation but to the world. YouTube captures statements, mistakes, and successes as quickly as they occur. The change in public address is obvious. Speakers must adjust to a vast audience. In many cases, that means using the "least common denominator" approach: offend as few as possible, assemble a majority.

As mentioned earlier, McLuhan highlighted a significant development—the medium itself transforms a message. The acceptance speeches of major political candidates at conventions provide excellent examples. Remember that the networks receive the texts of the speeches in advance; network personnel can choose to keep the camera on the speaker for the duration of the speech, a tactic most likely to be taken by C-SPAN. Alternately, a network can reinforce and enliven what the speaker is saying by showing pictures of audience members weeping, laughing, or cheering. If the speaker mentions children, a television camera focuses on a child. If the speaker mentions women, a television camera focuses on a woman. A network, however, can undercut the impact of a speech by showing images that are unfavorable to a speaker—the yawning member of Congress at the State of the Union address, the delegate at the convention wearing the silly hat. In short, the editorial options available to broadcasters have a rhetorical impact on audiences beyond what the content and delivery of the speech alone would have. Transmitted globally, the images chosen by broadcasters and bloggers can have enormous consequences for a political campaign.

Technological changes in the media have even resulted in changes in political careers. For example, black-and-white television with its cathode-ray tube revealed the dark stubble under Richard Nixon's first layer of skin in his 1960 debates with John Kennedy. Nixon looked like he had a constant five o'clock shadow, a visage of evil to some. Color television using different technology did not present the same image; it was one of the many factors contributing to Nixon's political comeback in 1968. Would the candidacy of the very fluent Bill Clinton have been as successful without the use of talk shows, MTV interviews, and previously unknown venues of public speaking? Would the Republican presidential race have ended more quickly and would the eventual outcome have been different in 2012 without the nineteen debates preceding the primary in Florida?

The personal computer, with its access to the World Wide Web, has increased independent contracting, work in the home, telecommuting, and desocialization as a large number of computer users turn their work stations into fortresses of isolation. Yet, a high percentage of these people vote; therefore, contemporary politicians need to reach them. Hence, every major political candidate now has a home page on the Internet and appeals to voters through social media, which has become a forum for dialogue among individuals, organizations, and communities. Social media played a crucial role in coordinating demonstrations and messages during the Arab Spring of 2011 and the attacks on American embassies in the late summer of 2012. Furthermore, it allows pictures, videos, and commentary to be seen by millions of people all over the world.

The investigation of the impact of new media on rhetoric is a major area of research in the field. One of the pioneers in that venture was Marshall McLuhan, who was the first to see the potential for the media to influence the message in major ways.

McLuhan (1911–1980)

While many writers see technology as an alienating force in our lives, Herbert Marshall McLuhan believed that the electronic media extended humans and provided them with new sources of energy. McLuhan's distinguished career began with teaching at the University of Wisconsin (1936–1937) and St. Louis University (1937–1944). He received his doctorate from Cambridge University in 1942. He taught at Assumption University (1944–1946) before finally settling at St. Michael's College of the University of Toronto from 1946 until his death. When he had established his reputation, he did take a year off to fill the Albert Schweitzer Chair of Humanities at Fordham University for the 1967–1968 academic year, which gave him access to the media in New York City and helped popularize his theories.

McLuhan's most famous work, *Understanding Media: The Extensions of Man* (1964), traced the development of literacy in broad strokes, positing a determinism whereby particular technological developments alter the nature of human understanding.[36] The book begins with the preliterary period of myth, when orality was the only means of contact. Memorization, rituals, stories, and intimate participation in communal life provided the bonds for people in small villages. The tribe socialized all of the human senses: the smell from the fire, the touch of the hunt, the vision of the ceremony, the sound of the drum, and the taste of the communal meal.

Tribalism was severely eroded by the development of language, writing, and then printing. Books could be read alone, plus they provided links to a world outside of the village. Printing reduced the sense of tribe and in the process began to isolate human senses by emphasizing the mind. According to McLuhan, humans assumed a linear orientation—much like the sentence progressing across the page. We began to look for a "line of thought," to see whether an argument "follows from" the one preceding it. Humans became wedded to the notion of progress (moving forward), particularly measured by wealth, scientific discovery, and the development of new technology. Linearity became omnipresent: we work on assembly lines; cutting in a line is a sin.

The dominance of print began to wane with the arrival of new technology. The telephone and radio offered alternatives to written communication. The isolating aspects of reading the printed word could be replaced with shared listening to radio broadcasts and eventually television and other electronic media. The contemporary period with its heavy reliance on telecommunication is, according to McLuhan, eroding nationalism and moving us toward a "global village" with a meta-tribalism. McLuhan saw the rise of globalism long before other thinkers, perhaps because he was a devout Catholic, and therefore a member of a "universal" church.[37] Class distinctions dissolve when the rich and the poor enjoy the same programming on television, although various subaudiences may develop. McLuhan claimed, "With TV came the end of bloc voting in politics, a form of specialization and fragmentation that won't work since TV. Instead of the voting bloc, we have the icon, the inclusive image."[38] McLuhan believed that John Kennedy's successful run for the presidency in 1960 proved that icons can break down voting blocs. Ronald Reagan's, Bill Clinton's, and Barack Obama's abilities to attract voters from the opposition party provide more recent examples of this phenomenon.

McLuhan claimed that media alter the environment, which in turn causes different balances between sense perceptions:[39] "The extension of any one sense alters the way we think and act—the way we perceive the world. When these ratios change, men change."[40] The dominant medium of an age determines the balance between, for example, seeing and hearing. In the process, how and what we perceive is affected.

Print media elevated the visual senses and emphasized linear sequences. However, telecommunication has eroded linear thinking. Demonstrating the influence of his mentor Harold Innis, McLuhan argued that the reason many children have trouble reading is because they are organized for more sense participation by the electronic media than children who were raised in the print environment. Electronic media present patterns of dots or pixels instead of lines of words, which explains the desire for more graphics and less linearity on the Internet. Extending his analysis, McLuhan saw the electronic age and its ability to overwhelm the audience with endless images as erasing the Western tendency to classify and categorize. Rather, the overload of

instant communication requires the ability to reorganize patterns and to shift attention constantly. There is no time for linear sequencing and reflexivity.

The power of the medium to influence how we perceive and how we organize our
thinking led McLuhan to conclude somewhat hyperbolically that "the medium is the
message." What he meant, as he revealed in subsequent interviews, was that each new
medium is like a new language and, therefore, has a significant impact on the messages it carries.[41] Television, for example, emphasizes a quality picture and professional behavior. Speakers who fail to meet these standards will offend the viewing
public no matter what their message is. The stumbling sportscaster, the bumbling
anchorperson, and the inarticulate candidate have very short careers on television.[42]

The medium is also the message because most messages are really composed of
something else; that is, most messages are media themselves. Printed words are really
marks on a page; television is transmitted in pixels; newsprint pictures are a collection
of dots; speech is vibrations in the air. McLuhan divided media according to the sen-
sory data involved. He defined print as a "hot medium" because it extends a single
sense in high definition; that is, it fills in all the blanks with its description and argumentation, and relies mainly on sight to convey its message. The audience is not expected to
fill in much; *hot media require little participation*. Most novels qualify as hot because they
do a good deal of describing, and they provide detailed conversations that advance the
plot. "Cool media" extend several senses and do not fill in all the needed data. McLuhan used black-and-white television as his example of a cool medium; it appeals to
sight, hearing, and what he calls "tactility," the perceptual activity of the brain that connects the mosaic of dots on the television picture tube.[43] *Cool media require a high degree of
participation*. To make the difference between hot and cool media clear, McLuhan provided a number of comparisons. The cartoon is cool; the color photograph is hot. The
telephone is cool; the radio is hot. Television is cool; motion pictures are hot.[44] A seminar is cool; a lecture is hot. Thus, since McLuhan's time we have moved from low-defi-
nition black-and-white television to high-definition color television.

Furthermore, McLuhan argued that careful study would lead one to conclude
that certain themes are expressed better on one medium than another. Each medium
communicates in a unique way that may be more compatible with one message than
another. For example, we say that a picture is worth a thousand words. However,
radio blinds me to pictures, so they would be more suitable to television. However, if I
wish a reader to study and reflect upon my words, an editorial commentary or blog
might be a better medium for my message because the readers can take time with it,
read it at their own pace, and reconsider it.

Such a simple system is open to some criticism and correction. For example,
since a cool medium requires more mental participation, it is more inclusive or engaging. Since a hot medium requires less mental participation, it is less inclusive and less
engaging. The hotter the medium, the less chance for favorable or unfavorable distortion; the cooler the medium, the greater chance of distortion. Although McLuhan saw
radio as a hot medium because it provided high definition for the ear, it can be seen
also as a cool medium for the eye, where no sense data are provided—allowing for
imaginative participation in creating visual images quite impossible with television.
Politicians who face hostile audiences should address them directly and personally if
possible in the hottest medium to prevent negative distortion; politicians who have

Marshall McLuhan.

friendly followings should address them using the coolest medium in order to induce participation and to enhance their favorable image.

McLuhan referred to audience distortion as a "Freudian censor . . . which protects our central system of values" while also filtering material, or "cooling" what we perceive, so that we do not get "stressed out" from semantic overload.[45] Certainly, Americans who heard the fireside chats of Franklin Roosevelt on the radio did not "see" him as he actually was—sitting behind a desk speaking into a microphone. They *imagined* him sitting in a rocker by his fireside, speaking to them from his heart. In his 1968 and 1972 runs for the presidency, Richard Nixon made extensive use of radio both for speeches and advertisements because he had a good radio voice and did not want his image to get in the way of his positive perception, particularly on the issues, as measured by opinion polls.[46]

The implications of this theory for advertising are many. Certain products that have indelicate connotations (for example, deodorants, fungicides, or condoms) can be "warmed up" by placing them in contexts that are more attractive on various hot media. "Cooling down" an image might induce more participation and hence identification with the product. Icons, or trademarks, such as Pepsi-Cola's yin-yang in red and blue or Nike's swoosh, are cool because they require the viewer to fill in data to make the proper associations.

New work in the field of rhetoric on memorialization might also benefit from an infusion of McLuhanesque theory.[47] For example, the Lincoln Memorial in Washington, DC, might be seen as hot because it presents a larger-than-life Lincoln sitting in a well-defined chair surrounded by his greatest quotations. Not much is required from the observer, who would thus be less engaged and somewhat excluded. On the contrary, the Washington memorial is a simple, large obelisk with no reference to the first president on it. Its coolness requires mental participation to figure out how the stone monument represents George Washington. In this way, it is engaging and inclusive.

McLuhan's statements that the medium *determines* how perceptions are formed may be overstated, but he did focus attention on mediated reality. Whether form completely discounts content is debatable, but McLuhan's focus on form did open new avenues of exploration and suggested new aspects of context. Does information learned from a radio broadcast (aural context) differ from information learned from a magazine (visual context)? The phrase "the medium is the message" was sometimes altered to "the medium is the m*a*ssage." Do the media envelop us, manipulate our perceptions, and ease images into our consciousness? Does the capability of reaching large numbers of people—in different geographic locations, with varying levels of education, and from diverse socioeconomic groups—level some of those distinctions? What is filtered in or out of the images presented? How does the selection of a medium alter the credibility of the message? The proliferating media options available today are sufficiently influential to warrant a critical examination of the relationship between rhetoric and the media.

Anyone who has watched a televised presidential debate and then listened to the media coverage of it knows that there is great deal of distortion between the actual event and what gets reported. The news media present sound bites from the debates that they categorize as newsworthy—that is, dramatic, humorous, or attention getting. In 2008, Americans heard sound bites from speeches of Barack Obama that indicated all he talked about was change. However, the full texts of his speeches were replete with detailed discussions of various issues. In the 2012 Republican primary debates, the news media excerpted acerbic, nasty, and humorous exchanges between contenders, often ignoring thoughtful and detailed presentations of proposed solutions to problems. Mediated rhetoric is a fact of life, and rhetorical theorists need to take cognizance of it, since reporters and politicians and their advisors certainly do.

During the 1992 campaign, candidate Bill Clinton proved a master of the technique of using the media to his advantage. He circumvented the traditional news media (and their layers of mediation) and went to the voting public as directly as he could by appearing in such unorthodox political venues as MTV and talk shows. In his first year as president, he remarked at the Radio and Television Correspondents Dinner of March 18, "You know why I can stiff you on press conferences? Because Larry King liberated me by giving me to the American people directly." In 2008, Hillary Clinton appeared in a sketch on *Saturday Night Live* and later in the year, John McCain hosted the show. The illustrative example that follows attempts to show that politicians who try to manipulate the media often get manipulated themselves. In either case, the public receives a mediated message instead of a straightforward speech.

Mediated Rhetoric: Murphy Is the Message

On May 19, 1992, Vice President Dan Quayle gave a speech on family values which was billed as a response to the rioting that had occurred in Los Angeles earlier in the month.[48] Quayle believed "the lawless social anarchy which we saw is directly related to the breakdown of family structure, personal responsibility, and social order in too many areas of our society." He supported his contention with statistics and a specific program to solve the problem. The news media, however, focused on one sentence as Quayle moved toward his conclusion: "It doesn't help matters when prime-time TV has Murphy Brown—

a character who supposedly epitomizes today's intelligent, highly paid, professional woman—mocking the importance of fathers, by bearing a child alone, and calling it just another 'lifestyle choice.'" The sentence was played on all three major evening news broadcasts, and the speech soon was the subject of editorial scrutiny.[49]

Murphy Brown was a popular situation comedy starring Candice Bergen as an unmarried news personality. In the series of episodes to which Quayle referred, Murphy became pregnant by her former lover who popped into town only to leave for South America after their tryst. After anguishing over whether to have the child, Murphy gave birth on an episode that topped the ratings chart.

After his sensational remark, Quayle's staff carefully selected forums where he sought to awaken the need for "family values." On June 9, for example, Quayle delivered a speech to the Southern Baptist Convention in Indianapolis that the *New York Times* called "the sequel to his attack on the *Murphy Brown* television show." Two days later, he addressed the annual meeting of the National Right to Life Committee in Washington, DC, and advocated a "commitment to Judeo-Christian values." A few days later, he chastised Time Warner Incorporated for producing a record by rap singer Ice-T whose lyrics read, "I'm 'bout to dust some cops off. . . . Die, pig, die." In August, the "family values" theme was featured at the Republican Convention. Clearly, the speech on "family values" delivered in San Francisco in May touched a nerve, brought much more attention to Quayle's subsequent speeches, and shuffled the priority of issues being discussed in the presidential campaign.

Quayle's manipulation of the media sought to enhance his value to the Republican ticket going into his party's convention of August 1992. He soon learned that media manipulation is a two-way street. The media, which had taken great delight in ridiculing Quayle's gaffes, were quick to equate his attack on a cultural elite with former Vice President Spiro T. Agnew's attack on the media beginning in 1969.[50] Quayle followed Agnew's strategy of driving a wedge between the "average American" with whom Quayle hoped to identify and his antagonists. However, Quayle expanded the antagonistic group to include not only the news media but also the film and academic communities: "My friends, I know it can be discouraging playing David to the Goliath of the dominant cultural elite. In Hollywood and elsewhere, your opponents have a lot of money, a lot of glamour, a lot of influence." Like Agnew, Quayle also localized his enemy: "Talk about right and wrong, and they'll mock us in newsrooms, sitcom studios, and faculty lounges across America."

Thus, Quayle activated a much smaller, right-of-center segment of the public than Agnew and attacked a much larger segment of the media in his "cultural elite," which included such popular groups as professors and film and television stars. In post-Watergate America, society and its "cultural elite" were far more secular and cynical than they had been only a generation before.[51] Thus, Quayle did not immunize himself from attack; he invited it.

Second, while Spiro Agnew made sure the full text of his speech criticizing the media was broadcast directly to the American people in November of 1969, Dan Quayle's speech to the Commonwealth Club in 1992 was not. Instead, he left himself open to distortion because the media were allowed to select a sound bite taken out of context. Given Quayle's negative image, partially established by the very media he was attacking, the sound bite resulted in his meaning being distorted unfavorably by the public. Furthermore, Quayle developed a dialectical tension between values and vices that served to engage some in his target audience at the expense of alienating a great many others.

Quayle severed not only the "cultural elite" from his coalition but the "underclass"—non-Judeo-Christians, single parents, and those with alternative lifestyles. No doubt these groups watched when, in September, Candice Bergen won an Emmy for her portrayal of the character Murphy Brown and sarcastically thanked the vice president.[52] She had not only become the message but, as an actress in the real world, delivered another message directly aimed at the vice president's electoral chances.

A few weeks later, the season premiere of *Murphy Brown* was watched by approximately seventy million viewers and received a huge 41 percent audience share in the Nielsen ratings. At the end of the program, Candice Bergen implied that the vice president had taken a position antithetical to the single-parent families sitting on stage with her: "Perhaps it's time for the vice president to . . . recognize that, whether by choice or by circumstance, families come in all shapes and sizes. And ultimately what really defines a family is commitment, caring and love."[53]

She then introduced some families "who might not fit into the vice president's vision of a family." The enthymeme is not subtle: the people on stage with Bergen had been marginalized by the vice president. His exclusionary rhetoric gave credibility to Bergen's claim. Thus, while he succeeded in manipulating the media to elevate the issue of family values to national attention, which sustained the campaign for several months and consolidated the support of the right, Quayle failed to achieve a national consensus on the issue. Instead, he fell victim to the response of the fictional television character, which drove many undecided voters from the Republican ticket, which lost the election. In this case, concern for the power of a medium to convey images of particular lifestyles led to treating a fictional character as the embodiment of a harm to be addressed. Ironically, the very power that created the original concern concentrated its efforts and helped to defeat the attacker. Once again, the medium was the message.

CONCLUSION

We live in a crazy world where a situation comedy character can play an important role in national politics. That character might not have had such rhetorical clout if she had not been attacked by a real, live politician. In any case, it is clear that technology mediates communication in a way that distorts it. Yet, our built-in respect for science and the marvels of technology continue to give it credibility.

To avoid being overwhelmed by media and the "information" (infomercials, entertainment as news, blogs, etc.) they provide, we can build censors that filter this communication flow in responsible ways based on the theories presented in this chapter. Richards would have us understand that what we are hearing and seeing needs to be *contextualized* and that it does not mean the same thing to you as it does to your neighbor. When we listen to the evening news or indulge ourselves with rabid commentators of the left or right, we need to be careful that we pick up on the connotative meanings that are being attached to the words we hear and the images we see, images that have been highly edited to hold our attention and to make a point.

Perelman and Olbrechts-Tyteca would have us become part of the universal audience, an audience that might serve as the ideal jury in any law case. Being a member of this audience requires an education and an understanding of what reasonable people have concluded about the information being presented. It also requires that we understand how to reason, how to sift evidence, and how to make decisions in a rational way. As rhetors, we are instructed by Perelman and Olbrechts-Tyteca on the means of bringing our arguments to the fore.

Toulmin would have us examine each argument in terms of its functional parts. What serves as the data for the claim being made? Does that data provide sufficient grounding for the claim? What warrant does that claim derive from the data? Does the warrant or the data require further backing? Does the claim need to be qualified or is there a rebuttal to it?

McLuhan would have us examine the impact of the medium on the message it is carrying. Do we believe it just because we have seen it on television or YouTube? Is what we are imagining different than what is actually taking place during a radio broadcast? Did the persons to whom we are listening select a particular medium to color their message in some way? To which of our senses does the medium appeal? In what ways does it extend them?

These are not easy tasks to undertake. None of us are naive enough to believe that the average person in the average household will undertake all of these critical steps. Media distortion is a fact of life that must be taken into account in our theory. It will continue to dominate our consciousness, unless we become more critical of what we are reading, watching, and hearing. The theories presented in this text are important tools in our quest to analyze the endless stream of messages we encounter.

Study Questions

1. What is semiotics? How did I. A. Richards build on Augustine's theory of symbolism?

2. Draw a model of Richards' encoding and decoding system using a single sentence as your data.

3. Explain Bertrand Russell's theory of correspondence. Give an example from everyday conversation.

4. What is the difference between denotative meaning and connotative meaning? Provide some examples from your language use.

5. How do Perelman and Olbrechts-Tyteca separate formal logic from argumentation?

6. Why do Perelman and Olbrechts-Tyteca include tropes and figures in their theory of argumentation? What are *loci*?

7. What is the difference between "field variant" and "field invariant"? Give several examples of variant field arguments.

8. Break down an argument from a recent public speech using the Toulmin model.

9. What does McLuhan mean by "hot" and "cool" media?

10. What did McLuhan mean by "The medium is the message"? Select several political candidates and propose a media strategy for them based on McLuhan's theory.

Notes

[1] See Umberto Eco, *A Theory of Semiotics* (Bloomington: Indiana U. Press, 1976), p. 7.

[2] See Paul R. Corts, "I. A. Richards on Rhetoric and Criticism," *Southern Speech Journal*, 36 (1971): 115–26.

[3] See his *Philosophy of Rhetoric* (New York: Oxford U. Press, 1936) and *The Meaning of Meaning* (New York: Harcourt, Brace, 1923/1956) with C. K. Ogden. See also, I. A. Richards, *Speculative Instruments* (Chicago: U. of Chicago Press, 1955).

4 Moore (1873–1958) developed "ordinary language" philosophy.

5 Bertrand Russell, *Logic and Knowledge: Essays 1901–1950* (New York: Macmillan, 1968), p. 197.

6 At one time Russell was a student of Whitehead at Cambridge. Their collaborative roles were that Russell was the philosopher and Whitehead the mathematician.

7 For more on Olbrechts-Tyteca, see Barbara Warnick, "Lucie Olbrechts-Tyteca's Contribution to *The New Rhetoric*," in *Listening to Their Voices: The Rhetorical Activities of Historical Women*, Molly Wertheimer, ed. (Columbia: U. of South Carolina Press, 1997), pp. 69–85.

8 Latini was the teacher of Dante.

9 C. Perelman, "The Rule of Justice," in *The Idea of Justice and the Problem of Argument*, John Petrie, trans. (London, 1963), pp. 86–87.

10 The invitation for a visiting professorship was extended to Perelman by my dissertation advisor, Robert T. Oliver, and the outside member of my committee, Henry Johnstone of the Philosophy Department.

11 For a contemporary example of this kind of analysis, see my *First Amendment Profile of the Supreme Court* (Rome: John Cabot U. Press, 2011.)

12 C. Perelman and L. Olbrechts-Tyteca, *The New Rhetoric: A Treatise on Argumentation*, John Wilkeson and Purcell Weaver, trans. (Notre Dame, IN: U. of Notre Dame Press, 1969), p. 13. The book was first published in English in 1969.

13 Ibid., p. 4.

14 Robert E. Tucker, "Figure, Ground and Presence: A Phenomenology of Meaning in Rhetoric," *Quarterly Journal of Speech*, 87 (2001): 396–414.

15 Perelman and Olbrechts-Tyteca, *The New Rhetoric*, pp. 30–35.

16 Ibid., pp. 21–23.

17 As we have seen, the term is borrowed from Roman rhetorical theory, where it referred to associated arguments or parts of speeches with physical places. See chapter 5.

18 Perelman and Olbrechts-Tyteca, *The New Rhetoric*, pp. 411–459.

19 Ibid., p. 5.

20 Chaim Perelman, "Reflections on Justice," in *Revue de l'Institut de Sociologie*, 24 (1951): 281.

21 Perelman and Olbrechts-Tyteca, *The New Rhetoric*, p. 287; see also, pp. 83, 130.

22 Ibid., p. 33.

23 Ibid., p. 142.

24 Stephen Toulmin, *The Uses of Argument* (Cambridge: Cambridge U. Press, 1958), p. 7.

25 This differentiation can be traced back to the different approaches of Plato and Aristotle. Toulmin claimed that Plato's line separated fields and that Aristotle's line divided things up inside each field.

26 Backing is derived from the *epicheirema* of traditional Greek logic, in which one syllogism developed a premise for the next syllogism in a sequence.

27 Some might argue that I am extending Toulmin beyond his claims about field theory. However, in his presentation at the Second International Conference on Argumentation in Amsterdam in 1990, he said that he had wished he had made more of field theory in his early works and now embraced it completely. Toulmin loved teaching at various U.S. universities. For example, in 2007 he could be found teaching at the University of Southern California, where he resided in a student dormitory suite with his wife. He was quite accessible to students and writers.

28 See Wayne Brockriede and Douglas Ehninger's second edition of *Decision by Debate* (New York: Harper and Row, 1977) for a useful laying out of Toulmin's system.

29 See Toulmin's *Human Understanding* (Princeton: Princeton U. Press, 1972).

30 Ibid., p. 486.

31 He calls formal logic a Platonizing approach.

32 In his *Human Understanding*, Toulmin argues that Kuhn's claims are too relative and that the proper understanding of the evolution of science should not be based on radical paradigm shifts but on the arguments that are used to support the new theories. In short, it is not the paradigm shift that allows Galileo's theories to conquer others; it is his arguments.

33 Toulmin, *The Uses of Argument*, p. 253.

34 Toulmin, *Human Understanding*, p. 3.

35 Toulmin regularly acknowledges his debt to Aristotle. Among other things, Toulmin traces the argumentative skill of case making back to Aristotle and Hermagoras.

[36] Marshall McLuhan, *Understanding Media: The Extensions of Man* (New York: McGraw Hill, 1964). Parts of this work are based on McLuhan's doctoral dissertation on the verbal arts, starting with Cicero.

[37] McLuhan attended mass almost every day.

[38] Ibid., p. 321.

[39] Ibid., p. 90.

[40] Ibid., p. 53.

[41] See, for example, his "Interview" in *Playboy* (March, 1969): 61, where he said, "I'm not suggesting that content plays no role—merely that it plays a distinctly subordinate role."

[42] Recall from chapter 8 that Heidegger argued that technology transforms us. McLuhan would seem to agree with that.

[43] Stereophonic sound, colorization, and digital high definition will heat television up as less mental participation is needed to produce a realistic image on the screen.

[44] This difference is likely to change with high-definition television.

[45] McLuhan, *Understanding Media*, p. 24.

[46] Nixon's advisors were well aware of McLuhan's theories; pages from his books were tacked to the wall of the Nixon's headquarters during the 1968 campaign.

[47] See, for example, Carole Blair, Marsha Jeppeson and Enrico Pucci Jr., "Public Memorializing in Postmodernity: The Vietnam Veterans Memorial as Prototype," *Quarterly Journal of Speech*, 77 (1991): 263–88.

[48] For a more detailed version of this account see Craig R. Smith, "Dan Quayle on Family Values: Epideictic Appeals in Political Campaigns," *The Southern Communication Journal*, 60 (1995): 152–64. The quotations used here are taken from that article unless otherwise noted.

[49] On the June 9, 1994, NBC *Dateline* news magazine, Quayle continued to defend his comment and made clear it was no offhand remark. In his memoir, it is telling that he consistently refers to the address as the "Murphy Brown speech." *Standing Firm: A Vice Presidential Memoir* (New York: Harper Collins, 1994), pp. 323, 334.

[50] Agnew initiated his attack with an address in Des Moines, Iowa, on November 13, 1969, which was carried by all three major television networks. Agnew was an overnight sensation and went on to give many more speeches bashing the media as "nattering nabobs of negativism."

[51] Volvo even made a car commercial addressed to the vice president, asking, "What do you think of these family values?"

[52] *Murphy Brown*'s producer, Diane English, also attacked the vice president and put down Ronald and Nancy Reagan's ability to raise children. The attacks led to a direct response by the vice president while speaking in Kansas City on September 2. He called Hollywood a "stronghold of the adversary culture." He then defended again his speech of May 19 attacking the morality of encouraging women to raise babies without fathers. In a reference to the initial episode of *Murphy Brown* for the new season, Quayle said, "Winning an Emmy is not a license to lie." *Time*, among others, covered the controversy by putting a picture of Candice Bergen on its September 21, 1992, cover; on her blouse, Ms. Bergen wore a campaign button that read, "Murphy Brown for President."

[53] From the author's transcript of the broadcast.

Postmodern and Feminist Theories

I n the "postmodern" world, linearity is replaced with the cyclical nature of our being; objectivity is being replaced with subjectivity; multiple perspectives replace a single view. Television programs, such as *Modern Family, Glee,* and *Desperate Housewives* toggle seamlessly between comic and dramatic frames while revolving around several ongoing narratives, with many themes trailing through several episodes. Flashbacks as well as flash-forwards are not uncommon. Boundaries between disciplines are being erased as inter- and cross-cultural studies bring rhetoricians into contact with sociologists and anthropologists. Performance of literature blends into film, dance, music, and drama. Values are questioned; tolerance is privileged. Many voices in many forums, some of them quite fragmented, seek our attention. What is the impact of this postmodern condition on rhetorical theory?

We begin by defining postmodernism through the eyes of its chief spokespersons, Michel Foucault and Jean-François Lyotard. Postmodernism is framed as a backlash against the unitary, conformist, and hierarchical nature of "modernist" rationalism that posited a systematic division of knowledge into discrete categories and a hierarchy of universal values. The chapter also includes a review of the theories of Jacques Derrida and Jean Baudrillard, the former on deconstructing discourse and the latter on how communication is overwhelming us. The chapter then turns to the feminist critiques of society in order to deduce a feminist rhetorical theory in the postmodern world.

POSTMODERNISM: OXYMORON OR USEFUL CONSTRUCT?

The famous architect Philip Johnson was an unabashed advocate of the "modernist" style for many years; he admired the work that emerged after World War II, particularly that of Le Corbusier,[1] Ludwig Mies van der Rohe, and the Bauhaus School in Germany. Le Corbusier sought to tear down whole areas of the "Old World" and build new sprawling, modern housing areas; he was also chosen as one of the architects to plan the United Nations complex in New York City.

Trained by some of the same teachers as Le Corbusier, Mies van der Rohe was more popular in the United States in part because he inserted his buildings into landscapes that were already formed.[2] In 1951 his buildings emerged at 860 and 880 Lake Shore Drive in Chicago and stand aloof, ascetic, and strong against the Chicago winds on high and the swirling traffic below. They were two of the reasons he eventually got a contract to complete the Seagrams building on Park Avenue in New York City a few years later. Mies van der Rohe, with whom Johnson collaborated in the 1950s, believed "less is more" in architectural design. He was inspired by the rationalism of the Enlightenment, the science of technology, and the advent of a new age of democracy following the Second World War. Like other modernists, he sought to reform the medieval approach with its broad plazas used for congregating after mass at the cathedral or after the town hall meeting in the civic center. He deemed them inefficient in the cities where land was scarce.

The modernists imposed their style first in the massive effort to rebuild war-devastated Europe. The style spread to the United States. Mies van der Rohe's influence is readily apparent to this day. The geometric glass configurations along the Chicago River had their echoes in New York, Los Angeles, and many other cities. Modernism became the rage of new architecture from 1950 through the seventies.

Modernist buildings are intentionally unadorned to draw attention to the materials used in construction, often glass or concrete sheets. Mies van der Rohe hoped these buildings would not betray the function for which they were used; as a social democrat, he hoped they could be used for any purpose from banking to education. He was particularly critical of the habit in the United States of using Greek architecture for banks, Roman architecture for government buildings, and frontier architecture for public schools. His IBM building (1969–1971) in Chicago is typical of his style. It looks like a large, rectangular, black glass box. It could hold anything, but it inspired no romance or transcendence.

Johnson eventually came to believe that these structures were devoid of feeling, aesthetic justification, and originality. Johnson's admission was stunning; the emperor of American architecture confessed that he had no clothes. To correct the situation, Johnson, along with Michael Graves, developed a "postmodern" style that retained the best techniques of modern construction and materials but combined them with echoes from the great eras of architecture. Johnson's AT&T building (now the Sony building) in New York is a very tall, narrow box, but it also reflects a new contextualism by mirroring an environment of skyscrapers. It is capped with a Romanesque architrave and pediment. Postmodernism caught on quickly and became a major movement in architectural circles.

Postmodernism was also welcomed in artistic realms that had been badly beaten up by rationalism. The modernist critique of anything subjective, including the arts, had taken its toll on creators. Many welcomed a new outlook that restored their right to explore subjective realms. Ancient and traditional styles and models were re-interpreted and given new life in pluralistic approaches to art. Diversity became a hallmark of postmodernism as its followers mined different cultures, particularly postcolonial cultures, for new perspectives on art. Postmodernism became eclectic in its free-ranging exploration of ideas in multicultural contexts. In the academic community, postmodernism was quickly transformed to signify a kind of pastiche approach that did not recognize standard boundaries and categories; "Postmodern theory . . . rejects modern assumptions of social coherence and notions of causality in favour of multiplicity, plurality, fragmentation, and indeterminacy."[3] This trend was particularly noticeable in performance studies in Germany where dance, slides, music, and film might all be operating on stage at the same time.[4] Andrew Lloyd Webber invented a wonderful postmodern moment in his musical *Evita* when he showed a newsreel clip on the screen behind the characters of the musical. With their backs to the audience, the cast appears to be addressing the citizens of 1950 Argentina. Then the bridge holding them revolves to face the actual audience, which is treated as the people of Argen-

The Sony Building, formerly the AT&T Building, New York City.

tina. Thus, the imaginary plane between audience and stage is broken. The audience members are no longer merely observers; they are players in the drama.

From performance to criticism and from criticism to theory, postmodernism has evolved into a complex movement with many offshoots: "[I]n the contemporary high tech media society, emergent processes of change and transformation are producing a new postmodern society and its advocates claim that the era of postmodernity constitutes a novel stage of history and novel sociocultural formation which requires new concepts and theories."[5] To make sense of what sounds like an oxymoron—how can something be postmodern, after the now—we need to understand that "modern philosophy" refers to a certain type of thought. That is, postmodernism presupposes "modern" philosophy, which was an outgrowth of Enlightenment thinking, some of which we sampled in our examination of Francis Bacon, John Locke, René Descartes (see chapter 8), Friedrich Hegel and Immanuel Kant (see chapter 9). As we learned, the optimism of the modernists was battered in the twentieth century with the advent of two horrific world wars, the authoritarianism and failure of Marxism, and the discoveries of Freud.

Modernists believed in a hierarchical categorization of knowledge and values based on a universal imperative that could be *determined by reason*. They claimed that the rules of the universe were fixed and could be known using science and logic as guides. The project of modernism was to discover which values were the most important and how humans might best order them. The modernists believed that intellection, whether intuitive or reasoned, could discover or verify the truth and order our private as well as our public lives.[6]

Postmodernists are highly suspicious of the legacy of modernism because of its hierarchical nature and overreliance on science, technology, and logic. Ironically, postmodern thinking has gained an ally in some of the latest theoretical thinking in physics. Paul Davies argues that "The quantum microworld is not . . . linked by a tight network of causal influences, but more by a pandemonium of loosely obeyed commands and suggestions."[7] These theories have necessitated the development of "fuzzy logic" and "fuzzy physics,"[8] which search out the contradictions in the material world. Quantum theory acknowledges that a particle can be in two places at the same time; it can travel faster than the speed of light; that is, it can "communicate" with a fragment of itself.

Stephen Hawking's *A Brief History of Time* adds a major dimension to the postmodern view. He offers a reform of Albert Einstein's theory. Einstein's general theory of relativity, developed around 1915, held that space is produced by the presence of matter. The expansion of matter from the big bang to the present means that we are constantly traveling away from other galaxies as the universe expands. In fact, scientists have failed to determine how large the universe is. Reforming Newton's theory of gravity, Einstein's theory predicts certain effects in the solar system, in double stars, and in quantum mechanics.

Hawking points out that this theory is very difficult to understand because we perceive things on a scale by which we live—the size of a tree, a person, or a desk is measured from our perspective. Thus, such large notions as an ever-expanding universe of billions of stars, or that the light of stars billions of light years away is just reaching us even though the star may have already collapsed, are incomprehensible, as are such tiny particles as electrons and quarks. Science has developed its own rhetoric to deal with this problem. Quantum mechanics works at explaining the microlevel, while astrophysics works at explaining the macrolevel. The pragmatic results can be impressive. For example, the computer-chip industry would be nonexistent without quantum mechanics. The theory that the big bang occurred fifteen billion light years ago would be impossible without astrophysics. The fifteen-billion mark, explains Hawking, puts a "horizon" on how far back we can look into the universe; however, it puts no limit on the future. Furthermore, since science is built on the repeatability of experiments, the universe can't be understood by traditional science because it is a one-time, ongoing experiment. Einstein, Hawking, and others struggled with realities that are beyond the boundaries of our knowledge. In so doing, they undercut traditional science and logic—and provide support for the more random, fuzzy, and rhetorical approaches of the postmodernists. At the very least they recognize that rhetoric is crucial to exploring and explaining scientific theories.

Postmodernists recognize that we live in the midst of a fragmented culture in which it is essential to recognize certain facets of a postmodern era. This era is marked by new forms of knowledge and information as a result of computer and other media technology, significant changes in the socioeconomic system, increased cultural fragmentation, respect for diversity, changes in the experience of time and space, a trend toward subjective inquiries, and a breaking up of established ways of life and once stable social orders. The "normal family unit" containing a nonworking mother, an employed father, and children has become rarer. We are capable of receiving the news instantaneously from remote corners of the world, and the world itself can be viewed by humans in ninety-minute orbits. This "shrinking" of the world has pushed cultures up against one another, forcing them to observe and interact with others as never before. In some cases, this has led to greater degrees of tolerance; in other cases, it has led to a turning inward and protection of cultural traditions.

One need only look at situation comedies to see the difference between the modern and the postmodern. Family relations are at the margins of the stories; parents are ridiculed. The programs' themes are clearly postmodern; for example, equality among friends is more important than family; ethnic and gender diversity is more common than ever; traditional family values are often denigrated. We hear regularly about the "new normal," and a sitcom is even named that.

Christine Di Stefano, a feminist scholar, writes that postmodernism renders the conventional into the arbitrary; it promotes a politics and theory of disbelief toward the language of rationality, interests, and autonomy. These are questioned as characteristics of a humanistic self previously thought to provide the legitimizing foundation for modern social life.[9] Certainly, postmodernism uses different lenses than rationalism. The question is, what new insights does looking through these lenses provide?

Foucault (1926–1984)

Michel Foucault used the postmodern platform to criticize the master narratives of Marx and capitalism:

> Humanity does not gradually progress from combat to combat until it arrives at universal reciprocity, where the rule of law finally replaces warfare; humanity installs each of its violences in a system of rules and thus proceeds from domination to domination.[10]

Across his body of work, Foucault pursued the answers to three major questions: (1) How does knowledge sustain, define, rationalize, or undermine power? (2) How does power define, sustain, or undermine knowledge? (3) What role does discourse play in these relationships? Foucault believed that power was an inherent part of all social relations and that such relationships could be revealed in the rhetoric between the players.

In the process of answering these questions, he condemned the dialectical "blackmail" of Enlightenment thinking in an effort to expose the powers behind domination and to retrieve the density and relativity of language lost since the age of the Sophists.[11] The rationalist stripped language of its emotive, spiritual, and mythic force. He denigrated rationalism, arguing that there "was no external position of certainty, no universal understanding . . . beyond history and society."[12]

Foucault's first book, *Madness and Civilization* (1961), his doctoral dissertation in psychology, examined the role history and society played in diagnosing and/or inducing insanity in individuals. He claimed that the assessment of madness was discursively constructed and went through four phases. In medieval times, madness was framed by the religious era in which society was guilty for the fall of man and faced the apocalypse. The mad were possessed by devils; witches could change a human's fate. A rhetoric of exorcisms, incantations, and secret, magical symbols developed.

The church had a rich tradition of biblical literature from which to draw such a rhetoric. Jesus was said to have cast out devils and the apocalyptic Book of Revelation is full of signs and symbols with various layers of meaning.

In the Renaissance, madness was framed inside the folly of human life, which gave a tongue to madness in the character of the wise fool. Such characters can be seen in Shakespeare's play, such as King Lear's loyal fool or Romeo's friend Mercutio. At one point in the play Romeo takes Mercutio's head in his hands and says, "Peace, Mercutio, Peace. You speak of nothing." And Mercutio replies, "True, I speak of dreams, which are the children of an idle brain." Thus, a comical rhetoric that is often ironic emerged.

The modern age gave birth to confinement. In this third era, reason and bourgeois morality sought to marginalize madness instead of giving it a tongue. The resulting rhetoric often consisted of condemnation of those who could not "tell right from wrong." Speaking outside rational and/or moral boundaries led to condemnation and consignment, if not to an institution, to a place outside of moral society. The body thus became a target of power. Rhetoric often operated to make bodies docile; you could speak as long as you followed the rules. If you disrupted things, you would be removed and/or confined.

Michel Foucault.

With the emergence of Freud in the twentieth century (see chapter 10), the study of madness created the all-wise psychologist, whose credibility often carried over to other medical personnel in the fourth era. Foucault criticized the latter eras because by suppressing madness, they also suppressed creativity. He specifically cites the examples of the painter Vincent Van Gogh and the philosopher Frederick Nietzsche; Van Gogh witnessed the truth of being in his paintings, and Nietzsche produced truth in his philosophy. Both accomplished these feats despite bouts of insanity. The rhetoric of expertise was soon borrowed by commentators in general that were quick to identify hidden motivations, such as narcissism, neuroses, sexual desires, and the like.

Foucault extended this analysis in his next book by showing that there was a hidden grid that organizes scholarly discourse and defines what can or cannot be thought of and taught.[13] The power of language is reduced when it too becomes a subject of study, as in the work of Ferdinand de Saussure (see below), a structuralist who examined the *langue* (rules) and *parole* (words) of language use. Uncovering this grid becomes the task of Foucault's "archaeology." He unearths historically embedded codes that determine what we are allowed to think about and how we think and talk about it. He dubs these knowledge sets "epistemes," from the Greek word for knowledge.[14] Epistemes organize our thought. Think about the difference between a scholastic episteme and a humanistic episteme, which we have studied in this book in previous chapters. The scholastic would confine the production of knowledge to science and reason; the humanist would expand the production of knowledge to include the ancients, myths, and our own imagination.

To overcome these often unconscious rules and grids, Foucault proposed "counter-sciences" to open the dialogue about what is knowledge:

> I would like my books to be a kind of tool-box which others can rummage through to find a tool which they can use however they wish in their own area. . . . I would like the little volume that I want to write on disciplinary systems to be useful to an educator, a warden, a magistrate, a conscientious objector. . . . I write for users, not readers.[15]

He hoped these "users" would become critics.

Archaeology of Knowledge (1969) was Foucault's most important book for our purposes because he traced the role that speech plays in maintaining systemically unequal relationships. He wrote that "the production of discourse is at once controlled, selected, organized, and redistributed according to a certain number of procedures."[16] Foucault replaces his "epistemes" with discursive practices ("discourses") that situate speakers within disciplines and other social or workplace locations. These discourses follow certain rules. (1) They emerge from society and culture—that is, from the family, peers, fellow workers, and/or religion. "You can't talk that way on this job." "Don't use that tone of voice with me." (2) They are handed down by institutions of authority such as universities or the practices of medicine or law. "That study does not follow the proper statistical formulation." "That piece of evidence is inadmissible in a court of law." (3) They are generated by grids of specification (archaeological rules of formation) that relate one discourse to another. For example, medicine can relate biological and chemical discourses of science. This archaeology gives us an entry into the archives of acceptable discourses that underlie history and society: what is allowed and what is not allowed to be thought or said. Archaeologies also expose axes of truth, power, and discourse.

This investigation leads Foucault to a rather pessimistic picture of the ability of humans to overcome institutions and cultural structures. "Official knowledge" gives those in power the ability to keep those who are marginalized in place, and that is bad because the marginalized may have "subjugated knowledge" that is useful. It was not too long ago that psychiatric associations claimed that homosexuality was a mental abnormality, thereby marginalizing homosexuals and the knowledge they possessed. Foucault dealt with this "juridical" problem by making a differentiation between institutions that *govern* justice and institutions that are qualified to express the truth. For example, the president appoints the people who rule on scientific matters in many government agencies. They in turn express their opinions by ruling on scientific findings, such as the uses of stem cell research or the truth about climate change. These rulings may enforce the position of the president on these matters instead of the position of scientists, the ones more qualified to express the truth. Yet, we have seen, as with the psychiatric associations, that once the truth-sayers gain authority, they, too, become part of the institutions that govern. It is psychiatrists who decide whether suspects are sane enough to stand trial or whether they should be confined to a mental institution. Authorities are in a position of using rhetoric to transform others. Their "enouncements," as Foucault calls them, sanction a particular form of knowledge. For example, historically the deformed have been portrayed as monsters, like Quasimodo in *The Hunchback of Notre Dame*.

However, as a first corrective, Foucault hoped that his critique would "restore" speech as "event," a Sophistic notion. He begins by borrowing from the dramatist Euripides (484–407 BC), who wrote many tragedies that contain frank, honest, and often difficult speeches of the truth. He called these *parrhesia*. They were also used by the Cynic Diogenes as he searched for an honest man. Foucault revives the term in an attempt to strip discourse of all manipulation and adaptation. He establishes three categories for this type of speech: (1) the diatribe, or stern preaching; (2) the condemnation of bad behavior; and (3) the probing dialectic.[17] He acknowledges that *parrhesia* can be difficult to take; those who utter this kind of truth-speech are called *parrhesiastes*. There are many examples of such speakers in history, most notably the Greeks Socrates and Diogenes. However, there are also contemporary examples. Mary Fisher, the daughter of a wealthy Republican contributor, addressed the 1992 Republican Convention, calling on the party to support research on HIV/AIDS, and revealed that she had the disease. In 2011, Supreme Court Justice Samuel Alito was the lone dissenter in a freedom of expression case in which he argued that personal attacks that cause emotional distress should not be protected by the First Amendment.

As a second corrective, Foucault would also return speech to "performance" rather than informative report. If you perceive a speech to be an objective collection of facts, you are likely to give it too much credibility and ignore its subtext or subversive nature. You may fail to see how it is conveying power, a power that might not be deserved. By looking at discourse as "performance," he saw the way relationships come together in the speech, how institutions and social processes influence speakers, and vice versa. Most importantly, when speech is examined as "performance," it reveals for whom the speaker is speaking. Like the Marxists, he asks, what powers lie behind the speaker and whose agendas are being advanced? In the speaking situation, subjects "constitute" themselves and sponsors of events emerge. As they perform, speakers are "inventing themselves" using the "patterns . . . which are proposed, suggested, and imposed" by their cultures, societies, and social groups.[18]

As a third corrective, Foucault advised resisting forms of power. If nothing else, such a step would reveal the relationships of power and the methods used to sustain them. During the Occupy Movement at the University of California at Davis in 2011, students peacefully assembled and then refused to move when ordered to do so by the campus police. Instead of arresting and dragging the students away, the police sprayed the students with huge amounts of pepper spray. This cruel overreaction revealed the university to be an insensitive institution of power. Eventually, however, it paid reparations to the students.

Foucault argued that just as rhetoric can sustain these power relationships, it is also useful in resisting and exposing them, especially when it is used in "anarchistic struggles." However, Foucault's study of the history of rhetoric within various epochs reveals that much of this reformist rhetoric becomes "fragmentary" and "disordered" and, thus, unable to defeat the powerful forces that rule over it.[19] This lesson was born out by the disintegration of the Occupy Wall Street Movement in 2012.

His articles and lectures led to his appointment to the Collège de France in 1970 where he continued his work on power relationships and discourse. In *Discipline and Punishment*, first published in 1975, he analyzed the history of incarceration while he was actively involved in the prison reform movement in France. His book used "genealogy" as a starting point to develop a method that would "thematize relationships among truth, theory and values, and the social institutions and practices in which they emerge."[20] Again, Foucault was trying to unearth hidden networks of rules for discourse that govern knowledge and thereby us too. Thus, genealogy is more concerned with the present, while archaeology is more concerned with the past.

Using his genealogy, Foucault sought to reveal the biases of history and to destabilize meta-narratives. This move sometimes requires the creation of counter-memories, reconstructions of the past that present an antithesis to what traditional or standard history teaches us.[21] Counter-memories can lead to counter-publics, which can further challenge historic knowledge. The myth of the antebellum South, with its hoop skirts and happy servants presented in such fiction as *Gone with the Wind* can be destroyed by a factual narrative that reveals the cruelty visited on slaves and the poverty most white farmers endured. Using genealogies, counter-memories have the ability to unmask individuals by revealing their identities and relationships and trying to "dissipate" the historical roots of our identities. Foucault argued that space constituted individuals rhetorically in terms of their visibility and power; the more space one controlled, the more powerful one was. But there was also a power implied by placement within space. For example, the guard tower elevates the guard to a position where he or she can look over the prisoners who are assembled in the "yard" below, like children or animals. This panopticon is an architectural feature of the technology of power that Foucault borrowed from Jeremy Bentham, a late eighteenth-century British political philosopher. The prisoner cannot escape the gaze of the guard, but the guard can avoid the gaze of the prisoner.[22] The power equation is in part a function of space and placement that can be assessed through the gazes of the participants.

Foucault's lectures of 1975–1976 have been collected in a book called *Society Must be Defended*, which was released in 2003. These lectures begin with Foucault's move from French structuralism in language to the investigation of its strategic uses. For example, rhetoric can empower a subject area by transferring the credibility from one field to another. Science is credible. Thus, when we take certain subject areas that are not physical sciences, such as anthropology, sociology, communication theory, and call them "social sciences," we empower them with new credibility. The resulting disciplinary power consists of selection (editing out nonscientific approaches, editing in scientific approaches), normalization (how does it fit in with disciplines of science?), hierarchicalization (where does it fit in the scheme of things: is sociological theory more scientific than communication theory?), and centralization (how does it flow from the center of scientific research?). Furthermore, Foucault claimed that by reducing knowledge to various disciplines, academics control it and empower the disciplines. They then invent language to protect their subject areas. In communication theory, "stage fright" becomes "communication apprehension"; "mental rehearsal" becomes "imagined interactions"; "goodwill" becomes "caregiving."

Early in these lectures, Foucault was particularly interested in how history functions to filter human perceptions rhetorically. As I pointed out earlier, Greek and

Roman historians were trained in rhetoric before they were allowed to write history. The rhetorical filtering of modern historians is often obvious. David McCullough often heroizes his subjects: Harry Truman's low moments are minimized; John Adams' glee at the passage of the Alien and Sedition Acts is ignored.

Foucault continued to explore how power networks surround us and hold us down by imposing limits on speaking situations. In his *History of Sexuality*, first published in 1976, he claimed that "power and knowledge are joined together."[23] While he conceded that power could create knowledge, it was located in "the manifold relationships of force that take shape and come into play in the machinery of production."[24] Those who have knowledge have power, and knowledge is often encoded into a language of its own. Any novice trying to penetrate the language of computers, congressional parliamentary procedures, or Wall Street trading will understand Foucault's point.[25] Rhetoric encodes knowledge so that those who posses it share it only among themselves. This use of rhetoric is the opposite of its public making-known function that we examined in earlier chapters. It is instead a kind of tribal use of rhetoric to protect knowledge from those outside the tribe. It is employed by scientists as well as hip-hop rappers.

Further, Foucault told us, institutions often prioritize communication elevating one kind of rhetoric over another.[26] Some institutions prefer "team spirit" to "individual achievement." Others prefer the rhetoric of incentives to the rhetoric of equal pay. These preferences produce effects in the real world. Those who call for "free trade," for example, often overlook what that means internationally in terms of working conditions for laborers in other countries. Those who call for environmental preservation often overlook the effect on energy supplies or jobs. Thus, Foucault is a critic of the rhetoric of exclusion, secrecy, and myopia, because it supports domination, which squeezes freedom out of a society.

Finally, Foucault carried his analysis of powerful rhetorics to posit a theory on the rhetoric of space. Specifically, he advised being on guard for "heterotopias," closed off and arranged spaces that subvert or transform certain relationships in a society.[27] Heterotopias might be characterized by celebrating an aspect of culture or resituating it; they may bring together normally unaffiliated events, objects, or themes; they may be highly accessible, or not; they may bring a narrative, such as deviation, into focus; they may change perceptions over time. Hence they have become a tool of those who read architectural creations in general and memorials specifically as rhetorical texts.

Heterotopias speak to us about changes in our values. For example, when the Vietnam Memorial was commissioned for the National Mall in the late 1970s, American society had a much darker view of war than it did in 2004 when the World War II Memorial, located not far from the Vietnam Memorial, was completed. The Vietnam Memorial is a deep black gash into the earth off to the side of the Mall; it lists all those who died in the war, not the battles that were fought. The World War II Memorial includes fifty-six vertical columns and several waterfalls. It is a celebration of victories in the war; its central location interrupts the flow of the Mall running from the Lincoln Memorial to the Washington Memorial. It is not difficult to discern how American culture perceives these two wars. These heterotopias emphasize certain things, the list of those killed in one case, the list of the battles won in the other. These heterotopias also reflect certain moods, the sadness of a lost war, the pride of a just war. In this way, Foucault's "heterotopology" gives us yet another extension of his rhetorical theory.

Lyotard (1924–1998)

Jean-François Lyotard also wrote extensively on what he called the "postmodern condition." He argued that it moved at varying speeds in different locations, but that it was linked to globalization and such technological transformation as the "computerization" of a society. He clearly reflected the French penchant to move from the study of consciousness to the study of language. Within the study of language, Lyotard advanced the relative, poststructural approach. Structuralism is best represented in the work of Ferdinand de Saussure, who divided the study of language between *parole* (words, discourse, or utterance) and *langue* (grammar, systems of language, and games). Furthermore, Saussure argued that the empirical study of *parole*, the careful observation and analysis of discourse, helps us to infer *langue*, the rules of the language game. The investigation can be synchronous—a study of the *parole* at the moment—or it can be diachronous—a study of discourse over time.

In reaction, Lyotard began his poststructural analysis by arguing that "master narratives" should give way to local narratives. This shift would make universal rules about language almost impossible. Lyotard wrote, "I define *postmodern* as an incredulity toward meta-narratives."[28] He was particularly critical of science for treating narratives as "fables, myths, legends, fit only for women and children."[29] In other words, the sweeping explanations of how the world works advanced by modernists, particularly scientists, do not hold up. Any attempt to build a theory of language around such explanations is doomed to failure. Theories of language must be built on more specialized, localized fragments that can only be found using a microcultural approach. The microapproach reveals what Lyotard called the pragmatics of language, how it works in the everyday world.

Like Foucault, Lyotard separated himself from the structuralists by focusing on the performative in language rather than its construction. The project for Lyotard becomes the discovery of the differences between various viewpoints, and then the articulation of those differences as "case conflicts" *(differends)* in which "one side's legitimacy does not imply the other's lack of legitimacy."[30] This openness and tolerance of all stakeholders eliminates the possibility of predetermined judgments, those

Jean-François Lyotard.

foreordained by myth, master narratives, hierarchical structures, or social milieu. Because it believes that consensus is a myth and often totalizing, the *differend* becomes a prying dyad that won't go away. The *differend* is meant to create an imbalance, to throw the establishment off its game, as it were. For example, it might attempt to halt a court case by suggesting alternate narratives. If the U.S. Navy is being sued for damaging marine life with its sonar testing, the *differend* may argue that the real cause of damaged marine life is global warming.

The *differend* can also be invoked when conflicting parties can't find common rules on which to base a resolution. Monarchies operate differently than republics, but they often come in conflict with one other. Initiating a *differend* at the World Court at the Hague might help to resolve the conflict. In such cases, the *differend* can record and save different interpretations of events, rules, and procedures while transcending disputes.

Lyotard would have us reflect on the conflict at hand based on a respect for all disputants' positions and engage only in "temporary contracts." The same tolerance permits many conflicting views to surface in society and also leads to a multiplicity of theories built from the new openness. In fact in his work *Just Gaming*, Lyotard retrieved Aristotle's notion of contingent prudence, which "consists in dispensing judgment without models."[31] Each instance of assessment would be case specific; there would be no applicable precedents.

Lyotard's elimination of "determining criteria" reveals him to be a relativist who seeks to undermine normative standards. If, however, every position has validity, how do we decide among them? If every local rhetoric is valid, how do we talk to one another across localities, resolve differences, and find the truth? Did Lyotard mean to suggest as a kind of modern Sophist that the locality is the measure of all things?

To counter this criticism, Lyotard embraced certain standards that provide a sense of order within his system. For example, he endorsed openness and tolerance along with a respect for the language of disputants. Violence is to be avoided. Furthermore, Lyotard would eliminate any privileging of various classes and would give voice to those who have been marginalized. Once a voice is legitimized, it must make its case in Lyotard's world of jurisprudence. That is, disputants are allowed to use rhetoric, but ultimately a judgment will be handed down by a judge who is without bias. We are reminded of Perelman's universal audience (see chapter 12), but we need to remember that with Lyotard, having a voice guarantees a hearing, not acceptance.

Perhaps Lyotard's theory can be illustrated by the plight of Native Americans in the United States and Latin America.[32] For centuries their way of life, their language, and their values were marginalized by a Euro-American culture that attempted to remove, annihilate, Christianize, and finally absorb them. The Euro-American culture did these things in the name of such modern values as religious superiority, material wealth, technological progress, and geographic expansion. Furthermore, the Euro-American culture imposed its view of the law on Native Americans who embraced a wholly different view of the universe. The *differend* or case conflict here is represented on one side by a linear culture caught up with modern progress and on the other by a cyclical culture that believes that it is one with nature. For most Euro-Americans, perfection is rewarded beyond this world in a Christian heaven, while for most Native Americans the "Great Spirit" pervades this earth. The problem with this *differend* was that the Native American side of the dispute was not given a legitimate voice until recently. Euro-American exclusionary strategies visited a holocaust on Native Americans.

Lyotard's project involved making sure such tragedies are not repeated in a pre-scribed legal and political system. He suggested that each side in a dispute should have its claims treated "as if" they were true so that they could be evaluated reflexively in contemporary culture. In this way, Lyotard hoped to avoid the possible tyrannizing effects of metaphysical claims and laws, the very kinds of laws proposed by Hegel and Kant. Obviously, his system comes with a price. It requires society to deprioritize many values that provide stability, security, and order. It requires others to let go of their identities. It protects the voices of hate and evil that frequently enter into *differends*. Like Thomas Jefferson, Lyotard would tolerate any opinion as long as all voices were left free to combat it. However, Lyotard realized that by tolerating all voices, a society might create groupings that are counterproductive. The very act of banding together to produce a voice may incite the massive opposition of the powers that be:

> The resistance of communities banded around their names and their narratives is counted on to stand in the way of capital's hegemony. This is a mistake. First of all, this resistance fosters this hegemony as much as it counters it. Then, it . . . gener-ates the fear of falling back into legitimation through tradition, indeed into legiti-mation through myth, even if that legitimation also gives shape to the resistances of peoples to their extermination. Proud struggles for independence end in young, reactionary States.[33]

In *The Postmodern Condition: A Report on Knowledge* (1984), Lyotard explained where the sources of hegemony lie when he wrote that knowledge cannot be sepa-rated from its sponsors whether they be institutional structures, such as the church, or cultural formations, such as ecological groups. They influence the editing process by which knowledge is conveyed, giving it a contextual aspect that influences meaning. Furthermore, technology has become the new God-term, pushing out such Platonic universals as "the true, the just, or the beautiful."[34] By minimalizing the need for his-toric understanding, technology has undermined the grand narratives of the past such as Marx's dialectical materialism, the story of the enthronement of the proletariat.

Lyotard pulled together many of the theses we have been examining throughout this book. Recall that we started with an examination of the powerful rhetorical pull of mythology to make sense of the chaotic universe. Lyotard saw mythology as some-thing that legitimizes the rule of law in a way that marginalizes various groups. We also examined the Marxist critique of society and discovered its disdain for hege-monic rhetoric, which Lyotard also condemned. He hoped that these master narra-tives would die away.

Richard Rorty (1931–2007), a leading postmodern theorist in the United States, argued that our task is to keep "the conversation going rather than to find objective truth."[35] The mistake the modernists made was to assume that because science had given us objective knowledge of the material world, reason guided by the scientific imperative could give us objective knowledge of ethics, government, music, and other human pursuits. With the collapse of that project, postmodern theory has developed a rhetoric of pluralism to engage in and take account of the "conversation" of various participants in fragmented locations.[36] Thus, in reaction to the structural analysis of language of such thinkers as Ferdinand de Saussure, Charles Peirce, and Ludwig Wittgenstein, Lyotard and Rorty argue for a poststructural analysis that demonstrates that universal consensus can no longer be obtained and that, in fact, generalization is dangerous and conforming—that is, hegemonic.

In an effort to avoid these problems, Rorty makes the case that ideas are neither *noumenal*, as Plato claimed, nor rationally unified, as Kant claimed, nor a reflection of nature, as the Romantics claimed. Instead, *ideas are the constructions of human beings in a social context.* Only indigenous and parochial criteria for validity are able to formulate a "polytheism of values." While Foucault addressed the same issue by examining "a glance" that converts something diffuse, dispersed, and multiple into a subjected unity,[37] Lyotard looked for "case conflicts."

Derrida (1930–2004)

Jacques Derrida, a French philosopher of language, seeks out *différance,* the difficulties of signifying things and concepts with a language that has become self-referential, almost always metaphorical. In this linguistic environment, how can ideas and

Jacques Derrida.

objects be signified? How many meanings do they obtain over time? How does the context work to change the signification process? The answer is, *rhetorically as opposed to logically.* Thus, interpretations of meanings are required and such interpretations are necessarily persuasive. You must make a case for your interpretation, and case making is a rhetorical project. Derrida thus reveals that literary criticism is a rhetorical practice.

Derrida explores writing as the model of *différance* because it is more stable than speech in terms of placing meaning on things and concepts. Writing is more likely to acknowledge the distance and deferred nature of description than speech, which gets bound up in immediacy. This opinion arises out of his critique of Western metaphysics; Plato assessed writing to be inferior to speech and, worse yet, did not realize that language is separate from the things it references. Derrida claims that writing is superior to speech because it can more easily be separated from context. Things (referents) exist prior to their incorporation into language; thus, the

attempt to analyze knowledge by analyzing speech is difficult.[38] Language cannot transcend itself; it cannot reach beyond itself to the reality it names. However, rhetoric is epistemic because it reveals the weakness of logic and scientific discourse by revealing that knowledge, as most people mean it, is a linguistic construction. *Knowledge is as relative and self-deceptive as the discourse used to construct it.*

Derrida also criticizes dialectical logic for imposing an exclusive structure on what should be seen as multiplicity. Arguing that any attempt to sustain a unity in philosophy is doomed to failure, Derrida expresses "a desire to escape the combinatory . . . to invent incalculable choreographies."[39] Derrida's dance is Foucault's performance;[40] both prefer subjective creativity to rational objectivity in reading the world. In that way they provide new and different interpretations of discourses. However, Derrida's object is not to see things from another perspective just for the sake of it. Not every interpretation is valid. There are times when deconstruction produces a "right track" and/or a "better" reading. At the same time we must be wary of "false (that's right: false, not true) and feeble" readings, "a bad (that's right: bad, not good) and feeble reading."[41]

At the same time, we must also be on guard against exclusive readings. The discourse of most disciplinary theories, especially the sciences, is totalizing and thereby can exclude important meanings. Derrida is particularly worried about the use of methodologies, since they often simply find what they are looking for instead of being open to hidden or layered meanings. His attack on such structuralists as Saussure and Lévi-Strauss is well-known, as is his belief in the metaphorical nature of even scientific discourse. Derrida's brand of deconstructionism seeks *polysemy* (multiple meanings), thereby multiplying possible interpretations of texts.

Derrida's deconstruction demonstrates what a concept excludes and includes, empowers or weakens, retrieves or forgets. When it comes to texts, such as speeches, he argues that *every text implies another text* like the infinite regression of two facing mirrors, and thus, texts are delusions. Such a position undermines the purported objectivity of criticism because one can never quite finish the job and, particularly in the case of speech, can never re-create a single, enveloping context. Lincoln's Gettysburg Address borrows from Daniel Webster's Second Reply to Hayne, which borrows from George Washington's Farewell Address that was written in part by Alexander Hamilton, who wanted the president to endorse federalist values that can be found in the speeches of Edmund Burke, which are drawn from. . . . You get the idea. As Derrida writes, "it is not certain that what we call language or speech acts can ever be exhaustively determined by an entirely objective science or theory."[42] Hence *literary criticism is always a rhetorical act;* critics must justify their interpretations, their points of cutoff, their use of contexts. They are editors, who decide how much of a text and its progenitors are to be included in their analysis. They are constructionists, who must build a context for their analysis.

Derrida provides several ways out of this mirror chamber. First, his famous slogan, "there is nothing outside the text" can itself be deconstructed, as Derrida himself does, to mean "there is nothing outside context."[43] Our job then is to re-create the context of the text, which can be done—to cite just two approaches—using the hermeneutics of Martin Heidegger (see chapter 9)[44] or the dramatistic approach of Kenneth Burke (see chapter 11). While this construction of context may be subjective and relative because of the "incessant movement of recontextualization," it is not without meaning. Recontextualization opens the text to "solicitation" and destabilization, which helps in the interpretive process on the road to meaning. In his own critical work, Derrida often recontextualizes a work from the perspective of "marginalized" interpretations: How would the radical thinker view the text? What would the heretic say about the text? In this way, Derrida stages the problems he confronts again and again, turning them over, around, and inside out. Seeing the inaugural from the media context might reveal a concern for the size of the television audience and national ratings for the network. Seeing the inaugural from the point of view of the impoverished in the nearby ghettoes might reveal a concern for hypocrisy and empty promises. Seeing the inaugural from the perspective of those on the platform might reveal a concern for power or the implementation of promises.

Second, he argues that "quasi-transcendence" can help us form contexts that link the individual and the particular object and the action and the agent.[45] By getting a bit above the text, we are better able to perceive its context and relationships inside and outside that context. In this way, we can create our own text, one that makes sense out of the fragmentation that surrounds us, but it is important to understand that the construction of this text is a persuasive matter, not a logical one. In the process, we recognize that the things signified (objects, concepts), the signs (words), and the signifiers (speakers) have been configured in a certain way by society and/or the interpreter. We may wish to see these things from society's perspective or from other angles, again restaging events and problems.

Baudrillard (1929–2008)

Another of the postmodern French thinkers to have an impact on rhetorical theory was Jean Baudrillard, who loved films and playing games with language in his poetry and prose. He was born in Reims, France, of civil servants and was the first in his family to attend college. He taught high school and then returned to learning at the University of Paris, where he studied sociology. His *The System of Objects* (1968), written during the Paris riots, and *The Consumer Society* (1970) demonstrated how signs and symbols had converted us into capitalist consumers desirous of various commercial objects. He broke with his Marxist past by arguing that consumerism was more important than production in determining the history of a people. What we buy tells us who we are. He claimed that we are not in danger of having too little meaning in our lives; instead, we are being overwhelmed with meaning and it is killing us. He came to America in 1970 and spoke at the Whitney Museum of Art on American primitivism and developed a cult following. He became a kind of guru of postmodernism when the screenwriters of *The Matrix* films acknowledged his influence. (The Keanu Reeves character, Neo, opens a copy of one of Baudrillard's books and uses it to hide computer discs.)

Baudrillard was more comfortable as a critic than a theorist. For example, he attacked Foucault's take on the world. Baudrillard believed Foucault's search for knowledge as a function of power was a futile effort that led to delusion. If we try to understand an object, we are likely to be led away from its reality by its signification, its history, or its connotations. The web of meaning is too dense to penetrate because objects have so many attributes. This is particularly true when the object is a speech. They can be assessed as functional: the speech moves an audience. They can be assessed as having an exchange value: how much was the speech writer paid for the speech? They can be assessed in terms of their symbolic value: this speech is a eulogy in praise of the dead. They can be assessed in terms of their sign value: where does this speech reside in a system of speeches?

In 1983, Baudrillard rejected the "drama of alienation," that is, individuals who feel alienated discard their individualism to become part of the group, and claimed that we live in an "ecstasy of communication" in which "[e]verything is reduced to image, a celebration of the look. Instead of living under the 'sign of alienation,' we now live in a perpetual present that moves away from representation and private interiority."[46] He argued that the image had become reality.

Baudrillard once argued that the Gulf War of 1991 never occurred; it was instead a media creation, more like a video game than a real war. It was an example of the speed with which the media induce society to move. Baudrillard made this ironic point to try to illustrate that the public had lost the ability to tell the difference between reality and fiction; media have destroyed the linearity of history. In fact, films, in particular, and the media in general were responsible for this phenomenon. Reality no longer has the time to be real. There are many causes of this change. First, reality must be edited if it is to appear on the media; thus, it is already once removed from reality. Second, it is often presented in small, rapid bites to retain our attention. This emphasis on concise parts is another removal from reality. Third, it is often repeated in slow motion until an event sinks in. As a slow-motion, repeated event, it is not real and moves audiences away from reality. Thus, the public treats everything as if it were a game or a movie and cannot possibly act responsibly when it comes to governing. One good example of the distortion that can take place is the documentary. Michael Moore called his attack on President George W. Bush a documentary, *Fahrenheit 9/11*. But it was clearly a persuasive piece condemning the president. It was followed in 2008 by Citizens United's famous *Hillary: The Movie*, another pseudodocumentary that tried to destroy the credibility of the former First Lady. Then, in 2012, came *Obama 2016*, another persuasive attack attempting to pass itself off as a documentary. Many people were taken in by these deceptive labels.

The media have created this state of "hyperreality." One of its consequences is the massive increase in the number of so-called reality shows that permeate television. While the people on these shows are not actors, the shows are not real. They are staged. Watching the cable program *Big Brother after Dark* reveals that the prime time network hour-long version is highly staged and edited. Baudrillard had previously claimed that Disneyland attracts us because it is so superficial that it makes the rest of the world seem real. Disneyland is the model of "simulacrum," a copy of something that is more perfect than the original. Disneyland's Frontierland is more perfect than the original frontier. People, he claimed, could manufacture "simulacrums" of themselves, a perfected version living in their heads (a perfected persona that one maintains by performing it). It is a false representation of self, which is inauthentic and dangerous, just as a perfected false representation of a nation is dangerous. For example, in the section on civil religion in chapter 10 of this book, we saw that America has been portrayed as simulacrum by political leaders. Franklin Roosevelt claimed that America had a "rendezvous with destiny." Ronald Reagan echoed that thought and added that America was a shining city upon a hill, a reference to Jesus' Sermon on the Mount. Candidate Mitt Romney claimed that this is an American century and that the United States was created by God to lead the world.

It is not difficult to see the role of rhetoric in Baudrillard's theory. Rhetoric creates the desire to purchase objects. Rhetoric creates the context for reality shows so that we believe they are real, even though the actors or players are often reduced to puppets of the producers. The manipulation of events for the evening news is rhetorical, adjusting events for the media by adapting them to audience expectations that are generated by other media such as games, television, and films. Rhetoric is used to convince us that we know an object, when in fact, such knowledge is not possible. Self-persuasion induces us to believe in a false, perfected persona that we role-play in the world or project onto other perfected personas.

Feminism also seeks revisioning, making it in some ways a postmodern cultural movement that has provided fresh values and insights to rhetorical theory.[47] It represents a *differend* that has found voice and face. Thus, it provides us with postmodern thinking because it represents a definitive turn from the past.

FEMINISM IN THE POSTMODERN WORLD

Because of their pluralistic roots, feminist critiques result in a highly diverse corpus. Ecological feminists highlight earth cultures and natural preservation; socialist feminists seek to reveal oppression, achieve economic equity, and embrace nonhierarchical sharing; standpoint feminists endorse empirical studies of local narratives constructed at the margins of society;[48] contemporary feminists oppose the dichotomous approach of essentialist feminists who tend to be exclusive and hegemonic.[49] Feminist critiques of the legal system call for inclusion of personal narratives as evidence and punishment of offensive performative utterances. Since the feminist critiques are diverse, my approach will be more inductive than usual as I tease out common threads to weave a coherent theory.

We start at the end of World War II with Simone de Beauvoir, who was introduced in the section on existentialists in chapter 9, where she was pictured in Parisian coffee shops with her lover Jean-Paul Sartre. However, de Beauvoir was a major thinker in her own right. Her *The Second Sex* (first published in 1949) was considered a feminist manifesto because it argued that one is not born a woman, one is made into a woman by society. Part of that process is the rhetorical construction of sexuality. Thus, de Beauvoir started a second wave of feminism, the first being the suffragist movement, which originated in France in the late eighteenth century and cropped up in America following the Civil War: if African American men were going to get to vote, women wanted the same privilege. In the second wave, Monique Wittig (1941–2008) followed de Beauvoir's lead. Her prose poem of 1969 "Les guérillères" depicts female warriors who defeat a dominant male band after a fierce battle. It argued for women's liberation from the social con-

Simone de Beauvoir.

struction of gender. In her 1972 novel, *The Lesbian Body*, she played with pronouns to reveal how language can inhibit humans. In the story, two women literally deconstruct one another's bodies. In 1992, she composed a collection of essays dubbed *The Straight Mind* in which she argued that the notion of sexual differences is a mask for societal censorship of feminism. She sought an end to the classes of men and women and claimed that heterosexuality was a political regime that exploits women and keeps them inferior. This second wave of feminism was also propelled forward by such political activists as Gloria Steinem, Betty Friedan, and Congresswoman Bella Abzug.

Linda Nicholson and Nancy Fraser reveal many similarities between postmodernism and second-wave feminism:

> Both have offered deep and far-reaching criticisms of institutional philosophy. Both have elaborated critical perspectives on the relation of philosophy to the larger culture. . . . [B]oth have sought to develop new paradigms for social criticism which do not rely on traditional philosophical underpinnings. . . . They have tried to rethink the relation between philosophy and social criticism so as to develop paradigms of criticism without philosophy.[50]

Both movements share a profound skepticism of generalized claims, and both contribute new ways of looking at rhetorical theory, although postmodernism focuses on the dangers of modernist philosophy and feminism tends to focus on social criticism. Fraser, for example, endorses more inclusive political practices in our public speaking. She is particularly critical of Habermas' "public sphere" (see chapter 10) because in allowing only the rational speakers into the sphere, it may exclude some women, spiritualists, minorities, and members of the lower economic classes, among others.[51]

Despite their rejection of Marxist rationalism, that is, a systematic study of society that articulates universal principles of what is just and what is unjust, feminist critiques reflect Marxism's influence embodied in "radical," "Marxist," "Socialist," "liberal," "standpoint," "post-Marxist" and "eco-" feminism. These groupings sometimes represent deep and sharp divisions. Black feminists consistently have resisted hegemonic depictions of the movement as white. Audre Lorde in the late seventies and early eighties said she felt like an "outsider-within" the movement. She regularly commented on racism in feminist organizations. In 1980, speaking at Amherst College for women, she claimed, "There is a pretense to a homogeneity of experience covered by the word *sisterhood* that does not exist."[52] Another African American writer, bell hooks (previously known as Gloria Watkins) has attacked the white bias in some feminist writing and in classical literature in general.[53] She also said her work in the movement led her to an "oppositional world view."[54] Adrienne Rich has condemned a heterosexual bias in feminist writing. Nancy Hartsock warns fellow feminists to avoid postmodernism because it is "a dangerous approach for any marginalized group to adopt."[55] She believes that the ill repute in which postmodernism is held in some circles will tarnish the feminist approach.

Reflecting Derrida's call for multiplicity, Celeste Condit prefers a diverse perspective to one based on a dichotomy generated by gender. "Dichotomy feminism," she writes, "portrays male and female activities and ways of being as radically separate from one another and assigns rhetoric to the realm of the male."[56] Chicana writers such as Gloria Anzaldúa echo the existential call for creativity as a pathway to the soul:

"When I write it feels like I'm carving bone. It feels like I'm creating my own face, my own heart—a Nahuatl concept. My soul makes itself through the creative act."[57] She calls on marginalized groups to find their intersecting differences and embrace them. This can be done by investigating the way in which discursive practice fosters the oppression generated in the scenes of race, class, gender, religion, disability, nationality, ethnicity, and sexuality. In her studies, bell hooks reveals the intersectionality of these oppressions that Anzaldúa is trying to reverse. These intersections can be seen as ideological coordinates that enforce hegemonic thinking. While sometimes fracturing, this theory leads to a healthy de-essentializing of what it means to be a feminist.

Given this diversity, it is easy to understand why the postmodern rejection of objectivity is particularly strong among feminists who believe that women have been treated like objects, including objects of sex and objects of stares; they have been objectified as possessions. As we saw with Martin Heidegger, technology has the ability to reframe humans; seeing women as reproductive machines with parts that need to be enhanced or replaced is often a fault of the medical-scientific community. Shulamith Firestone was one of the first feminists to recognize this problem. In her book, *The Dialectic of Sex: The Case for Feminist Revolution*, she sought to liberate women from biological tyranny by creating a planned new world where fetuses were grown in artificial wombs and children were raised by the community, not the single family.[58]

By tracing the Marxist and postmodern themes in feminism, we can untangle the various feminist critiques and assess their contributions to rhetorical theory. Early political feminists used the Marxist critique to argue that women had been unfairly defined by their tasks—whether in the home as "housewives" or in the workplace as "secretaries." Reflecting Marxist materialism, they not only called for equality between genders throughout society but asked for a "space" of their own.[59] Betty Friedan, a self-described Marxist, redefined the family as a private locale, a feminist niche in space and time. Feminist writers had little difficulty establishing that the androcentric society privileged men and deprived women of space and power. It was time for women's liberation, a cry taken up by New Left feminists in the late sixties and early seventies.

By dipping into the well of Marxist theory, many of these feminists, particularly the Socialists, accepted the view that class distinctions and patriarchy were the chief causes of oppression. The material base of male domination derived from control of women's production. Working women were subject to a double shift, one on the job and one at home as "housewife." In the locales, women developed local narratives they could share, a concept that found resonance in the theories of Lyotard. While patriarchy is manifest in different ways in different cultures, it almost always results in the oppression of women. Thus, women needed to link across cultures to overcome these barriers. Socialist feminists called for working women of the world to unite. For example, in a commencement address at the Kennedy School of Government at Harvard in May of 2012, Christine Lagarde explored a "world of interconnections:"

> Borders, barriers, walls have come down to allow this degree of interconnection. And yet . . . you know that there are many more walls . . . being built of that people try to build—physical walls, political walls, mental walls.

In her address, she used a personal example to reinforce her point. After completing a law degree, she was offered a position with a law firm but told she would never be made a partner in the firm. She "walked out the door and never looked back." Eventually, she became the first female finance minister of a G7 nation (France), and then the first female managing director of the International Monetary Fund.[60]

Rich attacked patriarchy that she defined as

> the power of the fathers: a familial-social, ideological, political system in which men—by force, direct pressure, or through ritual, tradition, law, and language, customs, etiquette, education, and the division of labor, determine what part women shall or shall not play, and in which female is everywhere subsumed under the male.[61]

Gender-Based Communication

Though many different feminist approaches were developed, they were united in the quest to identify gender-based problems in the language. In the world of identity politics, consciousness raising is often followed by the development of a group language. Self-described "radical" feminists such as Shulamith Firestone alleged that various discursive "norms" were clearly "gender based."[62] She argued that males had defined truth, beauty, love, and justice since the beginning of time.

This androcentric domination tended to have, to use a Marxist term, a hegemonic effect: success meant conformance to masculine ideals that were often patriarchal, competitive, and hierarchical.[63] One need look no further than many television programs of the fifties, sixties, and seventies to see how patriarchal values were venerated. Fathers, despite portrayals as bumbling in some situation comedies, generally set the rules and established the rewards for competition.[64] Even women who broke through these patterns—Murphy Brown and Roseanne in situation comedies, the women in *Chicago Hope* and *ER* in dramatic series— were often depicted as unpleasant, disruptive, or aggressive.[65]

Worse yet, those values and characteristics associated with the feminine gender were deprecated, while those associated with the masculine gender were privileged.[66] The problem began in the "ideology" of Freud, who portrayed the psyche in sexist ways: The masculine is left-brained— rational, mathematical, and scientific; the feminine is right-brained—instinctive, intuitive, emotional, and spatial. Hence, the masculine is competitive and judgmental, while the feminine is cooperative and questioning. The masculine is hierarchical and permanent, while the feminine endorses equality and change. The masculine is

bell hooks.

individualistic and industrious; the feminine is interdependent and passive. The masculine is product-oriented and linear; the feminine is process-oriented and cyclical. The masculine seeks power and status in the hierarchy; the feminine seeks collective gain.

Karen Foss put it this way when discussing male and female realms: "Women's reality is characterized by such features as a sense of interdependence and connection with others and with the world . . . an egalitarian use of power, and a focus on process rather than product."[67]

Feminists demonstrated that most societies elevate masculine over feminine values because of the need to survive and because men were the agenda setters and reward givers.[68] Using a poststructuralist perspective, for example, Barbara Biesecker criticizes the practice of rhetorical criticism for being patriarchal.[69] She claims that the association of certain values with one gender and not the other is a strategy of suppression.[70] The culture needs to understand that since women experience things differently than men, privileging a male understanding of experience prejudices society against a female understanding while at the same time forcing women to live in a world dominated by masculine values.

If masculine understandings predominate in our communication, then feminine understandings are marginalized. To remedy this situation, some feminists call for a rhetoric of difference, one that rejects masculine hegemony and embraces a group-oriented discourse built around a unity among the marginalized.[71] This antithesis is strong enough to become part of a *differend* only if it is built out of unity among women.[72]

As the movement matured, some feminists argued that communication differences were biologically driven, reflecting a materialist influence,[73] while others argued they were psychological, reflecting a Jungian influence as modified in the work of Alice Miller.[74] Behavioral feminists believe language use is gender based; until that is understood, men and women will continue to fail to communicate effectively, and women will be disadvantaged in the marketplace of ideas. Such a position, as Celeste Condit makes clear, leads to gender dichotomy that needs to be tempered by postmodern multiperspectivalism; that is, we need to examine texts, speeches, and works of fiction, from many different points of view.[75]

To deal with this problem, feminists have advocated a major overhaul in language. For example, in the professional world "Miss" and "Mrs." have been replaced by "Ms." "Actress" has been incorporated into "actor," which now applies to women and men, as does "comedian," "hero," and "nurse." "Ess," "ette," "ix" and other forms of diminutive status have been abolished. "Suffragettes" have become "suffragists." Feminists have also worked very hard to eliminate metaphors that undermine women;[76] "truncate" is preferred to "emasculate"; "field-setting" is preferred to "seminal." These critics understand that language creates ideology and ideology determines the political environment and/or creates false consciousness.

Another group of critics has broken through traditional ideology by claiming that, regardless of cause, women communicate differently than men. Jean Miller, in *Toward a New Psychology of Women* (second edition, 1986), demonstrates that women use conversation to expand and understand relationships, while men talk to convey solutions. Women see people as mutually dependent; men view them as self-reliant. Women see the world as interrelated and contextual; men see the world as discrete. Sociologist Carol Gilligan reports that one root of these differences occurs at age four when boys begin to break their dependence on their mothers, while girls immerse themselves in intimacy and empathy with their mothers.[77] Using case studies, Gilligan concludes that women are defined by their ability to care, connect, and respond to others, while men are defined by competitive success.

Supporting this line of thought, Deborah Tannen, in *You Just Don't Understand: Women and Men in Conversation* (1990), observes that women face each other in conversation, while men tend to glance off. For example, in the 2008 campaign debates, Senator McCain tended to ignore his opponent Senator Obama, while Governor Sarah Palin often engaged her opponent Senator Biden. Women share stories about life; men assert independence and success. Young girls build relationships by sharing secrets and developing intimacy; young boys fight for status in hierarchical groups— by adulthood they are still playing king of the mountain. It is just that the "mountain" may be a Fortune 500 company instead of the sand hill up the street. The bottom line is that male communication tends to be task oriented while female communication tends to be more nurturing and intimate. That's why those embracing the feminist psyche talk more than those who embrace the masculine psyche. Men are modernists; women are postmodernists.

While these categories overly essentialize the differences between women and men, they can provide a grounding for an orientation to the feminist critiques. Some moves in that direction occur in the work of Karlyn Campbell, who has argued that archetypal values can inhere in male or female speakers and reveal either a masculine or feminine speaking style.[78] For example, George H. W. Bush's call for a "kinder, gentler nation" in his acceptance speech at the 1988 Republican convention and his subsequent calls for a "team effort" with Congress represented a feminine side to his rhetoric. His valorization of competition, playing by the rules, and working hard represent the masculine side. Displaying her understanding of the synergistic relationship between rhetorical theory and criticism, Campbell analyzes the speaking and writing of such early African American feminists as Sojourner Truth, Ida B. Wells, and Mary Church Terrell. In the process, she enhances feminist rhetorical theory in our own time while differentiating between black and white feminist styles of the past.[79]

Using Campbell's theory, it is possible to construct a continuum running from the masculine to the feminine. A critic could place speakers toward one end or the other and justify that placement in terms of the language used in their speeches. The masculine and feminine would become personas *separated from physical genders*. For example, Margaret Thatcher, who served as the prime minister of Great Britain for eleven years, would be placed toward the masculine end of the continuum due to her valuing of work, individualism, competition, and hierarchies. Her address calling for war with Argentina would probably be seen as her most masculine moment. Promotion of competition among cabinet members, use of masculine metaphors, and valuing individual achievements and objectivity were some of the characteristics that argue for her placement on the masculine end of the continuum—and resulted in Soviet leaders dubbing her the "iron lady." As we have seen, those feminists influenced by the postmodern movement attempt to complicate this continuum even further by providing for a more differentiated approach to any single individual's rhetorical style.[80]

Elevating Feminine Values

After the language had been sanitized of its masculine bias, some feminists argued that feminine values contrast with masculine values and would improve society if only they were allowed to surface. Gloria Steinem advised, "Our aim should be to humanize society by bringing the values of women's culture into it, not simply to put individual women in men's places."[81] Julia Kristeva contends that females are more value-oriented than males and that the proof of this thesis can be found in a linguistic analysis of the rhetoric of women.[82] These studies are often case specific and demonstrate that in many academic fields the work of white males has dominated scholarship to the exclusion of female writing, let alone values. A number of writers in rhetoric have attempted to overcome these difficulties.

Julia Wood's book, *Who Cares? Women, Care and Culture* (1994) and Nel Noddings' *Caring: A Feminine Approach to Ethics and Moral Education* (1984) reflect the interrelational existentialists' rejection of the modernist model and their embrace of dialogic relationships. Wood and Noddings explore human connections by arguing that they are more valued by women than by men. They fuse the call for equality and caring in communication with a request that humans build responsible partnerships not as "I" alone, but as "I" in a series of dependent relationships with others. Noddings claims that our notion of "goodness" should be derived from concrete relationships not abstract intellection. It is in acts of caring that we learn the most about others and develop our strongest sense of tolerance. Such a privileging of the feminist value of caring turns rhetorical theory away from public forums and brings it into interpersonal relationships. According to feminists, little attention in the field of public address was focused on this area.

The feminist orientation also aligns itself with postmodernism when it comes to rejecting positivism. Isaac Balbus, Nancy Chodorow, and Syla Benhabib, to take but three examples,[83] argue that logical positivism is the ultimate end of materialist intellection—that which cannot be objectively verified is "non sense." This modernist tenet has contributed to an ideology of scientism that privileges the masculine bias: that knowledge is based in objectivity and logic, that it is discovered not created, that it is a reflection of nature, not society.[84] Objectivity allows one to stand aside, to be uninvolved. Worst of all, it allows one to objectify others, to make women into objects—objects of sex, objects of adoration, objects of scorn.

In particular, Benhabib's quarrel with the modernists resides in their "order of representations in our consciousness (ideas or sensations), the signs through which these 'private' orders were made public, namely words."[85] She argues that knowledge can be obtained subjectively through emotionality. *We can learn by feeling*, a distinctly nonmodernist belief. She asserts that one's emotional quotient is as important as one's intelligence quotient (IQ).

Standpoint Feminism

Another postmodern orientation can be found in the theories of "standpoint" feminists such as Nancy Hartsock, Nancy Fraser, and Sandra Harding.[86] The feminist standpoint emerges from an examination of the conflict between male and female life activities in our culture from the perspective of the marginalized. Harding claims that "[W]e start our thought from the perspective of lives at the margin."[87] Since male and female *experiences* are different, they operate from different standpoints, which affect their attitudes and communication.[88] Harding endorses a feminist empiricism to observe and analyze this problem and to undermine "Enlightenment assumptions."[89]

Hartsock employs the relativity of postmodernism to explore gender in a way that avoids abstract individualism. She moves to case studies, that is, actual locales and narratives. Like Lyotard, Fraser attempts to keep feminist analysis focused on real contexts such as the workplace or the marketplace.

Together these theorists contend that due to women's past and continued marginalization from the political system, they have a unique perspective on it, one quite different from white males who have participated in politics since the founding of the country. Standpoint feminists contend that males generally defend the hierarchic and competitive nature of politics, while women tend to criticize those aspects and replace them with such values as cooperation and caring. This new realism in the feminist movement was reflected in the speech of Ann Romney to the Republican Convention in 2012:

> I want us to think tonight about the love we all share for . . . our brothers and sisters, who are going through difficult times, whose days are never easy, nights are always long, and whose work never seems done. . . . The working moms who love their jobs but would like to work just a little less to spend more time with the kids, but that's just out of the question with this economy.

These standpoint preferences can be revealed in several ways, all of which have rhetorical dimensions. First, using Harding's "strong objectivity," theorists have completed analysis in the context of the workplace based on observation. The case for change is argumentative in nature and created with the collected data used as evidence. Second, others have employed contextual narratives—stories in the workplace—to explicate the values that are contained in it. This method has the advantage of having a natural "congruence" because it is situated in the environment of the workplace. Third, from the feminist standpoint, Adrienne Rich "re-visions" the situation; like Derrida, she participates in re-creating a context by seeing it through new lenses and using new critical methods to find larger or hidden texts. One of the best practitioners of this approach is Patricia Hill Collins, who asks African American women to overcome their predilection for self-sacrifice, particularly to protect emasculated African American men, and model new roles for the next generation.[90] She urges women to carefully navigate through the matrix of domination, which she deduces from bell hooks' theory of intersectionality (see above), which reveals the interlocking systems of oppression in our society.

Judith Butler, who studied with Hans Georg Gadamer in Germany, was introduced to the theories of Foucault while attending Yale University. She became fascinated with the question of the "other" in gay and lesbian thinking. After teaching at Wesleyan and Johns Hopkins Universities, she became chair of the department of rhetoric at the University of California at Berkeley, a post she held until 2004. At this writing, she is the Elliot Professor of Rhetoric at Berkeley. In her 1990 book, *Gender Trouble*, Butler sought to incorporate the performative notions of Foucault and Lyotard to argue that we perform gender. Like Foucault, she objects to the way juridical systems censor gender to protect normality. Juridical systems often criticize anything that varies from the official definitions of gender. We become subjects before the law in the intelligibility—she uses Foucault's term—of courts. Institutions, in this case the courts, establish knowledge systems that maintain power. Butler claims that in such a system "queer" is not intelligible; it is excluded from what is normal—that, by necessity, homosexuals live in a world that they must resist in order to survive. They become the subject of societal power when they identify with what is described as normal, acceptable sexuality. They become unreadable on the social map of power.

In her 1993 book, *Bodies that Matter*, she extends her argument by claiming that one's performance must align itself with the expectations of society or face "abjection." One is either coerced into normalcy or relegated to the margins of society. Furthermore, even those on the map of power are disadvantaged because placement on the map determines how much power one has. White males dominate the center, and as one moves to the margins, one finds homosexuals, black males, lesbians, the physically and mentally challenged, and the "less normal." The map represents women as objects; this discursive formation disadvantages women politically. Butler traces her argument all the way back to Aristotle, who argued that women's bodies produced the matter for the fetus, while the male provided the form. Such thinking divests materiality from reason, and women pay the price for this disassociation.

Feminist Legal Theory

The legal community provides yet another forum for the development of a feminist rhetoric. For example, Jennifer Nedelsky seeks "new conceptions of self that are emerging in feminist rethinking of legal rights."[91] Reflecting a strain of the feminist movement that seeks an incorporation of its values, Robin West writes, "Feminist legal theorists need to show through stories the value of intimacy—not just to women, but to the community—and the damage done—again, not just to women, but to the community—by the law's refusal to reflect that value."[92] In her case, the narrative power of rhetoric should be used to advance the cause of equality and tolerance for women. The fly in the ointment is that narratives need to be "congruent" with an audience's perception of reality if the story is to be persuasive. As many feminists point out, the perception of reality has been distorted to the masculine, particularly in the legal field. Thus, even if courts were to allow uninterrupted narratives, the narratives might of necessity have to be adapted to the masculine judicial system.

Carol Smart, in *Law, Crime, and Sexuality* (1995), targets this bias in her postmodern analysis of feminist legal theory. She claims that even feminist narratives often use patriarchal terms and values to make their point. These narratives are "confining" and often support current laws instead of reforming them.[93] She calls for treating women more as individuals and less as entities that are hegemonically bound together in gender.

She also warns feminists to avoid conspiracy theories, that is, to not assume that male lawyers conspire with male judges to suppress women. She points out that men are subject to laws and are often convicted under them. If there were a male conspiracy, this would not be the case. Feminists who assume that there is a conspiracy also assume that they can identify male special interests. Smart concludes by showing that the feminist conspiracy theory ignores class struggles that transcend gender. That is, there is more likely a white conspiracy against blacks than a male conspiracy against women. She writes, "the idea that law simply serves the interest of men against women and that legislation and legal practice is commonly guided by these principles does not stand up to closer examination."[94] The task of feminism is not to hold men to the current laws—the laws they created—but to reform current laws to reflect all segments of society.

Other leading thinkers on this topic begin with the notion of "performative utterances" borrowed from the ordinary language of philosophers and complementary to Lyotard's and Foucault's performance orientation. Gloria Anzaldúa, for example, argues that "identity is more like a performance in progress" than a principle.[95] For legal feminists, however, a performative utterance is discourse that makes something happen. Using this theory of speech acts, some legal feminists have argued that verbal rape is as damaging as physical rape and should be punished in civil court if not criminal court. The leading strategist among these thinkers is Catharine MacKinnon of the University of Michigan Law School. She begins her critique by debunking the modernist legal myth that laws are a reflection of

Gloria Anzaldúa.

and discovered in nature.[96] She sees rights as constructions of humans, not as derived from some higher province. MacKinnon goes so far as to argue that treating each person as an "individual" is a way to "mask" and "obscure" collective realities and to defeat the unity of women.[97] She attacks the objectivist approach to the law as dehumanizing. Here she is supported by Carol Weedon, who builds on Foucault and Lyotard to "throw light on how gender power relations are constituted, reproduced, and contested."[98] Weedon denies the usefulness of "individual experience" in constructing civic virtue and turns to "socially constituted" frames "within discourse."[99]

MacKinnon has joined with Andrea Dworkin to take the debate to another level.[100] They argue that pornography is an act of sexual subordination that should be subject to legal penalties just like any other act of sexual discrimination. They proposed an ordinance for the city of Minneapolis, which defines pornography as "graphic sexually explicit subordination of women through pictures and/or words." If the production of such material results in discrimination or assault, the creator of such discourse would be subject to civil trial.[101] The First Amendment implications of this position are troubling, but it does provide for an interesting discussion of the problems surrounding what is intended by the speaker and what is perceived by the listener. How does one prove intent? Can a society write laws that are based on the perception of what is meant as opposed to what could have been meant?

MacKinnon tried to answer these questions in her 1993 book, *Only Words*. She extended her definition of pornography by adding that the material produced must be intended to make a profit and *can be shown to have resulted in damage to women*.[102] For MacKinnon, the profit motive reveals intent. She continued that since words are considered acts when they result in sexual harassment, they should also be considered acts when they degrade women.[103] In both cases, "social inequality is substantially created and enforced—that is, *done*—through words and images."[104] It is one thing to protect pure speech but quite another to protect the action of the speech when it violates the rights of others. She stated her position clearly, "To express eroticism is to engage in eroticism, meaning to perform a sex act. To say it is to do it, and to do it is to say it."[105] Speech is performance; performance is speech. These will, no doubt, not be the last words on this line of thinking.

A FEMINIST RHETORICAL THEORY

Feminist critiques have moved beyond their postmodern and Marxist roots into an ever-evolving analysis of society and a woman's place in it. Karen Offin, for example, advocates movement feminism to improve women's lives in an ever-changing culture.[106] Hence, it is clear that feminist rhetorical theory is critical in its outlook; it attempts to build a discourse that points out the dangers of hierarchies, of linear thinking, and of assuming that logic and science, particularly technology, can solve our problems. It seeks to correct the use of language by rooting out masculine biases in word choice, metaphor, labels, and the like. Feminist rhetorical theory emerges from its dialectical history as a movement. That history of empowerment is a complex process requiring an awakening of selfhood.[107] Like Marx, many feminists claim that everything, including sex, is pervaded by politics. The joining of politics and rhetoric has been a hallmark of the women's dialectic, which developed in several stages.

First, raising consciousness encouraged women to examine their condition and place. MacKinnon writes that "consciousness raising is the major . . . theory of social change of the women's movement."[108] Again reflecting the influence of Marxism, the second stage determines who is responsible for the current, oppressive condition. Such a step involves the rhetoric of attack and critique. Often the male and his society become the devil figures in this story. The third stage involves improving the lot of women in every aspect of their lives from equal pay for equal work to being valued in the home. This process includes elevating women to prominent places in the vocational and political world to serve as models for others. It also involves giving women a sense of place and sense of having their own space. In this sense, feminist rhetoric is largely localized.

The fourth stage often, but not always, results in identification between the leader of a movement and the women in it. By identifying with women on the stage, on camera, or in the legislature, women in the audience can become liberated and realize their potential.[109] Thus, feminist rhetoric reflects the Marxist threads in Kenneth Burke's notion of identification and redefinition.

One of the most accomplished women in the contemporary era is Condoleezza Rice, former national security advisor and secretary of state. At the Republican Convention in August of 2012, she tried to demonstrate how she embodied the American dream when she said:

> A little girl grows up in Jim Crow Birmingham, the segregated city of the South where her parents can't take her to a movie theater or to a restaurant, but they have her absolutely convinced that even if she can't have a hamburger at the Woolworth's lunch counter, she can be president of the United States. . . . And she becomes secretary of state.

What occurs here is *an enactment of a redefinition through transformation* that relies heavily on a personal narrative. Four years earlier, Hillary Clinton would attempt to make history—to penetrate the ultimate glass ceiling—in 2008. But Clinton's rhetorical style would differ from Rice's; Clinton's focus was more on her professional record. Instead of punctuating her speech with a *personal* description of defying the odds of achieving success, she spoke of others who did so.

Thus, the historic dialectic out of which feminist rhetorical theory is born features narratives, particularly personal ones. Master narratives, particularly patriarchal and hierarchical theses, are deemed oppressive. Individual, local, feminine narratives form the feminist antitheses—whether in the home, in the courtroom, or from the margins. These narratives are built from the unique standpoints of women and thereby become stories that have never been heard by those in power. They can provide the data from which new policies (syntheses) are made and new rhetoric is generated. Certainly this position contributes to feminist legal theory. Whether it be the call for the use of narratives for evidence in the courtroom or the call for treating certain phrases as performative utterances, feminist legal theory would reconfigure forensic speaking to take into account many of the postmodern themes of Foucault and Lyotard.

Another feature of feminist rhetorical theory is that the power equation needs to be carefully assessed in communicative settings. Feminists often rely on Foucault's critique to explore the relationship of power and knowledge and to demonstrate that by keeping important information from others, one participates in a kind of enslavement.[110] This theme is as old as Plato's *Phaedrus* wherein Socrates criticizes himself for withholding information from Phaedrus during Socrates' first speech on love in order to control Phaedrus. In modern times, the knowledge-is-power game has been played by politicians and corporate chiefs to suppress those below them.

By picking up various threads from these critiques and readings, it is possible to deduce contributions of these different contemporary feminist approaches to rhetorical theory and criticism. First, those critiques that build on Marxist and postmodern critical theories endorse a fluid discourse that points out the dangers of hierarchies, of linear thinking, and of assuming that logic and science, particularly technology, can solve our problems. These critiques are skeptical of grand narratives, preferring local or personal narratives from which truths can be induced. They ferret out "false consciousness," particularly the masculine and Enlightenment "false consciousnesses" because of the damage they have done to women.

Second, those critiques that see gender as constructed by discourse attempt to root out masculine biases in word choice, metaphor, labels, and the like. The impact on semantic usage has been significant as has the rhetorical implications of gender-based language. In fact, a whole segment of politically correct dialogue and discourse flows from the efforts of feminists to cleanse the arena of linguistic possibilities of its masculine biases.

Third, some feminist critiques seek to prevent reason from dominating the search for truth; instead spiritualism and emotion, to name just two alternatives, are given new influence. Like the postmodernist, some feminists recognize the failure of reason and science to solve society's problems. The optimism of Hegel has given way to the cynicism of world wars, civil wars, holocausts, and terrorism. To transcend such cynicism and find new solutions to old problems, some feminists expect such emotions as empathy to break through to new truths, while others embrace a rhetoric of spirituality that leads to an appreciation of the rhetorical corridors to transcendence.

Fourth, some feminist critiques attempt to endorse a new kind of forensic speaking. Whether it be the use of situated, local, and/or personal narratives for evidence in the courtroom, or the call for treating certain phrases as performative utterances, feminist legal theory would reconfigure forensic speaking to take into account many of the postmodern themes of Foucault and Lyotard. Such an undertaking also benefits from the "strong objectivity" of Harding's theory by grounding its evidence in reality and recognizing that social knowledge is constructed. The implications for research into connections between rhetoric and the law are significant.

Fifth, the feminist sensitivity to audience uncovers the power equation in communicative settings and more directly engages and includes audience members. Foucault's critique is often used to explore the relationship of power and knowledge to demonstrate that by keeping important information from others one participates in a kind of enslavement. Gaye Tuchman studied how the latter has worked in the news media symbolically to annihilate women. She focused on how the media rhetorizes, if you will, news with a masculine bias.[111] In essence she asked, How can we free women from the tyranny of media messages limiting their lives to hearth and home?[112] Feminist rhetorical scholars have answered this question by dialoguing with audience members, putting them on an equal par with speakers, and calling for more discursive space and inclusiveness in public address.[113]

In primary debates in 2008, Hillary Clinton often faced tougher questioning than did Barack Obama, and when she complained about such treatment, she was dubbed a "whiner," even though all she was requesting was equal treatment inside the discursive space created by the debate format. This problem was most notably explored by Audre Lorde in her book *Sister Outsider* where she famously claimed that "the master's house will never be dismantled with the master's tools."[114] She argues that rhetoric can make a difference by allowing a marginalized group to create their discursive space where their own identity can emerge. Such rhetoric allows the group's identity to emerge from themselves rather than from the perspective of others.[115] Such rhetoric may destabilize hegemonic discourse and create new identities of the formerly marginalized group. When in 1985 she became the first woman to head the Cherokee Nation, Wilma Mankiller (1945–2010) set out to destabilize hegemonic perceptions not only of Cherokees but of women within that nation. Over her ten years as chief, she was successful in rebuilding a sense of confidence and self-esteem among the Cherokees, whether male or female.

Sixth and related, some feminists infuse the public realm with consideration of interpersonal situations and relationships. The emphasis on the interpersonal brings to light the intimate, which means that feminist rhetoric focuses on different issues than masculine rhetoric. The importance of caring relationships also affects a speaker's relationship with her/his audience while at the same time empowering those who seek caring relationships or caregiving. The foregrounding endorsement of interpersonal communication establishes a rhetoric of difference that may exclude those who are not part of the experiential group or may include the outsider who empathizes. Audre Lorde, for example, emphasizes empathy and equality, and thereby embodies the oppositions within their own ranks. Borrowing from Lorde and hooks, Collins urges black women to use their position as "outsiders within" to reject imposed hierarchies and take up new positions that they define and determine.[116]

Seventh, the postmodern approach has also fostered a gender diversity perspective that is an outgrowth of "gender deconstructionists" and "third-wave" feminists.[117] They see neither man nor woman as isolated ontologically, or essentialized, and prefer a much more differentiated view of individuals.[118] They argue that each of us is unique, and any theory that overlooks our unique features is superficial and dangerous. Such theories bury our uniqueness in categories of objectivity.

In this way, third-wave feminism emerged to critique the ever-changing bases of opposition and requirements for identity. It insists on local identities and identity politics in its notion of personhood. It seeks to uncover personal existence in the intersections of sex, gender, race, class, ethnicity, and the like. From these intersections, third-wave feminist rhetoric creates its own definitions and significances of existence and spirituality. Sometimes, even the body itself becomes rhetorical when it is used to convey a personal message, as when a woman shaves her head to show solidarity with a sister who has cancer or to remove the look of the past, the hair of the feminine.

The seven preceding contributions to rhetorical theory are born of an assessment of the multiperspectival approach of feminist criticism of society. Feminist rhetorical theory seeks to discover ways by which the masculine value system has been privileged, seeks to give at least equal status to feminine values or in some cases to demonstrate their superiority to the masculine, seeks to rid the language of sexism, and develops new rhetorical theories that use gender as a way to expose and make us more open to different scholarly approaches and new female scholars. Such an approach requires a "revisioning" of culture so that male-centered premises and values can be rethought, synthesized with feminine values, and/or replaced.

The study of rhetoric can reveal what feminists call "intellectual conventions" (such as linear versus cyclical thinking, abstraction versus reality) that are manifest in public speaking. The study of rhetoric can reveal what feminists call "mythic conventions" because whether they are about the "sleeping beauty" or the "white knight," we can uncover the ideology that lies behind them. The study of rhetoric can reveal what feminists call "role conventions" because these conventions rely on certain personae that rhetorical analysis can unmask.[119] Women can be companions without taking on the persona of sexual partner. Women can be successful without taking on the persona of a power gatherer. Women can enact the personae of cops, doctors, and lawyers if that is what it takes to prove effective in those roles. As Campbell has noted:

> [S]trategic adaptation is common in early feminist rhetoric. It is characterized by these rhetoric[al] elements: personal tone, speaking as a peer, relying on examples, testimony, and enactment of evidence, inductive structure, and efforts to stimulate audience participation.[120]

Clearly, postmodern and traditional rhetorical theory can help us to see these possibilities as no other studies can. Perhaps by finding a way to build bridges between the two, we can provide a more complete look at our society while transcending the differences our bodies impose upon us.

CONCLUSION

Postmodernism does not rely primarily on empirical knowledge, and it rejects modernist themes, such as human reason is the basis for rational control of physical and social conditions. It will continue to be controversial for a number of reasons. First, it rejects a single, correct reading of a text just as it rejects a master narrative of history. New meaning can be found, argue the postmodernists, by reading a text in different ways, in different contexts, and from different perspectives. Second, it rejects the rational model for the settling of disputes. Recall that in Jürgen Habermas' public sphere, all sides were given a voice, but they had to act rationally. In Lyotard's *differend* all sides are given a voice, and they may use the rhetoric of their choice to express themselves. Local narratives, mythology, and emotional evocations are all part of the game.

Third, postmodernism sees the speaking situation as performative. Thus, the speaker is an actor on stage involved in a drama with the audience. The speaker is not merely the news bringer, the informer, the persuader.

Fourth, postmodernists recognize that knowledge is power and that rhetoric often functions to encode that knowledge in ways that keep it inside the tribe, whether the tribe be the United States Senate or a street gang.

Fifth, the postmodern notion of deconstruction argues that no text is ever complete. Each text implies another text, maybe an earlier one, maybe the one that could be crafted from what is left out of the current text.

Sixth, because speech is so localized in its impact and construction, a universal structure cannot be manufactured for speaking situations. Instead, language must be seen as indigenous, relative, laden with hidden meaning, metaphorical, analogical, and polysemic. To get at such language, one must tolerate many different theories and methods, not a single "methodology."

Not since the Sophists have we been presented with such a tolerant, controversial, and relative theory of language. Not since the existentialists have we seen such skepticism of reason and science. While the demise of postmodernism has been predicted in scholarly work for over two decades, it continues to flourish and to contribute new and meaningful readings of texts. For that reason, we need to monitor its progress and enjoy its product.

Study Questions

1. In what ways does the "postmodern" condition affect you?

2. Do you consider yourself a postmodernist or a modernist?

3. What is the relationship between power and rhetoric in Foucault's postmodern theory?

4. Why is Lyotard considered a poststructuralist?

5. Why do postmodernists want to look at speaking as performance instead of analyzing its structure?

6. How does Lyotard's system of *differends* work in the legal context? Who gets to act as judge?

7. To what extent can feminism be seen as postmodern?

8. To what extent does gender-based communication theory change rhetorical theory? Find examples of gender-based phrases that exist in common language. In what ways do women communicate differently than men?

9. Cite an example of a contemporary male speaker who uses the feminine rhetorical style. Cite an example of a contemporary female speaker who uses a masculine rhetorical style.

10. What is feminist value rhetoric, particularly as represented in the thinking of Wood and Noddings?

11. What is standpoint feminism? Find examples of it in contemporary public address.

12. How are feminists attempting to change legal rhetoric? What is their objection to individualized case law?

13. Through what stages does the feminist rhetorical movement travel? What is the role of ego in each stage?

Notes

[1] His actual name was Charles Edouard Jeanneret. His first famous piece was "Citrohan," a model for inexpensive housing. He was a major advocate of the modern style in the twenties, popularizing it as a concept in several architectural publications in France and in Switzerland, his native country.

[2] He had also immigrated to Chicago in 1938 and became a U.S. citizen in 1944.

[3] S. Best and D. Kellner, *Postmodern Theory: Critical Interrogations* (New York: The Guilford Press, 1991), p. 4.

[4] The recent documentary on dancer and choreographer Pina Bausch highlights this trend.

[5] Best and Kellner, p. 3.

[6] Jürgen Habermas (see chapter 10) clearly believes that normative standards for the "better argument" can be found; his attack on "conservative postmodernism" was an attempt to salvage communicative rationality. Habermas strongly disagreed with the approaches of postmodernists Foucault and Derrida. He deeply resented their attacks on Enlightenment thinking.

[7] Paul Davies, *Superforce* (New York: Simon and Schuster, 1984), p. 200.

[8] See, for example, Bart Kosko, *Fuzzy Thinking: The New Science of Fuzzy Logic* (New York: Hyperion, 1993).

[9] Christina Di Stefano, "Dilemmas of Difference: Feminism, Modernity, and Postmodernism," in *Feminism/Postmodernism*, Linda Nicholson, ed. (New York: Routledge, 1990), p. 63.

[10] Michel Foucault, *Language, Counter-Memory, Practice: Selected Essays and Interviews*, Donald Bouchard, ed. (Ithaca: Cornell U. Press, 1977), p. 151.

[11] See Paul Rabinow, ed., *The Foucault Reader* (New York: Pantheon, 1984), p. 43. Modernist dialectic was advanced by Arthur Schopenhaur (1788–1860), Immanuel Kant (1724–1804), and Georg W. F. Hegel (1770–1831) (see chapter 9).

[12] Ibid., p. 4.

[13] Michel Foucault, *The Order of Things: An Archaeology of Human Sciences* (New York: Pantheon, 1970).

[14] See, for example, Aristotle on various forms of wisdom in chapter 4 of this book.

[15] In "Prisons et Asiles dans le Mécanisme du Pouvoir," *Dits et Ecrits*, vol. II (Paris: Gallimard, 1994), pp. 523–24. My translation.

[16] Michel Foucault, *The Archaeology of Knowledge* (New York: Harper & Row, 1972), p. 216. Ironically, the term archaeology is borrowed from the modernist Immanuel Kant, mentioned earlier in this chapter and chapter 9 of the present book.

[17] See Carlos Levy, "From Politics to Philosophy and Theology: Some Remarks about Foucault's Interpretation of Parrhesia in Two Recently Published Seminars," *Philosophy and Rhetoric*, 42 (2009): 313–25.

[18] Foucault, *The Archeology of Knowledge*, pp. 139–64.

[19] Michel Foucault, *Power/Knowledge* (New York: Pantheon, 1980), pp. 81, 85–86.

[20] This quotation comes from interview with Foucault, and is printed in Michael Mahon, *Foucault's Nietzschean Genealogy: Truth, Power and the Subject* (Albany: State U. of New York, 1992), p. 102.

21 Michel Foucault, "Nietzsche, Genealogy, History," in *Language, Counter-Memory, Practice: Selected Essays and Interviews by Michel Foucault,* ed. Donald F. Bouchard (Ithaca: Cornell U. Press, 1977), pp. 160–64.

22 Michel Foucault, *Discipline and Punishment: The Birth of the Prison* (New York: Vintage, 1979), pp. 200–2. In 1963 he had published *The Birth of the Clinic: An Archaeology of Medical Perception.* In an attempt to advance his previous theory, he studied how "the gaze" of the professional could reinforce power and objectify an other.

23 Michel Foucault, *History of Sexuality: Volume I: An Introduction,* Robert Hurley, trans. (New York: Pantheon, 1978), p. 100.

24 Ibid., p. 94.

25 Foucault reinforced a turn toward "critical rhetoric" in scholarship. The object of such criticism is to unearth patterns of domination and to demystify the ideologies that lie behind them. See, for example, Raymie McKerrow, "Critical Rhetoric: Theory and Praxis," *Communication Monographs,* 56 (1989): 91–111; "Critical Rhetoric in a Postmodern World," *Quarterly Journal of Speech,* 77 (1991): 75–78.

26 See Michel Foucault, "The Order of Discourse," in *Untying the Text: Post Structural Reader,* R. Young, ed. (Boston: Routledge, 1981).

27 Michel Foucault, "Of Other Spaces," Jay Miskowiec, trans. *Diacritics,* 16 (1986): 24; *The Order of Things: An Archaeology of Human Sciences* (New York: Vintage, 1994), p. xxi.

28 See Jean-François Lyotard, *The Postmodern Condition: A Report on Knowledge,* G. Bennington and Brian Massumi, trans. (Minneapolis: U. of Minnesota Press, 1993), p. xxiv.

29 Ibid., p. 27. Later he writes, "Scientists, technicians, and instruments are purchased not to find truth, but to augment power." p. 46.

30 J.-F. Lyotard, *The Differend: Phrases in Dispute,* G. Van Den Abbeele, trans. (Minneapolis: U. of Minnesota Press, 1988), p. xi.

31 J.-F. Lyotard, *Just Gaming,* Wlad Godzich, trans. (Minneapolis: U. of Minnesota Press, 1985), p. 26.

32 Lyotard spent ten years teaching in the schools of Algeria where he saw the same kind of displacement.

33 Lyotard, *The Differend,* p. 181.

34 Lyotard, *The Postmodern Condition,* p. 44.

35 Richard Rorty, *Philosophy and the Mirror of Nature* (Princeton: Princeton U. Press, 1979), p. 377.

36 Ibid.

37 Michel Foucault, "The Ethic of the Care of the Self as a Practice of Freedom," in *The Final Foucault,* J. Bernauer and D. Rasmussen, eds. (Cambridge: MIT Press, 1988), p. 11.

38 See his *Of Grammatology* (1967) and *Dissemination* (1972).

39 Jacques Derrida and Christie V. McDonald, "Choreographies," *Diacritics,* 12 (1982): 76.

40 And both were preceded by Kenneth Burke's famous suggestion that "always beneath the dance of words there will be the dance of bodies." *The Rhetoric of Religion,* p. 288.

41 The parenthetical remarks are Derrida's, not mine. See Jacques Derrida, *Limited Inc.,* Samuel Weber, trans. (Evanston, IL: Northwestern U. Press, 1988), p. 146.

42 Ibid., p. 118.

43 Ibid., p. 136.

44 Heidegger brings context to textual situation by challenging the reader to discover the "fore-structure" of the author. The fore-structure includes the linguistic possibilities of the author of the text, his or her inherited attitudinal conceptualization, and his or her methodology.

45 Derrida, *Limited, Inc.,* see particularly pages 136–37.

46 "The Ecstasy of Communication" in *The Anti-Aesthetic: Essays on Postmodern Culture,* Hal Foster, ed. (Port Townsend, WA: Bay Press, 1983), pp. 128–30.

47 See, for example, F. Capra, "The Concept of Paradigm and Paradigm Shift," *ReVision,* 9 (1986): 11–12; J. Roberts, *Beyond Intellectual Sexism: A New Woman, a New Reality* (New York: David McKay Robert, 1976); Karen Foss and Sonja Foss, "The Status of Research on Women and Communication," *Communication Quarterly,* 31 (1983): 195–204; Karlyn K. Campbell and Kathleen H. Jamieson, eds., *Form and Genre: Shaping Rhetorical Action* (Falls Church, VA: Speech Communication Association, 1990).

48 See, for example, S. K. Foss, C. L. Griffin, and K. A. Foss, *Feminist Rhetorical Theories* (Long Grove, IL: Waveland Press, 2006/1999). Even within this substrata of feminist critique there is a great deal of difference. D. L. O. Hallstein, "A Postmodern Caring: Feminist Standpoint Theories, Revisioned Caring, and Communication Ethics," *Western Journal of Communication,* 63 (1999): 3–56, goes so far as to suggest that there is no solid standpoint theory.

49 For an example of rhetorical theorists attempting to derive a rhetorical theory from a single feminist writer, see S. Foss and C. Griffin, "A Feminist Perspective on Rhetorical Theory: Toward a Clarification of Boundaries," *Western Journal of Communication,* 56: 330–49. They compare Starhawk to the standards of Kenneth Burke.

50 L. Nicholson, "Social Criticism without Philosophy: An Encounter between Feminism and Postmodernism," in Nicholson, p. 19. In the same volume, Jane Flax writes that feminist theory belongs "within" postmodern philosophy. "Postmodernism and Gender Relations," p. 40.

51 N. Fraser, "Rethinking the Public Sphere: A Contribution to the Critique of Actually Existing Democracy," in *Habermas and the Public Sphere,* Craig Calhoun, ed. (Cambridge: MIT Press, 1992), pp. 109–42.

52 Audre Lorde, "Age, Race, Class, and Sex," *Sister Outsider: Essays and Speeches by Audre Lorde* (Freedom, CA: Crossing, 1984), p. 116.

53 See bell hooks, *Outlaw Culture: Resisting Representations* (New York: Routledge, 1992).

54 bell hooks, *Theory from Margin to Center* (Boston, MA: South End Press, 1984), p. ii.

55 Nancy Hartsock, "Foucault on Power: A Theory for Women?" in Nicholson, p. 160.

56 Celeste Michelle Condit, "In Praise of Eloquent Diversity: Gender and Rhetoric as Public Persuasion," *Women's Studies in Communication,* 20 (1997): 91–116.

57 Gloria Anzaldúa, "Tlilli, Tlapalli: The Path of the Red and Black Ink," in *The Graywolf Annual Five: Multi-cultural Literacy,* Rick Simonson and Scott Walker, eds. (Saint Paul: Graywolf Press, 1988), p. 38.

58 Shulamith Firestone, *The Dialectic of Sex: The Case for Feminist Revolution* (New York: Farrar, Straus and Giroux, 2003).

59 See, for example, Karlyn Kohrs Campbell, *Man Cannot Speak for Her: A Critical Analysis of Early Feminist Rhetoric,* vol. 1 (New York: Praeger, 1989); H. L. Steeves, "Feminist Theories and Media Studies," *Critical Studies in Mass Communication,* 4 (1987): 95–135.

60 Quotations are from Robert O'Neill, "The Value of Global Citizenship," Harvard Kennedy School, May 23, 2012. http://www.hks.harvard.edu/news-events/news/articles/the-value-of-global-citizenship (accessed July 11, 2012).

61 A. Rich, *Of Woman Born: Motherhood as Experience and Institution* (New York: W. W. Norton, 1986), p. 57.

62 Shulamith Firestone, *The Dialectic of Sex* (New York: Bantam, 1970). See also, for example, G. Pascall, *Social Policy: A Feminist Analysis* (London: Tavistock, 1986).

63 See, for example, C. Mouffe, "The Sex/Gender System and the Discursive Construction of Women's Subordination," in *Rethinking Ideology: A Marxist Debate,* S. Hanninen and L. Paldan, eds. (New York: International General, 1983), pp. 139–43.

64 See Muriel G. Cantor, "Prime-time Fathers: A Study in Continuity and Change," *Critical Studies in Mass Communication,* 7 (1990): 275–85.

65 For a study of the hegemonic impact of the media, see R. Williams, *Marxism and Literature* (New York: Oxford U. Press, 1977).

66 The "gendering of sex roles" is explored by H. Steeves and M. Smith, "Class and Gender in Prime-time Television Entertainment: Observations from a Socialist Feminist Perspective," in *Journal of Communication Inquiry,* 11 (1987): 43–63. See also Flax, p. 52.

67 K. Foss, "Feminist Scholarship in Speech Communication: Contributions and Obstacles," *Women's Studies in Communication,* 12 (1989): 1–10.

68 See Michelle Rosaldo, ed., *Women, Culture, and Society* (Stanford: Stanford U. Press, 1974), particularly pages 17–42.

69 See B. Biesecker, "Coming to Terms with Recent Attempts to Write Women into the History of Rhetoric," *Philosophy and Rhetoric,* 25 (1992): 140–61. See also S. Gearheart, "The Womanization of Rhetoric," *Women's Studies International Quarterly,* 2 (1979): 195–201; Spitzack and K. Carter, "Women in Communication Studies: A Typology for Revision," *Quarterly Journal of Speech,* 73 (1987): 401–23.

70 Also see M. Humm, *Feminist Criticism* (Brighton, GB: Harvester Press, 1986); Sonja K. Foss, *Rhetorical Criticism: Exploration and Practice,* 4th ed. (Long Grove, IL: Waveland Press, 2009).

71 See, for example, Cathy Schwichtenberg, "Introduction: Connections/Intersections," in *The Madonna Connection: Representational Politics, Subcultural Identities, and Cultural Theory,* Cathy Schwichtenberg, ed. (Boulder: Westview Press, 1993).

72 Note the melding of Marxism and postmodernism in this position.

73 Biologically based studies of language can be traced back at least to Susanne K. Langer. See, for example, her "The Origins of Speech and Its Communicative Functions," *Quarterly Journal of Speech,* 46 (1960): 121–34.

[74] See Steeves.

[75] Condit. I should add that the work of Margaret Mead, Anke Erhardt, Patricia Goldman, Sarah Hardy, Annelisa Korner, Eleanor Maccoby, and many female scientists have made foundational contributions to the study of gender communication.

[76] S. Foss.

[77] Carol Gilligan, *In a Different Voice: Psychological Theory and Women's Development* (Cambridge: Harvard U. Press, 1982). Gilligan's research has been severely criticized by a number of feminist scholars. Julia Wood, whose theories we'll examine later in this chapter, claims that Gilligan's work is based on "precarious generalization" and moves "from limited and unrepresentative data to quite broad generalizations of women," in "Gender and Moral Voice: Moving from Woman's Nature to Standpoint Epistemology," *Women's Studies in Communication*, 15 (1992): 3–4.

[78] See K. K. Campbell, "Style and Content in the Rhetoric of Early Afro-American Feminists," *Quarterly Journal of Speech*, 72 (1986): 434–45. See Campbell's *Man Cannot Speak for Her*, Bonnie Dow and M. B. Tonn, "Feminist Style and Political Judgment in the Rhetoric of Ann Richards," *Quarterly Journal of Speech*, 79 (1993): 286–303.

[79] See also Dow and Tonn.

[80] See particularly Condit.

[81] She made this comment to me in 1980 during a political campaign for a senator we both supported.

[82] Julia Kristeva, "Le Temps des Femmes," *Cahiers de recherche de sciences des textes et documents*, 5 (1979): 5–19.

[83] I. Balbus, *Marxism and Domination* (Princeton: Princeton U. Press, 1982); N. Chodorow, *The Reproduction of Mothering* (Berkeley: U. of California Press, 1978); T. Meisenhelder, "Habermas and Feminism: The Future of Critical Theory," in R. Wallace, *Feminism and Social Theory* (Beverly Hills: Sage, 1989), pp. 119–32. Syla Benhabib, "Epistemologies of Postmodernism: A Rejoinder to Jean-François Lyotard," in Nicholson.

[84] See also Nicholson, p. 5ff.

[85] Benhabib in Nicholson, p. 110.

[86] Nancy Hartsock, "Foucault on Power: A Theory for Women?" in Nicholson: 157–75; Nancy Fraser, *Unruly Practices: Power, Discourse, and Gender in Contemporary Social Theory* (Minneapolis: U. of Minnesota Press, 1989); Sandra Harding, "Feminism, Science, and the Anti-Enlightenment Critiques," in Nicholson, pp. 83–106.

[87] Sandra Harding, *Whose Science, Whose Knowledge: Thinking from Women's Lives* (Ithaca: Cornell U. Press, 1991), p. 269. I should note here that Harding did not immediately embrace standpoint feminism. In fact, in her 1986 work, she was rather critical of it.

[88] N. Hartsock, "The Feminist Standpoint: Developing the Groundwork for a Specifically Feminist Historical Materialism," in *Discovering Reality*, Sandra Harding and Merrill Hintikka, eds. (Dordrecht, Holland: D. Reidel, 1983), p. 303. See also C. Weedon, p. 8; Harding, *Whose Science*, pp. 128–29.

[89] Sandra Harding, "Feminism, Science, and Anti-Enlightenment Critiques," in Nicholson, p. 98.

[90] P. H. Collins, *Fighting Words: Black Women and the Search for Justice* (Minneapolis: U. of Minnesota Press, 1998).

[91] Jennifer Nedelsky, "The Practical Possibilities of Feminist Theory," *Northwestern University Law Review*, 86 (1993): 1286.

[92] Robin West, "Jurisprudence and Gender," *University of Chicago Law Review*, 55 (1988): 65.

[93] Carol Smart, *Law, Crime, and Sexuality: Essays in Feminism* (London: Sage, 1995), p. 87.

[94] Ibid., p. 142.

[95] In Dwight Conquergood, "Rethinking Ethnography: Toward a Critical Cultural Politics," *Communication Quarterly*, 58 (1991): 180.

[96] Catharine A. MacKinnon, "Feminism, Marxism, Method, and the State: An Agenda for Theory," *Signs: Journal of Women in Culture and Society*, 7 (1982): 515–44. Andrea Dworkin, "Law as Interpretation," *Texas Law Review*, 60 (1981–2): 527–50.

[97] Catherine A. MacKinnon, "Legal Perspectives on Sexual Differences," in D. L. Rhode, ed., *Theoretical Perspectives on Sexual Differences* (New Haven: Yale U. Press, 1990) p. 223.

[98] C. Weedon, *Feminist Practice and Post-structural Theory* (Oxford, UK: Blackwell, 1987), p. vii.

[99] Ibid., p. 125.

[100] Andrea Dworkin, *Woman Hating* (New York: E. P. Dutton, 1984) writes, "Intercourse with men as we know them is increasingly impossible. It requires an aborting of creativity and strength, a refusal of responsibility and freedom: a bitter personal death. It means remaining the victim, forever annihilating

all self-respect. It means acting out the female role, incorporating the masochism, self-hatred and passivity which is central to it" (p. 184). See also her *Ice and Fire* (New York: Weidenfeld and Nicholson, 1987), particularly pp. 54, 64, 84–85, 101–2.

101 The ordinance has not faced a court test because, while it was adopted by the city council, it was vetoed by the mayor on First Amendment grounds.

102 Catherine A. MacKinnon, *Only Words* (Cambridge: Harvard U. Press, 1993), p. 22.

103 Ibid., p. 45.

104 Ibid., p. 13.

105 Ibid., p. 33.

106 Karen Offin, "Feminism and Sexual Difference in Historical Perspective," in Rhode, pp. 13–20.

107 See Spitzack and Carter.

108 MacKinnon, "Feminism, Marxism," p. 5.

109 See Richard B. Gregg, "The Ego-Function of the Rhetoric of Protest," *Philosophy and Rhetoric*, 3 (1971): 71–91.

110 Michel Foucault, *Power/Knowledge* (New York: Pantheon, 1980).

111 Gaye Tuchman, *Making News* (New York: Free Press, 1978).

112 "Liberal feminist" leader Betty Friedan first raised this kind of question in her critique of the women's magazines in "Happy Housewife Heroine," in chapter 2 of *The Feminine Mystique*. She argued that these magazines assigned a persona to women in order to keep them in the service of capitalism. Like other feminist critics, Friedan employed a Marxist approach to her subject.

113 See for example Sonja Foss and Karen Foss, *Inviting Transformation: Presentational Speaking for a Changing World*, 3rd ed. (Long Grove, IL: Waveland Press, 2012).

114 Lorde, *Sister Outsider*, p. 110.

115 Ibid., pp. 114–23. Lisa Flores explores Lorde's notion of "discursive space" in "Creating Discursive Space through a Rhetoric of Difference," *Quarterly Journal of Speech*, 82 (1996): 142–56. She shows how Chicana feminists repudiated "mainstream discourse and [espoused] self- and group-created discourse" (p. 145). Such a strategy is available to all marginalized groups.

116 For both Lorde and Collins, see Collins.

117 While these authors have differences, they do prefer the diversity perspective to the gender dichotomous one. Among others, they include Gloria Anzaldúa, *Borderlands: La Frontera* (San Francisco: aunt lute, 1987); bell hooks, *Talking Back: Thinking Feminist, Thinking Black* (Boston: South End, 1989); Judith Butler, *Gender Trouble: Feminism and the Subversion of Identity* (London: Routledge, 1990); and Toril Moi, *Sexual/Textual Politics* (London: Routledge, 1985).

118 As Condit rightly concludes, "[W]hen most men and women have the same scores on a given biological measure, it can hardly be said that this measure is an indication of an essential, dichotomous variation between the genders," p. 110.

119 See, for example, Karlyn Kohrs Campbell, "Femininity and Feminism: To Be or Not to Be a Woman," *Communication Quarterly*, 31 (1983).

120 Ibid., p. 106. This theme is reflected in Campbell's two-volume work, *Man Cannot Speak for Her.*

Rhetorical Consciousness

Thistle book has explored the history of rhetorical theory in Western civilization. To be included, a theorist needed to have advanced our understanding of rhetoric or advanced the discipline by introducing it into a new language or culture, preserving it for a new era. In the United States, rhetoric has been respected. Our greatest orator, Daniel Webster, learned the art of rhetoric at Dartmouth College. John Quincy Adams taught rhetoric at Harvard University. In 1915, it was revived as a legitimate academic field by James Winans, who drew from the principles of William James to refine persuasion theory. A field of study was born and then nurtured by a host of researchers on rhetoric, who turned to the classics, poetics, and psychology to enrich the revived discipline. Charles Sears Baldwin, Harry Caplan, Lane Cooper, Hoyt Hudson (1893–1944),[1] Everett Lee Hunt (1890–1984),[2] Richard McKeon (1900–1985),[3] A. Craig Baird (1928–1952), and Herbert Wichelns (1894–1973),[4] to name just a few, established a workable definition of a scholarly specialty that was unique and deserved separate status from English, philosophy, psychology, and drama departments.

Their rationale for the discipline can be traced to ancient Greece; it constitutes a strong defense of the discipline to this day. Unlike poetics, the art of rhetoric concerns *specific* messages for *specific* audiences as opposed to universal messages and audiences. It is concerned with suasory discourse as opposed to discourse that merely informs or entertains. It is not consummatory like poetics; that is, it is not an end in itself. It invites further action and extension. In its constitutive role, it can bring a people into being; in its instrumental role, it can persuade them to further action; in its aesthetic role, it can carry audiences to the sublime. This art form often manifests itself in persuasive speaking, but books, plays, films, editorials, songs, theatre, performances, and paintings are not beyond its realm. They too have rhetorical dimensions. No other art looks at the persuasive elements of what it studies. No other art finds its generative principles in its audience—hence the important links to pragmatism in terms of goals and to psychology in terms of audience analysis. Like the Greeks and the Romans, contemporary rhetorical theorists understand that rhetoric serves as a nexus for other studies.

RHETORIC AS ONTOLOGICAL

In the course of this survey, I have tried to demonstrate that rhetorical theory reflects the evolution of human consciousness. Rhetoric is an ontological structure—that is, an innate way of being, a defining human characteristic. Because humans are decision makers and thinkers, and because they think in symbols, they use rhetoric at basic levels of consciousness to interpret what they sense and to make sense of what they experience. As Protagoras said, "[humans are] the measure of all things."

Rhetoric is ontological because the decisions we make define our character. *We are known and judged*, according to Aristotle, Cicero, and Kierkegaard, to name just three philosophers on the subject, *by the decisions we make and how we make them*. If we have been in the habit of making good decisions, our credibility and sense of self are strengthened. Since the most important decisions we make are based on probabilities, the arguments that surround them are often rhetorical in nature. Again, we are defined rhetorically if we are human.

Rhetoric is also ontological because unlike other forms of discourse it understands that humans are always in some frame of mind, emotional state, or mood. Aristotle codified the ways in which that frame of mind can be reinforced or altered by rhetoric in terms of the causes of emotional states being proximate in time and space. In fact, rhetoric can move a listener from one state of mind to an entirely different one. Often such a movement is necessary before a listener can hear logical instructions and make rational decisions. Ending a panic in a burning building is not done logically; the panic is ended with powerful rhetoric in terms of image, forceful delivery, and credibility. Only when the panic has been replaced by calm can rational steps to safety be presented. Thus, like no other art form, rhetoric takes cognizance of the listener's state of mind, playing to this basic ontological structure of human nature.

Innate human interpretation of sensed data, rhetorical arguments used to make decisions, assessment of human credibility based on decision-making ability, and strategic use of emotional states demonstrate that rhetoric operates at the core of the human psyche. It is a significant part of our way of being; thus, the history of rhetorical theory can be seen as a history of the evolution of our consciousness. As we have learned more about that consciousness, we have improved rhetorical theory. John Locke's view that the soul is *tabula rasa*—literally an "empty cabinet" but better understood as a "blank slate"—and informed by its experiences, led to a division of the mind into various faculties. George Campbell then investigated the impact of this discovery on the canons of rhetoric and saw new ways to integrate rhetorical theory to produce more effective and affective speeches. Sigmund Freud's description of the psyche led Kenneth Burke to develop a theory of rhetoric around identification between speaker and audience. As new discoveries are made about our consciousness, new theories of rhetoric will also be spun out.

RHETORIC AS AXIOLOGICAL

Rhetoric is also axiological. That is, it helps to create, study, and use values. Socrates was one of the first to examine whether rhetoric improved or debased society. Obviously, it can do both. In terms of axiology, it can serve values—such as materialism, free enterprise, spirituality, and individualism—that can be either good or bad depending on your perspective. Deciding which values are most important and relevant to a given situation is extremely important. For Socrates and his famous pupil Plato, values were most relevant to the way people led their lives. Socrates believed that the contemplative life would lead humans back to their souls where they could once again seek the knowledge of the *noumenal* world and share it with others. His noble rhetoric, outlined particularly in the *Phaedrus*, called for a dialogic inquiry into the soul, which respected the other member of the dialogue and shared all discovered information. The values of tolerance, respect, equality, and knowledge are embraced and advanced by such a rhetoric. The same dialectical themes are revived in the twentieth-century theories of such interrelational existentialists as Martin Buber and Karl Jaspers.

Augustine was the first to explore systematically the ways for a preacher to defend the faith and convert others to it. Able to practice what he preached, Augustine started a line of rhetorical theorists that included many of the great leaders of Christendom such as Thomas Aquinas, Martin Luther, Melanchthon, and John Calvin.

Karl Marx presented the world with an entirely different set of values. Always suspicious of religion's ability to mask ideology and caught up with the optimism in humans' ability to reason to the truth, Marx advocated a critique of society to unearth its material motivations and hidden dialectical tensions. In order to free humans from society's hierarchical structures, he sought to bring equality to the workers of the world. The Marxist critique of societal operations and values provided a new set of values that were advanced rhetorically by various groups in many nations around the world. While the communist movement appears to have fallen because of its own weight, it did provide an antithesis to established notions of capitalism; the emerging synthesis reformed capitalism, allowing for unions, providing welfare, and redistributing wealth through progressive taxes. It also provided a critical rhetoric, which questions the overt claims of institutions and groups and looks for the larger text in which a more representative message may be found. It inspired Kenneth Burke to develop a dialectical approach to rhetorical criticism that uncovered hidden motivations and ideologies.

RHETORIC AS EPISTEMIC

For each advance in the way we learn things, there has been a similar advance in the sophistication of rhetorical theory. Often these advances come with the give-and-take of the battle between various schools of thought. The relativists, that is, those who believe that absolute or definite truth is difficult to determine, have provided rhetoric with powerful tools with which to shape perceptions. Rhetoric is instrumental in the social construction of knowledge. The line running from Protagoras' claim that "[humans are] the measure of all things" through Kierkegaard's argument that reality must be understood from the perspective of the subject to Burke's dramatistic understanding of discourse has been enormously productive of new rhetorical theory. Postmodernism is the latest approach to contribute to this legacy. It helps speakers understand multiple audiences and shifting conceptions of reality. An analysis of rhetorical discourse from this relativist perspective demonstrates that it parallels the evolving epistemology of these thinkers. For example, if we cannot know the truth and can only build illusions, then rhetoric should be dedicated to building and defending the better illusions of our society. Protagoras would have us create the better illusion in order to make sense of the world; Kierkegaard would have us understand that how we decide is more important than what we decide; Burke would have us see speakers as actors caught up in a drama of enormous symbolic importance. Foucault would have us discover how those who have and define knowledge manipulate us.

The empirical line in epistemic thinking—running from Thales' reductionist theories through Aristotle's observation of effective practice to Locke's emphasis on sensed data—has also produced major advances in rhetorical theory. Scientists have examined how the voice works physiologically to explain variation in pitch, rate, and volume that can hold the attention of the audience. We have studied successful speakers to determine precisely what makes them so, and then added these elements to the rhetorical arsenal. We have examined speech as it is sensed by an audience to see how it changes emotions and moves the will to act. The ancient school of empirical observation has become the contemporary testing ground of communication theory. From "communication apprehension" to "perceived caregiving," the theories of rhetoric have generated the hypotheses for testing in the social scientific realm. It is a marriage of the perspectives of Vico and Locke.

Plato's epistemology argued that the truth is in the *noumenal* world that had once been glimpsed by the human soul. By questioning the soul, we could retrieve the perfect knowledge of the *noumenal* world that would in turn prepare our souls for their return to it. In such a philosophy, rhetoric becomes a dialectical tool engaged in earnest questioning and contemplation. This theme, with some modifications, is reinforced by Immanuel Kant, who also posits a *noumenal* world, and by many leading existentialists, who believe the human soul is capable of reaching transcendent spirit. They also endorsed rhetoric's ability to make known the truth of discoveries of the soul. Because of the dialectical nature of this rhetoric, these philosophers, from Plato to Heidegger, disdain its use in public address. In the process, they neglect one of rhetoric's most important functions.

RHETORIC, GOVERNANCE, AND POWER

Public address conditions the political world. One of the vital themes of this book has been the way in which rhetoric is bound up with temporal power. Socrates, who believed power corrupted the soul, accused the Sophists of training the youth of Athens in rhetoric so they could achieve power and become "men in the city." Aristotle, who served in the court of Philip of Macedon and observed the use of power in many forms of government, argued that rhetoric is essential in a contingent world. His advice in the *Rhetoric* certainly could be used to obtain and wield power on the political stage. Cicero was a rhetorical theorist who actually did gain power, being elected consul of Rome and having a long career in the Roman Senate. He believed that there was no way to avoid using power; thus, like Quintilian after him, Cicero wanted each speaker, each civic leader, to be well acquainted with philosophy and history so that they would use their power prudently.

In the Renaissance, the most important writer on the relationship between power in civic affairs was Machiavelli. Like some of the Sophists, he believed the end justified the means, and he endorsed rhetoric as one of the chief means by which a prince could obtain his goals. Machiavelli's cold-hearted theory taught princes that rhetoric could be used to instill fear in their subjects and to create a sense of nobility for themselves. He even advised on ways to corrupt certain human traits into vices that could serve the prince's goals.

Among those who provide helpful monitors on power, the existentialists are perhaps the most profound. In an effort to bring a sense of responsibility to the use of power, they endorse guides for speaker and audience alike that would help to prevent the abuse of power in the future. Reflecting the lessons of Socrates in Plato's *Phaedrus*, existentialists argue that speakers should not discuss topics with which they have little familiarity. They should take custody of what they say and understand the consequences. They should also have a sense of commitment to what they advocate and to their audiences. That is, they should exemplify what they preach. If they advocate action, they should make sure it is in the best interests of their audiences. These things should be done without deception; audiences should be treated as equals and all relevant knowledge should be shared. Speakers should demonstrate a sense of commitment not only to their audiences and their messages, but to their craft. Finally, speakers should not make decisions for their audiences (an action that can stifle the development of souls); instead, speakers should force audiences to make decisions because that process increases their sense of selfhood.

If speakers have their responsibilities, so do audiences. Chief among these is holding speakers accountable for what they advise. Too often we vote for the candidates who promise us the most, then we fail to hold them accountable when they fail to deliver on those promises. Audiences need to know enough to be able to tell when a speaker has sufficient knowledge of a topic. It is not enough to determine a speaker's knowledge from listening to a half-hour television or Web broadcast or from reading his or her blog and fail to do any background reading on topics of importance. Finally, we need to take responsibility for the decisions we endorse and the speakers we support. All of this effort requires commitment, care, a sound education, and a healthy sense of skepticism.

If speakers and audiences take these steps, they live what the existentialists call authentic existences. These existences embrace tolerance and equality, which is another way that rhetoric is linked to the pragmatic operation of society. Speech has been a powerful tool of those who seek to bring equality to all humans. Whether it is the call for self-determination in India by Gandhi or the call for equality among the races in the United States by Martin Luther King Jr., public address has served to advance the causes of good persons speaking well. We should also note that rhetorical theory itself seems to thrive in places where it is treated as an equal among the disciplines. The rhetorical criticism of public address has worked to enhance rhetorical theory while at the same time revealing its connection to the marketplace of ideas.[5] The best of these critiques has also given the discipline a legitimacy in other academic fields, such as political science and history. Where rhetoric is not tolerated, it often degenerates, and those who would advance equality and tolerance are deprived of it as a tool for good.

CONCLUSION

Robert Scott understood why rhetoric is critical to the viability of other studies:

> [T]ruth is not prior and immutable but is contingent. Insofar as we can say there is truth in human affairs, it is in time; it can be the result of a process of interaction at a given moment. Thus rhetoric may be viewed not as a matter of giving effectiveness to truth but of creating truth. . . . Men may have recourse to some universal ideas in which they are willing to affirm their faith, but these must enter into the contingencies of time and place and will not give rise to products which are certain.[6]

The instability of the world, the elusive nature of the truth, and the diversity of audiences in the public and private arena ensure that the practice of rhetoric will be around as long as humans are. It will continue to reflect our evolving consciousness as long as we give equal voice to all members of society. Few studies are more worthy of our time and effort.

Study Questions

1. Based on your experience, in what ways is rhetoric ontological? Axiological? Epistemological?

2. What are the links between rhetoric and political power? Between rhetoric and tolerance? Between rhetoric and equality?

3. Given the current global economic and environmental situation, how can rhetoric be used to promote and foster understanding among various nations in the world?

Notes

[1] See "The Field of Rhetoric," *Quarterly Journal of Speech*, 9 (1923).

[2] See "Rhetoric and Literary Criticism," *Quarterly Journal of Speech*, 21 (1935).

[3] McKeon brought together *The Basic Works of Aristotle* (New York: Random House, 1966) and the classics at the University of Chicago for many years.

[4] Wichelns' landmark essay, "The Literary Criticism of Oratory," was first published in 1925. See reprint in *The Rhetorical Idiom: Essays in Rhetoric, Oratory, Language and Drama*, Donald C. Bryant, ed. (Ithaca: Cornell U. Press, 1958).

[5] See for example, S. K. Foss, *Rhetorical Criticism: Exploration and Practice,* 4th ed. (Long Grove, IL: Waveland Press, 2009).

[6] Robert Scott, "On Viewing Rhetoric as Epistemic," *Central States Speech Journal*, 18 (1967): 13–14; see also Scott's "On Viewing Rhetoric as Epistemic: Ten Years Later," *Central States Speech Journal*, 27 (1976): 258–66; Michael J. Hyde and Craig R. Smith, "Hermeneutics and Rhetoric: A Seen but Unobserved Relationship," *Quarterly Journal of Speech*, 65 (1979): 347–63.

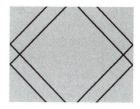

Appendix
A Timeline of Events

In the timeline that follows, events have been selected that influenced the relationship between rhetoric and knowledge. Learning was shaped by social surroundings and the development of new forms of social organization. Rhetoric became a powerful force in public affairs and education, evolving from stories that modeled desired behavior and reinforced values to arguments that convinced and persuaded. Some of the events sketched here are discussed in the text; others are listed to provide the contexts in which rhetoric evolved. A few events prior to the classical period of Greece and Rome mark the start of this journey. Encapsulating a time and place is a difficult enterprise, but it gives a sense of the complex inheritance of contributing influences.

HISTORICAL SYNOPSIS

Greece is a mountainous country in which tribal groups settled in small, isolated territories with sufficient natural resources to sustain small populations. Oligarchy—rule by a few leaders—was the standard form of government of these independent city-states. As populations increased, the sea provided opportunities for expansion. Trade increased and colonies were established. Because of their proximity to the great kingdoms of the East, the Greeks were exposed to the advanced culture of the Persians but were distant enough to avoid subjugation and became sufficiently strong to resist any such attempts. With the growth of wealth, tyrants vied with democracy for political control. Despite periods of alliances between the city-states, the classical period was marked by both civil wars and conflicts with outside powers.

Preliterate Greece was a culture of orality in which thinking was characterized by the juxtaposition of ideas. Concrete imagery that appealed to the senses and the emotions was mixed with ritualized references to authority through rhythmic proverbs. The invention of the alphabet separated language from the speaker. It became an object for analysis to be rearranged and reordered. One idea could be subordinated to another. Questions were asked rather than events described.

The juxtaposition of the beginning of humanist thought (the belief in human intellectual and moral capabilities and the motivation to use those abilities to achieve high standards) and brutal vying for power was eloquently summarized by Sophocles (496–406 BC) in *Antigone*. (Note that despite the accomplishments of the Greeks, the position of women—reflected in the exclusionary language in these two passages— was not advanced.)

> O clear intelligence, force beyond all measure
> O fate of man, working both good and evil.
> When the laws are kept, how proudly his city stands.
> When the laws are broken, what of his city then?

The poet Pindar (514–438 BC) phrased a similar sentiment:

> But brief is the season of man's delight.
> Soon it falls to the ground.
> Some dire decision uproots it.
> —Thing of a day! Such is man—a shadow in a dream.

In Rome, despite threats from enemies without and political struggles within, the empire grew steadily. Plebeian citizens battled patricians for equality of social, political, and religious rights. Yet, most Romans valued civic loyalty over personal interest. A reverence for public authority and responsibility primed them for excelling in tasks of law and government. Social and political life intertwined. The family was a training ground for civic patriotism. Distinctions in Roman society were based on the capacity for public service: leading armies in war, drafting legislation or adjudicating conflicts, and religious guidance. In the second century, glory in service of the state was replaced with self-interest. The powerful mix of kinship bonds, patronage, and duty eroded, and the new society was fragmented.

BC

1600–1200	Mycenaean culture dominates in Greece; settlements at Mycenae, Tiryns, Thebes, Pylos, Cnossus; culture develops in which Greek heroic myths are founded
1100–1000	Dorian Greeks arrive in mainland Greece
1050–950	Ionian Greeks migrate from mainland to Aegean islands and Asia Minor
825–730	Euboean settlements (primarily Chalcis and Eretria) become leading centers of trade and territorial expansion in Greece
814	Carthage established
776	First Olympic Games
753	Rome established by Phoenicians
750–700	Greek alphabet based on Phoenician model spreads throughout Greece
750–700	Homer; his works start the Greek emphasis on human achievement; versions of the *Iliad* and the *Odyssey* available in written form
750–700	Hesiod; poet, author of first mythology
735	Naxos founded; first Sicilian colony of the Greeks

733	Corinth establishes Syracuse in Sicily
730	Corinth most advanced city culturally and politically; Miletus, Athens, Samos, and Sparta rising in importance
720	Greeks move into Hellespont area
714–676	Archelochos of Paros invents iambic meter
664	Greeks arrive in Egypt for trade
650	Greek settlements in Black Sea region
624–548	Thales of Miletus; founder of Ionian philosophy; seeks physical rather than mythical explanations for events in nature; believes water is basic element of nature; predicts eclipse of sun in 585; systematic search for causes opens door for critical analysis
621	First written laws in Athens
611–547	Anaximander of Miletus; pupil of Thales; seeks source of nature; also omits any supernatural origins; Anaximenes, pupil of Anaximander, claims all substance can be reduced to air
593	Solon institutes legal code
580–507	Pythagoras of Samos; migrates to Greek colony in southern Italy; believes the origins of nature are inherently mathematical; begins line of thinking that runs through Newton and Einstein
546	Arrival of Persians in Mediterranean; conflicts for next 50 years
544–541	Heraclitus; believes flux and *logos* are only realities
540	Carthage and Etruscans (Romans) halt Greek expansion in western Mediterranean
515	Parmenides; believes in single God, the one permanence
509	Roman Republic established; survives until 27 BC when it becomes an empire
508–502	Democratic reforms of Kleisthenes in Athens

The Classical Age

Athens creates and loses an empire. Democracy is born and rhetoric prevails.

496–400	Sophocles; Greek dramatist explores the conflict between individual conscience and obligations to the state
492–479	Persia wars against Greek city-states
490	First Persian infiltration of mainland Greece; Battle of Marathon
485–411	Protagoras; earliest Sophist; antilogic; father of debate, teaches in Athens.
485–336	Rise of Sophists
485–380	Gorgias; arrives in Athens in 427 from Leontini, Sicily
484–425	Herodotus; writes about Persian wars; finds more to praise in Persian culture than most Greeks who put aside internecine quarrels in the face of a threat from "inferior" non-Greeks
480	Athens sacked by Persians; Carthage invades Sicily but is defeated
480–403	Critias; Sophist, early admirer of Socrates, later becomes one of the tyrants who brutally seizes control of Athens in 404
480(?)–411	Antiphon; Attic orator writes *Tetralogies*

478	Athens achieves prominence; leader in creating Delian League (478) of Greek city-states to combat Persia; creates empire that causes fears of Athenian imperialism among allies, especially Sparta
470–410	Aspasia of Miletus; left Miletus as its power faded and became one of the very few influential women in court of Pericles in Athens
469–399	Socrates; uses dialogue as means to retrieve knowledge in the soul
467	Syracuse in Sicily becomes democracy; the legendary Corax and Tisias teach rhetoric in Sicily
462	Ephialtes creates courts for lower levels of society
461	Conflict between Athens and Sparta begins
461–429	Age of Pericles; in his "Funeral Oration" he contrasts Athenian spirit and culture with Spartan discipline
460–377	Hippocrates; establishes medical school on Cos; seeks causes and cures for disease
460–399	Thucydides; elected general in Peloponnesian War; exiled in 424 for failing to rescue a city under attack from Sparta; spent time in exile (20 years) fashioning a history of the war to serve as a model for future historians; it includes many political debates and speeches
459–380	Lysias; prominent speechwriter and Sophist in Athens
451	Twelve Tablets establish Roman civil law in writing
451	Pericles issues law-defining citizenship
450–433	Empedocles explores power of language in Sicily; teaches Gorgias; Aristotle refers to him as first teacher of rhetoric
450	Zeno of Elea creates paradoxes
448–380	Aristophanes; comic playwright who uses *Lysistrata* to communicate his disgust for the Peloponnesian War. In the play, Athenian women seize the Acropolis and refuse relations with men until peace is achieved
447	Parthenon built in Athens
445	Canuleian law legalizes marriage between plebeian and patricians in Rome
443	Athenians establish Thurii in south Italy
436–338	Isocrates; Athenian student of Gorgias; first to establish school in 393
431–404	Peloponnesian War between Athens and Sparta, and their allies, destroys Delian League
427–347	Plato; student of Socrates, Athenian aristocrat; the Peloponnesian War, violence between oligarchs and democrats and execution of Socrates reinforces his distrust of democracy; believes society should be ruled by philosopher-kings
412	Revolt of Athenian allies; Persia joins struggle
404	Walls of Athens destroyed at end of Peloponnesian War; Sparta returns to dominance
399	Socrates executed for corruption of youths
395–386	Corinthian War—Sparta against Corinth, Thebes, Athens, and Argos—supported by Persia
390–354	Xenophon of Athens; writes first historical novel, *Cyropaedia*, which emphasizes moral leadership and is popular for centuries in Europe
387	Plato founds Academy

386	Plato writes *The Gorgias*
384–322	Aristotle; born in Stagira on Macedonian coast
384–322	Demosthenes; great orator who warns Athenians against takeover by Philip II of Macedonia
372–287	Theophrastus of Eresus; student of Aristotle, continues his Peripetetic School
370	Plato writes the *Phaedrus*
367	Aristotle enrolls at Plato's Academy; lecture notes assembled during his two stays in Athens (367–347 and 335–323) become basis for *Rhetoric*
359	Licinian-Sextian law in Rome grants limited ownership of lands
359	Philip II becomes king of Macedon; goes to war with Athens in 357
356	Philip's son, Alexander the Great, born
348	Plato dies
341–270	Epicurus established school in 306; advances philosophy that pursuit of pleasure is means to peace of mind
342	Aristotle tutors Alexander, now 14
338	Isocrates dies; Philip defeats Athens and Thebes; subjugates all Greece
337	Philip founds Corinthian League of Greek states and declares war on Persia
336	Alexander's father assassinated; at age 20 Alexander pursues his father's plan to invade the Persian Empire; creates the Hellenistic world, which extends as far as modern Russia and Afghanistan by 326
335	Aristotle founds the Lyceum (Peripatetic school); leading authority of his time in every area of knowledge
334–323	Alexander conquers Persia, Egypt, and marches to India; he dies in 323
330	Anaximenes produces *Rhetorica ad Alexandrum*
323–276	Alexander's empire splits into regions ruled by his generals who found royal dynasties: Greece (ruled by Antigonus), Macedon (ruled by Cassander), Thrace (ruled by Lysimachus), Egypt (ruled by Ptolemy), and the Seleucid Empire in Asia (ruled by Seleucus); last decades of Athenian prominence; gradual expansion of Rome results in an alliance of all parts of Italy south of the Po valley
322	Aristotle and Demosthenes die
304	Publication in Rome of handbook of legal phrases and posting of calendar in forum informing public of legislative dates
292	State supported library at Alexandria attracts Greek and Egyptian scholars who preserve Greek culture
264	Roman army arrives in Sicily to help in battle against Carthage; first Punic War; first gladiators compete in Rome; Carthage and the regions created from Alexander's empire are the four other powers in the Mediterranean
263	Syracuse allies with Rome
250	Demetrius writes *On Style*
246	Eratosthenes head of library at Alexandria; calculates circumference of earth correctly
229	Romans settle on eastern shores of Adriatic; admitted to Hellenic games
221	Hannibal takes command of Carthaginian forces in Spain at age twenty-five
218–201	Second Punic War won by Rome
204–122	Polybius; like Thucydides, believes historians should teach moral lessons

200   Rome develops its culture, borrowing heavily from Greek models

161   Romans expel Greek rhetoricians and philosophers

146   Carthage destroyed by Romans; Africa becomes province; Rome center of patronage; Latin literature flourishes

133   Roman senate fails to resolve domestic problems; senators consumed with their own prestige now that external threats from foreign enemies removed; Tiberius Gracchus had proposed land reform one year earlier. The Roman nobility view Gracchus as a threat to senatorial rule and kill him and 300 of his followers

116–27   Marcus Terrentius Varro; poet, grammarian, lawyer writes *De lingua Latina*

110–35   Philodemus; Roman Epicurean philosopher and rhetor

106–43   Cicero; eloquence overcomes class barriers, and he wins his election to series of political offices; believes rhetoric is an art that helps organize civilized life

105–23   Apollodarus of Pergamum; teacher of rhetoric for Augustus Caesar

89   Cicero writes *De inventione*

88   Sulla becomes ruler of Rome

84   *Rhetorica ad Herennium;* one of the most complete rhetorical manuals in Latin to survive into later epochs

79   Cicero travels to Athens to study philosophy at the Academy

70–19   Virgil; writes *Aeneid* consolidating Roman mythology

60   Pompey, Crassus, and Caesar form first triumvirate

55   Cicero writes *De oratore*

47–44   Dictatorship of Caesar

44   Caesar assassinated

43   Cicero assassinated for trying to prevent Antony from seizing power; political oratory suppressed; rhetoric serves entertainment function, focus on style

30   Antony and Cleopatra commit suicide; Egypt annexed by Rome

27   Octavian (Augustus); creative emperor who introduces reforms in provinces; his 41-year reign (27 BC to AD 14) is the start of Pax Romana, which lasts until AD 180

4(?)   Jesus of Nazareth is born

AD

14–37   Reign of Tiberius during which Jesus is crucified; Apostles Paul and Peter lead Christian movement.

37–41   Gaius Caligula comes to power only to be murdered by his own guards

41–54   Claudius rules as emperor, invading Great Britain

54–68   Reign of Nero, who blames Christians for major fire in Rome; Peter and Paul are crucified in 64

35–95   Quintilian; born in Spain, educated in Rome

69–79   Turning the siege of Jerusalem over to his son, Vespasian emerges as emperor from a civil war

70   Titus, son of Vespasian, destroys the Temple at Jerusalem that Herod the Great had created

79–81   Titus reigns as emperor

81–96	Titus' brother Domitian reigns as emperor employing Quintilian as a teacher
95	*Institutio oratoria* by Quintilian published
96–98	Nerva reigns, recalling St. John from exile on Patmos; John gives sermons that become the Book of Revelation
96–410	Second Sophistic; interest in etymology, grammar, and style
98–117	Reign of Trajan
117–138	Reign of Hadrian, who divides Britain and expands empire
150–219	Clement of Alexandria; theologian
155–225	Hermogenes of Tarsus; aide to Marcus Aurelius, writes books on rhetoric
161–180	Marcus Aurelius; last of the five "good" emperors; follower of stoic philosophy; during last fourteen years of his life while commanding legions on the frontier (Balkan peninsula) writes in Greek *Meditations*
165–167	Plague spreads through Roman Empire
172	Marcus Aurelius launches war against the Marcomanni tribes
175–250	Ammonius Saccas; teaches Origen
185–254	Origen; church father
200–258	Cyprian; church father
236	After a victory at Histria, Goths launch series of attacks around Black Sea
260–340	Lactantius Firmianus; theologian and orator
265–340	Eusebius of Caesarea; theologian and church historian
268–270	Goths attack Ephesus, Cyprus, Greece, and Macedonia
280–337	Constantine; Roman emperor allies with Christians; negotiates Nicean Creed (325); founds Constantinople (330)
313	Edict of Milan provides for toleration of Christians
340–397	Ambrose; Christian bishop and orator who teaches Augustine; argues emperor is *in* not *over* church
347–407	John Chrysostom; most prominent preacher of Patristic period; Archbishop of Constantinople
349–420	Jerome; translates the Hebrew and Christian scriptures into Latin; the *Vulgate* becomes the standard text in churches for one thousand years
354–430	Augustine; goodness ratified by religion not civic virtue; knowledge comes from revelation; holds chair of rhetoric at Milan 384–386; bishop at Hippo
376	Rome's frontier northeast of Black Sea collapses
376–380	Huns begin invasions pushing other tribes, such as Vandals, Alans, and Goths to the West
392	Paganism abolished in Roman Empire
395	Division of empire between East (Constantinople) and West (Rome); Huns raid Antioch
400–408	Vandals migrate across Germany and Gaul; Goths invade Italy
410	Led by Alaric, Visigoths sack Rome and move on to Gaul forcing Vandals and Alans into Hispania. Rome withdraws troops from Britain
410–427	Martianus Capella introduces Roman curriculum that became the seven liberal arts taught in Middle Ages
426–427	Augustine completes Book IV of *On Christian Doctrine*
430	Vandals surround Hippo; Augustine dies. Anglo-Saxons invade Britain
439	Vandals conquer Carthage and Africa

442–447	Huns invade Roman held Balkans
453	Attila the Hun dies; civil war ensues
470	Huns defeated and partially absorbed into Eastern Roman Empire
476	End of Roman Empire in the West as Theodoric leads Amal-Ostrogoths into Rome

Middle Ages

Education had begun to decline in the late Roman Empire. Schools closed and many literary works of the Hellenistic era were lost. Knowledge of Greek and Latin declined as the center of Western civilization moved north to Europe. Germanic tribes and Christian principles eventually forged a new culture. The early Middle Ages (500–1050) were marked by a breakdown of central authority, declining population, decaying cities, deaths from starvation or disease and Viking raids. Gradually large landowners began to exercise authority, and feudalism began. Christianity had become the religion of the Roman state. When the empire fell to the Germanic tribes, Christian Romans worked to convert the new rulers. Almost no one other than clerics could read or write Latin. Support for education shifted from secular to ecclesiastical patrons. Monasteries became the new centers of culture. Charlemagne revived classical Greek and Roman learning to maintain his empire and to further Christianity. He also ordered the copying of old manuscripts. The Carolingian Renaissance is responsible for the resurrection of texts that guided the formation of knowledge in the West. It also blunted the expansion of Islam, which had begun in 632.

The High Middle Ages (1050–1300) were marked by improvements in farming, a growing population, and a return to urban life and commerce. Merchants and artisans formed a new social class. The middle class centered around the marketplace rather than the church or castle. The power of kings grew as they extended their authority over more land and marked the beginning of the European state system. The kings resented papal interference in political life, while new knowledge was gained from contact with Middle Eastern and Asian cultures. Two branches of learning grew from the Augustinian trunk: scholasticism, with its focus on logic and form, and humanism, with its focus on reviving the classical ideal and the study of personal talent.

480(?)–524	Boethius; places invention of arguments under dialectic; preserves Aristotle's work
477–565	Cassiodorus; pupil of Boethius; writes *Institutes*—summary of the trivium and quadrivium
488	Ostrogoth kingdom established in Italy by Theodoric
511	Theodoric adopts Roman system of governance and expands his empire to south Gaul and Spain. Franks defeat Visigoths in north Gaul
526	Theodoric dies; Franks emerge as European leaders
527–565	Eastern Emperor Justinian defeats the Vandals and Ostrogoths, then institutes *Corpus iuris civilis* in 534, a compilation of the three types of laws developed by the Romans over centuries: civil law, law of nature, and law of nations; forms basis of common law in Eastern Roman Empire through Middle Ages and is reintroduced in the West in the twelfth century
529	Justinian closes Academy at Athens

570(?)–632	Muhammad; powerful speaker; teachings contained in Qur'an
570–636	Isidore of Seville; bishop who pursues seven arts, including rhetoric and dialectic
590–604	Pope Gregory the Great outlines art of letter writing
730–804	Alcuin of York; called by Charlemagne to reinstate education in his empire; writes *Disputatio*
732	Charles Martel defeats the Moors at Poitiers and builds Frankish Empire
752	Martel's son, Pippin II, installs Carolingian line by deposing the Merovingian king
768–814	Pippin's son Charlemagne; rules from Tours; becomes Holy Roman Emperor on Christmas 800 after defeating Lombards (775) and Avars (796); in 814 he is succeeded by his son Louis the Pius
793	Vikings begin raids on Britain
860	Vikings lay siege to Constantinople
878	King Alfred of Wessex turns back Vikings, some convert to Christianity
881	Vikings sack Aachen, Cologne, and Bonn
895	Magyars conquer the Great Hungarian Plain
950–1022	Notker Labeo; revives rhetorical theory in *De arte rhetorica*
993	Henry of Saxony claims Holy Roman Empire
955	Henry's son, Otto I, defeats invading Magyars
962	Otto II named Holy Roman Emperor
1000–1200	Seven liberal arts form basis of French cathedral schools, ancestors of modern universities
1079–1142	Peter Abelard
1095	First Crusade includes charismatic preacher Peter the Hermit
1096–1141	Hugh of St. Victor; writes *Didascalion*
1100–1180	John of Salisbury; aide to Becket; studies grammar, rhetoric, and logic in *Metalogicus*
1126–1198	Averroës; writes commentaries of the work of Aristotle; *Decisive Treatise*
1214–1292	Roger Bacon; writes *Opus maius* embracing empirical approach to science and the arts
1221–1274	St. Bonaventure; writes *Art of Preaching*
1225–1274	Thomas Aquinas; at University of Paris; works toward synthesis of faith and reason
1265–1321	Dante; writes *Divine Comedy* and a theory of rhetoric later expanded by Vico

Renaissance

After several fits and starts, the Renaissance finally took off in the fourteenth century. It was a product of several factors. First, the development of vernaculars created a stronger sense of nationalism, which in turn generated more nation-states, which could then develop their own cultures. Second, the rise of commercial centers such as Florence and Venice allowed for the accumulation of large amounts of money by individuals who could then fund artists. Third, inventions and explorations led to new visions of the world that inspired artists. Fourth, heretics and dissenters created a space for doubt about the teachings of the Catholic Church. Once the printing press was developed, these dissents culminated in the Protestant reformation.

All of these factors led to a revival of rhetoric. New languages meant new ways of saying things. New poetry and drama in these languages required rhetorical skill to develop plots, internal speeches, and rich imagery. Wealthy donors provided money to retrieve lost manuscripts of such rhetoricians as Cicero. Exploration and contact, particularly with Muslim states, led to further discoveries of ancient rhetorical texts including Aristotle's *Rhetoric*. Debates over political and religious issues stimulated the need for facility at verbal attack and defense. Public speaking moved beyond the pulpit to political venues. That caught the attention of such theorists as Niccolò Machiavelli, who wrote the innovative textbook on princely rhetoric.

1304–1374	Petrarch; discovers speeches and letters written by Cicero
1369–1415	John Hus; opposes sale of indulgences; burned at the stake
1386–1466	Donatello; Renaissance sculptor
1395–1472	George Trebizond; introduces Greek tradition of Aristotle in *Five Books of Rhetoric* (1440); arrives in Venice in 1416
1416	Poggio Bracciolini finds copy of Quintilian's *Institutes*
1434–1494	Medici rule Florence
1444–1485	Rudolph Agricola
1452–1498	Savanarola; Dominican monk who leads coup in Florence
1453	Turks conquer Constantinople; end of Eastern Roman Empire
1456	Guttenberg invents printing press
1465–1536	Desiderious Erasmus; disputes Luther's approach to reform; writes *Praise of Folly* (1509)
1469–1527	Machiavelli; writes *The Prince;* advances rhetorical theory with new *real politik*
1475–1564	Michelangelo; sculpture, painter, poet
1483–1543	Martin Luther; leads reformation; contends with Erasmus and Eck; disdains populist revolt
1484–1531	Ulrich Zwingli; endorses authority of the Bible over the authority of the church
1492	Ferdinand and Isabella fund Columbus; begin Inquisition
1497–1560	Philipp Melanchthon; writes *Confession of Augsburg* and *Elements of Rhetoric* (1521); ally of Luther
1509–1564	John Calvin; Swiss puritan
1515–1572	Peter Ramus; strips rhetoric of *inventio* and *dispositio;* publishes *Dialectique* (1521)
1517	Luther posts *Ninety-Five Theses*
1520–1601	George Puttenham; *The Arte of English Poesie*
1521	Henry VIII named "Defender of the Faith" by pope; later he creates Church of England
1523–1581	Thomas Wilson introduces five classical canons in English; publishes *The Arte of Rhetoric* (1553)
1530	Leonard Cox writes first book on rhetoric in English
1540	Ignatius Loyola founds the Jesuit Order, known for refined sense of argumentation and Catholic education
1545(?)–1630	Gabriel Harvey brings Ramus' theories to England in *Rhetor* (1577)
1550	Richard Sherry writes *A Treatise on Schemes and Tropes*
1558–1633	Abraham Fraunce; develops *Arcadian Rhetorike*
1561–1621	Francis Bacon; claims four "idols" corrupt communication; writes *On Advancement of Learning* (1605)

1572	St. Bartholomew's Day massacre in France results in defenestration of Peter Ramus
1577	Henry Peacham publishes *Garden of Eloquence*
1584	Dudley Fenner publishes *The Artes and Logike of Rethorike*
1588	Spanish Armada defeated
1637(?)	Thomas Hobbes publishes translation of Aristotle's *Rhetoric*
1596–1650	René Descartes; rationalist philosopher; posits mind-body duality in *Discourse on Method* (1637)

Enlightenment (Modern Period)

The term "Enlightenment" was popularized by Immanuel Kant to describe a philosophical movement that relied on reason to reach the truth; it also had faith that science could solve many of the world's problems. As the countries of Europe threw off the yoke of statist religions and loosened the hold of monarchs, thinkers were more free to come forward with new ideas about how knowledge could be obtained. John Locke, for example, revived reliance on the senses in his empirical approach, while expanding the rights of humans in his political tracts. At the same time, scientific discovery and invention continued and eventually led to an industrial revolution. Optimism about the future of humankind reached a peak in the writing of Friedrich Hegel, who believed each nation could find its innate spirit dialectically. His theory was hijacked by Karl Marx, who sought to spread the rights obtained by the middle class to the proletariat.

The Enlightenment was balanced by two new theories. The first reinitiated the development of beauty in language, culminating in the writing of Hugh Blair. The second was the existential movement launched by Søren Kierkegaard, which called for an examination of the individual as the proper study of philosophy.

1603	Elizabeth I dies
1632–1704	John Locke; empiricist philosopher; sees soul as blank slate and the path to transcendence
1643–1715	Reign of Louis XIV
1661	Claude Buffier publishes *Traité de l' eloguence* on style, using Aristotle and the Romans
1661–1741	Charles Rollin; treatise on Belles Lettres modeled on Quintilian
1662	Royal Society founded in London
1668–1744	Giambattista Vico; neo-humanist; posits theory of imagination
1711–1776	David Hume; develops "scepticism"
1717	Francois Fenelon's *Dialogues on Eloquence* are published posthumously
1718–1800	Hugh Blair; writes *Lectures on Rhetoric and Belles Lettres* in 1783
1719–1796	George Campbell; writes *Philosophy of Rhetoric* in 1776
1720–1785	Thomas Gibbons; noted historian who publishes a study of tropes and figures
1723–1790	Adam Smith; lectures on rhetoric; writes *Wealth of Nations*
1724–1804	Immanuel Kant; supreme rationalist; seeks moral imperatives
1733–1804	Joseph Priestly; scientist; publishes *Courses of Lectures on Oratory and Criticism*
1753–1837	Gilbert Austin; writes *Chironomia*
1762	Thomas Sheridan; publishes *A Course of Lectures on Elocution*

1770–1831	Georg Wilhem Friedrich Hegel; develops dialectical approach to reason and history
1776	American Revolution begins
1781	John Walker; publishes *Elements of Elocution*
1786–1869	James Rush; American; writes *The Philosophy of the Human Voice*
1787–1863	Richard Whately; resurrects rhetorical argumentation in *Elements of Rhetoric* (1828)
1806	John Quincy Adams holds Boylston Professorship in Rhetoric and Oratory at Harvard University
1813–1855	Søren Kierkegaard; father of existentialism
1818–1883	Karl Marx; father of communism and dialectical materialism
1818–1903	Alexander Bain; writes *English Composition and Rhetoric* in 1866
1856–1939	Sigmund Freud; father of modern psychology; develops theory of identification
1857–1913	Ferdinand de Saussure; French structuralist; develops semantics
1875	Alexander Graham Bell (arrived in U.S. in 1871 as teacher of speech to the deaf) invents telephone

Twentieth-Century Thinkers

After the death of U.S. President William McKinley in September of 1901, his assassin, Leon Czolgosz, was electrocuted. There to film the event was Thomas Edison, already known for his development of the phonograph and the lasting light bulb. When asked what he would call his new invention, Edison said, "The motion picture." And so began a media for persuasion, only one of many to flourish in the twentieth century. "Movies" would soon advance ideological themes that supported patriotic visions through many wars and consumerism during peace time. Radio, television, and the Internet would eventually follow.

However, if the twentieth century ushered in the media era, it also marked the collapse of rationalism. Sigmund Freud, who had begun his work in the previous century, became a household name in the twentieth century as he continued to privilege the irrational over the rational. Karl Marx's communist utopia calcified into the Soviet state that eventually entered into a "Cold War" with the United States. Two world wars, holocausts, and the rise and fall of fascist regimes called for new approaches to solving problems. Existentialism and the battle for civil rights had a resurgence after World War II; postmodernism and feminism emerged in the 1970s, soon to be followed by gay and lesbian protests. These events served as a backdrop for such writers as Kenneth Burke and Chaim Perelman, who sought to cure the world's ills with new rhetorics. And yet, despite the call for economic globalism in the 1990s and following, there seemed to be no cure for a continued primitivism grounded in religion among the peoples of the world.

As we were about to move into the twenty-first century, matters did not seem to improve when dire reports about global warming indicated that the planet might be at the tipping point toward permanent decline. People in such "civilized" countries as the United States, Japan, France, England, and Spain all had to deal with terrorist attacks. Rhetoric kept pace with all of these developments by altering and adding to its theory to facilitate new debates and needs. Marshall McLuhan alerted rhetoricians to the potential of media, while Jacques Derrida and Michel Foucault enhanced rhetoric with postmodern thinking. Rhetorical theorists borrowed from philosophers and public commentators to apply rhetoric to new circumstances and popular culture. From "fuzzy physics" to the impact of situation comedies, rhetoric found itself in the forefront of contemporary investigations. It is not too much of an exaggeration to say that almost all communication has a rhetorical dimension.

1878–1965	Martin Buber; interrelational existentialist writes *I and Thou* in 1923
1879–1931	Albert Einstein; theory of relativity
1883–1969	Karl Jaspers; interrelational existentialist writes three volume *Philosophy* in 1932
1889–1976	Martin Heidegger; builds hermeneutic theory of rhetoric in *Being and Time* (1927)
1893–1979	I. A. Richards; constructs modern sender-receiver model in *Philosophy of Rhetoric* (1936)
1897–1992	Kenneth Burke; develops dramatistic theory of rhetoric; publishes *Grammar of Motives* (1945), *Rhetoric of Motives* (1950)
1899–1988	Lucie Olbrechts-Tyteca; co-author of *The New Rhetoric* (1958)
1905–1980	Jean-Paul Sartre; atheistic existentialist writes *Existentialism and Humanism* in 1948
1906	Human voice transmitted by "wireless"
1908–1986	Simone de Beauvoir; leads feminist movement in France
1911–1980	Marshall McLuhan; examines effects of modern media in *Understanding Media* (1964)
1912–1984	Chaim Perelman; places philosophy under rhetorical argumentation in *The New Rhetoric* (1958)
1922–2009	Stephen Toulmin; develops "field theory" of argument in *Uses of Argument* (1958)
1924–1998	Jean-François Lyotard; leading postmodern advocate of poststructural analysis of language
1926–1984	Michel Foucault; advances postmodern theory of knowledge, power, and communication
1927	First U.S. demonstration of television at Bell Telephone Laboratories
1929–2008	Jean Baudrillard; developed theory of hyper-reality
1929–	Jürgen Habermas; calls for rational argument in public sphere in *Knowledge and Human Interests* (1968)
1930–2004	Jacques Derrida; leader of "deconstructionist" movement
1936	Televisions go on sale; coaxial cable developed
1942–2004	Gloria Anzaldúa; adds spiritual dimension to feminist theory
1945	United Nations founded
1946–	Catharine MacKinnon; develops feminist legal theory
1956–	Judith Butler; stresses notion of embodiment in performance studies
1962	First satellite to carry television broadcasts is orbited
1970	Contemporary feminist movement led by Betty Friedan, Gloria Steinem, and Bella Abzug begins
1973	American Vinton Cerf develops an internet of computer services for the Defense Department
1983	Direct satellite broadcasts are made available to public

1989	World Wide Web is developed for public use
1991	Soviet Union collapses

Twenty-First Century

2001	Terrorists launch an attack on U.S. soil
2008	Hillary Clinton and Barack Obama make historic runs for the democratic nomination for president of the United States; Barack Obama is the first African American elected president of the United States
2008–2009	The worst financial crisis in the U.S. since the Great Depression, with rippling effects worldwide throughout the ensuing years
2010	Arab Spring begins
2011	Osama bin Laden, founder of Al-Qaeda, killed in surprise attack
2012	President Barack Obama elected to a second term

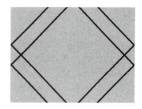

Bibliography

Abbott, Don Paul, "Mayans' Rhetorica and the Search for a Spanish Rhetoric," *Rhetorica,* 11 (1993): 162–73.

Aboulafia, Mitchell, *The Mediating Self: Mead, Sartre, and Self-Determination* (New Haven, CT: Yale U. Press, 1986).

Adams, John C., "Ramus, Illustrations, and the Puritan Movement," *Journal of Medieval and Renaissance Studies,* 17 (1987): 195–97.

Aland, Kurt, *Synopsis of the Four Gospels,* 3rd ed. (Stuttgart: Wurrtembergishe Bibelan Stalt, 1979).

Alter, Robert, *The Art of Biblical Narrative* (New York: Basic Books, 1981).

Altman, Joel B., *The Tudor Play of Mind: Rhetorical Inquiry and the Development of Elizabethan Drama* (Berkeley: U. of California Press, 1978).

Anderson, Fulton Henry, *The Philosophy of Francis Bacon* (Chicago: U. of Chicago Press, 1948).

Anderson, Raymond E., "Kierkegaard's Theory of Communication," *Speech Monographs,* 30 (1963): 1–14.

Anzaldúa, Gloria, "Tlilli, Tlapalli: The Path of the Red and Black Ink," in *The Graywolf Annual Five: Multi-Cultural Literacy,* Rick Simonson and Scott Walker, eds. (Saint Paul: Graywolf Press, 1988): 29–40.

Aquinas, *On Being and Essence,* Armand A. Maurer, trans. (Toronto: Pontifical Institute of Medieval Studies, 1949).

Aquinas, *Summa Theologicae,* Thomas Gilby, ed. (New York: McGraw-Hill, 1964).

Aquinas, "Commentary on the Politics," in *Medieval Political Philosophy,* Ralph Lerner and Muhsin Mahdi, eds. (New York: The Free Press, 1967): 297–334.

Aristotle, *The Nicomachean Ethics,* D. Ross, trans., in *The Basic Works of Aristotle,* Richard McKeon, ed. (New York: Random House, 1966): 935–1126.

Aristotle, *Poetics,* W. Rhys Roberts, trans. (New York: Modern Library Random House, 1954).

Aristotle, *Politics,* Benjamin Jowett, trans., in *The Basic Works of Aristotle,* Richard McKeon, ed. (New York: Random House, 1966): 1127–324.

Arthos, John, *The Inner World of Gadamer's Hermeneutics* (Notre Dame, IN: U. of Notre Dame Press, 2009).

Astell, Mary, *A Serious Proposal to the Ladies, Parts I & II* (London: Rich Wilkin, 1697).

Atwill, Janet M., *Rhetoric Reclaimed: Aristotle and the Liberal Arts Tradition* (Ithaca, NY: Cornell U. Press, 1998).

Augustine, *De doctrina Christiana,* J. F. Shaw, trans. (Chicago: Encyclopedia Britannica, 1952).

Aune, James Arnt, *Rhetoric and Marxism* (Boulder, CO: Westview Press, 1994).

Averroës, "On the Harmony of Religion and Philosophy," George F. Hourani, trans., in *Medieval Political Philosophy,* Ralph Lerner and Muhsin Mahdi, eds. (New York: The Free Press, 1967): 163–86.

Bacon, Francis, *De Augmentis* in *The Works of Francis Bacon,* 15 vols., James Spedding, Robert L. Ellis, and Douglas D. Heath, eds. (London: Longman, 1870): vol. 5.

Bacon, Francis, *The Works of Francis Bacon,* 15 vols., James Spedding, Robert Ellis, and Douglas Heath, eds. (London: Henry G. Bohn, 1883–93).

Bacon, Roger, "Opus Maius: Moral Philosophy," Richard McKeon, Donald McCarthy, and Ernest Fortin, trans., in *Medieval Political Philosophy,* Ralph Lerner and Muhsin Mahdi, eds. (New York: The Free Press, 1967): 355–90.

Bakewell, Charles M., *Source Book in Ancient Philosophy* (New York: Gordian, 1909).

Balbus, Isaac D., *Marxism and Domination* (Princeton, NJ: Princeton U. Press, 1982).

Baldwin, Charles Sears, *Medieval Rhetoric and Poetic* (New York: Macmillan, 1928).

Barrett, Harold, *The Sophists: Rhetoric, Democracy, and Plato's Idea of Sophistry* (Novato, CA: Chandler & Sharp, 1987).

Barthes, Roland, "Myth Today," in *A Barthes Reader* (New York: Hill and Wang, 1982): 93–149.

Basler, Roy P., *The Collected Works of Abraham Lincoln,* vol. 1 (New Brunswick, NJ: Rutgers U. Press, 1953).

Bate, Walter J., *Criticism: The Major Texts* (New York: Harcourt, Brace, 1952; reprint Wolf Den Books, 2002).

Baudrillard, Jean, "The Ecstasy of Communication," in *The Anti-Aesthetic: Essays on Postmodern Culture,* Hal Foster, ed. (Port Townsend, WA: Bay Press, 1983): 126–34.

Bedell, George C., *Kierkegaard and Faulkner: Modalities of Existence* (Baton Rouge: Louisiana State U. Press, 1972).

Bellah, Robert, "Civil Religion in America," *Journal of the American Academy of Arts and Sciences,* 96 (Winter 1967): 1–21.

Benoit, William L., "Isocrates and Plato on Rhetoric and Rhetorical Education," *Rhetoric Society Quarterly,* 21 (1991): 60–71.

Benoit, William L., "Isocrates on Rhetorical Education," *Communication Education,* 33 (1984): 109–20.

Benson, Thomas W., "Rhetoric as a Way of Being," in *American Rhetoric: Context and Criticism,* Thomas W. Benson, ed. (Carbondale: Southern Illinois U. Press, 1989).

Berry, Donald L., *Mutuality: The Vision of Martin Buber* (Albany: SUNY Press, 1985).

Best, Steven and Douglas Kellner, *Postmodern Theory: Critical Interrogations* (New York: The Guilford Press, 1991).

Betz, Brian R., "Eric Fromm and the Rhetoric of Prophecy," *Central States Speech Journal,* 26 (1975): 310–15.

Bevilacqua, Vincent, "Philosophical Influences in the Development of English Rhetorical Theory: 1748 to 1783," *Proceedings of the Leeds Philosophical and Literary Society,* 12.6 (1968): 198–208.

Bizzell, Patricia and Bruce Herzberg, eds. *The Rhetorical Tradition: Readings from Classical Times to the Present,* 2nd ed. (Boston: Bedford/St. Martin's, 2001).

Black, Edwin, "Plato's View of Rhetoric," *Quarterly Journal of Speech,* 44 (1958): 361–74.

Black, Edwin, "The Second Persona," *Quarterly Journal of Speech,* 56 (1970): 109–19.

Blair, Carole, Marsha Jeppeson and Enrico Pucci Jr., "Public Memorializing in Postmodernity: The Vietnam Veterans Memorial as Prototype," *Quarterly Journal of Speech,* 77 (1991): 263–88.

Blair, Carole and Mary L. Kahl, "Introduction: Revising the History of Rhetorical Theory," *Western Journal of Communication,* 54 (1990): 148–59.

Blair, Hugh, *Lectures on Belles Lettres* (London: J. Cranwell, 1838).

Blair, Hugh, *Lectures on Rhetoric and Belles Lettres,* Linda Ferreira-Buckly and S. Michael Halloran, eds. (Carbondale: Southern Illinois U. Press, 2005.)

Bliese, John, "Deliberative Oratory in the Middle Ages: The Missing Millennium in the Study of Public Address," *The Southern Communication Journal,* 59 (1994): 273–83.

Bliese, John, "The Study of Rhetoric in the Twelfth Century," *Quarterly Journal of Speech,* 63 (December 1977): 364–83.

Bolgar, Robert R., *The Classical Heritage and Its Beneficiaries* (Cambridge, UK: Cambridge U. Press, 1963).

Booth, Wayne, *The Rhetoric of Fiction,* 2nd ed. (Chicago: U. of Chicago Press, 1983).

Bormann, Ernest, "Fantasy and Rhetorical Vision: The Rhetorical Criticism of Social Reality," *Quarterly Journal of Speech,* 59 (1972): 396–407.

Botein, Stephen, "Cicero as a Role Model for Early American Lawyers: A Case Study in Classical 'Influence,'" *Classical Journal,* 73 (1978): 313–21.

Bourke, Vernon J., *Augustine's Quest of Wisdom: Life and Philosophy of the Bishop of Hippo* (Milwaukee, WI: Bruce, 1945).

Bowersock, Glen W., *Greek Sophists in the Roman Empire* (Oxford: Oxford U. Press, 1969).

Boyle, Marjorie O'Rourke, *Loyola's Acts: The Rhetoric of Self* (Berkeley: U. of California Press, 1997).

Brock, Bernard, ed., *Kenneth Burke and Contemporary European Thought* (Tuscaloosa: U. of Alabama Press, 1995; paper 2006).

Brockriede, Wayne and Douglas Ehninger, *Decision by Debate,* 2nd ed. (New York: Harper & Row, 1977).

Brown, Peter, *Augustine of Hippo* (Berkeley: U. of California Press, 1967; revised edition, 2000).

Brownstein, Oscar, "Plato's Phaedrus: Dialectic as the Genuine Art of Speaking," *Quarterly Journal of Speech,* 51 (1968): 392–98.

Brumbaugh, Robert S., *The Philosophers of Greece* (Albany: SUNY Press, 1981).

Bruns, Gerald L., *Heidegger's Estrangements: Language, Truth, and Poetry in the Later Writings* (New Haven, CT: Yale U. Press, 1989).

Buber, Martin, *I and Thou* (New York: Charles Scribner's Sons, 1954).

Bullinger, Ernest W., *Figures of Speech Used in the Bible: Explained and Illustrated* (Grand Rapids: Baker Books, 2003).

Burgess, Theodore Chalon, "Epideictic Literature," *Studies in Classical Philology,* vol. 3 (Chicago: U. of Chicago Press, 1902): 89–254.

Burke, Kenneth, *Attitudes Toward History* (Boston: Beacon Press, 1961).

Burke, Kenneth, *A Grammar of Motives* (Englewood Cliffs, NJ: Prentice-Hall, 1954).

Burke, Kenneth, *A Grammar of Motives and a Rhetoric of Motives* (Cleveland: Meridian Books/World Publishing, 1961).

Burke, Kenneth, *A Rhetoric of Motives* (Berkeley: U. of California Press, 1966).

Burke, Kenneth, "Colloquy: I. The Party Line," *Quarterly Journal of Speech,* 62 (1982): 62.

Burke, Kenneth, *Counter-Statement* (Berkeley: U. of California Press, 1968).

Burke, Kenneth, "Ideology and Myth," *Accent,* 7 (1947): 195–205.

Burke, Kenneth, *Permanence and Change: An Anatomy of Purpose* (Indianapolis: Bobbs-Merrill, 1965).

Burke, Kenneth, *The Philosophy of Literary Form* (New York: Random House, 1961).

Burke, Kenneth, *The Rhetoric of Religion: Studies in Logology* (Berkeley: U. of California Press, 1961).

Burke, Kenneth, "Shakespearean Persuasion," *Antioch Review,* 24 (1964): 19–36.

Burke, Kenneth, *Terms for Order,* S. G. Hyman, ed. (Bloomington: Indiana U. Press, 1964).

Bryant, Donald G., "Edmund Burke on Oratory," *Quarterly Journal of Speech,* 19 (1933): 1–15.

Bygrave, Stephen, *Kenneth Burke: Rhetoric and Ideology* (London: Routledge, 1993).

Butler, Judith, *Bodies that Matter* (New York: Routledge, 1993).

Butler, Judith, *Gender Trouble: Feminism and the Subversion of Identity* (New York: Routledge, 1999, 2006).

Cahn, Michael, "Reading Rhetoric Rhetorically: Isocrates and the Marketing of Insight," *Rhetorica,* 8 (1988).

Campbell, George, *Philosophy of Rhetoric,* Lloyd Bitzer, ed. (Carbondale: Southern Illinois U. Press, 1963).

Campbell, Karlyn K., "Femininity and Feminism: To Be or Not to Be a Woman," *Communication Quarterly,* 31 (1983): 100–10.

Campbell, Karlyn K., *Man Cannot Speak for Her* (New York: Greenwood, 1989).

Campbell, Karlyn K., "Style and Content in the Rhetoric of Early Afro-American Feminists," *Quarterly Journal of Speech,* 72 (1986): 434–45.

Campbell, Karlyn K. and Kathleen H. Jamieson, eds., *Form and Genre: Shaping Rhetorical Action* (Falls Church, VA: Speech Communication Association, 1990).

Cantor, Muriel G., "Prime-time Fathers: A Study in Continuity and Change," *Critical Studies in Mass Communication,* 7 (1990): 275–85.

Caplan, Harry, "Classical Rhetoric and the Mediaeval Theory of Preaching," in *Historical Studies of Rhetoric and Rhetoricians,* Raymond F. Howes, ed. (Ithaca, NY: Cornell U. Press, 1961).

Carlson, A. Cheree, "Aspasia of Miletus: How One Woman Disappeared from the History of Rhetoric," *Women's Studies in Communication,* 17 (1994): 26–44.

Carpenter, Ronald H., "A Stylistic Basis of Burkean Identification," *Today's Speech* (1972): 19–24.

Carr, David, *Time, Narrative and History* (Bloomington: Indiana U. Press, 1991).

Charland, Maurice, "Constitutive Rhetoric: The Case of the *Peuple Québécois,*" *Quarterly Journal of Speech,* 73 (1987): 133–50.

Chase, Kenneth R., "Constructing Ethics through Rhetoric: Isocrates and Piety," *Quarterly Journal of Speech,* 95 (2009): 239–62.

Chesebro, James W., ed., *Extensions of the Burkean System* (Tuscaloosa: U. of Alabama Press, 1993).

Chodorow, Nancy, *The Reproduction of Mothering* (Berkeley: U. of California Press, 1978; reprint 1999).

Chrysostom, Dio, *Dio Chrysostom: Discourses 1–11,* vol. 1, J. W. Cohoon, trans. (Cambridge, MA: Harvard U. Press, 1932).

Cicero, *Brutus,* A. E. Douglas, ed. and trans. (Oxford: Clarendon Press, 1966).

Cicero, *De inventione,* H. M. Hubbell, trans. (Cambridge, MA: Harvard U. Press, 1949).

Cicero, *De officiis,* H. G. Edinger, trans. (Indianapolis: Library of Liberal Arts, 1974).

Cicero, *De oratore,* 2 vols., E. W. Sutton and H. Rackham, trans. (Cambridge, MA: Harvard U. Press, 1959).

Cicero, *Orator,* H. M. Hubbell, trans. (Cambridge, MA: Loeb Library, 1962).

Cicero, *De partitione oratioria,* H. Rackham, trans. (Cambridge, MA: Harvard U. Press, 1942).

Cicero, *Rhetorica ad Herennium,* Harry Caplan, trans. (Cambridge, MA: Harvard U. Press, 2004).

Clark, Donald Lemon, *Rhetoric in Greco-Roman Education* (Westport, CT: Greenwood Press, 1977).

Clark, Norma, "The Critical Servant: An Isocratean Contribution to Critical Rhetoric," *Quarterly Journal of Speech,* 82 (1996): 111–24.

Classen, C. Joachim, "St. Paul's Epistles and Ancient Greek and Roman Rhetoric," *Rhetorica,* 10 (1992): 319–44.

Clayton, Edward W., "The Audience for Aristotle's *Rhetoric,*" *Rhetorica,* 22 (2004): 183–203.

Cogan, Marc, "Rudolphus Agricola and the Semantic Revolutions of the History of Invention," *Rhetorica,* 2 (1984): 163–94.

Cole, Thomas, *The Origins of Rhetoric in Ancient Greece* (Baltimore: Johns Hopkins Press, 1991; paperback edition 1995).

Collingwood, Robin G., *Speculum mentis* (Oxford: Clarendon Press, 1924).

Collingwood, Robin G., *Faith and Reason,* Lionel Rubinoff, ed. (Chicago: Quadrangle Books, 1968).

Collins, Patricia H., *Fighting Words: Black Women and the Search for Justice* (Minneapolis: U. of Minnesota Press, 1998).

Condit, Celeste Michelle, "The Functions of Epideictic: The Boston Massacre Orations as Exemplar," *Communication Quarterly,* 33 (1985): 284–99.

Condit, Celeste Michelle, "Post-Burke: Transcending the Substance of Dramatism," *Quarterly Journal of Speech,* 78 (1992): 349–55.

Condit, Celeste Michelle, "In Praise of Eloquent Diversity: Gender and Rhetoric as Public Persuasion," *Women's Studies in Communication,* 20 (1997): 91–116.

Connors, Robert J., "Greek Rhetoric and the Transition from Orality," *Philosophy and Rhetoric,* 19 (1986): 38–63.

Conquergood, Dwight, "Rethinking Ethnography: Toward a Critical Cultural Politics," *Communication Quarterly,* 58 (1991): 179–94.

Consigny, Scott, "Gorgias's Use of the Epideictic," *Philosophy and Rhetoric,* 25 (1992): 281–97.

Consigny, Scott, *Sophist and Artist* (Columbia: U. of South Carolina Press, 2001).

Copleston, Frederick, *A History of Philosophy: Medieval Philosophy,* V, Part II (New York: Image Books/Doubleday 1962).

Corts, Paul R., "I. A. Richards on Rhetoric and Criticism," *Southern Speech Journal,* 36 (1971): 115–26.

Coulson, John, *The Saints: A Concise Biographical Dictionary* (New York: Guild Press, 1958).

Crable, Bryan, "Distance as Ultimate Motive: A Dialectical Interpretation of *A Rhetoric of Motives,"* *Rhetoric Society Quarterly,* 39 (2009): 213–39.

Craig, Christopher P., *Form as Argument in Cicero's Speeches: A Study of Dilemma* (Atlanta: Scholars Press, 1993).

Cribiore, Raffaella, *The School of Libanius in Late Antique Antioch* (Princeton, NJ: Princeton U. Press, 2007).

Crick, Nathan, "The Sophistical Attitude and the Invention of Rhetoric," *Quarterly Journal of Speech,* 96 (2010): 25–45.

Crick, Nathan and John Poulakos, "Go Tell Alcibiades: Tragedy, Comedy and Rhetoric in Plato's Symposium," *Quarterly Journal of Speech,* 94 (2008): 1–22.

Crosby, Richard B., "*Kairos* as God's Time in Martin Luther King, Jr.'s Last Sunday Sermon," *Rhetoric Society Quarterly,* 39 (2009): 260–80.

Cusa, Nicholas of, *De docta ignorantia,* P. Rotta, ed. (Minneapolis: A. J. Banning, 1985).

Davies, W. D. and Dale C. Allison, Jr., *A Critical and Exegetical Commentary on the Gospel according to Matthew,* vol. 1 (Leiden, Netherlands: E. J. Brill, 1963).

Day, Joseph W., *The Glory of Athens: The Popular Tradition as Reflected in the Panathenaicus of Aelius Aristides* (Chicago: Ares Publishers, 1980).

Derrida, Jacques, *The Gift of Death,* David Wills, trans. (Chicago: U. of Chicago Press, 1995).

Derrida, Jacques, *Limited Inc.,* Samuel Weber, trans. (Evanston, IL: Northwestern U. Press, 1988).

Derrida, Jacques, *Of Spirit: Heidegger and the Question,* Geoffrey Bennington and Rachel Bowlby, trans. (Chicago: U. of Chicago Press, 1989).

Detienne, Marcel, *Les Maitres de la vérité dans le Grèce Archaïque,* 3rd ed. (Paris: U. of Paris Press 1993).

Detienne, Marcel and Jean-Pierre Vernant, *Cunning Intelligence in Greek Culture and Society* (Sussex, England: Harvester Press, 1991).

Diels, Hermann and Walther Kranz, *Die Fragments der Vorsokratiker,* 2, 10th ed. (Berlin: Nachträge, 1960).

Di Lorenzo, Raymond, "The Critique of Socrates in Cicero's *De oratore:* Ornatus and the Nature of Wisdom," *Philosophy and Rhetoric,* 22 (1978): 251–54.

Donawerth, Jane, "Conversation and the Boundaries of Public Discourse in Rhetorical Theory by Renaissance Women," *Rhetorica,* 16 (1998): 181–200.

Doughtie, Edward, "Words for Music: Simplicity and Complexity in Elizabethan Air," *Rice University Studies,* 51 (1965): 1–12.

Dow, Bonnie and Mary Boor Tonn, "'Feminist Style' and Political Judgment in the Rhetoric of Ann Richards," *Quarterly Journal of Speech,* 79 (1993): 286–302.

Duhamel, Pierre A., "The Function of Rhetoric as Effective Expression," *Journal of the History of Ideas,* 10 (1949): 344–56.

Durant, Will, *The Reformation: A History of European Civilization from Wyclif to Calvin: 1300–1564* (New York: Simon and Schuster, 1957).

Durant, Will, *The Renaissance: A History of Civilization in Italy from 1304–1576 AD* (New York: Simon and Schuster, 1953).

Eakins, Barbara and R. Gene Eakins, "Comparison: Proof or Ornament," *Central States Speech Journal,* 26 (1975): 99–106.

Eco, Umberto, *A Theory of Semiotics* (Bloomington: Indiana U. Press, 1978).

Edelman, Murray, *Political Language* (New York: Academic Press, 1977).

Edwards, Michael, "Antiphon and the Beginnings of Literary Oratory," *Rhetorica,* 18 (2000): 227–42.

Elias, Marilyn, "Revenge May Be All in Anticipation," *Los Angeles Times* (October 18, 2010). http://articles.latimes.com/2010/oct/18/health/la-he-revenge-20101018

Elrod, John W., *Being and Existence in Kierkegaard's Pseudonymous Works* (Princeton, NJ: Princeton U. Press, 1975).

Elshtain, Jean Bethke, *Augustine and the Limits of Politics* (Notre Dame, IN: U. of Notre Dame Press, 1995).

Engnell, Richard A., "Implications of Rhetorical Epistemology of Gorgias," *Western Journal of Speech Communication,* 37 (1973): 175–84.

Engnell, Richard A., "Otherness and the Rhetorical Exigences of Theistic Religion," *Quarterly Journal of Speech,* 79 (1993): 82–98.

Enos, Richard, "Epistemology of Gorgias' Rhetoric," *Southern Speech Communication Journal* (1976): 35–51.

Enos, Richard, *Greek Rhetoric Before Aristotle* (Long Grove, IL: Waveland Press, 1993).

Enos, Richard and Jeanne L. McClaran, "Audience and Image in Ciceronian Rome: Creation and Constraints of the Vir Bonus Personality," *Central States Speech Journal,* 29 (1978): 98–106.

Erasmus, *Collected Works of Erasmus,* 42 vols., Craig R. Thompson, ed. (Toronto: U. of Toronto Press, 1978).

Erasmus, *Erasmus: Man of Letters,* Lisa Jardin, ed. (Princeton, NJ: Princeton U. Press, 1993).

Everitt, Antony, *Cicero: The Life and Times of Rome's Greatest Politician* (New York: Random House, 2003).

Fantham, Elaine, *Comparative Studies on Republican Latin Imagery,* Phoenix Suppl. 10 (Toronto: U. of Toronto Press, 1972).

Fantham, Elaine, "Varietas and Satietas: *De oratore* 3.96–103 and the Limits of Ornatus," *Rhetorica,* 6 (1988): 275–90.

Firestone, Shulamith, *The Dialectic of Sex: The Case for Feminist Revolution* (New York: Farrar, Straus and Giroux, 2003).

Fisher, Walter R., "Communication and Community," *Halcyon 1993: A Journal of the Humanities,* 15 (Las Vegas: U. of Nevada Press, 1993): 73–86.

Fisher, Walter R., *Human Communication as Narrative* (Columbia: U. of South Carolina Press, 1989).

Fisher, Walter R., "Narrative Rationality and the Logic of Scientific Discourse," *Argumentation,* 8 (1994): 21–32.

Fisher, Walter R., "Rhetorical Fiction and the Presidency," *Quarterly Journal of Speech,* 66 (1980): 119–26.

Fletcher, Richard, *The Barbarian Conversion: From Paganism to Christianity* (New York: Henry Holt, 1998).

Flores, Lisa A., "Creating Discursive Space through a Rhetoric of Difference," *Quarterly Journal of Speech,* 82 (1996): 142–56.

Fortenbaugh, William W., "Cicero, *On Invention* 1.5–77 Hypothetical Syllogistic and the Early Peripatetics," *Rhetorica,* 16 (1988): 25.

Foss, Karen and Sonja Foss, "The Status of Research on Women and Communication," *Communication Quarterly*, 31 (1983): 195–204.

Foss, Sonja K., *Rhetorical Criticism: Exploration and Practice*, 4th ed. (Long Grove, IL: Waveland Press, 2009).

Foucault, Michel, *The Archeology of Knowledge* (New York: Harper and Row, 1972).

Foucault, Michel, *Discipline and Punishment: The Birth of the Prison* (New York: Vintage, 1979).

Foucault, Michel, *History of Sexuality*, Robert Hurley, trans. (New York: Pantheon, 1978).

Foucault, Michel, *Language, Counter-Memory, Practice: Selected Essays and Interviews*, Donald Bouchard, ed. (Ithaca, NY: Cornell U. Press, 1977).

Foucault, Michel, *Society Must Be Defended: Lectures at the College of France, 1975–1976* (New York: Picador, 2003).

Freud, Sigmund, *A General Introduction to Psychoanalysis* (New York: Pocket Books, 1952).

Freud, Sigmund, *A General Selection from the Works of Sigmund Freud* (New York: Liveright, 1957).

Freud, Sigmund, "On Narcissism: An Introduction," in *The Standard Edition of the Complete Works of Sigmund Freud*, vol. 14, James Strachey, trans. (New York: Basic Books, 1956): 73–102.

Frye, Northrop, *Anatomy of Criticism* (Princeton, NJ: Princeton U. Press, 1957; reprint 2000).

Frye, Northrop, "Prophecy and the Gospel," in *The Gospels*, Harold Bloom, ed. (New York: Chelsea House, 1988).

Gaines, Robert N., "Isocrates, Ep. 6.8," *Hermes* (1990): 165–70.

Gaines, Robert N., "Philodemus on the Three Activities of Rhetorical Invention," *Rhetorica*, 3 (1985): 155–63.

Gallop, David, *Parmenides of Elea* (Toronto: U. of Toronto Press, 1984).

Gaonkar, Dilip P., "The Idea of Rhetoric in the Rhetoric of Science," *The Southern Communication Journal*, 58 (1993): 258–62.

Gargin, Michael, *Antiphon the Athenian: Oratory, Law and Justice in the Age of the Sophists* (Austin: U. of Texas Press, 2002).

Garver, Eugene, *Aristotle's Rhetoric: An Art of Character* (Chicago: U. of Chicago Press, 1994).

Garver, Eugene, *Machiavelli and the History of Prudence* (Madison: U. of Wisconsin Press, 1987).

Gaundissalinus, Dominicus, *De divisione philosophiae*, L. Baur, ed. (Münster, Germany: BGPM, 1903).

Gay, Peter, *The Enlightenment: A Comprehensive Anthology* (New York: Simon & Schuster, 1973).

Gencarella, Stephen O., "Purifying Rhetoric: Empedocles and the Myth of Rhetorical Theory," *Quarterly Journal of Speech*, 96 (2010): 231–56.

Genette, Gérard, *Narrative Discourse* (Ithaca, NY: Cornell U. Press, 1983).

Genette, G., *Narrative Discourse Revisited* (Ithaca, NY: Cornell U. Press, 1990).

George, Ann and Jack Selzer, *Kenneth Burke in the 1930s* (Columbia: U. of South Carolina Press).

Gerl, Hanna-Barbara, "On the Philosophical Dimension of Rhetoric: The Theory of Ornatus in Leonardo Bruni," *Philosophy and Rhetoric*, 11 (1978): 178–90.

Gibbons, Thomas, *Rhetoric* (London: Oliver and Bartholomew, 1967).

Gilbert, Allan H., *Literary Criticism: Plato to Dryden* (Detroit: Wayne State U. Press, 1962).

Gilligan, Carol, *In a Different Voice: Psychological Theory and Women's Development* (Cambridge, MA: Harvard U. Press, 1982; 1983).

Goeglein, Tamara A., "'Wherein Hath Ramus Been So Offensive?': Poetic Examples in the English Ramist Logic Manuals (1574–1672)," *Rhetorica*, 14 (1996): 73–101.

Grassi, Ernesto, *Rhetoric as Philosophy: The Humanist Tradition* (University Park: The Pennsylvania State U. Press, 1980).

Greenblatt, Stephen, *The Swerve: How the World Became Modern* (New York: Norton, 2011).

Gregg, Richard B., "The Ego-Function of the Rhetoric of Protest," *Philosophy and Rhetoric*, 3 (1971): 71–91.

Grimaldi, William M., *Studies in the Philosophy of Aristotle's Rhetoric* (Wiesbaden, Germany: Steiner, 1975).

Grube, George M., *Plato's Thought* (London: Methuen, 1935).

Guthrie, William K. Chambers, *The Sophists* (Cambridge, MA: Harvard U. Press, 1971).

Habermas, Jürgen, *Between Facts and Norms: Contributions to a Discourse Theory of Law and Democracy,* William Rehg, trans. (Cambridge: MIT Press, 1996).

Habermas, Jürgen, *Communication and the Evolution of Society,* T. McCarthy, trans. (Boston: Beacon Press, 1976).

Habermas, Jürgen, "Further Reflections on the Public Sphere," in *Habermas and the Public Sphere,* C. Calhoun, ed./trans. (Cambridge: MIT Press, 1992): 466–68.

Habermas, Jürgen, *The Philosophical Discourse of Modernity,* F. Lawrence, trans. (Cambridge, MA: M.I.T. Press, 1987).

Habermas, Jürgen, *The Theory of Communicative Action,* T. McCarthy, trans. (Boston: Beacon Press, 1984).

Haidt, Jonathan, *The Righteous Mind: Why Good People Are Divided by Politics and Religion* (New York: Pantheon, 2012).

Hallam, Henry, *Introduction to the Literature of Europe in the 15th, 16th, and 17th Centuries,* vol. 1 (New York: Harper, 1854/1880).

Hampshire, Stuart, *The Age of Reason* (New York: George Braziller, 1957).

Harding, Sandra, *Whose Science, Whose Knowledge: Thinking from Women's Lives* (Ithaca, NY: Cornell U. Press, 1991).

Hariman, Robert, "Political Style in Cicero's Letters to Atticus," *Rhetorica,* 7 (1989): 145–58.

Hariman, Robert, *Political Style: The Artistry of Power* (Chicago: U. of Chicago Press, 1995).

Hart, Roderick, *The Political Pulpit* (West Lafayette, IN: Purdue U. Press, 1977).

Hart, Roderick and J. L. Pauley, *The Political Pulpit Revisited* (West Lafayette, IN: Purdue U. Press, 2004).

Hauser, Gerard A., "Aristotle's Example Revisited," *Philosophy and Rhetoric,* 18 (1985): 171–79.

Heath, M. *Hermogenes on Issues and Strategies of Argument in Later Greek Rhetoric* (Oxford: Clarendon, 1995).

Hegel, Georg Friedrich Wilhelm, *Introduction to the Lectures on the History of Philosophy,* T. M. Knox and A. V. Miller, trans. (Oxford: Clarendon Press, 1985).

Heidegger, Martin, *Being and Time,* J. Macquarrie and E. Robinson, trans. (New York: Harper & Row, 1967).

Heidegger, Martin, "Letter on Humanism," Frank A. Capuzzi, trans., in M. Heidegger, *Basic Writings,* David F. Kreil, ed. (New York: Harper & Row, 1977).

Heidegger, Martin, "Letter on Humanism," in *Phenomenology and Existentialism,* Richard Zaner and Don Ihde, eds. (New York: G. P. Putnam's Sons, 1973): 155–70.

Heidegger, Martin, *Plato's Sophist,* Richard Rojcewicz and André Schuwer, trans. (Bloomington: Indiana U. Press, 1997).

Heidegger, Martin, *Poetry, Language, Thought,* Albert Hofstadter, trans. (New York: Harper & Row, 1971).

Heidegger, Martin, *The Question Concerning Technology and Other Essays,* William Lovitt, trans. (New York: Harper & Row, 1977).

Heidegger, Martin, *What Is Called Thinking?,* Fred D. Wieck and J. Glenn Gray, trans. (New York: Harper & Row, 1968).

Henderson, Judith Rice, "Erasmian Ciceronians: Reformation Teachers of Letter-Writing," *Rhetorica,* 10 (1992): 273–302.

Henry, Madeleine, *Prisoner of History: Aspasia of Miletus and her Biographical Tradition* (New York: Oxford U. Press, 1995).

Hill, Forbes, "Conventional Wisdom—Traditional Form—The President's Message of November 3, 1969," in *The Practice of Rhetorical Criticism,* 2nd ed., James R. Andrews, ed. (New York: Longman, 1990): 127–39.

Hill Jr., Sidney, "Dictamen: That Bastard of Literature and Law," *Central States Speech Journal,* 24 (1973): 17–24.

hooks, bell, *Feminism Theory from Margin to Center* (Boston, MA: South End Press, 1984).

Hopper, Robert, "Speech Errors and the Poetics of Conversation," *Text and Performance Quarterly,* 12 (1992): 120–32.

Horace, *Ars poetica* (London: Dent, 1928/1961).

Howell, William S., *Logic and Rhetoric in England, 1500–1700* (New York: Russell & Russell, 1961).

Howell, William S., "Renaissance Rhetoric and Modern Rhetoric: A Study in Change," in *Poetics, Rhetoric and Logic* (Ithaca, NY: Cornell U. Press, 1975).

Hudson, Hoyt, "The Field of Rhetoric," *Quarterly Journal of Speech,* 9 (1923): 167–80.

Hull, John M., *Hellenistic Magic and the Synoptic Tradition* (London: SCM Press, 1974).

Hunt, Everett Lee, "Plato on Rhetoric and Rhetoricians," *Quarterly Journal of Speech,* 1 (1920): 35–56.

Hunt, Everett Lee, "Rhetoric and Literary Criticism," *Quarterly Journal of Speech,* 21 (1935): 564–68.

Hyde, Michael J., "Emotion and Human Communication: A Rhetorical, Scientific, and Philosophical Picture," *Communication Quarterly,* 32 (1984): 122–34.

Hyde, Michael J., "Existentialism as the Basis for the Theory and Practice of Rhetoric," in *Rhetoric and Philosophy,* R. Cherwitz, ed. (Hillsdale, NJ: Lawrence Erlbaum Associates, 1990): 213–51.

Hyde, Michael J. and Craig R. Smith, "Heidegger and Aristotle on Emotion: Questions of Time and Space," in *The Critical Turn: Rhetoric and Philosophy in Contemporary Discourse,* Ian Angus and Lenore Langsdorf, eds. (Carbondale: Southern Illinois U. Press, 1992): 68–99.

Hyde, Michael J. and Craig R. Smith, "Hermeneutics and Rhetoric: A Seen but Unobserved Relationship," *Quarterly Journal of Speech,* 65 (1979): 347–63.

Hyland, Drew A., *The Origins of Philosophy: The Rise in Myths and Presocratics* (New York: Putnam, 1973).

Innes, Doreen, "Cicero on Tropes," *Rhetorica,* 6 (1988): 307–25.

Innocenti, Beth, "Towards a Theory of Vivid Description as Practiced in Cicero's Verrine Orations," *Rhetorica,* 12 (1994): 355–82.

Isocrates, *Isocrates,* 3 vols., George Norlin, trans. (Cambridge, MA: Loeb Classical Library, 1954–56).

Isocrates, *Isocrates,* vol. 3., Larue Van Hook, trans. (Cambridge, MA: Harvard U. Press, 1945).

Jameson, Fredric, *The Political Unconscious: Narrative as a Socially Symbolic Act* (Ithaca, NY: Cornell U. Press, 1981).

Jardine, Lisa, "Distinctive Discipline: Rudolph Agricola's Influence on Methodical Thinking in the Humanities," in *Rudolphus Agricola Phrisius,* F. Akkerman and A. J. Vanderjagt, eds. (Leiden: E. J. Brill, 1988): 38–57.

Jardine, Lisa, *Francis Bacon: Discovery and the Art of Discourse* (Cambridge, UK: Cambridge U. Press, 1974).

Jarratt, Susan, *Rereading the Sophists: Classical Rhetoric Refigured* (Carbondale: Southern Illinois U. Press, 1991).

Jarrett, James L., *The Educational Theories of the Sophists* (New York: Columbia U. Teachers College Press, 1969).

Jaspers, Karl, *Philosophy,* 3 vols., E. B. Ashton, trans. (Chicago: U. of Chicago Press, 1970).

Jaspers, Karl, *Way to Wisdom,* R. Manheim, trans. (New Haven, CT: Yale U. Press, 1970).

Jebb, Richard C., *The Attic Orators from Antiphon to Isaeos* (New York: Russell, 1962).

Jerome, *Letters of St. Jerome,* Charles C. Mierow, trans. (London: Longmans, Green, 1963).

Johannesen, Richard L., Rennard Strickland, and Ralph T. Eubanks, eds., *Language Is Sermonic: Richard M. Weaver on the Nature of Rhetoric* (Baton Rouge: Louisiana State U. Press, 1970).

Johnson, W. R., "Isocrates Flowering: The Rhetoric of Augustine," *Philosophy and Rhetoric,* 9 (1976): 34–43.

Johnstone, Christopher Lyle, *Listening to the Logos: Speech and the Coming of Wisdom in Ancient Greece* (Columbia: U. of South Carolina Press, 2009).

Jones, Ernest, *The Life and Work of Sigmund Freud,* vol. 3 (New York: Basic Books, 1957).

Julian, Stephen, "Advancing a Theory of Redefinition: An Examination of Pat Robertson's 1988 Presidential Campaign." Paper presented at the Annual Meeting of the Speech Communication Association, San Antonio, November, 1995.

Jung, Carl G., *Man and His Symbols* (New York: Dell, 1978).

Kahn, Victoria, "Humanism and the Resistance to Theory," in *Rhetoric and Hermeneutics in Our Time,* Walter Jost and Michael Hyde, eds. (New Haven, CT: Yale U. Press, 1997): 149–70.

Kahn, Victoria, *Machiavellian Rhetoric: From the Counter-Reformation to Milton* (Princeton, NJ: Princeton U. Press, 1994).

Kahn, Victoria, *Rhetoric, Prudence, and Skepticism in the Renaissance* (Ithaca, NY: Cornell U. Press, 1985).

Kant, Immanuel, *The Critique of Judgment: Part I, Critique of Aesthetic Judgment,* James C. Meredith, trans. (Oxford: Clarendon Press, 1952).

Kant, Immanuel, *Critique of Pure Reason,* Werner S. Pluhar, trans. (Indianapolis: Hackett Publishing, 1996).

Kant, Immanuel, *Foundations of the Metaphysics of Morals,* L. W. Beck, trans. (New York: Liberal Arts Press, 1959).

Kaufmann, Walter, *Existentialism from Dostoevsky to Sartre* (New York: Doubleday, 1968).

Kennedy, George, *Classical Rhetoric and Its Christian and Secular Tradition from Ancient to Modern Times* (Chapel Hill: U. of North Carolina Press, 1980).

Kennedy, George, *New Testament Interpretation Through Rhetorical Criticism* (Chapel Hill: U. of North Carolina Press, 1984).

Kennedy, George, *Quintilian* (New York: Twayne Publishers, 1969).

Kennedy, George, ed. and trans., *Invention and Method: Two Rhetorical Treatises from the Hermogenic Corpus* (Atlanta: Society of Biblical Literature, 2005).

Kerber, Linda K., "Salvaging the Classical Tradition" in *Federalist in Dissent: Imagery and Ideology in Jeffersonian America* (Ithaca, NY: Cornell U. Press, 1970): 95–134.

Kerferd, George B., *The Sophistic Movement* (Cambridge, UK: Cambridge U. Press, 1981).

Kierkegaard, Søren, *Attack upon "Christendom,"* Walter Lowrie, trans. (Princeton, NJ: Princeton U. Press, 1968).

Kierkegaard, Søren, "Christ as a Pattern," in *For Self-Examination and Judge for Yourself!* Walter Lowrie, trans. (Princeton, NJ: Princeton U. Press, 1968): 161–221.

Kierkegaard, Søren, *The Concept of Dread,* Walter Lowrie, trans. (Princeton, NJ: Princeton U. Press, 1973).

Kierkegaard, Søren, *Concluding Unscientific Postscript,* David Swenson and Walter Lowrie, trans. (Princeton, NJ: Princeton U. Press, 1946).

Kierkegaard, Søren, *Either/Or,* vol. 2, Walter Lowrie, trans. (Garden City, NY: Doubleday, 1959).

Kierkegaard, Søren, *A Kierkegaard Anthology,* Robert Bretall, ed. (New York: Modern Library, 1946).

Kierkegaard, Søren, *The Present Age and of the Difference between a Genius and an Apostle,* Alexander Dru, trans. (New York: Harper & Row, 1962).

Kierkegaard, Søren, *The Sickness Unto Death,* Walter Lowrie, trans. (Princeton, NJ: Princeton U. Press, 1954).

Kierkegaard, Søren, *Training in Christianity,* Walter Lowrie, trans. (Princeton, NJ: Princeton U. Press, 1967).

King, Margaret L., "Thwarted Ambitions: Six Learned Women of the Italian Renaissance," *Soundings,* 59 (1976): 280–304.

Kirk, Geoffrey S. and John E. Raven, *The Presocratic Philosophers* (Cambridge, MA: Harvard U. Press, 1971).

Kirkpatrick, Andy, "China's First Systematic Account of Rhetoric: An Introduction to Chen Kui's *Wen Ze*," *Rhetorica,* 33 (2005): 103–52.

Kirkwood, William, "Studying Communication about Spirituality and the Spiritual Consequences of Communication," *The Journal of Communication and Religion,* 17 (1994): 13–26.

Kohut, Heinz, *The Analysis of Self* (New York: International U. Press, 1971).

Lactantius, *Divine Institutes,* Sister Mary Francis McDonald, trans. (Washington, DC: Catholic U. Press, 1964).

Lavasseur, David G., "A Reexamination of Edmund Burke's Rhetorical Art: A Rhetorical Struggle Between Prudence and Heroism," *Quarterly Journal of Speech,* 83 (1997): 332–50.

Lawson, John, "Boethius and the History of Medieval Rhetoric," *Central States Speech Journal,* 25 (1974): 134–41.

Lawson, John, "Burke's Ciceronianism," in *The Legacy of Kenneth Burke,* Herbert Simons and Trevor Melia, eds. (Madison: U. of Wisconsin Press, 1989).

Lawson, John, *Lectures Concerning Oratory,* E. N. Clauson and Karl R. Wallace, eds. (Carbondale: Southern Illinois U. Press, 1972/1758).

Lawson, John, "St. Augustine and Martianus Capella: Continuity and Change in Fifth Century Latin Rhetorical Theory," *Communication Quarterly,* 24 (1976): 2–9.

Leff, Michael and Gerald P. Mohrmann, "Lincoln at Cooper Union: A Rhetorical Analysis of the Text," in *The Practice of Rhetorical Criticism,* 2nd ed., James R. Andrews, ed. (New York: Longman, 1990): 155–63.

Lehrer, Ronald, *Nietzsche's Presence in Freud's Life and Thought: On the Origins of a Psychology of Dynamic Mental Functioning* (Albany: SUNY Press, 1995).

Leon, Judah Messer, *The Book of the Honeycomb's Flow,* Isaac Rabinowitz, trans. (Ithaca, NY: Cornell U. Press, 1983).

Lerous, Neil R., "Luther's Am Neujahrstage: Style as Argument," *Rhetorica,* 12 (1994): 1–42.

Levison, John R., "Did the Spirit Inspire Rhetoric? An Exploration of George Kennedy's Definition of Early Christian Rhetoric," in *Persuasive Artistry: Studies in New Testament Rhetoric in Honor of George A. Kennedy,* Duane F. Watson, ed. *Journal for the Study of the New Testament,* Suppl. series 50 (Sheffield, England: Sheffield Academic Press, 1991): 25–40.

Lévi-Strauss, Claude, "The Story of Asdiwal," Nicholas Mann, trans., in *The Structural Study of Myth and Totemism,* Edmund Leach, ed., *Association of Social Anthropologists Monographs* 5 (London: Tavistock, 1967): 1–47.

Levy, Carlos, "From Politics to Philosophy and Theology: Some Remarks about Foucault's Interpretation of Parrhesia in Two Recently Published Seminars," *Philosophy and Rhetoric,* 42 (2009): 313–25.

Locke, John, "Epistle to the Reader," An Essay Concerning Human Understanding, in *The Age of Enlightenment,* Isaiah Berlin, ed. (Boston: Houghton Mifflin, 1956): 30–112.

Locke, John, *Two Treatises of Government* (Cambridge, UK: Cambridge U. Press, 1988).

Longinus, *On the Sublime,* G. M. A. Grube, trans. (New York: Library of Liberal Arts, 1957).

Longinus, "On the Sublime," Rhys Roberts, trans., in *The Great Critics,* James Harry Smith and Ed Winfield Parks, eds. (New York: W. W. Norton, 1959): 65–111.

Lorde, Audre, *Sister Outsider: Essays and Speeches by Audre Lorde* (Freedom, CA: Crossing Press, 1984).

Lowry, Martin, *The World of Aldus Manutius: Business and Scholarship in Renaissance Venice* (Ithaca, NY: Cornell U. Press, 1979).

Lundy, Susan and Wayne Thompson, "Pliny, a Neglected Roman Rhetorician," *Quarterly Journal of Speech,* 66 (1980): 407–17.

Luther, Martin. *Selections from His Writings,* John Dillenberger, ed. (New York: Anchor Books, 1962).

Lyotard, Jean-François, *The Postmodern Condition: A Report on Knowledge,* G. Bennington and B. Massumi, trans. (Minneapolis: U. of Minnesota Press, 1984).

Lyotard, Jean-François, *Just Gaming,* Wlad Godzich, trans. (Minneapolis: U. of Minnesota Press, 1985).

Lyotard, Jean-François, *The Differend: Phrases in Dispute,* G. Van Den Abbeele, trans. (Minneapolis: U. of Minnesota Press, 1988).

Mack, Peter, *Renaissance Argument: Valla and Agricola in the Traditions of Rhetoric and Dialectic* (Leiden: E. J. Brill, 1993).

Mack, Peter, ed., *Renaissance Rhetoric* (New York: St. Martin's Press, 1994).

Mack, Peter, ed., *The Significance of Rhetoric in the Renaissance* (London: Macmillan, 1992).

Mahler, M., *On Human Symbiosis and the Vicissitudes of Individuation* (New York: International U. Press, 1968).

Mahon, Michael, *Foucault's Nietzschean Genealogy: Truth, Power and the Subject* (Albany: SUNY Press, 1992).

Maimonides, "Guide of the Perplexed," Ralph Lerner and Muhsin Mahdi, trans., in *Medieval Political Philosophy,* Ralph Lerner and Muhsin Mahdi, eds. (New York: The Free Press, 1967): 191–226.

Majoragius, Mark A., *Aristotelis Stagyritae De arte rhetorica libri tres cum M. Antonii Maioragii commentariis* (Venice, 1591).

Marrou, Henri I., *A History of Education in Antiquity* (Madison: U. of Wisconsin Press, 1948).

Mast, Gerald J., "Panhelenism and Patriarchy in Isocrates' Helen." Paper presented at the Annual Meeting of the Speech Communication Association, Chicago, November, 1990.

May, James, *Trials of Character: The Eloquence of Ciceronian Ethos* (Chapel Hill: U. of North Carolina Press, 1988).

McGee, Michael C., "The 'Ideograph': A Link between Rhetoric and Ideology," *Quarterly Journal of Speech,* 66 (1980): 1–16.

McGee, Michael C., "A Materialist's Conception of Rhetoric" in *Explorations in Rhetoric: Studies in Honor of Douglas Ehninger,* R. E. McKerrow, ed. (Glenview, IL: Scott Foresman, 1982): 23–48.

McGee, Michael C., "In Search of 'The People': A Rhetorical Alternative," *The Quarterly Journal of Speech,* 61 (1975): 245–47.

McGee, Michael C., "Text, Context, and the Fragmentation of Contemporary Culture," *Western Journal of Speech Communication,* 54 (1990): 274–89.

McGee, Michael C. and Martha Martin, "Public Knowledge and Ideological Argumentation," *Communication Monographs,* 50 (1983): 47–65.

McGuire, Michael, "Mythic Rhetoric in *Mein Kampf:* A Structural Critique," *Quarterly Journal of Speech,* 68 (1977): 1–13.

McGuire, Michael, "Ideology and Myth as Structurally Different Bases for Political Argumentation," *Journal of the American Forensic Association,* 24 (1987): 16–26.

McKenna, Stephen J., *Adam Smith: The Rhetoric of Propriety* (Albany: SUNY Press, 2006).

McKerrow, Raymie E., "Critical Rhetoric: Theory and Praxis," *Communication Monographs,* 56 (1989): 91–111.

McKerrow, Raymie E., "Critical Rhetoric in a Postmodern World," *Quarterly Journal of Speech,* 77 (1991): 75–78.

Meisenhelder, T., "Habermas and Feminism: The Future of Critical Theory," in *Feminism and Social Theory,* R. Wallace, ed. (Beverly Hills: Sage, 1989): 119–32.

Miller, Alice, *The Drama of the Gifted Child: The Search for Self,* R. Ward, trans. (New York: Basic Books, 1982; 1997).

Milovanovic-Barham, Celica, "The Levels of Style in Augustine of Hippo and Gregory of Nazianus," *Rhetorica,* 11 (1993): 1–25.

Misciattelli, Piero, *Savonarola* (New York: D. Appleton, 1930).

Mohrmann, Gerald P., "The Civile Conversation: Communication in the Renaissance," *Speech Monographs,* 39 (1972): 193–204.

Morreall, John, *The Philosophy of Laughter and Humor* (Albany: SUNY Press, 1987).

Moss, Jean Dietz, *Novelties in the Heavens: Rhetoric and Science in the Copernican Controversy* (Chicago: U. of Chicago Press, 1993).

Mouffe, Chantal, "The Sex/Gender System and the Discursive Construction of Women's Subordination," in *Rethinking Ideology: A Marxist Debate,* S. Hanninen and L. Paldan, eds. (New York: International General, 1983): 139–43.

Murphy, James, J., *Rhetoric in the Middle Ages: A History of Rhetorical Theory from Saint Augustine to the Renaissance* (Berkeley: U. of California Press, 1974).

Murphy, James J., "Saint Augustine and the Debate About Christian Rhetoric," *Quarterly Journal of Speech,* 46 (1960): 400–10.

Murphy, James J., ed., *Peter Ramus's Attack on Cicero: Text and Translation of Ramus's* Brutinae Questiones, Carole Newlands, trans. (Davis, CA: Hermagoras Press, 1992).

Murphy, James, J., ed., *Quintilian on the Teaching of Speaking and Writing: Translations from Books One, Two and Ten of the* Institutio Oratoria (Carbondale: Southern Illinois U. Press, 1987).

Nicholson, Linda, ed., *Feminism/Postmodernism* (New York: Routledge, 1990).

Nietzsche, Friedrich, *The Birth of Tragedy,* Walter Kaufmann, trans. (New York: Vintage Books, 1967).

Nietzsche, Friedrich, "On Truth and Lie in an Extra-Moral Sense," Walter Kaufmann, trans., in *The Portable Nietzsche* (New York: Viking Press, 1968): 42–46.

Nietzsche, Friedrich, *The Will to Power,* Walter Kaufmann and R. J. Hollingdale, trans. (New York: Vintage Books, 1968).

Nizolius, Mathias, *De veris principiis et vera ratione philosophandi contra pseudophilosophos* (Parma, 1553).

O'Banion, John D., "Narration and Argumentation: Quintilian on Narration as the Heart of Rhetorical Theory," *Rhetorica,* 5 (1987): 325–51.

Ochs, Donovan J., "Aristotle's Concept of Formal Topics," *Speech Monographs,* 36 (1969): 419–25.

Ochs, Donovan J., *Consolatory Rhetoric: Grief, Symbol, and Ritual in the Greco-Roman Era* (Columbia: U. of South Carolina Press, 1993).

O'Leary, Stephen D., "A Dramatistic Theory of Apocalyptic Rhetoric," *Quarterly Journal of Speech,* 79 (1993): 385–426.

O'Leary, Stephen D. and Michael McFarland, "The Political Use of Mythic Discourse: Prophetic Interpretation in Pat Robertson's Presidential Campaign," *Quarterly Journal of Speech*, 75 (1989): 433–52.

Olsen, Kathryn, "The Controversy over President Reagan's Visit to Bitburg: Strategies of Definition and Redefinition," *The Quarterly Journal of Speech,* 75 (1989): 129–51.

O'Neill, Robert, "The Value of Global Citizenship," Harvard Kennedy School, May 23, 2012. http://www.hks.harvard.edu/news-events/news/articles/the-value-of-global-citizenship

Ong, Walter J., "Ramist Method and the Commercial Mind," *Rhetoric, Romance, and Technology* (Ithaca, NY: Cornell U. Press, 1971): 165–89.

Ong, Walter J., *Ramus: Method, and the Day of Dialogue; from the Art of Discourse to the Art of Reason* (Cambridge, MA: Harvard U. Press, 1958), reprinted as *Ramus: Method, and the Decay of Dialogue* (New York: Farrar, Straus & Giroux, 1974).

Pascall, Gillian, *Social Policy: A New Feminist Analysis* (London and New York: Routledge, 1997).

Patrick, J. Max, *Francis Bacon* (London: Longmans, Green, 1961).

Payne, David, "Rhetoric, Reality, and Knowledge: A Re-examination of Protagoras' Concept of Rhetoric," *Rhetoric Society Quarterly,* 16 (1986): 167–79.

Pease, Arthur S., "The Attitude of Jerome toward Pagan Literature," *Transactions and Proceedings of the American Philological Association,* 50 (1919): 150–67.

Perelman, Chaim, *The Idea of Justice and the Problem of Argument,* John Petrie, trans. (London, 1963).

Perelman, Chaim and Lucie Olbrechts-Tyteca, *The New Rhetoric: A Treatise on Argumentation* (London: Notre Dame U. Press, 1968).

Piper, Paul C., "De arte rhetorica," in *Die Schriften Notkers und seiner Schule,* 1 (Tubingen, Germany: Freibur I.B., 1882): 675–86.

Plato, *The Dialogues,* 2 vols., Benjamin Jowett, trans. (New York: Random House, 1937).

Plato, *Gorgias,* W. C. Hembold, trans. (New York: Bobbs-Merrill, 1952).

Plett, Heinrich F., *Rhetoric and Renaissance Culture* (Berlin-New York: W. de Gruyter, 2004).

Plett, Heinrich F., ed., *Renaissance-Rhetorik, Renaissance Rhetoric* (Berlin-New York: W. de Gruyter, 1993).

Pocock, John G. Agard, *The Machiavellian Moment: Florentine Political Thought and the Atlantic Republican Tradition* (Princeton, NJ: Princeton U. Press, 1975).

Polak, Emil J., *Medieval and Renaissance Letter Treatises and Form Letters: A Census of Manuscripts Found in Eastern Europe and the Former U.S.S.R.,* Davis Medieval Texts and Studies 8 (Leiden: E. J. Brill, 1993).

Poster, Carol, "An Organon for Theology: Whately's *Rhetoric and Logic* in Religious Context," *Rhetorica,* 24 (2006): 37–78.

Potkay, Adam, *The Fate of Eloquence in the Age of Hume* (Ithaca, NY: Cornell U. Press, 1994).

Poulakos, John, "Hegel's Reception of the Sophists," *Western Journal of Speech Communication,* 54 (Spring, 1990): 161–68.

Poulakos, John, *Sophistical Rhetoric in Classical Greece* (Columbia: U. of South Carolina Press, 1995).

Poulakos, John, "Toward a Sophistic Definition of Rhetoric," *Philosophy and Rhetoric,* 16 (1983): 35–48.

Poulakos, Takis, *Speaking for the Polis: Isocrates' Rhetorical Education* (Columbia: U. of South Carolina Press, 1997).

Poulakos, Takis and David Depew, eds. *Isocrates and Civic Education* (Austin: U. of Texas Press, 2004).

Prideaux, John, *Sacred Eloquence: The Art of Rhetoric as it is Laid Down in Scripture* (London: George Sawbridge, 1659).

Primmer, Adolf, "The Function of *the genera dicendi* in *De doctrina christiana 4*," in *De docrina Christiana: A Classic of Western Culture,* Duane W. H. Arnold and Pamela Bright, eds. (Notre Dame, IN: U. of Notre Dame Press, 1995): 47–67.

Proust, Marcel, 1932. *Remembrance of Things Past,* vols. 1 and 2. New York: Random House.

Psaty, Bruce M., "Cicero's Literal Metaphor and Propriety," *Central States Speech Journal,* 29 (1978): 107–17.

Purcell, William M., "Eberhard the German and the Labyrinth of Learning: Grammar, Poesy, Rhetoric, and Pedagogy in Laborintus," *Rhetorica,* 11 (1993): 95–118.

Puttenham, George, *The Arte of English Poesie,* Gladys D. Willcock and Alice Walker, eds. (Cambridge, UK: Cambridge U. Press, 1936).

Quintilian, *The Institutes of Oratory,* E. Butler, trans. (Cambridge, MA: Harvard U. Press, 1959).

Rabe, Hugo, ed., *Hermogenis Opera* (Leipzig: Teubur, 1913).

Race, William H., "The Word Kairos in Greek Drama," *Transactions of the American Philological Society,* 111 (1981): 197–213.

Ramus, Petrus, *Dialectic* (Paris: 1576).

Ray, Angela, "Learning Leadership: Lincoln at the Lyceum, 1838," *Rhetoric and Public Affairs* 13 (2010): 349–88.

Rebhorn, Wayne A., "Baldesar Castiglione, Thomas Wilson, and the Courtly Body of Renaissance Rhetoric," *Rhetorica,* 11 (1993): 261–74.

Reid, Ronald F. and James F. Klumpp, *American Rhetorical Discourse,* 3rd ed. (Long Grove, IL: Waveland Press, 2005).

Remer, Gary, "Political Oratory and Conversation," *Political Theory,* 27 (1999): 39–65.

Richards, I. A., *Philosophy of Rhetoric* (New York: Oxford U. Press, 1936).

Richards, I. A., *Speculative Instruments* (Chicago: U. of Chicago Press, 1955).

Richards, I. A. and Charles K. Ogden, *The Meaning of Meaning* (New York: Harcourt, Brace, 1956).

Rivkin, Ellis, *What Crucified Jesus?* (Nashville: Abingdon, 1984).

Robinson, James M., ed., *The Nag Hammadi Library in English* (New York: Harper Collins, 1990).

Rohde, Erwin, *Psyche: The Cult of Souls and the Belief in Immortality Among the Greeks* (New York: Books for Libraries Press, 1920).

Rolfe, John C., *Cicero and His Influence* (New York: Cooper Square, 1963).

Romilly, Jacqueline de, *The Great Sophists in Periclean Athens,* Janet Lloyd, trans. (Oxford: Clarendon Press, 1992).

Romilly, Jacqueline de, *Magic and Rhetoric in Ancient Greece* (Cambridge, MA: Harvard U. Press, 1975).

Rorty, Richard, *Philosophy and the Mirror of Nature* (Princeton, NJ: Princeton U. Press, 1979).

Rosenfield, Lawrence W., "Central Park and the Celebration of Civic Virtue," in *American Rhetoric: Context and Criticism* (Carbondale: Southern Illinois U. Press, 1989): 221–66.

Rosenfield, Lawrence W., "The Practical Celebration of Epideictic," in *Rhetoric in Transition: Studies in the Nature and Uses of Rhetoric*, Eugene E. White, ed. (University Park: The Pennsylvania State U. Press, 1980): 131–55.

Ross, James Bruce and Mary Martin McLaughlin, *The Portable Medieval Reader* (New York: Viking, 1963).

Rowland, Robert C., "On Mythic Criticism," *Communication Studies,* 41 (1990): 101–16.

Rueckert, William H., ed., *Kenneth Burke and the Dawn of Human Relations* (Minneapolis: U. of Minnesota Press, 1963).

Russell, Bertrand, *Logic and Knowledge: Essays 1901–1950* (New York: Macmillan, 1968).

Safranski, Rudiger, *Martin Heidegger: Between Good and Evil,* Ewald Osers, trans. (Cambridge, MA: Harvard U. Press, 1998).

Saperstein, Marc, *Jewish Preaching from 1200–1800,* (New Haven, CT: Yale U. Press, 1989).

Sartre, Jean-Paul, *Existentialism and Human Emotions,* B. Frechtman and Hazel E. Barnes, trans. (New York: Philosophical Library, 1957).

Sartre, Jean-Paul, *Existentialism and Humanism,* Philip Mairet, trans. (London: Methuen, 1965).

Sartre, Jean-Paul, *Nausea,* Lloyd Anderson, trans. (New York: New Directions Publishing Co., 1964).

Schaeffer, John D., "Vico's Rhetorical Model of the Mind: *Sensus communis* in the *De nostri temporis studiorum ratione," Philosophy and Rhetoric*, 14 (1981): 152–67.

Schaff, Philip, *The Swiss Reformation* (Edinburgh, 1893).

Schiappa, Edward, *The Beginnings of Rhetorical Theory in Classical Greece* (New Haven, CT: Yale U. Press, 1999).

Schiappa, Edward, "Gorgias's Helen Revisited," *Quarterly Journal of Speech,* 81 (1995): 310–24.

Schiappa, Edward, *Protagoras and Logos: A Study in Greek Philosophy and Rhetoric* (Columbia: U. of South Carolina Press, 1991).

Schlatter, Adolf, *Der Evangelist Matthaus* (Stuttgart, Germany: Calwer, 1959).

Schrage, Wolfgang, *The Ethics of the New Testament* (Philadelphia: Fortress, 1988).

Scott, Robert, "On Viewing Rhetoric as Epistemic," *Central States Speech Journal,* 18 (1967): 13–14.

Scott, Robert, "On Viewing Rhetoric as Epistemic: Ten Years Later," *Central States Speech Journal,* 27 (1976): 258–66.

Seltman, Charles, *Approach to Greek Art* (London: Dutton, 1949).

Shildgen, Brenda Deen, "Petrarch's Defense of Secular Letters, the Latin Fathers, and Ancient Roman Rhetoric," *Rhetorica,* 11 (1993): 124.

Simons, Herbert W. and Aram A. Aghazarian, eds., *Form, Genre, and the Study of Political Discourse* (Columbia: U. of South Carolina Press, 1986).

Skinner, Quentin, *Reason and Rhetoric in the Philosophy of Hobbes* (Cambridge, UK: Cambridge U. Press, 1996).

Smith, Adam, *Lectures on Rhetoric and Belles Lettres,* J. C. Bryce, ed. (Indianapolis: Indiana U. Press, 1985).

Smith, Bromley, "The Father of Debate: Protagoras of Abdera," *Quarterly Journal of Speech,* 4 (1918): 196–215.

Smith, Craig R., "Actuality and Potentiality: The Essence of Criticism," *Philosophy and Rhetoric,* 3 (1970): 133–40.

Smith, Craig R., *Freedom of Expression and Partisan Politics* (Columbia: U. of South Carolina Press, 1989).

Smith, Craig R., "Martin Heidegger and the Dialogue with Being," *Central States Speech Journal,* 36 (1985): 256–69.

Smith, Craig R., "The Medieval Subjugation and the Existential Elevation of Rhetoric," *Philosophy and Rhetoric,* 5 (1972): 159–74.

Smith, Craig R., "Nixon's Acceptance: The Dual Audience Problem," *Today's Speech,* 9 (1971): 15–21.

Smith, Craig R., *Orientations to Speech Criticism,* 2nd ed. (Chicago: Science, Research, Associates, 1982).

Smith, Craig R., "A Reinterpretation of Aristotle's Notion of Rhetorical Form," *Western Speech Communication Journal* (1979): 14–25.

Smith, Craig R. and David Hunsaker, "Rhetorical Distance: A Critical Dimension," *Western Speech Communication Journal,* 37 (1973): 241–52.

Smith, Craig R. and Michael J. Hyde, "Rethinking the Public: The Role of Emotion in Being-with-Others," *Quarterly Journal of Speech,* 78 (1991): 446–66.

Smith, Craig R. and Scott Lybarger, "Bitzer's Model Revised," *Communication Quarterly,* 44 (1996): 197–213.

Smith, Craig R. and Paul Prince, "Language Choice, Expectation, and the Roman Notion of Style," *Communication Education,* 39 (1990): 63–74.

Solmsen, Friedrich, "The Aristotelian Tradition in Ancient Rhetoric," *American Journal of Philology,* 62 (1941): 35–50.

Solmsen, Friedrich, *Intellectual Experiments of the Greek Enlightenment* (Princeton, NJ: Princeton U. Press, 1975).

Spano, Shawn, "John Locke and the Epistemological Foundation of Adam Smith's Rhetoric," *The Southern Communication Journal,* 59 (1993): 15–26.

Spees, Richard, "John of Salisbury: Rhetoric in the Metalogicon," *Central States Speech Journal,* 20 (1969): 92–96.

Springborg, Patricia, ed., *Astell: Political Writings* (Cambridge: Cambridge U. Press, 1996).

Sproule, Michael, "The Psychological Burden of Proof: On the Development of Richard Whately's Theory of Presumption," *Communication Monographs,* 43 (1976): 115–29.

Steeves, H. Leslie and Marilyn C. Smith, "Class and Gender in Prime-time Television Entertainment: Observations from a Socialist Feminist Perspective," *Journal of Communication Inquiry,* 11 (1987): 43–63.

Struever, Nancy, *The Language of History in the Renaissance* (Princeton, NJ: Princeton U. Press, 1970).

Svoboda, Michael, "Athens, the Unjust Student of Rhetoric: A Dramatic Historical Interpretation of Plato's *Gorgias,*" *Rhetoric Society Quarterly,* 37 (2007): 275–306.

Szlezak, Thomas A., *Reading Plato,* Graham Zanker, trans. (New York: Routledge, 1999).

Tacitus, *Dialogue on Oratory,* Sir William Peterson, trans. (Cambridge, MA: Harvard U. Press, 1946).

Taylor, Jerome, *The Didascalicon of Hugh of St. Victor* (New York: Columbia U. Press, 1961).

Telegen-Couperus, Olga, ed., *Quintilian and the Law: The Art of Persuasion in Law and Politics* (Leuven, Netherlands: Leuven U. Press, 2003).

Thomas, Douglas, "Burke, Nietzsche, Lacan: Three Perspectives on the Rhetoric of Order," *Quarterly Journal of Speech,* 79 (1993): 336–55.

Timmerman, David and Edward Schiappa, *Classical Greek Rhetorical Theory and the Disciplining of Discourse* (New York: Cambridge U. Press, 2010).

Tindale, Christopher W., *Reason's Dark Champions: Constructive Strategies of Sophistic Argument* (Columbia: U. of South Carolina Press, 2010).

Too, Yun Lee, *A Commentary on Isocrates'* Antidosis (Oxford: Oxford U. Press, 2008).

Too, Yun Lee, *The Rhetoric of Identity in Isocrates: Text, Power, Pedagogy* (New York: Cambridge U. Press, 1995).

Toulmin, Stephen, *Human Understanding* (Princeton, NJ: Princeton U. Press, 1972).

Toulmin, Stephen, *The Uses of Argument,* 2nd ed. (Cambridge, UK: Cambridge U. Press, 2003).

Tucker, Robert E., "Figure, Ground and Presence: A Phenomenology of Meaning in Rhetoric," *Quarterly Journal of Speech,* 87 (2001): 396–414.

Tukey, David, "Toward a Spiritual Critique of Inter-subjectivist Rhetoric," The *Journal of Communication and Religion,* 10 (1988): 1–8.

Untersteiner, Mario, *The Sophists,* Kathleen Freeman, trans. (New York: Philosophical Library, 1964).

Vasaly, Ann, *Representations: Images of the Ancient World in Ciceronian Rhetoric* (Berkeley: U. of California Press, 1993).

Versenyi, Laszlo, *Socratic Humanism* (New Haven, CT: Yale U. Press, 1963).

Vico, Giambattista, *The New Science,* Thomas Goddard Bergin and Max Harold Fisch, trans. (Ithaca, NY: Cornell U. Press, 1948).

Vives, Juan Luis, *On Education: A Translation of the "De Tradendis Disciplinis,"* Foster Watson, trans. (Cambridge, UK: Cambridge U. Press, 1913).

Vogel, Cornelia J. de, *Greek Philosophy: A Collection of Texts,* vol. 1, Thales to Plato, 4th ed. (Leiden, Netherlands: E. J. Brill, 1963).

Walker, Jeffrey, "Before the Beginnings of 'Poetry' and 'Rhetoric': Hesiod on Eloquence," *Rhetorica,* 14 (1996): 243–64.

Walker, Jeffrey, *Rhetoric and Poetics in Antiquity* (Oxford: Oxford U. Press, 2000).

Wallace, Karl R., "The Substance of Rhetoric: Good Reasons," *Quarterly Journal of Speech,* 49 (1963): 239–49.

Wallraff, Charles F., *Karl Jaspers: An Introduction to His Philosophy* (Princeton, NJ: Princeton U. Press, 1970).

Wander, Philip, "The Ideological Turn in Modern Criticism," *Central States Speech Journal,* 34 (1983): 1–18.

Ward, John, *Systems of Oratory* (London, 1759).

Warnick, Barbara, "Judgment, Probability, and Aristotle's *Rhetoric,*" *Quarterly Journal of Speech,* 75 (1989): 299–311.

Warnick, Barbara, "Lucie Olbrechts-Tyteca's Contribution to *The New Rhetoric,*" in *Listening to Their Voices: The Rhetorical Activities of Historical Women,* Molly Wertheimer, ed. (Columbia: U. of South Carolina Press, 1997).

Warnick, Barbara, *The Sixth Canon: Belletristic Rhetorical Theory and Its French Antecedents* (Columbia: U. of South Carolina Press, 1994).

Weaver, Richard, *Ideas Have Consequences* (Chicago: U. of Chicago Press, 1948).

Weber, Max, *The Theory of Social and Economic Organization,* T. Parsons and A. M. Henderson, trans. (New York: Oxford U. Press, 1947).

Weedon, Chris, *Feminism, Theory and the Politics of Difference* (Oxford, UK: Blackwell, 2000).

Weedon, Chris, *Feminist Practice and Poststructural Theory* (Oxford, UK: Blackwell, 1987).

Wellek, Rene, *A History of Modern Criticism: 1750–1850,* vol. 1 (New Haven, CT: Yale U. Press, 1955).

Weisman, Avery D., *The Existential Core of Psychoanalysis: Reality, Sense and Responsibility* (Boston: Little, Brown, and Company, 1965).

Wess, Robert, *Kenneth Burke: Rhetoric, Subjectivity, Postmodernism* (Cambridge, UK: Cambridge U. Press, 1996).

Whately, Richard, *The Elements of Rhetoric* (Boston and Cambridge: James Munroe, 1855; rpt. Carbondale: Southern Illinois U. Press, 1963).

Wichelns, Herbert, "The Literary Criticism of Oratory," in *The Rhetorical Idiom: Essays in Rhetoric, Oratory, Language and Drama,* Donald C. Bryant, ed. (Ithaca, NY: Cornell U. Press, 1958): 5–42.

Wiethoff, William, "The Obscurantist Design in Saint Augustine's Rhetoric," *Communication Studies,* 31 (1980): 128–36.

Williams, Raymond, *Marxism and Literature* (New York: Oxford U. Press, 1977).

Wilson, Thomas, *Wilson's Arte of Rhetorique 1560,* G. H. Mair, ed. (Oxford: Clarendon Press, 1909).

Winnicott, Donald W., "The Theory of Parent-Infant Relationship," *International Journal of Psychoanalysis,* 41 (1960): 585–95.

Winterowd, Ross, "Kenneth Burke: An Annotated Glossary of His Terministic Screen," *Rhetoric Society Quarterly,* 15 (1985): 145–77.

Witt, Ronald G., *"In the Footsteps of the Ancients": The Origins of Humanism from Lovato to Bruni, Studies in Medieval and Reformation Thought,* vol. 74 (Leiden, Netherlands: E. J. Brill, 2000).

Wood, Ellen M. and Neal Wood, *Class Ideology and Ancient Political Theory: Socrates, Plato, and Aristotle in Social Context* (New York: Oxford U. Press, 1978).

Wood, Julia T., "Gender and Moral Voice: Moving from Woman's Nature to Standpoint Epistemology," *Women's Studies in Communication,* 15 (1992): 1–24.

Yunis, Harvey, *Taming Democracy: Models of Political Rhetoric in Democratic Athens* (Ithaca, NY: Cornell U. Press, 1996).

Zarefsky, David, "Lincoln's 1862 Annual Message: A Paradigm of Rhetorical Leadership," *Rhetoric and Public Affairs,* 3 (2000): 5–14.

Zimmerman, Michael, *Eclipse of the Self: The Development of Heidegger's Concept of Authenticity* (Athens: Ohio U. Press, 1981).

Zulick, Margaret D., "The Agon of Jeremiah: On the Dialogic Invention of Prophetic Ethos," *Quarterly Journal of Speech,* 78 (1992): 125–48.

Index

effective, essential elements of, 29, 31
  in feminist rhetorical theory, 395
  Fisher on, 20
  Islamic storytelling, 168
  Lyotard on, 377
  rhetoric of civil religion as, 309
  rhetorical dimensions of, 19–22
  transhistorical subject matter in, 308
Narrators, types of, 24
Natural signs, 161–162
Naturalist School, 34–39
Nausea (Sartre), 276
Necessity, rhetoric of, 318
Nedelsky, Jennifer, 392
Neoplatonists, 148, 154–155, 160
Nero, 146
New media, impact on rhetoric, 355–362
New Rhetoric (*Nova rhetorica*), Notker Labeo, 171
New Rhetoric, The: A Treatise on Argumentation (Perelman and Olbrechts-Tyteca), 347–350
New Science (*Scienza nuova*) (Vico), 237
Newman, Samuel Phillips, 251
Newton, Isaac, 235
Nicholas V, 194
Nicholson, Linda, 385
Nicomachean Ethics (Aristotle), 66
Ninety-Five Theses (Luther), 211
Nixon, Richard M., 120, 335, 356, 359
Nizzolius, 207–208
Noble rhetoric, 57, 146, 407
Noddings, Nell, 390
Normative theory of criticism, Plato's, 52
Notker Labeo, 171
Noumenal world, 36, 50, 56–57, 131, 269
Nous, 72
Novum Organum Scientiarum (*New Organon of Science*) (Bacon), 240
Nuñez, Pedro Juan, 223

Obama, Barack, 121, 253, 330, 360, 383
Observations on Man, His Frame, His Duty, and His Expectations (Hartley), 249

Occupy Movement, 374
Ockham, William of, 176, 243
Ockham's razor, 176
Octavian, 108
Oedipus Complex, 292
Offin, Karen, 394
Ogden, K. C., 344
Ogilvie, John, 251
Olbrechts-Tyteca, Lucie, 126, 343, 346–352
Olson, Kathryn, 335
Omission strategies, 303
On Analogy (Caesar), 106
On Formally Undecidable Propositions of Principia Mathematica and Related Systems (Godel), 346
On Humanistic Education (Vico), 237
On Nature (Parmenides), 40
On Rhetoric (Philodemus), 104
On Rhetoricians (Suetonius), 109
On the Marriage of Mercury and Philology (Capella), 155
On the Mode of Preaching (*De artificios modo predicandi*) (Alexander of Ashby), 158
On the Nature of Things (Anaximander of Miletus), 37
On the Nature of Things (*De rerum natura*) (Lucretius), 105, 195
On the Preacher's Art (*De arte praedicatoria*) (de Lille), 180
On the Shadows of Ideas (Bruno), 215
On the Soul (*De anima*) (Aristotle), 175
On the Sublime (Longinus), 131, 221
On the Way to Truth (Protagoras), 42
Ong, Walter, 208
Only Words (MacKinnon), 393
Onomatopoeia (*nominatio*), 128
Ontological rhetoric, 5, 314, 406
Opponent's words, argument from, 82
Opposites, argument from, 81
Opus maius (*Major Work*) (Bacon), 175
Opus tertium (Bacon), 175
Orator (Cicero), 125, 159
Organization (disposition/taxis), 85–89, 109
Organon (Aristotle), 66

Origen, 146
Origines (Isidore), 165
Ornatus, 125, 129–133
Ornatus/ornamenta verborum (beautiful order), 125
Ottoman Empire, 169
Ovid, 100
Oxymoron, 127

Paideia, 108
Panegyricus (Isocrates), 49
Parables, 27–28
Paradox, 130, 316
Parmenides, 40–41, 47, 105
Paroemia (proverbial expressions), 28
Parole/parola, 236, 377
Paromologia, 129
Parrhesia, 198, 374
Parts to the whole, argument from, 82
Pastoral Care (*Cura pastoralis*) (Pope Gregory the Great), 180
Pathé, 74–79. *See also* Emotion(s)
Pathos, 71, 74–79, 109, 175, 217, 256. *See also* Emotion(s)
Paton, Bartolomé Jiménez, 223
Patriarchy, 386–388
Patriotic appeals, 307–309
Patristic era, 145
Paul, 146
Paulhan, Jean, 347
Pax Romana (Roman Peace), 145
Peacham, Henry, 221
Peirce, Charles, 345
Peisistratus, 36
Pentad, Burke's, 325
Perception(s), 7
  Aristotle on, 77
  Bitzer on, 7
  exigence and, 7
  Foucault on, 375–376
  Hume on, 248
  importance in rhetoric, 4
  individual, truth based on, 36
  Machiavelli on, 202
  McLuhan on, 357, 360
  Protagoras on, 42–43
Perelman, Chaim, 126, 343, 346–352
Perfection, Burke on, 328
Performative utterances, 393, 396
Pericles, 40–41
Pericopes, 27–28, 30
Periodic style, 86